KW-550-673

CROSS-LINGUISTIC STUDIES OF TONAL PHENOMENA

Historical Development, Tone-Syntax Interface, and Descriptive Studies

Proceedings of the Symposium

CROSS-LINGUISTIC STUDIES

OF

TONAL PHENOMENA

Historical Development, Tone-Syntax Interface, and Descriptive Studies

Dec.14-16, 2004
Research Institute for Languages and Cultures of Asia and Africa (ILCAA)

Edited by
Shigeki Kaji

Research Institute for Languages and Cultures of Asia and Africa (ILCAA)
Tokyo University of Foreign Studies
2005

©Shigeki Kaji 2005

Research Institute for Languages and Cultures of Asia and Africa (ILCAA),
Tokyo University of Foreign Studies
3-11-1, Asahi-cho, Fuchu-shi, Tokyo 183-8534 Japan

Proceedings of the Symposium

CROSS-LINGUISTIC STUDIES OF TONAL PHENOMENA:
Historical Development, Tone-Syntax Interface, and Descriptive Studies

ISBN: 4-87297-917-6

Printed by Sanrei Printing Co., Ltd.
Cover design by Naganuma Design Office

Table of Contents

Session 3: Descriptive Studies

Acknowledgements

The papers collected in this volume were all presented at the fourth international symposium on tone entitled "Cross-linguistic Studies of Tonal Phenomena: Historical Development, Tone-Syntax Interface, and Descriptive Studies", which was held at the Research Institute for Languages and Cultures of Asia and Africa (ILCAA), Tokyo University of Foreign Studies, from December 14 to 16, 2004. Included in this volume are not only the papers presented at the symposium but also the commentaries to them.

The symposium was sponsored by the Ministry of Education, Science, Sports and Culture of the Government of Japan. We would like first to acknowledge our gratitude to thc Govcrnmcnt of Japan, whose generous sponsorship allowed the symposium to be realized and led to its successful ending. Our thanks go to the participants of the symposium, either as speakers, commentators, chairpersons or audience, and finally as the contributors to this volume.

We are also grateful to the administrative staff of the University, especially Ms. Mikiko Takizawa and Ms. Kyoko Hirano for their work, enabling us to have a pleasant, well-organized symposium as before. Most of the practical procedures were carried out by our doctoral course students and part-time researchers, for which we are very grateful. The editing of this volume was assisted by Dr. Ruth Roberts-Kohno, then research fellow at the Institute, without whose help this volume would not have been published so smoothly. I apologize for its delay, however, which is partially due to my affiliation change from ILCAA to Kyoto University, in the year 2004.

The cover design is, again, by Ms. Mika Naganuma and her group, with the same design but a different color, to assume the continuity of this tone symposium.

Shigeki Kaji

Preface

Tone is one of the common features of the world's languages. It is found not only in East and Southeast Asian languages, but in many languages of the world: native American, New Guinean, African, etc. If we include pitch-accent languages, quite a wide range of the world's languages can be seen to exploit this particular phonetic feature to a greater or lesser degree.

The Research Institute for Languages and Cultures of Asia and Africa (ILCAA) is an inter-university research center affiliated with Tokyo University of Foreign Studies. It has as its main role to organize and coordinate research projects relating to Asian and African studies in Japan.

It is on this basis that we organized international symposia on tone in 1998, 2000, and 2002, inviting foreign as well as domestic scholars working on various tone and/or pitch-accent languages. The main objectives were to exchange ideas among specialists of different language families and tone types (comparing, for example, Asian tone languages and African tone languages), and to make the research done by Japanese scholars on Japanese accent more widely known.

This fourth symposium was conceived as a natural succession to the first three, after evaluation and consideration of the outcomes. It was organized around three topics: historical development, tone-syntax interface, and descriptive studies. The term "historical development" was chosen rather than "tonogenesis" as the former has a wider coverage than the latter (tone change, tone loss, etc. in addition to tonogenesis). The topic "tone-syntax interface" was chosen because of the interaction which tone has in the syntax of languages (as seen in many African languages in particular). The other presentations were covered under "descriptive studies". However, this classification is an expedient of arranging the papers in three days, and should not be taken as categorical. Indeed, Hieda's paper on Kumam tone in "historical development" deals with the tone-syntax interface of the language, and Shintani's paper on Austroasiatic tone languages in "descriptive studies" could have been more properly put under the topic of "historical development".

Four or five papers were read each day, and each paper was followed by a commentary. A general discussion relating to each day's topic was programmed at the end of the session. However, the papers as well as the commentaries in this volume are not as they were presented at the symposium. The authors could incorporate comments in their text if they wished to. The editorial efforts are minimal except for some typographical adjustments.

I do not need to overview the papers contained in this volume. But it is interesting to observe that the same thing is said of different languages of the world. With respect to tonogenesis, for example, which always has been one of the central themes of our symposia, it is noteworthy that three researchers mentioned language contact as a possible factor in tonogenesis at the symposium. Donohue, in his comments on Ross' paper on the history of the Trans New Guinean languages, rather strongly suggested an areal phenomenon of tone. Nagano-Madsen also in her comments on Bradshaw's paper on Suma tone development, a Central African language, hinted at the influence of neighboring languages. Finally, Mazaudon in her survey of Sino-Tibetan tone reminded us of the existence of word-tone in Punjabi, an Indo-Aryan language adjacent to the Sino-Tibetan languages. This factor was also suggested by Hualde (2003) in his analysis of Basque tone.

What is said by the respective authors may not be new to the specialists of the circle, but can be very new to non-specialists. This is the main reason why this kind of symposium is necessary and useful. As I have repeatedly said, we know what we know, and we don't know what we don't know. So, we want to know what we don't know. Any theory obviously must be based on wide and accurate knowledge of the languages treated. From this perspective all the papers presented were very instructive.

It is to be recalled that our intention when we entitled the symposium "cross-linguistic studies" was that tone be discussed on a worldwide level by bringing together phenomena reported in individual languages. For this purpose, this fourth symposium, as well as the first three, were quite successful, because a variety of phenomena were presented and discussed by specialists of different languages families and tone types, and from various perspectives. I believe that our symposia are on the right track to pursuing our objective to understand the role of tone in human language.

Shigeki Kaji

Reference

Hualde, José I. 2003. "Some ways in which Basque is and is not like Japanese and how it got to be that way". In S. Kaji (ed.) *Cross-Linguistic Studies of Tonal Phenomena: Historical Development, Phonetics of Tone, and Descriptive Studies*, Tokyo: Research Institute for Languages and Cultures of Asia and Africa, Tokyo University of Foreign Studies. 2003, pp.291-309.

Session 1

Historical Development

Towards a reconstruction of the history of tone in the Trans New Guinea family

Malcolm Ross
Malcolm.Ross@anu.edu.au
Research School of Pacific and Asian Studies
and Centre for Research on Language Change,
The Australian National University

1 Introduction

The purpose of the research reported here was rather modest: to survey what is known about tone in TNG languages and to assess the degree to which tone might play a part in the reconstruction of Proto Trans New Guinea and later TNG interstage languages.[1]

The importance and typological range of tone in New Guinea became evident only with the groundbreaking publication of Donohue (1997), and Yip's (2002) recent textbook survey of tone makes no mention of tone in Papuan languages. My purpose here overlaps Donohue's insofar as I am reporting on what has been written about tone in TNG languages, and I have benefited greatly from his work (his typology covers all New Guinea tone languages, not just TNG).[2] But I have conducted this survey from a diachronic perspective, endeavouring to see what the geographic domain of tone looks like on the map and to understand how different tonal systems might be related to each other diachronically.

2 The Trans New Guinea family

The languages of the Pacific are usually divided into Austronesian, Papuan and Australian. The Austronesian languages form a definite phylogenetic group, but 'Papuan' and 'Australian' are cover terms for collections of languages whose phylogeny is not well understood. 'Papuan' essentially means 'spoken in the New Guinea region and not Austronesian or Australian'. There are perhaps 650 Papuan languages, and recent research suggests that they fall

---

[1] Revised draft of paper presented at the international symposium *Cross-linguistic Studies of Tonal Phenomena: Historical Development, Tone-syntax interface, and Descriptive Studies*, December 2004, Research Institute for Languages and Cultures of Asia and Africa (ILCAA), Tokyo University of Foreign Studies. Please do not quote without the author's permission.

[2] I am also indebted to him for personal communications and for Donohue (2004), in part a commentary on the symposium version of this paper, which have aided me greatly during revision. Needless to say, this revised version remains my responsibility.

into about 20 phylogenetic groups (Ross Forthcoming).[3] Phylogenetically, the New Guinea region is linguistically the most diverse on the planet (Nettle 1999: 116–117). Nonetheless, around 400 Papuan languages appear to belong to a single phylogenetic group, Trans New Guinea, whose putative boundaries are shown on the map.

There have been two main phases of historical research on the languages of the TNG family, both of them centred on the same location: the Department of Linguistics of the Research School of Pacific and Asian Studies at the Australian National University.[4] The first phase began in the early 1960s, when S.A. Wurm set about surveying the languages of New Guinea and collating the results. For Papuan languages, these were published as Wurm, ed. (1975b). The sheer immensity of the task meant that much of what appeared in this book was sketchy in the extreme, and Wurm's claim that he and his team had discovered a large 'Trans New Guinea phylum' covering much of mainland New Guinea was greeted with skepticism by commentators. In his survey of Papuan languages, Foley (1986: 3, 213) recognised upwards of 60 small groups and perhaps two dozen isolates related at a level on a par with Romance or Germanic, but he rejected the TNG phylum on the grounds that the necessary groundwork to allow the establishment of larger groupings under the comparative method had yet to be done.[5]

Only a few snippets of historical research on languages of the putative TNG family were published in the twenty years after 1975, and the second phase began almost by accident. The first, very modest version of the TNG hypothesis was McElhanon and Voorhoeve (1970). In 1995 Andrew Pawley and I were invited, at a few weeks' notice, to contribute to a festschrift in honour of C.L. Voorhoeve. In search of an appropriate offering, Pawley revisited McElhanon and Voorhoeve (1970) and found that there was a more plausible case for a TNG family than the critics had allowed. Consequently, I did a rough survey of the pronoun forms (mostly collected by Voorhoeve) in languages which Wurm had included in the TNG phylum to see if they supported a phylogenetic grouping. Pronouns were the only evidence spanning enough languages to allow a TNG-wide survey. I was surprised to discover that they supported a TNG hypothesis quite strongly, albeit a grouping somewhat smaller than Wurm's. Our papers were published as Pawley (1995) and Ross (1995).

Since then, Pawley has proposed a putative early TNG phoneme inventory and about 200 early TNG reconstructions, including the singular and dual members of a paradigm of verbal desinences (Pawley 1998, 2001, Forthcoming). My pronominal research had widened to include all Papuan languages for which I can find data, and I have examined the data more carefully, and proposed probable boundaries for the TNG family and its subgroups (Forthcoming, Ross In preparation a, In preparation b).

One fact that caused Wurm to spread his TNG net too wide was that an overwhelming majority of TNG languages share a set of structural features which through millennia of contact have been copied by members of other phylogenetic stocks, including Austronesian (Ross 1996). TNG languages are SOV and postpositional. Clauses typically have nominative–accusative alignment, but it is common to find the instrumental postposition also used to

[3] It may be that these groups were once related to each other, but some or all of these relationships lie back beyond the reach of the comparative method.

[4] The history of the TNG hypothesis is recounted in some detail by Pawley (Forthcoming).

[5] Foley (2000) indicates that he now accepts a reduced version of the TNG such as that discussed below.

mark the subject of a transitive verb (the so-called 'ergative' marker). TNG languages tend to suffix rather than prefix, and verbs often have complex paradigms of suffixed desinences which indicate subject person/number agreement, tense, aspect and mood.

At present TNG has (like Afro-Asiatic) the status of what Nichols (1997) calls a 'quasi-stock': a grouping of stocks with promising phylogenetic markers but no regular sound correspondences and few clear cognates. With careful work we hope to show it to be a 'stock' (Nichols 1992: 24–25), a grouping with a protolanguage that can be reconstructed by the comparative method (like Indo-European or Austronesian). However, this will be no mean task. Proto TNG may be a more ancient language than is customarily reconstructed by the comparative method. The 400 TNG languages show considerable diversity in lexicon and morphology. There are currently 33 groups of TNG languages recognisable by inspection or by the application of the comparative method (Ross Forthcoming),[6] and 8 isolates. Bellwood (Bellwood 1997; Diamond and Bellwood 2003) has argued that the expansion of some of the world's largest language families was an outcome of the Neolithic transition, i.e. the transition from foraging to agriculture, and it seems eminently likely that this is true of the TNG family. It seems likely that TNG expanded at the expense of earlier linguistic diversity because it was carried by a taro- and banana-based agricultural expansion following domestication in the Highlands of New Guinea. The Highlands warmed up after the last Ice Age about 14,000 years ago and the archaeological record shows that taro and bananas were being cultivated there by 10,000 years ago (Denham et al. 2003). The TNG expansion may well have begun within a millennium or so of their cultivation (Pawley Forthcoming). If so, then it is ancient in comparison with other protolanguages reconstructed by the comparative method.

3 The tonal typology of Trans New Guinea languages

We are probably reaching the limits of what can be done by a broad-brush, 'top-down' approach, and need to reconstruct more of the histories of the 33 constituent groups.[7] If Proto TNG was indeed spoken by early agriculturalists in the Highlands, then we would expect the Highlands to show the greatest phylogenetic diversity within the TNG family, and they apparently do. On the assumption that there have not been massive population displacements there in the intervening millennia, we might have at least a weak expectation that the Highlands language groups will provide us with more information about Proto TNG than will languages further away. A notable feature of Highlands groups is tone, and so there is a fair possibility that Proto TNG was also tonal. It would in any case be unwise to attempt a reconstruction which ignored a central feature of daughter languages.

Unfortunately, some descriptions of Highlands languages ignore tone, while others mention it but give few details, despite the attention drawn to Highlands tone by Pike (1964). There are a number of reasons for this. One has been that linguists working on these languages were not accustomed to looking for tone, and either did not recognise it or believed it to be so marginal that they could discount it.

---

[6] This number may well drop with more research.

[7] Some detailed work on local groups has been done (Kainantu–Goroka, Madang), but has yet to be written up and published.

As the map shows, languages with tone cluster along the flanks of the cordillera, mostly in the region where we think Proto TNG was spoken. There is also a smaller area of tone around Uhunduni, further west. To the south, southwest and west of the core region, as well as around Uhunduni, we find groups with pitch accent systems or systems which hover somewhere between tone and pitch accent. And further away still are groups with no vestige of tone that we know of.

Donohue divides New Guinea systems into three types:

syllable tone: the system 'assign[s] a separate tone to each syllable in a word';

word tone: 'the domain of each tone is the word as a whole';

pitch accent: 'there is one simply designated syllable that determines the shape of the pitch pattern on the rest of the word'.

However, he is careful to point out (i) that there is great diversity within these categories and (ii) that the boundaries between them are unsharp.

Papuan languages are arrayed along the whole continuum, but tonal TNG languages range from those which hover on the borderline between syllable tone and word tone through to straightforward pitch-accent languages. Between these points is a clustering of word-tone languages, of which Kewa is an example. Thoroughgoing syllable tone is to my knowledge not represented among TNG languages.

3.1 Word tone: East Kewa

Table 1 illustrates the noun system in East Kewa (Engan)[8]. East Kewa[9] has word tone, and the tone melody is in each case spread across the word as a whole. However, the shape of that tone melody is determined by the position of the word within an intonational phrase (ip). Table 1 shows the basic and derived melodies of each of the five tone classes of noun. The derived melody occurs when the final tone of the preceding word (the 'trigger') is H (for examples in context, see §4.1.1). Otherwise the basic melody occurs, with the proviso that ip-initial L and H are neutralised to M, i.e. basic L and HL become ip-initial ML, and basic LH becomes ip-initial MH.[10]

Word tone means, for example, that in the case of monosyllabic *máa* 'neck'[11] after a H

[8] I write the name of the group to which a language belongs in parentheses each time I begin discussion of a language.

[9] East Kewa data are from Apoi Yarapea of Mugumapu village and represent part of a piece of joint research on East Kewa tone. The analysis remains tentative. We have been aided by the Franklins' account of tone in West Kewa, but there are differences between the tone systems of the two dialects, and many differences in the assignment of individual words to classes.

[10] Other analyses are possible, but the fact that the ip-medial melody occurring after a low trigger also occurs in a predictable variant ip-initially suggests that it is basic, i.e. not subject to a trigger effect. Whatever analysis is chosen, the analyst cannot determine the class of a noun without knowing both its realisations.

[11] An acute accent indicates H, an overstrike M, no accent L (on the assumption that L is unspecified for tone). The minimal word is a monosyllable of two moras. In a curious asymmetry, there are five underlyingly monomoraic vowels /i e a o u/ and one invariably bimoraic vowel /aa/. However, when a phonological word is monosyllabic, its vowel spans two moras and the distinction in length between /i e a o u/ and /aa/ is neutralised. A quality distinction between /aa/ and bimoraic /a/ remains, but is not recorded orthographically here.

trigger there is a decided HL contour on the syllable, whereas in the case of *áda* 'house' and *rógōma* 'clay' H and L tones are allocated to first and last syllables. In a trisyllable the tone of the second syllable is non-contrastive and it is not clear what association convention, if any, applies to it.

TABLE 1: East Kewa nouns

tone class	syllables	basic tone melody		tone melody after H trigger		gloss
A	1	L	*maa*	H	*máá*	'taro'
	2		*pada*		*pádá*	'room'
	3		*lemogo*		*lémógó*	'bird type'
B	1	L^H	*maa*	HL^H	*máa*	'neck'
	2		*ada*		*áda*	'house'
	3		*rogoma*		*rógōma*	'clay'
C (rising)	1	LH	*eé*	LH	*eé*	'garden'
	2		*yasá*		*yasá*	'song'
D	2	HL	*kábu*	LH	*kabú*	'digging stick'
E (falling)	1	HL	*yáa*	HL	*yáa*	'bird'
	2		*kódo*		*kódo*	'scar'
	3		*lémōgo*		*lémōgo*	'pupil of eye'

The five classes are represented with varying frequencies in the data, and there are few three-syllable nouns: these facts lead to the absence of trisyllables from the rising tone class and of di- and trisyllables from the high class in Table 1.

Medial melodies of the tone class B are shown with a superscript H (L^H and HL^H) because nouns of this class have a floating H tone which functions as trigger for the following word (see (13)). This floating H is also sometimes already manifested on the final mora of the word if it has more than one syllable and if it is in a low-trigger environment, i.e. L^H becomes LH, so that *ada* 'house' and *rogoma* 'clay' become *adá* and *rogōmá* respectively. In ip-initial position L^H always becomes MH, i.e. the floating H tone docks on the final mora of the word, giving *māá*, *ādá* and *rōgōmá*. The citation melody of a noun is the same as the ip-initial melody, except in class B, where the citation form is M, not MH (i.e. floating H is deleted).

Floating H is probably the result of a diachronic tonal change whereby word-final H has been lost in certain environments without a concomitant change in the triggering process. However, if we assume that HL^H is derived from a melody with no more than two tones (the norm for East Kewa noun melodies), then the changes leading to it were more complicated than simple H-loss.

3.2 Word tone with complex association convention: Kairi

In Kewa the tone melody is spread across all the syllables of the word. In Kairi (Turama-Kikori)[12] the association convention is more complicated. There are four tone melodies, H, HL, LH and LHL. The H melody is mapped onto all syllables as in (1a). When the tone melody consists of more than one tone, it is associated with a lexically specified accent (i.e. an anchor-point) in an interesting way. By default, the accent falls on the final syllable of the word, the last two tones of the melody form a contour on that syllable, and all syllables before the last have the first tone of the melody. With the two-tone melodies HL and LH, this means that the first tone spreads across all non-final syllables **and** forms the first part of the final-syllable contour as in (1b) and (1c). With LHL it means that the first L spreads across all non-final (pre-accent) syllables and HL forms the final contour as in (1d). Further examples are shown in Table 2.

(1)

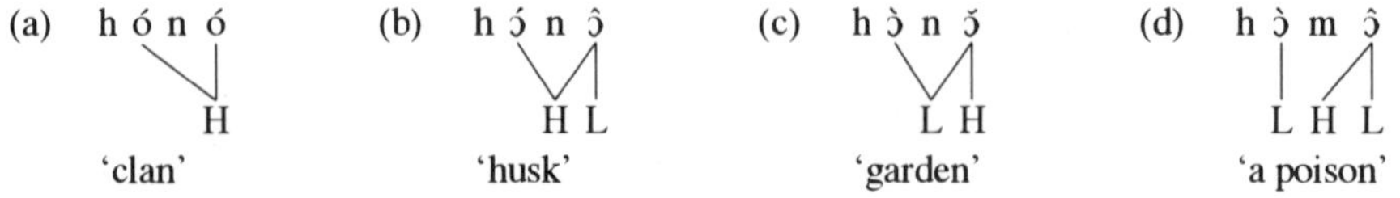

In a small number of words with LHL, however, the accent falls on the penultimate syllable. The three tones of the melody form contours on the penult (LH) and final (HL) syllables and the first L spreads across all pre-accent syllables as in (2).

(2)

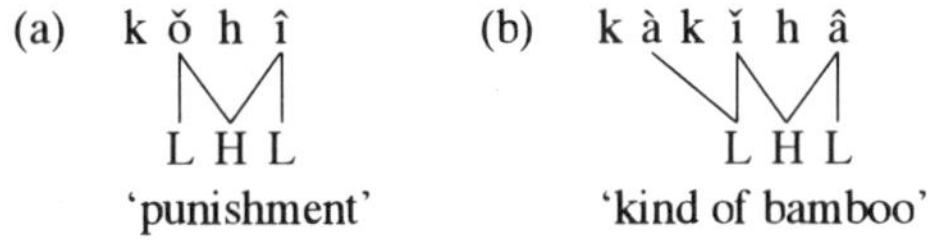

Note that there is a single association convention here. The tone melody is right-aligned with the end of the word, and tones are assigned to syllables from right to left but staggered so that they form a contour on each syllable as far as the accent (in practice the final or penultimate syllable). Pre-accent syllables have the first tone of the melody.

There are tone sandhi processes in Kairi but they are very different from those of the other languages discussed here, and it is unlikely that there is a diachronic relationship.

3.3 Between word tone and syllable tone: Fore, Usarufa, Telefol and Angaatiha

In a word-tone language like Kewa or Kairi, the number of tone melodies is the same regardless of the number of syllables in a word. In the ideal syllable-tone language, a word has T^S possible contrasting tone melodies, where T is the number of contrasting syllable tones, S the number of syllables in the word. For example, the number of tone melodies for, say, 3-syllable words is found by raising the number of syllable tones to the power of 3. So if a syllable-tone language has two tones, H and L, the possible tone melodies for one-, two-, three- and four-syllable words are as in (3).

[12] Gussenhoven (2004: 32) incorrectly situates Kairi in West Papua. It is located in the Gulf Province of Papua New Guinea.

TABLE 2: Kairi nouns

tone melody/ accent	one		two		three		four	
				number of syllables				
H	ké	'pitpit'	hónó	'clan'	kírímá	'k fish'	hárákánéá	'k prawn'
HL/final	kê	'crescent shell'	hɔ́nɔ̂	'husk'	éhénê	'fight'	pépéhérô	'peg'
LH/final	kě	'shellfish sp.'	hɔ̀nɔ̌	'garden'	ɛ̀mɛ̀hǐ	'breadfruit'	ràràkànĕ	'palate'
LHL/final	kě`	'tree sp.'	hɔ̀mɔ̂	'a poison'	èhìkô	'dish'	àràmèrâu	'k basket'
LHL/penult	—		kǒhî	'punishment'	kàkǐhâ	'k bamboo'	—	

(3)

one syllable	H				L			
two syllables	HH		HL		LL		LH	
three syllables	HHH	HHL	HLH	HLL	LLL	LLH	LHL	LHH
four syllables	HHHH	HHLH	HLHH	HLLH	LLLH	LLHH	LHLH	LHHH
	HHHL	HHLL	HLHL	HLLL	LLLL	LLHL	LHLL	LHHL

3.3.1 Fore

Scott (1978) analysed Fore (Kainantu-Goroka) as a syllable-tone language with H and L tones, but with gaps in the system as shown in (4).

(4) Fore: older analysis

one syllable	H				L			
newer two syllables	HH		HL		LL		LH	
three syllables	—	—	HLH	HLL	LLL	LLH	LHL	LHH
four syllables	—	—	HLHH	HLLH	LLLH	LLHH	LHLH	—
	—	—	HLHL	HLLL	LLLL	LLHL	LHLL	LHHL

The gaps were accounted for by two somewhat *ad hoc* constraints: (i) that no more than two adjacent H tones may occur; and (ii) that words of more than two syllables may not begin with the sequence HH. However, Scott (1990) provides a word-tone reanalysis of the system, shown in (5). This allowed him to deal with the uncertainties that had plagued his earlier analysis and were due to the difficulty of interpreting phonetically mid tone. For example, was [LMH] a realisation of LHH or of LLH? How did one distinguish one from the other? Scott's conclusion is that one doesn't, as [LMH] simply realises LH word tone, i.e. as in Kewa (§3.1) the middle syllable is non-contrastive.

Examples are shown in Table 3. In both (5) and the table I use a different notation from Scott's in order to facilitate comparison with other languages, particularly Kewa. The differences between Scott's and my notations are illustrated in (6). Scott cites words consisting of a stem and the predicate-marker suffix *-ne* or *-we*, in order to show docking of the floating tone of the melody on the predicate-marker.[13] Scott shows the tone of such

[13] The final N of *kí*N represents an underlying nasal that only surfaces when certain suffixes are added, as here. This convention is from Bee and Glasgow (1973), who use it for Usarufa, also a Kainantu-Goroka language. The phenomenon it represents is widespread in the family.

examples as H and HLH respectively, whereas I show the floating tone as a superscript, i.e. H^{H} and HL^{H}.

TABLE 3: Fore tone melodies

tone melody	number of stem syllables one		two		three	
H^{H}	*kíN*^{H2}	'maggot'	*nónóN*^{H1}	'breast'	*múyáaríN*^{H2}	'snake'
H^{L}	*káaN*^{L}	'one'	*á?noN*^{L}	'his head'	*káikena*^{L}	'about to rain'
HL^{H}	—		*áwa*^{H1}	'his tooth'	*nágaanto*^{H1}	'my elder brother'
HLH^{L}	—		—		*áataená*^{L}	'bad'
L^{L}	*kaoN*^{L}	'your friend'	*antaa*^{L}	'his intestines'	*kabaraN*^{L}	'bird'
L^{H}	*keN*^{H1}	'path'	*amaN*^{H2}	'his shadow'	*amaagiN*^{H1}	'his chin'
LH^{L}	—		*waníN*^{L}	'water'	*aenkáu?*^{L}	'at what place?'
LHL^{H}	—		—		*na?nánto*^{H1}	'my younger brother'

(5) Fore: newer analysis

one syllable	H^{H}				L^{L}			
two syllables	H^{H}	H^{L}			L^{L}	L^{H}		
three syllables	H^{H}	H^{L}	HL^{H}		L^{L}	L^{H}	LH^{L}	
four syllables	H^{H}	H^{L}	HL^{H}	HLH^{L}	L^{L}	L^{H}	LH^{L}	LHL^{H}

(6)

Scott			Ross		
ki-né	H	'it is a maggot'	*kíN*^{H2}	H^{H}	'maggot'
áwa-wé	HLH	'it is his tooth'	*áwa*^{H1}	HL^{H}	'his tooth'

Comparison of (5) and Table 3 shows an apparent mismatch, as H^{L} nouns are shown in the table with diacritics that appear to represent HL^{L}, e.g. *á?noN*^{L} 'his head' . However, this is manifested as, for example, *á?no-ne* 'it is his head', where the unmarked middle syllable is non-contrastive, i.e. phonetic [HML] reflects H^{L}.

Fore triggers operate quite differently from those in Kewa. In most Kewa cases, the final tone acts as trigger, and the triggered manifestation of the next word is determined by the tone class to which that word belongs. Fore is different. In Fore, as Table 3 shows, most triggers are floating tones which **differ** from the final tone. The only exceptions are the H^{H} and L^{L} melodies (which contrast with H^{L} and L^{H}).

To represent a trigger that is identical with the tone that precedes it, in for example H^{H}, appears redundant, but it is not entirely so, as superscript H actually represents two patterns, H1 and H2, as identified by Ford (1996). When the next item is a suffix, superscripted H1 and H2 have the same behaviour, as (6) shows. When the next item is a word in the same phrase, however, things are different. The rightmost column of (7) shows four nouns followed by the numeral /rara/ 'two' and the predicate marker in a clause meaning 'they are two [noun]s'. A noun with H1 trigger like *patari*^{H1} 'corncob' places a high tone on the **first** syllable of the following word, as in *patari rára-we* 'they are two corncobs', and a noun with H2 trigger like *tápaya*N^{H2} 'bat' places a high tone on the **second** syllable of the following word, as in *tápaya tará-we*. *Tápaya*N^{H2} might better be represented as *tápaya*N^{LH}, but this decision requires more extensive analysis than is at my disposal. Nouns with L trigger, on the other hand, *kegina*N^{L} 'ghost' and *wasaná*N^{L} 'person', cause the rest of the phrase to be low-toned. Whether a lexical item has a H1, H2 or L trigger is lexically determined.

(7)

gloss	melody	noun	noun-PRED	noun + 'two'-PRED
'corncob'	L^{H1}	*patari*^{H1}	*patari-wé*	*patari rára-we*
'bat'	HL^{H2}	*tápaya*N^{H2}	*tápaya-né*	*tápaya tará-we*
'ghost'	L^{L}	*kegina*N^{L}	*kegina-ne*	*kegina tara-we*
'person'	LH^{L}	*wasaná*^{L}	*wasaná-we*	*wasaná rara-we*

A crucial point revealed by Table 3 is that a stem of *S* syllables can only accommodate a tone melody with up to *S* + 1 tones. Thus a HLH or LHL melody occurs only on stems of 2 or more syllables, HLHL or LHLH only on stems of 3 or more syllables. In other words the number of contrasting tone melodies in words (stem + one-syllable suffix) of *S* syllables is 2*S*, since there are 2 tones. This means that Fore hovers somewhere between an 'ideal' syllable-tone language, where in a language with *T* tones the number of contrasting tone melodies in words of *S* syllables is T^S, and a 'normal' word-tone language like Kewa or Kairi where there is a small number of tone melodies, usually between 2 and 5. The difference in tonal arithmetic raises the diachronic question of whether Fore is descended from a Kewa-like language or Kewa from a Fore-like language, or both from a third type.

3.3.2 Usarufa

The Usarufa dialect of Auyana-Usarufa also belongs to the Kainantu-Goroka family and has a tonal architecture similar to Fore, as shown in (8) .

(8) Usarufa

one syllable	H	HL	L		
two syllables	H	HL	L	LH	
three syllables	H	HL	L	LH	LHL

Unlike Fore, Usarufa anchors its HL and LH movements to accent points, and these accent points vary from one word to another (Donohue 1997: 362–365). Unfortunately, Bee and Glasgow's (1973) description is rather algebraic and lacks contrastive examples, but they indicate, for example, that disyllabic HL may be realised as H-L or H-HL, and trisyllabic HL as H-H-L, H-HL-L, H-L-L or HL-L-L. Donohue (1997: 364–365) extracts examples from their work contrasting, for example, *anê-ma* 'bird species' with *aá-ma*, and *aríburiʔ-a* 'sweet potato species' with *umoiyám-ma* 'bad cough', all LHL but with differing accents.[14]

[14] The suffix in each case is the noun-phrase marker /-ma/.

3.3.3 Telefol

Donohue (1997) summarises data from two TNG languages that appear to have syllable tone, Chuave (Chimbu-Wahgi) and Telefol (Ok). Both are intriguing, Chuave because two of its close relatives have been shown to have word tone (Hardie 2003; Chida 2003), and Telefol because of the distribution of its tone melodies. In the case of Chuave, the data do not allow us to pursue the issue further.

The Telefol data are interesting because they perhaps provide some insight into a historical relationship between syllable-tone and word-tone languages. Telefol has two tones, which Healey (1964) labels UP and DOWN.[15] All possible combinations of the two tones are found in one-, two- and three-syllable words, with a maximum of one tone per syllable. However, for the distribution of tone combinations in monomorphemic disyllables Healey (1964: 27) gives the following percentages.

(9)	DOWN–UP	UP–UP	DOWN–DOWN	UP–DOWN
nouns, adjectives, verbal adjuncts	48	43	8	1
verb stems	16	77	6	0

Two things are striking. First, UP–DOWN hardly occurs, and DOWN–DOWN occurs relatively seldom. Second, the distribution of tone patterns on verb stems and non-verbs differs. This happens in TNG word-tone languages too. I return to these matters briefly in §5.

Telefol also has a sandhi phenomenon whereby the word-final DOWN tone of a phrase-initial word spreads to the rest of the phrase, whilst a word-final UP spreads just to the first syllable of the next word. This is reminiscent of trigger behaviour in Kewa and of the floating tones of Fore and Usarufa.

3.3.4 Angaatiha

Another language for which there are published materials and which is described as having syllable tone is Angaatiha (Angan) (Huisman and Lloyd 1981). However, a count of the attested tone melodies casts doubt on this characterisation. There are three tones, H, HL and L, and accordingly three monosyllabic melodies. With three tones we would expect 9 patterns on disyllables and 27 on trisyllables. We find 7 and 10 respectively, as in (10). Three-syllable patterns ending in -HL are placed on a separate line for convenience only.

(10) Angaatiha: as published

one syllable	H	HL		L			
two syllables	H-H	H-L	HL-H	L-L	L-H	L-HL	
		HL-L					
three syllables	—	H-L-L	H-L-H	L-L-L	L-L-H	L-H-L	L-HL-H
						L-HL-L	
			H-L-HL		L-L-HL		L-HL-HL

If HL sequences are regarded as anchored to more than one accent point, this reduces to the tone melodies in (11).

[15] Donohue (1997: 355–356) interprets these as L and H respectively, with a dissimilatory epenthetic tone.

(11) Angaatɨha: revised analysis

one syllable	H	HL			L				
two syllables	H	HL	HLH		L	LH	LHL		
three syllables	—	HL	HLH	HLHL	L	LH	LHL	LHLH	LHLHL

This organisation resembles that of Fore, insofar as three-tone melodies are mapped onto two-syllable stems, and four-tone melodies (and the seemingly anomalous LHLHL) are mapped onto three-syllable stems. The difference is that in Fore the final tone is realised only on a following morpheme, whereas in Angaatɨha it is realised on the stem itself.

One could speculate about the distribution of the patterns in (10), but this is not germane to my purpose, which is to show that Angaatɨha can be interpreted as a word-tone language.

3.4 Pitch-accent languages

If TNG tonal typology is viewed as a cline ranging from syllable tone through word tone to pitch accent, then pitch-accent languages are at the opposite extreme from Telefol.

No detailed accounts of TNG pitch-accent languages are accessible to me, but Donohue (1997) provides brief accounts of pitch-accent systems in Una (Mek), Marind (Marind), and Kaure (Kaure) and of systems intermediate between pitch accent and word tone in Fasu (West Kutubu) and the isolate Momuna.

In Una (Mek) the number of possible contrasts on a polysyllabic word is equal to the number of syllables. However, there is also a high/low contrast on monosyllables, perhaps a vestige of an earlier word-tone system.

Nearer to a word-tone system is Fasu (West Kutubu), where each word has one of two contrasting tone melodies, one with a H, the other with a L. The tone is anchored to an accent point which varies across lexical items. All other syllables are tonally unspecified. May and Loeweke (1965) are explicit about the fact that there is a H/L contrast between tonally specified syllables, and that these syllables vary in position. May and Loeweke's set of three-syllable examples is shown in (12).

(12)

	tonally specified syllable					
	1st		2nd		3rd	
H	*férepe*	'bushknife'	*sakáre*	'arrow'	*kenarí*	'tree type'
L	*èresa*	'dark'	*hiwàti*	'eyelash'	*kenarì*	'bamboo type'

In monsyllables, the contrast is limited to H and L, as expected: *mè* 'language', *mé* 'taro'.[16]

Momuna (Donohue 1997: 372-373) has a system similar to Fasu, except that there is a three-way contrast on monosyllables: high, mid, low. The Kaure (Donohue 1997: 370) system resembles Fasu in its architecture, but the contrast is between H and HL.

Foe (East Kutubu), sandwiched between Kewa and Fasu, appears to have word tone with just two melodies, high (HL when utterance-final) and low (LHL when utterance-final) (Rule 1993: 24–25). There is no mention of accent in the admittedly scanty account, and this language may form a typological bridge between the word tone of Kewa and the pitch accent of Fasu.

[16] Note that these are cognate with East Kewa *maa/máa* 'neck' and *maa/máá* 'taro' (Table 1).

3.5 Typology overview

The typological range, then, of tone in New Guinea is from Telefol, a syllable-tone language with some suggestion of word tone, through a variety of word-tone systems with and without variable accent, to pitch-accent systems which usually also have a high/low distinction.

For the purposes of the map, I have treated all tone languages as a single category and all languages with pitch-accent-like systems as a separate category. Where a family covers a small area and one language of a family is known to be tonal, I have marked the family as tonal. Where a family covers a small area and one language is known to have pitch accent (and none known to be tonal), I have marked the family as having pitch accent.

In the western half of the map, however, where families tend to cover larger areas, I have endeavoured to meet the concerns of Donohue (2004) and to mark tonal or pitch-accent regions within larger families. Thus in the west there is a small tonal area consisting of the isolate Uhunduni and the Wolani and Moni languages of the Wissel Lakes group within the West Trans New Guinea Linkage. On either side are two pitch-accent areas: (a) the Ekari language of the Wissel Lakes group and the Kamoro language of the Asmat family, and (b) Western Dani, also part of the West Trans New Guinea Linkage. There is also a pitch-accent area which spans the gap between the two tonal areas and includes North Asmat and Citak Asmat, languages on the northern edge of the Awyu-Dumut family, the Mek family, and the isolate Kaure. In the southwest, the Syiagha-Yenimu language of the Awyu-Dumut family bridges the gap between the two areas occupied by Marind languages.

The resulting distribution is interesting. Tone languages form two areas: a substantial continuous region in the east, and a much smaller region around Uhunduni in the west. Pitch-accent languages cluster around and between the two tonal regions. One pitch-accent region, consisting of East Strickland, Bosavi and West Kutubu, has the appearance of an enclave within the major tonal area. It is hard to avoid the inference that this geographic distribution is diachronically significant.

There are a number of groups for which I simply have no relevant information. These include several to the west and north-west of the Gulf of Papua. Since some Kiwai languages have pitch accent (Donohue 1997: 367–369) and Porome has some kind of low-functional-load tonal system (Martin Steer, pers. comm.), it would not be surprising if languages between them and other pitch-accent groups also had pitch accent.

Some of the decisions incorporated in the map have not been justified above. Groups with tonal members that are not discussed above are listed below:

Weri: This is a South-East Papuan language which is evidently a word-tone language (Boxwell and Maurice 1966).

Pawaian: Donohue (1993) classifies Pawaian as having syllable tone, but with the proviso that the sources (MacDonald 1973; Trefry 1969) are very limited.

Teberan: MacDonald (1973: 125, 128) says that Daribi is tonal, Polopa probably tonal.

Wiru: 'Phonologically, it is characterised by…a word-level tonal system with low functional load' (Wurm 1975a: 488).

Duna: Duna is tonal, probably with word tone (Lila San Roque, pers. comm.).

Awin-Pa: Voorhoeve (1975: 390) writes that there is some evidence that the language has contrastive pitch, possibly a high and a low tone.' This is one of the weakest cases on the map for counting a group as tonal.

Uhunduni: Voorhoeve (1975: 410) reports three tonemes: H, M and L.

Wolani and Moni: Voorhoeve (1975: 408–409) reports that the languages are tonal. Again, this is one of the weakest cases on the map for counting languages as tonal.

Groups with pitch-accent members that are not discussed above are listed below. The evidence tends to be rather flimsy.

Suena (Binandere): This language is simply reported to have a few minimal pairs based on tone or stress (Wilson 1969: 89–90).

Bosavi: Bosavi itself seems to have a system similar to Fasu (Schieffelin and Feld 1998).

East Strickland: Nomad is said to have 'contrastive pitch' (Voorhoeve 1975: 391).

Syiagha-Yenimu: Donohue (2004) notes that this Awyu-Dumut language has pitch accent.

Asmat: Donohue (1993) cites evidence from Drabbe (1953) and from his own fieldnotes suggesting that Kamoro has a system similar to Una. Northern and Citak Asmat varieties also seem to have pitch accent (Donohue 1997).

West Dani: Donohue (2004) reports evidence of possible pitch accent from his own fieldnotes.

Ekari: Donohue (2004) cites Drabbe's (1952: 4–5) brief account of a tonal phenomenon which appears to be some kind of pitch accent. Voorhoeve (1975: 407) says that the language is tonal.

Iha: Pitch accent in Iha is described by Donohue and Brown (1999).

4 A closer look

In this section I will take a closer look at word-tone systems in two TNG Highlands families: Engan, represented by East Kewa, and Kainantu-Goroka, represented by Fore, Move and Usarufa. In §4.3 I compare the two types of word-tone system represented by these families.

4.1 Engan

4.1.1 More on East Kewa

East Kewa nouns were introduced in §3.1. Three of the five tone classes of nouns have two basic realisations, one following a high trigger, the other elsewhere.

Since finite verbs are clause-final, they do not determine the realisation of the following word, but all other word-classes which are realised as phonological words do. For example, the otherwise homophonous temporal adverbs *ábálá* 'first (of all)' and *abala* 'yesterday' contrast in word tone. They carry H and L tone respectively.

(13) a. *ábálá rógōma áda-wa*
first clay see-1S-NRPAST
'First I saw the clay.'

b. *abala rogoma áda-wa*
yesterday clay see-1S-NRPAST
'Yesterday I saw the clay.'

The adverb *ábálá* in (13a) provides a high trigger which causes the following word to appear with its high-trigger HL tone melody as *rógōma* ('clay'). After *abala* in (13b) it occurs with its basic L melody as *rogoma* (cf. Table 1).

Verbs also have a high-trigger variant. The verb *áda-wa* in (13a) and (13b) is the high-trigger variant because the preceding noun *rogoma* 'clay' is a class B item with a floating H tone which serves as high trigger for the verb (§3.1). The basic variant is *ada-wa*, which occurs in (14) following *maa* 'taro', the basic (L) variant of a class A noun.

(14) *abala maa ada-wa*
yesterday taro see-1S-NRPAST
'Yesterday I saw the taro.'

Notice that the high-trigger effect is recursive. Thus in *ábálá máá áda-wa* 'First I saw the taro', *ábálá* 'first' triggers the high-trigger variant *máá* 'taro', and this in turn triggers the high-trigger variant *áda-wa* 'I saw'.

My research on East Kewa verbs is in its infancy, but there appear to be only three tone-melody classes of verb root, corresponding in their tone melodies to noun classes A, B and C (except that verbal class B has no floating tone). By default, the tone melody of a verbal desinence is determined by that of the root to which it is attached, and the resulting verb–desinence tonal combinations are shown in Table 4. Each tone pattern has two parts. The first represents the tone of the root, the second the default tone of its desinences.

TABLE 4: East Kewa verbs

tone class	verb	gloss	basic tone melody	tone melody after H trigger
A	*pona*	'cut'	LL-L(L)	HH-H(H)
	na	'eat'	L-L(L)	H-H(L)
B	*ada*	'see'	LL-L(L)	HL-L(L)
	ruma	'climb up'	LL-L(L)	HL-L(L)
C	*rubá*	'throw out'	LH-(H)L	LH-(H)L

Parentheses in the tonal representations of the desinences in Table 4 take account of the fact that some desinences have one syllable, others two. Two sets of desinences are shown in Table 5 (there are other sets: see Yarapea 2004). Singular desinences are monosyllabic and thus have the tone pattern indicated by the unparenthesised tones in Table 4. Non-singular desinences are disyllabic and have the tone pattern which includes the parenthesised tones.

TABLE 5: Verbal desinences		
person and number	NEAR PAST	PRESENT PROGRESSIVE
1S	*-wa*	*-lo*
2S	*-e*	*-le*
3S	*-a*	*-la*
1D	*-apa*	*-lepà*
2/3D	*-ape*	*-lepè*
1P	*-ama*	*-lemà*
2/3P	*-ame*	*-lemè*

Table 5 shows that the final syllable of present progressive non-singular desinences is low tone, marked here by a grave accent. This low tone is **not** overridden by the default non-singular -HH desinence melody following the high-trigger variant of a class A root like *pona* 'cut'.[17] Contrast (15a), with a -HH near past desinence, with (15b), where the final desinence tone of the present progressive remains low, giving HL.

(15) a. *ímú=mí póná-ámé*
FREE:3P=ERG cut-3P.NRPAST
'They cut (it).'
b. *ímú=mí póná-léme*
FREE:3P=ERG cut-3P.PRES
'They are cutting (it).'

Usually, the first syllable of a desinence has the same tone as the final syllable of the root, as illustrated in (16a), but verbs with a rising root, like *rubá* 'throw out', take singular desinences with L tone despite root-final H, as Table 4 shows and as illustrated in (16b).

(16) a. *né=mé ná=wá*
FREE:1S=ERG eat-1S.NRPAST
'I ate (it)'
b. *né=mé rubá=wa*
FREE:1S=ERG throw.out-1S.NRPAST
'I threw (it) out'

Each verb word, i.e. root + desinence combination, is a phonological word. There are combinations in Table 4 which diverge in two ways from the H, HL, L and LH melodies found in nouns. Class C combinations have an LHL tone melody, and these and the various high-trigger HL melodies require marking with an accent to show where the fall occurs. With roots of class A we find HHHL, as in *wárá́á-rípa* 's/he touched' in (17a),[18] but HLLL occurs with roots of class B, as in *rúma-leme* 'they are climbing' in (17b).

[17] Table 4 shows that not all class A roots have an -HH desinence melody after a high trigger. The root *na* 'eat' has -HL. This is not yet properly understood.

[18] The desinence *-rípa* belongs to a variant paradigm which occurs with roots in /-aa/.

(17) a. *ipú=mí* *wáráá-rípa*
FREE:3S=ERG touch-3S.NRPAST
's/he touched (it)'

b. *ímú=mí* *rúma-leme*
FREE:3P=ERG climb-3P.PRES
'they are climbing (it)'

Until this point, I have written simply of 'word tone'. This works fine for nouns, because an enclitic (e.g. the 'ergative' enclitic *=me*) simply takes the tone of the noun to which it is attached. But this classification (adopted by the Franklins in their analysis of West Kewa) can only be sustained with regard to verb roots, not the words formed from them.

There are several possible descriptive approaches to this situation. The simplest is to treat the tonal analysis of nouns and verbs separately, with five classes of nouns and three classes of verb roots, treating verb words as root + desinence combinations in which each constituent has its own tone melody, even though the desinence melody may be determined by the root melody.

Differences between noun and verb paradigms are crosslinguistically quite common. The larger the paradigm, the greater the burden on memory and the greater the probability of regularity. The smaller the paradigm, the less the memory burden and the greater the probabilities of more morphological and/or tonal subcategories and of irregularity and lexicalisation. Verbs tend to have larger paradigms than nouns, with the consequence that the two lexical categories go in different directions (Richard Rhodes 1987 and pers. comm.).

4.1.2 Other Engan languages

Kewa is a member of the Engan group of languages, which also includes Mendi, Sau, Huli, Ipili and Enga. There are dictionaries of West Kewa (Franklin and Franklin 1978), Huli (Rule 1971) and Enga (Lang 1978) and grammars of West Kewa (Franklin 1971), East Kewa (Yarapea 2004) and Huli (Rule 1974; Lomas 1988). The Huli and Enga dictionaries mark tone on entries, but the West Kewa dictionary doesn't. The West Kewa grammar, on the other hand, discusses tonal processes whereas the others don't.

The brief account in Lang (1978) indicates that Enga has three tone melodies, H, HL and LH. No information is available on how tone works with verbs or on other tonal processes.

For Huli, Rule (1974) describes three tones: level, high falling and low rising. He describes the level tone as 'a level mid tone over the whole word'. I take this to be H. Non-finally, his high falling tone is high, but utterance-finally it is high on all syllables except the last, which is low. I interpret this as HL. Non-finally, his low rising tone is low on all syllables except the last, which is high, but utterance-finally it remains low throughout. I interpret this as LH. These interpretations are strengthened by Lomas' (1988) findings, which are accompanied by mingograms. Lomas has a fourth tone, LHL, but this seems to me to reflect overdifferentiation of HL. His findings are largely based on citation forms, and this is problematic. Thus Huli, like Enga, probably has three tone melodies, interpreted here as H, HL and LH.

Franklin (1975) provides a comparative wordlist with 99 items as a starting point for reconstructing Proto Engan. Impressionistically, the degree of difference among the Engan lists is of a similar order to lists for the Romance languages, and the task of establishing sound correspondences and reconstructing Proto Enga would be a relatively straightforward one. However, only Enga items are marked for tone, and so the list cannot be used for tonal reconstruction.

TABLE 6: Engan tonal correspondences (nouns)

gloss	East Kewa	Enga	Huli
	Basic L	HL	H[a]
'man	aa	akáli	ágálí
'taro'	maa	máa	máá
'room'	pada	páda	árá
'we'	naa	—	náá
'hand'	kii	kíŋi	gî
'I'	ne	—	î
	Basic L^H	LH	??
'leg'	aa	kapé	—
'neck'	maa	maŋé	maá
'egg'	kapaa	kapá	hábane
'house'	ada	adá	ádá
'clay'	rogoma	—	dóŋómá
'maternal aunt'	papa	—	papá
	Basic LH	H?	??
'garden'	eé	éé	—
'banana'	kaí	—	háí
's/he'	ipú		íbú
'lizard'	kaú	—	gaú
'steam'	popó	—	pópo
	Basic HL	HL?	LH?
'bird'	yáa	yáka	egá

[a] HL on monosyllables.

Table 6 shows a few tonal correspondences for nouns in East Kewa, Enga and Huli, compiled from my East Kewa data and from the data in Lang (1978) and Rule (1971). There is a perfect tonal correspondence between East Kewa and Engan for the small number of available pairs, but no obvious correspondence between Huli and the other two languages. Unfortunately, verbs are given in the Enga dictionary in a form that is not appropriate for investigating correspondences.

4.2 Kainantu-Goroka

In §3.3 I discussed Fore and Usarufa. Both are members of the Kainantu-Goroka family, whose member languages, roughly from east to west, are Waffa, Tairora, Binumarien, Gadsup-Agarabi, Awa, Auyana-Usarufa, Fore, Gimi, Kamano-Yagaria, Benabena, Gahuku-Asaro, Yabiyufa and Siane. The first six are described in a set of articles published as McKaughan (1973b), and there are dictionaries of Awa and Fore with tones marked (Loving and Loving 1975; Scott 1980). It is not clear whether Waffa and Tairora are tonal (Tairora is said to have lexical stress), and the only one of these six languages for which tone and tonal processes have been reasonably well described is the Usarufa dialect of Auyana-Usarufa (Bee 1973; Bee and Glasgow 1973; Ford 1996). The remaining languages from Fore to Siane probably constitute a subfamily. Aspects of tone in Usarufa, Fore, Gimi and Kamano-Yagaria are variously described in comparative perspective in the largely unpublished work of Kevin Ford (see references). Fore tone is also discussed by Scott (1978, 1990) and Siane by James (1994).[19] Most of the data and analysis in this section are due to Ford, and are from Fore, from the Move dialect of Kamano-Yagaria, and from Usarufa.

As I foreshadowed in association with the description of the tonal system of Fore nouns in §3.3.1, there are a number of differences between the tone systems of East Kewa (Engan) and the Kaintantu-Goroka languages. Engan languages have a fixed set of tone melodies, regardless of the number of syllables in a root or word. The set of tone melodies increases in Kaintantu-Goroka languages with each additional syllable in a word (§3.3). Triggers in Kaintantu-Goroka languages work differently from East Kewa and so, in certain respects, do verb + desinence combinations.

The most complex of the Kainantu-Goroka systems for which data and analysis are available is the Move dialect of Kamano-Yagaria, as recorded by Ford (1996). Here there are four kinds of trigger: L, H1, H2 and Hf. The effect of L is the same as in Fore: the rest of the phrase is low tone, as in (18).

(18) *sóko*^{L} *kayále* > *sóko kayale*
nice pig
'a nice pig'

The effect of H1 and H2 is the same as in Fore, except that they not only place a high tone on the first or second syllable of the next word but also on all remaining syllables in the phrase.[20]

(19) a. *ve*^{H1}*-maʔ kayále* > *ve-má káyálé*
man-DEF pig
'the man's pig'

b. *yoʔ*^{H2}*-a-maʔ vitíʔ* > *yoʔ-a-má pítíʔ*
house-his-DEF from
'from his house'

[19] There are other descriptive materials on some of these languages, but none deals with tone.

[20] A further complication is that Move has an extra-high surface tone which occurs when an already high tone is affected by a H trigger.

The Move Hf trigger does not occur in Fore. Its effect is to place a high tone on the final syllable of the phrase:

(20) *aʔ*^{Hf} *kayále > a kayalé*
female pig
'a sow'

It is worth noting in passing that the effects of the various H triggers in Fore and Move bear some resemblance to those in certain Bantu languages reported by Kisseberth and Odden (2003: 62-63). They describe cases of both tone-spreading and tone-shifting, including unbounded rightward shift in Zigula, where H shifts to the penultimate syllable of the word in much the same way as Move Hf shifts to the final syllable of the phrase. However, the domain of the Bantu processes appears to be the word, whereas in Fore and Move it is the phrase. Consequently, the affected H occurs lexically on a syllable of the Bantu word, whereas in Fore and Move it floats.

Usarufa resembles Fore and Move and also has a lexicalised trigger (Ford 1996). The first lexical item of each of (21a)–(21c) has H tone, but the superscripted trigger differs and has different perturbation effects on the rest of the phrase. L and H1 are similar to Move L and H1. L renders all further syllables low tone in (21a) and (22a). H1 loses its own high tone, but places a high tone on the next and all following syllables in (21b) and (22b). H1x differs from H1 in that an item with an H1x trigger retains its own final H, as in (21c).

(21) Waigaʔ Usarufa (Ford 1996)

a. *pó*^{L} *bi ma > póbima*
pig DEF in
'in the pig'

b. *máN*^{H1} *yáa*^{H1} *bi ma > maʔyábímá*
this grave DEF in
'in this grave'

c. *yóN*^{H1x} *bi ma > yópímá*
garden DEF in
'in the garden'

(22) Kágu Usarufa (Bee 1973: 279)

a. *nokááN*^{L} *aáwaʔ-ma > nokáán-aawaʔa*
night food-N
'food for the night'

b. *miN*^{H1} *aáwaʔ-ma > min-ááwáʔá*
that food-N
'that food'

Ford shows that other dialects of Kamano-Yagaria, as well as the Gimi language, each have their own trigger patterns. James' (1994: 144-145) examples suggest that Siane has at least an H1f trigger. Otherwise, the remaining Kainantu-Goroka languages have yet to be investigated in this regard.

Verbs in Move show a pattern whereby the tone on some desinences is determined by a root trigger. At the same time, however, desinences have their own tone and vary as to whether this is changed by co-occurrence with a given root. The desinence may also determine the tone of the root.

A small sample from Ford (1991), who identifies four root classes, is given in Table 7. The fourth class, represented by *eli* 'take hold', has an H2 trigger which places a H on the second or only syllable of the desinence, unless the desinence is 'resistant', like the non-singular desinences of East Kewa (tonal superscript *res*). One desinence, 1S.PAST, has a retroactive L trigger which makes the root entirely low tone.

TABLE 7: Move (Kamano-Yagaria) verbs

verb	gloss	tone	1S.PAST ^{L}-HL^{res}	1S.FUT -HL^{res}	ANTERIOR -(L)L	PARTIC -L	1S.DESID -LLH	2S.IMPER -L
begí	'beat'	-H	*begi-dúe*	*begí-súe*	*begí-oge*	*begí-te*	*begí-sumená*	*begí-o*
hápái	'tell'	-HH	*hapai-dúe*	*hápái-súe*	*hápái-oge*	*hápái-te*	*hápái-sumená*	*hápái-o*
toló	'leave'	-LH	*tolo-dúe*	*toló-súe*	*tolo-ge*	*toló-te*	*toló-sumená*	*tolo*
eli	'grab'	-L^{H2}	*eli-dúe*	*eli-súe*	*eli-ogé*	*eli-té*	*eli-suména*	*eli-ô*

Two forms in the table do not adhere to these tone melodies. They are *tolo-ge* 'leave-PARTIC' and *tolo* 'leave-2S.IMPER'. The reason appears to be that the desinences are *-o-* initial and L, and that this vowel coalesces with the final H *-o-* of the stem, L winning out.

The interaction of stem classes and desinences in Usarufa is more complicated. A sample is shown in Table 8.[21] The data are from Bee (1973: 271–278), who call these forms 'diagnostic sets', i.e. the rest of the paradigm can be predicted if these forms are known. Bee's three classes are not defined by tone, and the only effect of stem tone here is in the 3S.PRES form in *-iye*, where a stem with no high tone places a H on the second syllable of the desinence, as in *a-iyé* 's/he is shooting' and *na-iyé* 's/he is eating'.

The criteria for the three classes are these. Class 1 stems place L tone on the PAST marker /-ra/ where Class 2 stems place H tone. Class 3 stems are considered 'constant' by Bee, but they are apparently resistant only to the retroactive H trigger of *-n-iye* 3S.FUT, and not to the retroactive L trigger of /-o/ 2S.IMPER.[22]

As Bee points out, cutting across the unpredictable lexical classification into Classes 1, 2 and 3 is another unpredictable classification, one which places either H or L on /-o/ 2S.IMPER.

The Usarufa system is similar to the Move system in that there is a tonal interaction between stem and desinence and that a desinence may have a tonal effect on the stem. It

[21] There are morphophonemic changes entailing stem truncation, interaction of a stem-final consonant -N or *-ʔ* with the affix-initial consonant, (including tone changes before *-kao* 2D.IMPER), and the replacement of stem-final *-o* by *-i* in 3S.FUT forms which lie beyond the scope of this discussion.

[22] The form *káráá-kao* 2D.IMPER probably receives H on the stem-final vowel as a result of the interaction of stem-final *-ʔ* with the desinence *-kao*, which also causes changes in the final vowel of other stems.

differs from it insofar as there is no tonal consistency among the stems of a trigger class (the classes are entirely lexical) and there are cross-cutting trigger classes.

Ford (1996) gives a number of noun cognate sets, marked for tone, for the Huva and Move dialects of Kamano-Yagaria, Gimi (a close relative of Fore) and Waigaʔ Usarufa. A sample is given in Table 9. I have generally chosen sets that include Usarufa cognates, but the level of cognation between Huva, Move and Gimi is considerably higher than between any of them and Usarufa. I have also added Awa and Tairora cognates from Bee (1971) and McKaughan (1973a) and some Awa cognates from Loving and Loving (1975). Awa and Tairora have even fewer items cognate with Huva, Move and Gimi than does Usarufa, in part a product of greater distance. Some of the Tairora items are difficult to recognise as cognate, but they display regular correspondences with Usarufa and Awa (Bee 1971; Ross 1997).

TABLE 8: Kágu Usarufa verbs

	verb	gloss	3S.PRES -LL	3S.PAST -L-LL	3S.FUT ^{H}-LL	2D.IMPER -LL	2S.IMPER ^{L}-L or ^{L}-H
1	*ámiN*	'give him'	*ámi-e*	*ámi-ka-iye*	*amí-n-iye*	*ámê-kao*	*ami-ó*
	íta	'hear'	*íta-iye*	*íta-ra-iye*	*itá-n-iye*	*ítáa-kao*	*itaa-o*
	agátá	'turn' TR	*agátá-iye*	*agáta-ra-iye*	*agatá-n-iye*	*agátáa-kao*	*agata-ó*
	káútóʔ	'burn' TR	*káút-íye*	*káú-ta-iye*	*kautí-n-iye*	*káútô-kao*	*kautu-o*
2	*atáeN*	'chop'	*atá-iye*	*ata-ká-iye*	*ataí-n-iye*	*atáe-kao*	*atai-ó*
	aa	'shoot'	*a-iyé*	*a-rá-iye*	*á-niye*	*aa-kao*	*aa-ó*
	púráN	'peel'	*púrá-iye*	*pú-ká-iye*	*purá-n-iye*	*púráá-kao*	*puraa-ó*
	na	'eat'	*na-iyé*	*na-rá-iye*	*ná-n-iye*	*naa-kao*	*naa-o*
3	*káraʔ*	'cut'	*kára-iye*	*kára-ta-iye*	*kára-n-iye*	*káráá-kao*	*karaa-o*

I have not worked out tonal correspondences for Table 9, but there is clearly a reasonable hope of reconstructing proto-etyma with tone and with triggers here. Ford does not show triggers for Huva, although Huva nouns divide into two classes on the basis of trigger, unrelated to their own tone. Their triggers behave like the H1 and H2 triggers of Move. Gimi has three triggers, L, H1 and H2, which behave like their Fore counterparts.

4.3 A comparison of the Engan and Kainantu-Goroka systems

The Engan and Kainantu tonal systems are similar to the extent that

- both have word tone;
- non-verb items in both have tonal triggers affecting the following items within a phrase;
- and verbs consist of stem + desinence combinations in which the tone class of the stem may affect the tone of the desinence.

Table 9: Kainantu-Goroka tonal correspondences (nouns)

gloss	Huva	Move	Gimi	Usarufa	Awa	Tairora
'path'	*kí?*	*kí?*^{H}	*?é?*^{L}	—	—	—
'rain'	*kó?*	*kó?*^{H}	*?aú*^{L}	*á?*^{H1}	*a?*	*á?u*
'tree'	*yá*	*yayá*^{H}	*yá*^{L}	*yáá*^{H1}	—	*katari*
'crack'	*kékópá*	*ekopá*^{H}	*?é?o*^{L}	*kekó?*^{H1}	—	—
'wife'	*náru?*	*nalú?*^{H}	*nalo*^{L}	*ná?*^{L}	—	—
'knee'	*-rá?ya*	*-léta*^{L}	*-láé*^{L}	*rayúɴ*^{H1}	*ərœu*	*tori*
'chicken'	*kokóre?*	*kokóle*^{L}	*?o?óle*^{L}	*kokóreɴ*^{L}	—	—
'cheek'	*-rámeta*	*-kálameta*^{L}	*-metá*^{L}	*-máráɴ*^{H1x}	—	—
'bird'	*mná*	*namá*^{H}	*nímí*^{L}	*numá*^{H1}	—	*numə*
'little finger'	*katré*	*katelé*^{L}	*a?así?*^{L}	—	—	—
'necklace'	*sesú*	*sesú*^{L}	*ásesú*^{L}	*padédu*^{L}	—	—
'bean pod'	*avoké*	*ávoka*^{L}	*abó?ea*^{L}	*kobáraɴ*^{L}	—	—
'egg'	*mú?*	*mú?*	*amú*^{Hf}	*ámú?*^{Hf}	—	—
'fly'	*ósí?*	*kosí?*^{H}	*?osí*^{Hf}	*wadí*^{H1}	—	—
'cockroach'	*hgánó?*	*hakanó?*^{H}	*a?anó*^{Hf}	*kawanó*^{H1}	—	—
'decoration'	*kónárí*	*konalí*^{H}	*onalí*^{Hf}	*konarirí*^{H1x}	—	—
'tree sp.'	*kraívá*	*kalaíva*^{L}	*alaibá*^{Hf}	*karawébá*^{L}	—	—
'sugarcane'	*éve*	*evé*^{H}	*yabí*^{Hf}	*yá?*^{H1}	*sà?*	*ká?ə*
'ear'	*-géta*	*-g′′eta*^{L}	*-?etá*^{Hf}	*-raraɴ*^{L}	*arĕ*	*ato*
'thigh'	*-rurú?*	*-lú*^{L}	*-ló?*^{Hf}	*-rú?*^{L}	*əru*	*-tədə*
'armpit'	*-kávé*	*-kavé*^{H}	*-?ábé*^{H1x}	*-ábéɴ*^{L}	*abé*	*akəmə*
'white'	*véyé?*	*veyé*^{H}	*béyé?*^{H1x}	*wayáɴ*^{H1x}	—	*e?ərə*
'star'	*óvú*	—	*óbú*^{H1x}	*wiyó?*^{H1x}	*wœyò?*	*vəho?ura*
'banana'	*égé*	*egé*^{H}	*yá?í*^{H1x}	*é?*^{H1}	—	*eta*
'tears'	*-aúni*	*-aúnú*^{H}	*-aúná*^{H1x}	*a?nú*^{H1}	*a?nu*	*əu?uru*

[a] HL on monsyllables.

There are, however, important differences between the systems:

- Engan languages have a fixed set of tone melodies, regardless of the number of syllables in a root or word. The set of tone melodies increases in Kaintantu-Goroka languages with each additional syllable in a word (§3.3).
- Tonal triggers in non-verb items and tonal conditioning of desinences by verb stems tend to be correlated with the tone of the final syllable of the trigger item or stem in East Kewa, but not in Kainantu-Goroka languages. There are two contrasting triggers, high and low, in East Kewa, which cause one of two tone melodies to be selected by the following word. The two available tone melodies are part of the phonological

structure of the word. In Kainantu-Goroka languages there are usually more than two contrasting triggers, and the effect of the trigger is not conditioned by the phonology of the affected word as it is in East Kewa.

- As far as I know at the moment, an East Kewa verb stem may condition the tone of its desinence, but not vice versa. In Move and Usarufa such retroactive conditioning does occur.

5 Concluding thoughts

More work is needed to do satisfactory reconstructions of Proto Engan and Proto Kainantu-Goroka, but there is no doubt that these tasks could be successfully undertaken. The same is true of the reconstruction of Proto Chimbu-Wahgi, the language ancestral to the group that intervenes geographically between Engan and Kainantu-Goroka.[23] What is much less clear is whether the detailed reconstruction of a language ancestral to all three groups is feasible and whether their most recent common ancestor is Proto TNG or a more recent interstage. Initial inspection shows cognacy in pronouns, some verbal desinences and a few basic verb roots, but not a great deal more. But I remarked earlier that little further progress can be made with this larger task before progress has been made with careful reconstruction of local groups.

Donohue (2004) reminds us that tone, whether word tone or syllable tone, is an areal phenomenon, and that maintenance or loss of tone in a given language depends on whether neighbouring languages are tonal or not. The map reflects this: it is significant that there are no tonal outliers and only two putative pitch-accent outliers, Iha to the west and Suena to the east. Donohue points out that syllable tone languages foster the genesis of syllable tone in their neighbours, presumably via multilingualism. However, tone systems which develop in this way are not arbitrary. When a language acquires tone, it does so through the transphonologisation of existing phonetic features. For example, phonetic high and low pitch following voiceless and voiced onsets respectively are reinterpreted as tone (and the onset voicing distinction may then be lost). This means that a tone system is not diachronically arbitrary. It may reflect an earlier tone system or it may reflect some other set of phonological contrasts from which tone developed. There is some risk, then, that if we reconstruct tone, we are actually reconstructing the set of features from which tone arose, rather than tone itself.

Bearing this caveat in mind, the fact that there are tonal subgroups located in the region where Proto TNG is most likely to have been spoken suggests that Proto TNG or quite an early TNG interstage was tonal or had a set of features ancestral to modern tone. This areality almost certainly reflects that fact that the presence of many tone languages cheek to cheek has fostered the maintenance of (mostly) word tone. The fact that pitch-accent languages occur in clusters adjacent to the main tonal area suggests that they are descended from tone languages but that their systems have been simplified as a result of being on the periphery of the region and having fewer tonal neighbours.

[23] A preliminary collection of Chimbu-Wahgi cognate sets shows a level of relationship similar to that of the Engan or Kainantu-Goroka languages.

Can we make any inferences as to what sort of system Proto or early TNG had? The evidence suggests that it was either word tone, or syllable tone with a tendency towards word-tone-like patterning like we find in Telefol, or a set of features ancestral to one of these.

We can also make inferences about Proto TNG grammar which have a bearing on tone. It is likely that it was SOV and postpositional, and that the first word of a phrase affected the tone of the rest of the phrase. Exactly how this worked, however, it is hard to say. Evidence from East Kewa suggests that trigger systems arise through the effect of a word-final H or L on what follows, but that this effect sometimes becomes lexicalised, such that when the tone of the triggering word changes over time, its lexicalised trigger effect remains unchanged, at least for a while. This in turn implies that trigger systems are not very stable, prone to change (internal comparison of Kainantu-Goroka languages suggests this) and unlikely to be reconstructable beyond quite shallow time depths.

It is also likely that Proto TNG had complex paradigms of suffixed desinences which indicated subject person/number agreement, tense, aspect and mood, and that the tonal behaviour of the verb was different from that of the noun. Since the verb was clause-final, it did not serve as a trigger. But since it was composed of stem + desinence combinations, one can reasonably infer that the tone of the stem would have affected the tone of the desinences. I suspect that we will never be able to do more than reconstruct elements of desinences, as the desinences themselves tend to be products of processes of grammaticisation and erosion which are repeated cyclically to maintain the system. And if we cannot reconstruct the desinences, then we cannot reconstruct their tones!

To pull the threads together, reconstructions of the histories of local groups within TNG, including tonal histories, are doable. Only when this work is well progressed will it be possible to determine how much higher-level reconstruction is possible, but I would be surprised if higher-level tonal reconstruction were possible because of the cyclic processes with which it is associated.

References

Bee, Darlene, 1971. Comparative and historical problems in East New Guinea Highland languages. *Pacific Linguistics*, A-6:1–37.

——, 1973. Usarufa : a descriptive grammar. In Howard McKaughan, ed., *The languages of the Eastern Family of the East New Guinea Highland Stock*, 225–323. Seattle: University of Washington Press.

——, and Kathleen Barker Glasgow, 1973. Usarufa tone and segmental phonemes. In Howard McKaughan, ed., *The languages of the Eastern Family of the East New Guinea Highland Stock*, 190–203. Seattle: University of Washington Press.

Bellwood, Peter, 1997. Prehistoric cultural explanations for the existence of widespread language families. In Patrick McConvell and Nicholas Evans, eds, *Archaeology and linguistics: Aboriginal Australia in global perspective*, 123–134. Melbourne: Oxford University Press.

Boxwell, Helen, and Boxwell Maurice, 1966. Weri phonemes. *Pacific Linguistics*, A-7:77–93.

Chida, Shuntaro, 2003. On the tone of the Dom language. Unpublished typescript.

Denham, T.P., S.G. Haberle, C. Lentfer, T. Fullagar, J. Field, M. Therin, and B. Porch. N.and Winsborough, 2003. Origins of agriculture at Kuk swamp in the Highlands of New Guinea. *Science*, 301:189–193.

Diamond, Jared, and Peter Bellwood, 2003. Farmers and their languages: the first expansions. *Science*, 300:597–603.

Donohue, Mark, 1993. Tone systems in New Guinea. Unpublished paper, Research School of Pacific and Asian Studies, Australian National University.

——, 1997. Tone systems in New Guinea. *Linguistic Typology*, 1:347–386.

——, 2004. Tone and the Trans New Guinea languages. Paper presented to the international symposium *Cross-linguistic Studies of Tonal Phenomena: Historical Development, Tone-syntax interface, and Descriptive Studies*, December 2004, Research Institute for Languages and Cultures of Asia and Africa, Tokyo University of Foreign Studies.

——, and Lea Brown, 1999. Ergativity: some additions from Indonesia. *Australian Journal of Linguistics*, 19:57–76.

Drabbe, P., 1953. *Spraakkunst van de Kamoro-taal.* The Hague: Martinus Nijhoff.

Drabbe, Peter, 1952. *Spraakkunst can het Ekagi.* 's-Gravenhage: Martinus Nijhoff.

Foley, William A., 1986. *The Papuan languages of New Guinea.* Cambridge: Cambridge University Press.

——, 2000. The languages of New Guinea. *Annual Review of Anthropology*, 29:357–404.

Ford, Kevin, 1991. Hua-Filigano tonal correspondences. Unpublished manuscript, University of Papua New Guinea, Waigani.

, 1996. Comparative study of the borderland of the East-Central and Eastern families of the East New Guinea Highlands Stock. Unpublished typescript, University of Papua New Guinea, Waigani.

Franklin, Karl J., 1971. *A grammar of Kewa, New Guinea.* Canberra: Pacific Linguistics.

——, 1975. Comments on Proto-Engan. In S.A. Wurm, ed., *New Guinea area languages and language study*, 263–275. Canberra: Australian National University. (Pacific Linguistics C-38.)

——, and Joice Franklin, 1978. *A Kewa dictionary, with supplementary grammatical and anthropological materials.* Canberra: Pacific Linguistics.

Gussenhoven, Carlos, 2004. *The phonology of tone and intonation.* Cambridge: Cambridge University Press.

Hardie, Peter, 2003. *Is Kuman tonal? An account of basic segmental and tonological structure the Papuan language Kuman.* M.A. thesis, Australian National University.

Healey, Alan, 1964. *Telefol phonology.* Canberra: Pacific Linguistics.

Huisman, Ronald, and Joy Lloyd, 1981. Angaatiha tone, stress and length. In Phyllis M. Healey, ed., *Angan languages are different: four phonologies*, 63–82. Huntington Beach CA: Summer Institute of Linguistics.

James, Dorothy J., 1994. Word tone in a Papuan language: an autosegmental solution. *Language and linguistics in Melanesia*, 25:125–148.

Kisseberth, Charles, and David Odden, 2003. Tone. In Derek Borse and Gérard Philippson, eds, *The Bantu languages*, 59–70. London: Routledge.

Lang, Adrianne, 1978. *Enga dictionary*. Canberra: Pacific Linguistics.

Lomas, G.C.J., 1988. *The Huli language of Papua New Guinea*. Ph.D thesis, Macquarie University.

Loving, Richard, and Aretta Loving, 1975. *Awa dictionary*. Canberra: Pacific Linguistics. (Pacific Linguistics C-30.)

MacDonald, George E., 1973. The Teberan language family. In Karl J. Franklin, ed., *The linguistic situation in the Gulf District and adjacent areas, Papua New Guinea family*, 118–148. Canberra: Pacific Linguistics.

May, Jean, and Eunice Loeweke, 1965. The phonological hierarchy in Fasu. *Anthropological Linguistics*, 7/5:87–97.

McElhanon, K.A., and C.L. Voorhoeve, 1970. *The Trans-New Guinea phylum: explorations in deep level genetic relationships*. Canberra: Pacific Linguistics.

McKaughan, Howard, 1973a. A study of divergence in four New Guinea languages. In Howard McKaughan, ed., *The languages of the Eastern Family of the East New Guinea Highland Stock*, 694–738. Seattle: University of Washington Press.

——, ed., 1973b. *The languages of the Eastern Family of the East New Guinea Highlands stock*. Seattle: University of Washington Press.

Nettle, Daniel, 1999. *Linguistic diversity*. Oxford: Oxford University Press.

Nichols, Johanna, 1992. *Linguistic diversity in space and time*. Chicago: Chicago University Press.

——, 1997. Modeling ancient population structures and movement in linguistics. *Annual Review of Anthropology*, 26:359–384.

Pawley, Andrew, 1995. C.L. Voorhoeve and the Trans New Guinea Phylum hypothesis. In Connie Baak, Mary Bakker, and Dick van, der Meij, eds, *Tales from a concave world: liber amicorum Bert Voorhoeve*. Leiden: Department of Languages and Cultures of South-East Asia and Oceania, Leiden University.

——, 1998. The Trans New Guinea Phylum hypothesis: a reassessment. In Jelle Miedema, Cecilia Odé, and Rien A.C. Dam, eds, *Perspectives on the Bird's Head of Irian Jaya, Indonesia: Proceedings of the Conference, Leiden, 13–17 October 1997*. Leiden: Department of Languages and Cultures of South-East Asia and Oceania, Leiden University.

——, 2001. The Proto Trans New Guinea obstruents: arguments from top-down reconstruction. In Andrew Pawley, Malcolm Ross, and Darrell Tryon, eds, *The boy from Bundaberg: Studies in Melanesian linguistics in honour of Tom Dutton*, 261–300. Canberra: Pacific Linguistics.

——, Forthcoming. The chequered career of the Trans New Guinea hypothesis: recent research and its implications. In Andrew Pawley, Robert Attenborough, Robin Hide, and Jack Golson, eds, *Papuan Pasts: Investigations into the cultural, linguistic and biological history of the Papuan speaking peoples*. Canberra: Pacific Linguistics.

Pike, Eunice V., 1964. The phonology New Guinea Highlands languages. In James B. Watson, ed., *New Guinea: the Central Highands*, 121–132. (American Anthropologist 66/4, Part 2.)

Rhodes, Richard, 1987. Paradigms large and small. *Berkeley Linguistics Society*, 13:223–234.

Ross, Malcolm, 1995. The great Papuan pronoun hunt: recalibrating our sights. In Connie Baak, Mary Bakker, and Dick van, der Meij, eds, *Tales from a concave world: liber amicorum Bert Voorhoeve*, 139–168. Leiden: Department of Languages and Cultures of South-East Asia and Oceania, Leiden University.

——, 1996. Contact induced change and the comparative method: cases from Papua New Guinea. In Mark Durie and Malcolm Ross, eds, *The comparative method reviewed: regularity and irregularity in language change*, 180–217. New York: Oxford University Press.

——, 1997. Preliminary report on the languages the Kainantu family. Unpublished typescript, Paupan Linguistics Project, Research School of Pacific and Asian Studies, Australian National University.

——, Forthcoming. Pronouns as a preliminary diagnostic for grouping Papuan languages. In Andrew Pawley, Robert Attenborough, Robin Hide, and Jack Golson, eds, *Papuan Pasts: Investigations into the cultural, linguistic and biological history of the Papuan speaking peoples*. Canberra: Pacific Linguistics.

——, In preparation a. Defining the Trans New Guinea family: preliminary evidence from pronouns. In Andrew Pawley, Malcolm Ross, and Meredith Osmond, eds, *Papuan languages and the Trans New Guinea family*. Canberra: Pacific Linguistics.

——, In preparation b. Pronouns as preliminary evidence for grouping Papuan languages. In Andrew Pawley, Malcolm Ross, and Meredith Osmond, eds, *Papuan languages and the Trans New Guinea family*. Canberra: Pacific Linguistics.

Rule, Murray, 1971. Huli-English English-Huli dictionary. Mimeo, The Huli Language Conference.

——, 1974. Statement of the phonology and grammar of the Huli language. Unpublished typescript, Asia-Pacific Christian Mission.

——, 1993. *The culture and language of the Foe-Lake Kutubu people of the Southern Highlands Province, Papua New Guinea*. Merewether, N.S.W.: The Author, for Chevron Niugini Ltd.

Schieffelin, Bambi B., and Steven Feld, 1998. *Bosavi–English–Tok Pisin dictionary (Papua New Guinea)*. Canberra: Pacific Linguistics.

Scott, Graham, 1978. *The Fore language of Papua New Guinea*. Canberra: Pacific Linguistics.

——, 1980. *Fore dictionary*. Canberra: Pacific Linguistics. (Pacific Linguistics B-62.)

——, 1990. A reanalysis of Fore accent. *La Trobe Working Papers in Linguistics*, 3:139–150.

Trefry, D., 1969. *A comparative study of Kuman and Pawaian, non-Austronesian languages of New Guinea*. Canberra: Pacific Linguistics. (Pacific Linguistics B-13.)

Voorhoeve, C.L., 1975. Central and western Trans-New Guinea phylum languages. In S.A. Wurm, ed., *New Guinea area languages and language study*, 345–459. Canberra: Pacific Linguistics. (Pacific Linguistics C-38.)

Wilson, Darryl, 1969. Suena phonology. *Pacific Linguistics*, A-18:87–93.

Wurm, S.A., 1975a. Eastern central Trans-New Guinea phylum languages. In S.A. Wurm, ed., *New Guinea area languages and language study*, 461–526. Canberra: Pacific Linguistics. (Pacific Linguistics C-38.)

——, ed., 1975b. *New Guinea area languages and language study*. Canberra: Pacific Linguistics.

Yarapea, Apoi Mason, 2004. *Morphosyntax of Kewapi*. Ph.D. thesis, Australian National University.

Yip, Moira, 2002. *Tone*. Cambridge: Cambridge University Press.

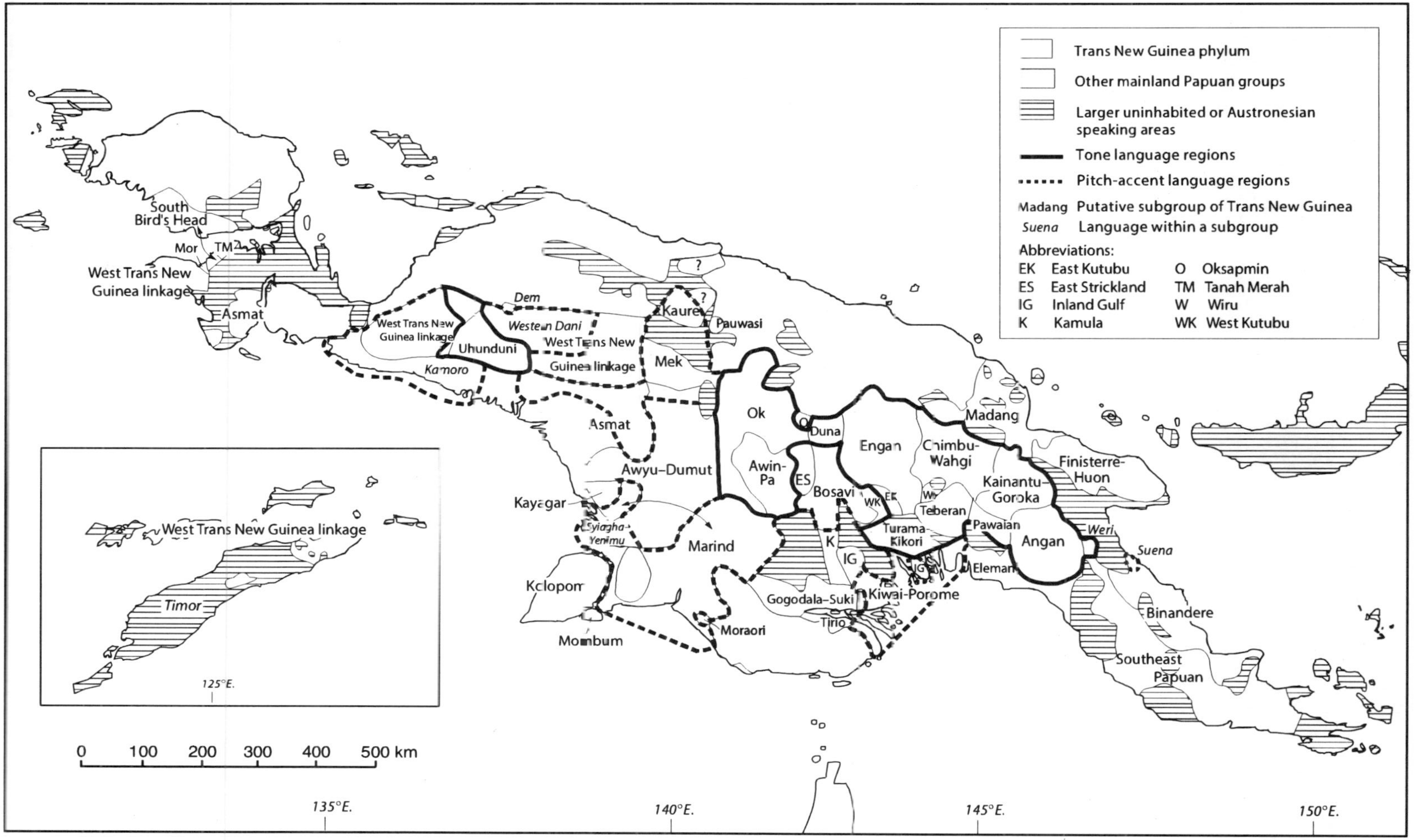

Map : Tone and pitch accent in the putative subgroups of the Trans New Guinea family

Tone and the Trans New Guinea languages

Mark Donohue

Centre for Research on Language Change, Australian National University

and

National University of Singapore

mark@donohue.cc

1. The distribution of tone in the Trans New Guinea family

In this paper I shall discuss mainly the question of categorising 'tone systems' into types, such as 'pitch accent', 'word tone' and 'syllable tone' (such as employed by Donohue 1997's examination of tone in New Guinea), and demonstrate that these 'types' are in fact arbitrary points in a multi-dimensional continuum that includes stress systems at one of its extremities. This finding is significant for an examination of tonality in New Guinea, since it implies that an attempt to map tonal distribution in New Guinea must also take account of the distribution of complex metrical systems.

In order to effectively make this point I must first address the geographic distribution of 'tone languages' in New Guinea, and offer some elaborations. Following a parametric account of tone language typology, I shall offer examples of the confusion between tone and stress systems in languages from New Guinea, or Trans New Guinea languages from the islands west of New Guinea.

Ross proposes that the distribution of different 'types' of suprasegmental systems in the Trans New Guinea family of New Guinea can be studied in isolation from the genetically unrelated non-Trans New Guinea languages of the area. This is a somewhat surprising approach to take, given the conclusions in Donohue (1997) which indicate that tone and pitch accent phenomena are, in New Guinea at least, not genetically stable features, but rather can mainly be predicted on the basis of areal membership, and being subject to tonogenesis on comparatively short notice, through the reinterpretation of existing phonological material, notably voicing contrasts and contrastive stress systems. Despite clear areal trends, to be exemplified in the sections that follow, Ross' study concludes that the distribution of different types in the Trans New Guinea family is far from random.

I shall not discuss the characterisation of Kewa or the other highland languages that Ross describes in depth, having no first-hand knowledge of these languages myself, nor of many of the descriptive conventions that Ross uses. Instead, I shall concentrate on the historical and geographical issues raised in the paper. I shall direct my comments towards three major points:

1. The distribution of different kinds of tone and pitch accent systems in the Trans New Guinea languages, and in New Guinea as a whole. This will in turn involve two things:

2. A revised typology of tone (/pitch accent) systems based on multiple binary features that better models the variation and apparent historical transformations we observe.
3. Discussion of the pitch accent / stress overlap, and (in some areas) reasons why there may be diachronic confusion between the two systems.

If a study should be restricted to one family, then Trans New Guinea would be the logical choice. The family is, even in its most conservative guise, spread over a much greater area of New Guinea than any other serious linguistic grouping, and so is most likely to show the kind of distance between component languages that can lead to differences of a historically interesting nature.

On the other hand membership in the Trans New Guinea phylum is controversial. For many of the languages outside the central(-east) cordillera the crucial regular correspondence sets in either bound morphological forms or core lexical items have not been demonstrated. I would support without hesitation approximately 80% of the proposed scope of the TNG family; but the edges, particularly in the west, are controversial. These discrepancies between family scopes are not obviously significant in terms of Ross' examination of the tonal behaviour of some specific 'core Trans New Guinea' language, an examination which centres about the main cordillera and the region to its south; but I suspect it should be significant. I shall return to this point in section 5.

More significantly, the distinction between 'tone' and 'pitch accent' systems is epiphenomenal, reflecting a set of terminologies that is left over from a period of phonological inquiry in which we had less understanding of the variation to be found across languages, and less appreciation of the extent to which different language 'types' simply represent descriptively convenient points on a continuum of variation. The variation extends to a treatment of the supposed divide between (metrical) stress languages and tonal languages. Showing this distinction to be epiphenomenal opens up the material to be investigated to the extent that a more meaningful characterisation of geographical and diachronic variation is possible.

2. The distribution of tone languages in (Trans) New Guinea

We know that the occurrence of different tone systems in New Guinea is not random, as Ross' map indicates. But it is not true that all tonal systems are on an equal footing with respect to areal behaviour and diachronic stability. Donohue (1997: 380-381) makes the following observations on the stability and borrowability of different types of prosodic systems:

> (1) Syllable tone systems both require areal support, and foster the spread of such systems in their contact with other languages.
>
> (2) Word tone systems require areal support from other tonal languages, and without it they change into other systems.

(3) Pitch accent systems can occur independently, not requiring the support of nearby tonality in surrounding languages. This is perhaps not surprising, given the formal similarity between pitch accent systems and stress systems, and the attested evolution of languages from one system to the other.

In short, we need to consider the following points in examining the distribution of pitch accent phenomena in New Guinea:

1. The location of attested 'pitch accent' languages.
2. The presence or absence in the area of languages described as having contrastive stress.
3. The presence or absence of languages in the area with other types of suprasegmental systems.

Crucially, these are all *areal* factors, not genetic ones. The processes of language change mean that the origin of a suprasegmental phenomenon such as tone in an area with what appears to be an exceptionally long history of contact is highly problematic, and that the reconstruction of these suprasegmental features is difficult, with multiple plausible rephonologisations available when we consider a range of languages and language families.

One example of such treatment can be found with Iria and Asienara, two languages of south-west New Guinea, found at the mouth of Arguni Bay.[1] These languages are part of the Asmat-Kamoro family, a family that shows tonal behaviour of the north-eastern languages, Kamoro and Citak Asmat (Drabbe 1953, 1958, Bromley 1973/1975, Voorhoeve 1965, 1980 and pc.). We would not, however, wish to assign these languages to a list of 'pitch accent' languages, since we do not have any data on their suprasegmental behaviour; all we do know is that they are separated from Asmat and Kamoro by the Mairasi and the other intrusive languages of the Etna Bay area; and that they are phonologically more conservative than their eastern relatives.[2] Since the more detailed reports of the languages neighbouring Iria and Asienara, namely Irarutu, Koiwai and Mairasi all indicate non-tonality, and since there is evidence of greater phonological and phonotactic complexity in the western Asmat-Kamoro languages than there is in the eastern languages, then the default assumption should be that they are not tonal

1 For geographic regions, see map 2.

2 Compare the following cognates, showing phonological reduction in Asmat and Kamoro compared to their western relatives Asienara and Iria:

	'pig'	'water'	'see'	'stone'	'hair'	'tree'	'leg'
Asienara	*oka*	*moya*	*borara*	*etara*	*fida*	*oyida*	*mavura*
Iria	*oʔa*	*moda*	*borara*	*etərə*	*hiə*	*ora*	*movura*
Kamoro	*oo*	*mi*	*(mam i-)*	*(omani)*	*wiri*	*ote*	*maw*
Asmat	*o*	*m(b)u*	*por*	*ek*	*fin*	*os*	*m(b)ay*

languages. The presence of suprasegmental pitch patterns in Kamoro and Citak Asmat must be an innovation of those languages, for whatever reasons.[3]

If we examine a distribution of contrastive pitch behaviour in the south-western New Guinea region, we find that, irrespective of genetic affiliation, languages can be expected to show pitch accent behaviour if one of the following conditions are met:

1. They are spoken in areas adjacent to the central cordillera, in the north of the south-west New Guinea area;
2. They are spoken in areas close to the (recent) Marind spread, in the south-west of the area (or they are themselves languages of the Marind family).
3. They are spoken in areas close to the (relatively recent) Ok spread, in the centre-east of the area (or they are themselves languages of the Ok family).

We find that the languages of the central area, the central and southern Asmat languages, all the remaining Awyu-Dumut languages, the Kayagar languages, and the far-flung western Asmat-Kamoro languages Iria and Asienara, do not show any pitch accent phenomena. On the other hand Kamoro and Citak Asmat are languages whose speakers have frequent contact with highlands peoples from the cordillera. Similarly, the northern Members of the Awyu-(N)Dumut family show clear pitch accent prosody, and are in contact with speakers of the western Ok languages to their immediate north (in the same area to which Citak extends), which the central and southern Awyu-(N)Dumut do not show suprasegmental phenomena. Clearly the presence of pitch accent in south-western New Guinea is best predicted on the basis of area, not genetic affiliation. This implies that pitch accent is not a stable marker of linguistic relatedness; the presence of pitch accent in those languages in this area show that it is best ascribed to contact, and not to being inherited from an ancestral language.[4]

Another area in which the characterisation of pitch phenomena in Trans New Guinea languages suggests areal effects is the south-east 'tail' of New Guinea. The Binandere family has not been thought of as showing any tonal behaviour. While Dutton (1975) shows that Koita is a language with contrastive stress, as are other languages of

---

3 Voorhoeve does not suggest that Central Asmat is tonal; as noted in Donohue (1997: 375), there are some words that appear to show pitch contrasts in Voorhoeve's data, but they are restricted to specialised ritual words (Voorhoeve, p.c.). This suggests strongly that pitch accent is not a part of the regular phonological inventory for Central Asmat. Similar non-phonemic contrastive segments are found in particular speech styles in other languages; for instance, the appearance of [ɬ] by Grizzly bears speaking in Takelma (Hymes 1979), or retroflex consonants being present only in the names of gods in the speech of Hindu Newaris.

4 Since there is such strong evidence of a central cordilleran pattern of pitch utilisation in word-tone systems, with a 'spillover' of pitch-accent to the south, it is surprising that Ross did not examine the languages to the north of the main range. The languages are not part of the TNG family, but are tonal with tone bearing a high contrastive load. Examples of such languages include Yetfa and Lepki, immediately north of, and in contact with, Mek languages from the highlands, and further away Kaure. See Map 3 for a complete picture of tonal patterns in New Guinea.

the South-east (such as Ömie: Austing and Upia 1975), Barai (closely related to Koita) is a problematic case. Olson (1975: 474) writes:

> Stress is contrastive on the word level and is defined as a combination of pitch, and either length or intensity. There are two contrastive pitch levels, high and low. To mark stress, high pitch combines with increased intensity and low pitch combines with length. Note the four possible combinations on the following two syllable words: **íko** *before*, **ikò** *sew*, **ìre** *food*, and **iré** *stand*.

This, combined with Wilson's (1971) description of pitch phenomena in Suena, and reports of the tonal behaviour found in Weri (Boxwell and Boxwell 1971, Goilala family – a possible historical link to the Koiari languages) (and the hesitations by Farr and Farr [1975], Farr [1999] on the analysis of pitch in Korafe), makes it appear that we cannot discount the role of pitch accent in the history of the languages of South-east New Guinea. As we go further south along the tail of New Guinea we find less and less evidence of any pitch accent or stress contrasts; the languages that do show these phenomena are all found in the centre and north of the 'tail'. That is, evidence of tone or pitch accent phenomena is found in areas (relatively, or historically) close to the main cordillera.

2.1 A revised picture of the distribution of tonal types in New Guinea

Taking the above comments into account we note the following major differences in a map of tonal behaviour in the Trans New Guinea languages:

- The domain of word tone languages extends from the far west of the main ranges to the far east, in the highlands (see, for instance, Drabbe 1952 and Doble on Ekari in the west, and papers such as Tida 2000, James 1994, and the collection in McKaughan 1973); only the Mek languages in the centre show any variation, being a family in which pitch accent patterns with a low functional load are probably found in all languages.
- Pitch accent behaviour is also found in the languages of the Bomberai peninsular, at the western edge of New Guinea.
- The TNG languages of the south-west of New Guinea are not tonal, except when individual languages are adjacent to language families with tonal phonologies.
- Some of the languages of the south-east tail, those close to the main cordillera, have pitch accent phonologies or else full tonal systems (most notably Weri, which appears to have one of the few unambiguous cases of syllable tone systems in New Guinea).

We can summarise this very simply: the distribution of pitch accent languages is entirely dependant on the distribution of word tone languages: amongst the TNG languages, tone is found in the central cordillera and in languages adjoining that area (a distribution that matches the appearance of tonal languages in otherwise non-tonal language families in New Guinea). That is, tonality in the TNG languages is very simply modelled by assuming the presence of tone systems in the central cordillera, with some spillage. Map 1 is reduced from Donohue (2003a).

Map 1. The distribution of Word tone and Pitch accent in the TNG languages

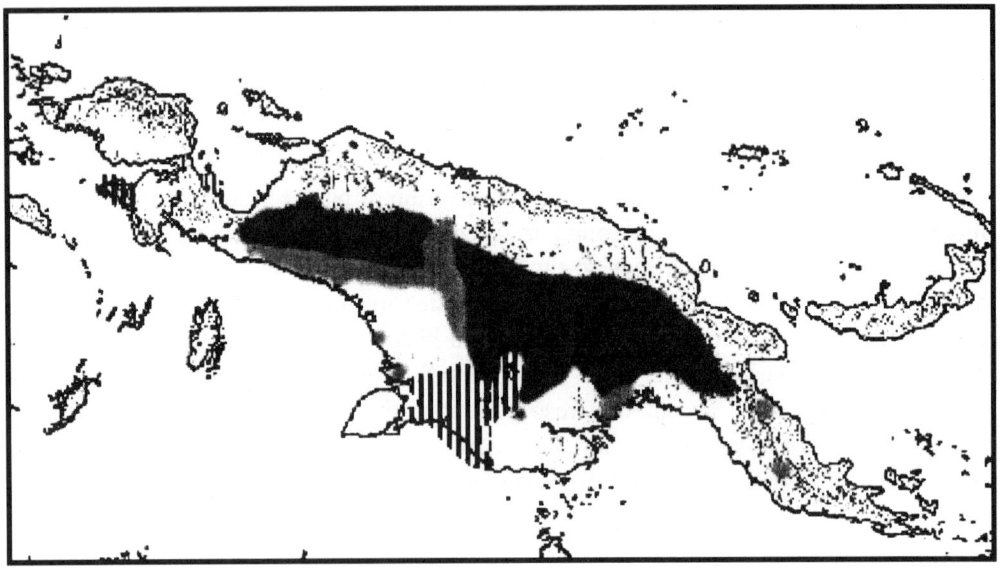

Dark: Trans New Guinea 'word-tone' systems
Light: Trans New Guinea 'pitch accent' systems
Vertical stripes: language families (Bomberai peninsula, Marind) with pitch accent systems, and whose status as Trans New Guinea languages is questionable.

Support for an areal, rather than genetic, model of pitch accent in TNG languages can be found in the presence of some as-yet unclassified tonal behaviour in the southernmost Madang group languages, and in the north-westernmost languages of the south-east. In these languages, members of genetic groupings that are not, on the whole, tonal, we find that the fringe languages, in contact with word tone languages of the central cordillera, have adopted tone systems.[5,6] The question we must ask is not why tone and tone-like phenomenon are borrowed, but why word tone systems are not borrowed. I return to this question in section 5.

---

5 The alternative hypothesis would be that, apart from the languages adjacent to the cordillera, all members of the low-level genetic groupings have lost tonal features. This second hypothesis requires a much greater number of independent innovations than does the first, but also relies on the areal support offered by the central cordilleran tone languages, and so still argues for areal factors dominating genetic ones as regards the distribution of tonal phenomena.

6 The only exception to this characterisation is the pitch-accent found in Bomberai languages. This reflects the complex mixed social-linguistic history of the Bomberai area, a point that I shall return to later in section 4.1.

3. Issues of analysis and categorisation

The distinction between languages with pitch accent systems and languages with tone systems has played a significant role in the mapping of tone in New Guinea. Donohue (1997) recognised three 'types', namely pitch accent, word tone and syllable tone, while acknowledging that there are intermediate cases between these descriptive 'norms'. Ross (2004) defined tone systems as including both 'word tone' and 'syllable tone' systems.

While it is sensible to distinguish between different kinds of suprasegmental behaviour, it is not so clear that this three-way dichotomy is the 'correct' division to make. As Ross notes, paraphrasing Donohue (1997), there are no sharp borders between 'pitch accent', 'word tone', and 'syllable tone' systems, with plenty of evidence being found to suggest that these are simply typologically stable (= cross-linguistically well attested) 'types' on a continuum of phonological association.

It is quite possible, indeed common, to find a language with a pitch accent system that shows a contrast between high and low pitch on monosyllables. All that is required, phonologically, is for words to allow for the possibility of being unaccented. Tokyo Japanese is one such language; if a word is not accented then the accentual HL melody will not be assigned, and in its stead a default H melody applies to the word (except for a left boundary tone). The following monosyllabic/monomoraic examples show contrasts between accented and non-accented words of minimal size.

Pitch contrasts on monomoraic words in Tokyo Japanese

(1)	+ accent (= HL melody) [˥]	– accent (= H melody) [˩]
se	'back'	'rapids'
ha	'edge'; 'tooth'	'leaf'
hi	'fire'	'day, sun'
ho	'ear of grain, crest of a wave'	'sail'
mi	'winnowing fork'	'body'

The contrast between the two words in each row is a regular consequence of the fact that words of *n* morae length in (Tokyo) Japanese show *n*+1 contrasts, allowing for the absence of a lexical accent.[7]

---

[7] The well-known rules for pitch realisation apply here: an accented mora is associated with the H of a HL melody, which spreads leftwards to all but the first mora in a word, where an automatic process applies a L tone. Following the accent the L tone is associated with all following morae. In the absence of an accented syllable a H melody applies to the word, except for the above-mentioned automatic initial L association.

The origins of many of the complexities of pitch accent systems such as that found in Japanese can be found in the reduction of the number of tone-bearing units in a word (Kortlandt 1993). Examples include *ame* 'rain', < *amai, and *hebi* 'snake', < *fembi < *paimpi, where the vowel contractions have left their mark with a high tone in modern Japanese varieties.

(2)	*hasi*	'edge, tip'	┘┐	+ *ga* 'nominative':	*hasi ga*	┘┐+┐
	hási	'chopsticks'	┐┘		*hási ga*	┐┘+┘
	hasí	'bridge'	┘┐		*hasí ga*	┘┐+┘

On the other hand, without a contrast on monosyllabic or monomoraic words, a distinction between 'pitch accent' and '(contrastive) stress' is not easy to maintain, formally. I take the following characteristics as being the defining ones for a prototypical pitch accent system:

1. lack of metrical iteration;
2. relative pitch heights specified phonologically in the lexicon, not prosodically;
3. possibility of a contrast on monosyllabic (/monomoraic) words;
4. possibility of the entire system being described with automatic phonological processes and maximally one single diacritic assigned lexically (McCawley 1978).

These describe a pitch accent prototype, in contrast to a stress prototype; some stress languages are not iterative, and not all pitch accent languages do allow contrasts on monosyllables.

I propose that when thinking about typological 'kinds' of tone languages, especially the differences from a diachronic perspective, it is more useful to examine the properties that led to the labels in Donohue (1997), rather than simply use the labels themselves. I propose the following relevant features.

Pre-linking: Does the language allow for tones to be prelinked to a particular tone bearing unit, or do tones simply associate across the domain of their tone bearing unit according to automatic processes, not lexical ones?

Tone spreading: Do tones associated with a particular phonological unit spread across the (phonological, prosodic) word in which they appear, or are they confined in some way?

Melodies: Is there more than one tone melody which may be associated with a given tone bearing unit?

If we examine the language 'types' reported for New Guinea in Donohue (1997) and in widespread use in the tonological literature we find they show the following behaviours with respect to these features.

Table 1. Tone system 'types' and tone behaviour

	pre-linking (option)?	tone spreading?	multiple melodies?
'Pitch accent'	+	±	±
'Word tone'	±	+	+
'Syllable tone'	(–)	–	+

Under this multiple binary typology we could describe Tokyo Japanese as a language with optional prelinking (since not all words require an accent), and with tone spreading (in that the H of a HL melody spreads over preceding morae). It should not be categorised as having multiple tone melodies, since a tone melody in the sense used here is a lexically assigned unit, and not phonological unit assigned by automatic process, and the H melody in Tokyo Japanese is a phonological default, not a lexically assigned melody.

Examples of 'prototypical' pitch accent languages, with prelinking, no tone spreading and only one 'melody' can easily be found in the New Guinea region. Una is one example, and Arigibi Kiwai another. Compare the following possibilities for pitch behaviour on words of up to three syllables (from Donohue 1997, drawing on Louwerse 1978, 1988 and Wurm 1973). The differences between the two systems are as follows: Arigibi Kiwai does not allow a contrast on monosyllables, but otherwise allows a contrast both in the placement of accent and the presence of an accent.[8] In Una, words of more than one syllable in length must bear an accent, but monosyllables are only optionally accented. In both cases there is no spreading of the tone unit associated with an accented syllable.

Table 2. Pitch contrasts in Una (Mek family, central cordillera) and Arigibi Kiwai (Kiwai family, northern Gulf)

		Una		Arigibi Kiwai	
One syllable	˥	kal	'tree sp.'	–	
	˩	kal	'marsupial sp.'	naʌ	'fish'
Two syllables	˥ ˩	bita	'truely'	nimo	'louse'
	˩ ˥	bita	'frogs'	umu	'dog'
	˩ ˩	–		tutuʌ	'long'
Three syllables	˥ ˩ ˩	kʉnkɑlyɑ	'joint'	ŋgiʔɛpu	'heart'
	˩ ˥ ˩	kʉnkalya	'pimple'	ivio	'sun'
	| | ˥	bilbilyi	'building materials'	mudɛbɛ	'claw'
	˩ ˩ ˩	–		vovoʔo	'bird'

Unlike Una, which REQUIRES at least one high pitched syllable in all but monosyllabic words, Kiwai has the restriction that at least one syllable per word must be low-pitched, and allows for words composed entirely of unaccented syllables. This is a restriction on the assignment of tones to syllables that is the opposite of the high tone requirement formulated to account for the Una data, with the requirement being that each word must contain at least one low-pitched syllable. The number of pitch contrasts

[8] Note that Arigibi Kiwai, a very northern variety, is the *only* Kiwai language for which pitch contrasts have been reported. The far-flung Kiwaian family stretches from the very non-tonal Trans-Fly area south of Daru in the south, to the very tonal northern Gulf at its other extreme. This is further support for the idea that pitch-accent, at least, is areally dominant.

in Arigibi Kiwai is thus equal to the number of syllables in a word, plus one, except that monosyllabic words display no contrasts.

The other elaboration of pitch accent systems comes when we find more than one contrast possible on an accented syllable. For instance, in Kaure accent falls on an unpredictable syllable, and additionally must be specified as high or falling (Dommel and Dommel 1991). The pitch of the non-accented syllables in a word is not affected by the location or identity of the accent. In Auye (data from Moxness 2000) an expression with all short syllables can only show tonal contrasts on the final syllable, but the tone melody spreads to all preceding syllables; and all post-tonic syllables (in following case markers) are specified as being low-pitched. Examples of disyllabic contrasts on disyllables are shown in Tables 3 and 4.[9]

Table 3. Kaure: complex pitch accent

	Kaure			
sialü	'path'	˩ ˥	o ó	H
daitai	'mouse's sago'	˩ ˥˩	o ò	HL
inhoi	'mountain site'	˥ ˩	ó o	H
daitai	'wife's footprints'	˥˩ ˩	ò o	HL

Table 4. Auye: simplex word tone

	Auye			
piya	'tree'	˥ ˥	o ó	H
wedo	'mammal'	˩ ˥	o ò	LH
geka	'pandanus'	˥ ˥	o ó	H
geka	'nest, web'	˩ ˥	o ò	LH

An example of a language from outside the New Guinea area with a very simple word tone system that can be used to illustrate this typology is Kagoshima Japanese (Kubozono 1999). In Kagoshima there are no options for accent placement in the word, simply the option of selecting a LH melody or a LHL melody, as with Tokyo Japanese. It is tempting to think of the initial L as being assigned by rule, leaving us with a contrast between H and HL alone. The melodies attach to the last syllable of the word (actually the phrase), and show no spreading.

Table 5. Tokyo Japanese and Kagoshima Japanese compared

		Tokyo			Kagoshima		
namida	'tear'	˥ ˩ ˩	ó o o	HL	˩ ˩ ˥	o o o	(H)
kokoro	'heart'	˩ ˥ ˩	o ó o	HL	˩ ˩ ˥	o o o	(H)
otoko	'man'	˩ ˥ ˥	o o ó	HL	˩ ˩ ˥	o o o	(H)
sakana	'fish'	˩ ˥ ˥	o o o	(H)	˩ ˥ ˩	o o o, HL	HL

9 Similar conditions on the domain of tonal realisation are common in tonal systems of New Guinea, applying across a range of language families in the north of the island, often restricting the tonal domain to the last two (potential) tone-bearing units of the word.

Table 6 repeats the information in Table 1, adding only a breakdown of the logically possible combinations of features, and illustrative examples of languages which instantiate the different types. Languages from New Guinea are shown with underlining.

I have listed 'Pitch accent 4' as being the same as 'Word tone 1', and 'Word tone 2' as being the same as 'Pitch accent 3', because they are essentially the same phonological systems. Any differentiation would be solely in terms of quantity: a 'Word tone 2' system might be represented by Barupu, which appears to be a pitch accent system with the complication that it shows four or five different melodies, which is more than we feel comfortable allowing into the description of a 'mere' pitch accent language.[10] Otherwise I have not let the number of tonal contrasts, beyond the fact of the presence of tonal contrasts, enter into the typology.

Ross also notes that in some cases, at least, the pitch description of verbs differs from that of nouns. This is, of course, entirely expected. I refer the reader to Smith (1998) for details of the argument, applied to Japanese varieties but equally applicable to the New Guinea context.

Table 6. Permutations of suprasegmental features and illustrative languages

		pre-linking (option)?	tone spreading?	multiple melodies?	Example
'Pitch accent'	1	+	–	–	Una, Arigibi Kiwai
'Pitch accent'	2	+	+	–	Tokyo Japanese, Isirawa
'Pitch accent'	3	+	–	+	Kaure, Fasu, Kyoto
'Pitch accent'	*4*	+	+	+	= word tone 1
'Word tone'	1	+	+	+	Skou, Auye
'Word tone'	*2*	+	–	+	Barupu (= pitch accent 3)
'Word tone'	3		+	+	Mae Enga, Mende, Shanghai
'Word tone'	4	–	–	+	Kagoshima
'Syllable tone'		–	–	+	Weri, Cantonese

Geographic and family information about the languages: Una, Mek (TNG) from Star Mountains; Arigibi Kiwai, Kiwai (TNG?) from northern Gulf; Isirawa, Kwerba from north-west New Guinea; Kaure: isolate? from NCNG; Fasu: TNG from southern New Guinea;

4. Pitch accent beyond the west of (Trans?) New Guinea

In section 2 I noted that the only occurrence of pitch accent phenomena in Trans New Guinea languages that are not found in areas contiguous with the word tone systems of the central highlands is in the West Bomberai languages, Iha and Baham (and possibly

10 Thanks to Miriam Corris for discussion on the tonal system of Barupu.

Karas, though there is not enough data to determine this for certain) (Coenen 1953, Donohue and Brown 1998, and own fieldnotes). In this section I propose a scenario that accounts for this fact, as well as going some way towards accounting for the presence of very unusual stress systems in the languages of Yapen island, in Cenderawasih Bay.

4.1 Proto Timor-Alor-Pantar stress (/accent?)

The languages of the far west of the proposed Trans New Guinea phylum are found in the centre and east of the predominantly Austronesian language-speaking island of Timor, and on a small number of islands nearby. The languages of Alor and Pantar for the most part regularly show final stress patterns: the last syllable of a word is stressed, with only a small number of enclitics proving exceptional to this. This is a pattern attested in a wide range of languages. Only in the far east of the island is this rule not regularly applicable. In Kolana we find surface contrasts in stress, such as those shown in (3). There are also superficial stress contrasts, seen in (4), but these arise only as a result of vowel epenthesis between consonants, and will not be treated here.

Kolana stress contrasts

(3)	[a'da]	['adol(ŏ)]	[ɛ'a]	['ɛa]
	'fire'	'bird'	'rain'	'your mother'

Kolana false stress contrasts

(4)	[mă'dã] (< /mdan/),	['madã]	(< madan/)
	'cook'	'wear clothes on upper body'	

Table 7 shows comparative evidence from other languages of the Timor area (Bunak, Oirata), Alor (Blagar, Retta, Kabola, Kafoa, Kui) and Pantar (Lamma, Tewa and Nedebang) that support the hypothesis that an earlier stage of proto Timor-Alor-Pantar showed segmental contrasts in these words.

Table 7. Comparative evidence for the Kolana contrasts

	'fire'	'fish'	'rice'	'bird'	'stand'
Lamma	ha'ra	hap	'harak	arel	-tar
Tewa	har	haf	ha'ra, 'arax	dal	tas
Nedebang	'ara	afiŋ	kara	*daya*	tasi
Blagar	had	hab	ara	*duŋ*	tasi, tahi
Retta	ad	ʔab	ha'lak	*duag*	*mate*
Kabola	haʔ	hab	hala	*hiw*	*tuh*
Kafoa	ara	ʔafuy	a'yaka	*hiʔ*	*mati*
Kui	ar	eb	a'rak	adol	teya
Bunak	hoto	–	aa	*tie*	–
Oirata	afa	ahi	–	asa	*na*-te
Kolana	[a'da]	[a'pi]	[a'rak(ă)]	['adol(ŏ)]	['tati]
pT-A-P	*haDa	*hapuy	*harak	*aD(?)ol	*tati

The Nedebang form *kara* involves metathesis of the proto-form *harak to *kara*; the *k* is not a reflex of the initial *h. Metathesis is sporadic but not uncommon in western Alor-Pantar.

The *a*-initial words that show final stress in Kolana are reconstructable as being *h-initial. The preceding sample cognate set shows that the initial h is preserved in the western Alor-Pantar languages, where stress has completely shifted to final position.

I suggest that, despite the fact that final stress is now regular in most of the languages of Alor and Pantar, this regularisation of stress assignment is a historically recent development, and a language ancestral to the Alor Pantar languages had regular penultimate stress. The presence of an [h] in the onset prompted the loss of voicing on the following vowel by assimilation. Following this the stress shifted to the final syllable, since there was now not enough acoustic material to support the perception of a stressed syllable. This in turn led to the loss of the onset in the now stressless syllable. Since the conditioning factor for the devoicing of the vowel was no longer present, regularisation of the output for the vowel worked to apply voicing to the vowel again. The final diachronic change we can hypothesise would involve the regularisation of stress to a final position for all lexical items; this would reflect the state of the suprasegmental systems in western Alor-Pantar, but does not logically follow from the chain of events that I have described, since it is precisely the languages of Pantar that provide the strongest evidence for the presence of the initial h; that is, they did not lose the unsupported onset. The different possible 'stages' of development are shown in (5). I suggest that while Kolana in eastern Alor has gone through stages 1 – 5, the other languages of Alor, and most of the languages of Pantar, show evidence of stages 1 – 3, and then 5 – 6.

This establishes a historical scenario for a stress contrast. We should note that the conditions that I have posited for the shift in stress (and the development of stress contrasts in some cases) are the same as those that have been postulated in some theories of tonogenesis. The relevance to a discussion of tonal behaviour is in the higher-order relatives of these languages, specifically Oirata.

A scenario for the development of stress/accent contrasts in proto Alor-Pantar

(5)

	vowel initial root	glottal-initial root	
Stage 1:	V́CV	hV́CV	
Stage 2:	V́CV	hV̥́CV	devoicing
Stage 3:	V́CV	hV̥CV́	stress shift
Stage 4:	V́CV	V̥CV́	unsupported onset loss
Stage 5:	V́CV	VCV́	regularisation of modal voicing
Stage 6:	VCV́	VCV́	paradigm regularisation

Oirata has a segmentally simple, yet prosodically complex phonology. De Josselin de Jong describes the stress as being regular, with there being a contrast between long and short vowels, but notes (1937: 174) that 'a double vowel is contracted to a single vowel', giving as an example '*tuure* may be contracted to *tū̆re* or *ture* etc.' (*tu(u)re*: 'heavy, heaviness, burden, fatigue, danger'). In my notes I find I have fluctuated between writing doubled vowels and an accent, this sometimes corresponding to a single vowel in de Josselin de Jong's transcription. For instance, I record both *kaa□ere* and *ká□ere*, where de Josselin de Jong writes *kadere* for 'chair'. I suspect that there is something non-metrical about Oirata, and that it has something resembling a pitch accent system, though only further investigation will show this hypothesis to be true or not. Regardless of the analysis of Oirata, the historical scenario sketched in (5) has all the elements necessary for tonogenesis.

The historical scenario I would like to posit for the Bomberai languages involves substantial contact with an ancestor of the modern Timor-Alor-Pantar languages. Independent evidence for this hypothesis comes from the numerous cognates (or at least apparent cognates) that are shared between the West Bomberai languages and the languages of the Timor-Alor-Pantar area. There are, additionally, a significant number of lexical items and paradigmatic forms that show resemblances to West Papuan forms or paradigms in the Timor-Alor-Pantar languages, minimally pointing to some extended period of contact with that language group.[11] I suggest that the Timor-Alor-Pantar languages are originally West Papuan languages that, having moved south to the Bomberai area, came into extensive contact with a Trans New Guinea influence in that region.

---

[11] This suggestion is substantiated by the evidence of the *kain timur* tradition in the Bird's Head area, through which cloth originally from Nusa Tenggara, in the vicinity of the Timor-Alor-Pantar area, is used for ceremonial purposes across the Bird's Head. This indicates that continued trade reaching between Nusa Tenggara and West Papua continued into the historical period. For further evidence of a Timor-Alor-Pantar/West Papua link, see various papers in Miedema, Odé and Dam (1998).

After arrival in the Timor-Alor-Pantar region, probably after the arrival of the Austronesians to the islands subsequent to the non-Austronesian Timor-Alor-Pantar spread, a period of creolisation-like change stripped the morphology from most verbs in the languages, resulting in the ongoing process of regrammaticalising pronominal and aspectual information, leading to few cognates in bound morphology other than pronominals. But importantly, I argue that, regardless of the ultimate genetic affiliations of the Timor-Alor-Pantar languages, they have had substantial input from the West Papuan languages, a family not related to Trans New Guinea, but one in which tonal contrasts are widely reported (Gravelle 2001 on Meyah, Odé 1995 on Mpur, Berry and Berry 1999 on Abun). Furthermore, the languages of Yapen, thought to be related to the West Papuan languages before Voorhoeve's removal of them in 1975, show stress behaviour that is challenging for metrical accounts, but which can easily be accounted for with an analysis employing tone melody-like notations (see the next section).

5. A diachronic model of the distribution of tonal languages in Trans New Guinea

If there is any justification for a diachronic model of tonality in TNG languages, one that ignores the vagaries of multiple independent reanalyses of stress into pitch accent and pitch accent into stress, and further complications with word tone, then it must take into account the following facts:

- Word tone languages are found all across the central cordillera, the only exception being the Mek languages (see below);
- Pitch accent languages are not found in any particular genetic groups; the distribution of pitch accent in TNG languages is best modelled in terms of the area in which the language is found, not the affiliation it shares.

  (syllable tone languages are vanishingly rare in New Guinea, and if they are definitely found they are in all cases outlier (or outlying) languages in a family that shows word tone features)[12]

Reasons for the spread of pitch accent systems through areal influence are not hard to find. While a syllable tone system is acquisitionally transparent (albeit potentially complex), the presence of complex tone sandhi phenomena, or of a word tone system with spreading, means that the location of pitch changes cannot be simply learned from one hearing. These factors alone would mitigate for borrowed phonological pitch to be realised in the form of a pitch accent system, or a syllable tone system. Given the frequently polysyllabic and agglutinate nature of words, especially verbs, in Trans New Guinea languages the pitch accent system is most likely.

---

12 Many languages previously analysed as syllable-tone languages turn out to be better represented as word-tone languages. See Tida (2000, 2003) for discussion of the Chimbu languages. Similarly, Iau, reported as showing eight contrastive tones on the syllable in Bateman (1987), is better analysed as a word-tone language, as are most of its other close relatives in the Lakes Plains family (Clouse and Clouse (1993).

I would like to conclude with remarks on the stress/accent cline, which tie in with the discussion of the West Bomberai languages' showing pitch accent systems possibly being the result of having a strong West Papuan element in their makeup, either original (substratal), or else borrowed. In the languages of Yapen island we find complex stress patterns, incorporating a number of features that are not normally found together in one language. Saweru, a Yapen island language, is not genetically related to the Trans New Guinea languages (it is probably related to the languages of the West Papuan Phylum). It does, however, have a complex, and metrical, prosodic phonology, illustrated briefly in the following examples (for more detailed discussion, see Donohue 2003b).

An analysis in terms of stress must allow each lexical item to appear with either a binary or a ternary foot, and furthermore specify the position of the prominent syllable in each foot. Kondo (2001) describes the stress system of Guahibo, a language of eastern Colombia, as involving both iambic and trochaic patterns, providing a precedent to having contrastive metrical patterns in the one language, but the added stipulation that foot length is lexical, and not phonological, makes this a complicated system indeed, one for which a metrical analysis is not overly helpful.[13]

Table 8. Stress contrasts in Saweru

	Binary foot		Ternary foot		
	Trochaic	Iambic	Initial	Medial	Final
σ[14]	*un* 'comb'	*-va* 'mouth'			*-tu* 'tooth'
σ σ	*ísi* 'cave'	*kamí* 'egg'			*taní* 'mat'
σ σ σ	*manúnu* 'squid'	*màmbadú* 'crowned pigeon'	*ámpara* 'morning star'		*kabarí* 'fog'
σ σ σ σ	*ùmanánay* 'hornbill'	*amìtabúɲ* 'weekday'	*wowénambe* 'swamp'	*a-miŋgámi* 'eyeball'	*ìnumisó* 'today'
σ σ σ σ σ	*atàriái* 'headwaters'		*andetáfuay* 'turtle (sp.)'	*àndamamúnay* 'stonefish'	
σ σ σ σ σ σ	*ànukòfafúri* 'mullet (sp.)'		*ànsanaŋgómiri* 'garfish'	*iŋgùmburaréa* 'dolphin'	

An alternative analysis would treat the different apparent foot types as involving either a simple H (for the 'binary' roots) or else HL or LH ('ternary' roots) melody.

13 The presence of languages with both binary and ternary feet is documented in Elenbaas (1999), describing Finnish and Sentani.

14 The stress patterns of short words can be checked by examining the possessive construction, in which the noun takes genitive prefixes of up to three syllables in length. Thus 'my mouth' is *ìnavá*, while 'my tooth' is *inatú* ~ *inàtú*, **ìnatú*, with different patterns of secondary stress.

Both patterns involve a condition on tone melody spreading, so that the melody repeats, associating from right to left, throughout the prosodic word. Furthermore, there is a constraint against lexically assigned tone units appearing on adjacent syllables (a variant of Dorsey's law) listed here as *TT (ban adjacent tonal units), and a default L assignment in the event of there being no lexical tone assigned to a particular syllable.[15] The application of these constraints to *amìtabúɲ* 'weekday' is shown in (6), presented derivationally for reasons of space.

(6) *amìtabúɲ* 'weekday'

a.	lexical material melody: H	σ	σ	σ	σ,
b.	R→L association				H
c.	Spreading	H	H	H	H
d.	*TT		H		H
e.	L insertion	L	H	L	H
	Emulates prosodic structure:	(σ	σ̀)	(σ	σ́)

A trochaic word simply has an additional stipulation that the final syllable is extrametrical (outside the domain of tone assignment). Extrametricality is independently required in the language to account for the treatment of the large number of Austronesian loanwords which have entered from Ambai, a neighbouring and economically dominant language, since the Saweru moved from the highlands of Yapen island to their island .

(7) *ùmanánay* 'hornbill'

a.	lexical material melody: H	σ	σ	σ	σ,
b.	Extrametricality				x
c.	R→L association			H	x
d.	Spreading	H	H	H	x
e.	*TT	H		H	x
f.	L insertion	H	L	H	L
	Emulates prosodic structure:	(σ̀	σ)	(σ́	σ)

When the melody is LH the effect is to emulate ternary feet. With no extrametrical syllable we have a final-prominent ternary foot, and with an extrametrical final syllable we have a medial-prominent ternary foot.

[15] We also require a principle of only one melody assigning to one syllable, and a precedence relationship, H » L, in the event of two melodies competing for association to the same syllable.

(8) *ìnumisó* 'today'	a. lexical material	σ	σ	σ	σ,
	melody: LH				
	b. Extrametricality				
	c. R→L association			L	H
	d. Spreading	L	H	L	H
	e. *TT	H		L	H
	f. L insertion	H	L	L	H
	Emulates prosodic structure:	(σ̀)	(σ	σ	σ́)

(9) *àndamamúnay* 'stonefish'	a. lexical material	σ	σ	σ	σ	σ,
	melody: LH					
	b. Extrametricality					x
	c. R→L association			L	H	x
	d. Spreading	L	H	L	H	x
	e. *TT	H		L	H	x
	f. L insertion	H	L	L	H	L
	Emulates prosodic structure:	(σ̀	σ)	(σ	σ́	σ)

A word with a HL melody can emulate either the common trochaic patterns, if there are no extrametrical elements in the word, or else appear as an initial ternary pattern, if there is an extrametrical final syllable. (10) presents a possibly alternative analysis of a trochaic pattern. The existence of two separate kinds of lexical specification that would both result in trochaic patterns might explain the fact that this is the overwhelmingly most common stress pattern in the language, both in loan words and in apparently native words. In (11) we can see the effects of a HL melody on a lexical item with an extrametrical final syllable.

(10) *ùmanánay* 'hornbill' (= (7)')	a. lexical material	σ	σ	σ	σ,
	melody: HL				
	b. Extrametricality				
	c. R→L association			H	L
	d. Spreading	H	L	H	L
	e. *TT	H		H	L
	f. L insertion	H	L	H	L
	Emulates prosodic structure:	(σ̀	σ)	(σ́	σ)

(11) *wowénambe* 'today'	a. lexical material	σ	σ	σ	σ,
	melody: HL				
	b. Extrametricality				x
	c. R→L association		H	L	x
	d. Spreading	L	H	L	x
	e. *TT		H	L	x
	f. L insertion	L	H	L	L
	Emulates prosodic structure:	(σ)	(σ́	σσ	)

The different melodies, combined with specifications for extrametricality on words, produce the prosodic patterns seen in Table 9.

Table 9. Melody and metricality specifications and observed stress patterns

		Extrametrical final syllable?	
		no	yes
Melody	H	iambic	trochaic
	HL	trochaic	ternary initial
	LH	ternary final	ternary medial

The point of this exposition on Saweru is to show that a language with what appears to be metrical (= iterative) structure can be productively analysed with the same terminology and methodology as are used to describe tone systems.[16] I suggest that the relationship that Saweru and Yawa, the non-Austronesian languages of the Yapen area, share with the West Papuan languages of the Bird's Head, albeit distant, historically, is what is reflected in the unusual and complex stress patterns found in these languages and, to a lesser extent, in the Austronesian languages with which they share complex and intimate bidirectional borrowing relationships. This is support for the contention that I raised in section 2.4 that the presence of contrastive stress systems should raise the suspicions of anyone trying to reconstruct the tonal history of an area. The evidence is that stress and pitch accent systems can evolve in either direction from the other, and the presence of contrastive stress systems can be as much evidence of prior tonality as it can be the first step towards acquiring a pitch accent system.

References

AUSTING, JOHN, and RANDOLPH UPIA. 1975. Highlights of Ömie morphology. In T.E. Dutton, ed., *Studies in languages of Central and South-East Papua*: 513-598. Canberra: Pacific Linguistics C-29.

Bateman, Janet. 1986. The tone morphemes and aspect in Iau. In Janet Bateman, Iau verb morphology. NUSA: Linguistic studies of Inconsian and other languages in Indonesia 25: 1-50.

BERRY, KEITH and CHRISTINE BERRY. 1999. *A Description of Abun: A West Papuan language of Irian Jaya*. Canberra: Pacific Linguistics B-115.

BOXWELL, HELEN and MAURICE. 1971 [1966]. Weri phonemes. *Papers in New Guinea Linguistics* No. 5: 77-93. Canberra: Pacific Linguistics A-7.

BROMLEY, MYRON. 1973 / 1975. *A progress report on suggested Citak orthography*. MS.

CLOUSE, HELJÄ AND DUANE. 1993. Kirikiri and the Western Lakes Plains languages: selected phonological phenomena. *Language and Linguistics in Melanesia* 24 (1): 1-18.

COENEN, JULES. 1953. *De Ihandin taal gesproken op het schiereiland Onin, aan de westkust van N-Guinea*. MS.

[16] I should mention that it is also possible to motivate a completely stress-driven account of Saweru prosody, involving lexically assigned extrametrical final syllables, and some words that lexically assign prosodic foot boundaries about specified syllables irregularly. It is not clear that either of the lexical melody analysis or the foot boundary analysis is less arbitrary than the other, and that is the point.

DE JOSSELIN DE JONG, J.P.B. 1937. *Oirata, a Timorese settlement on Kisar*. Studies in Indonesian culture I. Amsterdam: N.V. Noord-Hollandsche Uitgevers-Maatschappij.

DOBLE, MARION. 1987. A description of some features of Ekari language structure. *Oceanic Linguistics* 26:55-113.

DOMMEL, PETER R. and GUDRUN E. 1991. Kaure Phonology. In Hartzler & Woods, eds., *Workpapers in Indonesian languages and Cultures* Volume 9: 1-68. Jayapura: SIL.

DONOHUE, MARK. 1997. Tone in New Guinea. *Linguistic Typology* 1 (3): 347-386.

2003a. The tonal system of Skou, New Guinea. In Shigeki Kaji, ed., *Proceedings of the symposium Cross-linguistic Studies of Tonal Phenomena: historical development, phonetics of Tone, and descriptive studies*: 329-355. Tokyo University of Foreign studies: Research Institute for Language and Cultures of Asia and Africa.

2003b. *The variable foot in Saweru*. Paper presented to the Australian Linguistics Society. University of Newcastle. Newcastle, 28 September 2003.

DONOHUE, MARK, and LEA BROWN. 1999. Ergativity: some additions from Indonesia. *Australian Journal of Linguistics* 19 (1): 57-76.

DRABBE, PETER. 1952. *Spraakkunst van het Ekagi (Wisselmeren Ned. N. Guinea)*. 's-Gravenhage: Martinus Nijhoff.

1953. *Spraakkunst van de Kamoro-taal*. 's-Gravenhage: Martinus Nijhoff.

1958. Grammar of the Keenok dialect. MS, Mbi-Tsjiweu.

DUTTON, T.E. 1975. A Koita grammar sketch and vocabulary. In T.E. Dutton, ed., *Studies in languages of Central and South-East Papua*: 281-412. Canberra: Pacific Linguistics C-29.

ELENBAAS, NINE. 1999. *A unified account of binary and ternary stress: considerations from Sentani and Finnish (Een unificeerede analyse van binaire en ternaire klemtoon: overwegingen uit het Sentani en Fins)*. PhD thesis, Utrecht University.

FARR, CYNTHIA. 1999. *The interface between syntax and discourse in Korafe*. Canberra: Pacific Linguistics C-148.

FARR, JAMES, and CYNTHIA FARR. 1975. Some features of Korafe morphology. In T.E. Dutton, ed., *Studies in languages of Central and South-East Papua*: 731-770. Canberra: Pacific Linguistics C-29.

GRAVELLE, GILLES G. 2001. *Meyah morphology and syntax*. Northern Territory University MA.

HYMES, DELL. 1979. How to talk like a bear in Takelma. *International Journal of American Linguistics* 45: 101-106.

JAMES, DOROTHY J. 1994. Word tone in a Papuan language. *Language and Linguistics in Melanesia* 25 (2): 125-148.

KONDO, RIENA. 2001. Guahibo Stress: Both Trochaic and Iambic. *International Journal of American Linguistics* 67 (2): 136-166.

KORTLANDT, FREDERIK. 1993. The origin of the Japanese and Korean accent systems. *Acta Linguistica Hafniensia* 26: 57-65.

KUBOZONO, HARUO. 1999. *Nihongo no Onsei* (The Sound System of Japanese). Tokyo: Iwanami.

LOUWERSE, JAN/YAN. 1978. A tentative phonology of Una. *Irian: Bulletin of Irian Jaya development* 7 (3): 43-90.

1988. *The Morphosyntax of Una in relation to discourse structure: a descriptive analysis*. Canberra: Pacific Linguistics B-100.

MCKAUGHAN, HOWARD. 1973. *The languages of the eastern family of the east New Guinea highlands stock.* Seattle: University of Washington Press.

MIEDEMA, JELLE, CECILIA ODÉ and RIEN A.C. DAM, eds. 1998. *Perspectives on the Bird's Head of Irian Jaya, Indonesia.* Amsterdam: Rodopi.

MOXNESS, MICHAEL E. 2000. Auye phonology. MS, Sentani: Summer Institute of Linguistics, Papua Branch, Indonesia

MCCAWLEY, JAMES. 1978. What is a tone language? In Victoria A. Fromkin, ed., *Tone: a linguistic survey*: 113-131. New York: Academic Press.

ODÉ, CECILIA. 1995. Tones in Mpur (West Papuan phylum). *ICPhS 95 Stockholm*, Session 78.1, Vol. 4: 216-219.

OLSON, MIKE. 1975. Barai grammar highlights. In T.E. Dutton, ed., *Studies in languages of Central and South-East Papua*: 471-512. Canberra: Pacific Linguistics C-29.

SMITH, JENNIFER. 1998. Noun faithfulness: evidence from accent in Japanese dialects. In Noriko Akatsuka, Hajime Hoji, Shoichi Iwasaki, Sung-Ock Soh, and Susan Strauss, eds., *Japanese/Korean linguistics* 7: 611-627. Stanford: CSLI.

TIDA SYUNTARÔ. 2000. *On the tone of the Dom language*. Masters thesis, Kyoto University, Japan. English version translated by Yoshihiro Kawabata. (Original title: *Domugo no tôn ni kansuru kôsatu.*)

VOORHOEVE, C.L. 1965. *The flamingo bay dialect of the Asmat language.* Verhandelingen van het Koninklijk Instituut voor Taal-, Land- en Volkenkunde, deel 46. 's-Gravenhage: Martinus Nijhoff.

1975. Central and Western Trans-New Guinea phylum languages. In S.A. Wurm, ed., *New Guinea area languages and language study Vol. 1: Papuan languages and the New Guinea linguistic scene*: 345-459. Canberra: Pacific Linguistics C-38.

1980. *The Asmat languages of Irian Jaya*. Canberra: Pacific Linguistics B-64.

Wilson, Darryl 1971. Suena Phonology. In Papers in New Guinea Linguistics No. 9: 87-93. Canberra: Pacific Linguistics A-18.

WURM, S.A. 1973. The Kiwaian language family. In Karl Franklin, ed., *The linguistic situation in the Gulf District and adjacent areas, Papua New Guinea*: 217-260. Canberra: Pacific Linguistics C-26.

Map 2. Areas referred to

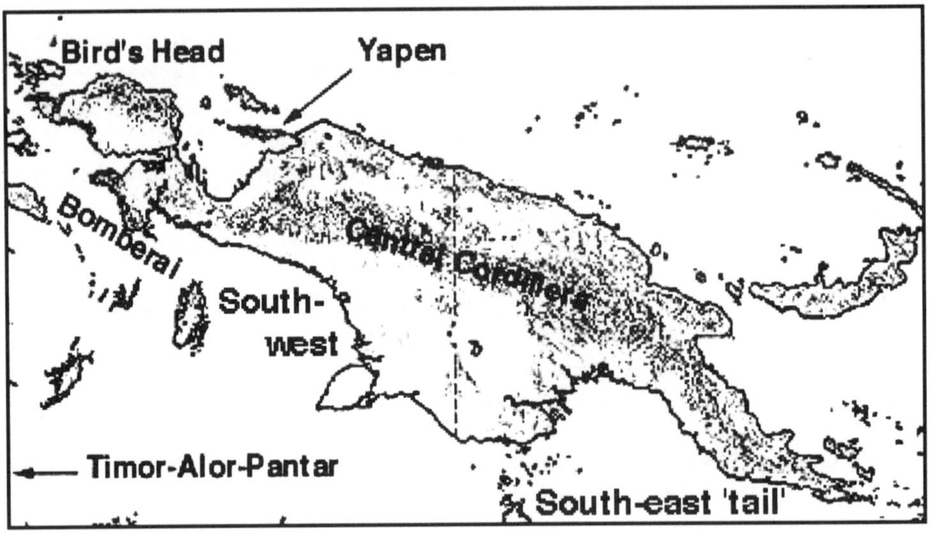

Map 3. Distribution of all tone languages (TNG or not) in New Guinea

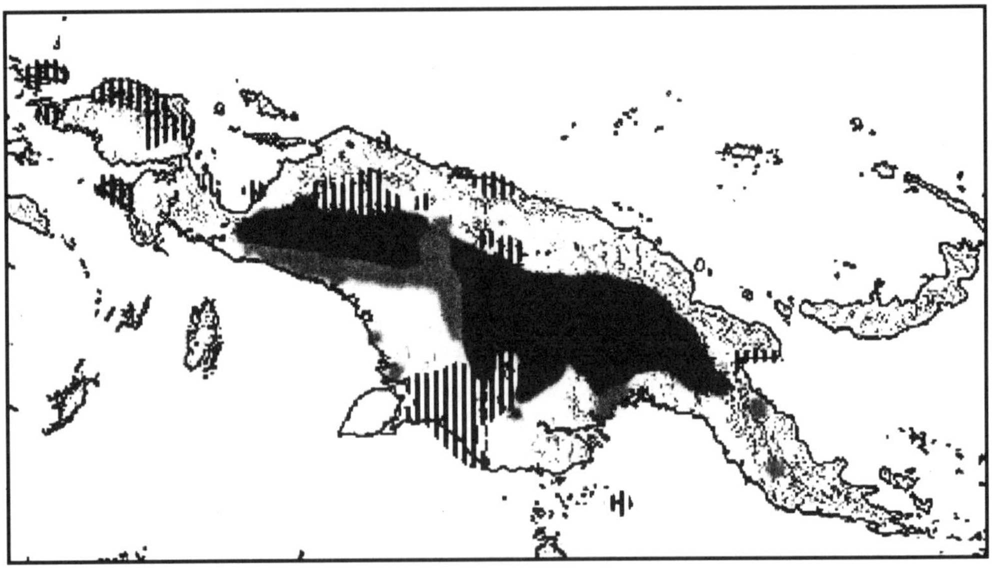

Dark: Trans New Guinea 'word-tone' systems
Light: Trans New Guinea 'pitch accent' systems
Vertical stripes: non-Trans New Guinea tonal systems (mostly pitch accent, with word-tone in the north of the island)

On the Functions of the Sino-Korean Accents

Chiyuki Ito
ILCAA
chiyukit@aa.tufs.ac.jp

1 Introduction

The Sino-Korean (SK) vocabulary discussed in this paper is attested to in the Middle Korean (MK) texts published in the 15th and 16th centuries. SK morphemes were as a rule loanwords from Middle Chinese (MC) roughly during the Sui 隋 and Tang 唐 dynasties, and the accents basically corresponded to the MC tones. Because of their origin, however, they showed unique features that were not seen in the MK native words. In this paper, we will clarify these unique features by examining the accentual functions of the SK morphemes.

1.1 The Phonological System of MK

The phonological system of MK was as follows:[1]

Table 1: MK Phonological System

	Consonants																		
Korean Alphabets	ㄱ	ㄴ	ㄷ	ㄹ	ㅁ	ㅱ	ㅂ	ㅸ	ㅅ	ㅿ	ㅇ	ㆁ	ㆆ	ㅈ	ㅊ	ㅋ	ㅌ	ㅍ	ㅎ
Transcriptions	g	n	d	r	m	w	b	v	s	z	'	ŋ	ʔ	j	c	k	t	p	h
Reconstructions	k	n	t	l/r	m	w	p	β	s	z	ɸ/ɦ	ŋ	ʔ	ts	ts^h	k^h	t^h	p^h	h

Consonant Clusters					
ㅺ	ㅲ	ㅳ	ㆅ	ㅴ	ㅵ
sg	sb	bd	hh	bsg	bsd

Vowels						
ㅏ	ㅓ	ㅗ	ㅜ	ㅡ	ㅣ	ㆍ
a	ə	o	u	ɨ	i	ʌ
a	ə	o	u	ɨ	i	ʌ

Complex Vowels				
ㅑ	ㅐ	ㅘ	ㅝ	ㆊ
ia	ai	oa	uə	iuiəi

Accents		
Even Tone	Departing Tone	Rising Tone
L	H	R

The first consonants were called *initial sounds* (初聲), the vowels and the semivowels *medial sounds* (中聲), and the final consonants *final sounds* (終聲).

1 Part of the consonant clusters and complex vowels are omitted in this table. Transcriptions are basically based on Fukui (1989).

In MK texts, the pitches of all syllables were recorded by *side dots* (傍點). There were 3 pitch types: the *Even Tone* (平聲), the *Departing Tone* (去聲), and the *Rising Tone* (上聲). The Even Tone was a low pitch, and the Departing Tone was a high pitch. The Rising Tone was a rising pitch occurring only in initial syllables; it has been analyzed by Korean linguists as a combination of the Even Tone and the Departing Tone.

In MK the first pitch in a verb stem or a noun was distinctive, and after that pitch seems to be governed by automatic rules of prosody.[2] That is, it is assumed that MK had an *accentual* system, not a *tonal* system like Chinese, although the pitches were called *tones*. For convenience, we will not use the MK tone names below. We will refer them as a low pitch, a high pitch, and a rising pitch.

1.2 The Phonological System of MC

1.2.1 Chinese Syllable Structure

Chinese syllable structure can be represented as *IMVE/T*.[3] The meaning is explained below.

I is the *initial* (聲母): the initial consonant of the syllable
M is the *medial* (介音): the semivowels which precede the principal vowel
V is the *principal vowel* (主母音): the nucleus of the syllable
E is the *ending* (韻尾): segments following the principal vowels
T is the *tone* (聲調): a tone contour superimposed over the whole syllable

In addition, all segments after the initial are called the *final* (韻母).

There were 4 tones in MC: the *Even Tone*, the *Rising Tone*, the *Departing Tone*, and the *Entering Tone*. It is assumed that the Even Tone was a low contour, the Rising Tone was a slightly rising contour, the Departing Tone was a rising contour, and the Entering Tone was a high contour.[4]

1.2.2 Correlations between the Initials in MC and the Initial Sounds in SK

The initials in MC corresponded to the initial sounds in SK as follows:[5]

---

[2] cf. Kadowaki (1976), Fukui (1985), etc.
[3] cf. Kōno (1968:350).
[4] cf. Kindaichi (1951), Rai (1951), Ito (1999).
[5] The reconstructions and the classification of series are basically based on Hirayama (1967:145-146). At the time of the rhyming dictionary *Qieyun* 切韻 (601), Light lip sounds were not independent from Heavy lip sounds. Light lip sounds were formed out of the old bilabials under certain conditions in the middle of the Tang dynasties. Initial *yun* 云 was partly derived from Old Chinese initial *xia* 匣 historically.

Table 2: MC Initials

Classification by Place of Articulation	Series	Phonation Types							
		Clear		Secondary Clear		Muddy		Secondary Muddy	
		MC	SK	MC	SK	MC	SK	MC	SK
Heavy lip sounds (重脣音)	*bang* 幫	幫 p	b (p)	滂 pʰ	p (b)	並 b	b (p)	明 m	m
[Light lip sounds (輕脣音)]	[*fei* 非]	[非 f]	b	[敷 fʰ]	b	[奉 v]	b	[微 ɱ]	m
Tongue sounds (舌音)	*duan* 端	端 t	d	透 tʰ	t	定 d	d	泥 n	n
	zhi 知	知 ȶ	d	徹 ȶʰ	t	澄 ȡ	d	娘 ȵ	N
Half-tongue sounds (半舌音)	*lai* 來							來 l	R
Front-tooth sounds (齒音)	*jing* 精	精 ts	j	清 tsʰ	c	從 dz	j		
		心 s	s			邪 z	s		
	zhuang 莊	莊 ʈʂ	j	初 ʈʂʰ	c	崇 ɖʐ	j c s		
		生 ʂ				俟 ʐ	s		
	zhang 章	章 ȶɕ	j	昌 ȶɕʰ	c	船 ȡʑ	s		
		書 ɕ	s			常 ʑ	s	羊 j	'
Half-front-tooth sounds (半齒音)								日 ɲ	z
Back-tooth sounds and throat sounds (牙喉音)	*jian* 見	見 k	g	溪 kʰ	g	羣 g	g	疑 ŋ	'
		曉 h	h			匣 ɦ	h		
		影 ʔ	'					[云 ɦ]	'

Initials were divided into 4 phonation types: Clear (全清, voiceless unaspirated consonants and ʔ), Secondary clear (次清, voiceless aspirated consonants), Muddy (全濁, voiced consonants), and Secondary muddy (次濁, nasals, liquids, approximants).

Basically, Clear and Muddy initials appeared in SK as unaspirated initial sounds, and Secondary clear appeared as aspirated initial sounds, although there were some exceptions, such as the initial *xi* 溪, which appeared as the unaspirated initial sound *g*, not aspirated *k*. The Even Tone morphemes with Muddy initials sometimes appeared as aspirated initial sounds in SK, reflecting the historical merger with the Secondary clear initials.

2 Basic Correspondences between the MC Tones and the MK Accents

One-syllable native nouns of MK had 3 accentual types—a low pitch, a high pitch, and a rising pitch, but the accentual distribution was uneven. That is, most monosyllabic native nouns had a high pitch, while few had a low pitch or a rising pitch. This aberrant distribution was established as a result of historical development.[6]

The accents of SK morphemes, however, corresponded quite regularly to the MC

[6] cf. Ramsey (1991).

tones. The correspondences researched in the several MK texts[7] are given below:[8]

Table 3: Accentual Distribution of the SK Morphemes

SK Accents	MC Tones				Totals
	Even Tone	Rising Tone	Departing Tone	Entering Tone	
L[9]	**1955**	19 (19)	31 (31)	11	2016 (2016)
L or R	27	23 (39)	13 (30)	0	63 (96)
L or H	29	2 (7)	2 (7)	39	72 (82)
L or R or H	2	3 (9)	4 (11)	2	11 (24)
R	18	**714 (663)**	**897 (836)**	1	1630 (1518)
H	12	**111 (106)**	**127 (120)**	**841**	1091 (1079)
R or H	3	60 (89)	96 (135)	13	172 (240)
Unknown	80	31 (31)	46 (46)	36	193 (193)
Totals	2126	963	1216	943	5248

As shown in Table 3, the accentual distribution of the SK morphemes was very different from that of native nouns.

The basic correspondences between the MC tones and the SK accents, then, were as follows:

---

[7] The MK texts researched in this paper are divided into 3 groups: (a) the texts with relatively accurate side dots, (b) the texts with inaccurate or unique side dots, and (c) the texts with few or no side dots. The accents of the SK morphemes which appeared only in the latter 2 groups are regarded as *unknown*.

(a) *Yukjo beppo dan-gyeong eonhae* (六祖法寶壇經諺解), *Jineon gwon-gong, Samdan Sisingmun eonhae* (眞言勸供, 三壇施食文諺解), *Beonyeok sohak* (飜譯小學), *Hunmong jahoe* (訓蒙字會)—Eizan (叡山) Library version, The version of General Library, The University of Tokyo, Sonkeikaku (尊経閣) Library version, Cabinet Library version, Kyujang-gak (奎章閣) version, Dong-guk syeorim (東國書林) version, *Sohak eonhae* (小學諺解)—Dosan seowon (陶山書院) version, Miyagi (宮城) Prefecture Library version, Mr. I Gyeomro (李謙魯)'s book, *Taehak eonhae* (大學諺解), *Jung-yong eonhae* (中庸諺解), *Noneo eonhae* (論語諺解), *Hyogyeng eonhae* (孝經諺解), *Bunmun onyeok yeokaebang* (分門瘟疫易解方).

(b) *Gyecho simhak inmun, Balsim suhaengjang, Yaun jagyeong se* (誡初心學人文, 發心修行章, 野雲自警序)—Song-gwang (松廣) temple version, *Mongsan beobeo eonhae* (蒙山法語諺解)—Song-gwang temple version, Korea University Central Library version, Ogura (小倉) Library version, *Sabeobeo eonhae* (四法語諺解)—Song-gwang temple version, Korea University Central Library version, Ogura Library version, *Revised version Beohwagyeong eonhae* (改刊法華經諺解)

(c) *Gani byeogonbang* (簡易辟瘟方), *Gyecho simhak inmun, Balsim suhaengjang, Yaun jagyeong se*—Sebong (瑞峯) temple version, *Jangsugyeong eonhae* (長壽經諺解).

[8] Even in the texts with accurate side dots, there were some mistakes of side dots, especially in the Rising and the Departing Tones (For the basis to judge the mistakes, see Ito (2002).). The values of the Rising Tone and the Departing Tone in this table are calculated by correcting these mistakes. The values including these mistakes are given in brackets. This is true of the following table.

[9] In the tables below, a low pitch, a high pitch, and a rising pitch are abbreviated to L, H, R respectively.

Table 4: Basic Correspondences between the MC Tones and the SK Accents

MC Tones	SK Accents
Even Tone	L
Rising Tone	R or H
Departing Tone	
Entering Tone	H

Almost one-to-one correspondences are seen between the Even Tone and a low pitch, and between the Entering Tone and a high pitch. On the other hand, the Rising Tone and the Departing Tone correspond to either a rising pitch or a high pitch, although the majority correspond to a rising pitch.

3 The Syllabic Inclination and the Syllabic Constraint

As Kōno (1968) has already pointed out, the aspirated initial sounds *p*, *t*, and *c* had a tendency to be in complementary distribution with the unaspirated initial sounds *b*, *d*, and *j*. For example, the rhyme *-a* tended to appear with the initial sound *p*, not with the initial sound *b*. The rhyme *-um* could appear only with the initial sound *p*. Kōno (1968) called this phenomenon the *syllabic inclination* (音節偏向).

Kōno (1968) referred to this phenomenon only in his treatment of the aspirated/unaspirated oppositions, but we can see that this syllabic inclination affected other aspects of the SK morphemes as well.

Let us look at one example. The initials *ni* 泥 and *niang* 娘 were basically represented by the initial sound *n* in SK, but in some SK morphemes, they also appeared as the initial sound *r*, which usually derived from the initial *lai* 來. This development has been thought to be the result of a hypercorrection, because in MK the initial sound *r* changed to *n* historically.

However, this is not true. This phenomenon was even seen in the texts where the phonetic change from *r* to *n* had not taken place. A further point to be noted here is that the SK morphemes derived from Chinese syllables with *ni* 泥 and *niang* 娘 initials had an initial *r* sound only in the cases of the following morphemes or syllables: 諾 *nag /rag*, 難 *nan /ran*, 念拈 *niəm /riəm*, 佞寧 *niəŋ /riəŋ*, 杻 *niu /riu*, 怒惱 *no /ro*, 餒 *noi /roi*, 農濃 *noŋ /roŋ*, 能 *nɨŋ /rɨŋ*, 你尼 *ni /ri*. This restriction was seen in all texts. Therefore, we cannot simply regard this phenomenon as a hypercorrection.

In this case, aberrant distributions in MC caused these Korean alternations. In MC, these rhymes originally had few characters with the initials *ni* 泥 and *niang* 娘, but many characters with the initial *lai* 來. Reflecting this systematic imbalance (=syllabic inclination), and because of the close relationship between *n* and *r* in MK, the initial sound *n* of the SK morphemes must have changed to *r*. It is not obvious what the close relationship was, but there may have been some phonetic similarity.

Thus, the syllabic inclination caused the pronunciation of some SK morphemes to change. We will call this function the *syllabic constraint*. This constraint must have been established gradually after SK had been introduced into Old Korean. The syllabic constraint affected various aspects of the SK morphemes.

Every language has conditions and constraints on the arrangements of its phonemes, so we can say that in a sense every language has this kind of syllabic constraint. However, what is unique about the syllabic constraint in SK is that there were what can be called strong and weak SK syllables, and that the weak syllables were forced to change their shapes by structural pressure.

We will examine the syllabic inclination and the syllabic constraint by taking some examples of SK accents, below.

3.1 The Syllabic Inclination—the Complementary Distribution between a Rising Pitch and a High Pitch

The Rising Tone and the Departing Tone in MC corresponded to a rising pitch or a high pitch in SK. However, the same SK syllable type rarely had both a rising pitch and a high pitch.[10] That is, a rising pitch was almost in complementary distribution with a high pitch. This is an example of the syllabic inclination.

The SK syllables derived from the Rising and the Departing Tones are classified based on the accents as follows:

(a) Syllables that had a high pitch

: cʌ, hə, ji, di, niə, pio, jiu, siu, co, to, pu, du, tiəi, niəi, goai, koai, gɨi, pan, 'in, min, bon, suən, 'ɨn, sʌiŋ, paŋ, siaŋ, niaŋ, ciəŋ

(b) Syllables that had both rising and high pitch

: jʌ, ci, ri, cio, dio, diu, ro, go, riəi, 'ui, piən, goan, riəŋ, giəŋ

(c) Syllables that had rising pitch

: sʌ, 'a, pa, ja, ta, sa, ga, ha, na, ma, 'ə, gə, 'i, bi, pi, ti, si, gi, mi, zi, 'ia, jia, cia, sia, zia, 'iə, jiə, ciə, diə, riə, siə, ziə, 'io, jio, rio, sio, gio, hio, nio, mio, zio, 'iu, ciu, riu, niu, ziu, 'o, bo, po, jo, do, so, ho, no, mo, 'oa, joa, coa, soa, goa, hoa, 'u, bu, ju, tu, ru, su, gu, hu, mu, bʌi, jʌi, cʌi, dʌi, tʌi, rʌi, gʌi, hʌi, nʌi, 'ai, pai, gai, hai, nai, mai, 'əi, gəi, 'iəi, piəi, jiəi, diəi, siəi, giəi, hiəi, miəi, ciui, ciuiəi, 'oi, joi, coi, toi, roi, goi, hoi, noi, soai, gui, guəi, huəi, 'ɨi, bɨi, sɨi, hɨi, jʌm, cʌm, 'am, jam, cam, dam, ram, gam, ham, 'əm, bəm, gəm, həm, cim, dim, rim, sim, nim, zim, 'iəm, piəm, jiəm, diəm, tiəm, riəm, siəm, giəm, niəm, ziəm, 'ɨm, rɨm, gɨm, hɨm, gʌn, hʌn, 'an, ban, can, dan, tan, ran, san, gan, han, nan, man, 'ən, gən, jin, cin, rin, sin, gin, zin,

---

[10] Gim Yeongman (1967a, b) has already pointed out this phenomenon, but his data are not completely correct.

'iən, biən, jiən, ciən, diən, riən, siən, giən, hiən, niən, miən, ziən, jiun, siun, 'on, jon, con, don, ron, son, gon, hon, 'oan, soan, hoan, 'un, bun, dun, gun, hun, mun, 'uən, guən, huən, cɨn, gɨn, hɨn, mɨn, jʌiŋ, rʌiŋ, gʌiŋ, hʌiŋ, mʌiŋ, 'aŋ, baŋ, daŋ, jaŋ, taŋ, raŋ, saŋ, gaŋ, haŋ, naŋ, 'iŋ, biŋ, ciŋ, 'iaŋ, jiaŋ, ciaq, diaŋ, tiaŋ, hiaŋ, 'iəŋ, biəŋ, jiəŋ, diəŋ, tiəŋ, siəŋ, hiəŋ, miəŋ, 'ioŋ, jioŋ, tioŋ, sioŋ, zioŋ, jiuŋ, diuŋ, 'oŋ, boŋ, joŋ, coŋ, doŋ, toŋ, roŋ, soŋ, goŋ, hoŋ, moŋ, 'oaŋ, goaŋ, hoaŋ, 'ɨŋ, jɨŋ, dɨŋ, sɨŋ, gɨŋ, hɨŋ, ziaŋ

(d) Syllables that could have either rising pitch or high pitch

: *ra, tiu, giu, 'ʌi, sʌi, mʌi, cai, dai, tai, sai, ni, ciəi, pum, jan, hən, bin, din, 'iun, ziun, caŋ, maŋ, riaŋ, niəŋ, puŋ, hui*

As shown above, in the SK syllables derived from the Rising and Departing Tones, few syllables had a high pitch. It is therefore assumed that a high pitch was an exceptional accent for them.[11]

It is difficult to explain high pitch only by phonetic conditioning. The high pitch must have been established by causes that included, but were not restricted to, phonetic conditions.[12] One of the phonetic conditions, however, seems to be aspirated consonants.

1. The high pitch tended to appear in the SK morphemes with aspirated initial sounds except for *h*.[13] Table 5 shows the number of the different morphemes with each accent.

---

[11] Some syllables of (a) were used for the only SK morpheme, so the reason for the high pitch may not have been directly relevant to their syllabic structures. Actually, the following examples had special reasons for high pitch: 胖 *paŋ* ^{H}, 鋪 *pu* ^{H}, 蒜 *suən* ^{H} were borrowed from Early Mandarin around the 16th century, so their accents reflected the Departing Tone of the period. 快 *koai* ^{H} was an exceptional syllable in that it had the initial sound *k*, so it may have been introduced later than the Tang dynasty. The character 泥 had the Even Tone and the Departing Tone in MC. In SK, The Even Tone variant (which meant 'mud') appeared as *ni* ^{L}, and the Departing Tone variant (which meant 'stagnate') appeared as *niəi* ^{H}. The pronunciation *niəi* ^{H} was probably an artificial SK morpheme based on the Chinese rhyme books, because it was rarely used in the MK texts. The SK morpheme 切 *ciəi* ^{H} normally appeared as the second element of the SK word 一 *'ir* ^{H} 切 *ciəi* ^{H}, and the accent was fixed as a high pitch, because there was a constraint against a rising pitch appearing within a word in MK.

[12] As to this problem, see Ito (2002), and 2.3 below.

[13] Gim Yeongman (1967a, b) has also pointed out this phenomenon, but he treated the aspirated consonants and the initial sound *h* equally, and his conclusion was based on the number of different syllables.

Table 5: Number of the Different Morphemes with High or Rising Pitch

Initial Sounds	R	H	Totals	Percentages of H
k	0 (0)	1 (1)	1 (1)	100.00 (100.00)
t	62 (62)	30 (37)	92 (99)	32.61 (37.37)
p	64 (64)	25 (28)	89 (92)	28.09 (30.43)
c	91 (91)	27 (34)	118 (125)	22.88 (27.20)
j	149 (150)	40 (46)	189 (196)	21.16 (23.47)
r	120 (120)	31 (36)	151 (156)	20.53 (23.08)
g	291 (291)	75 (92)	366 (383)	20.49 (24.02)
d	158 (158)	38 (40)	196 (198)	19.39 (20.20)
n	38 (38)	9 (11)	47 (49)	19.15 (22.45)
s	228 (230)	53 (59)	281 (289)	18.86 (20.42)
m	84 (84)	18 (22)	102 (106)	17.65 (20.75)
b	135 (135)	25 (28)	160 (163)	15.63 (17.18)
’	264 (265)	28 (34)	292 (299)	9.59 (11.37)
h	161 (162)	15 (28)	176 (190)	8.52 (14.74)
z	38 (38)	3 (3)	41 (41)	7.32 (7.32)

Although it is a problem that there was only one example of the initial sound *k*, we can say that aspirated initial sounds tended to have high pitch. The initial sound *h* seldom had a high pitchs despite being often considered an aspirated consonant in Korean.

Few native words with aspirated initial sounds had rising pitch in MK. These may have been established under the influence of the SK morphemes.

2. The Clear and the Secondary clear initials had more occurrences of high pitch than the Muddy and the Secondary muddy initials.

Table 6 shows the number of the different morphemes with each accent.

Table 6: Number of Different Morphemes with Each Accent

SK Accents	Rising Tone				Departing Tone			
	Clear	Secondary Clear	Muddy	Secondary Muddy	Clear	Secondary Clear	Muddy	Secondary Muddy
R	335 (335)	78 (78)	185 (185)	202 (201)	408 (410)	125 (125)	251 (251)	228 (228)
H	81 (97)	29 (32)	26 (38)	40 (45)	100 (117)	36 (38)	54 (69)	39 (49)
L	22 (36)	7 (8)	10 (14)	8 (16)	22 (33)	11 (16)	8 (18)	9 (13)
Unknown	15 (15)	2 (2)	4 (4)	10 (10)	19 (19)	7 (6)	8 (8)	12 (12)
Totals	453 (483)	116 (120)	225 (241)	260 (272)	549 (579)	179 (185)	321 (346)	288 (302)

Table 7 shows the percentages of each accent, except for unknown accents.

Table 7: Percentages of Each Accent

SK Accents	Rising Tone				Departing Tone			
	Clear	Secondary Clear	Muddy	Secondary Muddy	Clear	Secondary Clear	Muddy	Secondary Muddy
R	76.48 (71.58)	68.42 (66.10)	83.71 (78.06)	80.80 (76.72)	76.98 (73.21)	72.67 (69.83)	80.19 (74.26)	82.61 (78.62)
H	18.49 (20.73)	25.44 (27.12)	11.76 (16.03)	16.00 (17.18)	18.87 (20.89)	20.93 (21.23)	17.25 (20.41)	14.13 (16.90)
L	5.02 (7.69)	6.14 (6.78)	4.52 (5.91)	3.20 (6.11)	4.15 (5.89)	6.40 (8.94)	2.56 (5.33)	3.26 (4.48)

The Secondary clear initials had the highest percentage of high pitch. The difference in percentages may have been relevant to the contour influenced by the initials of MC. As already mentioned, the Rising Tone in MC was a slightly rising contour and the Departing Tone was a rising contour. Therefore, as a rule, most of them were represented by rising pitch in SK. However, the rising contours probably sounded like high tones when they had Secondary clear initials. On the contrary, the onset time pitch may have fallen when there was a Muddy or Secondary muddy initials.

3.2 The Syllabic Constraint—the Complementary Distribution of the Aspirated and the Unaspirated Initial Sounds when Classified by Accent

3.2.1 Complete Inclination and Partial Inclination

The complementary distribution of the aspirated and the unaspirated initial sounds that Kōno (1968) pointed out can be further classified into 2 types if we take the accents into consideration. For a given rhyme,

(a) the aspirated initial sound was in complementary distribution with the unaspirated initial sound regardless of the accents. (There was no opposition between aspirated and unaspirated initial sounds);

(b) the aspirated initial sound was (almost) in complementary distribution with the unaspirated initial sound when grouped according to the accents.

We will call the former case *complete inclination*, and the latter case *partial inclination*.

For example, the distribution of the SK morphemes with the initial sounds *d* and *t* was as follows (the values represent the number of different morphemes).

Table 8: Distribution of the SK Morphemes with the Initial Sounds *d* and *t*

Final sounds		-*Ø*			-*m*			-*n*			-*ŋ*		
SK Accents		L	R	H	L	R	H	L	R	H	L	R	H
d	*ʌ*												
t								1					
d	*a*	4			12	10		11	10		15	3	1
t		7	8	1	3			4	8	2	1	5	
d	*o*	25	18	2				6	5	1	12	9	
t		1		6							2	3	1
d	*u*	1	2	13				4	1				
t		7	3	1									
d	*ɨ*										10	4	
t													
d	*i*	6		3		1		3	1	3	2		
t		4	10	1	3								
d	*ʌi*	2	10	1									
t		6	3								1		
d	*ai*		2	1									
t			5	2									
d	*oi*												
t		6	3										
d	*ia*										4	5	
t												3	
d	*iə*	6	10	1		6	1	7	14		21	9	
t					5	3		1			2	1	
d	*io*	17	7	4									
t		4										2	
d	*iu*	12	7	4							2	4	
t		3	1	1							6		
d	*iəi*	19	9	2									
t			4	13									

Complete inclinations are indicated by bold lines, and the (almost) partial inclinations are shaded. For the concrete data, see the appendix.

Some rhymes showing partial inclinations were actually almost complete inclinations:

1. In the opposition *diən* /*tiən*, the almost complete inclination to *diən* had been established. In this rhyme, 天'heaven' was the only example that appeared as *tiən*. It is assumed that 天 retained its old sound because the morpheme 天 was basic and frequently used in the MK texts.
2. In the opposition *diəŋ* / *tiəŋ*, the almost complete inclination to *diəŋ* had been established. The morphemes 廳'office,' 聽'listen' as a rule appeared as *tiəŋ* in SK,

but in a one text, they appeared as *diəŋ* as well. These exceptions probably occurred because of the syllabic inclination (=syllabic constraint).

In some rhymes, complete complementary distribution occurred as a result of partial inclination. For example, tim^{L} and dim^{R} were in completely complementary distribution.

3.2.2 The Partial Inclinations in Tongue Sounds

In the rhymes where partial inclination took place, some interesting phenomena including syllabic constraints are observed. We will look at some examples of partial inclinations in the lingual sounds below.

(a) The opposition *da* / *ta* —*da* had only a low pitch

In the rhyme *-a*, all morphemes with a rising pitch and a high pitch appeared as *ta*. (See appendix). Therefore, the opposition *da* / *ta* was seen only with a low pitch. However, even with a low pitch, many morphemes appeared as *ta*. This implies that the inclination to *ta* was being established. Actually, the morphemes 多苶陀 da^{L} were unique exceptions[14] because they were often used to transliterate words in Buddhist texts. They retained their old sounds to transliterate faithfully the original sounds of MC or Sanskrit. And 陀 could also be pronounced as ta^{L}. This may have been the result of the syllabic constraint.

When these situations are taken into consideration, it is possible to think that the rhyme *-a* basically tended to incline to *ta*.

(b) The opposition *di* / *ti* —as a rule *di* did not appear in the Rising and the Departing Tones

In the Rising and the Departing Tones, *ti* mainly had a rising pitch, and *di* had a high pitch. (See appendix). Therefore, ti^{R} and di^{H} were almost in complementary distribution. Still, di^{H} was represented by only 3 morphemes 地知智. They may have been shaped by analogy with 池 di^{L} and 知 di^{L}, because they were respectively based on the same *xieshengfu* (諧聲符, phonetic signs). Alternatively, they may have had the old intact sound because they were often used in Buddhist texts. If so, it is assumed that at least in the Rising and the Departing Tones, *ti* was a default syllable and as a rule *di* did not appear.

(c) The opposition *dio* / *tio* —*tio* had only a low pitch

In the rhyme *-io*, *tio* did not have a rising or a high pitch. (See appendix). The initial

---

14 The morpheme 苶 had a low pitch although it derived from the Rising Tone in MC. This was by analogy with 多 da^{L}, which derived from the Even Tone.

sound *d* of the morpheme 眺糶 *dio*^{R} was exceptional because they had the initial *tou* 透. 眺 *dio*^{R} was shaped by analogy with 兆 *dio*^{L}/*dio*^{R}, which had the initial *cheng* 澄 in MC. 糶 *dio*^{R} was shaped either by contamination with 糴 *diəg*^{H}, which had the initial *ding* 定, or was the result of syllabic constraint, by which -*io*^{R} could not appear with the initial sound *t*.

(d) The opposition *do*/*to* — complementary distribution was being established, in a way that *do* tended to have either a low pitch or a rising pitch, while *to* tended to have a high pitch

In the rhyme -*o*, most morphemes with the initial sound *d* had either low pitch or rising pitch, and most morphemes with the initial sound *t* had high pitch (See appendix). The initial sound *d* of the morphemes 慆滔瑫韜饕 *do*^{L} was exceptional because there was an initial *tou* 透 in MC. 慆滔瑫韜 *do*^{L} was probably the result of analogy with 蹈稻 *do*^{R}, which had the initial *ding* 定 in MC. 饕 *do*^{L}, however, cannot be explained the same way. It is assumed that 饕 *do*^{L} occurred because of the syllabic constraint, by which -*o*^{L} could not appear with the initial sound *t*.[15]

(e) The opposition *du*/*tu* — complementary distribution was being established, in a way that *du* tended to have a high pitch, while *tu* tended to have a low pitch

In the rhyme -*u*, most morphemes with the initial sound *d* had high pitch, and most morphemes with the initial sound *t* had low pitch (See appendix). The morpheme 妬 'envy' appeared as either *tu*^{L} or *tu*^{R}. 妬 had the Departing Tone in MC, so *tu*^{L} was exceptional. This exceptional low pitch may have been caused by the syllabic constraint, which was based on the complementary distribution between *du* and *tu*. On the other hand, the morpheme 頭 'head' was the only example that appeared as *du*^{L}. This may have been caused by analogy with morphemes with the *xieshengfu* 豆, or it may have retained its intact sound because it was a basic morpheme.

3.3 The Exceptions to the Syllabic Constraint

Although the syllabic constraint had a strong influence on SK morphemes, there were some exceptions. As noted above, the morphemes used in transliterating Buddhist texts and frequently used morphemes were the exceptions. We will look at now other exceptions.

(a) Analogical accents

1. The morpheme 九 'nine' originally appeared as *gu*^{R}, but around the end of the 16th

---

15 The only exception 條 *to*^{L} was seen in some versions of *Hunmong jahoe* (訓蒙字會). In the other versions of *Hunmong jahoe*, 條 appeared as *tio*^{L}.

century, its accent tended to have a high pitch. The gu^H was caused by analogy with the numbers 六'six' $riug^H$, 七'seven' cir^H, 八'eight' par^H, and 十'ten' sib^H.[16]

2. It is assumed that the high pitch of the SK morpheme 出'go out' ciu^H was the result of analogy with another reading of the same character 出 $ciur^H$, which was derived from the Entering Tone. In the same way, the accent of 植'plant' ti^H was probably the result of analogy with 値'value' tig^H.

(b) Artificial accents

The SK morphemes derived from the Departing Tones had high pitch if they were rarely used in the MK texts. In the same way, the SK morphemes derived from Rising Tones had rising pitch. This phenomenon was often seen in the Chinese-Korean glossary, *Hunmong jahoe* (訓蒙字會); e.g. 硯'ink stone' *'iən*^{H}, 薊'thistle' *giəi*^{H}, 蟣'louse' *gıi*^{R}, 咫'a unit of length' *ji*^{R}.

The SK morpheme 去'leave' *gə* normally had a rising pitch, but in *Hunmong jahoe*, and only there, it had a high pitch, where it was used as a part of the SK word 去 *gə*^{H} 聲 *siəŋ*^{L} 'Departing Tone'. 去 in this case had a high pitch probably because in MK, a high pitch was called the *Departing Tone*. We can regard this phenomenon as either an artificial accent or an accentual splitting, as discussed below.

(c) Accentual splitting by meanings

Some SK morphemes had both a rising pitch and a high pitch to distinguish different meanings. Generally, a high pitch tended to appear in a specialized usage. At least in the SK morphemes derived from the Rising and the Departing Tones, a high pitch seems to have been a marked accent.

1. The morpheme 故 *go* had a high pitch when it meant 'reason', and it had a rising pitch when it meant 'old.'[17] The latter case may have been by analogy with 古 'old' *go*^{R}.
2. The morpheme 允 *'iun* had a high pitch when it was used as a personal name (高 *go*^{L} 允 *'iun*^{H}). It had a rising pitch when it was used as the adverb that meant 'really.'
3. The morpheme 大 appeared as *dai*^{R} when it meant 'big', and appeared as *dai*^{H} or *tai*^{H} when it was used as an honorific in the words like '大夫,' '士大夫,' '大宰,' '大師,' '大廟,' '大王.'
4. The morpheme 點'point' *diəm* normally had a rising pitch, but in *Hunmong jahoe*

[16] It was also by analogy that 八 with the initial *bang* 幫 appeared as *par*^{H} in SK. The syllable *par* was used only for 八. This is because 八 became aspirated by analogy with the neighboring morpheme 七 *cir*^{H}.

[17] cf. Nam Gwang-u (1984:41-42).

it had a high pitch in the meaning of 'side dots.'[18]

4 Conclusions

The accents of the SK morphemes had unique features that were not seen in the native words.

(a) The MC tones corresponded to the SK accents as follows: the Even Tone was realized as a low pitch; the Rising and the Departing Tones were mainly realized as rising pitch, but in some cases as high pitch; the Entering Tone was realized as a high pitch. Because of these correspondences, the accentual distribution of SK morphemes was quite different from that of native words.
(b) The SK morphemes derived from the Rising and the Departing Tones tended to have high pitch when the initial consonants were aspirated in MC or in MK.
(c) The SK accents were strongly influenced by syllable structure (the syllabic inclination).
(d) The syllabic inclination can be classified into 2 types according to both the aspirated/unaspirated oppositions and the accents: complete inclination and partial inclination.
(e) The syllabic inclination resulted in the syllabic constraint—the systematic, structural pressure on the canonical shape of each syllable.
(f) Some SK morphemes were not affected by the syllabic constraint for several reasons, including the transliteration of Buddhist texts, high frequency, analogy, artificial accents, and accentual splitting.

References

Fukui Rei. 1985. "Chūki chōsengo no akusento taikei ni tsuite" (A study of the Middle Korean accentual system). *Tokyo University Linguistic Papers '85*: 61-72.

———. 1989. "Chūki chōsengo bunken no denshi keisanki ni yoru shori" (Computer-processing of Middle Korean texts). *Meikai journal - Division of Modern Language 2*: 17-29.

Gim Yeongman. 1967a. "Ijo jeongi ui hanjjaeum ui unyul (seongjo) [I]" (A prosodic study of Sino-Korean morphemes in the early Yi (李) dynasty). *Hangeul 139*: 69-78.

———. 1967b. "Ijo jeongi ui hanjjaeum ui unyul (seongjo) [II]" (A prosodic study of Sino-Korean morphemes in the early Yi dynasty). *Hangeul 140*: 95-113.

Hirayama Hisao. 1967. "Chūko kango no onin" (A phonological study of Middle

[18] Still, the accent of 點 may have changed from a rising pitch to a high pitch because it was used as the second element of SK words such as 一點'one dot', 二點'two dots.'

Chinese), in *Chūgoku bunka sōsho 1, Gengo*. Tokyo: Taishūkan.

Ito Chiyuki. 1999. "Chūki chōsengo no kanjigo akusento taikei" (The Sino-Korean accentuation in Middle Korean). *Gengo Kenkyū* 116: 97-143.

———. 2002. "Chōsen kanjion kenkyū" (A study of Sino-Korean). Doctoral dissertation, the University of Tokyo.

Kadowaki Seiichi. 1976. "Chūki chōsengo ni okeru seichō kōtai ni tsuite" (A study of tonal alternations in Middle Korean). *Chōsen Gakuhō 79*: 17-54.

Kindaichi Haruhiko. 1951. "Nihon shishō kogi" (Original meaning of Japanese tones), in Terakawa Kishio, Kindaichi Haruhiko, and Inagaki Masayuki (eds.) *Kokugo akusento ronsō*: 627-703. Tokyo: Hosei University Press, 1951.

Kōno Rokurō. 1968. "Chōsen kanjion no kenkyū" (A study of Sino-Korean), in *Kōno Rokurō chosakushū 2*, 1979: 295-512. Tokyo: Heibonsha.

Nam Gwang-u. 1984. *Hangugeo ui baleum yeongu [II]* (A study of Korean pronunciation). Incheon: Inha University press.

Rai Tsutomu. 1951. "Kanon no shōmyō to sono seichō" (A study of tone of Kanon-shōmyō). *Gengo Kenkyū* 17-18:1-46.

Ramsey, S. Robert. 1991. "Proto-Korean and the Origin of Korean Accent," in *Studies in the Historical Phonology of Asian Languages*, Michael J. Shapiro and William J. Boltz, eds. Philadelphia: John Benjamins, 1991.

Appendix

The SK morphemes that had more than one accent or appeared with both *d* and *t* are given in brackets.

		-Ø			-m			-n			-ŋ		
		L	R	H	L	R	H	L	R	H	L	R	H
d	*ʌ*												
t	*ʌ*							呑					
d	*a*	多爹茶(陀)			眮潭潭蟫談痰澹莟壜(湛擔耽)	淡膽毯菼澹禫啖賺(湛擔)		單簞襌端丹湍猯坍壇檀團	旦疸鍛碫担短段但斷(袒)		搪煻唐塘糖堂棠螳膛螗幢甋襠瑭(當)	戇(當黨)	(黨)
t	*a*	他馱駝跎酡鼉(陀)	唾拖涶舵椃打墮惰	(朶)	探貪(耽)			攤灘攤彈	炭坦憚綻誕(嘆歎袒)	(嘆歎)	湯	蕩盪盪鍚帑	
d	*o*	都覩刀忉舠兜篼慆滔瑫韜饕圖塗屠徒途桃淘逃陶萄濤斂(賭)	倒到睹倒島擣道導渡鍍蹈稻幬棹盜(賭祷度)	(祷度)				敦墩驐暾豚魨	褪沌囤遯(頓)	(頓)	冬疼東蝀同桐銅筒童僮瞳彤	凍棟蝀董潼洞峒衕動	
t	*o*	條		土吐兔菟套討							通侗	痛統慟	桶
d	*u*	頭	(豆杜)	斗抖蚪蠧脰痘脰餖荳竇肚(豆杜)				屯臀飩窀	鈍				
t	*u*	偸投骰餖瘉牏(妬)	透(妬鬪)	(鬪)									
d	*ɨ*										藤騰疼籐滕澄登燈橙(鄧)	等鐙凳(鄧)	
t	*ɨ*												
d	*i*	蜘持遲墀池(知)		地智(知)		朕		珍塵(陳)	(鎭)	陣(陳鎭)	徵澄		
t	*i*	癡馳治(絺)	置致躓懥恥痔稚雉治(絺)	植	砧湛沈								

		-Ø			-m			-n			-ŋ		
		L	R	H	L	R	H	L	R	H	L	R	H
d	ʌi	臺擡	帶對碓貸代玳袋黛待(戴)	(戴)									
t		台胎苔炱(殆怠)	態(殆怠)								撐		
d	ai		歹(大)	(大)									
t			汰泰鈦薹(太)	(大太)									
d	oi												
t		鎚蓷瘄頹魋椎	退腿煺										
d	ia										張腸場(長)	丈仗杖帳(長)	
t												脹漲韔	
d	iə	瀦樗摴儲低除	詆著楮箸筯苧杼底邸(抵)	(抵)		店坫踮簟覘(點)	(點)	顛巔癲田廛傳(轉)	典靦顯殿澱電淀甸奠畋癜驏傳(轉)		丁釘疔汀鞓亭停聤廷庭蜓貞禎蟶檉頳呈程裎棖(廳)	飣頂鼎碇頲定艇鄭鋥	
t					添甜沾(忝諂)	舔(忝諂)		天			(廳聽)	(聽)	
d	io	凋琱彫雕鵰旦條跳蜩鰷淘嘲朝晁潮(調兆)	朓糶銚趙(調兆弔)	釣鳥蓧(弔)									
t		貂條齠超										塚寵	
d	iu	鍮株蛛誅輸廚櫥紬儔疇稠籌	拄柱宙冑(住晝肘)	紂(住晝肘)							(中重)	仲蚛(中重)	
t		追隊(錘)	墜	(錘)							忠衷椿沖翀蟲		
d	iəi	堤羝觝梯綈稊鵜醍題提踶蹄啼蕛荑猪篨低除	帝睼弟第悌娣底邸(諦)	(涕抵)									
t			髢(棣滯涕)	嚏蒂蝃替體遆逮禘彘(諦棣滯涕)									

Sino-Korean Accent and Ito Chiyuki's Research

S. Robert Ramsey
University of Maryland

It is remarkable how Sino-Korean vocabulary has preserved Chinese tonal distinctions. To be sure, these distinctions exist in Korea today only in a few regional dialects, but in those dialects, they are preserved with great consistency. Chinese tones are reflected with even greater transparency in Korean alphabetic materials of the fifteenth and sixteenth centuries.

And yet, perhaps because the standard Seoul dialect has no lexical pitch distinctions at all, Korean's preservation of Chinese tones has generally gone unnoticed. The first time I became aware of it was in 1972, when Mantaro Hashimoto first pointed the distinctions out to me. At the time, Hashimoto was doing research on Korea's southeastern dialects, and he had noticed the correspondences. He reported that when Taegu speakers recited the names of the Chosŏn kings, they invariably pronounced the names with pitches reflecting the Middle Chinese tones of the characters with which the names were written. (Cf. Hashimoto 1978, pp. 211-14.) In this serendipitous way, Hashimoto was able to show that the Chinese information was for the most part all there, reflected morphophonemically in the readings of the Sino-Korean compounds. It was a moment of revelation.

Hashimoto had been looking at speech in Korea's southeast, in Kyŏngsang. And so, not long after he told me of his discovery, I took a look at the accent systems of northeast Korea, in Hamgyŏng, where I also found morphophonemic evidence of Middle Chinese tones. The principal speaker of that dialect that I interviewed was an older woman, completely illiterate not only in Chinese characters but even in Hangul, and yet the Sino-Korean words in her vocabulary still preserved Chinese tones, albeit in a different form, and at a different level of abstraction. I wrote up my findings, but certainly not in the detail that they deserved.

Both Hashimoto's and my research was on Chinese tones in modern Korean dialects. (Hashimoto's findings on Korean dialect accent have been presented on pp. 133-94 of Hashimoto 1978; mine can be found in Ramsey 1977.) Of course, Korean scholars had already written on Sino-Korean tones at the time of Hashimoto's research. But there were not many such articles.

Now Ito Chiyuki has written an interesting and provocative paper on this very topic. I was glad to have seen her paper, first of all because it is well done. But I am also glad to find out about her research because the topic has been relatively neglected. By now a sizable literature on Korean tone and accent has accumulated over the past couple of decades, including many works on the tone marks of Middle Korean. But little has been said about the tones of Sino-Korean. In fact, before reading Ito's paper, my principal sources of information on the topic had been my own notes and notes from the lectures of Professor Kim Wanjin, as well as the same two 1967 articles by Kim Yŏngman that Ito cites. Why the neglect? I suspect it is mainly because the borrowing of linguistic features is ordinarily considered peripheral to what linguists usually look at. But it is also curious that although Sino-Xenic distinctions have been scrutinized carefully by those interested in reconstructing earlier stages of Chinese, tone has generally been left out of the picture. Dr. Ito shows that there is much more about that topic that deserves our attention.

The textual basis of Dr. Ito's research deserves elaboration. She writes that Sino-Korean vocabulary is attested in the Middle Korean texts of the 15th and 16th centuries, but that is only partially true. The great majority of MK texts—all of the early texts, in fact—reflect only the prescriptive, artificial readings found in the 1447 Korean rhyming dictionary *Tongguk chŏngun* ('The correct rhymes of the Eastern Country' 東國正韻). The *Tongguk chŏngun* is a six-volume dictionary of Chinese characters issued as an official standard for Sino-Korean pronunciations. The pronunciations that it contains are very much prescriptive and intended to "correct" the Chinese character pronunciations then in use in Korea. And though it ultimately failed to accomplish this objective, the artificial pronunciations the *Tongguk chŏngun* specified were followed carefully in the Hangul writings published over the next few decades. The readings it put forward were highly theoretical combinations of the phonological categories of Chinese rhyme tables and dictionaries with elements of Korean pronunciations. The transcription of tones, of course, followed Chinese categories. That was the Middle Korean tradition. All in all, the Chinese character readings given in these Middle Korean texts were thus neither fish nor fowl, and virtually unusable for most linguistic research.

The earliest Korean text to break with the *Tongguk chŏngun* tradition by transcribing actual Sino-Korean pronunciations was the Korean exegesis of the Tang poet Dù Fǔ's poems, the *Pullyu Tu kongbu si ŏnhae* (分類杜工部詩諺解), the title of which is customarily shortened to *Tusi ŏnhae* (杜詩諺解) (25 volumes). Compiled by the scholar Cho Wi at the king's command, the work was finished in 1481, but a complete copy of the first edition has as yet not been found. The problem, if it can be thought of as that, is that the *Tusi ŏnhae* does not usually give sound glosses for Chinese characters at all. Instead, our linguistic information comes from the transcriptions of words of Sino-Korean origin, which are believed to follow actual pronunciations. And so, since the researcher has to rely on etymological assumptions, the *Tusi ŏnhae* is difficult to use for establishing Sino-Korean readings.

The best place to start researching the Korean readings of Chinese characters is with the *Yukcho pŏppodan kyŏng ŏnhae* (六祖法寶壇經諺解) and the *Sisik kwŏn'gong ŏnhae* (施食勸供諺解), two texts published fifty years after the beginning of the period, in 1496. Dr. Ito of course knows this fact quite well, because those are the first sources that she used in her research. But the nature of the Korean written record, complex though it is, is something worth explaining a bit more. Although these are clearly Middle Korean texts, they postdate the earliest body of alphabetic materials.

A word might well be said about Dr. Ito's analytical framework. In explaining the system, she writes:

> "In MK the first high pitch in a verb stem or a noun was distinctive, and after that pitches seem to be governed by automatic rules of prosody. That is, it is assumed that MK had an *accentual* system, not a *tonal* system like Chinese, although the pitches were called *tones*."

In other words, what are called "tones" by the Korean authors of the texts were actually pitch accents instead. The distinction that Ito draws between the two types of systems is useful and natural.

Here's why. As Ito points out, none of the tones after that first high pitch in the word carried any lexical information. They were predictable and non-distinctive. Then there was the behavior of what was marked as the Rising Tone. As Ito says, that "tone" was a morphophonemic combination of a low pitch plus a high pitch—in other words, a Rising Tone consisted of a long, rising-pitched syllable, the second mora of which carried the locus of the morpheme's accent. From that fact other facts follow. For example, in describing the Rising Tone, Ito says that it occurred only in initial syllables. That was not always true, though, at least in the early textual record; for example, *tay*^{L}*Wem*^{R} 'great tiger' (with a Rising Tone marked on the second syllable) is found in the very first MK text, the 1447 *Yongbi ŏch' ŏn ka*. ('The Song of the Dragons Flying Through Heaven' 龍飛御天歌). What I believe was the case instead was a tendency to avoid rising pitch in non-initial syllables, especially in case the syllable was preceded by a high, or another rising, pitch. In other words, the distinctive element in a Rising Tone—that is, the high pitch it carried on its second mora—was lost when another accent preceded it. But whenever a "Rising Tone" was preceded by only low pitch, and thus not by an accent, the locus of the high pitch contained in the Rising-Tone syllable was crucial because it was distinctive.

Even better evidence for the naturalness of Ito's analysis can be found in the modern dialects where pitch distinctions have been preserved. In my work I have found that the pitch pattern of a modern reflex can be completely accounted for once we know where the accent locus is, and that accent locus in the modern word can be related directly to the locus of the first high pitch in the MK word. That is to say, what makes Ito's findings seem even more relevant is the fact that they have endured. The correspondences she points to in the Middle Korean textual record are also found in the language today.

Many questions about the MK system remain, of course. To what extent was its pitch system really like those found in the modern Korean dialects? Here is one obvious, but basic, question: In the modern dialects, the accent (or tone) of most monosyllables is morphophonemic—that is, it can only be detected if the word is followed by another element, a particle or the copula. For example, the syllable [pE] can mean either 'pear', 'boat', or 'belly' in Hamgyŏng. But when followed by the nominative particle, our Hamgyŏng speaker will pronounce it [pEGA] when it means 'pear' and [P€ga] if it means 'boat' or 'belly'. In other words, the system is in this respect like the familiar pitch accent system found in Tokyo Japanese. However, in MK texts, the tone of each syllable was marked, even when it appeared in isolation. What are we to conclude about the MK pitch system from this fact? Were MK scribes representing phonetic reality, or were they simply transcribing underlying lexical distinctions? It is difficult to know. Nevertheless, whatever conclusions we draw about such puzzles, I for one am convinced by all circumstantial evidence that Ito has analyzed the system correctly as one involving pitch accent.

Let me turn briefly to another problem, and that is the phonetic descriptions of the Middle Chinese tones. I am not sure what source Ito has used for these descriptions, but it seems to me there is no way to be sure about phonetic values when describing such changeable features. Even in modern varieties of Mandarin, tonal registers and contours vary widely; can we imagine that was not also the case 1,400 years ago? What were Chinese tones like then? There is very little we can say for sure. Most Sinologists now believe that Chinese tonal categories originally represented segmental distinctions, and many argue that these segmentals endured well into the Middle Chinese period. Note also that we are talking about a lapse of almost a thousand years from the beginning of the Middle Chinese period to the transcription of the MK texts. Other than noting the correspondences of distinctive categories, I do not believe there is much that can be concluded about Middle Chinese tones from the phonetic values of Korean pitch.

Ito has produced a careful study of SK tones that exceeds in detail anything else that has been written about them. She has taken the foundation provided by Kōno Rokurō's landmark study of Sino-Korean and built upon it. The explanations she provides for the correspondences between the SK values and the MC tonal categories are carefully reasoned and convincing. Some of the details she produces give provocative hints about future research extending well beyond SK tones. For example, she notes that the Korean initial consonant *h* does not pattern the way aspirated consonants do; is that perhaps a clue that the consonant had a separate historical origin? Her observation is a useful and provocative one.

Ito's research also raises more general linguistic issues. For one thing, let us remember that she is talking about the transfer of distinctions across language boundaries. We all know that Sino-Korean words and morphemes were not, strictly speaking, loanwords; they were borrowed systematically using the structure of rhyming dictionaries and rhyme tables as guides. What access did the Koreans have to the sounds of the Chinese sources, and to what extent did actual pronunciations shape what the Koreans came up with? How did the Koreans cope with the distinctions of tone using the phonological resources at their disposal? I have at various times speculated that the Chinese system itself acted as a catalyst for Korean tonogenesis; perhaps the weight of that Sino-Korean vocabulary effected phonological changes in native words that produced the pitch system we see in Middle Korean.

The question is, why are Sino-Korean tones different from Sino-Japanese tones? As is well known, Japanese had a well-developed pitch accent, or tone, system at least as early the 8th century, and almost certainly long before that. The Japanese system reflected a greater array of pitch distinctions than did Middle Korean, and the system was apparently much more stable and balanced. How is it, then, that Chinese tones are not reflected equally well in Sino-Japanese? The question makes the Korean correspondences all the more surprising, and at the same time, all the more fascinating.

REFERENCES

Hashimoto Mantarō. 1978. *Gengo ruikei chiriron* [言語類型地理論]. Tokyo: Kōbundō.

Kim Wanjin. 1973. *Chungse kugŏ sŏngjo ŭi yŏn'gu* [中世國語 聲調의 硏究]. Seoul University dissertation.

Kim Yŏngman. 1967a. "Ijo chŏn'gi ŭi hantcha-ŭm ŭi unyul (sŏngjo) I [이조 전기의 한자음의 운율(성조) I]". *Han'gŭl* 139:67-78.

Kim Yŏngman. 1967b. "Ijo chŏn'gi ŭi hantcha-ŭm ŭi unyul (sŏngjo) II [이조 전기의 한자음의 운율(성조) II]". *Han'gŭl* 140:95-113.
Ramsey, Samuel Robert. 1977. *Accent and Morphology in Korean Dialects*. Seoul:Tower Press.

On tone in Tamang and neighbouring languages: synchrony and diachrony

Martine Mazaudon
LACITO, Centre National de la Recherche Scientifique, Paris
mazaudon@vjf.cnrs.fr

It would be easy to believe that tone "languages" constitute by now a well defined typological category. Numerous books and articles have endeavoured to provide us with a reliable definition, with a list of characteristics. But there are at least two classes of powerful contenders for the title of prototypical tone language. These classes can be exemplified by (1) a Nilo-Saharan African language like Kunama, with its three level tones, assignable to each mora, and four contour tones analysable as 'tone-clusters' of level tones (Yip M., 2002:141-2) on the one hand, or (2) an Asian language like Vietnamese, with six melodic tones, assignable to each syllable.

Languages with a lower concentration of lexically distinctive pitches in the spoken chain were not traditionally assigned to the "tone language" category (Pike K. L., 1948), unless the interplay of a tone system with an accent system could be invoked to explain away the absence of pitch contrasts on unstressed syllables by neutralization (Martinet A., 1967:90-91). Some of these less than fully tonal languages were categorized as "pitch-accent" systems, with either Swedish, Norwegian or Serbo-Croatian acting as the prototype (Lehiste I., 1970:85).

Beside the tone-bearing unit, and the possibility of analysing contours as "tone-clusters" (as in Kunuma) or not (as in Vietnamese), a third aspect of tone systems which can be debated is "the interaction between tone and non-tonal (typically laryngeal) features," which can sometimes be interpreted as "a phonological condition on tone" or "even be a part of the definition of a tone, e.g. the low creaky tone of Vietnamese" (Hyman L., 2001:1371).

For the Tamangish (or TGTM) branch of Tibeto-Burman, and for the tonal dialects of Tibetan, in the neighbouring Bodish branch, we make two claims.

(1) The tone bearing unit is the morpheme, or the word.

(2) Cooccurring laryngeal features are best analyzed as features of the tones.

The historical origin of these tones in segmental material at the beginning and the end of words is consistent with these synchronic claims.

1. The tonal situation of languages of the Tamangish (TGTM) and Bodish (Tibetan) groups

Following Shafer's classification, the languages discussed here all belong to one division from among the six in Sino-Tibetan,[1] the Bodic division, a name formed from

[1] Shafer's six divisions of Sino-Tibetan, all bearing names in *–ic* are 1. Bodic,2. Burmic, a very large group containing, among others, Burmese, the Yi languages in China, and

bod, the name of Tibet in Tibetan. The Bodic division contains four sections, one of which, the Bodish section, contains two main branches, the Bodish branch, consisting of all the Tibetan dialects, and the Gurung branch, which I have renamed "Tamang" or "the Tamangish branch," in accordance with the speakers' autonym, or TGTM after the initials of its main languages, Tamang, Gurung, Thakali, and Manangke (Shafer R., 1955). No claim is made here concerning the higher level classification of the family, but the many dialects of Tibetan and Tamangish are definitely closely related.

Geographically, these two branches of the Tibeto-Burman (TB) family are located contiguously at the south-western edge of the Sino-Tibetan area, in contact with the non-tonal Indo-Aryan languages. If tonogenesis has spread from the east, it might be expected that this western edge would have been reached most recently, and that tone formation processes could still be observed, yielding typologically "less tonal" languages.

Languages of the Tamang branch are all tonal, and have very similar four-tone systems, in regular etymological correspondence. The bipartition of an earlier two-tone system is reconstructible, but the origin of these two tones is obscure. I have shown that Benedict's attempt to correlate the two old Tamang tones to the two tones reconstructed for Lolo-Burmese and Sino-Tibetan is not conclusive. (Benedict P. K., 1972; Mazaudon M., 1985).

Tibetan dialects on the other hand go from toneless, as in Ngaba Amdo, to marginally tonal with almost no functional load, as in Balti (Pakistan), to fully tonal as in Lhasa, Shigatse, or Dzongkha (Bhutan), although some redundancy with associated segmental features remains (Huang B., 1995 ; Sun J. T.-S., 1997, 2003). For Tibetan we are lucky to have a written form dating from the 7th century, predating tonogenesis. Tibetan tones are more recent than the two proto-Tamang tones. They can easily be traced to segmental material at the beginning and the end of words as reflected in the conservative Tibetan orthography. Tamangish is close to Tibetan, but their separation dates from before the period of Written Tibetan (WT). The reconstruction of the older Tamangish two-tone system has to be done by internal and comparative reconstruction inside the group of Tamangish dialects (Mazaudon M., 1978). This system is not shared by Old Tibetan, which appears to have been toneless.

2. The domain of tone

In a recent encyclopedia article Hyman proposes the following definition: "A language with tone is one in which an indication of pitch enters into the lexical realization of at least some morphemes" (Hyman L., 2001:1368). But Hyman specifically avoids saying that all languages that have tone (in the sense of his definition) are "tone languages" (ibid. 1376). The problem with Hyman's definition, for the languages we are concerned with, is that it contains an unspoken part, which is listed

---

the Kuki-Naga languages in India, 3. Baric, i.e. the group around the Bodo-Garo languages of Assam, 4. Karenic, the Karen languages in Burma and Thailand, 5. Sinitic, the Chinese so-called 'dialects', and 6. Daic, i.e. Thai Kadai and their group. The Daic division is not now generally considered to be a member of Sino-Tibetan. Tibeto-Burman is here used to designate divisions 1 to 4.

as a "property" of tone. The "tone bearing unit (TBU)" is said to be the mora, the vowel, or at most the syllable (ibid. 1368). Any assignment of a pitch pattern to a larger domain has to be worked out as an interplay of stress and tone. So Swedish type "pitch-accent" systems are considered as "hybrids" which mix properties of stress-systems and of tone-systems, while a system like Tokyo Japanese is regarded as a "restricted tone-system" (ibid. 1376). Himalayan tones are not considered.

I started working on Nepalese Tibeto-Burman languages in 1969, at about the same time as Kenneth Pike and some members of his team. Pike was the author of the famous early definition of a tone language as "a language having lexically significant, contrastive but relative pitch on each syllable" (Pike K. L., 1948:3). After a few months of working with Tamang, Gurung and Thakali, Pike was led to admit that the "foot" or "phonological word" was the domain in which pitch and voice quality (breathiness) contrasts had to be stated (Pike K. L., 1970). At this point the analysis was still in progress, and Pike's statement was made in terms of "restrictions". By mid 1970, however, he co-authored with Maria Hari and Doreen Taylor a paper on Western Tamang which plainly states that "the domain for each of these contrasts [of breathiness and pitch contour] is the morpheme or the morpheme followed by non-tonal suffixes" (Hari M., D. Taylor & K. L. Pike, 1970:82).

At the same time, I worked out the tonal system of a dialect of Eastern Tamang, which, unsurprisingly, had similar characteristics. The demonstration was done in my dissertation in 1971 and was published in 1973. (Mazaudon M., 1973b:61-92). I must say that, without the moral support of Pike, the official proponent of the one-tone-per-syllable theory, I would never, as a PhD student at the time, have dared to believe that my inability to break down the tonal patterns into successions of syllabic tones with sandhi or accentual restrictions was not simply due to my own incompetence. Of course a "solution" is always possible inside a theory, provided enough fudging is allowed. I believe the theory should rather be revised to allow for some languages with a TBU larger than the syllable.

I will briefly summarize the evidence for TGTM languages, then compare the structure of their tonal domain to that of some Tibetan dialects.

2.1 Word-tone in the languages of the Tamang group (TGTM)

In TGTM languages the tone bearing unit in the lexicon is the morpheme; in the sentence, it is the word, formed from a tonal lexical item plus its atonal grammatical affixes. The tonal melody which characterizes the tone of the lexical item fully determines the pitch of the suffix or string of suffixes. In many cases, the melody simply extends, or rather deploys itself over the number of syllables available.

All languages of the Tamang branch described until now[2] exhibit a four-tone system (Mazaudon M., 1978). Pitch values on monosyllabic words for eight of these dialects are represented in Figure 1,[3] using Chao Yuen-ren's notation (Chao Y.-r., 1933).

[2] There are two exceptions: Chantyal, which has borrowed 80% of its vocabulary from Indo-Aryan Nepali, and is reported to have lost its tone system (Noonan M., 2003) and an urban variety of Manangke spoken by young bilinguals in Kathmandu, which is

	TAMANG			THAKALI			GURUNG	MANANG
tone	Ris.	Sahu	Taglung	Tukche	Marpha	Syang	Ghachok	Ngawal
1.	54	44	55/44	54	43	43	33	33
2.	44	54	43	44/33	45	45	54	45
3.	33/22	11	33/22	11	33/22	11	11	54
4.	211	32	51	121	51	33/22	12	31

Fig. 1. Phonetic pitch of the 4 tones on monosyllables in 8 dialects of the TGTM group

2.1.1 Excursus on tonogenesis in TGTM: a case of tonal bipartition

Five of the eight dialects listed have a main split in their system between two high tones and two low tones. These are Risiangku and Sahugaon Tamang, Tukche and Syang Thakali, and Ghachok Gurung. Correlatively, the low tones are accompanied by a particular phonation type, which has been described as breathiness (shown by a grey background in the chart), while the two high tones are pronounced with modal voice.

Two more features are associated with low tone words in these five dialects, one phonological, one phonetic. First, and this is valid for all eight dialects, the obstruent initials, on which a contrast of aspiration exists under tone-1 and tone-2, do not contrast for aspiration under tone-3 and tone-4. In words of tones 3 and 4, only one laryngeal mode is found on word-initial consonants. In the five dialects with a main High/Low division, the resulting archiphoneme is unaspirated.

Secondly, phonetically, obstruent initials under the low tones in these five dialects can be optionally slightly voiced. Nowhere in the phonemic systems of the eight dialects is a voicing contrast pertinent:[4] initials on the high tones are either voiceless aspirated or voiceless unaspirated, phonetically and phonemically. In intervocalic position, unaspirated obstruents are voiced, and often spirantized. In dialects where the intervocalic aspiration contrast exists (Risiangku among them) the aspirated obstruents remain unchanged (no deaspiration, no voicing, no spirantization).

reported to have reduced its tone system to a simple high-low opposition (Hildebrandt K., 2003).

[3] Language cum ethnic names are on the first line, village names on the second line. Ris. is Risiangku, Sahu is Sahugaon.

[4] Nepali loans in Gurung are an exception.

Tone	*Voice quality*	*Phonemic contrast*
tone-1	modal voice	ph *vs* p ...
tone-2	modal voice	ph *vs* p ...
tone-3	breathy voice	*no contrast* [bɦ~b~p]
tone-4	breathy voice	*no contrast* [bɦ~b~p]

Fig. 2. Relationship of tones and initials in Risiangku, Sahu, Tukche, Syang, Ghachok

The relationship between pitch and laryngeal features on the vowel and the initial is a giveaway for the origin of the tones. We can readily reconstruct the redundant occasional feature of voice as belonging to the ancestral stage, while a tonal opposition developed later from what used to be redundant pitch lowering after proto-voiced initials. As devoicing of the obstruent initials progressed, the voicing contrast on continuants and sibilants disappeared, and tones were phonemicized. We can thus reconstruct an old system for Proto-TGTM with two tones, a three-way contrast (aspirated, voiceless, voiced) on obstruent initials, and a two-way contrast (voiced and voiceless) on continuant initials. For a step by step demonstration see (Mazaudon M., 1973a, 1978). This is the absolutely standard scenario of tonal bipartition which took place repeatedly all over Asia, as demonstrated by Haudricourt for Vietnamese and Chinese in his 1954 articles (Haudricourt A.-G., 1954b, 1954a), and which we can represent in the format he used in his detailed survey "Bipartition et tripartition des systèmes de tons dans quelques langues d'Extrême-Orient" (Haudricourt A.-G., 1961).

Initials ↓ *Tones* →	*A	*B
k,ts,t,p..., kh,tsh,th,ph..., s, *hm>m, *hn>n ..., *hl>l, *hr>r ...	1	2
*g>k, *dz>ts, *d>t, *b>p ..., *z>s..., m, n, ..., l, r, w...	3	4

Fig. 3. Bipartition of tones in proto-TGTM

We will return to the other three dialects in section 4.1, after considering the domain of the tones.

2.1.2 The domain of tone in TGTM

In all languages of the group, grammatical suffixes are reported to be devoid of distinctive tones, and to carry pitch patterns entirely conditioned by the tone of the root.

As an example, Figure 4 presents the four tonal contours of Risiangku Tamang as pronounced by a male speaker on verb roots followed by the suffix /-ma/. The contours are averaged over 38 different verbs in a carrier sentence. The carrier sentence — /X-ma X-ma ^{3}la:nan X-ci/ 'He X-ed a lot' (X-ing X-ing much X-ed) — provides three occurrences of the verb+suffix combination in three positions on the intonation curve. The second occurrence of /X-ma/ was chosen for the present calculation[5].

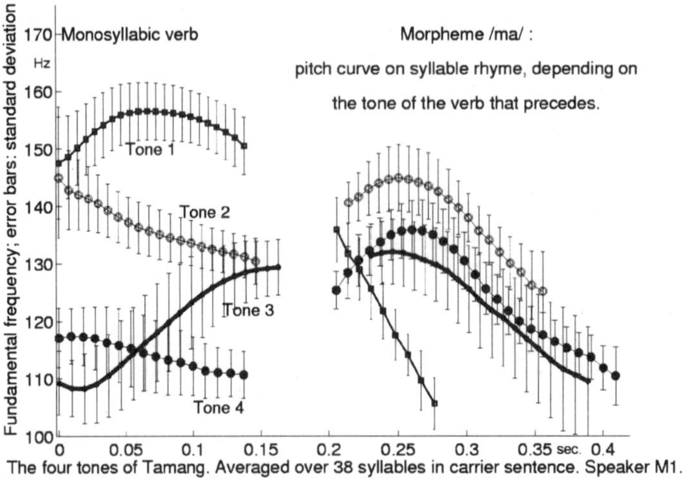

Fig. 4. The four tones of Risiangku on disyllabic bimorphemic verbal words

The same patterns occur on disyllabic monomorphemic nouns.

Except for some realignment in timing, and occasional loss of the extremities of the curve on short items, these patterns are the same four patterns that are realized on monosyllabic monomorphemic words. Thus in a language like Risiangku Tamang, which has an independent opposition between long and short vowels, we observe the same four tones on a short CV word, a long CVV word, a monomorphemic CVCV disyllable, bimorphemic CV-CV or CVCV-CV words, and so on up to trisyllabic morphemes, which are rare, or roots with strings of suffixes, which are frequent.

As an example, we can compare, in Figure 5, the fall-rise on the word 'horse' (resulting in the acoustic impression of a level tone), with the tone-2 pattern on verbal words in Figure 4, which falls on the first syllable and rises on the second syllable (before a phrase-final fall which is found with all tones). The sentence is : /^{2}ta ^{3}pi-pa/ 'he says horse'. Similarly, on a tone-2 trisyllabic word, the first syllable falls gently, the second is higher, and the third slightly lower than the second. (Fig. 6).

---

5 Thanks to Alexis Michaud for realizing this figure. The measures were done on open syllable verb roots with a long vowel exemplifying the different vocalic qualities. Data for individual syllables were interpolated linearly at 100 time points equally spaced between the beginning and end of the vowel, so that the results could be averaged over syllables. More technical detail on the method can be found in A. Michaud's article, "Final consonants and glottalization: new perspectives from Hanoi Vietnamese", *Phonetica* 61:119-146 (2004).

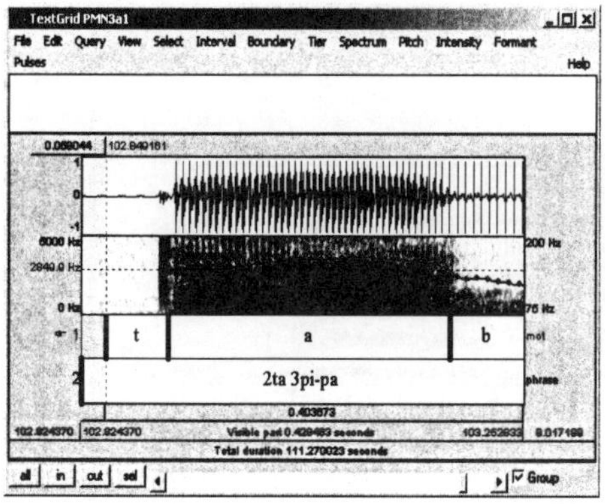

Fig.5. An example of tone-2 on a short CV word /^{2}ta/ 'horse' in Risiangku

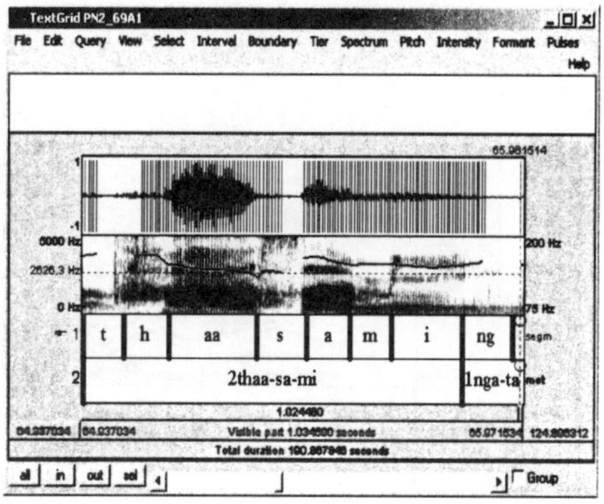

Fig.6. A tone-2 trisyllabic word in Risiangku /^{2}tha:-sa-mi/ 'if he cuts'

Tone-1, a high-falling tone in Risiangku, falls sharply, after an optional rise, on phrase-final monosyllables. In the tone-1 disyllabic words of Figure 4 this is realized by the sharp increase in the slope of the Fall on the suffix. Note also that brevity was described as a correlative character of tone-1 on monosyllables (Mazaudon M., 1973b:63). In Figure 4 we observe that the verb root is not significantly shorter for tone-1 than for the other tones, but the suffix is extremely short.

The same expansion-compression of the tonal melody can be observed in the other TGTM languages.

We will now take an example from Tukche Thakali, from a recording by Maria Hari (Hari M., 1971). Figure 7 compares two tone-4 monomorphemic words, /^{4}me/ (spelled 'meh) 'cow' and /^{4}came/ ('cahme) 'daughter' in the carrier sentence /cu nga-c -- ihmu/ 'this is my '.

It appears that the full pattern Fall-Rise-Leveling-and-Fall that is realized on the disyllable /^{4}came/ is simplified to almost only the Rise on the short vowel of the monosyllable /^{4}me/. If we were to consider the first syllable as the sole carrier of the tone, /^{4}me/ would be a rising tone, and /^{4}came/ would be a falling tone. When a final nasal lengthens the rime, as in /^{4}tim/ ('tihm) the overall melody on the rime (Fig 7c) resembles closely that on the disyllable /^{4}came/ (Fig 7b); the rise is delayed as compared to /^{4}me/.

7a
7b
7c

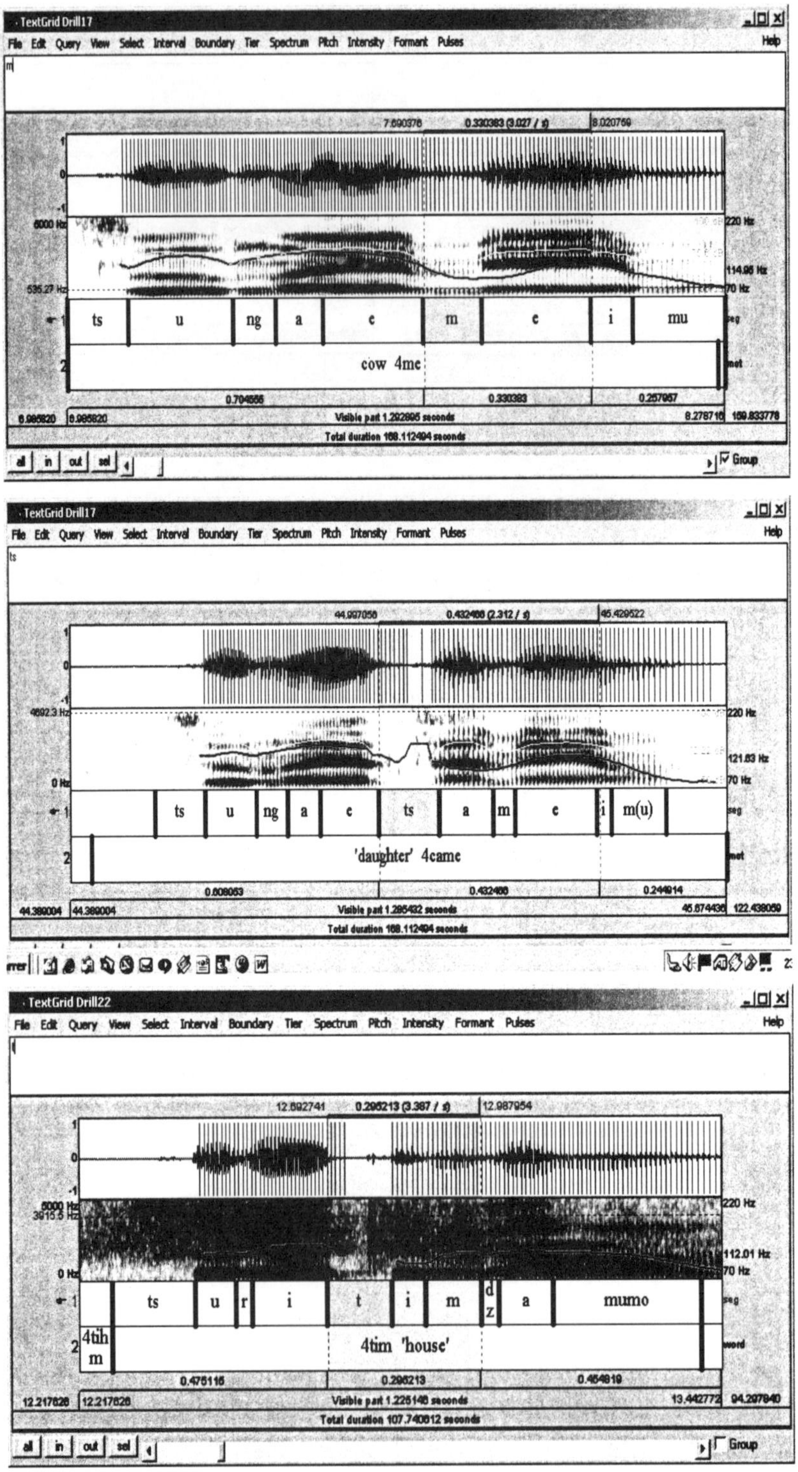

Fig.7. Tone-4 in Tukche Thakali on: a. short monosyllable b. disyllable c. VN rime

In Manangke, a recent paper by Kristine Hildebrandt presents tracings of tone contrasts on quasi-minimal sets, showing the spreading of tone patterns on monosyllables, disyllabic roots, and disyllabic words formed of verb stems + nominalizer suffix (Hildebrandt K., 2005:26-31). This can be shown for all languages of the group.

I have dwelt at length on the issue of the tone-bearing unit and presented some phonetic illustrations because this type of system is uncommon. It is likely connected to emergent tone systems (provided that emergence is understood as a process which can last for centuries), rather than to long established systems. Nonetheless it should be emphasized that it can be ascribed to the same consonant-based laryngeal origin which is at the source of so many Asian tones and not to "prosodic features such as length, stress, and intonational tones," as is postulated for pitch-accent languages (Ove L., 2004).

As a final remark, note that, in Risiangku Tamang, breathiness, which we will consider in Section 3, also extends over the whole morpheme[6] (maybe the word), unless it is stopped by a phonetically voiceless segment, that is, an aspirated stop or /s/.

2.2 The domain of tone in Tibetan languages

The tonal dialects of Tibetan also have word-tone systems. They differ from the TGTM type in that part of the word may fall out of the domain of the tone. These extrametrical syllables, short and unstressed, disappear in Dzongkha, leaving a compensatory fall in pitch.

2.2.1 Lhasa

In Lhasa Tibetan as described by Sprigg (Sprigg R. K., 1954, 1955), Chang and Shefts (Shefts B. C., 1968b, 1968a), Hu (Hu Tan, 1982), and many others, we can distinguish four prosodic entities on monosyllables: high, high falling-glottalized, low, and low-rising-falling-glottalized. A length distinction exists additionally on non glottalized syllables. Depending on the features that each analyst chooses to include as "tonal," this results in 2 (only HIGH and LOW) to 6 possible "tones" (if length is considered an attribute of tone).[7] Length can occur on initial or non-initial syllables, and I believe it is best treated as separate from the tone pattern. On longer items, whether etymologically compounds or formed of a root plus a derivational suffix, the same four patterns are encountered: the beginning of the word is high or low, the end is falling-glottalized or level-smooth, and the intervening syllables are high.

The segmental origin of these pitch patterns has been understood for over a century because the older form of non-tonal Tibetan is faithfully reflected in the orthography. As in TGTM, and possibly at roughly the same time, the loss of the voicing contrast on the initials (complicated by the simplification of initial clusters) gave rise to the high/low register contrast which all authors recognize. Note that this emergence of a tonal contrast occurred in a toneless language, whereas the TGTM

---

[6] In Tukche Thakali and Gurung it is reported to be limited to the first syllable.

[7] CV [54] and [12], CVV or CVN [55] and [113], CVc or CVNc or CVC [52] and [132] after (Hu Tan, 1982:18-20).

languages were already tonal. The two "falling-glottalized tones" are reported to have alternative pronunciations, without a noticeable fall when a final oral or glottal stop is actually pronounced (Sprigg R. K., 1955). Some other authors consider such pronunciations as a reflection of the orthography. Whatever the case may be, the transphonologization of the closure due to the presence of a final obstruent in a falling pitch pattern is a later development, still in progress.

From the point of view of the domain of tone, it should be noted that word-internally, whether syllable final consonants are present or not, there is no falling pitch, and whether syllable initials are spelled with voiced initials or not, there is no low tone.[8] It all works as if only the word-initial and word-final consonants had their features transferred to a tonal contrast. And I would like to suggest that this may indeed have been the case.

There is a typological difference, however, between Lhasa Tibetan and languages of the Tamang group. All Tamang syllables appear to be about equally stressed. In Lhasa Tibetan, inflectional (as opposed to derivational) suffixes, like case-markers and verbal suffixes, are de-stressed. Correlatively, they are "extrametrical" from the tonal point of view, "in that the host syllable they are attached to is characterized by domain-final contours, as if the enclitics do not count as part of the tonal domain" to quote J. Sun's formulation (Sun J. T.-S., 1997:503) (see also Mazaudon, 1977:82-83). These suffixes are written without tone marks in Chang and Shefts' transcription and marked low by Sprigg. They do not carry the distinctive features of the root tone, and play no role in its identification.

2.2.2 Dzongkha

A last type of tonal development I would like to touch upon occurred in Dzongkha, the national language of Bhutan. The languages of the Bodish section, and to a large extent TB languages in general, are poor in accentual contrasts. They do not generally give prominence, either by way of F0 or intensity, to one syllable per unit. Either all syllables have roughly equal prominence, as in the TGTM group, or one syllable per unit is weak. This last is the case of Burmese schwa syllables at the beginning of the word, a structure which Matisoff has named "sesquisyllable" (Matisoff J. A., 1999:11).

What we just mentioned about extrametrical suffixes in Lhasa points to the opposite pattern: a weak syllable at the end of the word. Dzongkha has pushed this characteristic one step further, and reduced disyllables to monosyllables. (Mazaudon M. & B. Michailovsky, 1988). In so doing it gave rise to a bipartition of its High/Low basic system (of the same origin as in Tibetan or TGTM) into a four-tone system. Monosyllables derived from old disyllables have falling pitch, while historical monosyllables have level pitch, except for old vowel + *r* and *l* rimes which also have falling pitch. Ex. WT *thag-pa* > thap [42] 'rope' , WT *thap* > thap [44] 'stove'. The

[8] The reported "spreading", in the Lhasa dialect, of an initial low tone into a second syllable if it is long (whence a phonetic rise) does not constitute counter evidence, since the low pitch realized in that context is non distinctive (Sun J. T.-S., 1997:501sqq ; 2003:40). This non coincidence of pitch patterns with syllabic boundaries actually makes Lhasa more similar to Tamang.

synchronic result is a four-tone system on all syllable types, except short open CV syllables.

2.3 The origin of word-tone in Bodish

The basic question in this domain is whether richer systems of syllabic tones existed before and were reduced through sandhi phenomena in polysyllabic words, or whether word-tone systems emerged as such. In recent compounds, across Bodish languages, both in the TGTM and in the Tibetan group, we find that two behaviours are possible depending on the degree of integration of the compound. Some compounds retain the tones of each component. This is often accompanied by other signs of the independance of the components, for instance, in Risiangku Tamang, retaining a long vowel in the second component, and failing to voice the initial of the second component. Composition in this case is only syntactic (no possible separation of the components without a change in meaning). Other compounds acquire a single tone. Some can oscillate between the two structures.

For those words which always have a single tone, the date of compounding cannot be ascertained for unwritten languages, but certainly a number at least of modern Tibetan compounds and words derived through suffixation are attested as such from the beginning of Written Tibetan. In such old polysyllabic items, I have heard from classical Tibetan scholars that many "spelling mistakes" occur in old texts between all three series of initials: voiced, voiceless and aspirated. This indicates that the three-way manner contrast which gave rise to tone in word-initial position was not present in intervocalic position at the time when tone started to develop, and explains why tone did not develop in non-initial syllables.

The other source of initial-based tonal contrasts in Tibetan was the reduction of initial clusters: this did not occur in word internal position, where the clusters are still found.[9] Thus a second potential source of tonal opposition was unavailable in internal position.

3. The non-F0 cues of tone, concomitant, successive, or alternative

3.1 Breathiness and Tamang tones

3.1.1 Phonation and melody: concomitant or successive

As we have already mentioned, breathiness on the initial consonant and the rime cooccurrs with low tone in most Tibetan dialects and in all TGTM dialects. This is not to say that the degree of breathiness or the implementation of breathiness is the same everywhere. According to Silverman, Tamang is an exception to a general rule he was able to establish according to which, in languages where a tonal system and a phonation contrast coexist, the implementation of features of tone and features of phonation (creak or breathiness) are sequential, not simultaneous. Typically, in a system which has tone, breathy phonation would occur at the beginning of the vowel, or on the end of an initial sonorant and the beginning of the vowel, leaving the end of the vowel free for tonal

[9] A more detailed argument is given in (Mazaudon M., 1974:36-38, and 1977:87-90).

contrasts, as in Mazatec, an Otomanguean language of Mexico (Silverman D., 1997:152-4), or alternatively it could occur later, after tonal contrasts, and be heard as post-vocalic aspiration, as in Jeh, a Mon-Khmer language of Vietnam (ibid. 144-6). Breathiness blurs tonal information, and thus the simultaneity of tone information and phonation information is less than optimal from an efficiency point of view.

Sequencing or "phasing", to use Silverman's term, is not the way TGTM languages treat this potential conflict. All sources report the presence of breathiness all through the vowel, often starting during a sonorant initial, and the occasional perception of a post-vocalic *h*-like sound. In Risiangku Tamang I have even observed that breathiness may extend to the following syllable if not arrested by an intervening phonetically voiceless consonant (an aspirate or /s/).

Silverman surmises (ibid. 194) that since Tamang uses tone and breathiness in a non-sequential manner, Tamang breathiness must be weak. This is indeed the case. There is much less noise in a Tamang breathy word than in a Nepali word starting with a so-called voiced aspirate.

But there is another consideration which will resolve Tamang's exceptionality. Maddieson (Maddieson I., 1984:132) reinterprets the Tamang four-tone system as the combination of two tones and two phonation types. This can be done mechanically from the charts in Figures 1 and 2, by analysing tone-3 as "tone-1 + breathy", and tone-4 as "tone-2 + breathy" (tone-1 being "tone-1 + clear", and tone-2 now being "tone-2 + clear"). However Mazaudon (1973: 79-84) has demonstrated at some length that any analysis of the four tones as combinations of binary features resulted in arbitrary choices, and concluded that the best interpretation was a scalar system of four tones from highest to lowest, each tone having idiosyncratic secondary cues. Breathiness is one of those secondary cues. In this interpretation Tamang is no longer an example of a "laryngeally complex language", defined as a language making independent phonological use of F0 and voice quality. Pitch and phonation cues to tonal oppositions in Tamang can be realized concomitantly because they are cues to a single tone rather than distinct entities.

Silverman observes that laryngeal features usually are formed with a "primary gesture", e.g. "lower vocal fold tension" for low tone and "higher glottal aperture" for breathiness. Each feature also has concomitant "enhancing gestures", which contribute to its audibility (ibid.:141-3). As it happens, breathy voice and low tone share some "enhancing gestures", like "lower larynx." The primary gesture for each of them also happens to be a member of the set of enhancing gestures of the other. So, if low tone and breathiness cooccur they reinforce each other. This actually is rather consistent with the details of Tamang phonetics. In Risiangku, tone-4, the lowest tone, is also the more breathy of the two low tones. Tone-3, which is less low and less breathy than tone-4, conversely retains more often and to a greater degree the etymological voiced (or lenis) character of the initial stop.

So if Silverman would employ my analysis of Tamang tones, tones 3 and 4 would be, like Mandarin third tone, cases of tonal melody with secondary phonation cues, and he would be left with only one exception to his generalization, the Mpi language of Thailand, whose use of creakiness is unresolved.

3.1.2 The alternative use of tonal cues

The alternative use of cues to a given phonemic entity constitutes the synchronic variation which allows historical change. During the evolution of TGTM languages, after a period when low pitch and breathy phonation increased together while the initial was becoming more and more voiceless, these two features started going their separate ways in some dialects, as we will see in Section 4. Thus when tone-4 in Taglung Tamang had become high falling (instead of very low[10]) the breathy phonation stopped being an "enhancer" and was dropped.

Synchronically, I noted in Risiangku that among variant realizations of tone-4, when the pitch fell to the bottom of the range, the initial was totally voiceless, and breathiness too was absent. When the tone is low enough, the additional cue of breathiness can be dispensed with.

Allophony, or allotony between pitch and non-pitch features is found in languages other than Tamang. In Latvian, for example, Lehiste says, "Laryngealization is the one consistent phonetic feature associated with the so-called third tone," (Lehiste I., 1970:90) and again, "Laryngealization [...] may also function [...] as an allotone of low pitch." In a similar manner, allophony between a final consonant and a melodic pattern is often claimed for Tibetan.

3.2 Breathiness and Tibetan tones

3.2.1 The high pitch of non-initial syllables

Yip (Yip M., 2002:196-9), following Duanmu (Duanmu S., 1992), proposes a synchronic analysis of Lhasa Tibetan which explains the High pitch on internal syllables as the spreading of a postulated High component which is postulated to be present in all initial tones. Thus high initial would be H, and a low initial would be LH. This is postulated to explain the high pitch of word internal syllables in Lhasa.

Sun convincingly refutes this argument by demonstrating that High in Lhasa (and in all other Tibetan dialects) is the neutral tone, and need not be posited underlyingly (Sun J. T.-S., 1997). He points out that his analysis is also consistent with history. The default tone is High synchronically because it was always high; it is unchanged from the non-tonal stage of old Tibetan. I would like to phrase this a little differently, following the same line of argument. Instead of saying that in old Tibetan "all syllables were normally produced in the high register" (Sun, 1997:508), I would prefer to say they were all produced with a modal voice (and no pitch register). The important point is that, as Sun rightly emphasizes, when pitch differences started to be phonologized, some syllables migrated to Low, and not the reverse. Thus the internal syllables, with their high pitch, represent the unchanged state historically, which is also the synchronic default tone (in a syllabic analysis) in modern Tibetan

---

[10] This kind of evolution of melodic tones is nothing miraculous. It is definitely not a one step process, as shown by dialect comparison (Mazaudon, 1978). When a Low cannot become any lower, it turns rising or falling (in a very similar way to *i > ai in the Great English vowel shift), after which any portion of the curve can become the prominent cue.

Sun draws an argument for his analysis of "High" as the default across all Tibetan dialects from two Khams dialects, Derge and Batang, where a proto-voiced initial, when unprefixed, yielded a voiceless initial with low tone (WT go > Derge ko (L) 'hear'), but where those proto-voiced initials which were originally prefixed remained voiced, and had a High tone (WT dgu > gu (H) 'nine'). So, says Sun, since voice phonetically lowers the pitch, if a High occurs after a voiced initial it has to be original. This case constitutes a good example, in my view, of how alternative cues which are used in a period of change get settled or not: in forms where voicing was retained, low pitch, even if it developed phonetically at the time, did not become established as a main cue, and it was eventually dropped in later evolution.

"Furthermore," Sun remarks, "register on syllables with **synchronically** [Sun's emphasis] voiced obstruent initials show variation in register which is apparently random in some dialects, e.g. Derge (Huang B., 1995), Chamdo (Liu F.-H., 1984)." This Khams data is a textbook case for a structuralist analysis: if there is no difference, there is no object. If Low does not exist after modern voiced initials, then High does not "exist" either. The observed random variation reflects the absence of a phonological contrast, in my terms an archiphoneme, in Sun's terms a neutral tone.

3.2.2 The role of breathiness

Historically I would recast the story, introducing breathy voice as a main actor, in the following terms. Unprefixed voiced initials started devoicing and became breathy, along with the following rime, at the same time as the pitch of the syllable became lower. We have already seen that breathiness and Low pitch are mutually reinforcing. Prefixed voiced initials had their voicing protected by the prevoicing due to the prefix. They may have had a slight depressing effect on pitch, as is reported universally for voiced initials, but that depression was not developed nor phonologized. So, eventually, depending on the dialect, when tone was phonemicized on breathy syllables,[11] voiced initial syllables, which were phonologically toneless,[12] either retained that 'neutral' status, as seen in the random variation in Derge and Chamdo, or lined up as a group with one of the two newly created tones. Or again, as in the example of Batang, quoted by Sun from Gesang (Gesang J., 1985), they split between High and Low according to some other small phonetic difference created by the point of articulation of their initial, as in Batang ndzee (H) 'rice' < WT *'bras vs* ndzee (L) 'to resent' < WT *'gras*.

The intermediate presence of breathiness seems certain. It exists synchronically in many if not most Tibetan dialects, probably in more dialects than has been reported. Mainland Chinese scholars, who are doing a thorough job of describing these dialects, are not in the habit of transcribing phonation differences which are analyzed as a redundant feature. Tone-as-pitch is considered the element to be noted. But for history you need those redundant features: they are the stuff that past and future are made of.

---

[11] That is, cognitively, when tone became the preeminent clue, and phonologically when at least one initial merged totally with another. The first candidate to look for in Bodish is always *z > s, and next the sonorants.

[12] As an unrepentent Prague school structuralist, I would say a neutralization context was created there.

Tibetan and TGTM display in their synchronic state, with their multi-clue tonal systems, an embodiment of the diachronic process. They demonstrate something which is not new but is sometimes forgotten, that phonetically "Voice" may give rise to low(ering) but phonemically it is "Voice merges with Voiceless" which gives rise to Low.

4. The evolution of tones in TGTM after the bipartition

As Haudricourt pointed out, "once it is constituted, the tonal system evolves without remembering its origins".[13] Thus, for example, the old *B-LOW and *B-HIGH tones, in the Popei dialect of Chinese, acquired a high and a low value, respectively, in the modern language.

4.1 Diachronic evolution

The evolution after the bipartition of the three TGTM dialects which we have not yet examined in detail demonstrates this point. In Figure 1 we can see that tone-4 in Taglung and Marpha has evolved from being a very low tone to being the highest tone in the system and sharply falling [51]. It has lost its breathy component at the same time. As an heir to the LOW tonal series, it has kept the neutralisation[14] of aspiration on initial stops, and only voiceless unaspirate stops occur.

In Manang, tone-4 has remained rather low [31], but tone-3 has soared to the top of the scale [54]. Both lost their breathy component, but both keep the trace of their LOW origin in the neutralization of aspiration on their initial stops. Interestingly, the archiphoneme is realized voiceless unaspirated under tone-3, as in Taglung and Marpha, but voiceless aspirated under tone-4. I believe this reflects the difference in the degree of breathiness that we noted in Risiangku Tamang. In Manangke, when devoicing of the initial was complete, the heavy breathiness of tone-4 was reinterpreted as aspiration on segments which allowed it (occlusive stops), and was lost on segments which did not allow aspiration (sonorants and /s/). The breathiness on tone-3, being lighter, was dropped whatever the initial. I noted an occasional extreme tenseness verging on a creak on very high realizations of tone-3. This is a phonetic reinforcement of the tense character of high tones (see Silverman) and not etymological.[15]

4.2 Synchronic evolution

The latest evolution of the Manangke tonal system in the speech of young urban bilinguals also displays an individual evolution of each tone: tones merge according to their phonetic proximity, not their etymological closeness. Hildebrandt shows that, across speakers, tone-1 (old *A-High series but modern *low* level) and tone-4 (old *B-

[13] "Une fois constitué, le système tonal évolue sans souci de sa valeur ancienne étymologique," (Haudricourt A.-G., 1961) (p.286 in the 1972 reprint).

[14] Remember that a "neutralization" is not a "merger". "Neutralisation" in its original meaning in the Prague school, is a synchronic relation, not a diachronic process. Diachronically, neutralisation can result from the loss of an opposition, but just as frequently from the failure to create an opposition.

[15] This might have been a "teaching" pronunciation used by my informants in the context of elicitation. Hildebrandt did not note it.

Low series, modern *low* falling) get closer and closer, and eventually merge for the most advanced speakers. (Hildebrandt K., 2003:177-182). Actually a very slight difference on the coda is still noted on monosyllabic nouns, and Hildebrandt remarks that verb roots followed by a suffix merge totally, but the suffixes following a tone-1 root and following a tone-4 root remain different. Thus the distinction seems to me to be temporarily maintained, although threatened, the timing of the modulation becoming more and more delayed, and being now totally realized on the suffix.

5. Conclusion

The Bodish languages are at the south-western edge of the vast tone-prone area of East and South-East Asia. Their neighbours to the west and south are non-tonal Indo-Aryan languages. It may thus be believed that they constitute the western frontier of the expansion of tone which started somewhere farther east. As such they are newly tonal languages, and they evidence features that may be attributed to that status. As a testimony of the areal spreading of tonality we should remember the presence of word-tone on Punjabi (Bahl K. C., 1956, 1957), a neighbouring Indo-Aryan language.

6. References

Bahl, Kali Chandra, 1956, Tones in Punjabi, *Indian Linguistics* 17:139-147.

—, 1957, A note on tones in Western Punjabi (Lahanda), *Indian Linguistics* 18:30-34.

Benedict, Paul K., 1972, The Sino-Tibetan tonal system., *in* Thomas, J. & L. Bernot (eds), *Langues et techniques, nature et société.* vol. 1, Paris, Klincksieck, p. 25-34.

Chao, Yuen-ren, 1933, A system of tone letters, *Le maître phonétique* 30:24-27.

Duanmu, San, 1992, An autosegmental analysis of tone in four Tibetan languages, *LTBA* 15.1:65-91.

Gesang, Jumian, 1985, [An analysis of the phonology of Batang Tibetan] (in Chinese), *Minzu Yuwen* 2:16-20.

Hari, Maria, 1971, *A guide to Thakali tone*, mimeo, SIL Nepal.

Hari, Maria, Doreen Taylor & Kenneth L. Pike, 1970, Tamang tone and higher levels, *in* Hale, A. & K. L. Pike (eds), *Tone systems of Tibeto-Burman languages of Nepal. Part I. Studies on tone and phonological segments*, Urbana, Univ of Illinois (OPWSTBL 3), p. 82-124.

Haudricourt, Andre-Georges, 1954a, Comment reconstruire le chinois archaïque, *Word* 10.2-3:351-364.

—, 1954b, De l'origine des tons en vietnamien, *Journal Asiatique* 242:69-82.

—, 1961, Bipartition et tripartition des systèmes de tons dans quelques langues d'Extrême-Orient, *Bulletin de la Société de Linguistique de Paris* 56.1:163-180.

Hildebrandt, Kristine, 2003, *Manange tone: scenarios of retention and loss in two communities*, PhD, U. of California at Santa Barbara, Linguistics.

—, 2005, A phonetic analysis of Manange segmental and suprasegmental properties, *LTBA* 28.1:1-36.

Hu Tan, 1982, Recherches sur les tons du tibétain (dialecte de Lhasa), *Cahiers de Linguistique Asie orientale* 11.1:11-46.

Huang, Bufan, 1995, Conditions for the genesis and diversification of tone in Tibetan dialects, *LTBA* 18.1:43-62.
Hyman, Larry, 2001, Tone systems, *in* Haspelmath, M. *et al.* (eds), *Language typology and language universals: an international handbook* vol. 2, Berlin and New York, Mouton de Gruyter (HSK 20.2), p. 1367-1380.
Lehiste, Ilse, 1970, *Suprasegmentals*, Cambridge, Massachusetts & London, U.K., M.I.T. Press, 194 p.
Liu, Feng-Hsi, 1984, Tones and tone sandhi in eastern Tibetan, *paper presented at the 17th ICSTLL, Eugene (Oregon).*
Maddieson, Ian, 1984, *Patterns of sounds*, Cambridge, London, New York, Cambridge University Press (Cambridge Studies in Speech Science and Communication), 1 vol., 422 p.
Martinet, André, 1967, *Eléments de linguistique générale*, Paris, Armand Colin (Collection U), 217 p.
Matisoff, James A., 1999, Tibeto-Burman Tonology in an Areal Context, *in* Kaji, S. (ed.), *Cross-linguistic studies of tonal phenomena. Tonogenesis, typology and related topics*, Tokyo, ILCAA, p. 3-32.
Mazaudon, Martine, 1973a, Comparison of six Himalayan dialects of Tibeto-Burmese, *Pàkha Sanjam* 6:78-91.
—, 1973b, *Phonologie du Tamang*, Paris, SELAF (Langues et Civilisations à Tradition Orale), 184 p.
—, 1974, Notes on tone in Tibeto-Burman, *LTBA* 1:27-54.
—, 1977, Tibeto-Burman tonogenetics, *LTBA* 3.2:1-123.
—, 1978, Consonantal mutation and tonal split in the Tamang subfamily of Tibeto-Burman, *Kailash* 6.3:157-179.
—, 1985, Proto-Tibeto-Burman as a Two-tone Language? Some Evidence from Proto-Tamang and Proto-Karen, *in* Thurgood, G., J. Matisoff & D. Bradley (eds), *Linguistics of the Sino-Tibetan Area: the state of the art. Papers presented to Paul K. Benedict for his 71st birthday*, Canberra, Australia, A.N.U. (Pacific Linguistics. Series C - 87).
Mazaudon, Martine & Boyd Michailovsky, 1988, Lost syllables and tone contour in Dzongkha, *in* Bradley, D., E. Henderson & M. Mazaudon (eds), *Prosodic Analysis and Asian linguistics : to honour R.K. Sprigg*, Canberra, The Australian National University (Pacific Linguistics. Series C - 104), p. 115-136.
Noonan, Michael, 2003, Chantyal, *in* Thurgood, G. & R. LaPolla (eds), *The Sino-Tibetan Languages*, London, New York, Routledge (Routledge Language Family Series), p. 315-335.
Ove, Lorentz, 2004, *Tonal variation in Scandinavian* (Actes du colloque «Tone and intonation in Europe», Santorini), (abstract).
Pike, Kenneth L., 1948 [1967], *Tone Languages*, Ann Arbor, U. of Michigan press, 187 p.
—, 1970, The role of nuclei of feet in the analysis of tone in Tibeto-Burman languages of Nepal, *in* Hale, A. & K. L. Pike (eds), *Tone systems of Tibeto-Burman languages of Nepal* vol. 1, Urbana, Dept of Linguistics, University of Illinois (OPWSTBL 3), p. 37-48.
Shafer, Robert, 1955, Classification of the Sino-Tibetan languages, *Word* 11.1:94-111.

Shefts, Betty Chang, 1968a, Glottalization and the Falling tone, *Monthly Internal Memorandum of the Berkeley phonetics laboratory* May 1968:10-20.

—, 1968b, Notes on length and tone in Tibetan, *Monthly Internal Memorandum of the Berkeley phonetics laboratory* March 1968:8-13.

Silverman, Daniel, 1997, *Phasing and recoverability*, New-York and London, Garland Publishing (Outstanding Dissertations in Linguistics Series), 1 vol., 242 p.

Sprigg, Richard K., 1954, Verbal phrases in Lhasa Tibetan, *Bulletin of the School of Oriental and African Studies* 16:134-156, 320-350, 566-591.

—, 1955, The tonal system of Tibetan (Lhasa dialect) and the nominal phrase, *Bulletin of the School of Oriental and African Studies* 17.1:134-153.

Sun, Jackson T.-S., 1997, The typology of tone in Tibetan, *Chinese languages and linguistics IV: Typological studies of languages in China*, Taipei, Academia Sinica (Symposium series of the Institute of History and Philology, number 2), p. 485-521.

—, 2003, Variegated tonal developments in Tibetan, *in* Bradley, D. *et al.* (eds), *Language Variation: Papers on variation and change in the Sinosphere and in the Indosphere in honour of James A. Matisoff*, Canberra, A.N.U. (Pacific Linguistics), p. 35-51.

Yip, Moira, 2002, *Tone*, Cambridge, UK, C.U.P. (Cambridge Textbooks in Linguistics), 341 p.

Polysyllabicity and Voice Quality of Other Tone Languages in the Sino-Tibetan Area"
Comments on Mazaudon paper

HAYASHI, NORIHIKO[1]
Graduate School of Letters, Kyoto Univ.
Japan Society for the Promotion of Science

0. Introduction

In Prof. Mazaudon's presentation, she claimed that in Tamangish languages, which are closely related to Tibetan languages, 'the tone-bearing unit (henceforth TBU) is the morpheme or the word', and 'the laryngeal feature is best analyzed as a feature of tone.' Since pitch is given greater attention in most of the analyses of tone languages in the world, and monosyllabicity in Asian tone languages is most common, her claim seems to be arguable. In this review, however, I would like to point out that her analysis may be applicable to other Asian tone languages. My claim is briefly summarized as follows.

(1) The TBU of some Sino-Tibetan languages is changing from the syllable to the word.

(2) The laryngeal feature of other Sino-Tibetan languages can also be analyzed as a feature of tone.

1. The domain of the TBU

Prof. Mazaudon's presentation has clearly shown that disyllabic words in Tamangic languages have four contrastive tones as in monosyllabic words. This means that the TBU of Tamangic languages is not the syllable but the word.

Let me move on to the other Tibeto-Burman languages, especially Lolo-Burmese (henthforth LB), which I am now studying. LB languages can be seen on the right side of Fig. 1 in Prof. Mazaudon's paper. The TBU of these languages has been considered to be the syllable. In fact, there are several monosyllabic words as seen in Table 1[2].

---

[1] e-mail: jinozu@yahoo.co.jp

[2] In Table 1, the correspondences in smooth syllables are shown. I quote the data from the following sources: Jino (my field notes), Hani and Achang (Huang 1992), Atsi (the example 'iron' from Huang 1992) and Written Burmese (Yabu 1982). /I/ is the transcription for / ˥ /. The notation of Written Burmese

Therefore, most Sino-Tibetanists can reconstruct proto-tones at the Proto-Lolo-Burmese (PLB) stage to some extent.

Tone of WB.	meaning	J.	H.	AC.	AT.	WB.	PLB.
Tone 1	'to die'	ʃi^{42}	sḭ^{55}	ʂɪ^{55}	šî-	sei-	*səy^{1}
	'iron'	ʃɛ^{42}	sɔ^{55}	ʂam^{55}	(ʃam^{51}to̱^{ʔ55})	sam	*syam^{1}
	'red'	a^{33}n̥ɤ^{55}	űɪ^{55}	na^{55}	nê̱/ʔănê̱	nii-/ a-nii	*ʔ-ni^{1}
Tone 2	'to wash'	tshi^{55}	tshi^{31}	(phɔp^{55})	chi-	chei:-	*ts(y)əy^{2}
	'to steal'	khju^{55}	xø^{31}	xau^{31}	khau-	kho:-	*kəw^{2}
	'bitter'	a^{55}khɔ^{55}	xa^{31}	xɔ^{31}	kho-	khaa:-	(*ka^{2})
Tone 3	'to open'	phɔ^{55}	phɔ^{33}	phɔŋ^{35}	phóŋ-	phwang.-	*pwaŋ^{3}
	'to know'	sɯ^{55}	xɤ̱^{33}	sɑ^{35}	sé-	si.-	*sey$^{2/3}$
	'to fall'	krɔ^{44}	ja^{33}	kʐua^{35}	kyó-	kya.-	(*gla^{3})

Table 1: Basic tonal correspondence in LB languages

It can be presumed that PLB is a monosyllabic language. However, it is safe to say that the tone system of some LB languages, especially Loloish, is changing from syllabic to word-tonal. According to Nishida (1988, 1993a, 1993b), Akha, Bisu and Lahu, spoken in Thailand, are some examples of LB languages. And on the basis of my analysis of the field data collected in Yunnan province, China, I regard Jino as a further example.

Some examples of Akha are taken from Nishida (1988). He observes that among Akha cardinal numbers, *'one'* to *'ten'* are monosyllabic and have their own tones, while all tonal patterns of the disyllabic numbers over *'eleven'* are neutralized to **LH** [11 (short) 55 (long)].

---

is based on Yabu (1982), but that of tones is slightly changed by me: Tone 1 /(unmarked)/, Tone 2 /:/ and Tone 3 /./.

All PLB forms are cited from Matisoff (2003), except for both of the words 'bitter' and 'to fall', whose proto-forms are tentatively reconstructed by me.

(1) a. *Monosyllabic cardinal numbers* in Akha
1 [ti: 33], 2 [ni: 33], 3 [sm̩55], ..., 10 [ts‘ɛ: 55]
b. *Disyllabic compounding numbers* in Akha
20 [ni 11 ts‘ɛ: 55], 30 [sm̩11 ts‘ɛ: 55], ...

This phenomenon is also true in Jino. In Jino, the numbers from *‘one’* to *‘ten’* are monosyllabic and have their own tones, while tonal patterns of the disyllabic numbers over *‘eleven’* are all neutralized to **LH** /33-55/[3]. The examples of Jino are seen in (2).

(2) a. *Monosyllabic cardinal numbers* in Jino
1 /thi^{55}/, 2 /ŋ̊i^{55}/, 3 /sø^{55}/ , ... , 10 /tshɤ^{42}/
b. *Disyllabic compounding numbers* in Jino
11 /tshɤ^{33}thi^{55}/, 12 /tshɤ^{33}ŋ̊i^{55}/, ... , 20 /ŋ̊i^{33}tshɤ^{55}/, 30 /sø^{33}tshɤ^{55}/ ...

In the previous literature, LB languages have been considered to be monosyllabic languages. However, it appears that polysyllabic words in LB have developed constraints on tonal sequences and that so-called ‘polysyllabicity’ is now occurring in some LB languages.

To grasp the phenomenon in detail, we may take the following two phonological approaches. The first one is in terms of pitch. According to Xu (1998), in Bisu spoken in China, the tone sequence /31-55/ becomes [31-22]. In other words, the tone /55/ becomes the low level tone [22] after the tone /31/ (see the Bisu example in (3). I conclude that the constraint, ‘the relative pitch difference should be reduced as much as possible,’ works in this language.

(3) mja^{55} *‘season’*: laŋ^{55}mja^{55} *‘spring’*, loŋ^{55}mja^{55} *‘summer’*, tsho^{31}**mja**$^{55\rightarrow 22}$ *‘autumn’*

Jino has a tone alternation rule as follows: tone /42/ changes into tone /33/ before /55/ (see (4)). The constraint, ‘the number of concave pitch patterns inside the word should be reduced as much as possible,’ may work in this case.

(4) ja^{42} *‘fowl’*: **ja**$^{42\rightarrow /33}$phɔ^{55} *‘cock’* (phɔ^{55} *‘male’*),
ja$^{42\rightarrow 33}$mɔ^{55} *‘hen’* (mɔ^{55} *‘female’*)

---

3 In Jino, the distinction between long and short vowels does not occur even in such compounds, though the second syllable becomes slightly stressed.

Considering the phonetic level, this type of constraint can be seen in other Sino-Tibetan languages. For example, Lin (1963) points out that the following tone sandhi phenomena in (5) are obligatory in Mandarin Chinese.

(5) a. tone sandhi of *shǎngshēng* (上声): 214 + 214→**35** + 214
    b. tone sandhi of *qùshēng* (去声): 51 + 51 →**[53-31]** (gentle falling)

With regard to pitch difference, we can state that there is a constraint of making rising or concave pitch patterns as simple as possible inside phonological words in those languages.

The second approach is in terms of stress. Needless to say, the tone of unstressed syllables varies more easily than that of stressed ones. As far as I know, the earliest analysis of tone sandhi in terms of stress in Asian languages may be of Chinese. In general, there are several stress patterns, such as trochaic (**S**W), iambic (W**S**) and so on. Chinese phonologists have not yet concluded whether Mandarin Chinese has either trochaic, iambic, or both stress patterns (Chen 2000). In Asian tone languages, one stress pattern seems to be fixed for each grammatical category.

As for nouns, Lhasa Tibetan and Mandarin Chinese basically have the trochaic stress pattern.[4] The tone of the first syllable in disyllabic words does not alter in these languages.[5]

On the other hand, we can suppose that most of the LB languages basically have the iambic pattern in the noun category. Using Mazaudon (1977)'s term, these languages can be divided into two groups: 'schwa languages' and 'non-schwa languages'. Spoken Burmese is in the former group, where the vowel in the first syllable changes into schwa and the initial consonant becomes voiced in compounds, while Jino is in the latter group, where the vowel of the first syllable in compounds does not become schwa, although it is unstressed. I consider that the stability of the tonal pattern depends on determining which stress pattern a given language takes.

Of course, an understanding of the morphology is necessary to grasp these

---

4 Some Sino-Tibetanists have already mentioned the stress patterns in the Sino-Tibetan area. Here I quote from LaPolla (2003: 32).

'Aside from these genetic groupings, and a split in prosodic type between a Southeastern iambic stress area and a Northern trochaic stress area, there are two other broader areas of language contact, the Indo-sphere and the Sino-sphere.'

5 In Lhasa Tibetan, except for the negative forms, verbs can also be considered to have trochaic patterns.

phenomena as in Chinese phonology. In any case, there is a need to investigate 'polysyllabicity' in Asian languages in a wide perspective.

Next, we will examine the other claim of Prof. Mazaudon.

2. Voice quality and tonal features

Prof. Mazaudon reported that in Tamangic languages, there is an opposition between voiceless aspirated and unaspirated initial plosives with a high tone, while the opposition is neutralized when bearing a low tone. And she observed that the vowels with low tone become breathy.

We can see this relationship between voice quality and the distribution of initial plosives in other Asian languages. For example, in smooth syllables of spoken Burmese, there are three tonemes: low-level (Tone 1), high-level (Tone 2) and high-falling (Tone 3).

According to most of the previous literature on Burmese, such as Yabu (1989), the creaky phonation accompanies the high-falling tone.

(6) SpB. /ka./ [ka̰^{41}] 'to dance', /la./ [la̰^{41}] 'moon'

In Burmese, we can recognize an interesting phenomenon. In the high-level tone, the ending of the vowel often becomes phonetically breathy[6] (Okell 1969: 11). Generally speaking, breathy vowels occur with a low tone[7], as in Tamang. Therefore, it is arguable that this is a peculiarity of Burmese.

Not only in Burmese, but also in Thai and Vietnamese,[8] laryngeal features (creakiness or breathiness) are elements of tone.

On the other hand, in some LB languages, it is not possible to say that creakiness is an element of tone, although the distribution of initial plosives varies with voice quality. Let us take the example of Hani, spoken in Yunnan, China (Dai & Duan 1995).

---

[6] Of course, many phoneticians and Sino-Tibetanists, including me, do not always agree with this point. Breathy feature can be more in low tone.

[7] Yip (2002) also says that breathy vowels usually occur in the low tone. Breathy vowels appear in low tones of Khmer, too.

[8] In both Thai and Vietnamese, a laryngeal feature is phonetically realized as an element of tone. Mitani (1989) reports that creaky phonation occurs in the third (High-Falling) or the fourth (High-Level) tone in Thai smooth syllables.

[Examples of Hani]

(7) a. pe^{31} 'to vomit', phe^{31} '(classifier)'

b. pe^{31} 'north' < Mandarin Chinese. běi「北」

As in most other LB languages, the opposition between the creaky and the non-creaky vowels exists in Hani. We cannot regard creakiness as a feature of tone because creaky vowels appear in all tonemes. However, voiceless initial plosives appear in complementary distribution in Hani native words[9], as in (7a). That is, voiceless unaspirates appear before creaky vowels, and voiceless aspirates appear before non-creaky ones. Recently, Hani has acquired a lot of Chinese loanwords, as in (7b), so that the initial aspiration opposition has appeared.

In Loloish languages, the phonological opposition between creaky and non-creaky vowels is mainly a reflex of *ʔ- in initial position and compensation for the loss of plosive endings of the proto language (Bradley 1979, Hayashi 2002, Matisoff 2003). Therefore, the status of laryngeal features in these languages seems to be rather different from that in Tamangic languages where the origin of the breathy feature can be traced back to voiced initials.

3. Conclusion

In her paper, Prof. Mazaudon claims that the domain of the TBU is the morpheme and that the laryngeal feature is best analyzed as a feaure of tones in Tamangic languages. However, as suggested in the above review, we can apply her observations to Jino, Hani, and other languages as well. Therefore, I think it is crucial to consider the applicability of given phenomena in a variety of languages in order to reach more convincing conclusions. Particularly in the present case of Sino-Tibetan languages, I suggest that it is not only important to look at laryngeal features and the TBU, but also the relationship between stress patterns and tonal sequences. This will definitely lead to more cross-linguistically applicable conclusions.

[9] This characteristics is true also of some Burmish languages, such as Atsi (Zaiwa), Pola.

Abbreviations

AC : Achang, AT: Atsi (Zaiwa), H.: Hani, J.: Jino, SPB.: Spoken Burmese, WB.: Written Burmese

REFERENCES

Bradley, David 1979. *Proto-Loloish.* London: Curzon Press.

Chen, Matthew Y. 2000. *Tone Sandhi —Patterns Across Chinese Dialects—.* Cambridge: Cambridge University Press.

Dài, Qíngxià (戴庆厦) and Duàn Kuànglè (段贶乐) 1995. *Hāníyŭgàilùn.* Kunming: Yúnnánmínzúchūbănshè. [*An introduction to the Hani language.* (in Chinese)]

Hayashi, Norihiko (林範彦) 2002. "Roro=Biruma sogo *ʔ ga gendai Tino-go ni ataeta eikyou ni tuite", *Kyouto Daigaku Gengogaku Kenkyuu*, Vol. 21: 311-335. Kyouto: Kyouto Daigaku Bungakubu Gengogaku Kenkyuusitu. ["On the influence of Proto-Lolo-Burmese *ʔ upon Modern Jino" *Kyoto University Linguistic Research* (in Japanese)]

Huáng, Bùfán (黄布凡) (eds.) 1992. *Zàngmiănyŭzúyŭyáncíhuì.* Beijing: Zhōngyāngmínzúxuéyuànchūbănshè. [*A Tibeto-Burman Lexicon.* (in Chinese)]

LaPolla, Randy J. 2003. "Overview of Sino-Tibetan Morphosyntax", Graham Thurgood and Randy J. LaPolla (eds.), *The Sino-Tibetan Languages*. pp. 22-42. London: Routledge.

Lín, Tāo (林涛) 1963. "Běijīnghuàliándúyīnbiàn" *Zhōngguóyŭwén* 1963. No.6 (reprinted in : Lín Tāo 2001 *LínTāoyŭyánxuélùnwénjí.* pp. 49-64. Beijing: Shāngwùyìnshūguăn.) ["Sandhi phenomena in Beijing Chinese" (in Chinese)]

Matisoff, James A. 2003. *Handbook of Proto-Tibeto-Burman —System and Philosophy of Sino-Tibetan Reconstruction—.* Berkeley: University of California Press.

Mazaudon, Martine 1977. "Tibeto-Burman Tonogenetics" *Linguistics of the Tibeto-Burman Area*: Vol.3, No.2.

Mitani, Yasuyuki (三谷恭之) 1989. "Tai-go" Takashi Kamei et. al. (eds.), *Gengogaku Daiziten*, Vol. 2: 529-545. Tokyo: Sanseido. ["Thai" (in Japanese)]

Nishida, Tatsuo (西田龍雄) 1988. "Aka-go" Takashi Kamei et. al. (eds.), *Gengogaku Daiziten*, Vol. 1: 137-142. Tokyo: Sanseido. ["Akha" (in Japanese)]

——————1993a. "Bisu-go" Takashi Kamei et. al. (eds.), *Gengogaku Daiziten*, Vol. 5: 313-322. Tokyo: Sanseido. ["Bisu" (in Japanese)]

——————1993b. "Rahu-go" Takashi Kamei et. al. (eds.), *Gengogaku Daiziten*, Vol. 5: 377-389. Tokyo: Sanseido. ["Lahu" (in Japanese)]

Okell, John 1969. *A reference grammar of colloquial Burmese.* London: Oxford University Press.

Xú Shíxuán (徐世璇) 1998. *Bìsūyǔyánjiū.* Shanghai: Shànghǎiyuándōngchūbǎnshè. [*A study on the Bisu language.* (in Chinese)]

Yabu, Shiro (藪司郎) 1982. *Atsi-go kisogoisyuu.* Tokyo: Institute for the Study of Languages and Cultures of Asia and Africa. [*A classified dictionary of the Atsi or Zaiwa language (Sadon dialect) with Atsi, Japanese and English indexes.* (in Japanese)]

——————1989. "Biruma-go" Takashi Kamei et. al. (eds.), *Gengogaku Daiziten*, Vol. 3: 567-610. Tokyo: Sanseido. ["Burmese" (in Japanese)]

Yip, Moira 2002. *Tone.* Cambridge: Cambridge University Press.

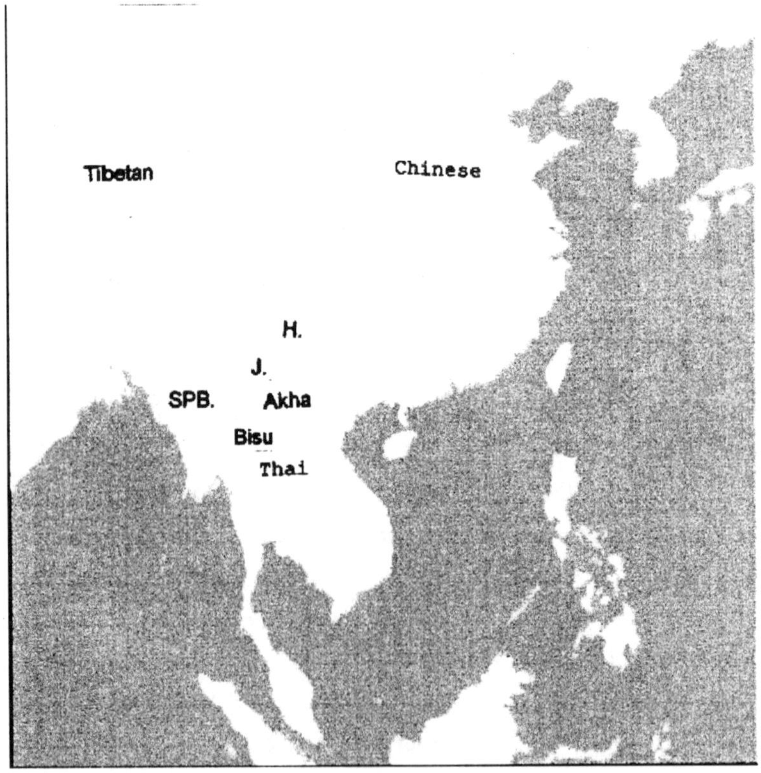

Map 1: Sino-Tibetan Linguistic Area

Tonal expressions of aspect in Kumam, a Western Nilotic language in Uganda: a historical consideration

Osamu HIEDA (Osaka University of Foreign Studies)

1. Introduction

Kumam is a member of Western Nilotic, which is a branch of the Nilotic languages in the Nilo-Saharan language phylum. The Western Nilotic languages are grouped into three major divisions : Northern West Nilotic, Nuer-Dinka and Lwo. Kumam belongs to the southern branch of the Lwo. The following sub-classification is based on Kohler (1955) and Greenberg (1963).

Table 1. Western Nilotic sub-classification

I.	Northern West Nilotic: Burun, Mabaan	
II.	Nuer-Dinka: Nuer, Dinka	
III.	Lwo: (a) Northern Lwo:	Shilluk, Anywa, Jur, Pari
	(b) Southern Lwo:	Luo (Kenya Luo), Adhola, Alur, Acoli, Lango, Kumam

Kumam is spoken in the north of Lake Kyoga in Lango province, central Uganda. The number of speakers is about 62,000.

Kumam is not yet documented. This is the first attempt to describe the tonal expressions of aspect in Kumam.

2. Tonal system in Kumam

In Kumam five phonetic tones (surface tones) are observed: high, low, falling, rising and down-stepped high. However, two level tonemes (underlying tones) are enough for all five phonetic tones to be generated. Contour tones (a falling and a rising tone) come about from the contraction of more than two tonemes. A falling tone is composed of a high toneme and a low toneme. A rising tone is composed of a low toneme and a high toneme. Moreover, a high toneme is lowered to a down-stepped high tone after a floating low toneme.

When an underlying high tone is assigned to a syllable, the syllable is phonetically pronounced with a high tone. When an underlying low tone is assigned to a syllable, the syllable is pronounced with a low tone. When an underlying high tone and an underlying low tone are assigned to a syllable, the syllable is pronounced with a falling tone. When an underlying low tone and an underlying high tone are assigned to a syllable, the syllable is pronounced with a rising tone. When an underlying high tone is preceded by an underlying low tone that is not assigned to a syllable, the underlying high tone is pronounced as a slightly lowered tone (cf. Table 2).

Table 2. Tonal system in Kumam

Phonetic tone (surface tone)	Transcription	Toneme (underlying low tone)
high tone	[h]	H
low tone	[l]	L
falling tone	[f]	HL
rising tone	[r]	LH
down-stepped high tone	[!h]	FL H (FL: floating low toneme)

This paper concentrates on a synchronic description and a historical consideration of tonal expressions of aspect. Therefore the following sections only discuss the tonal processes necessary to get from underlying tonal patterns to surface tonal expressions in the verbal morphology.

3. Aspect (imperfective / perfective) in Kumam

Indicative sentences always have the aspectual distinction of imperfective vs. perfective in Kumam. The two basic aspects have no segmental difference, but have distinctive tonal expressions. Tenses are expressed by auxiliaries or by adverbials peripherally. In (3c) the adverbial element *oudo* expresses the past tense. The auxiliary *a-tie*, 'to be (1st person singular)', bears the imperfective tonal expression. The imperfective tonal expression co-exists with an adverbial that represents the past tense. Therefore we can conclude that the basic tonal expressions distinguish aspects, not tenses.

The paradigms in (3a) and (3b) show the imperfective and perfective tonal expressions respectively. Personal pronominal prefixes must be attached to a verb stem. The imperfective verbal complex always bears the imperfective tonal expression low-high-high. And the perfective verbal complex always bears the perfective tonal expression low-high-low. The tonal expressions are constant for all verbs. When a nominal element that bears a low tone on the initial syllable follows the perfective verbal complex, the initial low tone alternates with a high tone in the nominal element. In (3b) the noun *cam*, 'food', bears a high tone because it is preceded by a perfective verbal complex.

Table 3. Imperfective and perfective (1): Transitive sentence

	(3a) Imperfective 'I cook food, etc.'	(3b) Perfective 'I cooked food, etc.'
sg. 1	a-tedo [lhh] cam [l]	a-tedo [lhl] cam [h]
2	i-tedo [lhh] cam [l]	i-tedo [lhl] cam [h]
3	e-tedo [lhh] cam [l]	e-tedo [lhl] cam [h]

	(3c) Past progressive 'I was cooking food, etc.'
sg. 1	oudo [lll] a-tie [lhh] tedo [hh] cam [l]
2	oudo [lll] i-tie [lhh] tedo [hh] cam [l]
3	oudo [lll] e-tie [lhh] tedo [hh] cam [l]

The imperfective and perfective tonal expressions are derived from hypothetical underlying tonal representations in (4a) and (4b). Subject prefixes bear a sequence of a low toneme and a high toneme underlyingly. Subject prefixes are pronounced with a rising tone, when Kumam speakers are required to pronounce them slowly. All verbs bear a high toneme underlyingly. In fact the infinitive form of the verb, *tedo* 'to cook', bears a high tone in (3c). The perfective aspect is marked suprasegmentally by a low toneme, and the imperfective aspect is marked by a suprasegmental zero toneme or a null.

When tonemes are assigned to syllables, from left to right, and one by one, the expected phonetic (surface) representations are obtained in (4a) and (4b). The noun *cam*, 'food', receives a high toneme on the surface in (4b), which is originally assigned to the verb stem *tedo*, 'to cook', at the underlying level [1].

Table 4. Tonal processes of imperfective and perfective (1) : Transitive sentence

```
                 (4a) Imperfective         (4b) Perfective
Underlying          a-   -tedo   cam          a-   -tedo   cam
                    /\     \/     |           /\     \/     |
                   L H  φ  H      L          L H L   H      L
Surface             a-   -tedo   cam          a-   -tedo   cam
                    /     | |     |           |      | |    |
                   L     (H H)    L          L      H L    H     L
                   I-imp.-cook food          I-perf.-cook food
                   'I cook food.'            'I cooked food.'
```

In order to confirm the hypothesis that the imperfective aspect is marked by a suprasegmental zero toneme and the perfective aspect is marked by a suprasegmental low toneme, we shall examine other examples.

The imperfective verbal complex always bears the tonal expression low-high, and the perfective verbal complex bears the tonal expression low-falling in intransitive sentences.

Table 5. Imperfective and perfective (2): Intransitive sentence

	(5a) Imperfective	(5b) Perfective
	'I come out.'	'I came out.'
sg. 1	a-wɔk [lh]	a-wɔk [lf]

A subject prefix bears a low toneme and a high toneme underlyingly. The imperfective aspect is marked by a suprasegmental zero toneme and the perfective aspect by a suprasegmental low toneme. All verb stems bear a high toneme. When tonemes are assigned to syllables, from left to right, one by one, the expected tonal representations are obtained in (6a) and (6b). Most intransitive verbs are monosyllabic and pronounced slightly long. When a sequence of a high toneme and a low toneme is assigned to a long syllable, the syllable is phonetically pronounced with a falling tone in (6b).

Table 6. Tonal processes of imperfective and perfective (2): Intransitive sentence

```
              (6a) Imperfective      (6b) Perfective
Underlying       a-    -wɔk             a-    -wɔk
                 /\      |              /\      |
                 LH  ϕ   H              LH L    H
Surface          a-   -wɔk               a-  wɔk
                 |      |               |    /\
                 L      H H             L    H L   H
```

The negative is represented by the adverbial *lika*, 'not', which precedes a verbal complex in (7a) and (7b). Vowel coalescence takes place between the end of the adverbial and the beginning of a verbal complex. The imperfective verbal complex in a negative sentence bears the imperfective tonal expression : down-stepped high-high. The perfective verb complex in a negative sentence bears the perfective tonal expression: down-stepped high-low.

Table 7. Imperfective and perfective (3): Negative sentence

	(7a) Imperfective 'I do not eat (it).'		(7b) Perfective 'I did not eat (it).'	
sg.1	lika [hh]	a-camo [!hh]	lika [hh]	a-camo [!hl]

The negative adverbial *lika*, 'not', bears a high toneme underlyingly. A subject prefix bears a sequence of a low toneme and a high toneme underlyingly. All verbs bear a high toneme underlyingly. The imperfective aspect is marked by a suprasegmental zero toneme, and the perfective aspect is marked by a suprasegmental low toneme. When vowel coalescence takes place between the end of an adverbial and the subject prefix, a vowel in the subject is lost, and a low toneme is assigned as in (8a) and (8b). When a low toneme loses the segment it is to be assigned to, the low toneme becomes a floating toneme. This floating toneme is referred to as a true floating toneme. The true floating low toneme is never assigned to any syllable. It lowers the following high toneme into a down-stepped high tone. The true floating low toneme behaves in a different way from the low toneme by which the perfective aspect is marked, although the low toneme in the perfective aspect is also not segmental.

Table 8. Tonal processes of imperfective and perfective (3): Negative sentence

	(8a) Imperfective 'I do not eat (it).'			(8b) Perfective 'I did not eat (it).'		
Underlying	lika	a-	-camo	lika	a-	-camo
	\/	/\	\/	\/	/\	\/
	H	LH ϕ	H	H	LH L	H
Surface	lik(a	a)-	-camo	lik(a	a)-	-camo
	\/		| /	\/		| /
	H	FL	(HH)	H	FL	H L H

When tonemes are assigned to syllables from left to right, one by one, the expected tonal expressions are obtained in (8a) and (8b). A high toneme is lowered into a down-stepped high tone after a floating low toneme.

Middle verb stems are derived by adding a suffix to verb stems in (9a) and (9b). The imperfective middle verbal complex bears the imperfective tonal expression : low-high-low. The perfective middle verbal complex bears the perfective tonal expression : rising-down-stepped high-low. The middle verb suffix, *-ere*, is always pronounced with a sequence of a high tone and a low tone.

Table 9. Imperfective and perfective (4): Middle sentence

	(9a) Imperfective	(9b) Perfective
	'We kick each other.'	'We kicked each other.'
pl. 1	o-gweere [lhl]	o-gweere [r!hl]

The middle verb suffix, *-ere*, bears a sequence of a high toneme and a low toneme underlyingly. The tonemes are assigned inalterably to the syllables of the middle verb suffix, since the suffix is always pronounced with a fixed tonal expression.

Table 10. Tonal processes of imperfective and perfective (4): Middle sentence

```
            (10a) Imperfective          (10b) Perfective
                  'We kick each other.'       'We kicked each other.'
Underlying         o-   -gweere              o-   -gweere
                   /\      / \  \            /\      |  \  \
                   LH  φ  H  H  L            LHL    H  H L
Surface            o-   -gweere               o-   -gweere
                   |      // |  \             /\      | \  \
                   L  (H H H) L              L H  FL(H H) L
```

A subject prefix bears a sequence of a low toneme and a high toneme underlyingly. The imperfective aspect is marked by a suprasegmental zero toneme, and the perfective aspect is marked by a suprasegmental low toneme. All verbs bear a high toneme underlyingly.

I argued before that tonemes are assigned to syllables, from left to right, one by one. But some morphemes violate this principle. Syllables in some morphemes are closely connected to tonemes. They do not allow tonemes to leave their syllables. Since rightmost tonemes are fixed to the right end of words, all other tonemes must be assigned to the preceding syllables in words.

Moreover, a sequence of tonemes of the same height can be counted as one toneme. This is explained by the fact that more than two tonemes are assigned to one syllable. For example, three high tonemes are counted as one high toneme, which is assigned to the penultimate syllable of the imperfective verbal complex in (10a), or two high tonemes are counted as one high toneme, which is assigned to the penultimate syllable of the perfective verbal complex in (10b).

Other tonemes are assigned to other syllables, from left to right, one by one. A high toneme is a salient toneme and is never lost through tonal processes. The first high toneme is assigned to the first syllable and constructs a rising tone with a preceding low toneme in (10b).

In (10b) the second low toneme becomes a floating toneme, because it is not assigned to any syllable. This true floating low toneme lowers the following high toneme into a down-stepped high tone.

Suffixes for benefactive pronominal objects are added to verb stems. The suffixes for benefactive pronominal objects bear an inalterable low toneme. The imperfective verbal complex bears the imperfective tonal expression: low-high-low. The perfective verbal complex bears the perfective tonal expression: rising-down-stepped high-low. The suffixes for benefactive pronominal objects are always pronounced with a low tone.

Table 11. Imperfective and perfective (5): Benefactive sentence

	(11a) Imperfective	(11b) Perfective
	'I cook for you.'	'I cooked for you.'
sg. 1	a-tɛd-ɪ [lhl]	a-tɛd-ɪ [r!hl]

Subject prefixes bear a sequence of a low toneme and a high toneme underlyingly. The imperfective aspect is marked by a suprasegmental zero toneme. The perfective aspect is marked by a suprasegmental low toneme. All verbs bear a high toneme underlyingly. The suffixes for benefactive pronominal objects bear a low toneme underlyingly.

Table 12. Tonal processes of imperfective and perfective (5) : Benefactive sentence

	(12a) Imperfective	(12b) Perfective
	'I cook for you.'	'I cooked for you'
Underlying	a- -tɛd-ɪ	a- -tɛd-ɪ
	/\			/\		
	LH ϕ H L	LH LH L
Surface	a- -tɛd-ɪ	a- -tɛd-ɪ
		/		/\		
	L (H H) L	L H FL H L

The final low toneme is attached to the last syllable. Tonemes of the same height are counted as one toneme. When tonemes are assigned to syllables, from left to right, one by one, the surface tonal expression is easily obtained in (12a).

In the case of (12b) a high toneme is selectively assigned to the penultimate syllable, because a high toneme is salient and obligatorily assigned to any syllable in Kumam. Then other tonemes are assigned to other syllables, from left to right, one by one. A sequence of a low toneme and a high toneme is assigned to the first syllable. The second low toneme changes into a floating toneme, because a high toneme is obligatorily assigned to any syllable and the following low toneme is not assigned to any syllable.

From the above examples we can conclude that the imperfective aspect is marked suprasegmentally by a zero or null toneme and that the perfective aspect is marked suprasegmentally by a low toneme. In the following sections the author will try to work out short comparative studies in order to find out the origin of the tonal expressions of imperfective aspect and perfective aspect in Kumam.

4. Origin of imperfective and perfective tonal expressions in Kumam

4.1. Non-past and past in Anywa[2]

Anywa, which belongs to the northern branch of the Lwo group, also distinguishes two basic tenses (aspects) : non-past and past.

Table 13. Non-past and past in Anywa

	(13a) Non-past	(13b) Past		
	'I cook, etc.'	'I drank milk, etc.'		
sg. 1	a-teedo [mlh]	caag [r]	a-maadh-a [mhh]	
	I-cook	milk	past:pass.-drink-I	
2	i-teedo [mlh]	caag [r]	a-maaddhi [mlh]	
3	e-teedo [mlh]	caag [r]	a-maadh-E [mhh]	
		(pass.: passive)		

Short forms of personal pronouns can be attached to verb stems, when verbal complexes have no tense/aspect marker, or if a tense/aspect marker is not segmental (Reh 1996: 191). When verbal complexes have a segmental tense/aspect marker, a subject suffix is attached to the end of a verbal complex, and a patient is located before a verbal complex.

Before we conclude that the tonal expressions of imperfective and perfective aspects in Kumam originated from the non-past and past tense markers in Anywa, we have a few queries to be solved. Specifically, we should explain the difference of affixation between Kumam and Anywa. If personal pronouns are dependent as well as independent, then verbal complexes can be analyzed as compositions of independent pronouns and verb stems as a result of contraction. Thus sentence types in Anywa are schematized as follows.

Table 14. Sentence types in Anywa

(14a) Non-past (Intransitive): S V
(Transitive): S V prep. O

(14b) Past (Intransitive): S T/A-V
(Transitive): O T/A-pass.-V S

(S: Subject, V: Verb, prep.: preposition, O: Object, T/A: Tense/Aspect)

Topic slot is located in sentence-initial position. Topicalization is obligatory. Topic shift exaggerates the distinction between non-past tense and past tense. When a sentence has two participants, the patient (object) is normally topicalized in past tense because of topic shift (cf. (13b) and (14b)). Then the sentence has OVS word order. Short forms of 'personal pronouns' are attached to the end of verbal complexes. They look like personal suffixes (cf. (13b)).

If a sentence has only one participant, namely, if it is an intransitive sentence, then a subject is topicalized even in the past tense. Personal pronouns have to be long forms, because short forms are not allowed to precede tense/aspect markers (cf. (15)). The result is that the sentence has SV word order.

Table 15. Long form of 'personal pronoun'

(15) Past
'I cooked.'
sg. 1 aan-a-teedo [mmlh]
I-past-cook

Topic shifting does not occur in non-past tense. Therefore subjects are topicalized and occupy sentence-initial position even in transitive sentences. When subjects are represented by short forms of 'personal pronouns', the short forms of 'personal pronouns' are attached to the beginning of verb stems. The short forms of 'personal pronouns' can be attached to verb stems when a tense/aspect marker does not intervene between them. The short forms and verb stems constitute verbal complexes as a result of contraction. The short forms of 'personal pronouns' behave like personal prefixes (cf. (13a)).

4.2. Sentence types in Western Nilotic

The Western Nilotic languages show varying patterns in word order (cf.Table 16).

Table 16. Word order in Western Nilotic

		Southern Lwo	Northern Lwo	Dinka	Nuer
Main Clause	Unmarked tense	SVO	SVO	SVO	VSO
	Marked tense	ST/AVO	OT/AVS	ST/AOV ~OT/ASV	T/ASOV
Interrogative		SVO	SVO~OVS	VSO	VSO
Subordinate Clause		SVO	VSO	VSO	VSO

The southern branch of the Lwo group shows a rigid SVO word order, and Nuer is a rigid VSO language. The northern branch of Lwo shows two sentence types in a main clause depending on the tense. The word order is SVO in a sentence that has no tense marker and OVS in a sentence that has a tense marker. SVO order and OVS order co-exist in interrogative sentences. In Dinka the word order is VSO in interrogative sentences and subordinate clauses. SVO order and OVS order co-exist in marked tense sentences in main clauses.

It is argued that word order change takes place in main clauses and then diffuses into interrogative sentences and subordinate clauses (Givón (1977), Vennemann (1973), (1975)). The proto-Western Nilotic originally had VSO word order. The word order change of VSO into SVO took place in the Western Nilotic languages except for Nuer.

In main clauses with a tense marker, the northern branch of Lwo shows some irregularities in word order.

4.3. Word order in the northern branch of Lwo

The northern branch of Lwo has a morphological passive, while the southern branch of Lwo has no morphological passive. A preposition can be attached to the preceding verb stem in morphological passive sentences (cf. (17b)). Moreover personal pronouns can be attached to the preceding verb stem together with a preposition in (17c).

Table 17. Passive sentences in Northern Lwo (Shilluk)[3]

(17a) ng'u a-nake ye en
lion past-pass.-kill by him
'The lion was killed by him.'

(17b) ng'u a-naki en
lion past-pass.-kill-by him
'The lion was killed by him.'

(17c) ng'u a-nage
lion past:-pass.-kill:by:him
'The lion was killed by him.'

When a verb stem ends in a voiceless stop consonant, the passive form is constructed by voicing the consonant in stem-final position (*nak* 'to kill' > *nago* 'to be killed') (Kohnen, 1938: 134). When verbs are preceded with a tense marker, the tense marker is changed into the passive form in a passive sentence (cf. (17a), (17b) and (17c)). The passive form of the past tense marker is only distinguished from the active form suprasegmentally[4].

Passivization is obligatory in marked tense sentences in the northern branch of Lwo. Therefore passive sentences have to be used, when sentences have more than two participants and a tense/aspect marker. Passivization is not obligatory in unmarked tense sentences, which have no tense/aspect marker. Passivization, that is, topic shifting, guarantees markedness of marked tense sentences.

Comparing the passive sentence in Shilluk (17c) with the past tense sentence accompanying a patient in Anywa (13b), it is easy to find the structural resemblance between them. The OT/AVS sentence type in Anywa originates from the passive sentence. The 'personal suffixes' in Anywa are originally composed of a preposition and personal pronouns as a result of contraction.

The northern branch of Lwo also has topicalization. A topic slot is located in sentence-initial position.

Table 18. Topicalization in Northern Lwo

(18a) dyel a-cam ye uthwon
sheep past:pass.-eat by hyena
'The sheep has been eaten by a hyena.'

(18b) uhwon dyel a-came
hyena sheep past:pass.-eat:by:her
'The hyena, the sheep was eaten by her.'

The sentence (18a) has to be a passive sentence, because it has a tense/aspect marker and has two participants. When an agent is topicalized, a topicalized noun phrase is located before a subject in (18b). The co-indexed pronominal element of the topic is attached to the end of the verbal complex.

4.4. Word order in Dinka[5]

Dinka also has passivization. When a sentence has a tense/aspect marker, the tense/aspect marker turns into a passive form as in Shilluk. A non-finite verb is separated from a tense/aspect marker, and located after an agent noun phrase (cf. (19c)), while in Northern Lwo, a non-finite verb always follows a tense/aspect marker. The passive form of the tense/aspect marker is morphologically and surprasegmentally marked (*a-ci* 'indicative marker-perfect' and *a-cii* 'indicative marker-perfect:passive') in (19c) (Nebel, 1948: 8).

Table 19. Passive sentences in Dinka

(19a)	cɔk	a-nak	ghɛɛn	
	hunger	ind.-kill	me	
	'Hunger kills me.'			
(19b)	ghɛn	a-nɛk	cɔk	
	I	ind.-kill:pass.	hunger	
	'I am killed by hunger.'			
(19c)	ghɛn	a-cii	cɔk	nɔk
	I	ind.-perf.:pass.	hunger	kill
	'I have been killed by hunger.'			

Topicalization is also obligatory in Dinka. The topic slot is located before a verbal complex. When sentences have a tense/aspect marker, pronominal suffixes are attached to the tense/aspect marker. When a topic slot is filled with an agent, a pronominal suffix represents a patient in (20a). When a topic slot is filled with a patient, a pronominal suffix represents an agent in (20b). A topic slot is obligatorily filled either with an agent or with a patient in Dinka. Consequently when a topic slot is filled with a patient, topicalization cannot be clearly distinguished from passivization in Dinka.

Table 20. Topic sentences in Dinka

(20a)	yin	a-caa	kony	apɛi
	you	ind.-past:me	help	very
	'You helped me very much.'			
(20b)	wamuth	a-ca	ting'	
	your brother	ind.-past:pass.:I	see	
	'Your brother was seen by me.'			

4.5. Word order in Nuer

Nuer has topicalization and passivization. Topicalization is not obligatory in Nuer. Topicalization is clearly distinguished from passivization by the location of participants in Nuer.

Table 21. Passivization and topicalization in Nuer

(21a)	che	ran	mɔkh	nɛkh		(Westermann, 1912: 103)
	perf.:he	man	buffalo	kill		
	'The man killed a buffalo.'					
(21b)	che	mɔkh	nɛkh	ke	ran	
	perf.:he	buffalo	kill	by	man	
	'The buffalo was killed by the man.'					
(21c)	wan	cɛ	rwacdhɪɛn	lɪn		(Hoffman, 1927: 62)
	fox	perf.:he	words-their	hear		
	'The fox heard their words.'					

A topicalized phrase is located in sentence-initial position, whether a subject or an object is topicalized (cf. (21c)). A passivized patient is located after a tense/aspect marker or a verb (cf. (21b)). When a patient is topicalized in Nuer, a topicalized noun phrase is easily distinguished from a passivized one because of its position. It is not, however, easy to distinguish a passivized noun phrase from a topicalized one in other Western Nilotic languages.

4.6. Passivization and topicalization in Western Nilotic

Passivization and topicalization in Western Nilotic languages are schematized in Tables 22 and 23 respectively.

Table 22. Passivization in Western Nilotic

Northern Lwo	S T/A V O	>	S T/A-pass. V A
	1 2 3 4		4 2 3 1
Dinka	S T/A V O	>	S T/A-pass. A V
	1 2 3 4		4 2 1 3
Nuer	T/A S O V	>	T/A-pass. S V A
	1 2 3 4		1 3 4 2

(A: Agent. Southern Lwo has no morphological passive.)

Table 22 shows passivization in a marked tense sentence. Passivization is obligatory in Northern Lwo, when a sentence has a tense/aspect marker and more than two participants.

Table 23. Topicalization in Western Nilotic

Southern Lwo	S T/A V O	>	To S T/A V-trace
	1 2 3 4		4 1 2 3
Northern Lwo	S T/A-pass. V A	>	To S T/A-pass. V-trace
	1 2 3 4		4 1 2 3

Nuer	T/A S O V	>	To T/A-trace O V
	1 2 3 4		2 1 3 4

(To = Topic. When a noun phrase is topicalized, its co-indexed pronominal element is left behind and is attached to the preceding element.)

Topicalization of an object is formalized in the southern branch of Lwo, because a subject is already located in a topic slot in normal word order. When a subject is topicalized, a cleft sentence should be used.

Topicalization of an agent in a passive construction is formalized in the northern branch of Lwo, because a marked tense sentence is always a passive sentence. A topic slot is located in sentence-initial position. And a subject fills the slot in normal word order.

Unless topicalization is applied, a topic slot is empty in Nuer. Consequently a topic slot can be filled by any element. Topicalization of a subject in Nuer is formalized in Table 23.

Topicalization in Dinka has been discussed in detail in section 4.4.

In summary, all Western Nilotic languages have topicalization. A topic slot is located in sentence-initial position. And a topic slot is always filled by a subject in pragmatically unmarked sentences in all Western Nilotic languages except for Nuer.

The Western Nilotic languages are divided into two groups in regard to the position of a main verb and a tense/aspect marker. No element can intervene between a tense/aspect marker and a verb in the Lwo group. A main verb and a tense/aspect marker can be separated by any element in Dinka and Nuer. Thus, it is difficult to determine which structure is to be reconstructed for the proto-language.

4.7. Topicalization and passivization in proto-Western Nilotic

The proto-Western Nilotic originally had *VSO word order. Probably there existed two dialectal groups. The one group had *T/AVSO word order in marked tense sentences, and the other *T/ASOV word order. The Lwo group originally had *T/AVSO word order in marked tense sentences. Topicalization is obligatory in the Lwo group. But topic shifting took place in marked tense sentences. Topic shifting was guaranteed by passivization.

It is possible to reconstruct topicalization in Table 24. However, the topicalization was in fact non-existent in marked tense sentences in the proto-language, because topic shifting took place in marked tense sentences. Passive sentences were obligatorily used in marked tense.

Topicalization was also obligatory. When a sentence had a tense/aspect marker, topicalization was applied to a passive sentence, namely, to the output in Table 25. The output in Table 26 has the same structure as the marked tense sentence in the northern branch of Lwo, which has more than two participants. A patient among participants is located in sentence-initial position. An agent follows a verb. Moreover a morphological feature of passive is attached to a tense/aspect marker. The final output in Table 26 is conclusively the origin of the marked tense sentence, which has more than two participants, in the northern branch of Lwo.

Table 24. Topicalization in Proto-Western Nilotic I

*(To) T/A V S O > **S T/A V O
1 2 3 4 5   4 2 3 5

Table 25. Passivization in Proto-Western Nilotic

*(To) T/A V S O > *(To) T/A-pass. S V A
1 2 3 4 5   1 2 5 3 4

Table 26. Topicalization in Proto-Western Nilotic II

*(To) T/A-pass. S V A > *S T/A-pass. V A
1 2 3 4 5   5 2 3 4

In the southern branch of Lwo the historical development of sentence structure went farther than that in the northern branch of Lwo. Tense/aspect markers transformed into segmental or suprasegmental affixes which cannot be separated from verb stems. Probably the loss of a segmental element made the historical development possible.

Table 27. Historical development of sentence structure in Southern Lwo

PWN   SBL
*(To) T/A V S O > *(To) T/A-V S O
(PWN: Proto-Western Nilotic, SBL: Southern Branch of Lwo)

Table 28. Passivization in Southern Lwo

*(To) T/A-V S O > *(To) T/A-pass.-V S A
1 2 3 4   1 2 4 3

Table 29. Topicalization in Southern Lwo

*(To) T/A-pass.-V S A > A T/A-pass.-V S
1 2 4 3   3 2 4

Topicalization was obligatory in the southern branch of Lwo. A topic is an agent that fills a topic slot in pragmatically unmarked sentences. The output in Table 29 has the similar structure of a marked tense sentence in the southern branch of Lwo. An agent is located in sentence-initial position, and a patient follows a verbal complex.

5. Origin of tonal expression of perfect in Kumam

The output in Table 29 is the origin of a marked tense sentence, which has more than two participants, in Kumam. In Kumam a tense/aspect marker lost its segmental element. When an agent is represented by a pronoun, a pronominal element is attached to a verbal complex. This fact reminds us that the short forms of 'personal pronouns' can be attached to the following verbal complex, when a tense/aspect marker is not segmental, or if there is no tense/aspect marker in the northern branch of Lwo.

The development of the tonal expression of perfective aspect in Kumam is schematized as follows.

Table 30. Historical development of tonal expression of perfect in Kumam

*A T/A-pass. V S > A- ϕ -pass.-V S

(ϕ means that it is not segmental, but that it bears a low toneme.)

The output in Table 29 becomes to be the input in Table 30. In Table 30 an agent is located in sentence-initial position. The subject has a patient role semantically. Perhaps no speaker recognizes that marked tense sentences originated from passive sentences. Consequently speakers can easily reanalyze passive sentences as active sentences during language acquisition.

Table 31. Origin of tonal expression of perfect in Kumam

*a-caa (?)	>	a-	>	- ϕ - (low toneme)
ind.-past:pass.		ind.-past:pass.		perf.

The tonal expression of the perfective aspect in Kumam originated from the indicative past passive marker, *a-*, in the northern branch of Lwo. The indicative past passive marker in Northern Lwo was originally the independent morpheme, *a-caa*, in proto-Western Nilotic, which represented the indicative past passive[6]. When the independent morpheme becomes a dependent one, and lost the segmental element, it was easily reanalyzed as a tense/aspect marker.

Notes

1 When a high toneme and a low toneme are assigned to a syllable, a long syllable is phonetically pronounced with a falling tone while a short syllable is phonetically pronounced with a high tone.

2 The data on Anywa is from Reh (1996).

3 The data on Shilluk is from Kohnen (1938).

4 Unfortunately a full description of tone in Shilluk is not yet available.

5 The data on Dinka is from Nebel (1948).

6 The independent morpheme can be reconstructed from the indicative past marker in Dinka. However the reconstruction of the vowel quality is tentative.

References

Givón, Talmy. 1977. 'The Drift from VSO to SVO in Biblical Hebrew: the Pragmatics of Tense-Aspect,' in C.N. Li (ed.), *Mechanisms of Syntactic Change,* New York: Academic Press.

Greenberg, Joseph H. 1963. *The Languages of Africa,* Bloomington: Indiana University Press.

Huffman, Ray. 1929. *Nuer-English Dictionary,* Berlin: Dietrich Reimer.

Hyman, Larry M. 1975. 'On the Change from SOV to SVO: Evidence from Niger-Congo,' in C.N. Li (ed.), *Word Order and Word Order Change,* Austin: The University of Texas Press.

Kohler, Oswin. 1955. *Geschichte der Erforschung der Nilotischen Sprachen,* Afrika und Ubersee, Beiheft, 28, Berlin: Dietrich Reimer.

Kohnen, Bernard. 1938. *Grammar of Shilluk,* Verona: Missioni Africane.

Nebel, Arturo. 1948. *Dinka Grammar,* Verona: Missioni Africane.

Noonan, Michael. 1992. *A Grammar of Lango*, Berlin : Mouton de Gruyter.

Reh, Mechthild. 1996. *Anywa Language, Description and Internal Reconstructions,* Köln: Rudiger Koppe.

Vennemann, Theo. 1973. 'Explanation in syntax,' in J.P.Kimball (ed.), *Syntax and Semantics* Vol. 2, pp.1-50, New York: Academic Press.

1975. 'An explanation of drift,' in C.N. Li (ed.), *Word Order and Word Order Change,* Austin: The University of Texas Press.

Westermann, Diedrich. 1912. 'The Nuer language,' *Mitteilungen aus den Seminar fur Orientalische Sprachen der Friedrich Wilhelms Universitat,* 15: 84-141.

Comments on "Tonal expressions of aspect in Kumam, a western Nilotic language in Uganda: a historical consideration" by Osamu HIEDA

Didier Demolin
Linguistics Department, Universidade de São Paulo & Phonology Laboratory, Université Libre de Bruxelles

First I will start this comment by some general remarks about the Kumam tone system and I will try to raise some comparative issues to follow Osamu Hieda's interesting presentation. The tonal system of Kumam appears to be a 'classical' case of a tone system in Nilotic languages and bears in addition some interesting similarities with other languages of the Nilo-Saharan phylum. In his presentation, Osamu Hieda mentioned that there are dowstepped high tones in the language. Since downstepping, although frequently reported in Nilotic, is not well documented, it would have been interesting to show in which environments downstepped high tones appear. For example, do downstepped high tones appear between affixes and roots or can they appear in other environments? Another important issue regarding tone is that Kumam has no mid tone but Anywa has. Can we understand this difference as the development from a HL system to a HML (i.e. the tone splitting) or is it a reduction of a HML to a HL system?

Some other general properties of tone in Nilotic languages have to be raised after this presentation. Osamu Hieda gave a historical perspective to Tense and Aspect markers (T/A) and to some issues about word order in Kumam and other related Nilotic languages. There are some issues related to those markers that need to be discussed. One of the most important ones is the relation between phonation types, affixes and tone. It is well known, since the fundamental work of Denning (1989) that the historical development of phonation types in Nilotic played a crucial role in the development of various features of these languages. This is the case for the evolution of [±ATR] vowel systems. Furthermore some tone splitting cases can be explained by the fusion of [±ATR] vowels (e.g. [e] and [ɛ]), their intrinsic pitch differences being retained to keep the semantic difference between words. [+ATR] vowels have in most, if not all, studied cases a higher pitch than the corresponding [-ATR] vowel. Andersen (1996) has reported some interesting cases in Dinka that has verb markers with different phonation types. The case reported by Andersen shows that there is an alternation between modal and laryngealized vowels. In most cases laryngealized vowels have a low tone. Nuer is also reported to mark T/A by phonation types but in this case it is between modal and breathy vowels. All this is to say that in addition to the careful morpho-syntatic observations of Osamu Hieda, a detailed investigation of issues related to phonation types could lead to a finer understanding of the historical development of tone in Kumam and Nilotic. This could lead to the understanding of pitch differences that are otherwise complicated to explain.

Another interesting aspect of Osamu Hieda's paper is in relation with the perfective and imperfective distinction. Kumam shows no segmental difference between perfective and imperfective but has distinctive tonal patterns.

(1) Kumam

```
                Imperfective                          Perfective

Surface         a- tedo cam    'I cook food'          a- tedo   cam      'I cooked food'
                |   |  |   |                          |   | |     |
                L   H  H   L                          L   H L     H
```

This is also true for many Central Sudanic languages (also from the Nilo-Saharan phylum). For example in Mangbetu (a Central Sudanic language spoken in Congo):

(2) Mangbetu

```
                Imperfective                          Perfective

Surface         ma- ngeku     'I leave'               ma- ngeku          'I left'
                 |    | |                              |    |  |
                 L    H H                              L    H  L
```

Past tenses are also expressed by a marker (not necessarily adverbial in the case of Mangbetu).

(3) Mangbetu

```
Surface         ma- ngeku    Bu     'I left yesterday'
                 |    | |    |
                 L    H L    L
```

This property of the T/A system is quite frequent in Nilo-Saharan languages. The facts reported by Osamu Hieda give more evidence that, for comparative purposes, morphological data are crucial to reconstruct this language phylum. This is important to enhance because when trying to do reconstruction on word correspondences, there are a lot of problems due to borrowings between various sub-groups of Nilo-Saharan languages and also between the latter and Niger-Congo or Afro-Asiatic.

Some final comments regarding the relation between tone and word other can also be made. An important feature of words and especially of verbs in Nilo-Saharan is that they have a tonal mark or even a tonal scheme. When there is movement of a constituent, such as in passivization, verbs retain their tonal characteristics and the results of the movements (e.g. the passive or relative marking) can be marked differently. Osuma Hieda showed that voicing differences can mark the passive in Shilluk nak 'to kill' > nago 'to be killed'. In Dinka, the passive is expressed suprasegmentally and segmentally on the tense marker, e.g. a-ci 'indicative-perfect' > a-cii 'indicative-perfect: passive'. Once again a possible origin for the development of tone can be that the loss of some segmental characteristic led to the reinforcement of the pitch level to mark T/A and other verb markers.

References

Andersen, T. (1996). Tone splitting and vowel quality: evidence from Lugbara. Studies in African Linguistics 17: 55-68.

Denning, K. (1989). The diachronic development of voice quality. Ph.D. Dissertation. Stanford University.

Session 2

Tone-Syntax Interface

Accent and Phrasing in Chimwiini

Charles W. Kisseberth
Tel Aviv University

0. Introduction

In this paper we examine the accentual system of Chimwiini, the northernmost variety of Kiswahili. This language was spoken in the town of Brava (=Mwiini) in southern Somalia for some centuries. The historical record indicates that some form of Kiswahili was spoken as far north as Mogadisho, but the subsequent expansion of the Somali language displaced the Kiswahili speakers on the mainland with the exception of the Bravanese (="wanthu wa mwiini"). After having successfully resisted the Somali linguistic advance, the Bravanese did not fare as well during the anarchy of the civil war in the 1990's, and it is reported that the people fled from Brava and relocated in refugee camps in Kenya or dispersed to a variety of locations. At present, the language must be regarded as "endangered."

This paper is based on material collected by Mohammad Imam Abasheikh (a native speaker-linguist) and myself in the 1970's while Mohammad was a Ph.D. student at the University of Illinois, and on a body of recorded narratives that Mohammad was able to provide and help transcribe on two subsequent brief visits to the United States. Unfortunately, a detailed understanding of the accentual system eluded us during the period of data collection, and it has only been very recently that I have been able to use the recorded texts to work out the system.

Before turning our attention to the accentual system, it is important to point out that since Kisseberth and Abasheikh (1974) [=K&A], it has been known that Chimwiini groups the words of a sentence into what we can call ***phonological phrases***. The evidence that K&A presented for this phrasing had to do with the restrictions on vowel length in Chimwiini and the phenomenon of vowel shortening that occurs in response to potential violations of these restrictions. Chimwiini shortens a vowel unless (a) it is located in the penult syllable of the phrase, or (b) is located in an antepenult syllable that is followed by a short penult syllable.

In a very important paper, Selkirk (1986) used the Chimwiini facts (mostly from K&A) to develop a theory of phonological phrasing. Specifically, she proposed that phonological rules may be restricted so as to apply inside phrases which are not themselves syntactic phrases, but rather are formed by aligning one of their edges with the edge of a limited range of syntactic phrase types. In the case of Chimwiini, she proposed that the right edge of a phonological phrase is aligned with the right edge of a word that stands at the end of a maximal projection (=X^{max}). As it turns out, the only maximal projections that are relevant are those which have lexical heads, i.e. what traditionally have been referred to as Noun Phrases, Verb Phrases, Prepositional Phrases, Adjective Phrases, and Adverbial Phrases.

Besides giving an algorithm for constructing phrases, Selkirk (1986) demonstrated that if one assumes a system of "abstract *phrasal* stress" that works like the Latin Stress Rule, then shortening may be seen to be a response to lack of abstract "stress". Although we prefer to avoid the use of the term "stress" in relationship to these facts, the relevance of the Latin Stress Rule to the Chimwiini vowel length facts is unquestionable.

Although Selkirk's proposal about how to form phonological phrases in Chimwiini is not sufficient, it is one of the principal factors in phrase formation. We have, in subsequent work, identified several other factors that affect phrasing and shall mention some of these in the course of this paper. But the broader purpose of this paper is to demonstrate that although K&A (1974) and Selkirk (1986) relied entirely on vowel length facts to determine the phrasing of sentences, there is actually a second data source that leads to postulating the same phrasing (and is in fact a more reliable signal, since there are structures where vowel length is not sufficient to determine phrase edges, whereas this second source of evidence *always* identifies the phrase edge). This second source is the accentual system, to which we now turn.

1. Accent at the word level in Chimwiini

The accent system in Chimwiini words is (almost) trivially simple. Accent, realized as high pitch, is either on the penult syllable or on the final syllable. Such systems are by no means unknown in the literature. For example, Kubozono has described the Kagoshima dialect of Japanese as having exactly this system (cf. Kubozono 2004a,b, and see the appendix to this paper).

But what determines whether Chimwiini words have penult accent or final accent? For example, in Kagoshima Japanese (mentioned above) the determination is a lexical matter. You must learn that some words have penult and others have final accent. It is not that way in Chimwiini. In Chimwiini, the default case is that every word in every word class has penult accent. Below are a few examples.

(1)	nouns:	m-búzi 'goat(s)', xáṯi 'letter', ma-waarḏíya 'guards', ḻ-waráxa 'paper'
	infinitive verbs:	ku-láala 'to sleep', ku-reebéla 'to stop for', ku-rebelána 'to stop for one another'
	adjectives:	súura 'good, nice', mú-le 's.o. tall'
	adverbs:	yána 'yesterday', kéesho 'tomorrow'

There is only one situation where the default penult accent is not possible: namely, when the word is monosyllabic. In that case, the only syllable available bears the accent. And thus, the contrast between penult and final accent is neutralized. There are very few such words in the language, examples of which are seen in (2).

(2) n-sí 'fish'   n-thó 'very'   n-ṯhí 'land'

So when do words have final accent? Final accent is largely a morphosyntactic matter. The following represent the major sources of final accent in Chimwiini. In two verb tenses, present and past, first person and second person subject verb forms are marked by final accent, while third person subject verb forms are marked by the default penult accent, as seen in (3).

(3)	n-jiilé	'I ate'	chi-jiilé	'we ate'
	jiilé	'you ate'	n-jiilé	'you pl. ate'
	jíile	'(s)he ate'	wa-jíile	'they ate'

(wé)/ na-ku-bigá 'you are beating' vs.
(yé)/ na-ku-bíga 'he is beating'
(The slash indicates a phrase edge. This is not relevant at the moment.)

Other verb tenses do not show this contrast. For example, all forms of the future tense are marked by default penult accent, as seen in (4).

(4) (wé)/ t̲a-ku-bíga 'you will beat' vs.
(yé)/ t̲a-ku-bíga 'he will beat'

Final accent is a characteristic feature of a relative verb. Such verbs usually are also signaled by a final vowel ***o***, but while there are circumstances where that vowel does not appear, there is no circumstance where the final accent does not appear. The final accent in the relative does not care what the subject of the relative verb is. Even in third person, the relative verb has final accent, as in (5a).

(5) a. someeló 'who read'
b. soméele 'he read'

There is a conditional verb form that governs final accent, again without respect to the nature of the subject marking on the verb, as seen in (6).

(6) ka-soomá 'if you, (s)he read'

Finally, the conjunction ***na*** (as opposed to the prepositional ***na***) has the property that it requires a final accent on a following noun. See (7).

(7) m-pháka 'cat' vs. naa m phaká 'and a cat'
m-phán̲a 'rat' vs. naa m-phan̲á 'and a rat'
kamaa m-pháka/ naa m-phan̲á 'like a cat/ and a rat'

Negative imperative verbs are also characterized by final accent.

(8) si-soomé 'don't read!'
si-somee=ní 'pl. don't read!'

From the preceding catalogue of cases where final accent is required, it is apparent that there is no morphosyntactic generalization covering all these instances.

2. Accent is a phrasal phenomenon

When examining Chimwiini sentences, the thing that immediately strikes one is that while sentences very often have two, three, or more accented words, they also often have many words that lack accent. Furthermore, whether a word has accent or does not have accent does not correlate with some distinction between lexical words and function words. The words that do have accent, have the accent in one of the expected places (penult or final), so it seems manifest that the same system that was observed in the word in isolation is also at work in the sentences. The empirical issue is simple: which words have accent, and which words do not?

It turns out that the answer to this question is already available to us on the basis of previous work on Chimwiini prosodic structure: ***the words that have the accent are all and only the words that stand at the end of phonological phrases that are postulated in order to account for the vowel length alternations.*** In other words, Chimwiini calculates where to locate the penult (or final) accent by looking for the right edge of the same phrases that are used to calculate the abstract "stressed" syllable (according to the Latin Stress Rule) that defines where length can occur (in Selkirk's analysis). We have never observed any contradictory data, i.e. we have never observed data where one edge seems to be used for accent and some other edge to calculate whether a vowel must be shortened. On the other hand, accent will often establish what the phrasing must be more precisely than do the vowel length facts.

In the data below, we take sentences where the phrasing follows the Selkirkian principle (the right edge of an X^{max} is the right edge of a phonological phrase). In each case, we see that the last word in the predicted phrase has accent, either penult or final according to the situation. We indicate a phrase edge by the symbol "/". We omit all discussion of how the vowel length alternations support the claimed phrasing structure. This discussion is omitted simply due to considerations of space.

The data in (9) illustrate that a subject NP is separated from its verb. This is true in main clauses and in subordinate clauses.

(9) *in main clauses, a subject is in a separate phrase from the verb*
ch-áayi/ chi-leesél̲a 'tea/ was brought'
m-phúunda/ chí-l̲a 'the donkey/ brayed'
mw-áana/ nii mule 'the child/ is tall'
mw-áana/ mú-le 'the child/ (is) tall' (with zero copular), cf. mwanaa mule 'the tall child'
qal̲bí=y-o/ i-na-x-fungóowa 'your heart/ is being locked (i.e. you are not showing feeling for my plight)'

in adverbial clauses, a subject is in a separate phrase from the verb
mux̲taa yé/ oloshelo barzaa=ní/ chi-wa-pa xabári/ ma-wazíiri…
'when he/ went (relative form of verb) to the royal parlor/ he gave (them) the news/ (to) the ministers'
mux̲ta n-théende/ zi-l̲aziló/ báaba/ chi-wa-vila w-aaná=w-e/ sít̲t̲a/ chi-wa-'ambíla/…
when the dates/ came out/ father/ called his children/ six/ (and) he said to them/…

complement clauses
t̲osheze kuwa Núuru/ file '(he) thought that Nuuru/ died'
Múusa/ hu-kahat̲a Núuru/ ku-ja xanzíiri 'Muusa/ hated (for) Nuuru/ to eat pork'

In all of these examples, we see that the last word in the subject NP is accented.

A non-subject XP located before the verb is separated from the verb phrasally. Any sequence of XP's, whether pre-verbal or post-verbal, are separated phrasally.

(10) ***pre-verbal non-subject XP***
ka nasiibú=y-e/ ku-waa m-bóvu/ mu-kée=w-e/ ntha-x-shíika/ míimba/ muxt̲aa yé/ waliko mubjaaná 'his luck/ being bad/ his wife/ did not give/ birth/ while he/ was a young man'

preverbal XP sequences
báaba/ marádhi/ ya-chi-m-zíid̲a/ chí-fa 'father grew sicker and died – lit. father/ sickness/ increased with respect to him/ he died'
báaba/ máa-t̲o/ ya-chi-m-fuungúka/ chi-wa hu-wóna 'father/ eyes/ opened (to) him/ it was then that he could see'
Áli/ múl̲o/ u-m-zukil̲íil̲e 'Ali/ the fire/ was able to be revived for him (due to his own efforts or someone else's)'

sku móoyi/ Hasíibu/ chi-m-uza maamá=y-e 'one day/ Hasiibu/ asked his mother…'
Heréédho/ l̲-kóombe/ pakulishilize ch-aakúja 'Hereedho/ spoon/ (she) used it to dish out food' (='Hereedho, a spoon, she used (one) to dish out food')

postverbal XP
somel̲el̲e mw-áana/ ch-uwo '(s)he read to the child a book' **(NP-NP)**
húuri/ i-wa-'oleze w-áana/ shati z-áawo 'sweat/ soaked the children/ their shirts' **(NP-NP)**
m-t̲ind̲il̲il̲e mw áana/ n̲áma/ kaa chí su 'he cut for the child/ meat/ with a knife' **(NP-NP-PP)**

kakanyize m-ayi ma-múl̲o/ ch-ungúu=ni 'she poured boiling water/ in the pot' **(NP/AP-LOC.)**
wowi íyi/ i-t̲a-ku-waa n-khávu/ kéesho 'this river/ will become dry/ tomorrow' **(AdjP-AdvP)**
yé/ bishile páasi/ jisa súura 'he/ ironed (lit. hit iron)/ well' (NP-AdvP, although /paasi/ is actually part of a fixed idiom) **(NP-AdvP)**
chi-wa-pakul̲il̲a w-áana/ mbal̲mbáli 'she dished (food) to the children/ separately' **(NP-AdvP)**
Heréedho/ m-pakulishize m-píshi/ ch-aakúja/ ka l̲-kóombe 'Hereedho/ caused the cook to dish out/ food/ with a spoon' **(NP-NP-PP)**
n-guwó=z-e/ z-a ku-laal̲íl̲a/ zi-bishil̲a páasi/ na mu-kée=w-e 'his clothes/ of sleeping in/ were ironed (lit. hit iron)/ by his wife' **(NP-PP (agent phrase))**

Heréedho/ m-pakulishilize Haalíma/ mw-áana/ ch-aakúja/ ka ḻ-kóombe 'Hereedho/ caused to dish out Haliima's/ child/ food/ with a spoon (=Hereedho caused Haliima's child to dish out food with a spoon)' **(NP-NP-NP-PP)**

Again, in each of these cases, the last word in the XP bears the accent.

Another important example of an XP sequence is conjoined NP's, shown in (11):

(11) ***conjoined NP's***
m-pháka/ naa m-phaṉá 'a cat/ and a rat'
Núuru/ na Jáama 'Nuuru/ and Jaama'
uzilee ṉáma/ na m-katí 'he bought meat/ and bread'
sku móoyi/ síimba/ mphúunda/ na bakayḻé/ waḻazile kuwíinḏa] 'one day/ lion/ donkey/ and hare/ left to go hunting'

The claim that the right edge of an XP will be phrasally separated from the next word also predicts that (in the absence of any additional principles) no break will occur between a word that is not XP-final and the next word. Although there are additional relevant principles, in the absence of the applicability of those principles, Selkirk's proposed phrase-formation principle will correctly ***not*** place a phrase break in the following locations:

(12) ***between a verb and a following NP, PP, AdvP that is inside the VP***
mí/ n-ṯhinzilee ṉamá 'I cut the meat' (no PP break between verb and its object NP ***ṉama***)

maskíini/ ch-ondoka ka chi-ḻíi=ni/ chi-m-zubazuba éelo/ chí-ḻa 'the poor man/ got up from bed/ (and) hugged the gazelle/ (and) cried' (no PP break between first verb and the prepositional phrase ***ka chi-ḻii=ni*** 'from bed' nor between second verb and its object ***eelo*** 'gazelle')

úyu/ m-weno=po eeló/ ch-uulúka/ chi-m-zubazuba ka furáha 'this one/ when (he) gazelle/ he jumped up /(and) embraced him with joy' (notice that the last verb is marked with object agreement for the noun ***eelo*** which is not otherwise expressed in the clause, but the prepositional phrase ***ka furaha*** is still grouped with the verb – i.e. the null object has no effect on phrasing)

ḻ-ṯépe/ ḻ-zubiḻa mu-tíi=ni 'a strip of cloth/ was wrapped around the tree' (no PP break between a verb and a following locative noun, ***mu-tii=ni*** (from ***mu-ti*** 'tree'))

chi-mw-ambila ki-ḻ-léeta 'he told him to bring it (e.g. **ḻ-paanga** 'sword')' (no PP break between verb and a following infinitival phrase, the verb here agrees with an object that is not expressed in the clause)

between a noun and its modifiers
mw-anaa mú-le 'a tall child'
mw-ana úyu 'this child'

mw-ana oloshelǿ 'the child (who) went'

between the head of an associative phrase and the associative phrase (-a NP)
d̲awa yaa múl̲o/ nii múl̲o '[prov.] the remedy for fire/ is fire (lit. medicine for fire/ is fire)'
mw-ana w-a Núuru 'Nuuru's child (lit. child of Nuuru)'
xissa y-a Hasíibu/ na sul̲tani w-aa n̲oká 'the story of Hasiibu/ and the king of snakes'

between an adjective and its modifiers
mu-lee nthó 'very tall'

In all these varied cases, a word that is ***not*** at the end of the phrase bears no accent.

Let us now turn to a crucial point. Selkirk (1986) suggested that the proposed algorithm for forming phrases predicts that the phonological phrase is derived from syntactic phrase structure, but is not itself necessarily a syntactic phrase. By placing a phrase edge at the right edge of each X^{max}, one does not predict that the material between two phrase edges will itself have any syntactic cohesion. The evidence that Selkirk was able to cite to support this claim was not overwhelming. The examples below will, we think, strengthen her argument considerably. (It cannot be ruled out, of course, that there might be some approach to syntactic structure that would claim one of these cases do have the status of a syntactic phrase. We do not think that any approach would explain all of these examples as actually being syntactic phrases.)

The first example that we will discuss involves conjoined NP's. Look at the example in (13).

(13) uzile chi-búuku/ na meezá '(s)he bought a book/ and a table'

First of all, let me make a note about accent location. In a third person past tense verb, the accent is on the default penult syllable. This is why in the phrase ***uzile chi-buuku*** 'he bought a book,' the accent is on the penult syllable. The conjunction ***na***, however, requires a final accent on the NP in which it occurs. This is why there is final accent in the phrase ***na meeza*** 'and a table'. The phrasing observed in this sentence is that predicted by the Right-Edge-of-XP hypothesis. The verb does rest at the right end of an XP, but ***chi-buuku*** does since it is a NP. As a consequence, there will be a phrasal break at the right edge of ***chi-buuku***. The word ***meeza*** also rests at the right end of an XP (in particular, it is a NP, and it is also the final word in the VP. If it is the case that the members of a conjoined NP count as a syntactic phrase, then it is clear that ***uzile chi-buuku*** is not a syntactic phrase, but only a phonological phrase. ***uzile chi-buuku*** consists of a verb plus ***part*** of a syntactic phrase.

A second example of the misalignment of phonological phrases and syntactic phrases comes from the relative clause construction in Chimwiini.

(14) mw-ana w-a Núuru/ m-someleeló/ laazíle 'the child who Nuuru/ read to (him)/ fell asleep'

In Chimwiini, when the head of a relative clause is not the subject of the relative clause, the head and the subject are joined by means of the so-called "associative" marker ***–a***, which agrees with the noun class of the head. The relative verb (actually, all the phonological phrases in the VP that the relative verb heads) is marked by a final accent, regardless of the tense or the person of the relative verb. The subject of the relative verb is not marked by final accent, but rather exhibits default accent. A third person past tense verb form such as ***laziile*** has default accent.

In (14), the phrasing follows from the Right Edge of XP hypothesis. The noun ***mw-ana*** is not an NP, but rather the head noun of an NP that also includes its relative clause modifier. The associative particle ***wa*** is also obviously not at the end of an XP. The subject of the relative clause, ***Nuuru***, is a NP and thus its right edge will coincide with the right edge of a PP. The verb ***m-someelo*** is at the end of a VP, and also at the end of the NP that has ***mw-ana*** as its head. Therefore, the relative verb will be at the end of a PP. The main verb of the sentence, ***laazile***, is at the end of a VP and thus will be at the end of a PP. Notice that a consequence of the Right Edge of XP hypothesis is that ***mw-ana w-a Nuuru*** will constitute a PP. But "child who Nuuru" is obviously not a syntactic phrase of any sort.

Another example of the misalignment of phonological phrases with syntactic phrases has to do with complement clauses embedded inside a verb phrase. The following two examples are illustrative:

(15) wó/ wa-na-x-t̠araja kuwa Núuru/ t̠a-mw-and̠ikila Hasáni/ xát̠i
'they/ hope that Nuuru/ will write to Hasani/ a letter'
vs.
mí/ n-na-x-t̠araja kuwa Nuurú/ t̠amwand̠ikila Hasaní/ xat̠í
'I hope that Nuuru/ will write to Hasani/ a letter'

The first thing to notice about these two sentences is that the main verb is in the present tense, which is a tense that exhibits an accentual contrast between first/second person subject forms and third person subject forms. Since third person forms represent the default accent type, they are less significant to the analysis than the first or second person forms that require final accent. In the second example in (15), notice that the final accent (triggered by the first person verb form) is marked throughout the verb phrase. (Other data show any pre-verbal material is not marked with the final accent. In the present example, because the subject is monosyllabic and thus the penult/final contrast is neutralized, we cannot see that this is the case.)

In any case, what is crucial in the present contrast are the phrases in terms of which the accent is realized. The phrase edges fall, as predicted, at the right edge of each maximal projection (the subject NP, the subject NP in the complement clause (***Nuuru***), the first NP object of the verb in the complement clause (***Hasani***), and the second NP object (***xat̠i***) which is also the end of the VP of both the lower clause and the higher clause. In the second example in (15) what we see is that one of the phrases is: **n-na-x-t̠araja kuwa Nuurú** 'I hope that Nuuru'. From a syntactic point of view, however, the main verb, the sentential complementizer, and the subject of the embedded clause do ***not*** constitute a phrase. They are a phrase only from the phonological point of view.

3. X^{max} is not everything!

Although there is no doubt that the alignment of phonological phrases with the right edges of maximal projections is a major factor in Chimwiini phonological phrasing, it is certainly not the only factor. The additional factors, however, all seem to have the characteristic that they may require phrases to be smaller than expected according to the Selkirkian principle. There seem to be no cases where a phrase inexplicably crosses an X^{max} edge. (We should note that there are some cases where it might be claimed that an X^{max} edge has been crossed, but it would appear to us plausible to deny the existence of such an edge in the examples in question. It is not the purpose of this paper to explore these matters.)

The first example of the need to invoke further phrasing principles has to do with verbs that are marked morphologically for negation. Such verbs are (generally) required to be at the end of a phonological phrase, even if the verb has a complement that would be expected to group with it by the Selkirkian principle.

(16) ***obligatory separation of a morphological negative verb from whatever follows in the clause***

marṯi w-íitu/ ile numbáa=ni 'our guest/ went home' vs.
marṯi w-íitu/ nth-aa-kú-ya/ numbáa=ni 'our guest/ did not go/ home'

mu-kée=w-e/ shishile míimba 'his wife/ became pregnant' vs.
mu-kée=w-e/ nth-a-x-shíika/ míimba 'his wife/ did not become/ pregnant'

úyu/ ṯa-k-infa káazi 'this one/ is suitable for the job' vs.
úyu/ h-a-ṯa-k-íinfa/ káazi 'this one/ is not suitable for/ the job'

In each of these examples, we see that whereas in the affirmative sentence, the first complement to the verb (***numbaani, miimba, kaazi***) is grouped into a phrase with the verb, no such grouping occurs when the verb is negative. Although a few examples that we have encountered suggest that there must be some situations uder which the negative verb groups together with a following complement, there are countless examples in our materials establishing that the norm is for separation to occur.

A second example is one that merits much more detailed research, but has to do with the phrasing of a nominal and a following modifier. In the course of our elicitation of data, modifiers were regularly grouped together with the noun that they modified. But at one point, MIA pointed out that it is possible to use a phrasing difference to convey a distinction between definite and indefinite nouns. Specifically, when an adjectival modifier is phrased with the nominal, the interpretation is that the nominal is definite. When the adjectival modifier is separated into a different phrase from the nominal, then the interpretation of the nominal is an indefinite one. Here are some examples:

(17) ***separation of a noun from an adjective is used to signal indefiniteness of the noun***

chi-wa-wene w-ana wa-wovú 'we saw the bad children' vs.
chi-wa-wene w-aaná/ wa-wóvu 'we saw some bad children'

n-uzile mezaa n-khulú 'I saw the big table' vs.
n-uzile meezá/ n-khúlu 'I saw a big table'

In Chimwiini, definiteness is not morphologically marked in any way. There are different strategies for conveying the distinction. For example, indefinite subjects may be postposed. Definite objects may govern object agreement on the verb. From the preceding examples, it appears that phrasing may also be employed to make the distinction.

When one looks at Chimwiini texts, there are many examples of modifiers being separated from the noun that they modify. These examples typically involve an indefinite noun.

(17) Mwíini/ ni múu-yi/ chi-hába 'Mwiini (=Brava)/ is a town/ small'
wé/ t̠a-ku-zala mw-áana/ mw-iimbíli 'you/ will bear a child/ male'
numbáa=ni/ i-waliko bárza/ n-khúlu 'in the house/ there was a reception room/ large'
barzáa=ni/ zi-walimoo zí-ti/ z-íingi 'in the reception room/ there were chairs/ many'
ni-wa-wene waa-nthú/ w-íingi/ suxúu=ni 'I saw people/ many/ in the market'
waliko múu-nthu/ móoyi/ d̠axt̠ári/ m-kúlu 'he was a man/ one/ doctor/ great (i.e. he was a great doctor)'

The issue that these data pose for the Selkirkian hypothesis is this: do the above data illustrate the need for an additional principle of phrase-formation, or do they represent cases where the syntactic XP structure is the reason for the phrasing? That is, perhaps indefinite nouns are in a separate maximal projection from the adjective that modifies them. If this were the case, then the phrasing would follow from the syntax and not require any additional principle.

(It is perhaps worth noting that the adjective, although isolated phrasally from the noun, is itself at the end of a PP. If one took the position that in these examples, the noun is actually at the end of the NP syntactically, then it would be necessary to assume that the adjective, for example, projects a maximal projection so as to ensure that it is at the end of an XP.)

Despite the relevance of definiteness to phrasing, it is certainly not the case that a modifier is always separated from an indefinite noun. The following examples illustrate:

(19) nunguu n-khúlu/ ha-y-kósi/ i-kóoko
pot large/ does not fail to have/ crust
'[prov.] A large pot/ never fails to have/ rice stuck to the bottom.'

niya n-jéema/ hu-t̠abíiba/ niyaa m-bóvu/ hu-xaríba
'[prov.] a good intention/ cures/ a bad intention/ spoils'

The phrasing of N-Adj sequences clearly encompasses more than the definite/indefinite contrast. For that reason, we expect that a syntactic explanation (definite nouns include the adjective in their maximal projection, while indefinite nouns do not) will fail. Most likely, the use of phrasing to convey a definite/indefinite contrast is not entirely unconnected to the next very broad range of cases where the Selkirkian principle does not predict the data.

The third example is the most far-reaching in its effects and involves what we shall loosely call *emphasis*, where this term will function as a cover-term for quite diverse phenomena such as contrastive stress, focus, stylistic emphasis. These phenomena share similar characteristics: the emphasized element stands at the end of a PP. There also is a disturbance in the 'neutral' sentence intonation. In the neutral case, Chimwiini sentences show what we can refer to as "downdrift" intonation (declination). The initial accent is realized at the highest pitch level, and each subsequent accent is somewhat lower in pitch. Putting some sort of focus, or emphasis, or contrastive stress on a word serves to distort this downdrift intonation; the focused or emphasized or contrastively stressed word is marked by an elevation of its pitch level. This elevation may be different from one form of emphasis to another. Furthermore, this elevation may occur in conjunction with other, non-neutral intonation patterns (yes-no questions, negative verbs). We do not pretend to have undertaken a complete and systematic study of these matters, but their consequences can be readily perceived in the examination of the recorded narratives.

The verb, when emphasized, is separated from the following XP in the verb phrase.

(20) ***verb separated from a sentential complement***

chi-lóota/ kuwaa yé/ wene ruuhú=y-e/ u-ko maha<u>l</u>a súura/ na na-ku-m-ṅesha moojé/ xámri 'he dreamed/ that he/ saw himself/ in a lovely place/ and he was serving his master/ liquor'

wó<u>tt</u>e/ báaba/ máama/ na mku<u>l</u>azé/ <u>t</u>éena/ wachoondóka/ ka n<u>t</u>ʰi ízo/ wachéenda/ xkala na Yuusúfu 'all/ father/ mother/ and his older brothers/ then/ MOVED/from these lands/ (and) they went/ to live with Joseph

n-jiilé/ <u>n</u>áma 'I ATE meat' (vs. nj-jilee <u>n</u>amá 'I ate the meat; I ate the MEAT')

textual examples lacking such a separation:

mw-iingíne/ chi-há<u>d</u>a/ <u>l</u>á/ si-chi-m-úβ<u>l</u>e/ walá/ si-chi-m-ru<u>d</u>e chi-simáa=ni 'another one/ said/ no/ let us not kill him/ neither/ let us not return him back into the well'

In elicitation, a demonstrative element is routinely grouped with the noun that it modifies. But in texts we can find examples where the noun is separated phrasally from the demonstrative.

(21) ***noun separated from following demonstrative***

XABÁRI/ ízi/ zi-m-komele su<u>lt</u>áani '[lit.] NEWS/ these/ reached the king ' (it is being emphasized here that some definite news that was the topic of discussion reached the king – the phrasing is not being used here to indicate indefinite news)'

Although in elicitation, the head of the associative phrase is regularly grouped together with the associative phrase, there are many examples in our material where phrasal separation occurs. Various examples follow.

(22) ***head of associative phrase separated from the associative phrase***
mu-kée=w-e/ m-bigiḻiḻe páasi/ n-guwó=z-e/ z-a ku-laaḻíḻa
'his wife/ ironed (lit. hit iron)/ his clothes/ of sleeping in (i.e. his pyjamas)'
(perhaps the possessive marking on the head plays a role in the phrasal separtation)

mw-íizi/ m-ḏafkile ṯaajíri/ chi-wóvu/ ch-a péesa
'the thief/ snatched from the rich man/ a bag/ of money'

chi-wóvu/ ch-a péesa/ ch-a ṯaajíri/ chi-ḏafkiḻa na mw-íizi
the bag/ of money/ of a rich man/ was snatched by the thief'

Yuusúfu/ chanza xfaṯísha/ mizígo/ ya mkuḻáze/ qabḻa ya mzígo/ waa muṉé] 'Joseph/ began to inspect/ the bags/ of his older brothers/ before the bag/ of his younger brother'

Because of the interweaving of phrasing and emphasis (as very broadly conceived), there are many sentences in the narrative texts where every word constitutes a separate phrase in clear contrast to what the Selkirkian principle would lead us to expect.

(23) yé/ mlowéele/ mwanáamke/ móoyi/ msúura/ nt^{h}ó] 'he/ married/ a woman/ one/ beautiful/ very'

The phrasing discussed above, which is at variance with what the Selkirkian algorithm predicts, always involves phrasing that is *smaller* than what the right edges of maximal projections would predict. A natural question to ask is whether there are any examples of phrasing that crosses a maximal projection. An answer to this question depends ultimately on syntactic analysis. It is worth noting however that it appears that any post-verbal XP is part of the same phrase as the verb, no matter what the grammatical relations are taken to be.

(24) suukári/ y-ingile n-ṯhúungu 'lit. sugar- entered- ants = ants got into the sugar'
(***sukari*** is the grammatical subject, but ***nṯhuungu*** seems to be the logical subject)

wa-léele '[cl.2] slept'
wa-lele wáa-nthu/ m-ṯanáa=ni 'people slept/ in the room'
m-ṯanáa=ni/ wa-lele wáa-nthu 'in the room/ (they) slept people'

m-ṯeka chiléma/ huṯekowaa yé/ amo waaké [prov.] the one who laughs at a cripple [lit. the laugher-at cripple/ is laughed at he/ or one of his (i.e. a relative) is'
in this example, the passive subject ("ye" = [cl.1] him,her) is postposed after the verb ***huṯekoowa*** *'[cl.1] is laughed at' – it is clear that "ye" is grouped into the same PP as the verb*

chi-búuku/ t̲a-x-powa mw-anáamke/ náa=mi 'a/the book, the girl was given one/it by me'

There are some aspects of phrasing that seem to be ***lexically*** determined. Specifically, certain non-lexical words seem to carry a requirement that they always stand at the right edge of a phonological phrase. Below we cite the examples that have come to our attention.

(25) ***the conjunction /l̲aakini/ 'but'***
l̲-pépo/ l̲vumíile/ l̲aakíni/ mlaangówa/ nt^{h}awuxfuungúka] 'the wind/ blew/ but/ my door/ did not open'

the quantifier /-ot̲t̲e/ 'all'
yé/ chi-waa d̲áwa/ z-ót̲t̲e/ na chi-wa maráði/ y-ót̲t̲e] 'he/ was medicine/ all/ and he was sickness/all (i.e. he was concerned with nothing but medicine and sickness)'

the conjunction /walá/ 'nor'
ha w d̲irkíki/ walá/ hawshiikíki 'it cannot be reached/ nor/ can it be touched [a riddle, the answer to which is ***mooshi*** 'smoke']'

4. The "scope" of final accent

There is one aspect of accent in Chimwiini that clearly goes beyond the phonological phrases that we have discussed in this paper (but is in no way independent of these phrases). A theoretical treatment of this aspect of pronunciation is not possible given the space restrictions on the present paper. But we would like to make clear the nature of the problem, and to suggest the deep connection between this problem and the phrasing matters we have dealt with.

We have already discussed that certain morphosyntactic forms "impose" the final accent on the phrase in which they occur. The technical mechanism for achieving this will depend on the theory of metrical structure that one assumes, and is not a matter that will be dealt with here. However, it is important to realize that in Chimwiini, the imposition of the final accent is not confined to the phonological phrase in which the relevant word is located. This raises a rather thorny issue: does the scope of final accent itself reflect a need for an appeal to syntactic structure, or can it too be seen as linked to the phonological phrasing. A definitive answer to this problem will not be attempted here, but possible lines of attack will be briefly sketched.

We will confine our attention here to two cases where the verb imposes its final accent on more than one PP: person-marking final accent in the past and present tenses, and relative verb induced final accent. We concentrate on these two cases because they are ones where we did attempt to elicit relevant material back in the 1970's, and they also occur with some frequency in our text collection.

We have argued that accent in Chimwiini is phrasal. This means that the final accent which is triggered by morphosyntactic aspects of the word is not realized on the word that triggers it, but on a larger unit. Some simple examples follow.

(26) ***person-marking final accent (first/second person, past and present verb tense forms)***
n-jilee ṉamá 'I ate meat'
ni-m-pele mw-aaná 'I gave it to the child'

elative-clause final accent (all relative verbs, independent of person of subject or tense)
karka majḻisi áyo/ ntháku/ jasiriḻo xkoodhá 'in that meeting/ there was no one/ who dared to talk'
bakáyle/ chimwambila nḏíiwa/ nimtambiilé/ múunthu/ xambilo jawabu izí/ nii ḏáfa]
'the hare/ told the pigeon/ I recognize/ that the one/ who told you these words/ is the crow'

At first glance, one might think that the appropriate generalization is the following: final accent appears on the final word of the phrase in which the triggering element is located. This generalization fits the data in (26) above. If this were in fact the entire story, then the only theoretical matter facing us would be to determine precisely what the mechanism is for getting the verb to impose final accent on the phrase in which it appears. But the appropriate generalization is rather different. Look at the data in (27).

(27) ***person-marking final accent (first/second person, past and present verb tense forms)***
n-m-ṯinḏiḻiḻe mw-aaná/ ṉamá 'I cut for the child/ meat'
ni-m-ṯinḏiḻiḻe mw-aaná/ ṉamá/ kaa chi-sú 'I cut for the child/ the meat/ with a knife'
ni-m-lisile mw-eenziwá/ ḏeení 'I paid my friend/ the debt'
ni-m-kasize siimbá/ na-ku-goroomá 'I heard the lion/ roaring'

relative-clause final accent (all relative verbs, independent of person of subject or tense)
zi-bishiḻa paasí/ na mu-kee=w-é/ ni n-guwó=z-e/ z-a ku-laaḻíḻa
'what was ironed/ by his wife/ are his clothes/ of sleeping-in (i.e. pyjamas)'

mí/ nḏi mí/ nimṯamaniiló/ na nsuḻiḻoo yé/ xfanya jawabuu mbovú
'me/ it is me/ who longed for him (sexually)/ and wanted him/ to commit bad acts'

At first glance, one might suppose that the mechanism for assigning final accent must take direct account of syntactic structure. Specifically, the person-marking final accent and the relative verb-induced final accent occurs ***at the end of every phonological phrase in the VP***. But this cannot be true, at least in the case of the person-marking accent. Consider the following examples.

(28) ni-m-ṯinḏiḻiḻe mw-aaná/ ṉáma 'I cut for the CHILD/ the meat'
ni-m-ṯinḏiḻiiḻé/ mw-áana/ ṉáma 'I CUT for/ the child/ the meat'

What we see from these examples is that if we use a principle other than "align-PPedge-with-right edge of X^{max}" to form a phrase – specifically, if we align the PP-edge with an emphasized word, then the person-marking goes no further than the emphasized word. Assuming that the emphasized word is not syntactically picked out, then we have evidence that the scope of final accent is not syntactically-based but based on the phonological phrase. From this we can conclude that phonological phrasing is relevant to the projection of final accent from the morphosyntactic element. We are currently exploring an account based on two ideas from Truckenbrodt (1999): the notion of a constraint called XP-Wrap may play a role in phonological phrasing in addition to aligning with the edges of maximal projections and the notion that phonological phrasing may be recursive. Developing these ideas here is not possible.

5. Intonation and final accent

The problem of the contrast between final and default accent is not confined to morphosyntactic considerations. It assumes a role in the intonational system as well. Again, space factors do not permit a full survey of the facts. Nevertheless, even limiting ourselves to some basic data will illustrate the influence of intonation on accent placement.

Consider the following data:

(29) wó/ wa-lele ma-sku ma-zíma 'they/ slept the whole night'
wó/ ↑wa-léele/ ma-sku ma-zíma 'they/ slept/ the whole night'
wó/ wa-lele ma-sku ma-z↑ímu 'did they/ sleep the whole night?'
wó/↑wa-léele/ ma-sku ↑ma-zimú 'did they/ sleep/ the whole night?'

The intonation of a neutral declarative sentence in Chimwiini is one whereby the pitch is highest on the first accented syllable and descends on each successive accented syllable. When the verb is separated from its following complement, this entails some raising of the pitch level on the emphasized verb, contra to the usual downdrift intonational pattern (the up-arrow indicates this raising in our transcription). Yes-no questions (of the type illustrated above) require a special raising of the final accented syllable. Examination of the data in (29) above shows that when the verb is prosodically separated from its complement, there is a difference in the placement of accent between the statement and the yes-no question. Specifically, in statements, the "default" accent is assigned to the material separated from the verb. In the yes-no question, the "final" accent type is assigned. These observations are confirmed by the data in (30) below.

(30) sí. chi-lele ma-sku ma-zimá 'we/ slept the whole night'
sí/ chi-leelé/ ma-sku ma-zíma 'we/ slept/ the whole night'
sí/ chi-lele ma-sku ↑ma-zimá 'did we/ sleep the whole night?'
sí/ ↑chi-leelé/ ↑ma-sku ma-zimá 'did we/ sleep/ the whole night?'

The verb in these examples triggers final accent. When the verb is separated from its complement, the final accent does not pass beyond the verb. In the statement, we find default penult accent on the following prosodically-separated phrase. In the case of the yes-no question, we find that the separated material exhibits final accent.

These data illustrate that final accent is not just a function of morphosyntactic considerations, but also of the intonational system (as it involves the formation of yes-no questions).

6. Conclusion

In this paper, we have examined the accentual system in Chimwiini. We have shown that at the word-level, it is extremely simple. However, the accent is assigned not to the word, but rather to the phrase. As such, the accent assignment provides overwhelming evidence in support of the notion that Chimwini utterances are parsed into phrases. Earlier this conclusion was arrived at on the basis of the facts about vowel length. Now we see that a completely independent system yields the same conclusion.

However, understanding accent in Chimwiini requires going beyond the facts about the phrasing that derive also from the vowel-length data. Specifically, the scope of final accent is beyond the phonological phrase as narrowly conceived. Second, the triggers of final accent turn out to be both morphosyntactic and intonational.

Appendix

Kagoshima dialect of Japanese

A precise parallel to the Chimwiini accent system can be found in the pitch accent system of the Kagoshima dialect of Japanese. In Kagoshima, a word either has penult accent or final accent, just as in Chimwiini. The choice between whether it has penult or final accent is a lexical one in Kagoshima (in contrast to Chimwiini). One simply must learn for any given word whether there is high pitch on the penult or on the final mora. Some examples:

(1) final accent:
así 'foot, leg', umí 'sea', amé 'rain', narú 'to achieve', harerú 'to clear'
namidá 'eyedrop', kokoró 'heart', otokó 'man', Ameriká 'America'

penult accent:
áme 'candy', íwa 'rock', náru 'to ring', haréru 'to swell up'
sakána 'fish', Indonesía 'Indonesia'

It is worth noting that the Kagoshima dialect of Japanese is very similar to Chimwiini in that the system is phrasal and not bound to the word proper. Recall that one must learn in Kagoshima whether a word has penult or final accent. However, the accentual type of the word is "transferred" to the phonological phrase based on that word. We shall indicate the accented syllable by putting it in capital letters.

(2)	indoneSIa 'Indonesia'	ameriKA 'America'
	indonesiAga 'Indonesia-NOM'	amerikaGA 'America-NOM'

indonesiaKAra 'from Indonesia'	amerikakaRA 'from America'
indonesiakaRAmo 'from Indonesia too'	amerikakaraMO 'from America too'

(All data come from Kubozono, personal communication.)

References

Kisseberth, Charles W. and Mohammad Imam Abasheikh. 1974. "Vowel length in Chi-Mwi:ni – a case study of the role of grammar in phonology." In M. W. la Galy, R.A. Fox, and A. Brock (eds.), *Papers from the parasession on natural phonology*. Chicago Linguistic Society.

Kubozono, Haruo (2004a) Tone and syllable in Kagoshima Japanese. *Kobe Papers in Linguistics* 4, 69-84. Kobe Papers in Linguistics.

Kubozono, Haruo (2004b) What does Kagoshima Japanese tell us about Japanese syllables? In T. Kageyama and S. Kishimoto (eds.) Nihongo no Bunseki to Gengo Ruikei (Analysis of Japanese and Language Typology), pp.75-92, Kurosio Publishers, Tokyo.

Selkirk, Elisabeth. 1986. "On derived domains in sentence phonology," *Phonology Yearbook* 3, 371-405.

Truckenbrodt, Hubert. 1999. "On the relation between syntactic phrases and phonological phrases," *Linguistic Inquiry* 30, 219-255.

Comments on Kisseberth Paper:
Accent and Phrasing in Chimwiini

by D. J. Mkude

0. Introduction

As a linguist interested in syntax I was gratified to read Kissebeth's paper which is basically an attempt to highlight the problem of relating phonological and syntactic phrasal units in Chimwiini and possibly other languages operating like it. Chimwiini, as the paper rightly points out, is one of the fifteen or so traditional Swahili dialects spoken along the eastern African coast. Standard Swahili (SS), which I am familiar with, is derived from one of these dialects, namely Kiunguja. Kiunguja is spoken in the central part of the Swahili coast whereas Chimwiini is spoken in the extreme north of that coast. Besides the commonality of numerous lexemes and basic grammatical structure, there are also a number of significant prosodic features that Chimwiini has in common with Standard Swahili. In my commentary I intend to highlight such features within the context of this paper, and also point out difficulties that some of the proposed analyses might raise in order to stimulate and guide further investigation. Excluding the introduction and the conclusion, this paper is divided into the following five sections, and my comments will be ordered accordingly.

1 Accent at the word level
2 Accent as a phrasal phenomenon
3 X-max is not everything
4 The 'scope' of final accent
5 Intonation and final accent

1. Word level accent

According to the paper on Chimwiini, 'accent is either on the penult syllable or on the final syllable'. In SS accent is always on the penult syllable. In cases of monosyllabic words, unlike in Chimwiini where the monosyllable word is accented, SS has a mechanism of providing a supportive syllable in order to safeguard the penult syllable accent rule.

(1)	-la (eat)	=>	ku-la	(verb)
	-nzi (fly)	=>	n-nzi	(noun)

The paper also points out that, with the exception of a few monosyllabic words, as well as a few weak disyllabic words, cf: Appendix in Kisseberth paper, final syllable accent is largely morphosyntactic: i.e. certain morphosyntactic forms 'impose' the final accent on the phrase in which they occur regardless of whether that phrase is syntactically cohesive or not.

2. Phrasal accent

It is claimed that at the level above the isolated word, accent in Chimwiini is phrasal in the sense that 'the final accent that is triggered by morphosyntactic aspects of the word is not realized on the word that triggers it, but on a larger unit' (Section 4). In elaborate speech, not every word gets accentuated as though it were standing alone. Certain words get accentuated, while others do not. The question that the section tries to address is: in an elaborate Chimwiini utterance, which words have accent and which ones do not? The nutshell answer given is "the words that have the accent are all and only the words that stand at the end of phonological phrases that are postulated in order to account for the vowel length alternations".

What is not very clear is whether phonological phrasing can be established independently of syntactic phrasing. Selkirk (1986) is said to have developed a theory of phonological phrasing in Chimwiini, and according to her theory 'phonological phrases are formed by aligning the right edge of a phonological phrase with the right edge of a word that stands at the end of a maximal projection'. For all practical purposes the maximal projections in question are syntactic phrases such as NP, VP, PP, etc. In the same vein of reasoning, it is claimed elsewhere in the paper that 'by placing a phrase edge at the right edge of each X-max, one does not predict that the material between two phrase edges will itself have any syntactic cohesion'. The paper cites three examples of misalignment between phonological and syntactic phrasing, one of which is given in (2).

(2) Uzile chi-buuku/ na meeza '(s)he bought a book/ and a table' (Kisseberth: (13))
(SS Alinunua kitabu na meza)

Syntactically, this sentence is ambiguous. One of the functions of prosody is precisely to disambiguate it by putting a juncture or disjuncture after *chi-buuku*. The argument put forward here therefore can only hold if the two objects must in Chimwiini be read conjointly, which need not be the case in SS, for example.

The placement of prosodic pause in Kisseberth's next two examples (14) and (15) looks rather suspicious too. One of the purposes of phonological clustering is to aid understanding. There is no clear reason why *Nuuru* should be clustered with *mwana* in (14) unless the relativisation rules in Chimwiini require it to do so. More information about relativisation might help. Likewise, there is no reason why *Nuuru* should be clustered with verb + *kuwa* in (15) to form a phonological phrase unless the rules of complementation in Chimwiini so dictate. A break after *kuwa* would be plausible, even if syntactically one might not recognize the unit as cohesive. Could these be idiosyncrasies of a particular speaker? Indeed, phonological boundaries need not correlate with syntactic boundaries, but they should at least reflect abstract clusters reflecting defensible and manageable 'thought units'. Clustering should be seen to aid rather than impede understanding.

3. X-max is not everything

In this section the paper admits that although the alignment of phonological phrases with the right edge of maximal projections is a major factor in Chimwiini phonological phrasing, there are other factors that must be invoked in order to account fully for the facts of the language data under study. Again the paper cites three areas where it is clear that the alignment rule alone would not suffice to account for the prosodic features found in the data. The first area is negation: a complement NP gets disjunctured from its verb, contrary to what obtains in the affirmative. In syntax, negators, like quantifiers, are known to be rather tricky largely because of lack of clarity of their operational scope. Although negation is marked on the verb, its operational scope could cover either the verb alone or the verb along with its complement or even the complement alone. It is therefore useful to understand more broadly how different facets of negation operate in Chimwiini. The seco nd area relates to the unexpected disjuncture between a noun and its modifier. The paper suggests that this might be a way of signaling the indefiniteness of the noun; but one might want also to consider whether it is not a way of signaling different situational functions of a modifier, i.e. whether it is restrictive or non-restrictive (appositional/ giving additional information rather than characterizing the noun). Disjuncture would suggest non-restrictiveness. Examples in (19) appear to represent the norm, i.e. restrictive and therefore no disjuncture! The third area covers a wide range of structures in which phonological phrasing is at variance with what is expected by Selkirk's formula. But perhaps we could reduce them to three points: namely, disjuncture of syntactically cohesive units, i.e. sentential complement from verb, demonstrative from noun and associative phrase from head-noun; subject-Object reversal construction; and lexically determined end-phrase elements such as conjunctions and complementizers. In SS emphasis usually entails a re-configuration of the entire grammatical structure rather than giving special prominence to a specific element in the structure, as appears to be the case in Chimwiini. My main observation here is that prosody is a complex aspect of human language. To appreciate its complexity and unravel it correctly it is important to try and situate it in the broader context of language use so as to distinguish idiosyncrasies from established and regular phonological patterns.

4. Scope of final accent

This section emphasizes further the need for more principles of establishing phrasal boundaries in Chimwiini. In this respect, the paper's reference to the XP-Wrap idea as an additional tool in the task should be a welcome suggestion. Unfortunately, examples (28) are missing from my version of the paper. Also the use of the abbreviation PP (presumably for phonological phrase) might be confused with the syntactic PP, which refers to Prepositional Phrase in this same document. The fundamental question that eludes a clear answer is the same throughout: can the scope of the final accent be established without appealing to syntactic structure? Perhaps more needs to be done to identify and define consistently linguistically relevant properties of speech, such as pause, juncture, stress, and pitch, without being constrained by syntactically established units. It is also important to develop and promote the consistent use of terminology.

5. Intonation and final accent

Intonation serves to distinguish discourse functions of an utterance rather than to cut up an utterance into meaningful clusters. It involves a change of pitch and encompasses the entire utterance as its basic operational unit. However, it can sometimes significantly impact the micro-units constituting it as is being suggested here.

Indeed the interaction between vowel lengthening, phrasal accent and intonation is a very complex process in Chimwiini. Our deeper understanding of it might possibly lie in knowing more about how other aspects of the language work, and whether its prolonged contact with the Somali language, and perhaps also Italian, has had any significant prosodic impact on it.

On the Kikamba Tone-Syntax Interface

R. Ruth Roberts-Kohno
Research Institute for Languages and Cultures of Asia and Africa
Tokyo University of Foreign Studies, Tokyo, Japan

I. Introduction

Kikamba is a Bantu language spoken in Kenya, classified as E55 (Guthrie 1971). The data in this paper was gathered from a speaker of the Machakos dialect of Kikamba. Kikamba has a robust pattern of interaction between Super-Low tone and syntax. In order to understand this interaction, we need to understand two things. The first is that Kikamba is a four-tone language. That is, there are four phonemic tones. The second is that the highest and lowest tones form a natural class, thus indicating the need for the feature [+extreme] which characterizes tones at the periphery of the tonal space. In this paper, I will provide evidence for these two claims, and show how Super-Low tone interacts with the syntax.

A. Kikamba Tones

The four tones in Kikamba are Super-Low (SL), Low (L), High (H), and Super-High (SH). Examples are seen in (1). (1a-d) are examples of nouns, and (1e-h) are examples of verbs.

(1)	a. SL (`)	e.i.à	'lake'	ke.emà	'hill'
	b. L (unmarked)	e.i.o	'banana'	ngatata	'wildebeest'
	c. H (´)	nda.á	'louse'	e.imá	'hole'
	d. SH (˝)	e.i.a̋	'weed'	kethi̋ma̋	'well'
	e. SL	kokonà		'hit' (infinitive)	
	f. L	nɔ̀ɔtő̈konɛ		'that we may hit' (subjunctive)	
	g. H	toi̋kaakoná		'we will not hit' (future)	
	h. SII	koya̋		'eat' (infinitive)	

These examples demonstrate that all tones may appear, and contrast, word-finally. The major restriction on Kikamba tone is that the SL tone is restricted to occurring at the right edge of a word or phrase, as seen in the SL Alignment constraint in (2).

(2) SL Alignment: Align (SL, R,X ^{MAX}, R)
The right edge of a SL tone must be aligned with the right edge of X-Max.
X-Max = maximal projection

B. Kikamba Tone Features

Kikamba tones can be characterized by the tone features [+/- upper] and [+/- extreme], as seen in (3). [+upper] is a feature indicating a tone is in the upper half of the tonal register. [+extreme] is a feature indicating a tone is at the periphery of the tonal space.

(3)	SH	=	[+ upper, + extreme]	L	=	[- upper, - extreme]
	H	=	[+ upper, - extreme]	SL	=	[- upper, + extreme]

This paradigm of tone features is based on the fact that SH tone and SL tone pattern together to the exclusion of H tone and L tone. When two tones pattern together, it is evidence that they share a feature and can be grouped together into a natural class.

II. The Tone-Syntax Interface in Kikamba: Lexical SL tone, Grammatical SL tone, and Phrasal SL tone

In Kikamba, the SL tone is the tone which interacts with the syntax. This interaction is complicated by the fact that there are three types of SL tone in Kikamba. It is precisely the behavior of the SL tone at different levels in the grammar which leads to the postulation of three different SL tones. The first type of SL tone is a lexical SL tone. A lexical tone is a tone which is underlyingly associated with a lexical item. The second type of SL tone is a grammatical SL tone. In this paper, I use the term grammatical to refer to a tone which has been assigned to a verb as part of the verb tense pattern. The final type of SL tone is Kikamba is a phrasal SL tone. This SL tone is assigned to a verb which is a main clause, affirmative verb. I will discuss each type of SL tone below, and provide examples of the SL tone interacting with the syntax. We will see that the different SL tones employ different strategies to avoid violating the SL-Alignment constraint, but all remain true to the fact that a SL tone may occur only at the right edge of X-Max.

A. Lexical SL tone

A lexical SL tone can be found in a large number of Kikamba nouns, and always occurs at the right edge of the word, as seen in (4).

(4)	a. mo.emì	‘farmer’ (cl. 1)
	b. matù	‘clouds’ (cl. 6)
	c. kebɛtì	‘wife’ (cl. 7)
	d. ibɛtì	‘wives’ (cl. 8)
	e. ñoñì	‘bird’ (cl. 9)
	f. andò	‘people’ (cl. 2)
	g. kalolò	‘little leg’ (cl. 12)
	h. tololò	‘little legs’ (cl. 13)

However, if a noun ending in a SL tone is followed by a modifier, the SL tone must move or delete so that it is not in violation of the SL-Alignment constraint. For lexical SL, the resolution is for the SL tone to delete: SL tone deletes at the end of a noun if the noun is followed by a modifier as seen in (5).

(5)	a. **mo.emi** moitɔ̋	'heavy farmer' (cl. 1)
	b. **matu** maníiní	'small clouds' (cl. 6)
	c. **kebɛti** cháakwa	'my wife' (cl. 7)
	d. **ibɛti** ndwá.ú	'sick wives' (cl. 8)
	e. **ñoñi** yaakwá	'my bird' (cl. 9)
	f. **ando** mɛ́ána	'how many people' (cl. 2)
	ando aíngé	'many people'
	ando máa-motábányá	'people of the preacher'
	g. **kalolo** ká-.á̋	'this little leg' (cl .12)
	kalolo ká-ángé	'another leg'
	kalolo káa-moɛma	'leg of Moema'
	kalolo káatólékilɛ́	'leg that broke'
	h. **tololo** tw-íingé	'many legs' (cl. 13)
	tololo tw-eebá	'which legs'
	tololo tw-éána	'how many legs'

In (6a), we see an example of a noun that has a SL tone not only on the final mora, but also on the penultimate mora. A SL tone will only surface on the penultimate syllable if the penultimate syllable is long and if there is also a SL on the final mora. When such a noun is followed by a modifier, both SL tones delete, as seen in (6b), because the SL tone is not at the right edge of X-Max. The fact that both SL tones delete indicates that the SL tone was linked to both moras. This provides evidence for the rule of [+extreme]-Spread1 in (6c): [+extreme] spreads leftward to a long penultimate syllable.

(6)	a. moȍndȍ	'person' (cl. 1)
	b. **moondo** moitɔ̋	'pregnant person'
	moondo mokó.ó	'old person'
	moondo mwá̋á̋thɛ̋	'evil person'

c. [+extreme]-Spread1
SL tone spreads leftward to the second mora of a long penultimate syllable.

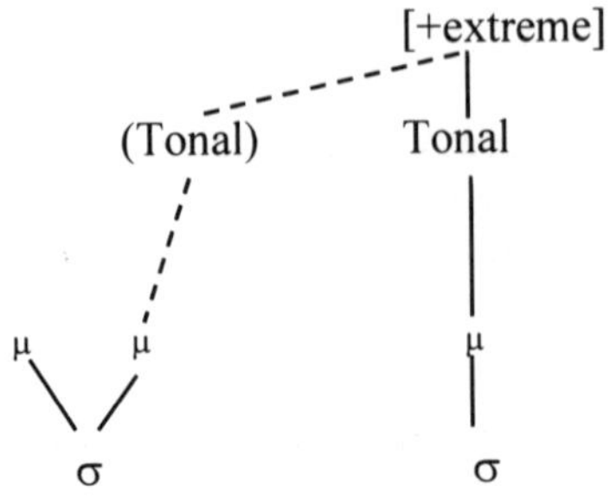

Moreover, if the first half of the penultimate syllable of a noun bears a H tone, and is followed by a SL tone, the SL tone will spread leftward to the H-tone mora and the H surfaces as SH, as in (7a). We know this because when the noun is modified, the lexical SL of the noun deletes since it is not at the right edge of X-Max, and the SH surfaces as a plain H. This provides evidence for the rule of [+extreme]-Spread2: [+extreme] spreads leftward to the first mora of a H-tone penultimate syllable. The result is the SH/SL/SL pattern seen in (7a).

(7)	a. kebe̋èlà	'chair' (cl. 7)
	b. **kebéela** kenɛ̋nɛ̋	'big chair'

c. [+extreme]-Spread2
SL tone spreads leftward to an adjacent, H-tone mora.

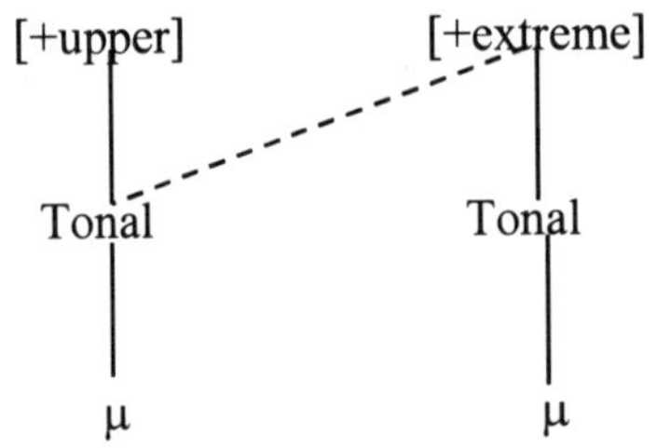

A third tone pattern for nouns is to end in two short SH syllables, as seen in (8a). When a modifier is placed after the noun, a HL pattern is realized on the two short syllables, as in (8b). The SL tone on the final syllable deletes because it is not at the right edge of X-Max. These nouns with 2 SH tones provide evidence for a further rule of [+upper]-Spread which spreads the H tone rightward to a SL tone syllable just in case the two final syllables are short.

(8)	a. ngi̋tɛ̋	'dog' (cl. 9)
	ekűnő	'mushroom' (cl. 5)
	b. **ngíte** nɛ̋nɛ̋	'big dog'
	ekúno enɛ̋nɛ̋	'big mushroom'

c. [+upper]-Spread

H tone spreads rightward to an adjacent, SL tone mora.

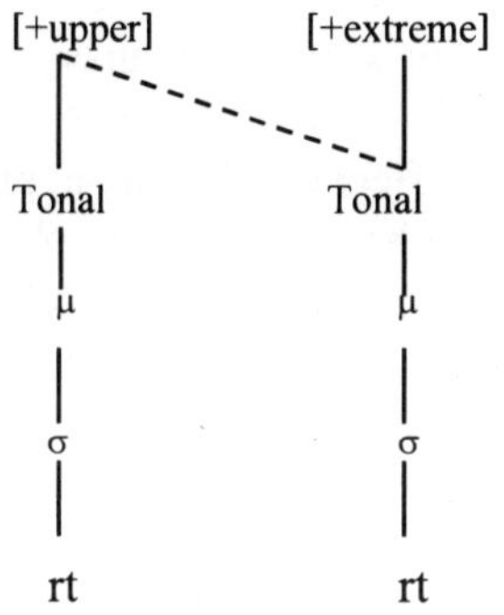

A final tone pattern is one in which only the final syllable bears a SH tone, as in (9a). In (9b), we see that just in case a modifier follows, the SH surfaces as a plain H tone. In other words, SH tone must be the combination of H and SL tone. When the SL component deletes, only [+upper] is left and the final vowel in the examples in (9b) surface with a H tone. Thus, the SL-Alignment constraint is one which restricts the tone feature [+extreme] to occurring exclusively at the right edge of an X-Max.

(9)	a. kotő	'ear' (cl. 15)
	ñamő	'animal' (cl. 9)
	ekwaasɛ̋	'sweet potato' (cl. 5)
	motẅí̋	'fruit-picker' (cl. 1)
	atẅí̋	'fruit pickers' (cl. 2)
	b. **kotó** konɛ̋nɛ̋	'big ear'
	ñamó níiní	'small animal'
	ekwaasé enɛ̋nɛ̋	'big sweet potato'
	motẅí mothwi.ì	'rich fruit picker'
	motẅí mokó.ó	'old fruit-picker'
	motẅí waa-moɛma	'fruit picker of Moema'
	atẅí mɛ́ána	'how many fruit pickers'
	atẅí aíngé	'many fruit pickers'

The SL tone in Kikamba is not just a phonetic effect of being in phrase-final position. If so, all nouns ending in L phrase-medially would end with SL phrase-finally, and they do not. There is no alternation of the final L tone of the nouns in (10) based on whether there is a following modifier or not. The final vowel of these nouns always surfaces as L.

(10)	a. ngusu	'pocket' (cl. 9)
	ngusu nɛ̋nɛ̋	'big pocket'
	b. ngatata	'wildebeest' (cl. 9)
	ngatata ngó.ó	'old wildebeest'

c. maio	'bananas' (cl. 6)
maio ma.asá	'long bananas'
maio mɛ́ú	'ripe bananas'
maio mɛ́ána	'how many bananas'

Furthermore, if SH tone were just a phonetic effect of a H tone in phrase-final position, all nouns which end in H tone phrase-medially should have a SH tone phrase-finally, and they do not. There are nouns which end in plain H tone regardless of the presence of a following modifier. (11) shows nouns ending in a H tone which do not alternate when followed by a modifier.

(11)	a. ngókó	'chicken' (cl. 9)
	ngókó nɛ̋nɛ̋	'big chicken'
	b. mabaatá	'ducks' (cl. 6)
	mabaatá manɛ̋nɛ̋	'big ducks'
	c. motábányá	'preacher' (cl. 1)
	motábányá mothwi.ì	'rich preacher'
	d. atábányá	'preachers' (cl. 2)
	atábányá mɛ́ána	'how many preachers'
	atábányá aíngé	'many preachers'

The rest of the examples in this section show nouns in various syntactic contexts. In each case, the data shows that if a noun ending in a SH or a SL tone is not phrase-final, the [+extreme] feature deletes and a plain H or a plain L surfaces on the final vowel of the noun. On the other hand, if the noun ending in a SH or a SL tone *is* phrase-final, the [+extreme] feature is at the right edge of X-Max, and does not need to delete.

In (12), we have a noun in subject position. The SL or SH tone remains, because the noun is final in its phrase, the NP subject position, as illustrated in (12f). In phrase-final position, the feature [+exteme] is at the right edge of X-Max, and thus, does not delete.

(12)	a. **andò** némábálókilɛ̂	'people fell'
	b. **moòndò** nóónaatálilɛ	'a person counted'
	c. **atwı̋** némábálókilɛ̂	'fruit-pickers fell'
	d. **motwɛ̋** nóónaabálokilɛ	'a head fell'
	e. **ngítɛ̋** nookwí.ɛ́	'a dog died'

f.

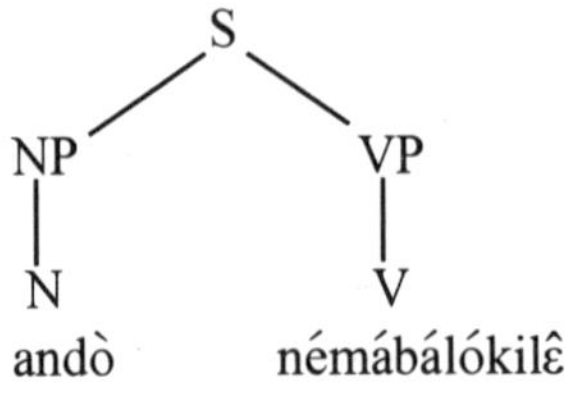

In (13a-c), a noun ending in a lexical SL tone is the first of two objects in a row after the verb. The SL tone does not delete because it is final within its NP, i.e., at the right edge of X-Max, as illustrated in (13d). Contrast these examples to (13e-g) where the first object ends in a lexical L tone, and not a SL tone. Thus, in phrase-final position, the lexical distinction between final SL and final L tone nouns is maintained.

(13) a. tóya̋a̋ꜜnɛ́ɛnga **moȍndȍ** maio — 'we didn't give the person bananas'
b. tóya̋a̋ꜜnɛ́ɛnga **mo.ɛnȉ** mokátɛ́ — 'we didn't give the guest bread'
c. tóya̋a̋ꜜtálela **mo.emȉ** ngókó — 'we didn't count chickens for the farmer'

d.

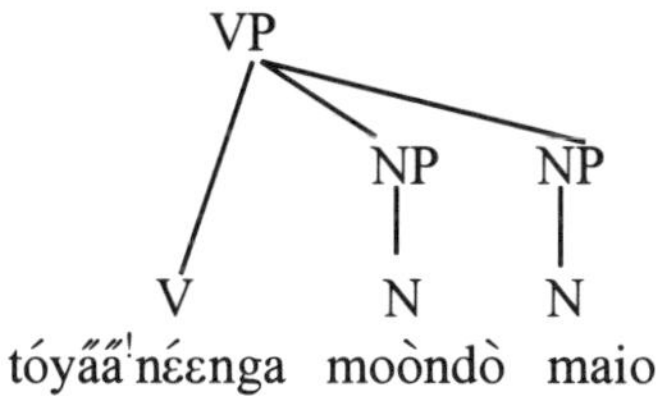

e. tóya̋a̋ꜜnɛ́ɛnga **moɛma** maio — 'we didn't give Moema bananas'
f. tóya̋a̋ꜜnɛ́ɛnga **moɛma** mokátɛ́ — 'we didn't give Moema bread'
g. tóya̋a̋ꜜtálela **moɛma** ngókó — 'we didn't count chickens for Moema'

Another syntactic environment is the conjoining of two NPs. First note that (14a, b) are the singular and plural of a noun ending in a SH tone. When the noun is followed by a modifier, [+extreme] deletes and final SH surfaces as plain H. But in (14c, d), the SH tone at the end of the first noun does not delete. This is because the noun is final in its NP, as seen in (14e). Therefore, since the constraint on SL-Alignment is not violated, the feature [+extreme] does not delete and SH remains.

(14) a. ekwaasɛ̋ — 'sweet potato' (cl. 5)
ekwaasé yáakwa — 'my sweet potato'
b. makwaasɛ̋ — 'sweet potatos' (cl. 6)
makwaasé masɛ́ɔ́ — 'good sweet potatos'
c. **ekwaasɛ̋** na-maio — 'sweet potato and bananas'
d. **ekwaasɛ̋** na-mosɛ̋ɛlɛ̋ — 'sweet potato and rice'

e.

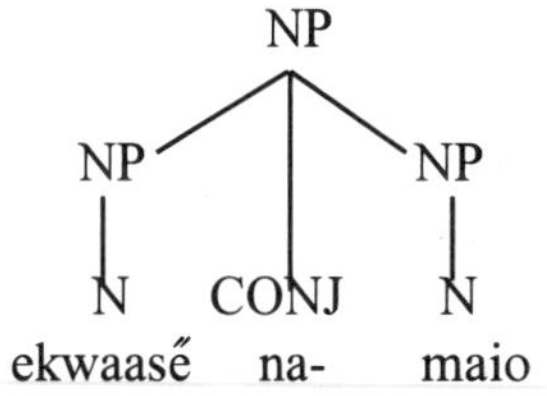

However, if the conjoined noun is followed by a modifier as in (15a-b), then the noun is no longer final in its NP. SL-Alignment is violated and the tone feature [+extreme] deletes, leaving a plain H tone at the end of the first noun in (15a-b). (15c-d) show the different syntactic structures for nouns ending in SL and SH tones. (15c) represents a noun at the end of its phrase and [+extreme] does not delete. In (15d), a modifier follows, leaving the noun medial in its phrase, therefore causing [+extreme] to delete.

(15) a. **ekwaasé** yáakwa na-mosɛ̋ɛ̋lɛ̋ 'my sweet potato and rice'
b. **makwaasé** ma.aasá na-maio 'long sweet potatoes and bananas'

c. [NP [N a.emì / ekwaasɛ̋]]

d. [NP [N a.emi / ekwaasé] [AP mɛ́ána / yáakwa]]

Another syntactic environment is when the noun is modified by a number. SL deletes at the end of a noun which is modified by the numbers 1-5, as seen in (16). Note that these are also the numbers which agree with the head noun: the number takes an agreement prefix which agrees with the class of the noun.

(16)	a. kalolò	'little leg' (cl. 12)
	kalolo ká-mwɛ̋	'1 little leg'
	b. tololò	'little legs' (cl. 13)
	tololo tw-éélé	'2 little legs'
	tololo tó-ta̋tű	'3 little legs'
	tololo tő-na̋	'4 little legs'
	tololo tó-ta̋ànɔ̀	'5 little legs'

However, when the same noun is modified by any other number, the final SL on the head noun does not delete. Interestingly, it is exactly the numbers 1-5 and no others which take an agreement prefix. Therefore, the lack of agreement prefix and the fact that the SL does not delete in exactly this environment is an indication of the internal syntactic structure of phrases indicating number. In phrases with the numbers 1-5, the number is part of the NP including the noun. In phrases containing numbers greater than 5, the number is outside the NP. Thus SL Alignment is not violated, and the SL on the noun in (17) does not delete.

(17)	a. tololò	'little legs' (cl. 13)
	b. tololò tháanthátő	'6 little legs'
	c. tololò mɔ.ɔ̋ɔ̋nza̋	'7 little legs'
	d. tololò ñááña̋	'8 little legs'
	e. tololò kɛ.ɛnda̋	'9 little legs'
	f. tololw'eekőmí	'10 little legs'
	g. tololò e.anà	'100 little legs'
	h. tololò ngélé	'1,000 little legs'

A final syntactic environment we will look at for nouns is the possessive phrases in (18). When the adjective *moaasá* 'tall' modifies *moòndò* 'person' in (18d), SL tone deletes on 'person.' *Moòndò* is not at the right edge of X-Max and violates the SL Alignment constraint. When the adjective *ndaasá* 'tall' modifies *ñamő* 'animal' in (18e), the SL tone on *moòndò* 'person'does not delete. *Moòndò* is final in its NP, since it is not modified by *ndaasá,* and the SL Alignment constraint is not violated. In all cases, the SH on 'animal' becomes plain H. The [+extreme] feature deletes leaving plain H on *ñamő* because 'animal' is not final in the NP.

(18)	a. ñamő	'animal' (cl. 9)
	b. moòndò	'person' (cl. 1)
	c. ñamó [yáa-moòndò]$_{NP}$	'animal of a person'
	d. ñamó$_9$ [yáa-**moondo**$_1$ moaasá$_1$]$_{NP}$	'animal of a tall person'
	e. ñamó$_9$ [yáa-**moòndò**$_1$]$_{NP}$ ndaasá$_9$	'tall animal of a person'

One exception worth noting is the modifier 'all' in (19), which agrees with the head noun, and should be in the same NP with its preceding head noun. However, [+extreme] does not delete from a noun ending in SL or SH which is followed by the modifier 'all.' This indicates that the modifier 'all' is in fact in a separate phrase. Thus, a final SL or SH remains on the head noun.

(19)	a. tololò tw-ɔ́ɔnthɛ̋	'all little legs' (cl. 13)
	b. makwaasɛ̋ ɔ́-ɔnthɛ̋	'all sweet potatoes' (cl. 6)

In summary, morphological agreement of modifiers with their head nouns indicates phrase structure, and interacts with tone insofar as SL tone, i.e. [+extreme], is sensitive to the right edge of a phrase, i.e. X-Max.

B. Grammatical SL tone

The examples in (20) to (23) show that there is a SL tone which is assigned by the tense/aspect system to all infinitives. This grammatical SL tone is also sensitive to syntactic structure. The SL tone on the final vowel of the infinitives in (20) deletes when the verb is followed by a complement.

(20)	a. kokonà	'to hit'
	kokona maio	'to hit bananas'
	b. kobulyà	'to grab'
	kobulya ngókó	'to grab chickens'

In the examples in (21), the SL tone spreads leftward to the second mora of a long penultimate syllable by the rule of [+extreme]-Spread1 (see 6c). But when followed by a complement, the SL tone deletes: it is no longer at the right edge of X-Max. Note that the tone spreading rules applicable for nouns are also applicable for verbs as well.

(21)	a. kosuùngà	‘to guard’
	kosuunga maio	‘to guard bananas’
	b. kokuùsyà	‘to pull’
	kokuusya ngókó	‘to pull chickens’

In the examples in (22), the SL tone spreads leftward by the rule of [+extreme]-Spread1, and then spreads leftward to an adjacent H-tone mora by the rule of [+extreme]-Spread2 (see 7c), resulting in a SH/SL/SL pattern. But when such a verb is followed by a complement, and is no longer at the right edge of X-Max, the SL tone deletes, and the SH surfaces as plain H on the antepenultimate mora.

(22)	a. kosyőòlà	‘to peel’
	kosyóola maio	‘to peel bananas’
	b. kokɛ̋ɛ̀thyà	‘to greet’
	kokɛ́ɛthya ngókó	‘to greet chickens’

In the examples in (23), not only does SL spread leftward by [+extreme]-Spread 2, but the H tone spreads rightward by [+upper]-Spread (see 8c), resulting in two short SH syllables. And when a complement follows, SL deletes since it is not at the right edge of X-Max, and SH surfaces as H on the penultimate syllable.

(23)	a. kota̋la̋	‘to count’
	kotála maio	‘to count bananas’
	b. kobi̋tha̋	‘to hide’
	kobítha ngókó	‘to hide chickens’

C. Phrasal SL tone

A third type of SL tone is associated with affirmative, main clause (henceforth, assertive) clauses. The behavior of this tone provides the most interesting tone-syntax interface data in Kikamba. Pre-pausally, the tone marking assertive clauses may surface as a SL tone or as the second half of a Falling tone. However, when an object follows an assertive verb, the verb is no longer final in its X-Max and the SL Alignment constraint is violated. This conflict is resolved *not* by deleting the phrasal SL tone (as was the case with lexical and grammatical SL tone), but by shifting the SL tone to the object so that it appears at the right edge of X-Max, and thus, no longer appears on the verb.

In the data in (24), examples of 5 assertive tenses are given. For each tense, three forms of the verb are given: phrase-final position, with the following final-L tone object (24a) *maio,* and with the following final-H tone object (24b) *ngókó*. In each case, the phrasal SL surfaces on the phrase-final verb, or shifts to a following object which is contained within the verb phrase.

(24)	a. ma.i.o	‘bananas’	b. ngókó	‘chickens’
	c. nétónáa[**koni.ȅ**		‘we hit’ (yesterday)	

d. nétónáa[koni.ɛ **ma.i.ò** | 'we hit bananas'
e. nétónáa[**tálilɛ̀** | 'we counted'
f. nétónáa[tálilɛ **ngókô** | 'we counted chickens'

g. tokáa[**konâ** | 'we will hit'
h. tokáa[koná **maiò** | 'we will hit bananas'
i. tokáa[**tálâ** | 'we will count'
j. tokáa[tálá **maiò** | 'we will count bananas'
k. tokáa[tálá ngókô | 'we will count chickens'

l. nétwáa[**koníɛ̂** | 'we hit' (remote)
m. nétwáa[koníɛ́ **maiò** | 'we hit bananas'
n. nétwáa[**tálílɛ̂** | 'we counted'
o. nétwáa[tálílɛ́ **maiò** | 'we counted bananas'
p. nétwáa [tálílɛ́ **ngókô** | 'we countd chickens'

q. nétwáa[**konâ** | 'we just hit'
r. nétwáa[koná **maiò** | 'we just hit bananas'
s. nétwáa[**tálâ** | 'we just counted'
t. nétwáa[tálá **maiò** | 'we just counted bananas'
u. nétwáa[tálá **ngókô** | 'we just counted chickens'

v. nétó[**kona.â** | 'we (always) hit'
w. nétó[kona.á **maiò** | 'we (always) hit bananas'
x. nétó[**tála.â** | 'we (always) count'
y. nétó[tála.á **maiò** | 'we (always) count bananas'
z. nétó[tála.á **ngókô** | 'we (always) count chickens'

The data in (25) and (26) are provided as a contrast to (24). They are examples of non assertive verb tenses (negative or subordinate clauses) which end in a H or L tone. Notice that in each case, there is no addition of a phrasal SL at the end of the verb.

(25) a. moond'oola twaatáléílɛ́ | 'person who we counted (remote) for'
b. toíkaatálá | 'we won't count'
c. moond'oola tókaatálelá | 'person who we'll count for'
d. moond'oola tótákaatálelá | 'person who we won't count for'
e. moond'oola totálela.á | 'person who we count for'
f. moond'oola totatálélá.á | 'person who we don't count for'
g. moond'oola tótálé.éetɛ́ | 'person who we have been counting for'
h. moond'oola tótátálé.éetɛ́ | 'person who we have not been counting for'
i. tóyaa̋tálééte̋ | 'we hadn't counted (remote)'
j. moond'oola twáatálé.éétɛ́ | 'person who we had counted for (remote)'
k. moond'oola tótáatálé.éétɛ́ | 'person who we hadn't counted for (rem)'
l. nɔ́ɔtɔ̋talɛ | 'we may count'

m. toyá̋átálá.á	'we didn't used to count'
n. moond'oola twáatálélá.á	'person who we used to count for'
o. moond'oola tótáatálélá.á	'person who we didn't used to count for'
p. tála	'count!'

(26) shows the non-assertive verbs in (25) with a following object placed after the verb. The following object does not acquire a SL tone, since there was not a phrasal SL tone on the verb to shift, and the final tone of the verb does not change. Thus, we see that the phrasal SL tone occurs only in assertive clauses.

(26)	a. moond'oola twaatáléílɛ́ maio	'person who we counted bananas (rem) for'
	b. toíkaatálá maio	'we won't count bananas'
	c. moond'oola tókaatálelá maio	'person who we'll count bananas for'
	d. moond'oola tótákaatálelá maio	'person who we won't count bananas for'
	e. moond'oola totálela.á maio	'person who we count bananas for'
	f. moond'oola totatálélá.á maio	'person who we don't count bananas for'
	g. moond'oola tótálé.éetɛ́ maio	'person who we've been counting bananas for'
	h. moond'oola tótátálé.éetɛ́ maio	'person we've not been counting bananas for'
	i. tóyaá̋táléétɛ́ maio	'person we hadn't counted bananas (remote)'
	j. moond'oola twáatálé.éétɛ́ maio	'person who we had counted bananas for (rem)'
	k. moond'oola tótáatálé.éétɛ́ maio	'person we hadn't counted bananas for (rem)'
	l. nɔ́ɔtɔ̋talɛ maio	'we may count bananas'
	m. toyá̋átálá.á maio	'we didn't used to count bananas'
	n. moond'oola twáatálélá.á maio	'person who we used to count bananas for'
	o. moond'oola tótáatálélá.á maio	'person we didn't used to count bananas for'
	p. tála maio	'count bananas!'
	q. moond'oola tótáatálélá.á ngókó	'who we didn't used to count chickens for'
	r. tála ngókó	'count chickens!'

The next set of data show that the phrasal SL tone at the end of the verb in (27c) shifts to a following object in (27d), but does not shift further than *moema* in (27e, f), since *moema* is at the right edge of an NP, as well as at the right edge of the higher VP. In other words, the phrasal SL has found the right edge of a phrase, X-Max, and does not shift further.

(27)	a. chá̋í	'tea'
	b. moɛma	(proper name)
	c. **nénékénɛ́ɛ́ngiɛ̂**	'I gave it'
	d. nénékénɛ́ɛ́ngiɛ́ **moɛmà**	'I gave it to Moema'
	e. nénénɛ́ɛngiɛ́ **moɛmà** chá̋í	'I gave tea to Moema'
	f. nénékénɛ́ɛngiɛ́ **moɛmà** kwáachá̋	'I gave it to Moema this morning'

In (27), phrasal SL shifts to a noun ending in a L tone, but in (28) the phrasal SL shifts to two nouns ending in a H tone: (28a) *kemiiná* and (24b) *ngókó*. If the phrasal SL shifts to a noun ending in a H tone, a H/SL Fall will surface, as in (28b). But, if SL has reached the right edge of a phrase, as in (28c), and the Falling tone is phrase-medial, H/SL surfaces as SH. This is because phrase-medial Falling tone is prohibited in Kikamba. It is resolved by delinking a tonal node and spreading [+extreme] to the tonal node bearing [+upper], resulting in a SH tone.

(28)	a. kemiiná	(proper name)
	b. nénékénɛ́ɛngiɛ́ **kemiinâ**	'I gave it to Kemiina'
	nétwáatálá **ngókô**	'we just counted chickens' (imm past)
	c. nénénɛ́ɛngiɛ́ **kemiinа̋** chái	'I gave tea to Kemiina'
	nétwáatálá **ngókő** kwáachа̋	'we just counted chickens this morning'

Examples from the copulative construction follow the same pattern, as seen in (29). (29a) shows an adjective which ends in a H tone. The adjective 'long' acquires a SL tone in the assertive copula in (29b), and surfaces with a Falling tone phrase-finally. When an adverb is added in (29c), the SL does not shift to the adverb, indicating that the SL has already reached the end of an X-Max. Since the Falling tone is no longer pre-pausal, and thus prohibited, H/SL Fall surfaces as SH.

(29)	a. mo.asá	'long' (referring to firewood)
	mbɔɔsɔ nda.asá	'long beans'
	b. okő né **mo.asâ**	'firewood is long'
	mbɔɔsɔ né **nda.asâ**	'beans are long'
	c. okő né **mo.asа̋** byo	'firewood is very long'

However, if the object the SL has shifted to is further modified, phrasal SL must shift to the next modifier. In (30c), phrasal SL stops on *maio* 'bananas,' since this is the right edge of X-Max. In (30d), phrasal SL may not stop on 'bananas' because it is further modified. Thus, SL shifts to the next modifier *motábányâ*, which surfaces with a final H/SL fall since *motábányá* ends in a lexical H tone. In fact, phrasal SL continues to shift throughout a string of modifiers until it finds the right edge of X-Max. This is illustrated in (30l). (30i-k) are examples of SL shift through a modifier string in the copulative construction.

(30)	a. maio	'bananas'
	b. motábányá	'preacher'
	c. nénɔ́ɔ́níɛ́ **maiò**	'I saw bananas (remote)'
	d. nénɔ́ɔ́níɛ́ maio **máa-motábányâ**	'I saw bananas of a preacher'
	*nénɔ́ɔ́níɛ́ **maiò** máa-motábányá	

e. nénɔ́ɔ́níɛ́ maio máa-motábányá **mo.aasâ** 'I saw bananas of a tall preacher'
f. nénɔ́ɔ́níɛ́ maio máa-motábányá **wa-moɛmà** 'I saw bananas of Moema's preacher'

g. masaakó (place name)
h. nénɔ́ɔ́níɛ́ maio máa-motábányá wa-moɛma **wa-masaakô**
I-saw bananas of preacher of Moema of Masaako

'I saw bananas of the preacher of Moema of Masaako'

i. kobétoka 'too'
j. okő né **mo.asâ** 'firewood is long'
k. okő né mo.asá **kobétokà** 'firewood is too long'

l. Recursive shift of Phrasal SL throughout a VP

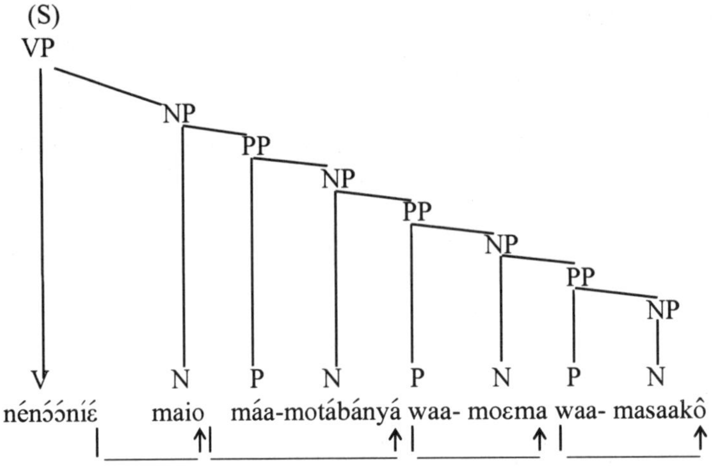

In (31a), the assertive verb ends in a Falling tone: the combination of a H tone and phrasal SL. (31b, c) are examples with postposed subjects. In (31c), the phrasal SL has shifted to the object *ngókó,* but stops there, surfacing as a SH tone. It stops shifting in both (31b) and (31c) because phrasal SL may not shift to a postposed subject: SL has reached the right edge of X-Max, and will shift no further, as illustrated in (31e, f). (31d) shows that a postposed subject, which is not part of the VP, may not be inserted in the VP between a verb and its object.

(31) a. moɛma **akáabálókâ** 'Moema will fall'
b. **akáabálókã̋** moɛma 'Moema will fall'
c. akáatálá **ngókő** moɛma 'Moema will count chickens'
d. *akáatálá moɛma ngókó 'Moema will count chickens'

e.
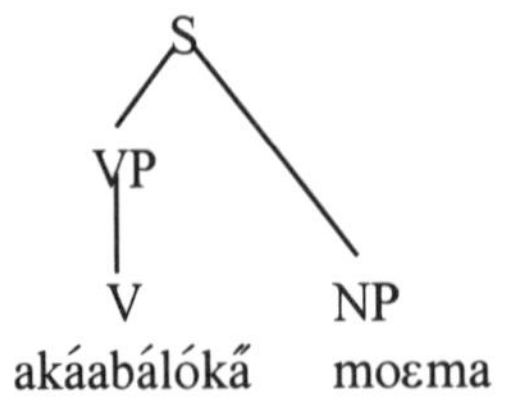

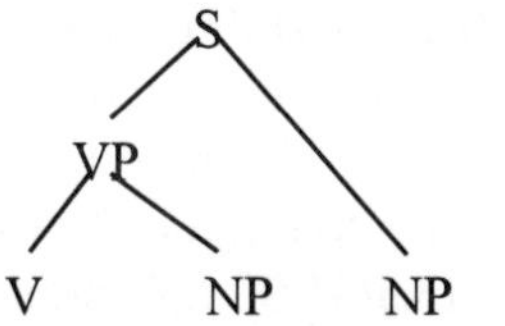

f. akáatálá ngókő moɛma

Examples with non-agreeing modifiers and the modifier 'all' are given in (32). Phrasal SL shift stops at a modifier which is not part of the VP. We have already seen that numbers greater than 5 do not agree with a head noun and are not part of the VP, and that 'all' agrees with the head noun but is not included in the VP. And since the H/SL Falling tone, which may not spread to the modifier, is phrase-medial, it surfaces as a SH tone.

(32) a. nénɔ́ɔ́níɛ́ maio **má.-atábányá̋** kɛɛndá̋ 'I saw bananas of nine preachers'
b. nénɔ́ɔ́níɛ́ maio **má.-atábányá̋** ɔ́ɔnthɛ̋ 'I saw bananas of all the preachers'
c. nóonɔ́ɔ́siɛ **ngókő** ekőmí 'he took 10 chickens'
d. nóonɔ́ɔ́siɛ **ngókő** kɛɛndá̋ 'he took 9 chickens'

Phrasal SL will shift into a locative phrase as well, as in (33c-f), but stops shifting when it reaches a non-agreeing modifier, as seen in (33d, f), which is an indication that the non-agreeing modifier is in a separate phrase.

(33) a. ñoombá 'house' b. nîinî 'small'
c. nemetilé.ilɛ mbɛ.ɛ waa **ñoombâ** 'I cut it in front of a house'
d. nemetilé.ilɛ mbɛ.ɛ waa **ñoombá̋** !kɛ.ɛndá̋ 'I cut it in front of 9 houses'
e. nemetilé.ilɛ mbɛ.ɛ waa ñoombá **nîinî** 'I cut it in front of a small house'
f. nemetilé.ilɛ mbɛ.ɛ waa ñoombá **nîinĭ** !kɛ.ɛndá̋
'I cut it in front of 9 small houses'

More locative examples are found in (34). (34c, d) show the shift of phrasal SL into the locative, just as in (33c-f), all of which are examples of agreeing locatives which take *waa*. However, the locatives in (34e-h) take *naa* before the noun and are non-agreeing locatives. These locatives do not allow shift of phrasal SL into the object of the locative. The SL stops on the locative, which is phrase-medial in (34g, h), and H/SL surfaces as SH.

(34) a. eolú waa-ñoombá 'above the house'
b. mbɛɛ waa-ñoombá 'in front of the house'
c. nekétiléilɛ eolú **waa-ñoombâ** 'I cut it above the house'
d. nekétiléilɛ mbɛɛ **waa-ñoombâ** 'I cut it in front of the house'
e. baasá naa-ñoombá 'far from the house'
f. bakóbé naa-ñoombá 'near the house'
g. nekétiléilɛ **baasá̋** naa-ñoombá 'I cut it far from the house'
h. nekétiléilɛ **bakóbé̋** naa-ñoombá 'I cut it near the house'

Two more locatives are found in (35a, c). Both allow shift of phrasal SL, which surfaces on the noun *ñoombâ*. However, if the alternate word order of noun followed by preposition is allowed, the shift of phrasal SL stops on the noun, as in (35b, d), indicating the following preposition is not part of the same X-Max. SL has already reached the end of X-Max, and may not shift further into the preposition. Once again, we see phrase-final H/SL fall surfaces as SH phrase-medially.

(35) a. nétwáamíbóέέ etíná **wa-ñoombâ** 'we washed it behind the house'
b. nétwáamíbóέέ **ñoomb' ɛ̋**ɛtína̋[1] 'we washed it behind the house'
c. nétwáamíbóέέ nthéené wa-**ñoombâ** 'we washed it inside the house'
d. nétwáamíbóέέ **ñoomba̋** nthéenɛ̋[2] 'we washed it inside the house'

The data have shown that phrasal SL shifts through modifier strings until it finds the right edge of X-Max. (36) shows phrasal SL will also shift through a series of relative clause modifier strings until it finds the right edge of X-Max as well. First, compare (36a) to (36b, h). (36a) is a negative clause and (36b, h) are assertive, and end in phrasal SL. Notice that the general tone rules are applicable here: SL has spread leftward twice in (36b) and the H on the verb surfaces as SH. In (36h), the relative clause modifier ends in a H tone and the addition of the phrasal SL creates a Falling tone.

When the relative clause modifier is further modified, as in (36d, e, i), phrasal SL shifts to the modifier. Compare (36d) to the negative clause in (36c) where no SL surfaces on the modifier *maio*. (36f) shows that phrasal SL will continue to shift through the modifier string until it reaches the right edge of X-Max, in this case *maníinî*. However, notice that in (36g) the phrasal SL will not shift to the non-agreeing modifier *kɛɛnda̋*: SL has already reached the right edge of X-Max.

(36) a. ndénɛ̋ɔ́na ngókó **ékɛ́ɛ́ngɛ́ɛ́tɛ́ɛtɛ** 'I didn't see a clucking chicken'
b. nénénɔ́ɔ́niɛ ngókó **ékɛ́ɛ́ngɛ́ɛ́tɛ̋ɛ̀tɛ̀** 'I saw a clucking chicken'
c. ndénɛ̋ɔ́na ngókó etoméetɛ **maio** 'I didn't see a chicken who has pecked bananas'
I-didn't see chicken rel-peck bananas

d. nénénɔ́ɔ́niɛ ngókó etoméetɛ **maiò** 'I saw a chicken who has pecked bananas'
I-saw chicken rel-peck bananas

e. nénénáakaathiɛ twáána tókuéetɛ́ **maiò** 'I praised children carrying bananas'
f. nénénáakaathiɛ twáána tókuéetɛ́ maio **maníinî**
'I praised children carrying small bananas'
g. nénénáakaathiɛ twáána tókuéetɛ́ **maiò** kɛɛnda̋ 'I praised children carrying 9 bananas'
I-praised children rel-carrying bananas 9

h. bɛ́ɛ ngókó **ngaatálâ** 'there's a chicken I'll count'
i. bɛ́ɛ moondo ngáatálelá **ngókô** 'there is a person I'll count chickens for'

In (37), phrasal SL continues to shift through the modifier string, searching for the right edge of X-Max. If the right edge of X-Max happens to be phrase-medial, H/SL Fall surfaces as SH, as in (37f).

(37) a. nétwáamɔ́ɔ́níɛ́ **maítálâ** ‘we saw them counting’
b. nétwáamɔ́ɔ́níɛ́ maítálá **ngókô** ‘we saw them counting chickens’
c. nétwáamɔ́ɔ́níɛ́ maítálá moondo **moníinî** ‘we saw them counting a small person’
d. nétwáamɔ́ɔ́níɛ́ maítálá ando **máa-moɛmà** ‘we saw them counting Moema’s people’
e. nétwáamɔ́ɔ́níɛ́ maítálá ando máa-moɛma **moníinî**
‘we saw them counting little Moema’s people’
f. nétwáamɔ́ɔ́níɛ́ maítálá ando máa-moɛma **moníiní̋** ɛ́ɛ́lé
we-them-saw they-counting people(Cl. 2) of- Moema(Cl 1) small (Cl. 1) two(Cl. 2)
‘we saw them counting little Moema’s 2 people’

Phrasal SL shifts not only into nominal modifier strings and relative clause modifier strings, but also into infinitival modifier strings, as seen in (38). (38a) is a negative clause and does not have a phrasal SL, whereas the phrasal SL in the assertive clause in (38b) surfaces on the object. And if the infinitival complement is modified in a chain of overlapping head-modifier relations, SL shifts to the end of that phrase.

(38) a. ndáel’ɔ́ɔtɛ́ma **maio** ‘I shouldn’t cut bananas’
b. nénáel’ ɔ́ɔtɛ́ma **maiò** ‘I should cut bananas’
c. nénáel’ɔ́ɔmotɛ́ɛthy’ ɔɔtɛ́ma **maiò** ‘I should help him cut bananas’
d. nénáel’ɔ́ɔmotɛ́ɛthy’ ɔɔtɛ́ma maio **mɛ́ɛ́wiɛ̂** ‘I should help him cut bananas that ripened’
e. nénáel’ɔ́ɔmotɛ́ɛthy’ ɔɔtɛ́ma maio mɛ́ɛ́wéiɛ́ **moondá̋ànè**
‘I should help him cut bananas that ripened in the garden’
f. nénáel’ɔ́ɔmotɛ́ɛthy’ ɔɔtɛ́ma maio mɛ́ɛ́wéiɛ́ mondáane **wáa-moɛmà**
‘I should help him cut bananas that ripened in the garden of Moema’

A further environment for the shift of phrasal SL tone is into subordinate clauses. Subordinate clauses vary as to whether they allow phrasal SL to shift into them. Interestingly, subjunctive subordinate clauses do not allow phrasal SL to shift into them, as seen in (39). In (39a, b), SL shifts to the object: *moɛmà*, but stops at the subjunctive verb. In (39c-e), the phrasal SL remains on the assertive verb. Since the resulting H/SL is phrase-medial, a SH tone surfaces. (39f) shows that the SL on the assertive verb is already at the right edge of a VP and is not required to shift further. Since the right edge of X-Max is found, the phrasal SL does not shift into the subjunctive verb.

(39) a. ne.ebíɛ **moɛmà** [áemɛ] ‘I paid Moema to dig’
b. ne.ebíɛ **moɛmà** [kemiiná áemɛ] ‘I paid Moema so Kemiina would dig’
c. **nemoebíɛ̋** [áemɛ] ‘I paid him to dig’
d. **tweɛndá̋** [moɛma átalɛ] ‘we want that Moema count’
e. **netálílɛ̋** [moɛma ábaandɛ] ‘I counted so that Moema may plant’

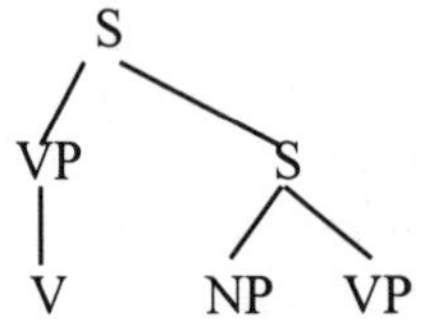

f. netáli̋lɛ̋ [moɛma ábaandɛ]

However, infinitival and When-clause subordinate clauses *do* allow shift of phrasal SL, as seen in (40). In (40a, b), SL surfaces on *moɛmà* because it has reached the right edge of X-Max. In (40c, d), phrasal SL shifts to the infinitive but cannot stay there, because it has not yet found the right edge of X-Max, so then shifts to the object following the infinitive. In (40e, f), SL stops on the the noun following the verb: it has found the right edge of X-Max. However, when no overt object follows the assertive verb, the SL tone may shift into the subordinate verb as seen in (40g), and will continue shifting to the right edge if the subordinate verb is further modified, as in (40h).

(40)	a. néándékíɛ **moɛmà** [kobaàndà]	'I hired Moema to plant'
	b. néándékíɛ **moɛmà** [kobaanda maio]	'I hired Moema to plant bananas'
	c. némoándékíɛ [kobaanda **maiò**]	'I hired him to plant bananas'
	d. tweɛndá [kobaandea **moɛmà**]	'we want to plant for Moema'
	e. nénémɔ́ɔ́níɛ́ [**moɛmà** aítálá]	'I saw them while M was counting'
	f. nénɔ́ɔ́níɛ́ **kebéésɛ̋** [keítálá]	'I saw the boy counting'
	g. nénɔ́ɔ́níɛ́ [**keítálâ**]	'I saw him counting'
	h. nénɔ́ɔ́níɛ́ [keítálá **maiò**]	'I saw him counting bananas'

This can be explained assuming two different structures for subordinate clauses. Infinitival and When clauses can be classified as IP clauses and are permeable to the shift of phrasal SL. Subjunctive clauses are classified as CP clauses and are impermeable. This is illustrated in (41).

(41) IP clauses are permeable — CP clauses are impermeable

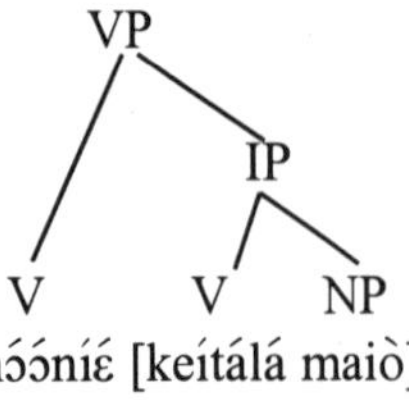

nénɔ́ɔ́níɛ́ [keítálá maiò]
'I saw him counting bananas'

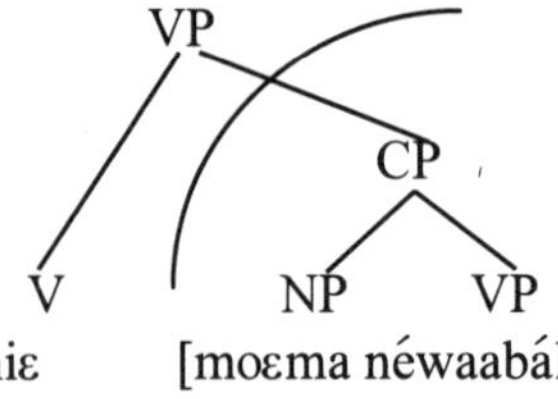

nénɔ́ɔ́niɛ [moɛma néwaabálókîlɛ̂
'I saw that Moema fell'

Evidence for a distinction between CP and IP clauses is that CP clauses allow optional complementizers and IP clauses do not. This is exactly what is found in Kikamba. Phrases that block SL shift may optionally have an overt complementizer, as demonstrated in (42a). Phrases that allow SL shift are prohibited from having an overt complementizer, as in (42b).

(42) CP clauses allow complementizers

a. neɔ́ná (*kaná)* moɛma néwaabálókílɛ̂ 'I see that Moema fell'

IP clauses do not.

b. *nénɔ́ɔ́níɛ́ *kaná* keítálá maiò 'I saw him counting bananas'

Furthermore, there is a third pattern with respect to the shift of phrasal SL tone. There are two environments where phrasal SL shift is neither blocked nor allowed. In (43) are examples of subordinate That-clauses. If there is no post-verbal noun for the phrasal SL to shift to, as there is in (43a), the SL simply deletes, as seen in (43b-g).

(43)	a. tokɛ́.ɛ́á **moɛmà** [kebéésé kɛ̋talɛ]	'we will tell Moema that the boy should count'
	b. tokáamɛ́á [mȁtalɛ]	'we will tell them that they should count'
	c. tokáamɛ́á [moɛma ȁtalɛ]	'we will tell them that Moema should count'
	d. nénɔ́ɔ́niɛ [moɛma néwaabálókílɛ̂]	'I saw that Moema fell'
	e. nénáasɔ́ɔmiɛ [moɛma néwaakwíɛ̂]	'I read that Moema died'
	f. kweɔ́nɛ́kánа́ [moɛma néwaatálílɛ̂]	'it seems that Moema counted'
	g. naísyɛ́ [moɛma néwaatálílɛ̂]	'I said that Moema counted (remote)'

The other environment is WH-questions. A phrasal SL may shift into a following complement from the assertive verb, as in (44a, c, e, g, i, k). But if there is no overt object, the SL deletes, as seen in (44b, d, f, h, j, l). Phrasal SL may not shift into a WH-word.

(44)	a. áűéí' **ɛ́iò** o.o	'who did he cook a banana for?'
	b. áűéí' ɔ́.ɔ	'who did he cook for?'
	c. waakuíɛ́ **maiò** ende.e	'when did you carry bananas?
	d. waamákuí' ɛ́ɛnde.e	'when did you carry them?
	e. wɔ́áíɛ́ **ngókő** bá	'where did you kill the chicken?'
	f. waakɔ́míɛ́ bá	'where did you sleep?'
	g. waɛ́tíɛ́ **maiò** nao	'who did you bring bananas with?'
	h. waɛ́tíɛ́ nao	'who did you bring with?'
	i. waɛ́tíɛ́ **moɛmà** mɛ́ána	'how many did you bring for Moema?'
	j. waɛ́tíɛ́ mɛ́ána	'how many did you bring for'
	k. waɛ́tíɛ́ **moɛmà** máo	'whose did you bring for Moema?'
	l. waɛ́tíɛ́ máo	'whose did you bring for?'

III. Conclusions

Kikamba provides a fascinating case of the tone-syntax interface. In order to understand this interaction, I have provided evidence that Kikamba is indeed a four tone language, and that it requires a tone feature [+extreme], which correctly predicts that tones at the periphery of the tonal space may form a natural class. Kikamba also provides evidence for lexical-level, grammatical-level, and phrase-level tones which interact with syntactic phrasing. In other words, the same tone assigned to a lexical item may interact with the syntax differently than if the tone is assigned at the grammatical or phrasal level, which is exactly what happens to SL tone in Kikamba. Moreover, SL tones know when the end of a phrase is reached and whether the morphological agreement or lack of it in a following word will allow the tone to shift further, block the tone shift, or cause the tone to be deleted. Thus, the interaction of SL tone with the syntax in Kikamba is a robust phenomenon which will contribute further to our understanding of the phonology-syntax interface.

IV. References

Odden, David and R. Ruth Roberts-Kohno. In Press. Constraints on Super-Low Tone in Kikamba.

Roberts-Kohno, R. Ruth. 2000. Kikamba Phonology and Morphology. The Ohio State University Dissertation.

[1] The SH tone on the final vowel of 'house' surfaces on the first vowel of the locative due to vowel coalescence between the two words. For more on Kikamba vowel coalescence, see Roberts-Kohno (2000).

[2] The locatives *etínã̈* and *nthéenẽ̈* have lexical SH tones on their final vowels, thus their tone is not determined by the presence of phrasal SL.

Comments on Ruth Roberts-Kohno paper "On the Kikamba Tone-Syntax Interface"

by André Motingea

This paper of Ruth Roberts-Kohno deals with Kikamba, a Bantu language spoken in Kenya. The author tries to demonstrate that Kikamba is a four-tone language: High, Low, Super-High and Super-Low. She argues "that the highest and lowest tones form a natural class, thus indicating the need for the feature [+extreme] which characterizes tones at the periphery of the tonal space".

We should say that this is an important contribution not only to general linguistics but also to Bantu linguistics. In fact, tonal phenomena observed in many presentday languages support the idea that they have not all developed from a simple system as reconstructed by Meeussen (1967: 84, 85): PB should have been a language with a complex tone system (in term of tonal rules), which is reduced in some present-day languages (Kisseberth and Odden 2003: 60). Facts one observes here in Kikamba are widespread in several languages in Central Bantu (where we are working ourselves) as well as in Western and Southern Bantu (Kisseberth and Odden 2003: 62-70). If one takes those features as innovations, then they will maybe help for the understanding of the Bantu expansion better than sound changes.

However, in our point of view there are two basic tones, which surface according to different rules of word structure and syntax order as well of prosodic order:

a. Word (and NP) level: Downstep (HH > HM), Falling tone, Upstep, High Tone Spread (left to right), etc.

b. Phrasal phonology: Topic/Focus on a member of the P, see Kohno's example (12) = Subject, (13a/b) = COP.NEG + Object, etc.

c. Prosodic: intonational phrase (Low from a High as a Pause marking): **-á > -a]ϕ.**

Tiene (Motingea 2003: 121)

ndzɔ́ ɪ mɪ	'my house' (house of me)
lɪ-kʊnɪ lɪ́ ndzɔ	'stake of the house'

Questions and general comments

1. Are SL and SH really phonemic or phonetic? Otherwise, is it possible to provide meaningful examples (minimal pairs) in isolation of contrast SL vs. L, SH vs. H, SL vs. SH with a distribution V_1 and V_2?

Grammatical tone (SL) with infinitives only = more or less *métatonie* (Meeussen 1967: 111): can the final vowel ***á > *-a,** if the infinitive is not at the edge of P?

Tiene (Motingea 2003: 121)

ʊ-túk-a			'to insult'
INF.15-insult-FV			

ʊ-kuk-á	**ʊ-túk-á**	**mɪ**	'you can insult me'
2SG-can-FV	INF.15-insult-FV	me	

2. The bearing of complex tones seems also to be explained by a phonological process: a kind of deletion compensation.

Historically: *l > ø, *n > ø

(30) **okő né mo.asâ** 'firewood is long'
[PB: *-**kóni** CS.1218]

(9) **mokó.ó** 'old'
[PB: *-**kódo** CS.1197]

Synchronically: **ngusu nɛ̋nɛ̋** (10a) < *n-nɛ́+n-nɛ́ cl.9 'big pocket'

In some languages, the compensation is shown by lengthening: keeping the mora (Hyman 2003: 48).

3. The way of writing Kikamba (many other authors are doing the same) seems to be responsible for hiding some tonal aspects: word boundaries are not clearly defined.

(30) **nénɔ́ɔ́níɛ́ maiò** 'I saw bananas' (remote)

né	ná-ɔ́n-í	ɛ́	maiò
ASR	1SG-see-FV	REMOTE	bananas

(35) **nétwáamíbóéɛ́ ñoombá̋ nthéenḗ** 'we washed it inside the house'

né	tó-áa	mí-bó-é	ɛ́	né	ñoombá̋	nthéenḗ
ASR	1PL-COP(?)	it-wash-FV	REMOTE	ASR	house	inside

4. Tone use in Kibamba seems to provide a good intermediate system (a step) to explaining the loss of tone in some languages (Swahili dialects).

References

Hyman, Larry M., 2003: Segmental phonology. In *The Bantu languages*, ed. by Nurse Derek and Gérard Philippson, pp.42-58. London and New York: Routlege.

Kisseberth, Charles and David Odden, 2003: Tone. In *The Bantu languages*, ed. by Nurse Derek and Gérard Philippson, pp.59-70. London and New York: Routlege.

Meeussen, Achille E. 1967: Bantu grammatical reconstructions. In *Africana Linguistica III.* (Annales, 61.) pp.80-121. Tervuren: Musée Royal de l'Afrique Centrale.

Motingea Mangulu, 2003: Kitiene, petite unité du bantou B.80. *Journal of Asian and African Studies* 67: 105-150.

Verbal Tone in Buli: a Morphosyntactic Analysis*

Michael Kenstowicz

MIT

In languages where tone or accent is lexically contrastive there is often an asymmetry in the lexical categories that display the contrast. Typically roots have a greater range of distinctions than affixes. Within roots nominals often make more distinctions than verbs. For example, in both Spanish and Italian nominals contrast the location of stress within the three-syllable window at the right edge of the word. Italian retains this contrast in verbal inflection (cf. *m'acin-a* 'grinds' vs. *lav'or-a* 'works') while it has been lost in Spanish. For pitch accent systems, Tokyo Japanese verbs lack the contrasts for accent location found in nouns while retaining the accented vs. unaccented lexical contrast. In the Fukuoka dialect (Smith 1999) verbs fall uniformly in the accented class (realized on the syllable containing the penultimate mora). Similar asymmetries are found in the Bantu languages. In many of these languages the absence of lexical contrasts in the verb is compensated for by complex accentual and tonal alternations as a function of the tense/aspect of the verb. These cases are particularly challenging analytically because often the underlying morphological structure is not clear and hence there is no direct connection between accentual/tonal location and tense-aspect exponence.

In this paper we look at another example of this phenomenon -- this time from a language with a richer inventory of lexical tonal contrasts. We will argue that rather than invoking rules of allomorphy, inflectional tone is best treated as the reflex of preverbal particles that, lacking any segmental exponence, find their tones realized on the following verb. In this analysis the tonal patterns on the verb reflect obliquely tonal particles that are the true exponence of the tense/aspect distinction. As we shall see, the burden of describing the tonal patterns on the verb is borne primarily by morphosyntactic rules that control the distribution of the tonal particles. Tonal particles are familiar from the associative construction in many West African languages where the pivot morpheme in Noun of Noun phrases is often just a tone that is realized on an adjacent noun or otherwise makes its presence felt (e.g. through downstep). More directly pertinent to our case, Elsa Gomez-Imbert (1997, 2002) has documented a striking precursor of the phenomenon in Barasana where inflectional prefixes marking subject agreement have lost their segmental exponence forcing their tones to associate with the following verb, where they displace the verb's original tone further to the right.

* Thanks to Masao Okazaki for helpful comments on this paper.

Our language is Buli, a Gur language of Northern Ghana. The analysis is based on previous collaboration with George Akanlig-Pare, a native speaker linguist of the Central dialect (Akanlig-Pare & Kenstowicz 2002, 2003; Akanlig-Pare forthcoming). This paper is divided into three parts. After a brief review of the language's general tonology, we survey the tone patterns in the verbal inflection, developing our analysis along the way. We then turn to the patterns of verbal tone found in serial verbs and subordinate clauses.

1. Background

Buli nouns and adjectives (argued to be a subset of nominals by Matushansky 2002) as well as particles contrast for three tonal levels: H(igh), M(id), and L(ow).

(1)	s^{y}úk	'path'	s^{y}ūk	'navel'	s^{y}ùk	'fish sp.'
	f í:k	'small'	pjēlūk	'white'	wɔ̀ŋ	'large'
	ká	'focus	sī	'if'	tì	subject relative complementizer

The syllable is the tone-bearing unit in Buli. The language has two very general tonal processes illustrated in (2). The first spreads a L tone to a syllable with a following H to create a Rising tone (2a). If that Rising tone itself occurs before another H then it is simplified to L by deletion of its H component (2b). In (2c), although the H on 'child' becomes a Rising tone, it does not simplify to L since the following tone is not H.

(2)	a. bí:k	'child'	wà bǐ:k	'his child'
	f í:k	'small'	bàŋ f ǐ:k	'a small lizard'
	b. wà bǐ:k	'his child'	wà bì f í:k	'his small child'
	c. bí màŋ	'good child'	wà bǐ màŋ	'his good child'

We state these rules in (3).

(3)

The derivations in (4) illustrate how these two rules apply.

(4)	/wà bí:k/	/wà bí f í:k/	
	wà bǐ:k	wà bǐ f í:k	Low Tone Spread
	---------	wà bì f í:k	Rising Tone Absorption

In order to discern the underlying tonal patterns in the verbal inflection, the effects of Low Tone Spread and Rising Tone Absorption must be undone.

2. Verbal Inflection

Verbs in Buli do not contrast lexically for tone. For example, when adjectives are turned into stative verbs, their inherent tones are replaced by Mid, thereby neutralizing tonal contrasts: cf. *wòŋ* 'tall', *wōn-ā* 'is tall'; *nālɛ̄ŋ* 'nice', *nāl-ā* 'is nice'. This property is shared by Konni -- Buli's close neighbor (see Cahill 1999) and appears to be an innovation. Other Gur languages such as Dagare (Bodomo 1997) have lexical tone contrasts on the verb. Buli is an SVO language. Subject pronouns are Low in tone. Direct-object pronouns are enclitic to the verb and alternate in tone as a function of the tense/aspect inflectional particles that precede the verb.

Let us preview our analysis. The verb's tone alternates between HL and L in certain tenses and is M otherwise. Mid is pretty clearly the default tone. HL is the reflex of an Inflectional particle whose semantic contribution to the utterance is varied. It has the flavor of a "force to" morpheme. This particle is restricted to main clauses. When added to certain tenses it imparts an emphatic sense to the verb. In other tenses it is part of the normal inflection. But whether its tones appear on the verb depends on what other particles accompany it in the INFL position. Three different realizations of this morpheme will be discussed. First, it is systematically missing after third person subjects. Second, when another morpheme intervenes between it and the subject, then its deletion is blocked. Finally, it can be attracted to a "heavy" verb: one with a cliticized direct object. We now turn to an illustration of these points and develop the analysis along the way.

In (5) we show the inflection in the perfect tense for the intransitive verb [la] 'laugh' and the transitive [nag] 'hit'. Verbal roots are underlyingly monosyllabic. When they end in a consonant they are normally followed by an epenthetic vowel that copies the tone of the preceding syllable. For certain complications see Akanlig-Pare & Kenstowicz (2002).

(5)	ǹ lǎ	'I laughed'	tì lǎ	'we laughed'
	fì lǎ	'you laughed'	nì lǎ	'you pl. laughed'
	wà là	'he laughed'	bà là	'they laughed'
	ǹ nàgí	'I hit'	tì nàgí	'we hit'
	fì nàgí	'you hit'	nì nàgí	'you pl. hit'
	wà nàgì	'he hit'	bà nàgì	'they hit'

Recalling the rules of Low Tone Spread and Rising Tone Absorption, it is clear that the verb has an underlying High tone in the first and second person /lá/, /nágí/ but a Low in third person /là/, /nàgì/. In (6) we see the perfect form of [nag] accompanied by the cliticized direct object *-wa*. Once again a different tonal contour emerges as a function of the subject. In the first and second person the verb has an underlying H and a L appears on the object suffix. But in the third person, the verb is Low and the object suffix is Mid.

(6) ǹ nàgí-wà	'I hit him'	tǐ nàgí-wà	'we hit him'
fǐ nàgí-wà	'you hit him'	nǐ nàgí-wà	'you pl. hit him'
wà nàgǐ-wā	'he hit him'	bà nàgǐ-wā	'they hit him'

Our analysis of these data runs as in (7) . We postulate a morpheme (call it Agr) consisting of HL followed by a Tns-Asp L tone. Lacking any segmental material to support its tones, the INFL node's HL maps to the verb pushing aside the L Tns-Asp morpheme. When the subject is third person [-participant], we postulate a morphosyntactic rule that deletes the Agr morpheme. The L of Tns-Asp remains and it maps to the verb. The object suffix then receives a default Mid.

(7) $[\text{Agr Tns}]_{\text{INFL}}$ Verb
HL L

AGR -> Ø / [-participant] ____

default: Ø -> M

The derivations in (8) illustrate the proposed analysis.

(8) morphosyntax

wà	$[\text{HL}]_{\text{Agr}}$ $[\text{L}]_{\text{Tns}}$	nag-wa	underlying
wà	$[\text{L}]_{\text{Tns}}$	nag-wa	Agr Deletion

phonology

wà	nag-wa $[\text{L}]_{\text{Tns}}$	Tone Association
wà	nàg-wā	Default Mid
wà	nàgǐ-wā	Epenthesis
wà nàgǐ-wā 'he hit him'		output

morphosyntax

fǐ	$[\text{HL}]_{\text{Agr}}$ $[\text{L}]_{\text{Tns}}$ nag-wa	underlying
	inapplicable	Agr Deletion

phonology

fǐ	nag-wa $[\text{HL}]_{\text{Agr}}$ $[\text{L}]_{\text{Tns}}$	Tone Association
fǐ	nágí-wà	Epenthesis
fǐ	năgí-wà	Low Tone Spread
fǐ nàgí-wà		Rising Tone Absorption

'you hit him'

Given this general analytic scheme, consider now in (9) the corresponding negatives marked by *àn*. The alternation between first and second vs. third person is leveled out. A reflex of the HL Agr appears on all forms of the verb. The intransitive [la] 'laugh' takes the factitive [ya] suffix that appears in the slot where clitics occur.

(9)	màn lǎ-yà	'I did not laugh'	tì àn lǎ-yà	'we did not laugh'
	fì àn lǎ-yà	'you did not laugh'	nì àn lǎ-yà	'you pl. did not laugh'
	wà àn lǎ-yà	'he did not laugh'	bà àn lǎ-ya	'they did not laugh'

The simplest analysis is that the negative particle *àn* intervenes between the HL Agr and the subject blocking the rule of Agr deletion.

(10) morphosyntax

wà àn [HL]$_{Agr}$ [L]$_{Tns}$ nag-wa	underlying
inapplicable	Agr Deletion

phonology

wà àn nag-wa [HL]$_{Agr}$ [L]$_{Tns}$	Tone Association
wà àn nágí-wà	Epenthesis
wà àn nǎgí-wà	Low Tone Spread
wà àn nàgí-wà	Rising Tone Absorption

'he did not hit him'

Now consider stative verbs. They lack any INFL node marking tense/aspect and hence receive a default Mid (11).

(11)	mì nal-a	'I emph. am nice'	tì nāl-ā	'we are nice'
	fì nāl-ā	'you are nice'	nì nāl-ā	'you pl. are nice'
	wà nāl-ā	'he is nice'	bà nāl-ā	'they are nice'

But when an emphatic sense is intended then the stative shows a HL falling contour (12). However, this tonal contour cannot occur in the third person, where no contrast between a plain and emphatic sense is possible. This of course is precisely the distribution of the Agr morpheme in the perfect seen in (5) and (6).

(12)	ǹ nǎl-à	'I *am nice*'	tì nǎl-à	'we *are nice*'
	fì nǎl-à	'you *are nice*'	nì nǎl-à	'you pl. *are nice*'
	wà nāl-ā	'he *is nice*'	bà nāl-ā	'they *are nice*'

The parallel with Agr is strengthened when we look at the corresponding negatives. Under the nonemphatic reading the stative verb retains the mid tone. But under emphasis the HL is leveled through the paradigm--just as in the perfect (cf. (9)).

(13)	mí àn nāl-ā	'I emph. am not nice'	tì àn nāl-ā	'we are not nice'
	fì àn nāl-ā	'you are not nice'	nì àn nāl-ā	'you pl. are not nice'
	wà àn nāl-ā	'he is not nice'	bà àn nāl-ā	'they are not nice'
	mà:n năl-à	'I *am not nice'*	tì àn năl-à	'we *are not nice'*
	fì àn năl-à	'you *are not nice'*	nì àn năl-à	'you pl. *are not nice'*
	wà àn năl-à	'he *is not nice'*	bà àn năl-à	'they *are not nice'*

It thus appears that the HL Agr morpheme--normally absent from stative verbs due to morphological impoverishment--can be inserted for emphasis--a striking analogue to the famous *do*-support phenomenon in English: cf. *I like it* vs. *I dó like it*.

(14) morphosyntax

fì $[HL]_{Agr}$ $[L]_{Tns}$ nal-a	underlying
fì nal-a	Infl Deletion (Impoverishment)

phonology

fì nāl-ā	Default Mid
'you are nice'	

morphosyntax

fì $[HL]_{Agr}$ $[L]_{Tns}$ nal-a	underlying
blocked under emphasis	Infl Deletion

phonology

fì nal-a $[HL]_{Agr}$	Tone Association
fì năl-à	Low Tone Spread
'you *are nice'*	

Imperative verbs show a similar impoverished inflection. The verb has default Mid (15a). When negated (15b), the imperative takes a different Neg morpheme (*kan*) compared to the perfect (*àn*). Furthermore, this particle imparts an emphatic sense to the verb--shown by the telltale HL tonal contour.

(15) a.	lā	'laugh!'	nāgī-wā	'hit him!'
b.	kán là	'do *not laugh*! '	kán nàgì-wā	'do *not hit him*!'

In this case, the HL mapping starts with the negative particle *kan*. We assume that this negative particle appears immediately before the verb and thus provides the first tone-bearing unit for the HL emphatic morpheme.[1] The L appears on the verb and any object suffix receives a default Mid.

(16)	<u>morphosyntax</u>		
	$[HL]_{Agr}$	nag-wa	underlying
		nag-wa	Infl Deletion
	<u>phonology</u>		
		nāg-wā	Default Mid
		nāgī-wā	Epenthesis
	<u>morphosyntax</u>		
	$[HL]_{Agr}$	kan nag-wa	underlying
	$[HL]_{Agr}$	kan nag-wa	Infl Deletion (blocked under emphasis)
	<u>phonology</u>		
		kan nag-wa	Tone Association
		$[H+L]_{Agr}$	
		kán nàg-wa	Default Mid
		kán nàgì-wā	Epenthesis

The future tense is marked by the particle *lì*. The following verb uniformly has the default Mid tone.

(17)	àtì:m l ì lā	'Atim will laugh'
	àtì:m l ì nāgī-wā	'Atim will hit him'
	f ì l ì lā	'you sg. will laugh'
	f ì l ì nāgī-wā	'you sg. will hit him'

We assume that the future particle appears in the Tns-Asp slot in the INFL node. Under standard assumptions in Autosegmental Phonology the HL Agr morpheme--if present in the structure to begin with--will be unable to associate to the verb across the future particle. Hence, the verb will receive the default Mid tone.

(18)	<u>morphosyntax</u>		
	f ì $[HL]_{Agr}$	$[l\ ì]_{Tns}$ la	underlying

---

[1] Cahill (1999:22) notes that the negative particle in Konni has variable positioning among the preverbal particles sometimes appearing at the beginning after the subject and other times preverbally.

phonology

f ì [HL]$_{Agr}$ [l ì]$_{Tns}$ la	Tone Association (blocked)
f ì l ì lā	Default Mid
'you will laugh'	

We now turn to the most puzzling piece of the verbal inflection. In the present tense the verb is preceded by a particle *à* which we assume occupies the Tns-Asp slot. Like the future *lì,* it is also Low in tone. Given the analysis in (18), we expect the verb to appear with the default Mid tone. This prediction is correct, as shown by the paradigm in (19).

(19) àtì:m à lā 'Atim laughs'
mí à lā 'I emph. laugh'
wà à lā 'he laughs'

àtì:m à nāgī ná:b 'Atim hits a cow'
mí à nāgī ná:b 'I emph. hit a cow'
wà à nāgī ná:b 'he hits a cow'

In the present tense negation is signaled by the particle *kàn* which we recall appeared preverbally in the imperative. Here it appears in place of the *à* and has a low tone.

(20) àtì:m kàn lā 'Atim does not laugh'
mí kàn lā 'I emph. do not laugh'
wà kàn lā 'he does not laugh'

àtì:m kàn nāgī ná:b 'Atim does not hit a cow'
mí kàn nāgī ná:b 'I emph. do not hit a cow'
wà kàn nāgī ná:b 'he does not hit a cow'

It makes sense to analyze *kàn* as the fusion of negation and the Tns-Asp particles. It also appears preverbally. Like *lì* and *à, kàn* also blocks any association of the HL Agr and so the verb receives a default Mid.

The surprise is that when the present tense verb has an enclitic pronoun then the HL contour systematically appears on the verb (21a). The same thing happens when the verb is negated (21b).

(21) a. àtì:m à nàgí-wà 'Atim hits him'
mí à nàgí-wà 'I emph. hit him'
mà: nàgí-wà 'I hit him'
wà à nàgí-wà 'he hits him'

b. àtì:m kàn nàgí-wà — 'Atim does not hit him'
mí kàn nàgí-wà — 'I emph. do not hit him'
ŋ̀ kàn nàgí-wà — 'I do not hit him'

Evidently the Agr morpheme has jumped over the Tns-Asp particle *à* (and its negative counterpart *kàn*) to lodge on the verb.[2] We postulate the morphosyntactic rule of affix hopping in (22). The [+present] feature encompasses the particle *à* as well as the fused negative *kàn*. The rule does not apply in the imperative since it plausibly lacks a Tense node.

(22) Agr + [+present] + [verb+pro]
1 2 3 -> 2 1 3

This rule precedes the one that deletes the Agr morpheme after third person subjects. By placing the Agr after the *à* and *kàn* Tns-Asp particles, Agr is no longer adjacent to the third person subject and so will escape deletion.

(23) morphosyntax

wà $[HL]_{Agr}$ $[\grave{a}]_{Tns}$ nag wa	underlying
wà $[\grave{a}]_{Tns}$ $[HL]_{Agr}$ nag-wa	Agr Lowering
inapplicable	Agr Deletion

phonology

wà à nag-wa H L	Tone Association
wà à nágí-wà	Epenthesis
wà à nǎgí-wà	Low Tone Spread
wà à nàgí-wà	Rising Tone Absorption

'he hits him'

To summarize, our analysis of Buli verbal inflection has postulated two tonal particles: a HL marking Agr followed by a L marking Tns-Asp. The latter receives segmental expression in the future and present tenses *lì* and *à* respectively, in which case the verb takes a default Mid tone. When the Tns-Asp slot is not segmentalized then the tones comprising the inflection are free to associate to the verb. When both Agr and Tns-Asp are available to associate to the verb preference seems to be given to the Agr. We have not encountered a context where both morphemes are clearly expressed on the verb.[3] Our analysis has consolidated the various realizations of the HL contour as exponents of an Agr morpheme. Three factors control its distribution. It is deleted after third person subjects. It

---

[2] An alternative analysis in which object pronouns are syntactically high and attract the verb is more problematic because the Tns-Asp particle must move with the verb and so the *à* will still intervene between the AGR and the verb.

[3] Barasana has examples in which two tonal prefixes precede the verb. Only the innermost one is realized. See Gomez-Imbert & Kenstowicz (2000) and Gomez-Imbert (2001) for discussion.

is also absent in contexts of impoverishment (stative and imperatives). But in the latter cases it can be resuscitated under emphasis--a reflex of the emphatic *do* syndrome. Finally, the Agr particle is attracted to a heavy verb+pro hopping over the present tense morpheme.

3. Other Constructions

We briefly survey several grammatical contexts which alter the makeup of the [Agr + Tns-Asp] INFL slot and hence, given our analysis, affect the tonal pattern of the verb in predictable ways.

3.1 Serial Verbs

The serial verb construction consists of two verbs that share an intervening object. (See Lee 2002 for analysis of serial verbs in Buli). Typically, the first verb displays the verbal inflection while the second appears in some nonfinite form. This is largely but not entirely true for Buli. Our paradigms use the canonical serial verb composed of *tūsī* 'push' and *l^{w}ānsī* 'drop'. When combined into a serial verb, the meaning changes to 'push down'.

The paradigm in (24) shows some serial verb constructions in the perfect tense.

(24) a. ǹ tùsí bāŋ l^{w}ànsǐ — 'I pushed down a bangle'
b. àtǐ:m tùsǐ bāŋ l^{w}ànsǐ — 'Atim pushed down a bangle'
c. àtǐ:m àn tùsí bāŋ l^{w}ànsī yà — 'Atim did not push down a bangle'

The first verb shows the agreement alternation. It takes an underlying H when the subject is first or second person (24a) and L when it is third person (24b). Low Tone Spread and Rising Tone Absorption apply to derive the *tùsí* alternant. V_1 is also where negation is expressed (24c). In the perfect tense V_2 is consistently low in tone. This suggests that the underlying structure of the IP in the serial construction is [Subj-Agr-Tns/Asp-V_1-Obj-Tns/Asp-V_2] with both verbs inflected for tense/aspect.

(25)

morphosyntax		
ǹ [HL]$_{Agr}$ [L]$_{Tns}$ tus bāŋ [L]$_{Tns}$ l^{w}ans	wà [HL]$_{Agr}$ [L]$_{Tns}$ tus bāŋ [L]$_{Tns}$ l^{w}ans	underlying
inapplicable	wà [L]$_{Tns}$ tus bāŋ [L]$_{Tns}$ l^{w}ans	Agr Deletion
phonology		
ǹ tus bāŋ l^{w}ans [HL]$_{Agr}$ [L]$_{Tns}$	wà tus bāŋ l^{w}ans [L]$_{Tns}$ [L]$_{Tns}$	Tone Association
ǹ túsí bāŋ l^{w}ànsǐ 'I pushed down a bangle'	wà tùsǐ bāŋ l^{w}ànsǐ 'he pushed down a bangle'	Epenthesis

There is one complication. In the serial construction when the subject is first or second person, encliticization of an object pronoun is blocked and the strong form of the pronoun (with a High tone) must be used instead. This means that we are unable to demonstrate an example in which the Low component of the HL Agr appears on the verb.

(26) wà tùsì-mə̄ lʷànsì	'he pushed me down'
wà tùsì mì lʷànsì	'he pushed me emph down'
f ì tùsí mí lʷànsì	'you pushed me emph down'
*f ì tùsí-mə̀ lʷànsì	'you pushed me down'

In the present each verb takes a segmentally lexicalized tense morpheme: Tns-V_1 Tns-V_2.

(27) a. àtì:m à tūsī mí á lʷānsī	'Atim is pushing me emph down'
b. mí à tūsī bí:k á lʷānsī	'I emph am pushing down a child'
c. mí túsí bí:ká á lʷānsī	'I emph push down the child'
d. àtì:m tùsì mì á lʷānsī	'Atim pushes me emph down'

V_2 consistently has a High-toned *á* particle. The verb itself carries a default Mid. When the serial verb has the progressive sense, then V_1 is preceded by the Low tone tense-aspect particle *à*. V_1 has the default Mid. This is what we expect since the *à* particle blocks the association of the tones of the AGR morpheme on V_1. Since the verb cannot take an enclitic pronoun in the first and second person, we cannot test whether the Agr morpheme can skip over the present tense particle in the serial verb construction. Finally, when the serial verb has an habitual sense then V_1 has no segmental preverbal particle. In this case, the H(L) agreement morpheme can appear on V_1 when the subject is not third person (27c). In the third person, the Agr is deleted and so only the Tense L survives; it docks to the verb (27d).

3.2 Subordinate Clauses

We mentioned that the Agr morpheme is barred from subordinate clauses. We briefly make this point here with several examples. In (28) we show the verb [nag] 'hit' in a relative clause. (See Hiraiwa 2002 for an analysis of Buli relatives). Relatives are marked by a final particle *lá*. Subject relatives take the complementizer *ĺī* while nonsubject relatives take *tì*. In the perfect tense the verb shows a uniform Low tone regardless of the person of the subject. This is the L of the Tns-Asp particle. In main clauses it is pushed aside by the Agr HL with first and second person subjects.

(28)	àtì:m nyà bì:ká tì mì nàgì lǎ	'Atim saw the child that I emph hit'
	àtì:m nyà bì:ká tì ǹ nàgì lǎ	'Atim saw the child that I hit'
	ǹ nyà bí:ká tì àtì:m nàgì lǎ	'I saw the child that Atim hit'

Since the agreement morpheme is banned from the relative clause, there can be no Agr Lowering (22) that we find in the main clause of present tense verbs. We can ask what tone an object pronoun will receive in the absence of the Agr morpheme. Other things being equal, we expect a default Mid to appear. This is a correct prediction, as shown by the paradigm in (29).

(29) a. ǹ nyà bí:ká lī nàgì-mə̄ lá 'I saw the child that hit me'
b. ǹ nyà bí:ká lī à nāgī-bā lá 'I saw the child that hits them'
c. àtī:m à nàgí-bà 'Atim hits them'

In (29a) the verb of the relative clause is in the perfect tense. Thus, the verb takes the Tns L tone and the enclitic object suffix takes default Mid tone. But in (29b) the tense node is lexicalized as *à*. The INFL node thus has no tone to contribute to the verb, which consequently surfaces with default Mid. Compare the present tense of the corresponding main clause verb in (29c). Here the Agr HL skips over the Tns-Asp à to show up on the verb.

Buli has several constructions in which the verb of the subordinate clause appears in a nonfinite form. (See Norris 2002 for discussion). One of these is as complement to the main clause verb *yā:lī* 'want'. If a clause lacks inflection and if inflection is the source of the tone for the verb, then we expect the verb to appear in the default Mid tone in this context. The paradigm in (30) shows that this expectation is confirmed.

(30) mà: yā:lī (àyǐn) àtī:m nāgī-mə̄ 'I want (that) Atim to hit me'
àtī:m à: yā:lī (àyǐn) ǹ nāgī-wā 'Atim wants (that) me to hit him'

4. Summary and Conclusions

We have proposed an analysis of the tonal alternations found in the verbal inflection of Buli. Once the general processes of Low Tone Spread and Rising Tone Absorption are factored away, the verb displays an alternation between HL ≈ L and M melodies. The Mid is a default while HL and L are treated as reflections of two inflectional particles: Agr and Tns-Asp. The body of the analysis involves morphosyntactic rules that delete, insert, and shift the location of these particles.

While internally consistent, the analysis requires further research on three fronts. First, more descriptive work on the grammar of Buli is required to test the basic premises of the analysis. An alternative analysis in terms of different tonal melodies in a verb's paradigm is certainly worth exploring. Second, if the tonal particle analysis is correct, then we expect to find other Gur languages in which the postulated Agr and Tns-Asp particles are segmentally realized. Here again much further research is required. At present we can only point to two parallels from Konni. First, Cahill (1999) documents the alternation between L in third person and HL in first and second in the perfective and imperfective tenses. In the paradigm in (31) for the verb [sɪ] 'bathe' the L portion of the HL is floating and triggers downstep on the *-á* suffix.

(31)	ǹ sí'-á mı̀ŋ	tì sí'-á míŋ
	sí'-á míŋ	nì sí'-á mı̀ŋ
	ù sì-á mı̀ŋ	bà sì-á mı̀ŋ

Second, Konni allows a greater range of adverbial particles to stand between the subject and the verb: for example *ù yà ɓɔ̀b-á mı̀ŋ* 'he is still tying' vs. *ǹ yá bɔ̀b-á mı̀ŋ* 'I am still tying'. Here we see the alternation showing up on the adverb immediately following the subject pronoun; the following verb is stable.

Finally, theoretically the interface among syntax and phonology on the one hand and morphosyntax and phonology on the other is still poorly understood. As mentioned at the outset, tone and accent seem to be particularly susceptible to expressing this relation. Intonation and phrasing are signaled suprasegmentally through variation in F0 and timing rather than through segmental changes. In this study we have invoked tonal particles as the bridge between the syntax and the verbal inflection. But undoubtedly in other languages this is not a viable option and the tonal patterns are part of a verb or noun's paradigm structure. How is this to be described formally? What are the morphological categories that are expressed tonally? Tense-aspect, singular vs. plural (at least in nouns in many Slavic languages), and person (Gur, Barasana) are well attested. What are the mechanisms for expressing these differences? Is agreement on the verb appropriate? If so, where are these features encoded and how does the grammar refer to them? These are questions of general interest that can only be addressed in the context of detailed analyses of individual languages.

References

Akanlig-Pare, George & Michael Kenstowicz. (2003) Tone in Buli. MIT Working Papers on Endangered Languages 4, 1-33. Revised version in Studies in African Linguistics 35, 55-96.

Bodomo, Adams. 1997. The Structure of Dagare. Stanford, Ca. Center for the Study of Language and Information.

Cahill, Michael. 1999. Aspects of the Morphology and Phonology of Konni. Columbus, Ohio: Ohio State University Ph.D. dissertation.

Gomez-Imbert, Elsa. 1997. Morphologie et phonologie barasana: approche non-linéaire. Doctorat d'État, Université Paris, 8, Saint-Denis.

Gomez-Imbert, Elsa. 2001. More on the Tone versus Pitch Accent Typology: Evidence from Barasana and Other Eastern Tukanoan Languages. Proceedings of the

Symposium Cross-Linguistic Studies of Tonal Phenomena: Tonogenesis, Japanese Accentology, and Other Topics, edited by Shigeki Kaji. Tokyo: Tokyo University of Foreign Studies, Institute for the Study of Languages and Cultures of Asia and Africa, 369-412.

Gomez-Imbert, Elsa and Michael Kenstowicz. 2000. Barasana tone and accent. International Journal of American Linguistics 66, 419-63.

Hiraiwa, Ken . 2002. Relativization in Buli. MIT Working Papers on Endangered Languages 4, 45-84.

Lee, Younghoo. 2002. Serial verb constructions in Buli. MIT Working Papers on Endangered Languages 4, 97-116.

Matushansky, Ora. 2002. Adjectives in Buli. MIT Working Papers on Endangered Languages 4, 117-30.

Norris, Rebecca. 2002. Embedded clauses in Buli. MIT Working Papers on Endangered Languages 4, 131-46.

Smith, Jennifer. 1999. Noun faithfulness and accent in Fukuoka Japanese. Proceedings of the 18th West Coast Conference on Formal Linguistics, edited by Sonya Bird, et al. published by Cascadilla Press, Somerville Ma. WCCFL 18, 519-31.

Comments on the Paper by Kenstowicz

Masao Okazaki
Ibaraki University
okzk@mx.ibaraki.ac.jp

I

The most interesting aspects of Buli verbal tone patterns can be summarized as follows.

(1) a. Tone is not lexically contrastive in Buli verbs.
b. The tonal patterns of Buli verbs are determined by tense, aspect, and the person of the subject.

Kenstowicz examines the tone patterns of the perfect, present, imperative, future, and stative forms of the verbs in affirmative and negative sentences and observes that there are three tonal patterns in non-emphatic affirmative sentences. The patterns are (i) L(M) in perfect sentences with a third person subject, (ii) H(L) in perfect sentences with either a first person or a second person subject, and (iii) M(M) in present, imperative, future, and stative sentences.

The surface tone patterns of Buli predicates are seen as unusual and are in sharp contrast with the surface tone patterns of nouns and adjectives, which are lexically contrastive. They cannot be captured by any system proposed by previous studies of phrase-level tone patterns. Kenstowicz tries to capture their unusual aspect with the following hypotheses.

(2) a. Abstract morphosyntactic elements in INFL like Agr and Tns are (underlying) tone bearing elements.
b. The surface tone patterns of sentences are derived through the application of rules, both morphosyntactic and phonological.

In particular, Kenstowicz proposes the underlying Buli morphosyntactic structure in (3), and the relevant rules in (4).

(3) $[\text{Arg Tns}]_{\text{INFL}}$ Verb
H+L L

(4) a. Agr $\rightarrow \phi$ /[third person subject] __ (morphosyntactic rule)
b. INFL $\rightarrow \phi$ (in some sentence types) (morphosyntactic rule)
c. $\phi \rightarrow$ M (default tone insertion (phonological rule))

The structure in (3) and the rules in (4) correctly derive the three surface realizations of verbal tonal patterns. Take the examples in (5).

(5) a. wà nàgì-wā 'he hit him'
b. f ì nāl-ā 'you are nice'

The tone patterns in (5a, b) are derived as in (6) and (7), respectively.

(6)
(4a) tone association
wà $[HL]_{Agr}$ $[L]_{Tns}$ nag-wa → wà $[L]_{Tns}$ nag-wa → wà nàg-wa

(4c) epenthesis
→ wà nàg-wā → wà nàgì-wā (output)

(7)
(4b) (4c)
f ì $[HL]_{Agr}$ $[L]_{Tns}$ nal-a → f ì nal-a → f ì nāl-ā (output)

II

Kenstowicz's analysis of verbal tone patterns in Buli attracts our interest, for it assumes that INFL elements like Agr and Tns are (abstract) tone-bearing elements. His analysis is also empirically plausible in that, as far as the data in his paper are concerned, it correctly captures the surface distribution of verbal tones in a coherent way. More importantly, the analysis raises additional issues concerning the interface between phrasal tone and syntax/semantics. I will comment on the following aspects of Kenstowicz's paper: (i) the fact that non-emphatic present, imperative, future, and stative sentences form a natural class concerning tone realizations, (ii) the proposal that abstract elements like Agr and Tns are (underlying) tone bearing elements whose tones have different surface realizations through either morphosyntactic or phonological operations, and (iii) facts about tones in serial verbs and their implications.

III

- Non-emphatic present, imperative, future, and stative sentences form a (natural) class with respect to tone realizations

This fact is quite natural and has a firm semantic basis which in fact strengthens Kenstowicz's arguments. He observes in another paper on Buli verbal tone that present tense sentences in Buli have a habitual interpretation. They are generic sentences, which do not describe events which have taken place in the real world. The same seems to apply to the stative sentences. The adjective *nal* 'nice' in the stative sentence examples belongs to the class of so-called 'individual-level predicates' and describes a permanent property of its subject from the point of view of the speaker. In addition, imperative and future sentences universally share a semantic property in that both types of sentences have a future sense. Imperative sentences, like future sentences, describe an event which has not taken place but will happen in the future.

From the above argument follows the conclusion that present, imperative, future, and stative sentences constitute a semantic class in that none describe events which have actually happened in the real world. The basic generalization is that, in Buli, sentences expressing an event that has not been accomplished in the real world lack the INFL elements. The conclusion further implies that Kenstowicz's morphosyntactic way of deriving surface tone patterns of the relevant sentence types has a firm semantic basis which validates the existence of the proposed process.

A semantic characterization of surface tone realizations receives a piece of (indirect) support from prosodic facts in other languages. For example, the eventive/noneventive distinction enters into surface prosodic realizations in Germanic languages like English and German, as the following examples illustrate.

(8) a. Your SHOES are muddy. (eventive, stage-level interpretation)
    b. Your son is INTELLIGENT. (noneventive, individual-level interpretation)

(9) a. FIREMEN are available. (eventive, stage-level interpretation)
    b. Firemen are AVAILABLE. (noneventive, individual-level interpretation)

It is therefore not unnatural that the same distinction regulates surface prosodic realizations in other languages which do not have any direct typological relation to Germanic languages.

The shared semantic property of the four relevant sentence types also serves as evidence for a possible semantic alternative to Kenstowicz's morphosyntactic analysis. However, the arguments for a semantic analysis are not strong enough to take the place of his morphosyntactic analysis. This may enable us to simplify the mechanism of Buli verbal tone realizations, but tone varieties which stem from the stage-level/individual-level distinction are not observed in Buli sentences with adjectives. Even if Kenstowicz's INFL deletion has a semantic motivation and is identified as a natural process on semantic grounds, further factual descriptions are required in order to decide whether INFL deletion is to be characterized as a rule applying at the semantics-phonology interface.

IV

• Abstract INFL elements like Agr and Tns are (underlying) tone bearing elements whose tones have different surface realizations through either morphosyntactic or phonological operations

This proposal is an unusual and inspiring aspect of Kenstowicz's analysis of verbal tone patterns in Buli. It is not a simple abstract analysis but is seen to be an analysis which has an empirical basis. The existence of the underlying HL of Agr is supported by the fact that eventive sentences with either a first-person or a second-person subject and negative and emphatic sentences exhibit the surface HL pattern. By contrast, eventive sentences with a third person subject do not exhibit the pattern. Evidence for postulating the L tone of Tns comes from the surface alternation between the presence and the absence of the future morpheme *lì*, which is associated with the L tone. Thus, postulating the underlying INFL elements associated with tones is a legitimate way of explaining the seemingly complex verbal tone patterns in Buli.

The next issue to be discussed is whether or not a semantic characterization of the above tonal alternation can be formulated as a possible alternative to Kenstowicz's morphosyntactic analysis. Given the possibility that the shared tonal behavior of non-emphatic present, imperative, future, and stative sentences has a semantic basis, the tonal alternations under consideration could also possibly be characterized as a phenomenon that takes place at the interface between the semantic and the phonological modules.

A likely candidate is the theory of the semantics-phonology interface wherein the basic distribution of phrasal tones is determined through a process which maps the existence of Agr and Tns in the semantic representation corresponding to respective tones. Surface tonal patterns are derived through the application of pure phonological rules which adjust tone patterns generated by the mapping. If a semantic theory in which Agr and Tns are both represented in its semantic or conceptual structure as essential elements, the semantic analysis can be formulated as a possible alternative to Kenstowicz's morphosyntactic analysis.

A clue to formulating such a semantic analysis lies in the nature of INFL deletion. Recall, as I have suggested above, that the rule is likely to have a semantic motivation. If it has a semantic motivation, then it also has the possibility of being reformulated as a rule applying at the level of the semantics-phonology interface. The elements in INFL have corresponding elements in some version of semantic representation, so that an alternative semantic version of the rule can be formulated as a semantics-phonology correspondence rule, roughly stated in (10).

(10) a. The Arg element corresponds to HL when it is syntactically realized.
b. The Tns element corresponds to L when it is syntactically realized.

This semantic analysis has the same empirical validity as Kenstowicz's morphosyntactic analysis, as far as the facts in section II are concerned. However, it does not work well when we consider the tonal patterns of the serial verb construction. The basic fact about the construction is that its predicate consists of two verbs and that it has the following IP structure.

(11) Subj-[[Agr-Tns-Asp-V_1]-Obj-[Tns-Asp-V_2]]

Characteristic of the construction is that, as shown in (11), an object NP is preceded by a verb and followed by another verb. More importantly, the two verbs have their own respective Tns morphemes and exhibit respective tone patterns, although they denote a single event in a combinatory manner.

The possible semantic analysis mentioned above cannot capture the tonal behavior of two verbs in the serial verb construction. The semantic representation of the construction exhibits a sort of syntax-semantics mismatch in that the two verbs combine into a single predicate, roughly as represented in (12a).

(12) a. [Predicate (Subj, Obj)] semantic representation
b. Subj V_1 Obj V_2 syntactic representation

If the basic tone distribution in the serial verb construction stems directly from a semantic representation, the surface tonal patterns in the construction cannot be captured. There would be no way to associate a single semantic predicate with two separate syntactic verbs, each with their respective tones. Direct access to the morphosyntactic structure seems to be the only way of accounting for the tone pattern of the serial verb construction.

V

The above discussion leads us to the following tentative conclusions:

(i) Buli verbal tone patterns can be captured by Kenstowicz's morphosyntactic analysis.
(ii) The fact that some sentence types exhibit the default Mid can be characterized as a morphosyntactic phenomenon which has a semantic motivation.
(iii) Buli verbal tone patterns can be treated within a theory of the semantics-phonology interface. However, the tone realizations in the serial verb construction are highly likely to defy conceivable semantic analysis.

It seems that both morphosyntactic and semantic factors are relevant to the surface realizations of Buli verbal tones. It is not easy to determine which factor counts most, and case-by-case examinations of tonal facts are necessary. As Kenstowicz himself points out, the whole picture of the interfaces between phonology, syntax, and morphosyntax is still poorly understood in Buli. It is true, however, that Buli verbal tone patterns raise interesting issues for the field of the interface among phonology, syntax, and morphosyntax. Further relevant facts need to be accumulated for the purpose of clarifying the overall picture of the interface between the various grammatical components in Buli.

Phonology-syntax interfaces in Busan Korean and Fukuoka Japanese*

Tomoyuki KUBO (Kyushu University)
kubo@lit.kyushu-u.ac.jp

0. Introduction

Busan Korean, henceforth BK, and Fukuoka Japanese, FJ, show striking similarity in neutralizing all accentual distinctions in words that occur in the domain between WH words on one hand, and [+wh] complementizers binding them on the other.[1]

Kim (1980) first pointed out that in Gyeongsangdo dialects, in which BK is included, tone sandhi occurs after WH words. However, his observation that syntactic structure is irrelevant to the WH-triggered accentual phenomenon (Kim 1980, p.153) is totally different from mine.

Hayata (1985, pp.25-27) first pointed out the FJ WH phenomenon. But his observation was limited to simple WH-COMP relation (direct and indirect WH questions), and interactions of multiple WH scopes were not treated.

Below, I will present further data and descriptive generalizations which foregoing studies have not given.

1. Brief sketch of the phenomenon

In BK, underlying accentual distinctions are neutralized between WH and COMP (including these elements), forming a minor phrase, and LHL (convex) pitch pattern is

---

* I would like to thank the following language consultants:
LEE Hwa-Seon: born in 1984 and brought up in Busan.
JUN Ho-Kyung: born in 1974 and brought up in Busan.
JO Mi-E: born in 1958 and brought up in Busan.
HASHIMOTO Hideko: born in 1957 and brought up in Fukuoka.
The Fukuoka data are mainly from the present author, KUBO Tomoyuki: born in 1957 and brought up in Fukuoka.
My deepest gratitude is due to Prof. Jennifer Smith of the University of North Carolina, who gave many valuable comments. I would also like to thank the participants of the conference for their comments and suggestions. All remaining errors are my own.

[1] This striking similarity, of course, does not directly lead to the genetic relationship of the two languages. It maybe an areal phenomenon (Sprachbund) or just coincidence; this question does not concern us here.

assigned both in main and embedded WH question (WH-Q) sentences, as schematically shown in (1). If a focused element intervenes between WH and COMP, underlying accent surfaces from that element onward, i.e. WH-triggered minor phrase formation and flat high pitch stops before that element.

In the schemata and examples below, " ' " stands for an underlying accent and (   ) represents a minor phrase. Pitch contour is roughly shown by free-hand lines, leaving accent reduction and downdrift out of consideration. In both languages, only high and low pitch are distinguished phonologically, which is derived based on the position of underlying accent.

(1) BK:

	minor phrase formation		tone assignment	
Syntax	→ (')(')( )	→	(')(')( )	/ non-WH-Q
	→ (WH COMP)	→	(WH COMP)	/(embedded) WH-Q
	→ (WH)(fo'cus)(COMP)	→	(WH)(fo'cus)(COMP)	/ WH-Q + focus

In FJ, similar to BK, underlying accentual distinction is neutralized between WH and COMP, forming a minor phrase, and LHR (in a main WH-Q) or LHL (in an embedded WH-Q) pitch pattern is assigned, as in (2). Unlike BK, focus construction does not affect the WH-triggered minor phrase formation (accent neutralization).

(2) FJ:

	minor phrase formation		tone assignment	
Syntax	→ (')(')( )	→	(')(')( )	/ non-WH-Q
	→ (WH COMP)	→	(WH COMP)	/ main WH-Q
	→ (WH COMP)	→	(WH COMP)	/ embedded WH-Q

Below we will see this phenomenon in detail.

2. Accentual distinction

Both BK and FJ have accentual distinctions except FJ verbs and adjectives. In BK, n-syllable nouns basically have n+2 accentual patterns. Below are four accentual patterns of disyllabic nouns. In the examples below, a dot represents syllable boundary.

(3) BK: a. yaŋ.nyəm[2] 'spice' yaŋ.nyə.m-i 'spice-NOM'

b. 'ə.lɨn 'adult' 'ə.lɨ.n-i 'adult-NOM'

c. ul.mul 'well' ul.mu.l-i 'well-NOM'

d. na.mu' 'tree' na.mu'-ga 'tree-NOM'

In BK, verbs show three accentual patterns in monosyllabic stems and four accentual patterns in disyllabic stems. Below are four accentual patterns of disyllabic-stem verbs:

(4) BK: a. nɨl.li.-da 'increase (transitive)'

b. 'nol.la.-da 'be astonished'

c. mi.lu'-da 'put off'

d. man'na.-da 'meet'

In FJ, *n*-syllable nouns have *n* accentual patterns:

(5) FJ: a. otoko' 'man' otoko'-ga 'man-NOM'

b. kokoro 'mind' kokoro-ga 'mind-NOM'

c. i'noti 'life' i'noti-ga 'life-NOM'

In FJ, verbs and adjectives always have a default accent pattern, with the accent assigned to the syllable including the penultimate mora. That is, verbs and adjectives do not have a lexical accent, and default pitch pattern is assigned to them.

---

2 The surface accentual pattern of BK is specified as follows:
(i)If there is no accent (" ' ") in a word, the initial two syllables are high, and the following syllable(s) is/are low.
(ii) The syllable followed by accent is high. When the second syllable is high, the initial is low.
(iii) The syllable(s) following accent is/are low. When a word has a pre-accent, only the initial syllable is low, the second and third are high, the following syllable(s) is/are low.

(6) FJ: a. nom-u "drink" non-da 'drank' nom-oo 'let's drink'

b. tabe-ru "eat" tabe-ta 'ate' tabe-roo 'let's eat'

In the declarative and yes/no question sentences, underlying accent surfaces in both languages.

3. Main [WH … COMP] clause

In [WH … COMP] main clauses in both languages, accentual distinctions are neutralized, forming a single minor phrase, and flat high pitch prevails between WH word and COMP.

In BK, sentence-final *-na* and *-no* are complementizers of yes/no and WH question respectively. In (7a) and (7e) below, there is no WH word, so the underlying accent of each word surfaces. In (7b), (7c), and (7f), accentual distinction is neutralized, forming a single minor phrase, and flat high pitch prevails between WH word and COMP. In (7d), *nuga* 'somebody' is not bound by [+wh] COMP, and its underlying accent (no accent, in this case) surfaces.

(7) BK a. (o'n⬀l)(gal'bi) (mu'un-na)?
today kalbi ate-YNQ
'Do you eat kalbi today?'

b. (o'n⬀l)(**nuga** galbi muun-**no**)?
today WHO kalbi ate-WHQ
'Who ate kalbi today?'

c. (**nuga** on⬀l galbi muun-**no**)
WHO today kalbi ate-WHQ
'Who ate kalbi today?'

d. (nuga) (o'n⬀l) (gal'bi) (mu'un-na)
someone today kalbi ate-YNQ
'Did someone eat kalbi today?'

e. (o'n⬀l)(yəŋ'mi-laŋ)(na'm⬀n)(gal'bi-yaŋnyəm) (mu'un-na)?
today Yəŋmi-COM remained kalbi-spices ate-YNQ
'Did you eat the leftover kalbi-spices with Yəŋmi today?'

f. (**nuga** on'l yəŋmi-laŋ nam'n galbi yaŋnyəm muun-**no**)?
WHO today Yəŋmi-COM remained my kalbi-spices ate-WHQ
'Who ate my leftover kalbi-spices with Yəŋmi today?'

In the FJ WH-Q, LHR pitch pattern is assigned, unlike in BK. We assume that in the FJ main-clause WH-Q, WH word is bound by sentence final ↑, or a phonetically null complementizer with the feature [+wh], as (8b), (8c), and (8e) show.

In (8a) and (8d), there is no WH word, so the underlying accent of each word surfaces. In (8b), (8c), and (8e), accentual distinctions are neutralized, forming a single minor phrase, and flat high pitch prevails between a WH word and a complementizer.

(8) FJ a. (kyo'o) (bi'iru) (nonda).
today beer drank
'I drank beer today'

b. (kyo'o)(**dare**-ga biiru nonda)?
today WHO-NOM beer drank ØCOMP
'Who drank beer today?'

c. (**dare**-ga kyoo biiru nonda)?
WHO-NOM today beer drank ØCOMP
'Who drank beer today?'

d. (bi'iru)(nomina'gara)(yo'ru-mo)(nerande)(nagai)(ronbun)(yonda-to)?
beer drinking night-also not-sleeping long paper read-nominalizer
'Did you read a long paper drinking beer, without sleeping at night?'

e. (**dare**-ga biiru nominagara yoru-mo nerande nagai ronbun yonda-to)?
WHO-NOM .... read-nominalizer ØCOMP
'Who read a long paper drinking beer, without sleeping at night?'

From the data in (7) and (8), we can make the following generalization for both languages.

(9) Generalization 1: In a main-clause WH-Q, the accentual distinctions of all of the constituents between a WH word and a complementizer are neutralized, forming a single minor phrase, and flat high pitch prevails between the WH word and the complementizer, although BK and FJ show slightly different phonetic realizations in sentence-final position.

[(..'...)(..'..)(WH ... COMP)] ([ ] represents clause boundaries)

4. Scope Interaction

Below, data from multiple [WH…COMP] constructions will be given for both languages.

4-1. Embedded [WH … COMP] clause

In BK, an embedded [WH … COMP] clause shows the same pitch pattern as a main [WH … COMP] clause, as in (10a) below. A minor phrase should be formed between the WH word and the COMP which binds it. Otherwise the sentence is ungrammatical, as (10b) shows.

In a WH-embedded WH construction, i.e., [WH … [WH … COMP] … COMP] construction, WH with wider scope takes precedence. Among three consultants, only one judged (10c) as ?, and the other two as ??. This may be due to the avoidance of a [*nuga nuga*] sequence, which is usually interpreted as a dvandva compound, with the meaning of 'who and who'. It is crucial, however, that the two consultants, who judged (10c) as ?? and (10d) as ?, reported that (10d) is far better than (10e). This means that, aside from the [*nuga nuga*] problem, a single minor phrase is formed that extends beyond the inner [+WH] COMP *-ji*. (10f) has the [*nuga nuga*] dvandva construction, in which both of the WH words are the constituents of the embedded clause.

(10) BK a. ([**nuga** galbi munn◇n-**ji**])(algo in'-na)?
WHO galbi ate-COMP know-YNQ
'Do you know who ate kalbi?'

*b. ([**nuga** galbi munn◇n-**ji**] algo in-na)?
WHO galbi ate-COMP know-YNQ
'Do you know who ate kalbi?'

?? or ? c. (**nuga** [**nuga** galbi munn◇n-**ji**] algo in-no)?
WHO WHO kalbi ate-COMP know-WHQ
'Who knows who ate kalbi?'

? or ok d. (**nuga**)([**nuga** galbi munn◇n-ji] algo in-no)?
WHO WHO kalbi ate-COMP know-WHQ
'Who knows who ate kalbi?'

*e. (**nuga**)([**nuga** galbi munn◇n-ji])(algo in-no)?
WHO WHO kalbi ate-COMP know-WHQ
'Who knows who ate kalbi?'

f. ([**nuga nuga** galbi munn-n-ji])(algo in'-na)?
WHO WHO kalbi ate-COMP know-YNQ
'Do you know who and who ate kalbi?'

In FJ, an embedded WH-Q shows the same pitch pattern as a main WH-Q except that there is final lowering, as in (11a) below. This final lowering can be regarded as the same default lowering observed in verbs and adjectives seen in (6). In a WH-embedded WH construction, i.e., [WH [WH COMP] COMP] construction, WH with wider scope takes precedence, as in BK, as seen in (11c).

(11) FJ a. [**dare**-ga biiru nonda-**ka**] sitto'o?
WHO-NOM beer drank-COMP know
'Do you know who drank beer?'

*b. ([**dare**-ga biiru nonda-**ka**] sitto'o)?
WHO-NOM beer drank-COMP know
'Do you know who drank beer?'

c.(**dare**-ga [**dare**-ga biiru nonda-**ka**] sittoo)?
WHO-NOM WHO-NOM beer drank-COMP know ØCOMP
'Who knows who drank beer?'

*d.(**dare**-ga [**dare**-ga biiru nonda-**ka**])(sitto'o)?
WHO-NOM WHO-NOM beer drank-COMP know ØCOMP
'Who knows who drank beer?'

From the data in (10) and (11), we can derive the following generalization for both languages:

(12) Generalization 2: In a WH-embedded WH construction, WH with wider scope takes precedence.

[(**WH** [WH COMP] **COMP**)]

When the embedded WH clause is extraposed, embedded and main WH-Q surface as two separate minor phrases both in BK and FJ.

(13) BK = scrambled version of (10c) and (10d)

([**nuga** galbi munnɁn-**ji**]) (**nuga** algo in-**no**)?
WHO …….. - COMP WHO … - COMP

(14) FJ =scrambled version of (11c)

([**dare**-ga biiru nonda-**ka**]) (**dare**-ga sittoo)?
WHO ……….. - COMP WHO …ØCOMP

4-2. Echo WH

In WH echo questions, echo WH takes precedence in both languages. In the examples below, speaker B asks speaker A an echo question.

(15) BK A: (yə'ŋi-ga)(mie-e'ge) [(**məəl** bullənnɁn-ji)] (mu'lədda).
Yəŋi-NOM Mie-DAT WHAT+ACC sang-COMP asked
'Yəŋi asked Mie what she/he sang'
B: (**nuga** mie-ege məəl bullənnɁn-ji mulədda-go?).
WHO ………………………………. -quotation marker ØCOMP
'WHO asked Mie what she/he sang?'

(16) FJ A: (yu'mi-ga) (na'oya-ni) (**nani**-o nonda-**ka**) (kiita).
Yumi-NOM Naoya-DAT WHAT-ACC drank-COMP asked
'Yumi asked Naoya what he drank.'

B: (**dare**-ga naoya-ni [nani-o nonda-ka] kiita-tte)?
WHO …………………………………… -quotation marker ØCOMP
'WHO asked Naoya what he drank?'

Data in (15) and (16) further support (12) Generalization 2, repeated in (17).

(17) [(**WH** [WH COMP] **COMP**)]

4-3. Multiple WH-Q

In a multiple WH construction, where multiple WH words are bound by the same complementizer, the WH word which is nearer to the complementizer takes precedence in both languages. In the beginning of the scope of the WH word which is nearer to the complementizer, a new minor phrase is formed:

(18) BK a. (**nuga** ole) ([**nuga** bul⁷n] nole bullən-**no**)?
WHO this year WHO sang song sang-WHO
'Who sang the song [which who sang] this year?'

b.(**nuga**)[(o'le)(nuga bul⁷n] nole bullən-**no**)?
'Who sang the song [which who sang this year]?'

(19) FJ a. (**dare**-ga kinoo) ([**dare**-ga nonda] biiru nonda-to)?
WHO-NOM yesterday WHO-NOM drank beer drank-nominalizer ØCOMP
'Who drank the beer which [who drank] yesterday?'

b. (**dare**-ga) [(kinoo)(**dare**-ga nonda] biiru nonda-to)?
'Who drank the beer which [who drank yesterday]?'

From the data in (18) and (19), we can derive the following generalization for both languages:

(20) Generalization 3: In a multiple WH construction, the WH word which is nearer to the complementizer takes precedence. At the beginning of the scope of the WH word which is nearer to the complementizer, a new minor phrase is formed.

a. [(**WH**......)(**WH** .... **COMP**)]

b. [[**WH**... [(.......) (**WH** .... **COMP**)]

5. Differences between BK and FJ

Besides the similarities above, BJ and FJ WH constructions also have some differences.

5-1. Binder

In FJ, every WH word should be bound by a [+wh] complementizer or other binders, as in Standard Japanese.

(21) FJ a. (**da**rega biiru nonde-**mo**) (iiyo).
WHO beer drink-also ok

'It does not matter whoever drinks beer,' or, 'Anyone can drink beer.'

b. (bi'iru)(**da're**ga nonde-**mo**) (i'iyo).

c. Na'oya-wa Ma'ri-ga **na'ni**-o nonde-**mo** yu'mi-ni iw'an-to?
Naoya-TOP Mari-NOM WHAT-ACC drink-also Yumi-DAT not-say-nominalizer
'Whatever Mari drinks, Naoya will not tell it to Yumi?'

d. Na'oya-wa Ma'ri-ga **nani**-o non-de-mo yumi-ni iw-an-to?
WHAT ……………………….. ØCOMP

In BJ, unlike FJ, WH words are interpreted as indefinites when not bound by a [+wh] complementizer. In (22) below, underlying accent surfaces in WH words.

(22) BK a. (**o'de**)(ga'ja).
somewhere let's go
'Let's go somewhere!'

b. (**nugu**) (ga'ja)
somebody let's go
'Somebody, Let's go!'

c. (**mə'ɒ**) (məg'ja).
something let's eat
'Let's eat something!'

5-2. Focus

In BK, focus constructions interact with the WH-triggered accent neutralization seen above. (23a1) is an unmarked WH-Q in that it is a simple interrogative sentence, asking who ate kalbi. (23a2) is marked in that it is an echo YN-Q, asking whether the word that speaker B heard in the utterance of speaker A is kalbi or not. (23b) is also marked, in that it is a rhetorical question meaning that no one should have eaten kalbi.

Prosodically, extra-high pitch is assigned to *galbi* in (23a2) and *nuga* in (23b), and underlying accent surfaces from these words onward. I assume that these two words have focus, and from these focused elements onward, underlying accent surfaces, i.e., WH-triggered accent neutralization does not occur.

(23) BK a1. speaker A: (**nuga** galbi muun-**no**)?
WHO kalbi ate-WHQ?'

a2. speaker B (**nuga**)(**gal'bi**)(muun-**nyago**)?
WHO kalbi ate-echo question
'Did you say who ate "**kalbi**"?'

b. (**nuga**)(galbi)(muun-**no**)?
WHO kalbi ate-WHQ?'
'**Who** ate kalbi?' = 'No one should have eaten kalbi.'

In FJ, focus constructions do not affect WH-triggered accent neutralization, although focus-triggered accent reduction similar to Tokyo Japanese (TJ) is observed. Thus, the following generalization can be made for BK only.

(24) Generalization 4 for BK: If there is a focused element in a WH-Q, WH-triggered accentual neutralization does not occur from that element onward.

(WH)(focus)(...COMP)

5-3. Extraposed WH word

In FJ, a main-clause constituent cannot intervene between the subordinate WH word and COMP. In (25) below, the WH word is extraposed from the embedded WH clause, and a main-clause constituent intervenes between the WH word and COMP. In such a construction, the pitch pattern (25b) is better than (25a), and in (25b) the scope of the WH word widens to the main clause.[3]

(25) FJ *a. (**nani**$_i$-o Yumi-wa [Naoya-ga t_i nonda-**ka**)] (oboetoo-to)?
WHAT-ACC Yumi-TOP Naoya-NOM drank-COMP remember-nominalizer
'Does Yumi remember what Naoya drank?

[3] *-ka* is a [+WH] complementizer, but in (25b) it is interpreted as a [-WH] complementizer, like *-kadooka*. A sentence in which *-kadooka* is substituted for *-ka* is also judged as ?.

?b. (**nani**$_i$-o Yumi-wa [Naoya-ga t_i nonda-ka] oboetoo-to)?
WHAT .... ØCOMP
'What does Yumi remember whether Naoya drank (it)?'

As Ishihara (2002) pointed out, in TJ, accent reduction occurs between the WH word and COMP, and the TJ equivalent of (25b), in which the reduction domain extends from *nani* to the end of the main clause, is better than that of (25a). Although the domain of the phenomenon in the two dialects is the same in this case, TJ has accent reduction and FJ accent deletion.

Contrary to FJ, in BK, (26a) is better than (26b).

(26) BK ?a. (**məəl**$_i$ yəŋi-nɨn [mie-ga t_i bullənnɨn-**ji**]) (algo in-na)?
WHAT+ACC Yəŋi-TOP Mie-NOM sang-COMP know-YNQ
'Does Yəŋi know what Mie sang?'

*b. (**məəl**$_i$ yəŋi-nɨn [mie-ga t_i bullənnɨn-ji] algo in-**no**)?
WHAT+ACC .... -WHQ
'What does Yəŋi know Mie sang (it)?'

From (25) the following generalization can be made for FJ.

(27) Generalization 5 for FJ: If the WH word in an embedded clause is extraposed beyond a main-clause constituent, the WH word is not associated with the complementizer of the embedded clause, but with the complementizer of the main clause:

*a. [(**WH**i ... [... ti ..**COMP**)] .... COMP]

?b. ([**WH**i ... [... ti ..**COMP**] ...... COMP])

6. Concluding remarks

In this paper, several generalizations common to BK and FK are made, which are repeated below.

Generalization 1: In a main-clause WH-Q, the accentual distinctions of all of the constituents between a WH word and a complementizer are neutralized, forming a single minor phrase, and flat high pitch prevails between the WH word and the complementizer, although BK and FJ show slightly different phonetic realizations at the sentence-final position:

[(...)(...)(**WH** ... **COMP**)] ([ ] represents clause boundaries)

Generalization 2: In a WH-embedded WH construction, WH with wider scope takes precedence:

[(**WH** [WH COMP] **COMP**)]

Generalization 3: In a multiple WH construction, the WH word which is nearer to the complementizer takes precedence. At the beginning of the scope of the WH word which is nearer to the complementizer, a new minor phrase is formed:

a. [(**WH**......)(**WH** **COMP**)]

b. [[**WH**... [(...) (**WH** **COMP**]

The following generalizations hold only for BK or FJ:

Generalization 4 for BK: If there is a focused element in a WH-Q, WH-triggered accentual neutralization does not occur from that element onward:

(WH)(focus)(...COMP)

Generalization 5 for FJ: If the WH word in an embedded clause is extraposed beyond a main-clause constituent, the WH word is not associated with the complementizer of the embedded clause, but with the complementizer of the main clause:

*i. [(**WH**i ... [... ti ..**COMP**)] ... COMP]

?ii. ([**WH**i ... [... ti ..COMP] ...... **COMP**])

I have shown that in BK and FJ, WH-triggered accent neutralization (accent deletion) and minor phrase formation occurs based on the positions of a WH word and the complementizer which binds it. In addition to this phenomenon, both BK and FJ have focus-triggered accent reduction, but this interacts with WH triggered accentual neutralization only in BK.

Bibliography

Hayata, Teruhiro. 1985. *Accent and Morphology of the Hakata Dialect* (in Japanese). Fukuoka: Kyushu University Press.

Ishihara, Shinichiro. 2002. Invisible but Audible Scope Marking: WH-Constructions and Deaccenting in Japanese. In: Line Mikkelsen and Chris Potts, eds., *WCCFL 21 Proceedings*. Somerville, MA: Cascadilla Press, pp.180-193.

Kim, Ca-Gyun. 1980. *The Tonal System of the Gyeongsangdo Dialects* (in Korean). Seoul: Gwa-hag-sa.

Kubo, Tomoyuki. 1989. The Pitch Patterns of Sentences Containing Wh-words in the Fukuoka-City Dialect (in Japanese). *Studies in Japanese Linguistics*, vol.156. pp.1-12.

Kubo, Tomoyuki. 1994. Flat High Pitch and the Scope of WH-words — Notes on the Pusan and Chinju Dialects of Korean — (in Japanese). *Grammatical Studies on Asian and African Languages* 22. pp.93-108.

Kubo, Tomoyuki. 2001. Syntax-Phonology Interface in the Fukuoka Dialect (in Japanese). *Journal of the Phonetic Society of Japan*, vol.5, No.3, pp. 27-32.

Kubo, Tomoyuki. 2002. Phonological Phrase, Syntax, and Focus (in Japanese). Paper read at The symposium on phonological domains, the 125th meeting of the Linguistic Society of Japan, Tohoku Gakuin University, Sendai.

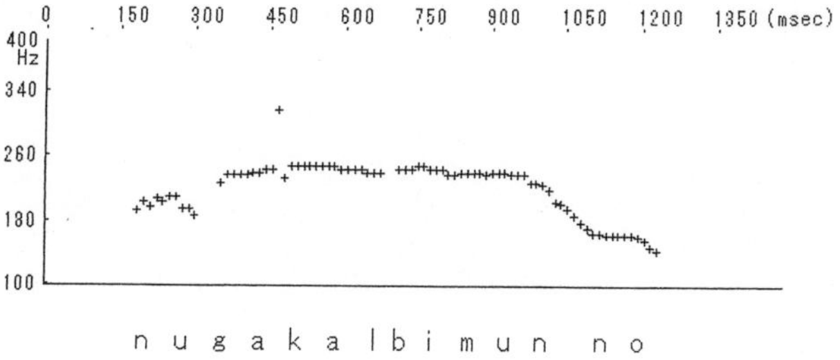

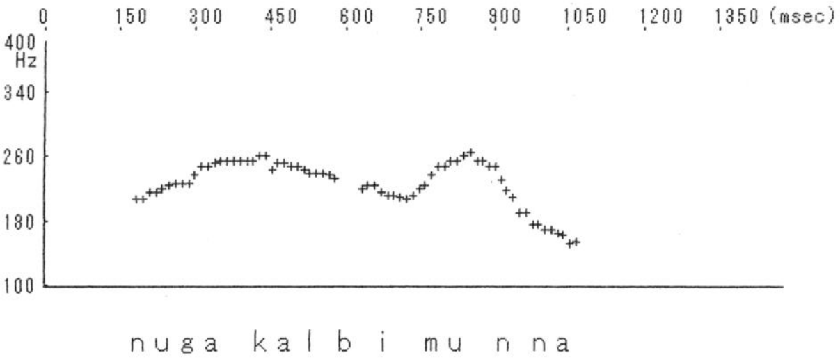

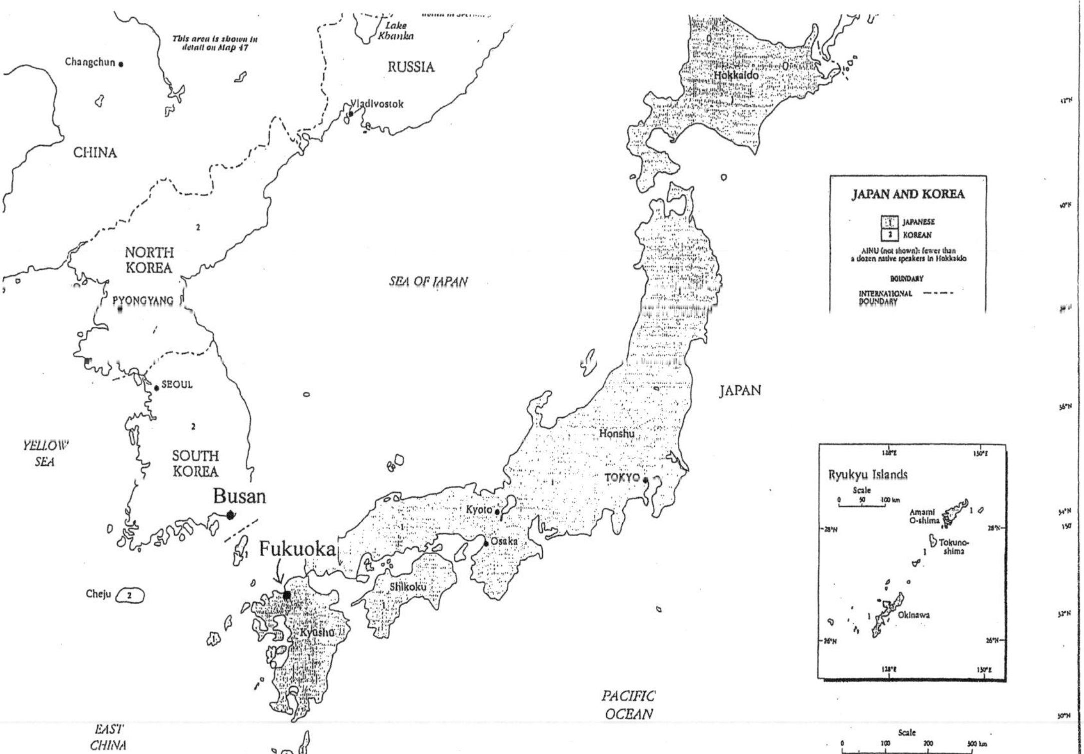

Moseley, Christopher and R. E. Asher eds. 1994. Atlas of the world's languages. London: Routledge.

Comments on "Syntax-phonology interfaces in Busan Korean and Fukuoka Japanese" by Tomoyuki Kubo

Jennifer L. Smith
University of North Carolina, Chapel Hill
jlsmith@email.unc.edu

The Busan Korean and Fukuoka Japanese patterns that Tomoyuki Kubo has presented in his paper raise significant questions that any formal model of the prosody-syntax interface must address. In these comments, I would like to focus on one such question: how can we account for the fact that intonation is sensitive specifically to the location of a [+WH] complementizer that *binds,* or is *syntactically and semantically associated* with, a particular WH-phrase? In other words, what characteristics must a formal model of the phonology/syntax interface have in order to represent this kind of correlation between WH-scope and intonational contour?

Ishihara (2004) develops an analysis of a very similar WH-scope/intonation correlation in the Tokyo dialect of Japanese, the Mutiple Spell-Out (MSO) account. An advantage of MSO is that it reduces the Tokyo WH-intonation pattern to a subcase of more general patterns of focus phonology, requiring no WH-specific extensions to the formal model of the prosody-syntax interface. If MSO could serve as a general, cross-linguistic model of WH-scope/intonation relationships, this would allow all apparent effects of WH-scope on prosodic phrasing to be modeled with existing mechanisms that relate focused constituents to prosodic structure (e.g., Truckenbrodt 1995, 1999; Selkirk 2003). On the other hand, MSO relies on cyclic syntactic derivation to account for the correlation between WH-scope and (focus) intonation, a position that is not straightforwardly compatible with constraint-based, parallel models of prosodic phonology.

In these comments, I show that while MSO can model certain aspects of the Busan Korean and Fukuoka Japanese patterns, it leaves other points unaccounted for. This finding has two implications. First, it may indeed be necessary to allow the prosody-syntax interface access to additional information beyond focus and syntactic edges; specifically, information about WH-elements and their scope. Second, the derivational MSO account has no clear advantage over a parallel approach to the prosody-syntax interface.

1. The BK/FJ pattern and its significance

Prof. Kubo demonstrates that in both Busan Korean (BK) and Fukuoka Japanese (FJ), when there is a WH-element bound by a complementizer, a prosodic constituent (minor phrase, MiP) is formed. This MiP begins at the WH-element; ends at the complementizer that binds the WH-element; and triggers the loss of all pitch accents associated with the morphemes that it contains, receiving default penultimate accentuation. Thus, the phonology of accent and intonation in BK and FJ appears to be sensitive to the syntax of WH-scope.

There is a formal approach to the prosody-syntax interface that holds that the prosodic system has access to only a very limited amount of syntactic information. In particular, it has been claimed that only information about edges of syntactic constituents and information about the morphosyntactic location of focus are accessible for prosodic structure, while detailed information about syntactic phrase structure is not (Chen 1987; Selkirk 1986, 2000, 2003; Truckenbrodt 1995, 1999). In the context of such proposals, it is important to determine whether the WH-scope/intonation correlation in BK and FJ can also be accounted for in terms of syntactic edges and focus features alone. If not, we will need to incorporate additional factors into the prosody-syntax interface.

2. The MSO account of the Tokyo Japanese WH-scope/intonation correlation

The MSO account of Ishihara (2004) is a formal model of a WH-scope/intonation correlation in Tokyo Japanese (TJ) that is very similar to the intonational patterns in BK and FJ described by Prof. Kubo. The MSO account of the TJ pattern does not require explicit reference to WH-scope or coindexation within the phonological system. This raises the question of whether the BK and FJ patterns can also be modeled with the MSO, in which case there would be no need to make the phonological component explicitly sensitive to WH-scope for these systems either.

The fundamental insight of MSO is that the WH-related intonational contour begins at a WH-phrase and extends to the end of the utterance. Crucially, however, at certain stages of the syntactic derivation, only the embedded clause is visible to the phonology, which means that the "end of the utterance" may in fact only be the end of an embedded clause as far as the phonology is concerned. On this view, the WH-scope/intonation correlation is indirect; it is a consequence of the cyclic nature of the syntactic derivation.

The close similarity between TJ on the one hand and BK and FJ on the other is the way in which a certain intonational domain closely correlates with WH-scope.[1] However, it is important to note that the characteristics of the WH-related intonational contour itself are quite different in TJ. The BK/FJ pattern involves *deaccenting* of the WH-element and the rest of the WH-domain, with default penultimate accent assignment on the WH-related MiP. In TJ, the WH-element receives *focus* intonation (Tomioka 1997; Deguchi & Kitagawa 2002; Ishihara 2002). The accent on the WH-element is realized at a particularly high pitch level, and then the remainder of the WH-domain undergoes post-focus reduction (PFR); that is, intrinsic pitch accents are not lost in the PFR domain (Ishihara 2002, 2004), but the pitch range is greatly lowered and compressed, making the difference between H and L tones very small. (For general discussion of non-WH focus intonation and PFR in TJ, see, e.g., Nagahara 1994; Sugahara 2003, 2005.)

---

[1]Hirotani (2003, 2004ab) has shown in production and perception experiments with Tokyo speakers that the WH-scope/intonation correlation is a *preference* rather than an absolute requirement. Based on these findings, Hirotani argues that the Tokyo pattern arises from a processing strategy and is not a matter for the formal grammar of the syntax-phonology interface. However, the WH-scope/intonation correlation in BK and FJ does seem to be unambiguous (T. Kubo, p.c.), and thus a matter for the grammar — so even if MSO turns out not to be appropriate for TJ, it is still potentially applicable to the BK/FJ pattern.

The relationship between WH-scope and intonational contour in TJ is illustrated by the examples in (1), from Ishihara (2004: 82, 84). Here and in subsequent examples, pitch accents are indicated with ‘ ' ’ at the location of the pitch fall, ‘ ^ ’ represents sentence-final rising intonation, and the WH-element and its associated complementizer are marked with **bold underline**. For the TJ examples, ‘*focus*’ represents the pitch-accent boost on the WH-element, and ‘__’ indicates the extent of the low-pitch domain associated with PFR.

(1) WH-scope/intonation correlation in TJ

(a) Na'oya-wa [Ma'ri-ga **na'ni-o** nomi'ya de no'nda to] i'mademo omo'tteru **no** ?

focus ______________________________________ ^

Naoya-TOP Mari-NOM what-ACC bar at drank COMP even.now think C_{+WH}

‘What$_i$ does Naoya still think that Mari drank t_i at the bar?’

(b) Na'oya-wa [Ma'ri-ga **na'ni-o** nomi'ya de no'nda **ka**] i'mademo obo'eteru.

focus ____________________

Naoya-TOP Mari-NOM what-ACC bar at drank C_{+WH} *even.now remember*

‘Naoya still remembers what$_i$ Mari drank t_i at the bar.’

In these examples, the WH-element is inside the embedded clause in both cases; the difference is that it is bound by the matrix complementizer in (1a), but by the embedded complementizer in (1b). Thus, the right edge of the WH-related intonational contour correlates with the WH-scope. The contrast in (1) with respect to the size of the WH-related intonational domains is strikingly similar to the difference between matrix and embedded scope for an embedded WH-element in BK and FJ (see examples (7b) vs. (10a,b) and (8b) vs. (11a,b) in Prof. Kubo’s paper).

The MSO account of TJ (Ishihara 2004) is based on the proposal that Spell-Out — i.e. the transfer of information from the syntactic component to the phonology — happens phase-by-phase (Chomsky 2000, 2001ab). A *phase* is any subpart of a clause that constitutes “the closest syntactic counterpart to a proposition: either a verb phrase in which all θ-roles are assigned or a full clause including tense and force” (Chomsky 2000: 106). Essentially, whenever a complementizer phrase (CP) is constructed, its tense phrase (TP) complement becomes available to the phonology. But a WH-element does not receive its [+WH] feature until the [+WH] complementizer that binds it has also been incorporated into the derivation (Ishihara 2004: 87). So a WH-element in an embedded CP will only appear with a [+WH] feature at Spell-Out — triggering formation of the WH-related intonational domain — if its associated complementizer is also in the embedded CP.[2]

[2]Ishihara (2004: 91) points out that because it is TP, not CP, that is sent to Spell-Out, this account would seem to predict — incorrectly — that the complementizer itself is excluded from the WH-related intonational domain. He suggests that complementizers and other WH-particles are phonologically cliticized to the preceding prosodic word (PrWd), and therefore surface phonologically as part of that PrWd’s intonational contour.

Specifically, an embedded WH-phrase that is associated with the complementizer (C) of the embedded clause will have its [+WH] feature assigned at the point where only the embedded clause has been sent to Spell-Out. Because the [+WH] feature is already present, a WH intonational domain is created at this stage of the derivation.

(2) MSO: Embedded WH-element bound by embedded C

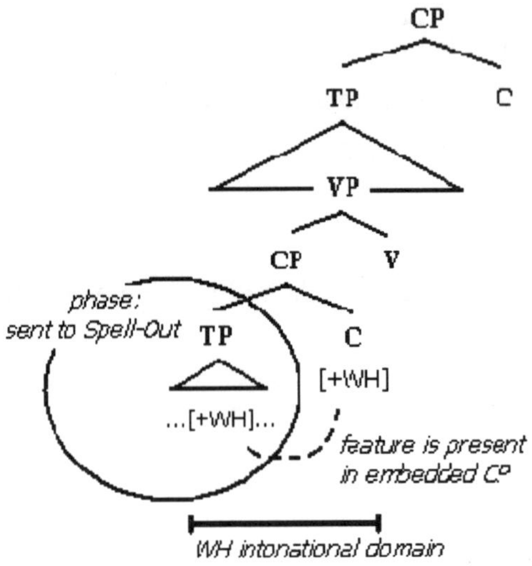

This is why the intonational domain extends no further than the embedded CP — material that is not included in this phase can not be phonologically manipulated at this instance of Spell-Out.

However, an embedded WH-phrase that is associated with the C of the matrix clause has no [+WH] feature when the embedded clause is sent to Spell-Out on its own. This means that no WH-related intonational domain is created at this stage. Only later in the derivation, when the whole matrix clause is sent to Spell-Out, does the embedded WH-element bear a [+WH] feature. But by that point, the whole matrix clause is visible to the phonology, so the WH-related intonational domain extends all the way to the end of the matrix clause.

(3) MSO: Embedded WH-element bound by matrix C

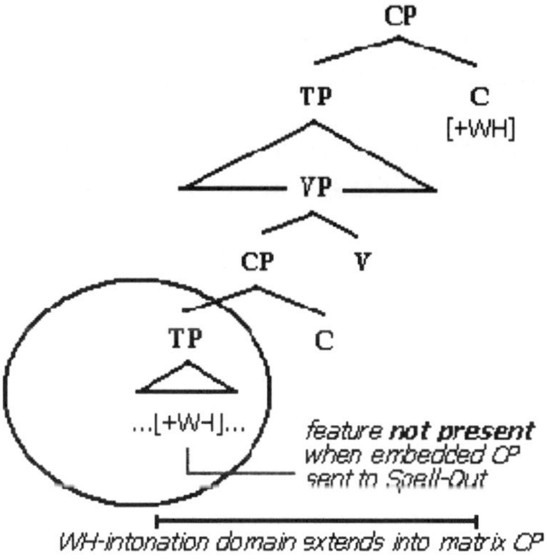

As these examples demonstrate, the MSO is able to account for the difference in intonational domains between sentences with main-clause and embedded-clause WH-scope, a difference that is also important in BK and FJ. However, the next section shows that other data discussed in Prof. Kubo's paper present problems for the MSO account.

3. Testing a prediction of the MSO account: Embedded WH-element scrambling
If the WH-related intonational domain is indeed assigned according to MSO, phase-by-phase, this predicts that the scrambling of an embedded WH-element up into the matrix clause should interact with the intonational contour in a particular way. This scrambling construction is in fact one of the contexts where the BK and FJ patterns differ, but crucially, neither one seems to match the predictions of the MSO acount.

According to the assumptions laid out by Ishihara (2004: 95-96), when an embedded WH-element is scrambled into the matrix clause, it first moves through the Spec, CP position of the embedded clause. This position is outside the embedded clause's TP, so when that TP is sent to Spell-Out, the WH-element is not included. As a result, no WH-related intonational domain can be created at this cycle of Spell-Out — even if the WH-element is bound by a [+WH] complementizer in the embedded CP. Therefore, MSO predicts that a WH-element scrambled out from the embedded clause should correlate with a WH-domain that extends to the end of the matrix clause, independent of the semantic scope of the WH-construction. Ishihara (2004: 108) presents the following example of scope mismatch, in which semantically, the WH-construction has embedded scope, but prosodically, the WH-related intonational contour extends to the end of the matrix clause. (Sentences with scrambling of an embedded WH-element tend to be somewhat "unnatural" (Ishihara 2004: 113, note 27), below this effect is observed for FJ and BK as well.)

(4) WH-scope/intonation mismatch in TJ:
Matrix intonational domain, embedded WH-scope

? **na'ni$_i$-o** Na'oya-wa [Ma'ri-ga t_i nomi'ya de no'nda **ka**] i'mademo obo'eteru.
focus ____
what-ACC Naoya-TOP Mari-NOM bar at drank C_{+WH} even.now remember
'Naoya still remembers [what$_i$ Mari drank t_i at the bar.']

As demonstrated in Prof. Kubo's example (25), given here in (5), FJ bears out the MSO account's prediction that the scrambling of an embedded WH-element is incompatible with ending the WH-related intonational domain at the embedded complementizer. In this scrambled structure, the only possible intonation is one in which the WH-related intonational contour extends to the end of the matrix clause. However, the semantic interpretation of this example is crucially different from that of the TJ example given in (4) above; in FJ, the WH-construction can only take *matrix* scope. (For FJ and BK examples, the WH-related intonational domain is indicated with '{ }', and the H-tone span inside this domain is marked '‾‾‾'.)

(5) No WH-scope/intonation mismatch in FJ:
Matrix intonational domain —> matrix WH-scope (=Kubo's (25b))

? { **nani$_i$-o** Yumi-wa [Naoya-ga t_i nonda **ka**] oboetoo-to ? }
what-ACC Yumi-TOP Naoya-NOM drank COMP remember-NOMINALIZER
'What does Yumi remember [whether Naoya drank (it)]?'

The pattern that Prof. Kubo describes for BK is even more problematic for the MSO account. In BK, when an embedded WH-element bound by the embedded complementizer is scrambled up into the matrix clause, the WH-related intonational domain still extends only as far as the *embedded* complementizer.

(6) No WH-scope/intonation mismatch in BK:
Embedded WH-scope —> embedded intonational domain (=Kubo's (26a))

? { **məəl$_i$** yəŋi-nɨn [mie-ga t_i bullənnɨn-ji] } algo in-na ?
what.ACC Yəŋi-TOP Mie-NOM sang C_{+WH} know-YNQ
'Does Yəŋi know what Mie sang?'

The MSO account fails to allow for this possibility, because it predicts that the WH-related intonational domain must extend to the end of that portion of the structure that is available at the current cycle of Spell-Out. If the intonational domain is initiated by an element that occupies a surface position in the matrix CP, then there is no way to prevent the intonational domain from extending to the end of the matrix CP.[3]

[3]Interestingly, Ishihara (2002) and Kitagawa & Fodor (2003) report a BK-like intonational contour for this type of sentence for TJ as well, although Ishihara (2004) subsequently argues that the results of his controlled production experiment with TJ speakers differ and do in fact support

In summary, the semantic and intonational consequences of scrambling an embedded WH-element up into the matrix clause are different in BK and FJ, but both patterns show a tighter connection between the semantic scope of the WH-construction and the size of the WH-related intonational domain than the MSO account predicts. Moreover, the intonational pattern observed in BK is one that MSO simply cannot generate, under any interpretation of the semantic WH-scope.

4. Conclusions and implications

Several aspects of the data presented by Prof. Kubo are not easily compatible with MSO as an account of the WH-scope/intonation correlations observed in BK and FJ. One such case is the embedded WH-element scrambling construction discussed in §3 above. There are additional characteristics of BK and FJ that seem to require mechanisms beyond MSO as well. For example, MSO is successful for TJ in part because WH intonation can be equated with focus intonation. However, this does not appear to be the case for BK and FJ, where the WH-related intonational contour involves accent deletion (even on the WH-element itself) rather than focus intonation.

The fact that the MSO is not fully able to account for the BK and FJ data has implications for our understanding of the nature of the syntax-prosody interface. For one thing, this means that it is still an open question as to whether the types of information accessible to the prosodic phonology will need to be expanded to include [+WH] features (see also Kisseberth, this volume, on the apparent sensitivity of prosodic structure in Chimwiini to semantic factors such as negation and definiteness). Additionally, the MSO account, with its reliance on cyclic, derivational construction of prosodic structure, would seem to be incompatible with constraint-based, parallel models of the syntax-prosody interface (e.g., Selkirk 1995, 2003; Truckenbrodt 1995, 1999); future research may determine whether a parallel approach to BK and FJ would be more successful than MSO.

More generally, Prof. Kubo's paper on the syntax-phonology interface in BK and FJ has both expanded the inventory of data related to the interface between prosody and syntax, and presented new challenges for formal models of that interface to address.

Acknowledgements

Some of the points raised here are also discussed in Smith (2005). Many thanks to Tomoyuki Kubo, Shosuke Haraguchi, and other participants at the 2004 Symposium, as well as to Randy Hendrick, Mako Hirotani, Shigeto Kawahara, Elliott Moreton, Lisa Selkirk, and Mariko Sugahara, for helpful comments and discussion. As always, the author is responsible for any remaining errors or inadequacies.

---

the predictions of MSO. The disparity between TJ speakers' intuitions and Ishihara's experimental results may support Hirotani's (2003, 2004ab) claim that the WH-scope/intonation correlation in TJ is more a processing strategy than a categorical requirement. As Ishihara (2004: 113, note 27) observes, the fact that these scrambled constructions are somewhat degraded in acceptability may also be contributing to the discrepancies.

References

Chen, Matthew. 1987. The syntax of Xiamen tone sandhi. *Phonology Yearbook* 4: 109-149.

Chomsky, Noam. 2000. Minimalist inquiries: The framework. In Roger Martin, David Michaels, and Juan Uriagereka, eds., *Step by Step: In Honor of Howard Lasnik.* Cambridge, Mass.: MIT Press, 85-155.

Chomsky, Noam. 2001a. Derivation by phase. In Michael Kenstowicz, ed., *Ken Hale: A Life in Language.* Cambridge, Mass.: MIT Press, 1-52.

Chomsky, Noam. 2001b. *Beyond Explanatory Adequacy.* MIT Working Papers in Linguistics (MITWPL) 20. Cambridge, Mass.: MITWPL.

Deguchi, Masanori, and Yoshihisa Kitagawa. 2002. Prosody and wh-questions. In Masako Hirotani, ed., *Proceedings of NELS 32,* vol. 1. Amherst, Mass.: GLSA, 73-92.

Hirotani, Masako. 2003. Prosodic effects on the interpretation of Japanese wh-questions. In Luis Alonso-Ovalle, ed., *On Semantic Processing.* UMOP 27. Amherst, Mass.: GLSA, 117-137.

Hirotani, Masako. 2004a. Does prosodic phrasing correlate with wh-scope in Japanese? Poster presentation at the Ninth Conference on Laboratory Phonology; University of Illinois at Urbana-Champaign, June 25.

Hirotani, Masako. 2004b. Prosodic boundaries in the comprehension and production of wh-questions in Tokyo Japanese. Paper presented at the 17th Annual CUNY Conference on Human Sentence Processing; University of Maryland, College Park, March 27.

Ishihara, Shinichiro. 2002. Invisible but audible Wh-scope marking: Wh-constructions and deaccenting in Japanese. In Line Mikkelsen and Chris Potts, eds., *Proceedings of WCCFL 21.* Somerville, Mass.: Cascadilla Press, 180-193.

Ishihara, Shinichiro. 2004. Prosody by phase: Evidence from Focus intonation–Wh-scope correspondence in Japanese. In S. Ishihara, M. Schmitz, and A. Schwarz, eds., *Interdisciplinary Studies on Information Structure 1.* Potsdam: University of Potsdam, 77–119.

Kisseberth, Charles W. This volume. Accent and phrasing in Chimwiini.

Kitagawa, Yoshihisa, and Janet Dean Fodor. 2003. Default prosody explains neglected syntactic analysis in Japanese. In William McClure, ed., *Japanese/Korean Linguistics 12.* Stanford: CSLI, 267-279.

Nagahara, Hiroyuki. 1994. *Phonological Phrasing in Japanese.* Doctoral dissertation, University of California, Los Angeles.

Selkirk, Elisabeth O. 1986. On derived domains in sentence phonology. *Phonology Yearbook* 3: 371-405.

Selkirk, Elisabeth O. 1995. The prosodic structure of function words. In Jill N. Beckman, Laura Walsh Dickey, and Suzanne Urbanczyk, eds., *Papers in Optimality Theory.* UMOP 18. Amherst, Mass.: GLSA, 439-469.

Selkirk, Elisabeth O. 2000. The interaction of constraints on prosodic phrasing. In Merle Horne, ed., *Prosody: Theory and Experiment.* Dordrecht: Kluwer, 231–263.

Selkirk, Elisabeth O. 2003. Bengali intonation revisited: an Optimality Theoretic analysis in which FOCUS stress prominence drives FOCUS phrasing. In Angela

Carpenter, Andries Coetzee, and Paul de Lacy, eds., *Papers in Optimality Theory II.* UMOP 26. Amherst, Mass.: GLSA, 305-335.
Smith, Jennifer L. 2005. On the WH-question intonational domain in Fukuoka Japanese: Some implications for the syntax-prosody interface. In Shigeto Kawahara, ed., *Papers on Prosody.* UMOP 30. Amherst, Mass.: GLSA, 219-237.
Sugahara, Mariko. 2003. *Downtrends and post-FOCUS intonation in Tokyo Japanese.* Doctoral dissertation, University of Massachusetts, Amherst.
Sugahara, Mariko. 2005. Post-focus prosodic phrase boundaries in Tokyo Japanese: Asymmetric behavior of an F_0 cue and domain-final lengthening. *Studia Linguistica* 59, 144-173.
Tomioka, Satoshi. 1997. Wh-in situ, subjacency, and LF syntax. Handout from LSA Summer Institute, Cornell Univesity, Ithaca, NY.
Truckenbrodt, Hubert. 1995. *Phonological Phrases: Their Relation to Syntax, Focus, and Prominence.* Doctoral dissertation, MIT.
Truckenbrodt, Hubert. 1999. On the relation between syntactic phrases and phonological phrases. *Linguistic Inquiry* 30(2): 219-255.

The Tone-Syntax Interface in Chinese: Some Recent Controversies*

San Duanmu
University of Michigan
Symposium on Cross-Linguistic Studies of Tonal Phenomena
Revised February 2005

The main question I explore in this paper is whether there is a general theory of the phonology-syntax interface that applies to all Chinese dialects. I first review three types of tone sandhi in Chinese, those in Mandarin, Xiamen, and Shanghai. Then I review the interaction between syntax and the domain of tone sandhi in these dialects. Next I discuss the analysis of the tone-syntax interface. In particular, I compare several current approaches to foot formation in Chinese and argue for the view that foot formation depends on stress assignment. The stress-based analysis applies to all the Chinese dialects in question, as well as better-known stress languages such as English.

1. Introduction

Chinese is a tone language, in which tones are lexically specified. In general, all full syllables (or heavy/bimoraic syllables) carry a lexical tone, whereas weak syllables (or light/monomoraic syllables) do not. In addition, a full syllable can usually carry at most two tones (LH or HL); more complex tone patterns (LHL or HLH) can occur only in final (or pre-pausal) position, where the syllable is extra long. This suggests that each mora can carry at most one tone (H or L).

When two (or more) syllables occur next to each other, their tones may undergo change. This is referred to as tone sandhi, which occurs in many Chinese dialects (and languages). In addition, whether tone sandhi takes place between two syllables or not often depends on the syntactic structure. It is fairly well understood what kinds of tonal changes will take place within a given sandhi domain. However, there is less agreement on how sandhi domains are formed, even though most scholars believe that they are sensitive to syntax. The focus of this paper will be on the relation between syntax and sandhi domains.

In section 2 I review three types of tone sandhi, those in Mandarin, Xiamen (also called Southern Min or Amoy), and Shanghai. In section 3 I discuss how sandhi domains interact with syntax. In section 4 I review current analyses of tone sandhi in the three dialects. In section 5 I compare several approaches to foot formation in Chinese, a crucial process in understanding domains for tone sandhi, and I will argue for a stress-based approach. In section 6 I offer some concluding remarks.

2. Three types of tone sandhi

It is common in Chinese dialects that when syllables occur next to each other, their tones undergo change, or tone sandhi. In this section I review three types of tone sandhi. The first occurs in Mandarin, known as Tone 3 Sandhi (T3S, also called Third Tone Sandhi). T3S is discussed at length first in Cheng (1968) and subsequently in many other works. In T3S a T3 becomes a T2 when it precedes another T3. The rule is given in (1) and exemplified in (2). Unless otherwise noted, transcription is given in Pinyin, where 0 indicates lack of lexical tone and 1-4 indicate the four full tones in Mandarin (or Standard Chinese).

(1) T3 T3 → T2 T3

(2) mai3 ma3 → mai2 ma3   mai2 ma3
buy horse   bury horse
'to buy a horse'   'to bury a horse'

As far as the listener is concerned, T3S neutralizes the difference between T3 and T2 and can create ambiguities, because T2-T3 and T3-T3 are both realized as T2-T3 on the surface. For example, although *mai3* 'buy' and *mai2* 'bury' have different tones underlyingly, 'to buy a horse' and 'to bury a horse' sound the same to the listener.

Because T3S neutralizes the distinction between T2 and T3, it is tempting to assume that T3S is a reduction process in which the first syllable loses its original tone because it has less stress than the second (Iwata 1999, 2001, Dell 2004). However, there are some problems with this assumption. First, T3S applies regardless of which syllable has more stress. For example, in trisyllabic structures such as *[[zhan3-lan3] guan3]* 'exhibition hall', there is good evidence that the first syllable has more stress than the second (Chao 1968, Hoa 1983, Yan and Lin 1988, Yang 1992), yet T3S still applies. Similarly, in a bisyllabic expression, T3S applies even if the first syllable has contrastive or emphatic stress. For example, in *bu shi [hao3 jiu3], shi [mi3 jiu3]* 'not GOOD wine, but RICE wine', the underlined syllables have contrastive stress, yet they still must undergo T3S. Second, there is a difference between merger and reduction. A reduction is a change from a contrastive form to a non-contrastive form, such as from a full vowel to a schwa. On the other hand, a merger can be a change from one contrastive form to another contrastive form. Because T2 is not a neutral tone but a full tone, which contrasts with other tones, T3S is not a true reduction rule, but a conditioned merger from one contrastive form to another, similar to [s→ʃ/__i] in English (e.g. *this year*) or Japanese, where both /s/ and /ʃ/ are contrastive sounds.

It is also tempting to consider T3S as a dissimilation rule. In particular, because T3 is a low tone (in nonfinal positions), T3S seems to be a dissimilation between two low tones (L-L). On the other hand, there is no dissimilation between the H's in T1-T1 (H-H), or between the L's in T4-T2 (HL-LH), or between L's in T4-T3 (HL-L). So the nature of T3S remains unclear. In any case, why T3S occurs is independent from the question of how the domains for T3S are formed. Since our main interest is in the latter, I do not pursue the nature of T3S any further.

The second type of tone sandhi occurs in Shanghai (and many other dialects in the Wu dialect family), whereby the tones of non-initial syllables are lost and the tone of the initial syllable determines the pitch contour of the entire domain. In particular, if we ignore the effect of onset voicing on the vowel, there are two syllable tones in Shanghai, LH and HL (Duanmu 1999 argues that the underlying syllable tones in Shanghai are L and H and they surface as LH and HL respectively by a polarity rule). Their influence on the tonal pattern of the domain is abbreviated in (3), where S is a stressed syllable and s an unstressed one, and where a hyphen separates tones on different syllables.

(3)	S	Ss	Sss+
	HL	H-L	H-L-L…
	LH	L-H	L-H-L…

The fact that the initial syllable has more stress is not always obvious to the native speaker (Selkirk and Shen 1990), but phonetic studies show that the rime of the initial syllable is nearly twice as long as that of non-initial syllables (Zhu 1995), in support of the view that the initial syllable has more stress. Some examples are shown in (4), transcribed in phonetic symbols.

(4)

HL-HL→ H-L
se + pe
'three cups'

HL-LH→ H-L
se + bø
'three plates'

LH-HL→ L-H
sz + pe
'four cups'

LH-LH→ L-H
sz + bø
'four plates'

It can be seen that the output tone pattern depends entirely on the first syllable, regardless of the underlying tones on the second syllable.

The third type of tone sandhi occurs in Xiamen and many other Min dialects. In this case, every full syllable has two lexically specified tone patterns: a final pattern, which is used when the syllable occurs in isolation or in the domain final position, and a nonfinal pattern, which is used when the syllable occurs in a nonfinal position. The final and non-final tones in Xiamen are shown in (5), according to the transcription of Chen (2000) (in Chao digits, where 1 is the lowest pitch and 5 the highest).

(5)	Categories	A	B	C	D	E	F	G
	Final tone (T)	44	24	53	21	22	32	4
	Nonfinal tone (T')	22	22	44	53	21	4/53	21

The nature of tonal alternations in Xiamen is not very clear. Chen (2000) suggests that the tonal alternation in (5) forms a music-chair like 'cycle' or 'clock'. However, any clock one might see is probably an accident and cannot be extended to other Min dialects. In any case, such issues need not concern us. In (6) are some examples of tonal alternations, from Chen (2000: 433), transcribed in Roman letters, where A-C are final tones and A'-C' are non-final tones. Tonal alternations are seen in the underlined words.

(6)

A
tsin p^hang
'very fragrant'

A'
p^hang tsui
'fragrant water (perfume)'

B
p^he we
'leather shoe'

B'
we tua
'shoe lace'

C　　　　C'
wi pĩ　　　　pĩ lang
'stomach illness'　　　　'ill person'

Tonal alternation is not limited to bisyllabic expressions. For example, the compound in (7) has four syllables; three have non-final tones (T') and one has the final tone (T).

(7) T' T' T' T
bi-kok sio-tsia
'America Miss (Miss America)'

It is worth noting that the final tone is used for the last stressed syllable. Consider the examples in (8), where 0 refers to lack of tone on an unstressed syllable.

(8) T' T' T　　　　T 0 0
bue nng kun　　　　bue nng kun
buy two pounds　　　　buy two pounds
'buy two pounds'　　　　'buy some'

When *nng kun* means 'two pounds', the syllables are stressed, and the final tone occurs on *kun*. When *nng kun* means 'some', the syllables are unstressed, and the final tone occurs on the preceding syllable.

Strictly speaking, since each syllable is choosing between its own two tones, the alternation in Xiamen should not be called tone sandhi (i.e. the choice is determined by the position of a syllable and not by the tone pattern of a neighboring syllable). However, I follow the tradition and use tone sandhi loosely to include the Xiamen case.

I have not discussed tone sandhi in other dialects, such as Tianjin, Danyang, and Wenzhou, which are still different cases. However, those in Mandarin, Shanghai, and Xiamen offer a rich body of data on the tone-syntax interface.

3. Interaction between syntax and sandhi domains

The interaction between syntax and domains of tone sandhi is well known in the three dialects we are looking at. First, consider the tone sandhi (T3S) in Mandarin (see Duanmu 2000, chapter 11 for more details). In (9) we see that T3S is sensitive to syntactic branching. A left-branching structure usually has just one pattern, but a right-branching structure can have two or more.

(9) Left-branching　　　　Right-branching

[[3 3] 3] → 2 2 3 only　　　　[3 [3 3]] → 3 2 3 or 2 2 3
[[mai hao] jiu]　　　　[mai [hao jiu]]
buy good wine　　　　buy good wine
'finished buying wine'　　　　'to buy good wine'

[[[3 3] 3] 3] → 2 2 2 3 only	[3 [3 [3 3]]] → 2 3 2 3, 3 2 2 3, or 2 2 2 3
[[[zhan-lan] guan] li]	[xiao [zhi [lao-hu]]]
exhibition hall inside	small paper old-tiger
'inside of exhibition hall'	'small paper tiger'

The difference is due to the cyclic application of T3S, moving from inner brackets to outer brackets. The analysis of left-branching structures is shown in (10), where underline shows the syllables to which T3S applies at each step.

(10) Left-branching: one output pattern
[[3 3] 3] → [[2 3] 3] → 2-2-3
[[[3 3] 3] 3] → [[[2 3] 3] 3] → [[[2 2] 3] 3] → 2-2-2-3

For right-branching structures, there is an additional factor, namely, a T3 before a T3 that has already changed into T2 can still change into T2 optionally (Shen 1994). This is stated in (11), where the double-underlined 2 is changed from an underlying T3.

(11) 3-2 → 2-2 (optional)

Two right-branching structures are analyzed in (12).

(12) Righ-branching: many output pattern
[3 [3 3]] → [3 [2 3]] → 3-2-3 or 2-2-3

[3 [3 [3 3]]]→[3 [3 [2 3]]] →[3 [3 [2 3]]]→2-3-2-3
→[3 [2 [2 3]]]→3-2-2-3 or 2-2-2-3

It is also known that tree structure alone is insufficient for predicting the outcome of T3S. For example, the two expressions in (13a) have the same tree structure and input tones, but the first can become [2 3 3 1] and the second cannot (* indicates a bad form). Similarly, each other pair in (13) have the same tree structure, but they do not have the same surface tone patterns (only relevant patterns are shown).

(13)	a.	3 3 3 1 → 2 3 3 1	3 3 3 1 → *2 3 3 1
		[wo [xiang [mai shu]]]	[xiao [zhi [lao-ying]]]
		I want buy book	small paper old-eagle
		'I want to buy a book'	'small paper eagle'
	b.	3 3 3 3 → *?3 2 2 3	3 3 3 3 → 3 2 2 3
		[wo [xiang [mai jiu]]]	[xiao [zhi [lao-hu]]]
		I want buy wine	small paper old-tiger
		'I want to buy wine'	'small paper tiger'
	c.	3 3 3 3 → 2 3 2 3	3 3 3 3 → *2 3 2 3
		[gou [[bi ma] xiao]]	[gou [[hen hao] yang]]
		dog than horse small	dog very good raise
		'Dogs are smaller than horses'	'Dogs are very easy to raise'

d. 3 3 3 4 → 2 3 3 4 [gou [[bi ma] kuai]] dog than horse fast 'Dogs are faster than horses'

3 3 3 4 → *2 3 3 4 [gou [[hen hao] kan]] dog very good watch 'Dogs are very easy to watch'

The above examples show that T3S is sensitive to not only the branching structure of syntactic trees but also additional information, either syntactic labels for the trees or information on a compound-phrase distinction, as well as information on word categories, to be discussed below.

Next consider the case in Shanghai. The example in (14) shows that tone sandhi is sensitive to syntax. The domains of tone sandhi are indicated by parentheses.

(14) LH LH → L-H
(ts^{h}o ve)
fry rice
'fried rice' (noun)

LH LH → LH-LH or L-LH
(ts^{h}o) (ve)
fry rice
'to fry rice' (verb phrase)

A bisyllabic NN (noun-noun) or AN (adjective-noun) can only form one tonal domain, where the output tonal pattern is determined by the first syllable. In contrast, a bisyllabic VO (verb-object) phrase forms two tonal domains, where each syllable keeps its own tones. A non-final monosyllabic domain, such as 'fry' in the VO phrase, usually takes just L or H in Shanghai, instead of LH or HL. According to Duanmu (1999), the full metrical analysis of the VO phrase in (14) is (mm).[(mm).m], where 'fry' forms a bimoraic foot (mm) and 'rice' is lengthened to three moras, which are equivalent to a bisyllabic foot [(mm).m]. A bimoraic foot (mm) usually takes one tone, whereas a bisyllabic foot [(mm).m] can take two tones.

Finally, consider the effect of syntax in Xiamen. Some examples are shown in (15), from Chen (2000: 433-434). The domains of tone sandhi are indicated by parentheses.

(15)	(hong-ts^{h}e)	(pang hong-ts^{h}e)	(hong) (ts^{h}e) (hɔ) (ak)
	wind blow	fly wind blow	wind blow rain pour
	'kite'	'to fly kite'	'wind blows and rain pours'

As shown, a domain may contain one, two, or three (or more) syllables. In addition, the same adjacent words 'wind' and blow' may belong to the same or different domains depending on the syntactic structure, to be explained below.

It is interesting to note that the sandhi domains in the three dialects are often different even for the same syntactic structure. Some examples are shown in (16)-(19), where domain boundaries are indicated by vertical lines. The words given are from Mandarin. Shanghai and Xiamen may use different words in certain cases (for example, Shanghai uses 'eat' instead of 'drink' for wine), but as long as the words have the same number of syllables, the domains boundaries remain the same. Also, not all Mandarin syllables in these examples are T3, so the domain boundaries cannot always be tested in terms of T3S. However, current researchers generally agree on the domains for T3S, and so I did not try to make up sentences that consist of T3 syllables only. Finally, tonal domains can be affected by speech rate, in that faster speech has fewer domains. The examples below show the domains for normal speech rate only.

```
(16)              [[Old Li] [often [drink [rice wine]]]]
                  [[老 李] [经常 [喝 [米 酒]]]]
     Shanghai     |        |      |      |          |
     Mandarin     |        |      |                 |
     Xiamen       |        |                        |

(17)              [[Old Li] [like  [Shaoxin's [rice wine]]]]
                  [[老 李] [喜欢 [绍兴 的 [米 酒]]]]
     Shanghai     |        |      |          |          |
     Mandarin     |        |      |          |          |
     Xiamen       |        |                 |          |

(18)              [Sarajevo  [is-in  Yugoslavia]]
                  [萨拉 热窝 [在 南斯 拉夫]]
     Shanghai     |    |    |    |    |    |
     Mandarin     |    |    |         |    |
     Xiamen       |         |              |

(19)          a.  fry  rice (phrase)      b. fry rice (compound)
                  炒 饭                      炒 饭
     Shanghai     |  |  |                    |     |
     Mandarin     |     |                    |     |
     Xiamen       |     |                    |     |
```

The example in (18) shows that, unlike what is suggested by Selkirk and Shen (1990), a tonal domain cannot be a prosodic word, because a polysyllabic word such as 'Sarajevo' or 'Yugoslavia' is one prosodic word, yet it can form two domains in Shanghai and Mandarin.

4. Current analyses of sandhi domains

I first discuss how each dialect has been analyzed. Then I discuss whether a general approach to the three dialects can be found.

4.1. Xiamen

The most detailed discussion of Xiamen is probably Chen (1987, 2000), according to which the sandhi domain in Xiamen is the phonological phrase (p-phrase). Adopting a suggestion from Lin (1994), Chen (2000: 459) defines the phonological phrase boundary as in (20).

(20) Xiamen p-phrase
{Right, X^{max}}, X^{max} not lexically governed

The right-hand boundary of a phonological phrase occurs at each right-hand boundary of a syntactic phrase (the maximal projection of an element X, or X^{max}), unless the X^{max}

is governed by a lexical word. The term 'govern' is a formal syntactic notion; it can be loosely understood as 'being next to'. For example, in an SVO (subject-verb-object) sentence, there are four right-hand X^{max} boundaries, labeled as 1-4 in (21), where I is the Inflection node (INFL), which is null in this sentence. The X^{max} boundaries that trigger phonological phrase boundaries are underlined.

(21) [[NP]$_{\underline{1}}$ I [V [NP]$_2$]$_{\underline{3}}$]$_{\underline{4}}$
(Ting sio-tsia) (pang hong-ts^{h}e)
(Ting miss) (fly kite)
'Miss Ting flies a kite.'

The first right-hand X^{max} boundary is that of the subject NP; since this NP is governed by I, which is not a lexical word, the right-hand boundary counts as a phonological phrase boundary. The second right-hand X^{max} boundary is that of the object NP; however, since the object is governed by the verb (a lexical word), its boundary does not count. The third right-hand X^{max} boundary is that of the verb phrase; since verb phrase is governed by I (not a lexical word), its right-hand boundary counts as a phonological phrase boundary. The fourth right-hand X^{max} boundary is that of the sentence, which is governed by either I or C (complementizer); since neither I or C is a lexical word, the right-hand boundary of the sentence counts as a phonological phrase boundary, which happens to coincide with that of the verb phrase.

To see more examples of domain formation, consider the difference between (22) and (23), adapted from Chen (2000: 459-460). The point of interest is the adverb, which forms a domain of its own in (23) but not in (22)

(22) [[NP] I [[AP] V]]
(Ting sio-tsia) (k^{h}un-lat t^{h}ak-ts^{h}eq)
(Ting miss) (diligent study)
'Miss Ting studies hard.'

(23) [[NP] [AP] I [V [NP]]]
(Ting sio-tsia) (kai-tsai) (tse tsit pan ki)
(Ting miss) (fortunately) (take this one flight)
'Fortunately, Miss Ting took this flight.'

In (22) the adverb is governed by the verb (a lexical word), so it does not form an independent domain. In (23) the adverb is supposedly governed by I (not a lexical word), so it forms an independent domain.

Chen's analysis of Xiamen is clearly superior to that of Duanmu (1995), which claims that the sandhi domain is a right-headed metrical foot. Criticisms of Duanmu (1995) are given in Chen (2000: 436-437) and not repeated here.

There is, however, a possible alternative to Chen's analysis. First, what seems to be at work is probably not a *domain* for tone sandhi, but rather the *positions* that trigger the final tone. Second, these positions seem to need two conditions, stated in (24).

(24) Conditions for the use of the final tone
a. The syllable should be stressed
b. The syllable should be followed by a pause or an unstressed syllable

The conditions can be seen in the examples in (25), from Chen (2000: 280), where T is a final tone, T' is a non-final tone, and 0 indicates lack of tone on an unstressed syllable.

(25)	T' T' T	T 0 0
	(bue nng kun)	(bue nng kun)
	buy two pounds	buy two pounds
	'buy two pounds'	'buy some'

In the first case, all syllables are stressed, but only the final one is before a pause, hence it alone takes the final tone. In the second case, when *nng kun* means 'some', the two syllables have no stress; the initial syllable is the only one that has stress, and it is before an unstressed syllable, and thus, it takes the final tone.

The conditions in (24) may also explain why the X^{max} in Chen's definition cannot be lexically governed. In most cases, being 'not lexically governed' means that the X^{max} is before a functional element (which is either unstressed if it is present or a pause if it is absent). Consider the difference between [Adverbial I] and [Adverbial V]. In [Adverbial I], the last syllable of the adverbial takes the final tone, because it is before a pause (if I is empty) or an unstressed syllable (if I is present). In [Adverbial V], the last syllable of the adverbial takes the non-final tone, because it is before a lexical word (not a pause or an unstressed syllable).

Finally, let us consider two additional facts. First, in a compound made of two bisyllabic nouns, familiar expressions tend to use one domain, whereas unfamiliar expressions tend to use two domains. This is consistent with the alternative analysis: a familiar expression tends to be spoken faster, and so there is usually no pause between the two nouns, and hence the final tone does not occur in the middle. In contrast, in an unfamiliar expression there tends to be a pause between the two nouns, and so the final tone can occur in the middle. The second fact is what Chen (2000: 471) calls the 'rhythmic effect'. An example is shown in (26).

(26) 'woman dressed up as man; nobody suspected'

woman	dress-up	male	attire	no	person	know	
lu	ban	lam	tsong	bo	lang	gi	
( )	(		)	(	)	( )	Regular
(	)	(	)	(		)	Rhythmic

The rhythmic reading can alter the regular tonal domains probably because it can reduce pauses in the regular reading (such as the one after 'woman') as well as adding new pauses (such as the one after 'dress up').

4.2. Shanghai

There are two approaches to tonal domains in Shanghai. According to the first, a tonal domain is a phonological word (Selkirk and Shen 1990). According to the second, a tonal domain is a left-headed metrical foot (Duanmu 1997, 1999).

In the analysis of Selkirk and Shen, a phonological word starts from the left edge of a lexical word and extends until the left edge of the next lexical word. Also, for Selkirk and Shen a compound is a single lexical word. Consider the examples in (27).

(27)	(ts^{h}o ve)	(ts^{h}o) (ve)	(tɕ^{h}i^{ʔ} i^{ʔ} pe)(zo)
	fry rice	fry rice	drink a cup tea
	'fried rice'	'to fry rice'	'to drink a cup of tea'

The compound 'fried rice' is one lexical word, and so it forms one domain. The verb phrase 'to fry rice' has two lexical words, and so it forms two domains. In 'to drink a cup of tea', 'a' and 'cup' are both thought to be non-lexical words, which do not start their own domains. Therefore there are two domains.

There are four problems with the above approach. First, it cannot explain why only lexical words (nouns, verbs, and adjectives/adverbs) can start a tonal domain but grammatical words (pronouns, classifiers, determiners, prepositions, and tense/aspect markers) cannot. Second, it cannot explain why a polysyllabic word can form two or more domains. Some examples are shown in (28).

(28)	(ko-r-fu)		'Golf'
	(ɲi-k^{h}a^{ʔ}-sõ)		'Nixon'
	(ʔo-ta-)(li-ja)	(ʔo-ta-li-ja)	'Australia'
	(nø-sz-)(la-fu)	(nø-sz-la-fu)	'Yugoslavia'
	(ku-r-)(pa-tɕo-fu)	(ku-r-pa-tɕo-fu)	'Gorbachev'
	(ʔe-se^{ʔ}-)(ŋu-pi-ja)	(ʔe-se^{ʔ}-ŋu-pi-ja)	'Ethiopia'
	(dʑe^{ʔ}-k^{h}a^{ʔ}-)(sz-lu-)(va^{ʔ}-ka^{ʔ})	(dʑe^{ʔ}-k^{h}a^{ʔ}-sz-lu-va^{ʔ}-ka^{ʔ})	'Czechoslovakia'

In fast reading, all the words in (28) can form one domain. However, in careful reading a word can form two or three domains. If a tonal domain is a phonological word, all the words should form one domain only. The third problem is that a compound can also form more than one domain. Consider the examples in (29).

(29)	(sã ɦo^{ʔ}-y)		*(sã)(ɦo^{ʔ}-y)
	business school		
	'business school'		
	(ɲy-ji ɦo^{ʔ}-y)	or	(ɲy-ji)(ɦo^{ʔ}-y)
	language school		
	'language school'		

If the expressions are compounds, they should both form one domain only, yet the second can form two domains. If the expressions are not compounds, they should both form two domains, yet the first cannot form two domains. The fourth problem is that contrastive stress can create a new domain. Consider the examples in (30).

(30)	Normal	Contrastive
	(lo-fu tɤ)	(lo-fu)(tɤ)
	'tiger head'	'tiger HEAD'

In normal reading, the compound ‘tiger head’ forms one domain. When there is contrastive stress on ‘head’ (as in ‘not tiger TAIL, but tiger HEAD’), it starts a new domain. If tonal domains are unrelated to stress, as Selkirk and Shen assume, additional assumptions are needed to explain why contrastive stress can start a new tonal domain.

Let us now consider the analysis that a tonal domain in Shanghai is a left-headed foot, based on Duanmu (1999). This analysis explains a number of things right away. First, it explains why it is the first syllable whose tone is kept: there is a general rule that in all Chinese dialects only stressed syllables can keep their underlying tones. Second, it agrees with the phonetic fact that the domain-initial syllable is phonetically much longer than non-initial syllables (Zhu 1995). Third, it explains why polysyllabic words can form bisyllabic domains from left to right: a common process of foot formation is to count syllables, rather than words. Fourth, it explains why contrastive stress can start a new domain: since a domain is a left-headed foot, every stress starts a new domain. Finally, it explains why grammatical words do not start a tonal domain. The reason is that grammatical words are not assigned stress, owing to independently motivated stress rules. In particular, in Duanmu’s analysis, Shanghai has the same rule as English for compounds and phrases, which is called Nonhead Stress, stated in (31).

(31) Nonhead Stress: A syntactic nonhead is stressed
Examples: In [X N] compounds, X is stressed
In [V O] phrases, O is stressed

Grammatical words are unstressed because they are mostly syntactic heads; for example, a classifier is the head of a classifier phrase. In addition, there is a rule for assigning stress to polysyllabic words and other free syllables, given in (32).

(32) Left-to-right foot formation (for polysyllabic words and free syllables):
Form syllabic trochees from left to right.

Now consider the examples in (33), where Ø is an empty syllable (Burling 1966, Liberman 1975, Giegerich 1985, Burzio 1994, and Hayes 1995).

(33)	x	x	(x) x
	(ts^{h}o ve)	[ts^{h}o] (ve Ø)	(tɕ^{h}i^{ʔ} i^{ʔ} pe)(zo Ø)
	fry rice	fry rice	drink a cup tea
	‘fried rice’	‘to fry rice’	‘to drink a cup of tea’

In the compound ‘fried rice’, Nonhead Stress is assigned to the first word, so there is one domain. In the phrase [V O] ‘to fry rice’, Nonhead Stress is assigned to ‘rice’, which can form a binary foot with an empty syllable (a pause). The first word ‘fry’ will form another kind of domain by itself—a bimoraic foot as a heavy syllable (instead of a bisyllabic foot); its tone will also be somewhat shorter than that on ‘rice’. In ‘to drink a cup of tea’, ‘a’ is the syntactic head of the determiner phrase and ‘cup’ is the syntactic head of the classifier phrase, so neither gets stress. In contrast, 'tea' is the syntactic nonhead of the classifier phrase, so it has stress. The verb 'drink' is not assigned stress either; however, the first three syllables can form a foot by the left-to-right foot formation rule.

Finally, compare (34) and (35). In (34), 'a cup' does not form its own domain when preceded by a verb, but does when it is in initial position. In contrast, 'one cup' always forms its own domain.

(34)	(x) x	(x) x
	(tɕ^{h}i^{ʔ} i^{ʔ} pe) (zo Ø)	(i^{ʔ} pe) (zo Ø)
	[drink [[a cup] tea]]]	[[a cup] tea]
	'to drink a cup of tea'	'a cup of tea'

(35)	x x	x x
	tɕ^{h}i^{ʔ} (i^{ʔ} pe) (zo Ø)	(i^{ʔ} pe) (zo Ø)
	[drink [[one cup] tea]]]	[[one cup] tea]
	'to drink one cup of tea'	'one cup of tea'

In the present analysis, 'a cup' forms a domain via the left-to-right foot formation process. In contrast, 'one' is the nonhead of the classifier 'cup', so 'one' has stress and 'one cup' always stars a domain.

I am not aware of a better alternative to the stress-based analysis of Shanghai. This analysis is also adopted by Chen (2000) and is consistent with Yue-Hashimoto's (1987) classification of Shanghai as an initial-dominance language.

4.3. Mandarin

There seems to be little disagreement that some kind of domains must be formed before the T3S rule applies in Mandarin. For example, most analyses (e.g. Shih 1986, Chen 2000, Duanmu 2000, Feng 2004, Wang 2004) seem to agree with the domain boundaries in the following examples, where domain boundaries are indicated with a vertical line '|'.

(36)	Word	|ma3yi3| → 2 3	'ant'
	Compound	|mi3-jiu3| → 2 3	'rice-wine'
	Phrase	|ni3 hao3| → 2 3	'you good (How are you?)'

(37)	Left-branching	Right-branching
	| [[[3 3] 3] 3] |→ 2 2 2 3 only	| [3 [3 [3 3]]] |→ 2 3 2 3, 3 2 2 3, or 2 2 2 3
	[[[zhan-lan] guan] li]	[xiao [zhi [lao-hu]]]
	exhibition hall inside	small paper old-tiger
	'inside of exhibition hall'	'small paper tiger'

(38)	Two Domains	One Domain
	| [wo [xiang | [mai shu]]] |	| [xiao [zhi [lao-ying]]] |
	I want buy book	small paper old-eagle
	'I want to buy a book'	'small paper eagle'

| [gou [[bi | ma] xiao]] | — dog than horse small — 'Dogs are smaller than horses'

| [gou [[hen hao] yang]] | — dog very good raise — 'Dogs are very easy to raise'

(39) | wu-wu-| wu-wu | — 'five-five-five-five'

| qi-wu-| wu-qi | — 'seven-five-five-seven'

(40) No emphasis
| xiang mai | gu-piao |
want buy stock
'want to buy stocks'

Emphasis on 'buy'
| xiang MAI gu-piao |
want buy stock
'want to BUY stocks'

In (36) we see that any bisyllabic structure can form a domain, since T3S applies to all of them. In (37) we see that even though all the structures form one domain, alternative patterns are possible in some but not in others; this indicates that cyclic application of T3S is needed within a domain (Shen 1994, Chen 2000, Duanmu 2000). In (38) we see that expressions that have the same branching structures can form one or two domains, and therefore additional information (such as syntactic labels or word categories) is needed to account for the difference. In (39) we see that flat structures can also form multiple domains. Finally in (40) we see that emphasis or contrastive stress can affect domain boundaries.

The domain boundary is primarily determined on the basis of whether T3S is obligatory. In particular, T3S must apply to adjacent 3-3 within a domain, but is optional for adjacent 3-3 between two domains. For example, consider the examples in (39), repeated in (41).

(41) a. | wu3-wu3-| wu3-wu3 | → 2 3 2 3 (*3 2 2 3)
'five-five-five-five'

b. | qi1-wu3-| wu3-qi1 | → 1 3 3 1 (or 1 2 3 1)
'seven-five-five-seven'

In (41b), the medial 3-3 need not change, which indicates that they are in separate domains. This is confirmed in (41a), where the first and third T3 must change, which indicates that the initial 3-3 are in one domain, so are the final 3-3. Similarly, consider (40), repeated in (42).

(42) a. No emphasis
| xiang3 mai3 | gu3-piao4 | → 2 3 3 4 (or 2 2 3 4)
want buy stock
'want to buy stocks'

b. Emphasis on 'buy'
| xiang3 MAI3 gu3-piao4 | → 3 2 3 4 (*2 3 3 4)
want buy stock
'want to BUY stocks'

In (42a), the medial 3-3 need not change, which indicates that they are in separate domains. In (42b), the medial 3-3 must change (i.e. the tone on 'buy' must change), which indicates that they are in the same domain. In addition, a single syllable does not form its own domain (unless it has phrasal stress and is in final position); therefore all the syllables in (42b) are in the same domain. (42b) also shows that, unlike what is suggested in some studies (e.g. Iwata 1999, 2001, Dell 2004), the syllable that changes its tone under T3S cannot be thought of as having less stress; in (42b) 'buy' has emphatic stress, yet it still must change its tone.

While most analyses agree on where domain boundaries should be, there are different views on how the boundaries are determined. I discuss this in the next section.

5. Foot formation in Chinese

Most analyses agree that T3S in Mandarin is sensitive to foot formation. However, opinions are divided on how feet are formed in Chinese. In addition, there is the question of whether T3S domains are identical to foot domains. In this section I argue for an approach in which foot formation is based on stress assignment and T3S domains are not always identical to foot domains. I also compare the stress-based analysis with three other approaches, those of Chen (2000), Wang (2004), and Feng (2004).

5.1. The stress-based analysis

The analysis I offer is a revised version of what is proposed in Duanmu (2000). The main claim is that, while languages can differ in word stress, all languages have the same rule for compound and phrasal stress. I present a general theory of stress first. Then I discuss foot formation.

5.1.1. A general theory of stress

The idea that word stress can be variable is not controversial. For example, English has many lexically idiosyncratic stress patterns, such as *Canada-banana*, *Alabama-America*, and *alpine-sardine*. However, the claim that all languages have the same rule for compound and phrasal stress may seem counter-intuitive; for one thing, many languages are often thought to have no stress. For example, in Hyman's (1977) survey of 444 languages, 113 are thought to have no stress, including Chinese. So what is the reason to think that all languages have stress, and that they all have the same rules for compound and phrasal stress? Let us begin with contrastive stress. I assume that all languages have contrastive stress, even in those that do not seem to have lexical stress. An example in Chinese is shown in (43), where contrastive stress is shown in uppercase.

(43) Wo xing HUANG, bu xing WANG
I name HUANG, not name WANG
'I (am) named HUANG, not named WANG.'

I assume further that in all languages the word under contrast has extra stress. But why is it so? Apparently, the word under contrast carries more information of interest. In other words, we give more stress to words with more information and less stress to words with less information. This may seem common sense, but I will show that it explains many well-known stress effects. So let us state the principle explicitly in (44).

(44) The Information-Stress Principle:
A word or phrase that carries more information than its neighbor(s) should be stressed.

The Information-Stress Principle explains two well-know facts right away. First, pronouns usually do not carry stress, because pronouns are used for entities that are either obvious or have already been mentioned, and so they usually do not carry much information. Second, as pointed out by Hayes (1995: 373) and many others, phrasal stress is often quite flexible. In the present analysis, it is because the information load of a word is not fixed but is dependent on the context, including the speaker and the listener.

Next consider how information load is determined. Following Information Theory (Shannon 1948), the information load of a form is defined in terms of its probability of occurrence, given in (45).

(45) Information load:
The more predictable a form is, the less information it carries.

Consider a simple phrase [Art N] (article-noun), such as *the car*. In English, there are only two choices for an article before a singular noun, *the* or *a*. Each has a probability of ½ in this environment. In contrast, English has thousands of nouns, and so each has a very small probability of occurring after an article. Therefore, in this structure the article carries far less information than the noun. Not surprisingly, if we omit the article, there is not much loss of information, but if we omit the noun, the information loss is more serious. Similarly, consider the difference between prepositions and verbs. Suppose that a language has six prepositions and 1000 verbs (and suppose that we can determine the category of a word through syntactic context). Their information load is analyzed in (46).

(46)

	P	V
Number of words	6	1,000
Probability of each word	1/6	1/1,000
Information of each word	low	high

In this case, the information load of an average verb far exceeds that of an average preposition. The example explains a well-known stress difference between functional (or closed-class) words and lexical (or open-class) words. A functional word is usually unstressed, because its information load is low. In contrast, the information load of a lexical word is high, and so it is usually stressed.

The Information-Stress Principle can also explain a well-known correlation between frequency and reduction, namely, frequent word tend to undergo stress loss and vowel reduction more often than infrequent words (Bybee 2001). For example, the second syllable is unstressed and reduced in *information* but not in *importation*, because *information* is a frequent word while *importation* is not. Similarly, the word *trombone* is an infrequent word for non-musicians, and so the first vowel is stressed and unreduced; for trombonists, on the other hand, the word is frequent and so the first vowel is unstressed and reduced. In the present analysis, a frequent word has less information, and so it tends to have less stress and is more likely to undergo reduction.

The Information-Stress Principle also points to a default rule for compound and phrasal stress. Consider phrasal stress first. A typical phrase has the structure [X YP] (or [YP X]), where X is the syntactic head and YP the syntactic nonhead. In standard X-bar syntax, the head is an element at the word (or affix) level, and the nonhead is an element at the phrase level. Since there are more possible phrases than possible words (or affixes), the occurrence of a nonhead (phrase) is less predictable than the occurrence of a head (word or affix). For example, consider a hypothetical language that has 1000 verbs and 1000 nouns. In a verb phrase [V NP], supposing the NP is made of up to two words (say an [N N] compound), the probabilities of an average V and an average NP can be calculated and are shown in (47).

(47)

	V	NP (up to [N N] compounds)
Number of forms	1,000	1,000 x 1,000
Probability of each form	1/1,000	1/1,000,000

Clearly, the probability of an average NP is far smaller than that of an average V, and so the information load of an average NP is far greater than an average V (in a real language the difference is even greater, because a real language typically has more nouns than verbs, and an NP can contain more than two words). By the Information-Stress Principle, therefore, the default phrasal stress should go to NP, which is the case in English (and in Chinese, to be exemplified below). By the same argument, in any phrase [X YP], phrasal stress should go to YP.

The analysis of compound stress is similar. In English, an [N1 N2] compound is parallel to a [YP X] phrase, where N1 is the counter-part of YP and N2 the counter-part of X. Therefore, N1 should receive compound stress, which is true in typical [N N] compounds in English.

The phrasal stress rule and compound stress rule are originally given as two separate rules in Chomsky and Halle (1968), which are also assumed in Halle and Vergnaud (1987). In the present analysis, they are related, namely, in both cases the syntactic nonhead is assigned stress. The unified rule is called Nonhead Stress, first proposed in Duanmu (1990) and repeated in (48), which ultimately derives from the Information-Stress Principle.

(48) Nonhead Stress:
In the syntactic structure [X YP (or [YP X]), where X is the syntactic head and YP the syntactic nonhead, YP should be stressed.

In (49) I compare Chomsky and Halle's analysis with the Nonhead Stress analysis. For clarity syntactic heads are underlined and relative stress among stressed elements is ignored.

(49)	Syntax	Nonhead Stress	Chomsky and Halle
	[V N]	buy CARS	(same)
	[P N]	in SCHOOL	(same)
	[N N]	WRIST-watch	(same)
	[N [N N]]	GOLD WRIST-watch	(same)
	[[N N] N]	WRIST-watch store	WRIST-watch STORE
	[N [V N]]	COWS eat GRASS	(same)
	[N [A [V N]]	COWS OFTEN eat GRASS	(same)
	[D N]	the CAR	(same)
	[N's N]	JOHN 's FRIEND	John's FRIEND
	[A (F) N]	RED (F) CARS	red CARS

In some cases, such as [N [N N]] and [N [V N]], Chomsky and Halle assign stress to more than one word. In the first seven structures, the syntactic heads are as traditionally understood. In [D N] the syntactic head is D, following Abney (1987). In [N's N] the syntactic head is the possessive {*s*}. The noun phrase [A N] is [A (F) N], where the syntactic head is the inflectional element {F}. This follows from the view that noun phrases are headed by a functional element, not always present in English but required in some other languages (Ritter 1991, Cinque 1993). For example, the Chinese counterpart to an English [A N] phrase is [A *de* N], where the head *de* is a functional element (Dai 1992, Duanmu 2000).

In most cases the analyses predict similar results. Where they differ, the Nonhead Stress analysis seems to be more accurate. For example, in [N's N] and [A N], both words have stress in the Nonhead Stress analysis, in agreement with the traditional judgment (Kenyon and Knott 1944, Jones 1950). Similarly, as Hayes (1995: 373-382) argues, in structures like [[N N] N] and [[[N N] N] N], no stress should be assigned after the main stress (here the first N). Finally, the present analysis agrees with the observation that verbs are less likely to be stressed than nouns (Ladd 1980: 90-92, Hayes 1995: 376). This is because (a) verbs often occur as syntactic heads, which do not receive Nonhead Stress, and (b) there are usually more nouns than verbs in a language, and so an average noun carries more information than an average verb.

The idea that there might be a universal rule for compound and phrasal stress has been proposed in different forms by Cinque (1993) and Zubizarreta (1998). According to them, the degree of stress is related to the depth of a syntactic tree: the deeper a branch, the more stress it has. Since a syntactic head generally does not branch, and the syntactic nonhead is a phrase, which can always branch, the syntactic nonhead is generally deeper and has more stress than the syntactic head. Thus, their theories predict similar stress patterns as Nonhead Stress.

5.1.2. Stress in Chinese

As in English, word stress in Chinese is unpredictable. For example, Mandarin has stressed monosyllabic words, such as *ma3* 'horse', and unstressed monosyllabic words, such as the progressive marker *zhe0* 'be doing'. Stress in bisyllabic words is also unpredictable. For example, some Mandarin words are heavy-heavy (both stressed), such as *fan1-qie2* 'tomato' and *ku3-gua1* 'bitter melon', whereas others are heavy-light (stressed-unstressed), such as *luo2-bo0* 'turnip' and *huang2-gua0* 'yellow melon (cucumber)'. Indeed, there are minimal pairs that are distinguished by stress alone, such as those in (50). The vowel difference in the monosyllabic pair is due to reduction in the unstressed word.

(50) Minimal pairs contrasted by stress

Monosyllabic	Heavy	Light
	zhao2 着	zhe0 着
	'contact'	'be doing'
Bisyllabic	Heavy-Heavy	Heavy-Light
	da4-yi4 大意	da4-yi0 大意
	'main idea'	'careless'
	bao1-han2 包含	bao1-han0 包涵
	'include'	'forgiving'

Moreover, word stress can vary from speaker to speaker, or from dialect to dialect. For example, As Li (1981: 37) points out, 'cotton' can be heard as *mian2-hua1* (heavy-heavy) or *mian2-hua0* (heavy-light) from Mandarin newsreaders. Similarly, *xi1-gua0* 'watermelon' is heavy-light in Beijing Mandarin, but *xi1-gua1* or heavy-heavy in Taiwanese Mandarin. (Some studies, such as Hoa 1983, further distinguish two kinds of heavy-heavy patterns: medium-heavy vs. heavy-medium. However, I agree with Chao 1968 that such a distinction is hard to verify.)

One might argue that the difference between the word pairs in (50) is not due to stress but due to the presence or absence of tone. If so, Chinese does not have lexical stress. This proposal has two shortcomings. First, it must explain why toneless syllables are phonetically unstressed (see below). Second, stress must be assumed for Chinese anyway, if not for word stress, at least for phrasal stress. So there is little theoretical gain in not recognizing word stress.

The phonetic difference between stressed and unstressed syllables in Chinese is very clear to native speakers. Indeed, the phonetic cues are similar to those in English (Fry 1955, 1958). Consider the examples in (51) and (52).

(51) English heavy-light

	Pe-	*ter*	'Peter'
Length	long	short	
Reduction	no	yes	
Tone	yes	no	

(52) Mandarin heavy-light (Pinyin: *ba4-ba0*, via reduplication of *ba4*)

	paa-	*pə*	'dad'
Length	long	short	
Reduction	no	yes	
Tone	yes	no	

In English, the heavy syllable is longer, has an unreduced vowel, and a tone (what is called 'pitch accent' in intonational phonology; Pierrehumbert 1980). In contrast, the weak syllable is short, has a reduced vowel, and no pitch accent. Similarly, in Chinese, the heavy syllable is longer, has an unreduced vowel, and a lexical tone, whereas the weak syllable is short, has a reduced vowel, and no lexical tone (Lin and Yan 1988). Thus, in both languages the difference between the two syllables is clear.

If the manifestation of stress is similar in English and Chinese, why then is there a popular view that Chinese has no stress? There seems to be three reasons. First, many words in Chinese are monosyllabic, and stress is usually more obvious in a polysyllabic word (i.e. when stressed and unstressed syllables occur next to each other). Second, minimal pairs in which stress is contrastive are not many. According to Li (1981: 37), there are some 30,000 bisyllabic words (including compounds) in a large Mandarin dictionary, and about 2,000 are clearly heavy-light. Of those about 100 pairs are contrasted by stress, and only half of those show 'large semantic differences' between each pair (for example, 'wife/woman' probably shows a small semantic difference and 'include/forgiving' probably shows a large semantic difference). In other words, stress contrast plays only a minor role in the Chinese lexicon. The third reason is that the stress difference between the two syllables in a heavy-heavy word is often not as obvious as that in English. Consider the examples in (53) and (54).

(53) English heavy-heavy: stress is clear

	meat	*ball*
Length	long	long
Reduction	no	no
Tone	yes	no

(54) Mandarin heavy-heavy: stress is less clear

	'meat	ball'
	rou4	*wan2*
Length	long	long
Reduction	no	no
Tone	yes	yes

In English, both syllables are long and have unreduced vowels. However, the first syllable also has a pitch accent, whereas the second does not. Thus, the stress difference is still quite clear. In Mandarin, both syllables are long and have unreduced vowels. In addition, both have lexical tones. Thus, the stress difference is much less obvious than that in English. It is interesting to compare the Chinese example in (54) with the English example in (55).

(55) English heavy-heavy: stress is less clear

	Red	*Cross*
Length	long	long
Reduction	no	no
Tone	yes	yes

In this case both words have pitch accents, and so their stress difference is less obvious than that in *meat ball*. According to Kenyon and Knott (1944) and Jones (1950), in expressions like *Red Cross* and *real deal*, the two words have equal stress, which is similar to the case of heavy-heavy words in Mandarin.

There is a further similarity between English and Chinese that is worth pointing out. Some scholars, such as Chomsky and Halle (1968), consider the second syllable in *Red Cross* to have more stress when the expression occurs in final position, but not when it occurs in non-final position. This is shown in (56).

```
(56)                                  x
              x             x         x
          x   x             x    x    x
        Red Cross          Red Cross office
```

Interestingly, the same proposal has been made for Mandarin (Chao 1968, Xu 1982, and Hoa 1983), which is illustrated in (57).

```
(57)                                  x
              x             x         x
          x   x             x    x    x
        rou4 wan2          rou4 wan2 tang1
        'meat ball'        'meat ball soup'
```

According to Hoa (1983), examples like (57) involve a rule that reverses the stress in a syntactic unit that is not final. In particular, Hoa assumes that compound and phrasal stress in Chinese is right-headed, or MS (medium-strong), following Chao (1968). The underlying stress for 'meat ball soup' is [[MS] S]. However, a nonfinal syntactic unit must undergo stress reversal, so that [[MS] S] becomes [[SM] S], where the final S is stronger than the initial S. Similarly, in *Beijing Daxue* 'Peking University', [[MS][MS] becomes [[SM][MS]]. One might suggest that perhaps stress reversal is unnecessary; all we need is a template MS or MWS (medium-weak-strong), regardless of inner syntax. Thus, 'meat ball' is MS, 'meat ball soup' is MWS, and 'Peking University' is MWWS. However, as Hoa (1983) argues, inner syntax is clearly relevant. For example, *Beijing Dongwuyuan* 'Peking Zoo' is [MW MWS], not [MW WWS] (unless in fast speech, perhaps), and *dongwuyuan damen* 'zoo entrance' is [MWW MS], not [MWW WS].

It is obvious that most people agree that stress is left-headed except for the final syllable. I suggest that the perceived extra stress on the final syllable is due to the pause that follows (and perhaps also to the boundary tone), which can lengthen the final syllable (Klatt 1975, 1976 for English; Lin et al 1984, Yan and Lin 1988, Yang 1992 for Chinese). It is worth noting that in Chinese, although the final syllable has longer duration, the first syllable has greater amplitude and higher F0 peak (Lin et al 1984, Yan and Lin 1988, Yang 1992). In view of such considerations, I analyze (57) in (58).

```
(58)   x                  x                        Foot stress
       ( x    x+  )       ( x    x    x+   )       Syllable stress
       rou4 wan2 Ø        rou4 wan2 tang1 Ø
       'meat ball'        'meat ball soup'
```

In both expressions, compound stress goes to the initial syllable (the syntactic nonhead), and so there is one syllabic foot, shown in parentheses. In addition, since each syllable is heavy, it is a moraic trochee and has its own stress (this is the 'dual-trochee' analysis introduced in Duanmu 1999). The final syllable is longer (indicated as x+) because of the following pause Ø. Now x+ may be perceived as having more stress than the initial syllable, even though the initial syllable has greater amplitude and F0 peak, but the difference is small. On the other hand, both the initial syllable and the final syllable should be perceived as being stronger than the medial syllable.

There is a popular assumption that stress (or accent) is an abstract notion that can be realized differently in different languages (e.g. Hayes 1995:5, Kaji 1999: 217). The above discussion shows that, as far as English and Chinese are concerned, there is no evidence for this assumption, because there is no fundamental difference in the phonetic realization of stress.

5.1.3. Foot formation and T3S

Let us now consider the formation of syllabic feet in Chinese (ignoring moraic feet for now) and the application of T3S. I assume the analysis in (59) and (60).

(59) Syllabic foot formation in Chinese:
In compounds and phrases, assign Nonhead Stress.
A foot has at least two syllables, with stress on the first syllable.
For free syllables and flat structures, build binary feet from left to right.

(60) Application of T3S:
Apply T3S cyclically from within each foot and upward.
T3S is optional between two cyclic domains.

The analysis predicts that a bisyllabic word or compound forms a foot, and a polysyllabic word or a sequence of digits form binary feet from left to right. Next consider a [V O] phrase, shown in (61), where parentheses indicate foot boundaries and vertical lines indicate the cyclic domain of T3S.

```
(61)          x
      | mai3  (hao3    shu1) |     →     2 3 1
       [buy   [good    book]]
      'to buy good books'
```

In the object, Nonhead Stress goes to 'good'. In [V O], Nonhead Stress goes to the object, which already has stress. Now consider T3S, which starts from within the foot; since 'book' is not T3, T3S has no effect. Next, T3S applies to the next node up, which is between 'buy' and 'good', giving [2 3]. The analysis shows that for T3S to apply, the two syllables need not be in the same foot. However, all three syllables are in the domain of T3S, even though the first is outside the foot. Next consider the example in (62), where | is a cyclic domain boundary.

```
(62)  x                       x
      (wo3  xiang3)  | mai3  (hao3  jiu3) →    2 3 3 2 3 (or 2 2 3 2 3)
      [I    [want     [buy   [good  wine]]]]
      'I want to buy good wine'
```

In ‘good wine’, Nonhead Stress goes to ‘good’. In ‘buy good wine’, Nonhead Stress goes to ‘good wine’, which already has stress. In ‘want buy good wine’, Nonhead Stress goes to ‘buy good wine’, which is already stressed. The subject ‘I’ is a pronoun, which may or may not receive Nonhead Stress. If it does not, it can still form a foot with the next syllable, via the left-to-right foot formation rule. Next consider T3S. The first foot forms its own domain. For the second foot, T3S produces 2-3 in the first step; the next step up is between ‘buy’ and ‘good book’, where T3S need not apply, because ‘hao’ has already changed to T2. This ends the second domain. Now, both ‘want’ and ‘buy’ are still T3, but they are in different domains. Therefore, T3S occurrs optionally between them. Next consider the compounds in (63) and (64).

(63)   x
     | (zhan-lan   guan   li) |
     [[exhibition   hall]   inside]
     ‘inside of exhibition hall’

(64)   x   x   x   x
     xiao   zhi   lao-hu   → | (xiao zhi lao-hu) |
     [small [paper [old-tiger]]]
     ‘small paper tiger’

In (63) the word ‘exhibition’ has initial stress. On the next two cycles, the syntactic nonhead is on the left, so stress should be on the left, which is already true. The result is one foot, which coincides with a cyclic T3S domain. In (64), the compound ‘old tiger’ first gets initial stress. On the next two cycles, the syntactic nonhead is on the left, so stress should be assigned to the left. This gives three adjacent stresses. However, since a foot needs at least two syllables, the three stresses cannot all remain. I assume that in this case only the initial stress is kept, because it is the ultimate syntactic nonhead. It is worth noting that in (63) and (64) there are no free syllables. Next consider the phrases in (65) and (66).

(65)   x   x
     |(gou   bi) | (ma   xiao) |
     [dog   [[than   horse] small]]
     ‘Dogs are smaller than horses’

(66)   x   x   x   x   x
     gou   hen hao   yang → |gou (hen hao yang)| or |(gou Ø)|(hen hao yang)|
     [dog [[very good] raise]]
     ‘Dogs are very easy to raise’

In (65), the innermost structure is ‘than horse’, where Nonhead Stress goes to ‘horse’. In the VP, V is the syntactic head, so Nonhead Stress goes to the adverbial, which is already stressed. Finally, the subject is not the syntactic head of the sentence, so it has stress, too. The two stresses create two feet. In (66), the innermost structure is ‘very good’, where Nonhead Stress goes to ‘very’. In the VP, V is the syntactic head, so Nonhead Stress goes to the adverbial, which is already stressed. Finally, the subject is not the syntactic head of the sentence, so it has stress, too. Furthermore, 'dog' is a monosyllable and cannot form a foot by itself. It can either lose its stress, or it can keep its stress and form a foot with a pause (which is available between the subject and the object, I assume). Either way, the domains are different from those in (65). Finally, consider the effect of emphatic (or contrastive) stress, shown in (67) and (68).

(67)
x　　　　　x
| (xiang mai) | (gu-piao) |
[want [buy stock]]
'want to buy stocks'

(68)
　　　x　　x　　　　　　　　　x
xiang MAI gu-piao → | xiang (MAI gu-piao) |
[want [buy stock]]
'want to BUY stocks'

In (67), 'stock' forms a foot, with stress on the first syllable. In 'buy stock', Nonhead Stress goes to 'stock', which is already stressed. Finally, 'want' gets stress from left-to-right foot formation. So there are two feet. In (68), 'want' has emphatic stress, which can override that on 'stock'. Thus, there is one foot. The verb 'ant' is outside the foot, yet it is in the same cyclic domain, because T3S can apply beyond the foot.

5.1.4. Comparison of domains

I have shown earlier that the domains of tone sandhi are often different in Shanghai, Mandarin, and Xiamen. Now if compound and phrasal stress are the same for all languages, as I have suggested, foot formation should be, too. How then do we explain the differences in the tone sandhi domains? I suggest that the same set of information is present for all the dialects, but Shanghai, Mandarin, and Xiamen make use of different aspects of the information for their tone sandhi. In particular, I suggest (69).

(69) Boundaries for tone sandhi:

Shanghai:	Foot boundaries
Mandarin:	Cyclic domain (a foot plus adjacent free syllables)
Xiamen:	Pre-pause heavy syllable

The examples below show the analysis of sandhi domains for the three dialects, where parentheses indicate foot boundaries, Ø indicates a functional element or a pause, and | indicates boundaries in Mandarin and Xiamen.

(70)
[[Old Li] [often [drink [rice wine]]]]
　x　　　x　　　　x
[[老 李] Ø [经常 [喝 [米 酒]]]] Ø
Shanghai ( ) ( ) ( )
Mandarin | | | |
Xiamen | | |

```
(71)                [[Old Li]  [like  [Shaoxin's [rice wine]]]]
                      x          x     x          x
                    [[老  李] Ø [喜欢 [绍兴  的 Ø [米  酒]]]] Ø
      Shanghai      (        )  (    )(        )  (      )
      Mandarin      |        |        |        |         |
      Xiamen        |        |                 |         |

(72)                [Sarajevo     [is-in  Yugoslavia]]
                      x    x            x    x
                    [萨拉 热窝 Ø [在    南斯 拉夫]] Ø
      Shanghai      (    )(    )       (    )(    )
      Mandarin      |    |     |            |     |
      Xiamen        |          |                  |

(73)             a.  fry  rice (phrase)        b.  fry rice (compound)
                           x                        x
                     炒  饭 Ø                       炒  饭  Ø
      Shanghai         (   )                       (      )
      Mandarin       |     |                       |      |
      Xiamen         |     |                       |      |
```

The above analysis differs from the view that dialects can have different rules for foot formation. Instead, all dialects have the same foot formation process. Dialects can use different boundaries for tone sandhi not because there is a typology of foot formation but because the dialects have different kinds of tone sandhi. In particular, the tone sandhi in Shanghai involves tone deletion from unstressed syllables, and therefore the domains are strictly foot-based. (The fact that tone deletion happens in Shanghai but not in Mandarin or Xiamen is due to another reason. According to Duanmu (1990, 1999), Shanghai syllables are all CV and not inherently heavy. They receive stress primarily through Nonhead Stress. In contrast, most Mandarin and Xiamen syllables are inherently heavy (CVX), and each can form a bimoraic foot and has its own stress even without Nonhead Stress.) The tone sandhi in Mandarin does not involve tone deletion, and so it can continue beyond a foot. Finally, the tone sandhi in Xiamen does not depend on the tones of neighboring syllables but only on whether a position is pre-pausal. Therefore, except when foot boundaries create pauses in a deliberated style, feet are mostly irrelevant.

5.1.5. Further evidence for the stress-based analysis

The present analysis can also account for a number of word length effects, discussed in Duanmu (2000). A peculiar property of Chinese is that many words have two forms, a long bisyllabic form and a short monosyllabic form. Some examples are shown in (74), where the redundant word in the long form is shown in parentheses in the gloss.

(74)

Long	Short	Gloss
ji-shu	ji	'skill-(trick)'
gong-ren	gong	'worker-(person)'
shou-biao	biao	'(hand)-watch'

gong-chang	chang	'(work)-factory'
zhong-zhi	zhong	'to plant-(plant)'
da-suan	suan	'(big)-garlic'
shang-dian	dian	'(business)-store'
shu-cai	cai	'(vegetable)-vegetable'

If each word has two forms, a two-word compound should have four combinations. However, in a noun-noun compound, only three of the combinations are good. An example is shown in (75), where 1 is a monosyllabic word and 2 is a bisyllabic word.

(75) [noun noun]
 2-2 ji-shu gong-ren
 2-1 ji-shu gong
 *1-2 * ji gong-ren
 1-1 ji gong
 'skilled worker'

Similarly, in a verb-object phrase, three combinations are generally good and one is bad, as shown in (76), where '?' indicates a marginal form.

(76) [verb object]
 2-2 zhong-zhi da-suan
 *2-1 zhong-zhi suan
 1-2 zhong da-suan
 ?1-1 zhong suan
 'to plant garlic'

In the present analysis, the word length effects are due to foot structure. Consider the analysis in (77), where S is a stressed syllable and s is an unstressed syllable. By Nonhead Stress the first noun is always stressed. The second noun is stressed if it is bisyllabic.

(77) [noun noun]
 2-2 (Ss)-(Ss)
 2-1 (Ss-s)
 *1-2 (S)-(Ss) first foot not binarity
 1-1 (S-s)

The problematic case is [1-2], where the first syllable has stress but is too short to be a foot (it is possible to delete the stress from the second noun so that the compound forms one foot, but the preferred solution seems to be to choose a bisyllabic first noun, or to choose a monosyllabic second noun). Next consider [V O], analyzed in (78). By Nonhead Stress the object is always stressed. The verb is stressed if it is bisyllabic.

(78) [verb object]
 2-2 (Ss)-(Ss)
 *2-1 (Ss)-(SØ)
 1-2 s-(Ss)
 ?1-1 s-(SØ)

Here the problematic case in [2-1]. Intuitively, the problem is that the object has more stress than the verb (because the nonhead has more information than the head), and so the object should not be shorter than the verb (because length is a major aspect in the manifestation of stress). Another way to look at it, suggested by Burzio (1994), is that a strong foot (one with two or more syllables) has greater attraction for stress than a weak foot (one with one syllable), and so the object will lose main stress to the verb.

Another set of word length effects are also discussed in Duanmu (2000) and illustrated in the examples in (79), where VV is a bisyllabic verb, V a monosyllabic verb, OO a bisyllabic logical object of the verb, and O a monosyllabic logical object of the verb.

(79)

[[OO VV] NN] xiao-mai shou-ge ji-qi wheat harvest machine 'wheat-harvesting machine'	*[[VV OO] NN] shou-ge xiao-mai ji-qi
[[V O] NN] ge mai ji-qi harvest wheat machine 'wheat-harvesting machine'	*[[O V] NN] mai ge ji-qi
*[[VV O] NN] shou-ge mai ji-qi harvest wheat machine 'wheat-harvesting machine'	*[[O VV] NN] mai shou-ge ji-qi

In general, when the verb and the object are both bisyllabic, their order must be [OO VV]. When they are both monosyllabic, their order must be [V O]. When the object is monosyllabic and the verb bisyllabic, neither word order is good. Some exceptions can be found; for example, when N is *zhe3* 者 'person/the one', both [OO VV N] and [VV OO N] can be used (He 2004). But for most N and NN the general patterns are as in (79).

In the present analysis (slightly different from that of Duanmu 2000), [[VV OO] NN] is bad because [VV OO] is a phrase, which should not occur inside a compound. On the other hand, [V O] can form a foot (as most bisyllabic structures can), and hence a compound, because a foot can shield the syntactic information inside it, so that it is treated as a word. This is called the 'Foot Shelter' effect in Duanmu (2000), which is supported by the fact that exocentric compounds, such as *huo-shao* 'fire-burn (baked wheaten cake)' and *kai-guan* 'open-close (switch)', occur only in bisyllabic structures. Next, [[VV O] NN] is bad because [VV O] is a phrase (and a bad phrase, see above), which is too long for a foot to shield its internal structure, and so it cannot occur inside a compound. Finally, [[O VV] NN] is bad because [O VV] is [1-2], which is a bad length structure for compounds (see above).

5.1.6. Summary

I have offered an analysis in which all dialects have the same foot formation process. Therefore, there is no need to assume that there are different foot types in Chinese dialects (Duanmu 1995, Iwata 2001). It is also worth pointing out that the predicted stress positions (the first syllable of a foot) agree with phonetic facts and other intuitive descriptions. For example, Zhu (1995) found that the rime of the foot initial syllable in Shanghai is phonetically nearly twice as long as that of noninitial syllables. In addition, Chao (1968), Xu (1982), and Hoa (1983) give similar judgments for stressed positions in Mandarin as the present analysis predicts (except for the pre-pause syllable, which is influenced by boundary effects). Finally, the present analysis follows a general theory of stress, and there is no need to make additional assumptions for grammatical words, pronouns, or the influence of emphatic/contrastive stress.

5.2. Chen (2000)

The analysis of Chen (2000) is an extension of Shih (1986) and is shared by Dell (2004). It makes the assumptions in (80) and (81).

(80) Foot formation in Mandarin (ordered steps):
  a. Grammatical words cliticize to the nearest lexical words.
  b. Feet are formed cyclically for compounds.
  c. Form a binary foot for the innermost bisyllabic unit.
  d. Start a foot boundary before emphatic/contrastive stress.
  e. Form feet left-to-right for free syllables.
  f. Join stray syllables with the nearest foot.

(81) Application of T3S:
  A T3S domain is a foot.
  T3S is optional between two feet.

The main difference between Chen's analysis and mine is that for Chen foot formation does not depend on stress. For example, in Chen's analysis a foot can be (s S), (S s), (s S s), (S s S), etc., where S is a stressed syllable and s is an unstressed one. For this reason, Chen introduces a new term—the 'minimal rhythmic unit' (MRU)—for what is traditionally called a syllabic foot (e.g. Chen 1979, Shih 1986), but it does not change the fact that the MRU is a new phonological entity. In addition, Chen needs separate assumptions to account for the difference between grammatical words and lexical words, and for the influence of emphatic/contrastive stress.

It can be shown that if we omit (80f), then Chen's MRUs mostly correspond to the feet in my analysis. Consider the examples in (82).

(82)

	Present analysis	Chen's analysis
	| mai (hao shu) |	(mai (hao shu))
	[buy [good book]]	[buy [good book]]
	'to buy good books'	'to buy good books'

| (wu-wu)-wu | ((wu-wu)-wu)
'five-five-five'   'five-five-five'

In the [V O] case, both analyses build a foot for 'good book'. In the present analysis, the verb remains outside the foot; it undergoes T3S not because it is in the same foot as the object but because T3S can apply beyond a foot. In Chen's analysis, the foot can have two (or more) layers; the object is in the inner layer and the verb is in the outer layer. Similarly, in 'five-five-five', both analyses build a foot for the first two syllables. In the present analysis, the third syllable remains outside the foot, but in Chen's analysis it is in the outer layer of a nested foot. In summary, Chen's analysis assumes that all syllables must belong to a foot; as a result, foot types are rather complicated. In contrast, the present analysis assumes that some syllables can remain unfooted, and all feet are consistently left-headed.

5.3. Wang (2004)

Wang (2004) does not discuss T3S but does discuss foot formation. Her analysis of is summarized in (83), which echoes a similar proposal by Lu (1989).

(83) Syllables form feet according to their syntactic 'closeness'.
Syllables that are syntactically close belong to the same foot.
Syllables that are not syntactically close belong to different feet.
A final syllable may appear to have more stress, owing to boundary effects.

Wang argues that in languages like English, stress is lexically distinctive, and so foot formation is based on stress assignment. In contrast, in languages like Chinese, stress is not lexically distinctive, and so foot formation is not based on stress assignment, but based on the syntactic closeness between syllables. Some syllables may appear to have more stress, such as those before a pause, but the stress effect is secondary and has no bearing on foot formation.

There are some problems in this analysis. First, it probably overstates the fact that stress is lexically distinctive in English. For example, it can be argued that pairs like *import-import* are not distinguished by stress but by word categories (noun vs. verb), and word categories in turn has affected stress. If so, there are not many word pairs in English that are distinguished by stress alone. Second, it downplays the fact that stress can be lexically distinctive in some Chinese word pairs. Third, it does not explain how feet are formed in polysyllabic words or flat structures (such as a string of digits). Fourth, it seems to overlook the many similarities between English and Chinese that I have discussed above. In any case, Wang does not offer many examples and so it is hard to evaluate her analysis in detail.

5.4. Feng (2004)

Like Chen (2000) and Wang (2004), Feng (2004) does not believe that stress plays a role in foot formation in Chinese. His analysis is given in (84).

(84) Every bisyllabic unit forms a foot, whether it is a word or a phase.
In words and compounds, build bisyllabic feet from left to right.
In phrases, build bisyllabic feet from right to left.

Feng does not discuss T3S, but does discuss some word length effects. His analysis of [N N] and [V O] are shown in (85) and (86), where S represents a syllable and # is a word boundary.

(85) [N N] compounds: L→R foot formation

2-2	(SS)#(SS)	
2-1	(SS)#S	
*1-2	(S#S)S	foot boundary not aligned with word boundary (?)
1-1	(S#S)	

(86) [verb object]: R→L foot formation

2-2	(SS)#(SS)	
*2-1	S(S#S)	foot boundary not aligned with word boundary (?)
1-2	S#(SS)	
?1-1	(S#S)	

Feng says that [1-2] does not fit left-to-right foot formation and [2-1] does not fit right-to-left foot formation. However, the precise reason for the violation is not discussed. Clearly, it is not because the foot contains a word boundary, since [1-1] is fine. Perhaps the foot boundary must be aligned with a word boundary? The answer is also no, because in polysyllabic words the foot boundary need not align with a word boundary, as shown in (87).

(87) (duomi)(nijia) 'Dominica'
(jieke)(siluo)(fake) 'Czechoslovakia'

Consider also the example in (88), which is an actual name of a park.

(88) (Shijing#Shan)#(Gongyuan) *(Shijing)#(Shan#Gong)yuan
[[Shijing Mountain] Park]

If we apply left to right foot formation, the result is (SS)#(S#S)S, which is incorrect. The correct foot structure is (SS#S)#(SS). Perhaps what Feng wants to say is something like (89).

(89) Feet are built cyclically, first for words and then for compounds and phrases.
In words and compounds, there cannot be a free syllable on the left.
In phrases, there cannot be a free syllable on the right.

But why is there such a difference between words and phrases? Feng (1998) suggests that left-to-right foot formation is the most 'natural' process for words, but one wonders why it is not the case for English words (consider *potato, America, Chicago, Japan*, etc.), where the foot does not start from the left. Nor is there an obvious reason why foot formation for phrases should be right-to-left. On the other hand, if foot formation is based on stress, there is an explanation. In a compound, Nonhead Stress is on the left, and so it should start with a bisyllabic foot. In [V O], Nonhead Stress is on O, and so it should end in a bisyllabic word.

Feng (2004) raises two questions for the stress-based analysis. First, Feng points out that some bisyllabic compounds have initial stress, such as *zhuo1-zi0* 'table', and some have final stress, such as *ying2-hang2* 'bank'. If they both form one foot, stress cannot be relevant. However, as I have discussed above, compounds like *ying2-hang2* 'bank' are heavy-heavy, which appear to have final stress only before a pause. Otherwise, they have initial stress, as do heavy-light compounds, such as *zhuo1-zi0* 'table'. It is worth noting that there are no light-heavy compounds, which follows from an analysis that assumes left-headed feet, but not from an analysis that allows right-headed feet. Second, Feng points out that in a [[V O] NN], compound, [V O] is a foot, yet according to Nonhead Stress, O has more stress, which is inconsistent with left-headed feet. The answer to this problem is that a foot can shield its internal syntax, so that the bisyllabic [V O] is treated as a word in this environment, and thus Nonhead Stress does not apply. The supporting evidence is that, while in a [V O] phrase O indeed has more stress than V, in [[V O] NN] V has more stress than O. Thus, neither of Feng's criticisms of the stress-based analysis seems compelling.

6. Concluding remarks

I have discussed some patterns of tone sandhi in Chinese and argued that a full understanding of tonal phenomena requires an understanding of stress. In addition, I have offered a general stress theory and shown that it plays a key role in foot formation and the syntax-phonology interface, without additional assumptions for grammatical words, pronouns, or the influence of emphatic or contrastive stress. Moreover, I have argued that different kinds of tone sandhi need not imply different rules for foot formation. Rather, different kinds of tone sandhi may be conditioned by different parts of a general prosodic structure, which are present in all dialects.

Many linguists still doubt that foot formation in Chinese is based on stress, but there seems to be little evidence for the alternatives (See Duanmu 2004 for more discussion). It is worth noting that the predicted stress positions in the present analysis agree with phonetic facts and other intuitive descriptions. If the present analysis is correct, it supports the view that tone and stress can exist in the same language (Liberman 1975, Pierrehumbert 1980, Goldsmith 1981), and offers a demonstration in a true tone language. Hopefully, it can help resolve similar controversies in Japanese and African languages (Odden 1999, Kaji 1999), and offer an alternative approach to the syntax-phonology interaction within them (Odden 1987, 1995).

*Acknowledgments: For helpful comments and discussions, I thank the audience at the 2004 *Symposium on Cross-Linguistic Studies of Tonal Phenomena* in Tokyo, and in particular my discussant Professor Ray Iwata. I also thank Professor Shigeki Kaji and other organizers for hosting the symposium.

References

Abney, Steven. 1987. *The English noun phrase in its sentential aspect.* PhD dissertation, MIT.

Burling, Robbins. 1966. The metrics of children's verse: a cross-linguistic study. American Anthropologist 68: 1418-1441.

Burzio, Luigi. 1994. Principles of English stress. Cambridge, UK: Cambridge University Press.

Bybee, Joan. 2001. Phonology and language use. (Cambridge Studies in Linguistics 94.) Cambridge: Cambridge University Press.

Chao, Yuen-Ren. 1968. *A Grammar of Spoken Chinese*. Berkeley, California: University of California Press.

Chen, Matthew. 1979. Metrical structure: Evidence from Chinese poetry. Linguistic Inquiry 10:371-420.

Chen, Matthew. 1987. The syntax of Xiamen tone sandhi. Phonology Yearbook 4:109-149.

Chen, Matthew. 2000. *Tone Sandhi: Patterns across Chinese Dialects.* Cambridge Studies in Linguistics, No. 92. Cambridge, UK: Cambridge University Press.

Cheng, Chin-Chuan. 1968. English stress and Chinese tones in Chinese sentences. *Phonetica* 18:77-88.

Chomsky, Noam, and Morris Halle. 1968. *The sound pattern of English.* New York: Harper and Row.

Cinque, Guglielmo. 1993. A null theory of phrase and compound stress. Linguistic Inquiry 24.2:239-297.

Dai, John Xiangling. 1992. *Chinese morphology and its interface with the syntax*. PhD dissertation, Ohio State University, Columbus.

Dell, François. 2004. On unwarranted claims about stress and tone in Beijing Mandarin. Cahiers de Linguistique Asie Orientale (Paris). 33.1: 33-63.

Duanmu, San. 1990. A formal study of syllable, tone, stress and domain in Chinese languages. Doctoral dissertation, MIT, Cambridge, Mass. Distributed by MIT Working Papers in Linguistics.

Duanmu, San. 1995. Metrical and tonal phonology of compounds in two Chinese dialects. Language 71.2: 225-259.

Duanmu, San. 1997. Recursive constraint evaluation in Optimality Theory: evidence from cyclic compounds in Shanghai. NLLT 15: 465-507.

Duanmu, San. 1999. Metrical Structure and Tone: Evidence from Mandarin and Shanghai. *Journal of East Asian Linguistics* 8.1: 1-38.

Duanmu, San. 2000. *The Phonology of Standard Chinese*. Oxford: Oxford University Press.

Duanmu, San. 2004. Left-headed feet and phrasal stress in Chinese. *Cahiers de Linguistique Asie Orientale* 33.1:65-103.

Feng, Shengli. 1998. Lun Hanyu de "ziran yinbu" [On "natural feet" in Chinese]. Zhongguo Yuwen 1998.1 (262): 40-47.

Feng, Shengli. 2004. Dong bin daozhi yu yunlu goucifa [Verb-object inversion and prosodic morphology]. Yuyan Kexue [Linguistic Science] 3.3 (May 2004): 12-20.

Fry, Dennis B. 1955. Duration and intensity as physical correlates of linguistic stress. JASA 27:765-768.

Fry, Dennis B. 1958. Experiments in the perception of stress. Language and Speech 1:126-152.
Giegerich, Heinz. 1985. Metrical phonology and phonological structure: German and English. Cambridge, UK: Cambridge University Press.
Goldsmith, John. 1981. English as a tone language. *Phonology in the 1980's*, ed. by Didier L. Goyvaerts, 287-308. Ghent, Belgium: E. Story-Scientia.
Halle, Morris, and Jean-Roger Vergnaud. 1987. *An Essay on Stress*. Cambridge, Mass.: MIT Press.
Hayes, Bruce. 1995. *Metrical Stress Theory: Principles and Case Studies*. Chicago: University of Chicago Press.
He, Yuanjian. 2004. The loop theory in Chinese morphology. Contemporary Linguistics 6.3: 223-235. [何元建 2004, "回环理论与汉语构词法",《当代语言学》第 3 期.]
Hoa, Monique. 1983. *L'accentuation en pékinois*. Paris: Editions Langages Croisés. Distributed by Centre de Recherches Linguistiques sur l'Asie Orientale, Paris.
Hyman, Larry. 1977. On the nature of linguistic stress. *Studies in stress and accent*, ed. by Larry Hyman, 37-82. Southern California Occasional Papers in Linguistics 4. Los Angeles: Department of Linguistics, University of Southern California.
Iwata, Ray. 1999. Comments on Prof. Shi's paper "A tone sandhi in Chinese northern dialects". In Proceedings of the Symposium "Cross-Linguistic Studies of Tonal Phenomena: Tonogenesis, Japanese Accentology, and Related Topics", ed. Kaji, Shigeki, 121-125. Tokyo: Institute for the Study of Languages and Cultures of Asia and Africa, Tokyo University of Foreign Studies.
Iwata, Ray. 2001. Tone and accent in the Chinese dialects. In Proceedings of the Symposium "Cross-Linguistic Studies of Tonal Phenomena: Tonogenesis, Japanese Accentology, and Other Topics", ed. Kaji, Shigeki, 267-291. Tokyo: Institute for the Study of Languages and Cultures of Asia and Africa, Tokyo University of Foreign Studies.
Jones, Daniel. 1950. *The pronunciation of English*. 3rd edition. Cambridge: Cambridge University Press.
Kaji, Shigeki. 1999. Comments on David Odden's paper. In Proceedings of the Symposium "Cross-Linguistic Studies of Tonal Phenomena, Tonogenesis, Japanese Accentology, and Related Topics", ed. Kaji, Shigeki, 217-219. Tokyo: Institute for the Study of Languages and Cultures of Asia and Africa, Tokyo University of Foreign Studies.
Kenyon, John Samuel, and Thomas Albert Knott. 1944. *A pronouncing dictionary of American English*. Springfield: Merriam.
Klatt, Dennis H. 1975. Vowel lengthening is syntactically determined in a connected discourse. Journal of Phonetics 3.3:129-140.
Klatt, Dennis H. 1976. Linguistic uses of segmental duration in English: Acoustic and perceptual evidence. Journal of the Acoustical Society of America 59.5:1208-1221.
Ladd, Dwight Robert. 1980. The Structure of intonational meaning: evidence from English. Bloomington: Indiana University Press.
Li, Weimin. 1981. Shi lun qingsheng he zhongyin [A preliminary discussion on stressless and stressed syllables]. Zhongguo Yuwen 1981.1:35-40.
Liberman, Mark. 1975. *The Intonational System of English*. Cambridge: MIT dissertation.

Lin, Jo-wang. 1994. Lexical government and tone group formation in Xiamen Chinese. Phonology 11: 237-275.
Lin, Maocan, and Jingzhu Yan. 1988. The characteristic features of the final reduction in the neutral-tone syllable of Beijing Mandarin. *Phonetic Laboratory Annual Report of Phonetic Research*, 37-51. Beijing: Phonetic Laboratory, Institute of Linguistics, Chinese Academy of Social Sciences.
Lin, Maocan , Jingzhu Yan, and Guohua Sun. 1984. Beijinghua liangzizu zhengchang zhongyin de chubu shiyan [Preliminary experiments on the normal stress in Beijing disyllables]. Fangyan 1984.1:57-73.
Lu, Bingfu. 1989. Jiegou, jiezou, songjin, qingzhong zai Hanyu zhong de xianghu zuoyong [The interactions among structure, rhythm, closeness, and heaviness in Chinese]. Hanyu Xuexi 3:25-29.
Pierrehumbert, Janet. 1980. The phonetics and phonology of English intonation. Doctoral dissertation, MIT, Cambridge, Mass.
Odden, David. 1987. Kimatumbi phrasal phonology. Phonology 4.13-36.
Odden, David. 1995. Phonology at the phrasal level in Bantu. In Bantu phonology and morphology, ed. Francis Katamba. München: LINCOM EUROPA.
Odden, David. 1999. Typological issues in tone and stress in Bantu. In Proceedings of the Symposium "Cross-Linguistic Studies of Tonal Phenomena, Tonogenesis, Japanese Accentology, and Related Topics", ed. Kaji, Shigeki, 187-215. Tokyo: Institute for the Study of Languages and Cultures of Asia and Africa, Tokyo University of Foreign Studies.
Ritter, Elizabeth. 1991. Two functional categories in noun phrases: evidence from Modern Hebrew. In Susan D. Rothstein (ed.) *Perspectives on phrase structure: heads and licensing*. Syntax and Semantics 25. San Diego: Academic. 37-62.
Selkirk, Elisabeth and Tong Shen. 1990. Prosodic domains in Shanghai Chinese. *The Phonology-Syntax Connection*, ed. by Sharon Inkelas and Draga Zec, 313-337. CSLI, Stanford University, Stanford, Calif. Distributed by University of Chicago Press.
Shannon, Claude E. 1948. The mathematical theory of communication. *Bell System Technical Journal* 27: 379-423 and 623-656, July and October.
Shen, Jiong. 1994. Beijinghua shangsheng liandu de diaoxing zuhe he jiezou xingshi [Tonal patterns and rhythmic structure in successive third tones in the Beijing dialect]. Zhongguo Yuwen 1994.4: 274-281.
Shih, Chi-lin. 1986. The prosodic domain of tone sandhi in Chinese. Doctoral dissertation, University of California, San Diego.
Wang, Hongjun. 2004. Shilun hanyu de jiezou leixing—songjin xing [On the metrical type of Modern Standard Chinese—a type based on looseness]. Yuyan Kexue [Linguistic Science] 3.3 (May 2004): 21-28.
Xu, Shirong. 1982. Shuangyinjie ci de yinliang fenxi [A quantitative analysis of disyllabic words]. Yuyan Jiaoxue Yu Yanjiu 1982.2: 4-19.
Yan, Jingzhu, and Maocan Lin. 1988. Beijinghua sanzizu zhongyin de shengxue biaoxian [Acoustic characteristics of the stress in Beijing trisyllables]. Fangyan 1988.3: 227-237.
Yang, Shun-an. 1992. Beijinghua duoyinjie zuhe yunlu tezheng de shiyan yanjiu [An experiment on the prosody of polysyllables in the Beijing dialect]. Fangyan 1992.2: 128-137.

Yue-Hashimoto, Anne O. 1987. Tone sandhi across Chinese dialects. In Wang Li memorial volumes: Chinese volume, ed. by Chinese Language Society of Hong Kong, 445-474. Hong Kong: Joint Publishing Co.
Zhu, Xiaonong. 1995. *Shanghai Tonetics*. Canberra: Australian National University dissertation.
Zubizarreta, Maria Luisa. 1998. Prosody, Focus, and Word Order. [Linguistic Inquiry Monograph 33] Cambridge, MA: MIT Press.

Comments on "The Tone-Syntax Interface in Chinese: Some Recent Controversies" by San Duanmu

IWATA, Ray (Kanazawa University)

1. Introduction

Since scientific studies on Chinese dialects restarted in 1979 in Mainland China after a long term of absence, so called "tone sandhi" has been an issue of great concern among linguists. Reflecting a growing amount of descriptive studies on this issue, two papers were presented at earlier symposiums of *Cross-Linguistic Studies of Tonal Phenomena*. At the first symposium, Shi Feng demonstrated that Third Tone Sandhi (T3S), a well known tone sandhi in Beijing Mandarin (BM), has spread all over north China (Shi 1999). At the second symposium, I discussed the typology of Chinese tone sandhi from the aspect of tonal neutralization (Iwata 2001a, and subsequently in Iwata 2001b). I argued that almost all tone sandhi phenomena so far witnessed in the Chinese dialects come under one of four types of tonal neutralization. There are other important works which attempt to describe tone sandhi typology for various Chinese dialects, notably, Yue-Hashimoto (1987) and Wei (2000). But a crucial problem unanswered in these studies, as well as in my own, was how sandhi domains are formed; in other words, how can we predict the domain of tone sandhi in terms of the tone-syntax interface. In this respect, it is worth referring to two distinguished works in the field of theoretical linguistics: one is by Matthew Chen (notably Chen 2000), and another, by the present author, San Duanmu.

2. Left-headed feet

The kernel notion of Duanmu's present paper, "left-headed foot theory", was extensively discussed for BM in the book, *The Phonology of Standard Chinese* (PSC). Two basic assumptions proposed are the following.

1) A polysyllabic word forms syllabic trochees from left to right.
2) Stress in compounds and phrases is determined cyclically by Nonhead Stress, which requires the syntactic nonhead to have more stress than the syntactic head.

The present paper is an extension of this theory to cover such dialects as Shanghai and Xiamen, aimed at proving the universal role of stress in foot formation and the phonology-syntax interface. Duanmu's arguments are accessible to readers who are unfamiliar with the evidence in Chinese dialects as well as to those who are unfamiliar with the theoretical issues of contemporary phonology. Indeed, this is a simple theory, but it still requires setting up such extra devices as empty syllables (empty beat; zero syllable), and even more crucially, my concern is that this theory may give the readers a somewhat different image of Chinese prosody from that we Chinese linguistic students have learned up until now. For the readers in the theoretical field, it is worth referring to the recent criticism on PSC offered by François Dell as well as to the rejoinder by Duanmu (Dell 2004, Duanmu 2004). In this commentary, I would like to offer some evidence which may be contradictory to the author's theory and to propose alternative accounts from typological perspectives. Readers are warned that my approach to Chinese prosody is based on traditional structuralism and does not involve a metrical analysis, but at relevant points, I will discuss the issues in metrical terms.

Hereafter, example numbers appearing on Duanmu's paper will be indicated in italics, and these will be rearranged together with my examples.

3. Stress in Beijing Mandarin (BM) [1]

Although all Chinese dialects have phonetic stress, the use of lexical stress does not seem to be that widespread in modern dialects.[2]

Let us begin with examining the case of the BM monosyllables cited in (*50*).

	Heavy	Light
(1)	zhao2 着	zhe0 着
	'contact'	'be doing'

The author treats this pair as being distinguished by stress alone. But we are equally privileged to ascribe this distinction to a tone difference, namely, to consider the progressive marker "zhe0" as having *zero tone*. A light syllable cannot carry a full tone but can carry a default tone (conventionally called "neutral tone" or "light tone"). Yip (1980) argues for the phonetic feature of the neutral tone syllable as having [-Upper] register, and to my knowledge, this feature is shared by many Chinese dialects (Iwata, 1999, 2001a).

Morphologically, "zhao2" is either free or bound while "zhe0" is always a bound enclitic to the verb or adjective. Here are two more parallel instances, among many others.

---

1 The term "Mandarin" seems to be employed by Duanmu rather loosely to cover such a variety as "Taiwanese Mandarin", but it should not be confused with Beijing mandarin (BM) and the other Mandarins. Otherwise, we are not speaking from the same basis. In line with Dell (2004: fn.2), I will use the term BM to avoid confusion.

2 In Iwata (2001a, b), I argued for the distinction between right-stressed and left-stressed types, and argued for the coexistence of both types in the majority of Chinese dialects. This stress typology was proposed mainly in view of comparative tonology and accentology, assuming that the main contributor to producing the difference in the type of tone sandhi is stress accent. However, this assumption was apparently faulty in terms of synchronic phonology, and the role of stress should be examined for each dialect. A revised version of my view appeared in Iwata (2004).

(2) “tou2” 头 ‘head’ e.g., “tou2 teng2” ‘head ache’, “ma3 tou2” ‘horse head’
“tou0” 头 ‘suffix’ e.g., “shi2 tou0” ‘stone’, “ma3 tou0” ‘harbor’

(3) “sheng1” 生 ‘to live’ or ‘to cause’ or ‘raw’
e.g., “sheng1 bing4” ‘to get sick’, “sheng1 yu2” ‘raw fish’
“sheng0” 生 ‘suffix’ e.g., “xue2 sheng0” ‘student’, “yi1 sheng0” ‘medical doctor’

Note that the author treats the Xiamen expression “bue nng kun” in a similar way as I do here ((*8*) and (*25*)).

(4)	T’ T’ T	T 0 0
	bue nng kun	bue nng kun
	‘buy two pounds’	‘buy some’

Likewise, the BM disyllabic minimal pair cited in (*50*) can be presented as follows.

(5)	T’ T	T 0
	da4 yi4	da4 yi0
	‘main idea’	‘careless’

Phonetically, in “da4 yi4”, the second syllable is stressed and an iambic *MS* pattern is formed (M: medium, S: strong); whereas in “da4 yi0”, the second syllable is unstressed with its tonal feature reduced, resulting in a trochaic *SW* pattern (W: weak). Note that previous studies dealing with stress in BM, including Duanmu (2000), distinguish at least three stress levels, S, M and W.

According to Duanmu, “da4 yi4” in (5), as well as “ma3 tou2” ‘horse head’ in (2), will be analyzed as follows (refer to the analysis shown as (*58*)).

(6)
X
(X X+)
da4 yi4 Ø

Due to the requirement of the syntactic nonhead stress rule, the compound stress in this case goes to the first syllable “da4” ‘main’, but the actual output is “medium-strong”. The author believes that this contradiction is resolved by setting up the empty syllable Ø. However, the setup of such a technical device will be problematic, as pointed out by Dell (2004:55-56). Phonetically, although it is true that phrase or sentence-final positions are often associated with some characteristic laryngeal gestures indicating end of utterance, such features are likely to be influenced by such factors as speech tempo and *real* phonetic pause, and consequently, are unstable (Iwata et al.,1990).

The alternative assumption proposed here does not assume any extra device, neither stress nor empty syllable. It treats "da4 yi0" as a phonological word and treats "da4 yi4" as a phonological compound. As for the latter, there is no need to argue for syntactic nonhead stress, rather it is assumed that the formation of the iambic *MS* pattern is an automatic process in BM disyllabic compounds. As a matter of fact, this particular pattern is consistently observed regardless of the syntactic construction of the given expression. For instance, "da4 yi4" 'main idea' is a [MN] compound (M: modifier; N: modified noun), while "mai3 ma3" 'to buy a horse' is a [VO] phrase, but evidently both show the MS pattern.

In trisyllabic compounds, there usually appears a *MWS* pattern, again regardless of the structure of the given expression (examples from Duanmu's (*9*)).

(7) [[zhan3 lan3] guan3] 'exhibition hall' [MN] compound (Left branching)
[[mai3 hao3] jiu3] 'finished buying wine' [VO] phrase (Left branching)

Here, however, the difference in the branching type is salient and in the right branching structure the stress pattern could be rearranged so that stress is occasionally put on the second syllable, conforming to Duanmu's theory (example (*62*)).

X
(8) [mai3 [hao3 jiu3]] 'to buy good wine' (Right branching)

Importantly, this difference is reflected in that of T3S realization, as is demonstrated in the examples *(9)-(13)*. However, a normal and much more frequent stress pattern in BM is MWS, if there emerges no such syntactic factor blocking its realization (Chao1968:35). Let us compare the [MN] compound "[[zhan3 lan3] guan3]" (exhibition hall) with the following compound, which has the same construction [MN] but shows right branching.

(9) [da4 [xue2 sheng1]] 'university student' (Right branching)

The stress pattern in this expression is identical with that in "zhan3 lan3 guan3", namely the MWS pattern. What is of interest here is the fact that the word for 'student' is usually uttered as "xue2 sheng0", with a reduced second syllable, if it stands alone. Then, the question becomes how the left stressed "xue2-sheng0" can succeed in being converted into the right stressed "da4 xue2 sheng1". According to Duanmu's theory, the only possible output of (9) will be left stressed, (10), and this does not conform to the evidence.[3]

---

[3] This expression (9) would be realized as left stressed only when an occasional contrastive stress is put

(10) X

X X

[da4 [xue2 sheng1]]

Parallel instances are not scarce (from Hirayama 1992:247).

(11) "zhi1 <u>dao0</u>" 'to know' → "bu4 zhi1 <u>dao4</u>" 'not know'

(12) "kan4 <u>jian0</u>" 'to see' → "kan4 bu0 <u>jian4</u>" 'unable to see'

In both cases, the right stressed MWS pattern is derived from the disyllabic left stressed SW pattern, by adding a negative "bu4" in initial position for (11), and for (12) by inserting this morpheme "bu4" between the first verb "kan4"('look') and the complement "jian4"('see'). This indicates that the stress pattern is blind to the internal constructions of compounds and phrases and that the formation of the MWS pattern is an automatic process in trisyllabic sequences (refer to Duanmu's discussion concerning his example (57)). This rule is also applicable to quadrisyllabic expressions, where a *MWWS* pattern is formed (Chao 1968: 206).

(13) "gan1 <u>jing0</u>" 'clean' → "gan1 gan0 jing0 <u>jing4</u>" 'perfectly clean'

The disyllabic form "gan1 jing0" can also be uttered in the MS pattern "gan1 jing4". But whether the stress pattern of the disyllabic adjective XY is SW or MS, it always acquires the pattern MWWS in the derivation process into the reduplicated XXYY. Here second and third syllables undergo a considerable degree of tonal and segmental reductions.

These are just some typical instances, and there is a strong tendency in BM that compounds and phrases are uttered in the M(W)(W)S pattern. This particular stress pattern is phonologically interpreted as /W(W)(W)S/, where the initial syllable automatically resumes its stress to medium degree, the so-called *determined feature* in structural linguistics (Hockett 1947, Matsumoto 1960).

Based on these observations, and if we follow a metrical analysis, the afore-cited assumptions proposed by Duanmu for BM are fully modified as follows.

(i) Polysyllabic words are always left-stressed; in other words, where there is a left-stressed foot (mostly trochaic or dactylic), it is a word.

(ii) A polysyllabic compound or phrase forms a right stressed foot, in which the initial syllable automatically resumes its stress.

---

on the first syllable, namely, 'not a high school student but a UNIVERSITY student'.

It is necessary to add three notes here.

1) The distinction between *word* and *compound* is salient. A word is defined phonologically either as a monosyllabic syllable which has a full tone of its own (T) or a polysyllabic sequence which has one full tone followed by one or more zero (default) tones (T...). This implies that (T) and (T...) are phonological equivalents and both carry *word tones*. All the other sequences are treated as phonological compounds.

2) Phonologically, there is no need to argue about the syllable weight since the stressed syllable is always heavy and the unstressed one, always light. Furthermore, since the stressed syllable always stands in initial position in words and it always stands in final position in compounds, we need not assume the phonological role of stress either.

3) A polysyllabic word is predictable to a certain extent by its morphological structure. For example, such sequences containing enclitics are words (refer to Xu 1956 for details). But there are many others which are unpredictable, just as monosyllabic words, and have to be recorded individually in the lexicon, e.g., (11) "zhi1 dao0", (12) "kan4 jian0" and (13) "gan1 jing0". It is worth noting that all polysyllabic words could potentially be compounds, i.e., right-stressed. Thus, the final morphemes in (11), (12), (13) resume their original tones when they meet with any morphological or syntactic requirement, namely, addition or insertion of the negative marker "bu4" for (11) and (12), reduplication for (13), so that the final syllable in "xue2 sheng0" resumes its original tone by adding the non-head "da4" ('big').

Consequently, a conclusive statement is that assumption (ii) predominates assumption (i). That is to say, the formation of phonological compounds is a fundamental process that could change even the stress pattern of the inner structure of the compound.

The assumptions stated above are based on the *word tone* theory proposed by Hayata (1999a, b), which can well account for the tonal and accentual phenomena observable in East Asia, including Japan, Korea and China. A word tone language is defined by Hayata as having an invariable number of tones, regardless of the length of the word. BM has four lexical tones, so four tones always appear in polysyllabic phonological words. In Kagoshima Japanese, there are always two tones regardless of the number of syllables contained in a word. The same is true for Kyoto Japanese, but the accentual distinction is coexistent with the tonal distinction.

The *word tone* theory also points out a general tendency of accentual shift observable in these languages, as defined by A1+A2 →A2, which means a predominance of the final component in the accentual realization in compounds. My assumption stated in (ii) above conforms to this typological evidence.

This commentary so far has focused on demonstrating that stress is not employed distinctively in BM. In fact, BM seems to be a language that uses compound stress distinctively. The fact that Duanmu seems to have disregarded or underestimated is the existence of the opposition between "medium-strong" vs. "strong-medium". He mentioned that such a distinction is hard to verify. Indeed, the distinction is hard to perceive in tone languages, where the F0 contour, the most important cue for stress distinction, is masked, as pointed out by Duanmu (Duanmu 2000:143). But this can not be equated with denying the existence of a such contrast. I myself have never observed the opposition between "medium-strong" and "strong-medium", but it must not be a mere accident that researchers in various areas, Matsumoto (1960), Xu (1980), Yin (1982), Hoa (1983) and Kratochvil (1987), share a common view with regard to the particular opposition. The following pair is from Matsumoto (1960:5).

(14) Medium-strong "ban4 tian1" 'half day'
Strong-medium "hou4 tian1" 'the day after tomorrow'

From a comparative point of view, there are grounds that Common Mandarin and Common Wu used compound stress distinctively, as was argued by Hirayama (1992) and Iwata (1999), and the distinction has disappeared or is going to disappear as *word tone* develops in these dialects. Therefore, the present topic needs to be investigated synchronically in a socio-linguistic perspective.

4. Stress in Shanghai (SH)

The two assumptions, (i) and (ii), stipulated for BM in the preceding section, are applicable to SH, though a certain modification is needed.

To begin with, a minimal pair in SH appearing in (15) is treated the same way as BM *without* assuming the role of stress (Duanmu's example (*14*)).

(15) ts^ho3 ve0 'fried rice'(noun) / ts^ho3 ve2 'to fry rice'(verb phrase)

It is assumed that SH tone sandhi rather faithfully reflects such information as the distinction between MN and VO constructions, namely, the former generally forms phonological words while the latter forms compounds. So in (15), the first expression "ts^ho3 ve0" (MN) is a word, while the second expression "ts^ho3 ve2" (VO) is a compound.

In SH, the tones of all non-initial syllables within a word, (usually less than three), automatically change to zero, and phonetically the polysyllabic word tone exhibits the five tone system, corresponding to the monosyllabic word tone.[4] A difference between SH and BM word tone is shown below with the actual tone contours indicated in a five point scale.

[4] In mainstream SH, phonetically there exist five lexical tones, but there are only two phonological tones. Firstly, this is due to the retention of the voice/voiceless distinction in the initial consonants, which enables us to erase the distinction between Tones 2, 4 and Tones 3, 5; and secondly, it is due to the retention of syllable final glottal stop, which enables us to erase the distinction between Tones 1,2,3 and Tones 4,5. Phonetically, Tone 2 and Tone 3 are MH and LM, respectively, but Duanmu describes Tones 2 and 3 likewise as LH or L in his example (*14*), probably due to this consideration. But note that Duanmu's L and H are the underlying representations corresponding to LH and HL, not denoting the default tone.

(16) BM "xue2 sheng0" 'student' /high-rising/-o → [35-2]
SH "ts^{h}o2 ve0" 'fried rice' /high-rising/-o → [33-44]

In SH, the tonal feature of the first syllable spreads into the second syllable (actually not to the third syllable and after that, the syllables assume the default value), while in BM it generally remains within the first syllable. But note that Tone 3 in BM evidently behaves like the tones in SH (refer to Iwata 1999: 278, for details).

(17) ma3 tou0 'harbor' /low-rising/-o → [21-4]

SH compounds have a peculiarity, which seems to be disregarded in Duanmu's presentation. Concerning the compound "ts^{h}o3 ve2" ('to fry rice'), an important fact is that the tone of the first syllable usually assumes the default pitch level (i.e., zero tone) and does not take the original [LH] or [L] (to be precise, [MH], cf. fn.4). According to Xu & Tang (1988), the exact tone contour for 'to fry rice' is [**44** 23]. Seemingly, this evidence does not attract the attention of the theoretical linguists engaging in SH phonology, but it is exactly the phenomenon reported by Kennedy (1953) for the Tangxi dialect and is witnessed in many other Wu dialects as well (Wang 1996:55-58). Duanmu says, "The first word 'fry' will form another kind of domain by itself – a bimoraic foot as a heavy syllable (instead of a bisyllabic foot)". However, the fact is that the first word takes the default tone; therefore, it is unlikely that the first syllable "ts^{h}o" forms a bimoraic foot by itself. I do not necessarily support the moraic analysis of Chinese. However, logically a more appropriate account would seem to be the foot formation [m.(mm)] for the compound "ts^{h}o3 ve2" ('to fry rice'), in contrast with that of [(mm).m] for the word ts^{h}o3 ve0 'fried rice'. Thus, it would seem there must be two types of metrical feet in SH, left-stressed and right-stressed.

(18)			
	X	X	
	|ts^{h}o ve|	|ts^{h}o | ve|	Word boundary
	(ts^{h}o ve)	(ts^{h}o ve)	Foot boundary
	'fried rice'	'to fry rice'	

Though it is still unclear what factors trigger the pre-attached default tone, it eventually signals the word boundary, as does the formation of a phonological compound. In this case, it reflects the formation of a [V O] compound. It is noted, however, that the compounds with VO construction have a tendency to be uttered with a word tone as well, conceivably reflecting a tendency of change from compound to word, so that the expression for 'to fry rice' has two alternative readings, right-stressed [44 23] and left-stressed [33 44] (Xu & Tang, 1988: 49).

It seems that any sequence of two words could trigger the pre-attached default tone. The following sentence is a quotation from the transcription of a colloquial conversation cited in Xu & Tang (1988:551).[5]

(19) ŋo | iɪʔ zəʔ | ɕiaN | lA | ɦA | məʔ | zən kuɑN | lE   Word boundary
ŋo (iɪʔ zəʔ) (ɕiaN lA) ɦA (məʔ zən kuɑN) lE   Foot boundary
{ŋo} {iɪʔ zəʔ} {ɕiaN lA} {ɦA} {məʔ zən kuɑN} {lE}   Compound boundary
'I' 'all the time' 'want' 'come' 'yet' ' no' 'time' 'come'
'I have long wanted to come, yet have had no time to come'

The disyllabic word "iɪʔ zəʔ" forms the left-headed foot, while the succession of the two monosyllabic words "ɕiaN" and "lA" forms the right-headed foot. In the expression "məʔ zən kuɑN", the negative marker "məʔ", which in metrical terms is a *heavy syllable* if it stands alone, is changed to a light syllable carrying the default tone, once it is added to the word "zən kuɑN" 'time'. The tone contour in this phrase is [**22** 22 44], in which the tonal realization of "zən kuɑN" is unaffected, but the tone of the first syllable assumes the default value [**22**].[6] The only possible account for the evidence is to assume a metrical foot (. X .), which, however, is not permitted according to Duanmu's principles (*31*) and (*32*).[7]

Much longer compounds can be formed in SH, as illustrated in Duanmu's examples (*28*) and (*29*). Two more examples are quoted from Xu & Tang (1988: 42, 46). Here, I will not adopt the metrical analysis. T, T' and 0 denote the full tone, modified tone and the zero tone (default tone) respectively, and the phonetic outputs are shown in a five point scale with the pre-attached default tone indicated in bold.

(20) T | T | T | T | T → {0 0 0 0 T} [**44 33 44 44** 23]
"iɪʔ | liɑN | sE | sɿ | ɦŋ" 'one, two, three, four, five'

(21) T 0 | T 0 | T 0 | T 0 | T → {T' 0 T' 0 T' 0 T} [55 **33** 22 **33** 22 **33** 55]
"tsoŋ ɦo | zən min | goŋ ɦu | koʔ" 'People's Republic of China'

Example (20) demonstrates the leveling effect which is caused by the sequence of default

---

5 Due to the font problem, the nasalization of vowel is indicated here by adding syllable final "N".

6 This value [22] is actually a conditional variant of [44] appearing in the first syllable of the phrase 'to fry rice'. The pre-attached default tone in SH is realized phonetically either as [44], [33] or [22]. It is realized as a higher pitch, [44], if it is associated with the syllable initiated by voiceless initials, while it is either [33] or [22], if it is associated with the syllable initiated by voiced initials (see fn. 4). In the case of voiced initiation, it is [22] in the staccato syllable ending in glottal stop (e.g., "məʔ"), while it is [33] in the legato syllable not ending in glottal stop (e.g., "liaN", which will appear in the example (20) below). It is also variable depending on the position of its appearance within a compound. See Xu & Tang (1988: 26 -27) for details.

7 Parallel examples with this are not scarce in BM, e.g., "da4 gu1 niang0" ('unmarried woman'), which shows the MSW pattern of stress.

tones emergent in the non-final syllables. What is phonologically relevant here is the role of the final full tone "T".

Example (21) is the case of the pre-attached default tone which blocks the right spreading of the tone "T" in each word. If this expression "tsoŋ ɦo | zən min | goŋ ɦu | koʔ" is realized as a simple succession of four feet, the output values must be [55 **21** | 22 **44** | 22 **44** | 55], but actually it can be uttered as [55 **33** 22 **33** 22 **33** 55], in which only the tone of the final word keeps its underlying form and the rest are modified. Here, each pre-attached default tone functions in combining the two words before and after it, so that eventually all four words become integrated into one compound. Along these lines, it will be worth referring to the expression "iʔ pe zo" 'a cup of tea', which is cited in Duanmu's example (*34*). Duanmu analyzes this as (X .)(X Ø). But the unstressed syllable "pe" (classifier) *could* be uttered in the pre-attached default tone, so that the tone of this phrase can surface as [33 **33** 23], instead of [33 **44** 23], which is the only output predictable from Duanmu's analysis.

Based on these analyses, the afore-mentioned assumptions are modified as conformed to the evidence in SH.

(i) Polysyllabic words are always left-stressed; in other words, a left-stressed foot indicates a word.
(ii) A polysyllabic compound *could* form a right-stressed foot, in which the non-final syllable(s) assume(s) the default tone.
(iii) The compound boundary is indicated by the occurrence of a full tone (final tone), which can be followed by the zero tone(s).

Here again, I argue for the view that there is no need to assume the role of stress, for which we cannot find any reliable phonetic grounds in SH. A widely prevailing view for SH, i.e., the stress-sensitive nature of SH tone sandhi, should be reexamined by taking the pre-attached default tone into account.

5. Other issues

5.1. Neutralization and tone sandhi

Duanmu rejects the view that tone sandhi is a tonal neutralization process occurring with unstressed syllables. Indeed, some types of neutralization occur at unreduced positions. A typical instance is a well-known consonant neutralization in BM, where the three-way distinction of the syllable initial consonants, /z,c,s/,/zh,ch,sh/ and /g,k,h/, is neutralized into one /j,q,x/ on the condition that they precede the glide /-i-/ or /-y-/. In contrast, the German distinction between voiceless and voiced stops is neutralized to voiceless in word-final position, which apparently reflects a general tendency of syllable reduction toward the end of a word. T3S in BM belongs to this latter type of neutralization.

Based on the fact that the first syllable has more stress than the second one in a trisyllabic structure such as [[zhan3 lan3] guan3], Duanmu argues that T3S applies regardless of which syllable has more stress. However, his argument is misleading since trisyllabic compounds usually assume the MWS stress pattern (phonologically /WWS/) and the fact that both first and second syllables are relatively weaker than the final one may well explain the reason why they undergo T3S.

Duanmu also mentions that T3S applies even if the first syllable has contrastive or emphatic stress. However, this is the evidence that is compatible with the neutralization theory. It is taken for granted that the tone sandhi rule is usually applied prior to occasional stress, since it is a more intrinsic prosodic feature in the language.

5.2. Tone sandhi domain

In section 5.1.4, Duanmu compares sandhi domains for the three dialects, BM, SH and Xiamen, and suggests (*69*).

Boundaries for tone sandhi:

Shanghai:	Foot boundaries
Mandarin:	Cyclic domain (a foot plus adjacent free syllables)
Xiamen:	Pre-pause heavy syllable

Duanmu mentions, “Dialects can use different boundaries for tone sandhi not because there is a typology of foot formation but because the dialects have different kinds of tone sandhi”. Indeed, what we see here are three types of tone sandhi that are quite different from each other. What is of relevance is to show the nature of such differences, and even more importantly, to see if any common mechanism is at work across the dialects.

First of all, what Duanmu calls “foot boundaries” for SH are word boundaries in my theory, and differ from the other two which are concerned with compound boundaries. Duanmu mentions, “In particular, the tone sandhi in Shanghai involves tone deletion from unstressed syllables, and therefore the domains are strictly foot-based”. However, BM and Xiamen words also involve tone deletion, as I discussed in the preceding section. All these are a matter of word tone.

Note that Duanmu’s SH tone sandhi refers exclusively to that of his left-stressed type; and that “final tone type”, namely the pre-attached default tone, is disregarded. This latter type, as well as tone sandhi in BM and Xiamen, is involved in the formation of phonological compounds. In these types, the length of a compound by definition is equal to the domain of the tone sandhi.

In the context-dependent type of tone sandhi, including T3S in BM, since tonal behaviors are sensitive to adjacent tones, tone sandhi domain is constructed cyclically from left to right unless any syntactic information blocks it. In the context-free type of tone sandhi, including the final tone type in SH and that in Xiamen, since tonal behaviors are not sensitive to adjacent tones, the tone sandhi domain has much reason to follow the constraints of syntactic information.

Readers will notice that SH compounds, as analyzed above, are actually analogous with the Xiamen p-phrase (*20*). A difference between the two dialects is that Xiamen tone sandhi is compulsory but that compound formation in SH depends heavily on the choice of how speakers demarcate the given utterance.

I surmise that such a difference may be better understood by examining the dialects, which lie somewhere in between Shanghai and Xiamen, and which show the characteristic features of the right dominant type of tone sandhi. It is expected that the "left-headed foot theory" will focus on accounting for the tone evidence in these dialects.

Acknowledgments: My sincere thanks to San Duanmu, from whom I learned a lot about contemporary theoretical phonology.

[REFERENCES]

Chao, Yuen-Ren (1968). *A Grammar of Spoken Chinese*. University of California Press (Berkeley).

Chen, Matthew (2000). *Tone Sandhi: Patterns across Chinese Dialects*. Cambridge Studies in Linguistics, No. 92, Cambridge University Press.

Dell, François (2004). On unwarranted claims about stress and tone in Beijing Mandarin. *Cahiers de Linguistique Asie Orientale* (Paris). 33-1.

Duanmu, San (2000). *The Phonology of Standard Chinese*. Oxford: Oxford University Press.

------------- (2004). Left-headed feet and phrasal stress in Chinese. *Cahiers de Linguistique Asie Orientale* 33-1.

Hoa, Monique (1983). *L'accentuation en pékinois*. Editions Langages Croisés (Centre de Recherches Linguistiques sur l'Asie Orientale, Paris).

Hayata,Teruhiro (1999a). Accent and Tone: Towards a General Theory of Prosody. S. Kaji ed., *Proceedings of the Symposium, Cross-Linguistic Studies of Tonal Phenomena, Tonogenesis, Typology, and Related Topics*, ILCAA (Tokyo University of Foreign Studies).

----------- (1999b). *Oncho no Typology*. [Typology of Tonal and Accentual Phenomena], Taishuukan Press.

Hirayama, Hisao (1992). Cong lishi guandian lun Wuyu biandiao he Beijing hua biandiao de guanxi. [On the relationship between tone sandhi in the Wu dialects and the neutral tone in Mandarin, from a historical perspetive], *Zhongguo Yuwen*, 1992-4.

Hocket, Charles (1947). Peiping Phonology. *Journal of the American Oriental Society* 67.

Iwata, Ray (1999). Lun Beijing Fangyan he Lianyungang Fangyan de Gaojiang Qingsheng ji qi Lishi Hanyi. [On the high falling neutral tone in the dialect of Beijing and Lianyungang: synchronic characteristics, historical implications and its typological affinity with the Wu tone sandhi], In S.Wang et al., eds., *Selected papers from the Fifth International Conference on Chinese Linguistics*, The Crane Publishing. Co. (Taipei).

----------- (2001a). Tone and Accent in the Chinese dialects. S.Kaji ed., *Proceedings of the Symposium, Cross-Linguistic Studies of Tonal Phenomena, Tonogenesis,Japanese, Accentology and Other Topics*, ILCAA(Tokyo University of Foreign Studies).

----------- (2001b). Chuugokugo no Seicho to Accent. [Tone and Accent across the Chinesedialects], *Journal of the Phonetic Society of Japan*, Vol.5, No.1.

----------- (2004). Hanyu Fangyan Ci-shengdiao de Xingcheng ji Fazhan. [On the formation of the "word tone" and its development in Chinese dialects], F.Shi & Z-W. Shen ed. *The Joy of Research: A Festschrift in Honour of Professor Wiiliam S-Y.Wang on his Seventieth Birthday*, Nankai University Press.

Iwata, Ray, M. Sawashima, H. Hirose and S.Horiguchi (1990). Syllable final "glottal stop" in Chinese dialects -- A fiberoptic and electromyographic study. *Annual Bulletin, RILP*, No.24.

Kratochvil, Paul. (1987). Beijing hua Zhengchang Huayu li de Qingsheng. [The neutral tone in normal speech of the Beijing dialect], *Zhongguo Yuwen*, 1987-5.

Matsuomoto, Akira (1960). Pekingo Accent ni Kansuru Ichi Kousatsu. [A study on the accent in Pekinese], *Chuugoku Gogaku*, 100.

Shi, Feng (1999). A Tone Sandhi in Chinese Northern Dialects. S.Kaji ed., *Proceedings of the Symposium, Cross-Linguistic Studies of Tonal Phenomena, Tonogenesis, Typology and Related Topics*, ILCAA(Tokyo University of Foreign Studies).

Wang, Ping (1996). *Suzhou Fangyan Yuyin Yanjiu*. [A phonetic study of the Suzhou dialect], Huazhong University of Science & Technology Press.

Wei, Gang-Qiang (2000). Diaozhi de Qingsheng he Diaolei de Qingsheng. [The neutral tone in terms of phonetic value and of phonological category], *Fangyan*, 2000-1.

Xu, Shi-Rong (1956). Shuangyinzhuici de Zhonyin Guize. [Stress rules in disyllabic words], *Zhongguo Yuwen*, 1956-2.

------------ (1980). *Putonghua Yuyin Zhishi*. [Fundamental knowledge in Standard Chinese Phonetics], Wenzi Gaige Press.

Yin, Zuo-Yan (1982). Guanyu Putonghua Shuangyin Changyongci Qingzhongyin de Chubu kaocha. [A preliminary study of stress accent in disyllabic basic words in standard Chinese], *Zhongguo Yuwen*, 1982-3.

Yip, Moira (1980). *The tonal phonology of Chinese*. MIT dissertation.

Yue-Hashimoto, A. (1987). Tone sandhi across Chinese dialects. *Wang Li memorial volume*, Joint Publishing, Hong Kong.

Session 3

Descriptive Studies

Austroasiatic Tone Languages of the Tai Cultural Area

— From a typological study to a general theory of their tonal development —

Tadahiko L. A. Shintani
Research Institute for Languages and Cultures of Asia and Africa, Tokyo

Ⅰ. Introduction

The area we have named the "Tai Cultural Area" contains within it four major language groups: Tibeto-Burman (including Brakaloungic), Austroasiatic, Tai, and Chinese. (Maps 1 & 2) The area may also be home to an abundant number of languages which are still scientifically unknown. Our data-collecting activities, which began in 1974 and are still underway, have provided us with a lot of useful data to improve this situation, and it has now become possible to review the former studies done on the languages of the area within a new scientific framework. Since we already provided new perspectives on the Brakaloungic (Karenic) languages at this symposium two years ago[1], we will take this occasion to reconsider the existing published data through reference to the new materials we have collected on a certain number of Austroasiatic languages of the area, which we presume to recognize as tone languages, for the purpose of giving a tentative overview of the origin of tones among these languages.

Two main groups of the Northern Austroasiatic languages are found in the Tai Cultural Area: the Khamu and Palaung-Wa groups. In the Khamu languages, a two tone system developed through the transphonologization of an initial voiceless / voiced opposition to a tonal high / low opposition. Since this information was presented by Suwilai at this symposium two years ago[2], we will limit the following discussion to the Palaung-Wa language group.

II. *Tones* of the Palaung-Wa languages reexamined through new data

II.1. Riang

There exist two languages in the Riang group (Black Riang and White Striped Riang) around the areas of Panglong, Loi Lem, Nam Can, and Mong Nai, and these two dialects were recorded with tone marks for the first time by G. H. Luce[3]. Since these two dialects seem to be very close to each other at least with respect to tone, we will treat here only the Black Riang dialect on which we have new data of our own. Luce states in his paper that this language has two tones, high level and falling, which descend from original voiceless and voiced initials, respectively. Our data agrees with Luce on the matter of the number of tones (two tone system), almost agrees with him concerning the origin of these two tones, but does not agree with his description of the falling tone. Our data shows that Luce's high level tone corresponds to our high level tone [55], but that his falling tone corresponds to our low level [11] or sometimes slightly rising [12] tone. Even though Luce does not show any minimal tonal pairs, we can easily recognize the existence of two phonemic tones with the following examples[4]:

---

[1] Tadahiko L. A. Shintani (2003), "Classification of Brakaloungic (Karenic) languages in relation to their tonal evolution", Shigeki Kaji (ed.) (2003), *Cross-Linguistic Studies of Tonal Phenomena*, ILCAA, Tokyo, pp.37-54.

[2] Suwilai Premsrirat (2003), "Khamu dialects: a case of register complex and tonogenesis", Shigeki Kaji (ed.) (2003), ibid., pp.13-36.

[3] G. H. Luce (1965), "Danaw, a dying Austroasiatic language", *Lingua*, No.14, pp.98-129.

[4] These examples are from our own data, and not from Luce.

(1) < *voiceless initials / < *voiced initials

< *voiceless initials	< *voiced initials
sətuʔ55 *vegetables*	sətuʔ11 *silk / to wash*
lɛm55 *Quelcus glandulifera Bl.*	lɛm11 *tree trunk*
plaʔ55 *hoe*	plaʔ11 *to regret*
səki55 *handbag*	səki11 *to measure (rice)*

The high tone normally descends from original voiceless initials and the low tone from original voiced initials just as described by Luce; this is a case of transphonologization from an initial voiceless / voiced opposition to a tonal high / low opposition which is widespread in Asian languages. The following comparison with Ta'ang, which retains original voiced initials, can demonstrate such a tonal development[5]:

(2)

meaning (tone class)	Riang	Ta'ang
tongue (H)	tak55	ka ɗaaʔ
tooth (H)	raaŋ55	hraaŋ
they (L)	kəʔ11	gɛ
house (L)	kaŋ11	gaaŋ
pig (L)	lek11	leʔ
fire (L)	ŋal11	ŋar
etc.		

We are aware that the same pattern of tonal development has also been attested in Khamu[6], P'u-Man[7] and Lamet or Khamet[8] in the Tai Cultural Area. We can find at the same time some doubtful examples among the words given by Luce, as follows[9]:

(3) ɲaaŋ55 *spittle* (No corresponding voiceless initial is found.)
num11 *urine* (hnum in Ta'ang)
kəcoʔ11 *bamboo shoots* (No corresponding voiced initial is found.)

---

5 Ta'ang data is provided by our graduate school student, a native Palaung speaker from Nam San.
6 Suwilai Premsrirat (2003), ibid.
7 Raleigh Ferrell (1978), "Le P'u-Man, Langue Austroasiatique", *Bulletin de la Société de Linguistique de Paris*, Tome LXVI, Fasc.1, pp.405-412.
8 Lamet was presented as a tone language for the first time by Karl G. Izikowitz, and its tone system was described later by Yasuyuki Mitani. Karl G. Izikowitz (1951), *Lamet, Hill peasants in French Indochina*, Göteborg. Yasuyuki Mitani (1965), "Kameetogo no onsotaikei no kijutsu to hikakugengogaku teki koosatsu" (A descriptive and Comparative Study of the Khamet Phonology), *Toonan Ajia Kenkyuu* (Jurnal of South-East Asian Studies), Vol.3, No.3, pp.22-51.
9 Riang forms given here are from our own data, and not from Luce.

lu?55 *thread* (No corresponding voiceless initial is found.)
səŋi?55 *sun* (No corresponding voiceless initial is found.)
laŋ55 *price* (No corresponding voiceless initial is found.)
pru?11 *village* (No corresponding voiced initial is found.)
rɛ?55 *house post* (roŋ in Dar'ang)
kɤn11 tsan11 *sword* (can in Ta'ang)

II.2. Plang (Tai Loi)

Plang language data is available on four dialects: two dialects (Xinman'e 新曼俄 and Guanshuang 關双) recorded by Li Daoyong 李道勇, Nie Xizhen 聶錫珍, Qiu Efeng 邱鍔鋒[10], and two dialects (Kontoi and Samtao) recorded by ourselves in Ceng Tung (Kengtung). These four dialects are all tone languages, but the number of recognized tones is different. Since the two dialects we recorded are identical on the matter of tone, we will explain the tone system of the Kontoi dialect first, and then we will review the tone systems of the two dialects recorded by the Chinese scholars.

The Kontoi dialect has two phonemic tones, high (high rising) and low (falling), which we can recognize through the following minimal pairs:

(4)	raŋ35 *tooth*	raŋ341 *pine tree*
	məl35 *round*	məl341 *upside down*
	mi?35 *sugar cane*	mi?12 *man (male)*

The realization of the tones differs according to the syllable type, as follows:

(5)	-zero, -nasals, -l, -r	-p, -t, -c, -k, -?	-h
H	35	35	55
L	341	12	33

H means the syllables having original voiceless initial consonants, and L means the syllables having original voiced initial consonants. We are aware from the above table (5) that this is again a case of tonal development through the transphonologization from an initial voiceless / voiced opposition to a tonal high / low opposition, which is the same as Khamu, Riang, P'u-Man, and Lamet. We can demonstrate such tonal development by the following

[10] Li Daoyong 李道勇, Nie Xizhen 聶錫珍, Qiu Efeng 邱鍔鋒(eds.) (1986), *Bulangyu jianzhi* 布朗語簡志(Outline of the Plang language), Beijing.

comparison[11]:

(6)	meaning (tone class)	Plang	Parauk	Ta'ang
	hulled rice (H)	ŋgo35	gao̲ʔ	rə koo
	thatch grass (H)	plɔŋ35	—	plɔŋ
	thorn (H)	kat35	ka̲t	—
	buffalo (H)	akrak35	kɣa̲ʔ	kraaʔ
	bear (H)	khreh55	kɣi̲h	kreh
	man / male (L)	miʔ12	ʃi̲ meʔ	me
	flower (L)	tai341	tai	—
	fire (L)	ŋoal341	ŋu	ŋar
	pig (L)	lek12	lik	leʔ
	foam (L)	pɤh33	bae	buh

There exists an important feature to be mentioned concerning the tones of this language. The tonal opposition displayed here is significant only on the last syllable of words, phrases, or sentences, i. e. at the syllable just before pause, otherwise the tones are neutralized and realized monotonically. For example, raŋ35 *tooth* and raŋ341 *pine tree* are tonally opposed when they are pronounced in isolation, but if they are followed by the word ən341 *he*, /raŋ35 ən341/ *his tooth* and /raŋ341 ən341/ *his pine tree* are pronounced the same: raŋ33 ən341 *his tooth* and raŋ33 ən341 *his pine tree*, respectively.

Another important feature to be noted is that the tonal opposition is significant in this language only in syllables having sonorant initials, because the other initials, in most cases, retain the original voiceless / voiced opposition.

Two dialects of the Plang language recorded by Chinese scholars contain more tones than the Kontoi dialect: four tones for the Xinman'e 新曼俄 dialect and three for the Guanshuang 關双 dialect. If we look into the tone correspondences among these three dialects, we can obtain *grosso modo* the following correspondences:

(7)		Xinman'e	Guanshuang	Kontoi
	(1)	35	55	35/55
	(2)	33	11	35/55
	(3)	33	11	341/12/33
	(4)	331	11	341/12/33

[11] Plang words are from its Kontoi dialect recorded in Ceng Tung and Parauk, one of the Wa languages, was also recorded in Ceng Tung. The original voiceless initials are always accompanied by creaky vowels in Parauk.

(5)	33	55	35/55

We have omitted here the fourth tone of the Xinman'e dialect [21] and the third tone of the Guanshuang dialect [13], since these two tones seem to appear only in certain contexts, and we wonder whether this phenomenon corresponds to the feature we mentioned with respect to the Kontoi dialect where the tonal opposition is only significant at the last syllable before pause. We can recognize a certain number of words that are marginal to the tone correspondence patterns displayed above, but it seems admissible to schematize the general trend as above. We can present some examples of each correspondence as follows[12]:

(8)	meaning	Xinman'e	Guanshuang	Kontoi
	(1) *moon*	khiʔ35	khiʔ55	che35
	rain	hlɛʔ35	lhɛʔ55	hli35
	eye	ŋai35	ŋai55	ŋai35
	(2) *stone*	muʔ33	hmɔʔ11	mo35
	sun	ŋiʔ33	hŋeʔ11	ŋai35
	(3) *pig*	lik33	lik11	lek12
	fire	ŋual33	ŋu11	ŋoal341
	(4) *tiger*	vai331	vai11	wai341
	mouse	kaŋ331	kaŋ11	kaŋ341
	(5) *nose*	muhl33	mɤlh55	məh55
	bridge	pɯk33	pɤk55	mpək55

We can observe from this table that category (1) corresponds to original voiceless initials and aspirated sonorant initials, category (2) to original voiceless sonorant initials, category (3) to original voiced sonorant initials, and category (4) to original voiced initials[13]. We cannot, however, determine for the moment the nature of the initials belonging to category (5). We know that the word "eye" has an original voiceless initial by its correspondence to a creaky vowel in Parauk of Ceng Tung which points to an original voiceless initial: ŋa̰e < *hŋae or *ŋhae. For the same reason, we know that the word "mouse" had an original voiced initial: kiaŋ in Parauk of

---

12 Xinman'e and Guanshuang dialect data is from Li Daoyong 李道勇, Nie Xizhen 聶錫珍, Qiu Efeng 邱鍔鋒(eds.) (1986), ibid. and Plang (Kontoi) data is from our data recorded at Ceng Tung. Voiceless m and voiceless l are transcribed here as hm and hl respectively for convenience in printing, and we have omitted presyllables.

13 "tiger" shows an original occlusive initial both in this language and in Va (II.4), but we don't know the reason of this anomaly for the moment.

Ceng Tung. We can still find a few examples of non-sonorant initials which belong to categories (2) and (3), but the majority of the examples can be classified as shown here. There exist both voiceless sonorants such as hm, hl, etc. and aspirated sonorants such as mh, lh, etc. and they are interchangeable from one language to another.

We can summarize from this table the schema of the tonal development that has taken place in these three dialects of Plang according to the manner of the initial consonants.

(9) Xinman'e dialect

H	voiceless initials + aspirated sonorant initials
M	non-aspirated sonorant initials
L	voiced initials

Guanshuang dialect

H	voiceless initials + aspirated sonorant initials
L	voiced initials + non-aspirated sonorant initials

Kontoi dialect

H	voiceless initials
L	voiced initials

The data provided by the Chinese scholars shows that not only the voiceless / voiced opposition, but also the aspirated / non-aspirated opposition for sonorant initials played a decisive role in the tonal development that took place in these two Plang dialects. This is a case of tonal tripartition which occurred only in syllables having sonorant initials; subsequently the tone system elaborated in this way influenced the other syllables having non-sonorant initials. Such a tonal development process may be the cause of the discrepancies in tonal correspondence among these three dialects.

II.3. Siam (Hsem)

Siam is a language mainly spoken in Ceng Tung, but we can find a certain number of migrants settled now in Thaton. Our first field trip to the village about ten years ago revealed that this language is a tone language having two tones, high and low[14]. We can recognize the existence of two tones by looking at the following minimal pairs:

[14] Tadahiko L. A. Shintani (1998), "Siam — A tonal language of the Wa language group —", Tadahiko L. A. Shintani (ed.) (1998), *Linguistic & Anthropological Study on the Shan Culture Area*, ILCAA, Tokyo, pp.7-30.

(10) jum55 *to plant* jum11 *to die*
num55 *young of age* num11 *year*
saoʔ55 *painful* saoʔ11 *to wash (clothes)*
siam55 *Shan people* siam11 *Siam people*

We are aware that the high tone of this language corresponds to original aspirated or voiceless fricative initials, and that this is a case of transphonologization from an initial aspirated / non-aspirated opposition to a tonal high / low opposition. We can demonstrate this tonal development by the following examples[15]:

(11)

meaning	Siam	Parauk	Ta'ang
blood	nam55	nham	hnam
tooth	ɣaŋ55	ɣhaŋ	hraaŋ
five	puan55	phuan	phan
rain	lieʔ55	lhɛʔ	—
good	muom55	mhɔm	—
light	caŋ55	khioŋ	—
painful	saoʔ55	saɯʔ	suu

As for the syllables having original non-aspirated initials, they take a low tone.

(12)

meaning	Siam	Parauk	Ta'ang
hand	taiʔ11	taiʔ	ɗii
to see	jaoʔ11	jaoʔ	jɯɯ
pig	lit11	lik	leʔ
neck	ŋoak11	ŋok	ka ŋɔh
fish	kaʔ11	kaʔ	kaa

This language has at present no aspirated consonants nor aspirated (or voiceless) sonorants.

II.4. Va (En)

En is but a name given by the neighboring Tai speaking people, and their autonym is Va [vaʔ55], which itself suggests us their possible relationship

15 Siam and Parauk words are from our own data. In Parauk, the voiceless initials including aspirated sonorants are always followed by creaky vowels.

with Wa. This language is very close to Siam both in vocabulary and phonology. Our field research revealed that this is a tone language of the Siam type with a high / low two tone system, but at the same time that the tonal correspondence is reversed for the syllables having occlusive initials. The original aspirated occlusive initials correspond to low tone and the non-aspirated to high tone.

(13)	meaning	Va (En)	Siam	Parauk	Ta'ang
	tree	kaoʔ11	kaoʔ55	khaoʔ	—
	shallow	tɔ11	tɔ55	thɔ	—
	head	kaiɲ55	kan11	kaiɲ	kiŋ
	tongue	dak55	dak11	dak	ka ɗaaʔ
	buffalo	kɣak55	krak11	kɣaʔ	kraaʔ
	tiger[16]	vai55	vai11	vai	rə vai

As for the syllables having aspirated (or voiceless) sonorants and voiceless fricatives, they take a high tone, and their non-aspirated counterparts take a low tone, just as in Siam.

(14)	meaning	Va (En)	Siam	Parauk	Ta'ang
	skin	hak55	hak55	haɯk	hur
	blood	nam55	nam55	nham	hnam
	lice	siʔ55	siʔ55	seiʔ	sii
	leaf	lak55	lak55	lhaʔ	hlaa
	pig	lik11	lit11	lik	leʔ
	to die	jum11	jum11	jum	jam
	neck	ŋoak11	ŋoak11	ŋok	ka ŋɔh

The reason why such opposite tonal developments took place in these two languages will be discussed later.

II.5. Parauk (Wa)

Paruk is one of the so called Wa languages found in Ceng Tung. Besides Paruk, Tung Va Wa data recorded with tone marks by G. H. Luce[17] and two dialects recorded by Chinese scholars[18] are at our disposal.

---

16 Tone anomaly is also observed in Plang (II.2).

17 G. H. Luce (1965), ibid.

18 Zhou Zhizhi (周植志), Yan Qixiang (顏其香) (eds.) (1984), *Wayu jianzhi* 瓦語簡志 (Outline of the Wa language), Beijing.

We will examine the data given by Luce first. He notes five tones, namely : (1) high level [55] (2) mid-high falling [42] (3) mid level [33] (4) low falling [31] (5) low level [11], but at the same time he recognizes that all these tones are conditioned by finals, initials or syllable type. The first tone is confined to syllables having occlusive finals with voiceless initials, the second tone to zero, lateral, or nasal finals, the third tone to occlusive finals with voiced initials, the fourth tone to minor syllables, and the fifth tone to syllables with final -h. Since the tones are conditioned by other elements as described by Luce, they are not phonemic at all. As far as his data is concerned, this Tung Va Wa language is not a tone language by our definition of tone language.

We will now examine our own Parauk data. This language has a series of creaky vowels which appear only in syllables having original voiceless initials:

(15)	meaning	Parauk	Ta'ang
	hulled rice	gao̱ʔ	rə koo
	tongue	da̱k	ka ɗaaʔ
	buffalo	kɣa̱ʔ	kraaʔ
	pig	lik	leʔ
	stone	si̱ maoʔ	mou
	tiger	si̱ vai	rə vai

If we admit tones, we cannot recognize creaky vowels, and if we recognize creaky vowels, then we cannot admit tones. It is just a question of choice. Another feature of this language worth mentioning is that there exists a certain melody attributed to each syllable according to the syllable final, something like what Luce observed about his Tung Va dialect: falling melody in syllables with zero and nasal final, high level with occlusive final, and mid level with -h final. But such differences can be observed only in the last syllable before pause, and otherwise the syllables are realized monotone, exactly the same phenomenon we have observed in Plang.

Chinese scholars provide us with data on three dialects: Bajianke, Wa, Awa, of which the first two have an ordinary / creaky vowel opposition which descends from an original voiced / voiceless initial contrast, just like we have observed in our Parauk data. But it seems that there exists no tonal opposition even in the Awa dialect which lost (or has never developed) an ordinary / creaky vowel opposition. We observed the same phenomenon in our brief fieldwork on the Wa language of Mong Nung which seems to have neither an ordinary / creaky vowel opposition nor a tonal opposition.

II.6. Palaung (Ta'ang, Dar'ang, De'ang, Da'ak, etc.)

About the languages classified as Palaungic, we have data on Ta'ang of Nam San provided by our students, Dar'ang of Ceng Tung, De'ang of Loi Le and Ceng Tung, and Da'ak of Kalaw. Besides this, Panku Palaung provided by G. H. Luce[19] and three dialects recorded by Chinese scholars[20] are at our disposal. Among these recordings, two languages are described as tone languages: Panku Palaung recorded by Luce and the Rumai (汝買) dialect recorded by Chinese scholars.

We will examine the data provided by Luce first. He notes three tones, namely: (1) high level [55] (2) mid falling [42] and (3) mid level [33]. However, he recognizes at the same time that these tones are conditioned by the syllable finals: tone (1) appears in syllables with occlusive finals, tone (2) with -zero, -nasal, or -r finals, and tone (3) with -h final. However, we can find a certain number of words which do not accord with his statement. All the words showing this discrepancy are attributed to tone (3) except for one example meaning "butterfly" attributed to tone (1), and most of them are presyllables or loanwords. This may mean that his falling tone does not fall when the syllable is followed by another syllable, a phenomenon just like what we found in the Plang and the Parauk languages. In any event, since these tones are always conditioned by the syllable final, these three tones are not phonemic, and we cannot therefore consider this language to be a tone language.

Our own Palaung data does not give us any evidence of tone, but there are two further remarks worth mentioning. Firstly, we note the existence of certain melodies according to the syllable final on the last syllable before a pause, the same phenomenon we observed in Plang, Parauk and Luce's Panku Palaung. Falling melody is attributed to the syllables with zero and nasal finals, high level or falling to occlusive finals, mid level to -h finals. Secondly, we find a complete set of nasal finals with preocclusion such as -pm, -tn, -cɲ, -kŋ in Dar'ang and De'ang, even though they are not phonologically opposed to the respective ordinary nasal finals[21]. It seems worth noting furthermore that these nasal finals with preocclusion appear only on the last

---

19 G. H. Luce (1965), ibid.

20 Chen Xiangmu (陳相木), Wang Jingliu (王敬留), Lai Yongliang (賴永良) (eds.) (1986), *De'angyu jianzhi* (德昂語簡志) (Outline of the Palaung language), Beijing.

21 These are realized phonetically as postnasalized occlusives, as in certain languages of New-Caledonia, but we consider them to be nasals with preocclusion due to their phonological status. The existence of similar consonants in Aslian languages is reported by Matisoff. James A. Matisoff (2003), "Aslian: Mon-Khmer of the Malay peninsula", *Mon-Khmer Studies* No.33, pp.1-57.

syllable before a pause. For example, "water" is pronounced [ʔɤpm], but "tear" is normally pronounced [ʔɤm ŋae] instead of [ʔɤpm ŋae] (ŋae means "eye"). Moreover, all the syllables with final -kŋ in these two dialects have a final -k in Da'ak of Kalaw as shown by its name.

We will now take up the Rumai dialect recorded by Chinese scholars. They note two tones: high level [55] and falling [51], but they offer only two minimal pairs, of which one is doubtful, because it involves a personal name. Among the words given by them, we can find another pair, making a total of two pairs, as follows.

(16) am55 *to stop breathing* am51 *rotten*
plaŋ55 *shiny* plaŋ51 *thatch grass*

Since we can find such oppositions, we are obliged to recognize this dialect as a tone language. What is then the origin of these tones? Let us see the corresponding forms in other dialects:

(17)

meaning	Rumai(汝買)	Ta'ang	Bulei (布雷)	Liang (梁)
to stop breathing	am55	ap	—	—
rotten	am51	am	—	—
shiny	plaŋ55	plaaŋ	plaaŋ	blaaŋ
thatch grass	plaŋ51	plɔŋ	plaŋ	blɔŋ

From these correspondences, we can take up syllable finals and vowel length as two possible factors in the origin of tones in this dialect, and develop two possible explanations: the first hypothesis is to attribute the origin of high level tone to an occlusive final, and the second one is to attribute it to a long vowel. Let us then reexamine the data with respect to these two factors. If we eliminate possible loanwords from Tai and Chinese languages, we can find a certain relationship between the tones and the two elements of syllable finals and vowel length. The falling tone appears either in syllables having -zero, -nasal, -glottal stop finals, or in syllables with a short vowel combined with -p, -t, -k, -h finals. The high level tone appears, on the other hand, in syllables with a long vowel combined with -p, -t, -k, -h finals.

(18)

	-zero	-nasal	-ʔ	-p	-t	-k	-h
short vowel	51	51	51	51	51	51	51
long vowel	51	51	51	55	55	55	55

ka51 *fish*
pjim51 *old*
tiim51 *nine*
a' ka?51 *left*
kaa?51 *to shave*

lep51 *to enter*	leet55 *to lick*
kik51 *to chop*	k' piik55 *to snap fingers*
tih51 *mushroom*	k' tiih55 *internal organs*

We can find, however, a certain number of exceptions, seven with -glottal stop finals, three each with the -zero, -m, -n, -k finals, and one with -h final. If we compare some of these exceptions to the corresponding words in other dialects, we find that the high level tone corresponds to the long vowel of the other dialects:

(19)	pih55 *to sweep*	ɓiih (Ta'ang)
	plaŋ55 *shiny*	plaaŋ (Ta'ang, Bulei), blaaŋ (Liang)
		blaakŋ (Dar'ang)

We cannot give any definitive conclusion at this stage concerning the origin of tones of this dialect, because the data at our disposal is far from sufficient, but we can suggest that the occlusion (including glottal stop) / nasal or zero opposition on the syllable final and/or vowel length may have played a decisive role. The existence of a complete set of nasal finals with preocclusion in Dar'ang and De'ang may be related to this tonal development.

II.7. Arva (La, Kha La)

La or Kha La is nothing but a name given by the neighboring Tai speaking people, and their autonym is Arva [ar va]. This name suggests a linkage to Wa, but its vocabulary does not show any close relation to the Wa languages. This language seems to be in a transitional or confused stage, and it is very difficult to formulate any clear principle about its phonetic evolution.

We can, however, regard this language as a tone language, provided that we can find a minimal tonal pair, even if only one for the moment, as seen below.

(20) kat55 *back* kat11 *hot*

This pair is no doubt a high / low tonal opposition. We will examine corresponding forms in other related languages.

(21) a. for "back"

kaʔ55 (Va) kal1 (Siam) qhɯʔ33 (Plang-Xinman'e)
kɹe55 (Plang-Guanshuang) kəi (Parauk) khaiʔ (Wa-Bajianke)

b. for "hot"

goan11 (Va) ɣuan55 (Siam)

It seems possible to say from these correspondences that "back" descends from an original voiceless initial and "hot" from an original voiced initial, and that this is again a case of transphonologization from an initial voiceless / voiced opposition to a tonal high / low opposition. This transphonologization may have occurred only in syllables having occlusive initials, because the other consonants normally maintain their original voiceless / voiced opposition.

The general trend of occlusive consonant mutations seems to be as follows:

(22) a.*voiceless non-aspirated occlusives > voiceless aspirated occlusives

meaning	Arva	Parauk	Ta'ang	Plang (Kontoi)
fruit	phle	pleiʔ	plee	pre35
egg	thap	tɔm	kaɗam	katɔm35
fish	khaʔ	kaʔ	kaa	kaʔ35

b.*voiced occlusives > voiceless or voiced non-aspirated occlusives

meaning	Arva	Parauk	Ta'ang	Plang (Kontoi)
foam	puih	bae	buh	pɤh33
breasts	pu	—	buu	bə35
horse	brak	bruŋ	brɔŋ	mrɔŋ341
jungle	pri	—	bri	phre35

c.*voiceless aspirated occlusives > non-aspirated or unchanged

meaning	Arva	Parauk	Ta'ang	Plang (Kontoi)
moon	giar	khiʔ	kiar	che35
sieve	khrəŋ	ghrɯŋ	rəkhrəŋ	khrɤŋ35
to prostrate	grup	gup	kuu	—

Among these correspondences, (22.a) is relatively certain and the other two are rather shaky. But even for correspondence (22.a), our different informants sometimes, but not very often, displayed different correspondences.

(23)	meaning	informant A	informant B	others
	muddy	gɤr	khɤr	kɤr35 (Plang-Kontoi)
	toilet	du vet	thu vet	ka te35 (Plang-Kontoi)
	female	bɤt	phɤt	bo̱n (Parauk)

We can still observe a common feature among these examples. All the words belonging to this category are pronounced relatively high regardless of which informant utters the word.

Even in such a confused situation, we can see that this is a case where the voiceless non-aspirated occlusives are strengthened and the others are, on the contrary, weakened. Therefore if a voiceless non-aspirated occlusive *accidentally* fails to be mutated to an aspirated one, it acquires stress which gives a high tone as a result. In such a case, the weakened one, either the original voiced or voiceless aspirated, takes the low tone. We can suppose that the tonal opposition shown above is the result of such a strengthened / weakened opposition and that the strengthened side accidentally failed to acquire aspiration. In fact, we can observe as a general trend in this language that syllables having original voiceless initials are pronounced relatively high and the others having original voiceless aspirated or voiced initials are pronounced low in most cases. It may therefore be possible that an original voiceless non-aspirated / aspirated opposition was transphonologized to a tonal high / low opposition, but we cannot find any such pairs at the moment.

It is worth adding two remarks about the syllable finals of this language. A falling intonation is attributed to syllables with -zero, -nasal, -r finals, a level intonation to those with -h final, a slightly rising one to those with -glottal stop final, and either a level intonation accompanied by a short vowel or a falling one accompanied by a long vowel to those with -p, -t, -k finals. Furthermore the nasal finals of other languages often correspond to the respective occlusive finals in this language.

II.8. Kanaw (Danaw)

Kanaw was recorded for the first time with tone marks by G. H. Luce[22]. He used the name of Danaw in his paper, but in fact, Danaw [thaʔnɔʔ] is but a Burmese appellation and their real autonym is Kanaw [kaʔnɔʔ]. Luce

[22] G. H. Luce (1965), ibid.

notes four tones, namely: (1) high level [55] (2) high falling [53] (3) mid rising [24] (4) low falling [21]. Our data approximately agrees with his findings, but the problem remains to determine whether they are really phonemic tones. Concerning the tones of this language, A. G. Haudricourt has mentioned on the basis of the data provided by Luce that the origin of the first tone of this language is from syllables with final glottal stops[23]. It is true that the syllables attributed to the first tone, high level tone, correspond normally to syllables with glottal stop or sometimes occlusive finals in other languages[24]:

(24)	meaning	Kanaw	Riang	Dar'ang
	dog	co55	soʔ55	ma sou
	leaf	la55	laʔ11	hlaa
	husked rice	ko55	koʔ55	rə gao
	tongue	ka taʔ55	tak55	sə ɗaʔ

We can therefore distinguish a high level tone from the other tones, and we can find the following minimal pair.

(25) le55 *penis* le53 *to go out*

Luce himself recognizes that the mid rising tone might be a variant of the high level tone, and indeed we cannot find any minimal pairs between the two. As for the remaining two tones, high falling and low falling, we can find a tendency for syllables with aspirated initials to be more likely to take a high tone than syllables with non-aspirated initials, but we cannot generalize this trend as a principle, because there exists a certain number of exceptions that we cannot neglect. We can also find certain differences between what Luce noted and what we ourselves have observed about these two tones. For example, we sometimes find low falling tone on the syllables on which Luce noted high falling tone and vice versa, and the same syllable is sometime pronounced differently according to the circumstances. It may be possible to conclude from this evidence that this language is a tone language with two phonemic tones, high level and falling, which are phonologically opposed to each other only in open syllables.

We find also that the falling contour appears only on the last syllable

---

[23] A. G. Haudricourt (1965), "Les mutations consonantiques des occlusives initiales en Mon-Khmer", *Bulletin de la Société de Linguistique de Paris*, Tome LX, Fasc.1, pp.160-172.

[24] The examples given here are from our data and not from Luce.

before a pause, otherwise syllables do not fall at all.

Luce classified this language in the Palaung-Wa group, but since our data shows significant distance from the other languages of the group, we may be obliged to change the classification of this language. However, we will save this matter for another occasion.

Ⅲ. Overview of the tones of the examined languages from a historical perspective

As we have seen above, there are three decisive factors for the origin of tones among the examined languages: (1) manner of initial consonant, (2) syllable finals, and (3) vowel length.

Ⅲ.1. Manner of initial consonant

There are two possible oppositions which can be transphonologized to a tonal high / low opposition: voiceless / voiced and aspirated / non-aspirated oppositions. The former is the case in Riang and Arva, and the latter is the case in Siam and Va. In the case of Plang, both oppositions are involved, but only for sonorant initials. In the case of Siam, the aspiration, being treated as stress, resulted in a high tone. In the case of Va on the other hand, the aspiration was treated as something like breathiness and resulted in a low tone. In other words, the aspirated / non-aspirated opposition was treated as a tense / lax opposition in Siam, and, in contrast, as a lax / tense opposition in Va. This different treatment explains the reversed tonal correspondences between these two languages.

Ⅲ.2. Syllable finals

The transphonologization from opposition on the syllable final to tonal opposition occurred in Kanaw. Haudricourt concluded that the high level tone of this language was from final glottal stop[25], but it seems better to say that it is a case of transphonologization from an occlusion / non-occlusion opposition at syllable final to a tonal high level / falling opposition, because it is not clear whether the glottal stop found in the related languages is original or secondary.

The case of the Rumai dialect of Palaung may be a transphonologization

[25] A. G. Haudricourt (1965), ibid.

from an occlusion / non-occlusion opposition at syllable final to a tonal high / falling opposition, as in Kanaw. In this respect, the existence of a complete set of nasal endings with preocclusion in Dar'ang and De'ang is very suggestive. Furthermore the fact that the nasal finals of other languages are often replaced in Arva by the corresponding occlusive finals may also support this idea.

Ⅲ.3. Vowel length

We are not very sure whether this factor alone can play a decisive role in tonal development of the languages we examined, and it may be related to the syllable final factor, as we have seen in the Rumai dialect of Palaung[26]. We can recognize many examples where the long vowel without any final consonant in Ta'ang often corresponds to a glottal stop final in other languages, and this evidence may also suggest a certain relationship between vowel length and occlusive finals.

Ⅳ. Conclusion

We have examined the tonal developments in eight languages belonging to the Palaung-Wa group, and we have deduced three possible factors which played a decisive role in each language. We can recognize after all a fundamental principle which regulates the tonal development that took place among these languages, i.e. a **tense / lax opposition**.

Both the voiceless / voiced opposition in Riang, Plang, Parauk, Arva, and the aspirated / non-aspirated opposition in Plang and Siam can be considered as a tense / lax opposition in the initial consonants. The aspirated / non-aspirated opposition in Va can likewise be considered a lax / tense opposition. In the case of Arva, it is more precisely voiceless non-aspirated vs. voiced aspirated opposition, where voiceless non-aspirated is attributed to the tense side, similarly to the case in Va.

---

26 But Svantesson reports two cases of tonal development from vowel length and vowel quality. Jan-Olof Svantesson (1988), "U", *Linguistics of the Tibeto-Burman Area*, Vol.11, No.1, pp.64-133. (1989), "Tonogenetic mechanisms in Northern Mon-Khmer", *Phonetica*, Vol.46, pp.60-79. (2001), "Tonogenesis in Southeast Asia — Mon-khmer and beyond", Shigeki Kaji (ed.) (2001), *Cross-Linguistic Studies of Tonal Phenomena*, pp.45-58.

(26) voiceless non-aspirated + tense > high tone (case in Va)
voiceless non-aspirated + tense > aspirated consonants (occasionally high tone) (case in Arva)

From another point of view, aspiration is treated differently according to the pole of opposition to which it is attributed. If it is attributed to the tense side, it takes high tone as in Siam, and if it is attributed to the lax side, it takes low tone as in Va. We can schematize these developments as follows:

(27) aspiration > tense > stress > high tone (case of Siam)
aspiration > lax > breathiness > low tone (case of Va)

The occlusion / non-occlusion opposition in the Rumai dialect of Palaung and Kanaw can be considered as a tense / lax opposition at syllable final.

As a result of the tense / lax opposition at initial consonant, the tense side acquires either high tone as in Riang, Plang, Siam, Va, and Arva, creaky vowel as in Parauk, or aspirated consonants as in Arva. As a result of the tense / lax opposition at syllable final, the tense side acquires high-level tone (more precisely non-falling tone) as in the Rumai dialect of Palaung and Kanaw. What is important here is the existence of an opposition, and not the existence of certain consonants themselves. When Haudricourt treated the origin of tones in Vietnamese[27], he stated that a glottal stop final led naturally to a rising melody, and a -h final to a falling melody, but as we have seen even in the languages examined here, the glottal stop final gives either high-level, falling, or low rising melody according to the languages concerned, and the -h final results in either a level or falling melody[28].

This tense / lax opposition principle may be widely applied either to other phonological phenomena or to other languages. We wonder whether it is possible to apply this principle to the origin of implosives. Let's compare the degree of mutation-to-implosive between Ta'ang and Dar'ang, two dialects of Palaung. In Ta'ang, p has become completely implosive, t has become implosive in most cases, but c and k remain unchanged. In Dar'ang, on the other hand, p, t, c have all become implosives, and k has become an

---

[27] A. G. Haudricourt (1954) "De l'origine des tons en vietnamien", *Journal Asiatique*, No.242, pp.69-82.

[28] A case of glottal dissimilation in Lahu is reported by Matisoff. James A. Matisoff (1970), "Glottal dissimilation and the Lahu high-rising tone: a tonogenetic case-study", *Journal of the American Oriental Society*, No.90-1, pp.13-44. Kingston points out that the existence of two kinds of glottal stop was the origin of two different tones, high and low, in Athabaskan. John Kingston (2003), "Mechanisms of Tone Reversal", Shigeki Kaji (ed.) (2003), *Cross-Linguistic Studies of Tonal Phenomena*, pp.57-120.

ordinary voiced g. Furthermore, these consonants remain unchanged as p, t, c, k in presyllables in Ta'ang, but in Dar'ang, on the other hand, the same implosives are observed both in presyllables and main syllables. This difference may be related to the devoicing movement that took place only in Dar'ang in which all the original voiced occlusives have become voiceless ones. In order to maintain the original voiceless / voiced opposition, the original voiceless ones were obliged to mutate either to aspirated ones or to implosives, giving high tone or creaky vowel. Among these choices, mutation to aspirated consonants was impossible, because the original aspirated consonants remained unchanged. The necessity for the original voiceless occlusives to mutate to implosives in Ta'ang was not so strong as in Dar'ang, as evidenced by the fact that the voiced ones remain unchanged in this dialect. We can therefore admit that the implosives in Palaung are the result of the tense / lax opposition, the implosives representing the tense side. The origin of implosives in Riang may be explained by the same argument. The origin of creaky vowel in Akha can be explained also by this tense / lax opposition principle, and in this case, the matter is the occlusion / non-occlusion opposition at the syllable final[29].

Our study of the Tai Cultural Area is not limited to tonal phenomena, and the more we accumulate data, the more problems arise.

As we have seen, most of the languages we treated here are tone languages in the strict sense of phonology, but there is something different about these languages compared to the languages of the other groups of the area. It is not easy to find minimal tonal pairs in these Austroasiatic languages, and any mistake in tones only rarely jeopardizes communication. We wonder whether we can call them tone languages in the same sense as the Tai languages, or we should call them "marginal" tone languages.

Among the languages treated here, Arva is rather distant from the others, and Kanaw is the most distant of all. It seems necessary to reconsider the classification of the Northern Austroasiatic languages as a whole on the basis of new scientific data.

---

[29] Tadahiko L. A. Shintani (ed.) (1999) *Basic Vocabularies of the Languages spoken in Phongxaly, Lao P. D. R.*, ILCAA, Tokyo, (2001) *Linguistic Survey of Phongxaly, Lao P. D. R.*, ILCAA, Tokyo.

References

Chen Xiangmu (陳相木), Wang Jingliu (王敬留), Lai Yongliang (賴永良) (eds.) (1986) *De'angyu jianzhi* (徳昴語簡志) (Outline of the Palaung language), Beijing.

Michel Ferlus (1974) "Les langues du groupe Austroasiatique-Nord", *Asie du Sud-Est et le Monde Insulindian*, Vol.5, No.1, pp.39-68.

Raleigh Ferrell (1978) "Le P'u-Man, Langue Austroasiatique", *Bulletin de la Société de Linguistique de Paris*, Tome LXVI, Fasc.1, pp.405-412.

André G. Haudricourt (1954) "De l'origine des tons en vietnamien", *Journal Asiatique*, No.242, pp.69-82.

— (1965) "Les mutations consonantiques des occulusives initiales en Mon-Khmer", *Bulletin de la Société de Linguistique de Paris*, Tome LX, Fasc.1, pp.160-172.

— (1972) *Problèmes de phonologie diachronique*, SELAF, Paris.

André G. Haudricourt, Claude Hagège (1978) *La phonologie panchronique*, PUF, Paris.

Karl G. Izikowitz (1951) *Lamet, Hill peasants in French Indochina*, Göteborg.

Shigeki Kaji (ed.) (2001) *Cross-Linguistic Studies of Tonal Phenomena*, ILCAA, Tokyo.

— (ed.) (2003) *Cross-Linguistic Studies of Tonal Phenomena*, ILCAA, Tokyo.

John Kingston (2003) "Mechanisms of Tone Reversal", Shigeki Kaji (ed.) (2003), *Cross-Linguistic Studies of Tonal Phenomena*, pp.57-120.

Li Daoyong 李道勇, Nie Xizhen 聶錫珍, Qiu Efeng 邱鍔鋒(eds.) (1986) *Bulangyu jianzhi* 布朗語簡志(Outline of the Plang language), Beijing.

G. H. Luce (1965) "Danaw, a dying Austroasiatic language", *Lingua*, No.14, pp.98-129.

James A. Matisoff (1970) "Glottal dissimilation and the Lahu high-rising tone: a tonogenetic case-study", *Journal of the American Oriental Society*, No.90-1, pp.13-44.

— (1973) *The Grammar of Lahu*, University of California.

— (2003) "Aslian: Mon-Khmer of the Malay peninsula", *Mon-Khmer Studies*, No.33, pp.1-57.

Yasuyuki Mitani (1965) "Kameetogo no onsotaikei no kijutsu to hikakugengogaku teki koosatsu" (A descriptive and Comparative Study of the Khamet Phonology), *Toonan Ajia Kenkyuu* (Jurnal of South-East Asian Studies), Vol.3, No.3, pp.22-51.

Tadahiko L. A. Shintani (ed.) (1998) *Oogon no yonkakuchitai* (Golden Quadrangle), Keiyuusha, Tokyo

— (ed.) (1999) *Basic Vocabularies of the Languages spoken in Phongxaly, Lao P. D. R.*, ILCAA, Tokyo.
— (ed.) (1999) *Linguistic & Anthropological Study on the Shan Culture Area*, ILCAA, Tokyo.
— (1999) "Siam — A tonal language of the Wa language group—", Tadahiko L. A. Shintani (ed.), ibid., pp.7-30.
— (ed.) (2001) *Linguistic Survey of Phongxaly, Lao P. D. R.*, ILCAA, Tokyo.
Suwilai Premsrirat (2003) "Khamu dialects: a case of register complex and tonogenesis", Shigeki Kaji (ed.) (2003) *Cross-Linguistic Studies of Tonal Phenomena*, ILCAA, pp.13-36.
Jan-Olof Svantesson (1988) "U", *Linguistics of the Tibeto-Burman Area*, Vol.11, No.1, pp.64-133.
— (1989) "Tonogenetic mechanisms in Northern Mon-Khmer", *Phonetica*, Vol.46, pp.60-79.
— (2001) "Tonogenesis in Southeast Asia — Mon-khmer and beyond", Shigeki Kaji (ed.) (2001) *Cross-linguistic Studies of Tonal Phenomena*, ILCAA, pp.45-58.
Zhou Zhizhi (周植志), Yan Qixiang (顔其香) (eds.) (1984) *Wayu jianzhi* 瓦語簡志 (Outline of the Wa language), Beijing.

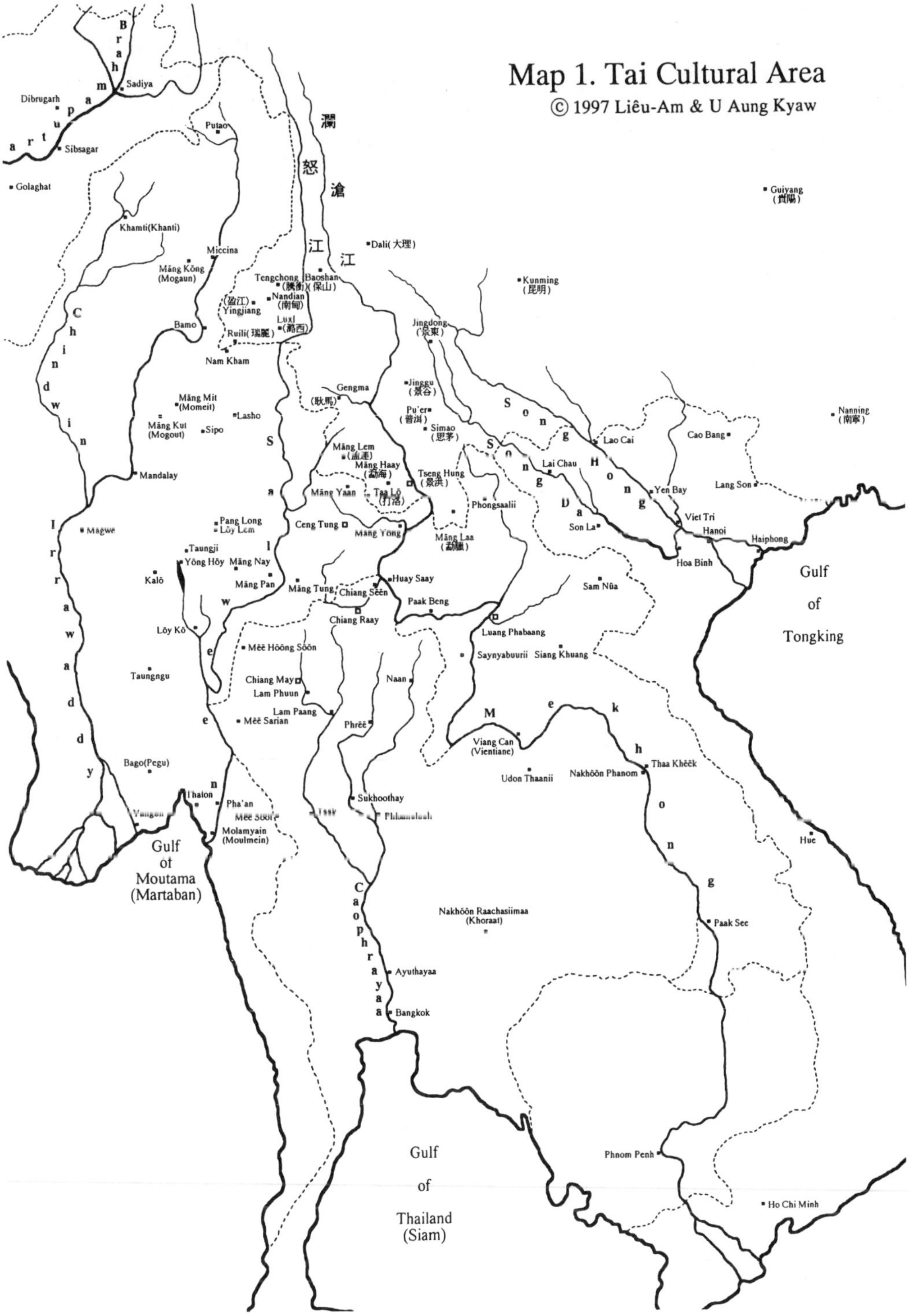

Map 1. Tai Cultural Area

© 1997 Liêu-Am & U Aung Kyaw

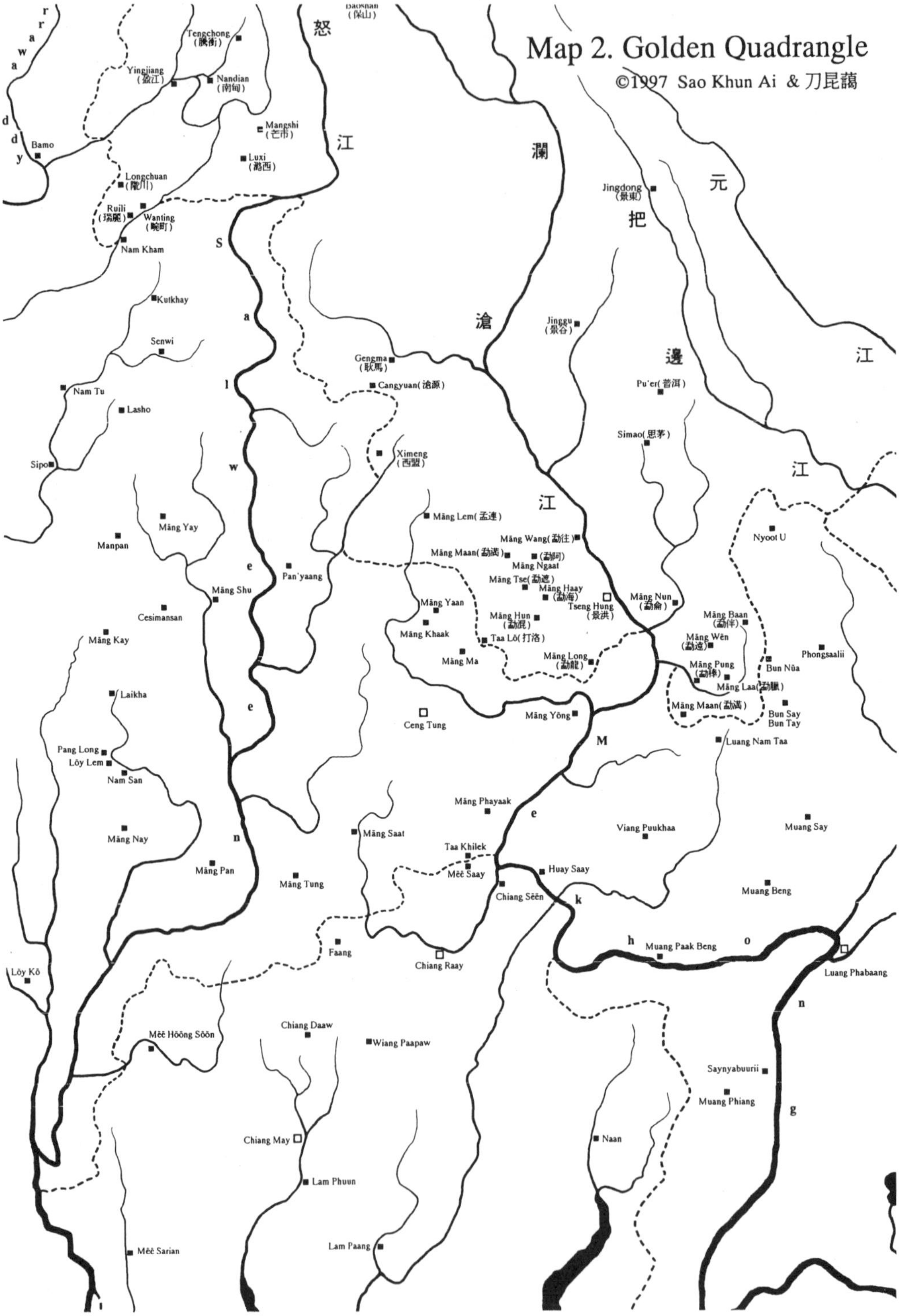

Map 2. Golden Quadrangle
©1997 Sao Khun Ai & 刀昆藹
(保山)
怒
江
Tengchong (騰衝)
Yingjiang (盈江)
Nandian (南甸)
Mangshi (芒市)
Luxi (潞西)
Bamo
Longchuan (隴川)
Ruili (瑞麗)
Wanting (畹町)
Nam Kham
Kutkhay
Senwi
Nam Tu
Lasho
Sipo
Mãng Yay
Manpan
Mãng Shu
Cesimansan
Mãng Kay
Laikha
Pang Long
Lôy Lem
Nam San
Mãng Nay
Mãng Pan
Lôy Kô
Mêê Hôông Sôôn
Mêê Sarian
Pan'yaang
Gengma (耿馬)
Cangyuan (滄源)
Ximeng (西盟)
瀾
滄
江
Jingdong (景東)
元
把
邊
江
Jinggu (景谷)
Pu'er (普洱)
Simao (思茅)
江
Mãng Lem (孟連)
Mãng Wang (勐往)
Mãng Maan (勐滿)
(勐阿) Mãng Ngaat
Mãng Tse (勐遮)
Mãng Haay (勐海)
Tseng Hung (景洪)
Mãng Nun (勐侖)
Mãng Yaan
Mãng Khaak
Mãng Hun (勐混)
Taa Lô (打洛)
Mãng Ma
Mãng Long (勐龍)
Mãng Yõng
Ceng Tung
Nyoot U
Mãng Baan (勐伴)
Mãng Wẽn (勐遠)
Mãng Pung (勐捧)
Mãng Laa (勐臘)
Mãng Maan (勐滿)
Bun Nũa
Bun Say
Bun Tay
Phongsaalii
Luang Nam Taa
Mãng Phayaak
Mãng Saat
Taa Khilek
Mêê Saay
Huay Saay
Chiang Sêên
Mãng Tung
Faang
Chiang Raay
Viang Puukhaa
Muang Say
Muang Beng
Muang Paak Beng
Luang Phabaang
Chiang Daaw
Wiang Paapaw
Chiang May
Lam Phuun
Lam Paang
Naan
Saynyabuurii
Muang Phiang
S a l w e e n
M e k h o n g

Comment on Tadahiko L.A. Shintani, "Austroasiatic tone languages of the Tai cultural area"

by James A. Matisoff, University of California, Berkeley

This paper is a convincing attempt to show that a wide variety of prosodic contrasts in the Palaungic branch of Mon-Khmer/Austroasiatic [1] can be ascribed to a single articulatory proto-opposition (TENSE vs. LAX), providing us with an excellent demonstration that widely different synchronic surface manifestations may be traced back to the same underlying cause.

Except for the anomalous case of Vietnamese, contrastive tone is not a widespread feature of the Austroasiatic family in general, undoubtedly because its characteristic syllabic structure is *sesquisyllabic*,[2] not strictly monosyllabic. Much more typical of Mon-Khmer is the exploitation of *registers* or *phonation types,* special voice qualities (especially "creaky" and "breathy") produced by altered configurations of the glottis. However, tones are definitely "in the air" in the Southeast Asian linguistic area, and the Palaung-Wa (= Palaungic) languages, spoken in the north of the Mon-Khmer area, find themselves surrounded by thoroughgoing tone languages of the "omnisyllabic" type, including Chinese, Tai, Tibeto-Burman, and Hmong-Mien.[3] It is not surprising then that much of Palaungic is undergoing tonogenetic influence from its neighbors.[4]

Shintani has studied a dozen more-or-less tonal Palaungic languages and dialects with a view to this problem. Almost all of them have developed true tonal contrasts, although their functional load still seems quite marginal, due apparently to the fact that in many cases the tonogenetic conditioning factors are still synchronically present, so that the nascent tonal contrasts are largely redundant; i.e. the transphonologization from segmental to suprasegmental contrasts has not yet been completed.

Shintani recognizes three types of tonogenetic factors: the manner of the initial consonant, the final consonant, and vowel length (the latter also noted for Khmuic). We can best appreciate the elegance of his analysis by presenting his results in tabular form:

[1] Specialists consider the Austroasiatic family to consist of the Munda languages of India on the one hand, and the dozens of Mon-Khmer languages (belonging to 8 or 9 subgroups) on the other.

[2] For the first use of this term, referring to forms which are "a syllable and a half" in length, see Matisoff 1973.

[3] It is somewhat strange that Shintani refers to this region as the "Tai cultural area", since so many other ethnolinguistic groups also live there. Perhaps a more suitable term would be "the Sinosphere", since they are all under the influence of Chinese civilization to some extent. See Matisoff 1999:5-11.

[4] The same is true of another northern Mon-Khmer branch, Khmuic. See Svantesson 1988, 1989, 1991.

Table I. Manifestations of the tense/lax opposition in Palaungic

Language	*tense manner*	*tense prosody*	*lax manner*	*lax prosody*	*conditioning factor*
Riang	*voiceless	HIGH	*voiced	LOW	proto-voice
Plang (Kontoi)[5]	*voiceless	HIGH	*voiced	LOW	proto-voice
Siam (Hsem)[6]	*aspirates *vless fricatives	HIGH	*non-aspirates	LOW	proto-aspiration
Va (En)	*unasp stops[7] *asp/vless sonorants *vless fricatives	HIGH	*asp stops *voiced sonorants *voiced fricatives	LOW	proto-aspiration in stops proto-voice in fricatives and sonorants
Parauk[8]	*voiceless	CREAKY VOICE	*voiced	MODAL VOICE	proto-voice
Palaung (Ta'ang & Dar'ang)	implosive		explosive		proto-voice
Arva[9]	*vless non-asp (> aspirates)	HIGH?	*voiced *aspirates	LOW	

The Plang dialects differ among themselves in the degree of tonogenesis they have undergone, and in the precise nature of the conditioning involved. The Xianman'e dialect shows a tonal tripartition, with both voicing and aspiration as conditioning factors; while the Guanshuang and Kontoi dialects have only undergone bipartition, with both voicing and aspiration playing a role in Guanshuang, while voicing alone seems to have determined the split in Kontoi (pp. 5-7). See Table II.

---

[5] With allotonic variants according to the final consonant, especially important in syllables with sonorant initials. There is considerable variation in the functionality of tone among the various Plang dialects; see Table II.

[6] This language has no synchronic aspirates or complex sonorants. There is no data provided concerning the fate of the simple *voiced series in Siam.

[7] This apparently includes voiced stops. Cf. Va **dak55** 'tongue' (p. 9).

[8] Tones are redundant in this language because of lack of consonant mutation. Luce recognizes five allotones, but the conditioning factors are still present. Cf. the situation in Naxi, a language close to the Lolo-Burmese nucleus of Tibeto-Burman, where the lack of the firm tonal contrast in stopped syllables that is typical of LB proper is attributable to incomplete mutation of its initial consonants. See Matisoff 1979, 1991.

[9] The prosodic situation in this language is confused; Shintani judges it to be in a transitional state.

Table II. Tonogenetic conditioning in Plang dialects

	HIGH	MID	LOW
Xianman'e	vless stops asp sonorants	non-asp sonorants	voiced

	HIGH	LOW
Guanshuang	vless stops asp sonorants (e.g. *hm)	voiced stops non-asp sonorants (e.g. *m, *ʔm)
Kontoi	voiceless stops and sonorants (e.g. *hm, *ʔm)	voiced stops and sonorants (e.g. *m)

Again, a chart is helpful in understanding the conditioning described by Shintani (pp. 12-13) for the development of true tone in the Rumai dialect of Palaung, as recorded by Chinese scholars.[10] Both vowel length and the nature of the final consonant are involved. See Table III.

Table III. Tonogenetic conditioning in Rumai

	Rumai	*Ta'ang*	*Bulei*	*Liang*	*Dar'ang*	*Proto-Palaung*
'stop breathing'	am 55	ap				*-p
'rotten'	am 51	am				*-m
'shiny'	plaŋ 55	plaaŋ	plaaŋ	blaang	blaakŋ	*-VVŋ
'thatch grass'	plaŋ 51	plɔŋ	plaŋ	blɔŋ		*-Vŋ

These Rumai data also illustrate differences between Mon-Khmer and Tai phonology. In Rumai syllables with long vowels, the zero, nasal, and glottal finals form a tonogenetic class; while final oral stops and -h form a separate class:

-V	-VN	-Vʔ	-Vp	-Vt	-Vk	-Vh	> Rumai 51
-VV	-VVN	-VVʔ					> Rumai 51
			-VVp	-VVt	-VVk	-VVh	> Rumai 55

One obvious difference is the lack of final –h in Tai. More significantly, in Tai -ʔ patterns tonally most like the three oral stops -p -t -k,[11] and not at all like vowel- and nasal-finals as in Rumai. Furthermore, in Tai -ʔ only occurs after short vowels, not after either long or short vowels as in Rumai. In this respect Tai -ʔ does behave differently from -p -t -k,

[10] The dialects of Palaung studied personally by Shintani have redundant tonetic variants, conditioned by the final consonant.

[11] In traditional Thai terminology, syllables with these four finals are called "dead" *(kham taaj)*, as opposed to "live" syllables with vowel, semivowel, or nasal finals *(kham pen)*.

which occur freely after either long or short vowels, with different tonal possibilities for each.[12] See Table IV.

Table IV. Tonal possibilities in Siamese (standard Thai) stopped syllables

				Siamese tone
-Vp	-Vt	-Vk	-Vʔ	short high
-Vp	-Vt	-Vk	-Vʔ	short low
-VVp	-VVt	-VVk		falling
-VVp	-VVt	-VVk		long low

Shintani wishes to stretch his tense/lax dichotomy to the Rumai case, by interpreting the proto-occlusive finals as tense, and the proto-non-occlusive ones as lax. Presumably 55 is the "tense" tone and 51 is the "lax" one.

Shintani has identified a number of hitherto unnoticed but theoretically interesting phenomena in these Palaungic languages.

•*Opposite tonogenetic effects of aspiration*

Shintani demonstrates that the feature of aspiration may exert two opposite tonogenetic effects: if aspiration is "attributed to TENSE", i.e. treated as a *stress*, it can lead to HIGH tone, as in Siam (Hsem); if it is "attributed to LAX", i.e. treated as *breathiness*, it can lead to LOW tone, as in Va.

•*Different tonal effects of final glottal stop*

A similar tonogenetic ambiguity seems also to be true with respect to final glottal stop. According to classic Haudricourtian theory, -ʔ leads to RISING tones, and -h to FALLING ones.[13] Yet Shintani provides counterexamples from Palaungic, where in one language or another -ʔ gives either high-level, falling, or low rising tone; while -h gives either a level or a falling contour.

This reminds one of the ambiguous status of the so-called MID series of Proto-Tai, comprising syllables with *voiceless unaspirated or *pre-glottalized initial consonants,[14] which sometimes pattern with the HIGH category (under tones *B and *C), and sometimes with the LOW class (under tone *A).[15]

[12] This same difference in tonal possibilities in stopped syllables according to vowel length is also characteristic of Cantonese, one phenomenon which has led scholars to posit a Tai substratum in Cantonese. See, e.g. Hashimoto 1976.

[13] Haudricourt 1954. In this seminal article Haudricourt already invoked the feature of TENSE to account for the raising effect of glottal stop, produced by what he called "une augmentation de la tension des cordes vocales". See also the descriptions of the TENSE-LARYNX SYNDROME vs. the LAX-LARYNX SYNDROME in Matisoff 1973:76, 1999a:5.

[14] Standard Thai (Siamese) syllables with voiceless unaspirated initials are often pronounced with a noticeable glottal accent. The *preglottalized initials /*ʔb *ʔd/ of Proto-Tai are now pronounced as implosive [bb] and [dd] in Siamese.

[15] See Haudricourt 1961.

Especially striking cases of opposite tonogenetic effects of glottal stop have been documented by Kingston, in his study (2003) of the tonally "high-marked" vs. "low-marked" members of the Athabaskan family. He concludes that there must have been two phonetically different varieties of glottal stop in the history of this language family.

•*Decomposed final nasals*

Shintani has discovered a series of syllable-final "nasals with preocclusion" [-pm -tn -cny -kŋ] in the Dar'ang and De'ang dialects of Palaung. This is an allophonic phenomenon, since this series does not contrast with simple nasal finals (p. 12). Shintani observes that similar consonants occur in certain languages of New Caledonia, where they are better treated as "postnasalized occlusives". Closer to home, all three branches of the Aslian subgroup of Mon-Khmer have such finals, noted long ago by Blagden, who referred to them as "disintegrated nasals".[16]

Because of this subphonemic articulatory habit in Palaung dialects, Shintani suggests renaming the whole Palaung-Wa subgroup of Mon-Khmer as *Paraukng*, though this seems a bit extreme in view of the unpronounceability of such a name by the typical English or Japanese speaker.[17]

•*The creaky vowels of Akha*

The Parauk dialect studied by Shintani has a register contrast between creaky and modal voice, which he also explains in terms of an original tense/lax opposition (pp. 10-11). He rightly observes that "the origin of the creaky vowel in Akha [a Tibeto-Burman language of the Southern Loloish group] can also be explained by this tense/lax opposition principle, and in this case, the matter is the occlusion/non-occlusion opposition at the syllable final" (p. 20).

Actually what is going on in Akha is a kind of *dissimilation* between the laryngeal features of aspiration and glottalization. The Proto-Lolo-Burmese *voiceless obstruents are realized as Akha aspirates in non-stopped syllables (< PLB syllables with final vowels or nasals), but as voiceless unaspirates in syllables with reflexes of PLB final stops */-p -t -k/, all of which have disappeared after causing glottalization of the vowel, e.g..

PLB *pa, *paŋ	>	Akha pha, phɔ
PLB *pak	>	Akha paʔ

In other words, aspiration and glottalization may not occur in the same Akha syllable.[18]

---

[16] Blagden judgmentally ascribed these sounds to "careless, slovenly articulation". See Matisoff 2003:18-22.

[17] Shintani is fond of introducing novel names for language groups, notably his term *Brakaloungic* for the Tibeto-Burman subgroup generally known as "Karenic" (p. 1). Besides its unfamiliarity, this designation bears an unfortunate resemblance to a kind of reclining armchair widely sold in the U.S. under the name *Barcalounger*. Nevertheless, one must sympathize with the innovative spirit which leads one to propose new names! I myself have taken a lot of criticism for my cover term *Kamarupan* for the Tibeto-Burman languages of Northeast India (see Matisoff 1999b).

[18] This is reminiscent of Grassman's Law, which formulated the constraint that aspiration could not occur in successive syllables of the same word in Sanskrit or Classical Greek. It is also quite similar to the "glottal

• *Implosive initial consonants*

Shintani proposes that the implosive initials which have developed from simple *voiceless unaspirates in Riang and in the Ta'ang and Dar'ang dialects of Palaung might also be explained as the tense members of an original tense/lax opposition (p. 20). This evolution has evidently proceeded further in Dar'ang than in Ta'ang. In Ta'ang implosives appear only in full syllables, while in Dar'ang they are also found in presyllables; in Dar'ang (but not in Ta'ang) palatal stops are affected as well as labials and dentals: [19]

Ta'ang:	*p > bb	Dar'ang:	*p > bb
	*t > t ~ dd		*t > dd
	*c > c		*c > jj
	*k > k		*k > g

From an areal point of view, it is not at all surprising that labials and dentals are more likely to acquire implosion than are palatals or velars. Such is the case, e.g., in Tai, Karenic, and Vietnamese.

• *"Marginal tone languages"*

Shintani applies this term to languages like Arva, where tonetic differences are noticeable but where they appear to have minimal functional load.[20] There are many more tone languages of this "marginal" type in Tibeto-Burman, and in Southeast Asia generally, than I had originally realized.[21]

One of the major contributions of Shintani's study is to put this type of transitional tone language into high relief in a language family where phonemic tone is not reconstructible for the proto-stage. Since Khmuic as well as Palaungic show strong tonogenetic tendencies, it seems irresistible to ascribe this Northern Mon-Khmer propensity to areal (Sinospheric) influence. Since even different dialects of the same Palaungic language may show great surface diversity in their prosodic systems, this family now takes its rightful place as a laboratory for the study of the tonogenetic process.

The prosodic systems of the Palaungic languages are particularly difficult to analyze at this transitional point in their history. Much more data will be welcome. Nevertheless, Shintani has largely succeeded in unifying an unruly mass of data in terms of a single underlying phonological opposition. He is to be congratulated for this insightful and provocative paper.

---

dissimilation" that prohibited the cooccurrence of a preglottalized initial and a glottal final in pre-Lahu, leading to the Lahu high-rising tone (Matisoff 1970).

[19] Due to typographic limitations we here write implosives with double consonants.

[20] This was one of the six types of Tibeto-Burman tone languages discussed in Matisoff 1999a:23.

[21] My slowness to recognize this was undoubtedly due to the fact that the first five tone languages I studied (Chinese, Jingpho, Thai, Lahu, Angami Naga) were all of the omnisyllabic type. (Jingpho is a rather special case, since it is largely sesquisyllabic in structure, with unstressed prefixal syllables; the full syllables of such words are all fully tonal, however.)

References

Hashimoto, Mantaro J. 1976. "Language diffusion on the Asian continent: problems of typological diversity in Sino-Tibetan." CAAAL 3:49-66.

Haudricourt, Andre-Georges. 1954. "De l'origine des tons en vietnamien." *Journal Asiatique* 242:69-82.

--------. 1961. "Bipartition et tripartition des systemes de tons dans quelques langues d'Extreme-Orient. BSLP 56.1:163-80.

Kingston, John. 2003. "Mechanisms of tone reversal." In Proceedings of CLSTP, 57-120.

Matisoff, James A. 1970. "Glottal dissimilation and the Lahu high-rising tone: a tonogenetic case study." JAOS 90.1:13-44.

--------. 1973. "Tonogenesis in Southeast Asia." In Larry Hyman, ed., *Consonant Types and Tone*, pp. 71-95. Southern California Occasional Papers in Linguistics, No. 1. Los Angeles: UCLA.

--------. 1979. "Problems and progress in Lolo-Burmese: Quo Vadimus?" LTBA 4.2:11-43.

--------. 1991. "Jiburish revisited: tonal splits and heterogenesis in Burmo-Naxi-Lolo checked syllables." Acta Orientalia 52:91-114.

--------. 1999a. "Tibeto-Burman tonology in an areal context." In Shigeki Kaji, ed., *Cross-linguistic Studies of Tonal Phenomena: tonogenesis, typology, and related topics*, pp. 3-32. Tokyo: ILCAA, Tokyo Unviersity of Foreign Studies.

--------. 1999b. "In defense of *Kamarupan*." LTBA 22.2:173-82.

--------. 2003. "Aslian: Mon-Khmer of the Malay Peninsula." *Mon-Khmer Studies* 33:1-58.

Svantesson, Jan-Olof. 1988. "U." *Linguistics of the Tibeto-Burman Area* 11.1:64-133.

--------. 1989. "Tonogenetic mechanisms in Northern Mon-Khmer." *Phonetica* 46:60-79.

--------. 1991. "Hu, a language with unorthodox tonogenesis." In Jeremy Davidson, ed., *Contributions to Mon-Khmer studies: essays in honour of Professor H.L. Shorto*, pp. 67-79. London:SOAS.

Synchronic Perspective on Diachronic Tone Change in Suma and Other Languages

Mary M. Bradshaw
Kyungpook National University
bradshaw@wmail.knu.ac.kr

1. Introduction

A perennial question that is being asked anew in recent conferences and literature is: what does phonology have to say about diachronic sound change? Perhaps we could ask just as profitably: what does diachronic sound change have to say about phonology? This paper is an attempt to provide a preliminary answer to these questions, especially as they relate to consonant-tone (CT) interaction.

McMahon 2000 suggests that in a lexical phonology framework sound change enters the phonology at the postlexical level, proceeds through the level 2 lexical level and then into level 1. The flaw in this reasoning, in my opinion, is related to another recent trend, the tendency to further blur the boundary between phonetics and phonology, a boundary which has never been entirely clear. The postlexical level at which sound change is said to enter the phonology is nothing more than the phonetic level, and the phonetic level is where sound change takes place. The position that sound change takes place on the surface, in the phonetics, is not new but it needs new support and that will be provided here with evidence from CT interaction.

The surface changes that occur are reinterpreted in the larger grammar resulting in lexical changes, changes to the phoneme inventory and sometimes changes in the system of productive phonological rules. There are important differences between these three results of sound change. Lexical change alone does not require changes in the phonology. Changes to the phoneme inventory and changes to the rule system are changes in phonology but there are differences between them. What they share in common is that they must be viable phonological entities, and phonological viability is modeled in the theory of phonological features. Changes to the phoneme inventory reflect what are possible phonemic contrasts as these are expressed in phonological features. Changes to the system of phonological rules express possible interactions, as these are expressed in phonological feature configurations. Furthermore, for a change to extend to the system of rules, there must be an alternation involving the change. That alternation can be a new one as the result of a change or it can be a modification to an existing alternation. Without a relevant alternation, even a change involving possible phonological interactions remains unexploited.

A comparison of sound change that enters and sound change that fails to enter the phonology has the potential to help clarify the boundary between phonetics and phonology. Sound change reflects what is possible in the phonetics, and that sound change which fails to enter the phonology in the form of a phonological rule reflects what is not possible in the phonology.

In this paper, the theoretical underpinning of phonological CT interaction, the feature [L/voice], is presented. Then, the diachronic tone changes of Suma are presented in order to illustrate their surface nature, as well as a typical case in which a diachronic change results in a change to the rule system of a language. Next, some atypical phonological cases of CT interaction are shown to fit neatly into the same theoretical framework as more typical cases. From there, the case of a language with lexical effects but no effects on the rule system is used to illustrate the importance of alternations in triggering the latter type of effect. The final sections of the paper present diachronic effects that have no parallel in synchronic CT interaction. The first of these effects involves three-way splits in the tonal manifestations and the second involves consonantal characteristics other than those represented by the [L/voice] feature. In the end, the picture that emerges is one in which diachronic CT interaction and synchronic CT interaction are theoretically different in nature despite their essential relationship. We might conclude that diachrony throws a lot of stuff at synchrony but very little sticks.

2. The Multiplanar Representation of CT Interaction

Featural representation is crucial to understanding CT interaction synchronically and its relationship to diachronic consonant-triggered tone change. Synchronically, CT interaction in productive phonological alternations can always be characterized in terms of a single monovalent feature, [L/voice], which is multiplanar in nature. It can associate on the segmental level to either the laryngeal node of the consonant or on the prosodic level to the mora. When this feature is associated to the laryngeal node, the segment is phonologically voiced. When it is associated to a mora, the corresponding vowel has L tone. When it is associated to both, CT interaction takes place.

(1)

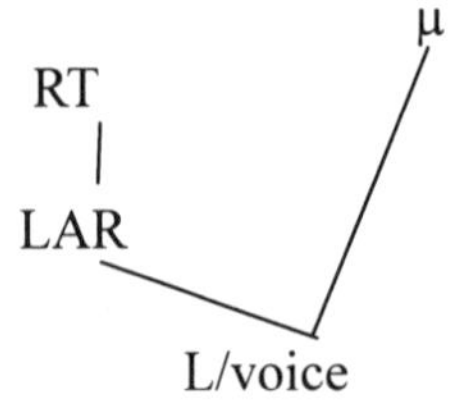

This is the featural configuration that crucially permits the interaction between a consonant and pitch on the phonetic level to become phonologized as a phonological rule of CT interaction.

Phonologically, the feature [L/voice] can spread from a mora to a following, or more unusually, a preceding consonant. Both of these are seen in Kotoko (Odden 2002), for example, and the former is seen in a range of languages some of which we will examine further. It can spread from a consonant to a mora, as in Yaka, Jabem and Jingpho. It can block a H tone from spreading, as in Siswati, Ikalanga, Bade and Ngizim.

The consonants involved in CT interaction can vary from language to language.

As is predictable from the relevance of the feature [L/voice], contrastively voiced obstruents are always depressor consonants in any language that displays CT effects. But other consonants may also be involved. These other consonants are never in contrast with a voiced counterpart and thus, may be assigned a L/voice feature without a change in their phonemic nature. Other consonants that may be involved include sonorants and, in at least one instance, implosives and glottal stop[1]. The latter case is found in Kotoko (Odden 2002) which has a number of unusual features in its CT interaction, none of which defies the generalization that phonological CT interaction is represented by multiplanar [L/voice]. Indeed, Kotoko supports that representation and the need for the separation of phonetic and phonological components of the grammar because of its nonconformity with phonetic expectations.

There has been some tendency in the literature to appeal to more than one feature in accounting for CT interaction. Halle & Stevens 1971 propose binary features [slack vocal folds] and [stiff vocal folds], while other phonologists suggest that there is a feature that combines H tone and voicelessness as well. There is no real evidence for this proliferation of features relating to the phenomenon of CT interaction as long as we recognize that there is a difference between phonological rules and lexical distribution or diachronic change. Without a recognition of the difference, we lose sight of a significant generalization. The need for the parsimonious use of features to describe phonological phenomena can help us to clarify the border between phonology and phonetics and lead to a clearer understanding of the relationship between phonology and diachronic sound change.

3. Tone Change in Suma[2]

Suma is a Gbaya language of the Adamawa Eastern group of the Niger Congo family which is spoken in the Central African Republic. It is a 3-tone language, and the history of its tone system involves two major changes. First, the introduction of mid tone, which differentiates Suma from its most closely related sister languages, eliminated the LH tone sequence, and, second, the effects of CT interaction reintroduced the LH sequence. These tone changes apparently have their origin in allotonic alternations[3] that are still evident in the closely related (and mutually intelligible) Gbaya

---

[1] Glottal stop as a depressor may come as a surprise to those who consider it to be a voiceless obstruent. Those who consider it to be a sonorant glide might find it less surprising. In the case of Kotoko, its nature as a glottalized sound is emphasized, although the lack of contrastive voicing is crucial.

[2] Data on Suma comes from my own notes. Thanks go to Namgbei Joel in particular for providing language information, along with other Suma speakers from Boguila.

[3] The relationship between borrowing of elements of the phonological and phonetic system and language internal change is not entirely clear. Suma, like many African languages, exists in a complex language environment and there could be a subtle pressure from surrounding three-tone languages to induce a change into a 3-tone system which, at the same time, could be based on the existing tonal patterns internal to the language. Although 2-tone languages are not uncommon and 4-tone languages are attested, a majority of the languages found in the CAR have 3 tones. For example, Sango, the national language which is used in the marketplace, in primary school education and in radio broadcasts, is a 3-tone language. However, the tones in Sango do not play a major contrastive role and Sango is spoken as a 2-

ɓozom where a H tone is realized as M after a L tone (Monino 1981).

3.1 Introduction of M tone

The first change, in which LH tone sequences were realized as M in tone took place both lexically and grammatically. This tone change deserves some attention because it is a clear case of the importance of the surface change from LH to M and the disregard for nonsurface information, such as the source of the surface sequence, whether derived or lexical, whether belonging to a single morpheme or a morpheme combination. Furthermore, it is of some interest as an alternative course that a language takes to add a third tone, even in a language that is moving towards some form of CT interaction. The important point to focus on is that where there was a LH surface tone, the tone is now realized as M, regardless of whether that LH surface tone is the result of a lexical tone pattern or whether it is the result of the placement of a grammatical tone. The significance of this indifference to the source of the LH pattern is that it tells us that the diachronic change is interested in surface events, the phonetic realm, and not with underlying events that belong to the phonological realm. The phonological realm is engaged when the surface tone changes require some kind of phonological interpretation.

The lexical tone changes can be seen in the following examples in which the LH tones seen in the 2-tone languages, which are the majority of the Gbaya languages. The Suma data is from my research, while the data on 2-tone Gbaya languages is from Monino 1981. Also given are other 3-tone Gbaya languages all from Monino's Eastern grouping. In that group, a M tone has also been introduced in the same environment as Suma's M tone. However, this innovation is a change from *H to M and is independent of the change in Suma's tone system, as is argued in Bradshaw 1996. As the following data shows, Suma's lexical H tone (*nú* 'mouth') corresponds to that of the 2 tone languages (*nú*) while the Eastern group's corresponding lexical tone is M (*nū*).

(2) *LH > M

	Suma	*2-tone*	*3-tone*
'hippo'	ŋgūɓū	ŋgùɓú	ŋgùɓū
'fog'	kūtū	kùtú	kùtū
'liquor'	dɔ̃̄ɔ̃̄	dɔ̃̀ɔ̃́, dɔ̃̀kɔ̃́	dɔ̃̀ɔ̃̄, dɔ̃̀kɔ̃̄
'side dish'	kpōō	kpòó	kpòō
'coldness'	gɛ̃̄ɛ̃̄	gɛ̃̀ɛ̃́	gɛ̃̀ɛ̃̄

There are 2 places in the proto-language in which LH tone patterns arise through grammatical tones. In one place, the LH tone pattern is the grammatical

tone language by native speakers of 2-tone languages (Samarin 1970). Another major influence on Suma is Gbɛya, a closely related (and mutually intelligible) language spoken in the prefectural capital of the Suma-speaking area, Bossangoa, where the closest high school is located. A full description of the language influences on Suma is beyond the scope of this paper and it is not clear that this would add any information worthy of note since the evidence of the language internal nature of the tone changes is convincing on its own.

morpheme signaling the perfective form of the verb. Verbs in the Gbaya languages are lexically toneless but bear grammatical tones indicating perfective, imperfective, nominalization, etc. In the perfective, the grammatical tone pattern for the closely related Gbaya languages of the Central group[4] is LH, while in Suma it is M. In this case, a grammatical morpheme that was *LH is reanalyzed as *M.

Roulon 1987 gives verbs in Gbaya kara ɓodoe in the perfective and they bear the LH tone pattern, as expected.

(3) *Perfective verbs in Gbaya kara ɓodoe (Roulon 1987)*

ɲɔŋ + Perf. → ɲɔ̀ŋá	'eat'
dɔk + Perf. → dɔ̀ká	'be numerous'
gbin + Perf. → gbìná	'break'

Similarly, the perfective verbs in Gbɛya have a L tone on the 'base' and a H tone on the suffix, resulting in a LH pattern.

(4) *Perfective verbs in Gbɛya (Samarin 1966)*[5]

kpà-á	'find (perfective)'
kùr-ó	'set off (perfective)'
rɛ̀m-á	'be sufficient (perfective)'
rɔ̃̀k-á	'be good (perfective)'

Suma verbs in the perfective bear a M pattern.

(5) *Perfective Verbs in Suma: Perfect = M*

a.	ĩŋ + Perfect → ĩ̄ŋã̄	'know'
	huy + Perf. → hũ̄yã̄	'release'
	pãŋ + Perf. → pã̄ŋ	'be bitter'
	ɓaa + Perf. → ɓāā	'peel'
	fũrĩ + Perf. → fũ̄rã̄	'spit'
	ɗafi + Perf. → ɗāfi	'make'
b.	dɛ + Perf. → dɛ̄ɛ̄	'do'
	dak + Perf. → dākā	'take out'
	duu + Perf. → dūrā	'be long'
	busi + Perf. → būsā	'become insipid'
	zuri + Perf. → zūrā	'languish'

A somewhat different situation underlyingly, but with the same result on the surface, is the case of the associative construction. Monino 1981 reconstructs the

[4] This group is proposed in Monino 1981. Suma was not included in his survey of Gbaya languages but segmental and lexical correspondences argue for its inclusion in this group (see Bradshaw 1996).

[5] I have taken minor liberties with the notation of Samarin's verbs, setting off the suffix with a hyphen and marking L tone with a grave accent when he leaves L unmarked.

following tone alternations for proto-Gbaya, a language with 2 tones. In the proto-language, a H tone is suffixed to the head word when there is a L tone on its right edge (and a L tone on the following word), resulting in a rising tone in words with a L pattern and in a level H tone in words with a HL tone pattern.

(6) *Proto-Gbaya (Monino 1981)*

a. L → LH/__L

*zù → *zǔ tòló	'dog's head'
*zàŋ → *zǎŋ tòló	'dog's insides'
*ɓàkà → *ɓàká tè	'tree branch'

b. HL → HH/__L

*kpánà → *kpáná lì	'jar of water'

This tone pattern, with a simple variation, can be seen in 2-toned Gbaya languages such as Gbaya kara ɓodoe from Monino's Northwest group in the data below from Roulon 1987. In this language, as in the reconstructed proto-language, the H associative morpheme is sensitive to the initial tone of the second word in the construction. Here we see that the associative H fails to surface when the second noun has an initial H tone. In addition, when the head word is monomoraic, only one tone is possible and so in the case where the H associative morpheme surfaces, the lexical L tone is eliminated. As expected for words with a H tone at the right edge, there is no alternation.

(7) *Gbaya kara ɓodoe (Roulon 1987)*

L	zù	'head'	L	zù wí	'man's head'
			H	zú tùà	'roof (top of house)'
L	tùà	'house'	LH	tùá tɛ̀ndɛ̀	'storage hut for cotton'
			L	tùà yé	'a village house'
L	zàŋ	'inside'	LH	zǎŋ ɗèlè	'surface of calebash'
			L	zàŋ wí	'stomach (inside of man)'
L	sùnù	'sesame'	LH	sùnú màì	'Mai's sesame'
H	nú	'mouth'	H	nú tùà	'door (mouth of house)'
HL	kûì	'egg'	HH	kűí kɔ̀rá	'chicken egg'
HL	kpánà	'pot'	HH	kpáná yì	'jar of water'

This tone patterning can also be seen in the two-toned Gbaya ɓiyanda from Monino's Southwest grouping. As in the reconstructed proto-language, a monomoraic word can bear a contour tone.

(8) *Gbaya ɓiyanda (Monino 1987)*

L	tè	'tree'	LH	tě kùmbɔ̀	'forest tree'
	tè		L	tè góŋ	'savannah tree'
	gùn	'trunk'	LH	gǔn tè	'tree trunk'
	gùn		L	gùn gásá tè	'trunk of big tree'

	tùà	'house'	LH	tùá gɔ̀lɛ́	'chicken house'
	tùà		L	tùà ʔɪ̀nì	'bladder (home of urine)'
	ɓàkà	'arm'	LH	ɓàká dàwà	'monkey arm'
	ɓàkà		L	ɓàkà wíwí	'man's arm'
H	kɔ́	'paw'	H	kɔ́ dàwà	'monkey paw'
HL	kûì	'egg'	HH	kűí gɔ̀lɛ́	'chicken egg'
	léɓè	'tongue	HH	léɓé gɔ̀	'panther tongue'

The pattern can also be seen in the associative construction of the Gbɛya language from Monino's Central group (where Suma also belongs) with data taken from Samarin 1966. In this case, when the word is monomoraic and there is a restriction on the number of tones it can bear, the result is an alternation from L to H tone, as in Gbaya kara ɓodoe.

(9) *Gbɛya (Samarin 1966)*

L	tè	'stem'	H	té gèɗà	'manioc stem'
	wèn	'affair'	LH	wèén kɔ̀fɛ̀[6]	'affair of the inlaws'
	saɗè	'animal'	LH	sàɗé gè	'what animal'
LH	dɔ̀ɔ́	'beer'	LH	dɔ̀ɔ́ kɔ̀fɛ̀	'beer for the inlaws'
HL	kpánà	'pot'	HH	kpáná rù kàmáà	'pot for mixing the food'

A look at the associative construction in Suma reveals a change in the pattern. Where the 2-toned Gbaya languages and the proto-language have a H associative morpheme, Suma has a M associative morpheme. Where the tone sequence LH is derived in the proto-language, it is replaced by M tone in Suma. The following data reveals that nouns with a L tone on the right edge alternate, while those with any other tone on the right edge do not. If the tone on a word is L, it becomes M and if the tone is HL, it becomes HH. The tones of the second noun in the construction have no effect on the tone alternations.

(10) *Alternations in the Associative Construction in Suma*

L	rì	'water'	M	rī bèrè	'breast milk'
	sàà	'game'		sāā bêm	'children's game'
	zã̀ŋ	'insides'		zã̄ŋ Bōnã̀m	'Bonam's insides'
	bèrè	'breast'		bērē bágàrà	'cow's teat'
	wɔ̀	'hunger'		wɔ̄ sàɗè	'hunger for meat'
	nĩ̀k	'tendon'		nĩ̄k gɛ̀ɛ́	'tendons of neck'
	mã̀rã̀	'tail'		mã̄rã̄ sàɗè	'animal's tail'
HL	kpã́nã̀	'pot, jar'	HH	kpã́nã́ rì	'water jar'
	kpárɛ̀	'seeds'		kpárɛ́ fón	'millet seeds'
	ɓólò	'pouch'		ɓóló nã́ŋã́	'animal skin pouch'

---

[6] Presumably the lengthening of the vowel in [wèén] is a phonetic phenomenon. The presence of a contour tone with a short vowel is licensed by the moraic nature of the final consonant, as in Suma.

kúrì	'egg'	kúrí gɔ̌k	'serpent's egg'
ndîŋ	'dirt, filth'	nɗíŋ wèn	'foul language'

When the head noun in the associative construction in Suma ends in a H or M tone, there is no alternation.

(11)	M	kōy	'remains'	kōy kàm	'leftover food'
		mbārā	'money'	mbārā zòrò	'price of fish'
		dɔ̄ɔ̄	'liquor'	dɔ̄ɔ̄ mbúrú	'palm wine'
	H	nṹ	'mouth'	nṹ Bōnã̀m	'Bonam's mouth'
		yéré	'basket'	yéré gɛ̀ɗã	'basket of manioc'
	LH	běy	'person'	běy àlà	'person of suffering'
	HM	ŋgéɗē	'turtledove'	ŋgéɗē zã̄ŋ zɔ̌	'bush turtledove'

The surface change that replaced *LH with M tone in the associative construction, as in the perfective construction, results in a reanalysis of the grammatical morpheme from a *H to a M tone. It is interesting that in the cases where the protolanguage derives *LH, the tone is now M, but where the protolanguage derives *HH, the tone has not changed. This case differs from that of the perfective in significant ways. In the perfective, the tonal morpheme was *LH, but in the associative construction, the tonal morpheme was *H. The derivation of a *LH surface pattern necessitated juxtaposing the *H morpheme with a lexical *L. Since the tone change was surface-oriented, only the presence of a surface *LH pattern was of any consequence. If the tone change was something other than surface-oriented, we would expect it to distinguish between the case in which a morpheme is underlyingly LH and the case where the sequence LH is the result of juxtaposing two morphemes.

It might be argued that the associative morpheme in Suma could still be a H tone and it simply lowers after a L tone. This is ruled out by data from longer words. Longer words are unusual in Suma and not often used in the associative construction, but when they are, the alternation is from L to M even in the case where there is a preceding H.

(12)	LLL → LMM			
	[yàwùndù]	'red peanut' (borrowed)	yàwūndū gèé?	'which red peanut?'
	LLLL → LMMM			
	[ã̀kã̀dèrè]	'toad'	ã̀kã̄dērē gèé?	'which toad?'
	LHL → LHM			
	[sìɪ́ɪ̀]	'ctn. insectivore'	sìɪ́ɪ̄ gèé?	'which insectivore?'
	[sùmã́rì̃]	'secret society' (from Banda)	sùmã́rĩ̄ gèé?	'which secret society?'
		HLL → HMM		
	[yã́kɔ̀ɓà]	'intestinal worm'	yã́kɔ̄ɓā gèé?	'which Ascaris?'

[nã́kã̀rã̀]	'shoe'	nã́kã̄rã̄ gèé?	'which shoe?'
[pã́pã̀nã̀]	'amniotic fluid'	pã́pã̄nã̄ gèé?	'which amniotic fluid?'
HHL → HHM			
[kpéɗésè]	'squirrel'	kpéɗésē zân	'bush squirrel'

No comparable long forms have been identified for the purposes of comparing Suma to the other Gbaya dialects, but it seems likely that in these cases the surface change from *LH to M no longer remains transparent. This might be attributed to the rarity of these types of words in the lexicon as well as their comparative rarity in individual usage. It is claimed that some of these words are borrowed forms (*yàwùndù* and *sùmã́rì̃*) and in those cases the surface change would not have been a factor. Given the unusual nature of these words, it is quite possible that all or most are words that were borrowed or created by compounding or other word formation processes after the sound change took place.

The reanalysis of the grammatical morpheme as a M tone in the associative construction, unlike the perfective case, entails some changes in tone rules precisely because there are relevant alternations. The alternation is no longer sensitive to the nature of the following tone and there is now a rule that raises the associative M tone to H after a H tone. The latter rule has to be sensitive to structural differences between an underlying HM tone and a derived HM tone as well as prosodic differences that relate to syllable count.

This excursus into the tone change in Suma which does not involve CT interaction has been undertaken to illustrate a larger point. Phonological tone change takes place on the surface, with different sources for the same surface pattern ignored in determining the pattern that emerges. This is not the introduction of a phonological rule LH → M. The rules that govern the alternations change in order to make phonological sense of the surface changes. This can be seen in the associative construction. What was at one time the simple association of a H morpheme has now become a more complex pattern with more complex rules, none of which is LH → M.

3.2 CT Interaction in Suma

At some point after the change *LH > M, another tone change occurred by which a L tone was introduced after a depressor consonant (*H > LH / D __, D = depressor consonant). The depressor consonants in Suma are the voiced obstruents, excluding the implosives and the prenasalized stops (which are allophones of the nasal consonants). Thus, it is only the consonants in Suma which are contrastively voiced that act as depressors.

This kind of tone change where a division in tones is triggered by voicing, with a low tone appearing after voiced obstruents and a high tone appearing after voiceless obstruents has been observed in Chinese, Karen, Tibeto-Burman, Austronesian, Tai, Miao-Yao, Vietnamese and Hottentot (sic), according to Hombert 1978. Siswati and Ewe could also be added to this list. This type of change can be illustrated with Lhasa

Tibetan. Here a voicing contrast is lost and a tone contrast is gained.

(13)

Classic Transcription:	kho	go	tho	do	sa	za
Present Pronunciation:	k^{h}ó	k^{h}ò	t^{h}ó	t^{h}ò	sá	sà
Gloss:	he	hear	number	two	mud	eat

(Hu 1980, cited in Duanmu 1990)

In Suma, unlike Lhasa Tibetan, the voicing contrast is retained and the sound change is not only lexical but also involves the introduction of a new phonological rule. Lexically, the LH tone contour which had been eliminated by the previous change now resurfaces in another context.

(14)

Suma (3 toned)	*2-tone Gbaya lgs.*	*Gbɛya*	
bı̀á	bı́á	bı́yá	'cane rat'
zɛ̀rɛ́	zɛ́ɛ́, zɛ́lɛ́, zɛ́rɛ́	zɛ́rɛ́	'disease'
gɔ̌k	gɔ́k, gɔ́ɔ́, gɔ́	gɔ́k	'serpent'
gàsá		gásá	'big'
gɛ̀ɛ́		gɛ́ɛ́	'neck'
zã̱̌ŋ		zã̌́ŋ	'different'
vũ̀'mɔ̱́		vṹ'mɔ̱	'fur'

This change had lexical consequences, as can be seen in the correspondences, but more importantly, it also resulted in the introduction of a phonological rule in which consonantal voicing and tone interact. We can distinguish the interaction in Suma from a phonetic effect in which tone is realized phonetically as L after voiced obstruents because there are cases in which a depressor consonant is followed by a H tone. In the following, nouns with depressor consonants bear an initial lexical H. It is not clear in every case why these exceptions exist, but monomoraic words like *zí* cannot bear two tones and *bágàrà* appears to be a borrowed form.

(15)

dúù	'bridge'	bêm	'child'	bɔ̱́ná̱	'kind of plant'
zí	'fly'	bágàrà	'cow'	dórò	'trail of small animal'

The phonological effects of the tone change show up in the imperfective form of verbs. This is not a lexical effect because the verbs are toneless, as mentioned in the discussion of verbs in the perfective, and their surface tone reflects the tone morpheme, which in this case is a H tone.

(16) *Suma Depressor Effects in Imperfective*

Depressor-initial		*Nondepressor*	
bǒm	'be blind'	'mɔ̱̃́sí̱	'compress'
dǐk	'be sonorous'	ɗúú	'be long'
gǎy	'reprimand'	éé	'leave behind'

gbǎk	‘borrow’	fɔ́ɗı́	‘stir briskly’
vǎy	‘bet’	páŋ	‘be bitter’
zùrı́	‘languish’	nɔ̃́y	‘boil’
bùsı́	‘be bland’	rɛ̃́m	‘be able to’
ɗìkı́lı́	‘tickle’	yárı́	‘unravel’
gɔ̀ɓı́	‘twist’	ŋgárı́	‘strengthen’
zìkı́ɗı́	‘delay’	níkı́rı́	‘exaggerate’

The phonological rule in Suma can be expressed as follows:

(17)

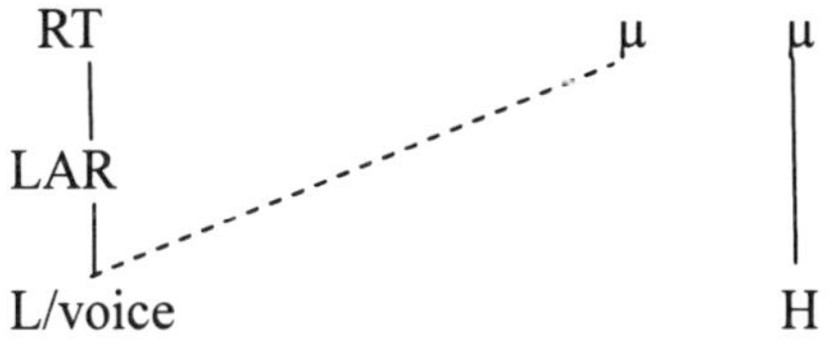

Verbs in the associative construction do not surface with LH when the initial consonant is not a voiced obstruent, as seen in the second column above. They also do not surface with a LH tone when the verb is monomoraic, even if the initial consonant is a depressor. This is due to the restriction, mentioned above, that does not allow more than one tone per mora. This pattern again makes clear that the depressor effect in Suma is not a surface effect, but the effect of a phonological rule.

(18) bɛ + H → bɛ́ ‘refuse’
dɛ + H → dɛ́ ‘do’

When these monomoraic verbs become bimoraic through suffixation, the depressor-induced tone pattern emerges, as in the nominalized form of the verb. As monomoraic verbs without depressors show, the grammatical tone for nominalization is H.

(19) a. bɛ+a +H → bɛ̀á ‘refusing’
dɛ+a +H → dɛ̀á ‘doing’
b. fo+a +H → fóá ‘agitation’
ɗu+a +H → ɗúá ‘collecting’

4. Additional Types of Synchronic CT Interaction

It turns out that there are a variety of phonological CT effects, all of which can be represented in terms of a multiplanar L/voice feature. One variation worth mentioning is the voicing of obstruents before a L tone. This occurs in Yaka, as shown in the following data. A noun which is class 5 in the singular and class 6 in the plural alternates between a LH and a H tone pattern. The class 5 prefix is a floating L tone.

(20) *Yaka (Kutsch-Lojenga 1998)*

ɓĭla	ma-ɓíla	'oil palm'
lŏi	ma-lói	'ear'
ndĭki	ma-ndíki	'wild yams'
yăká	ma-yáká	'Yaka language'

When the initial consonant is a voiceless obstruent, it becomes voiced just in the case where the floating L tone is affixed in class 5.

(21)

bŏɗi	ma-póɗi	'honey'
dăɗi	ma-táɗi	'sun'
dʒŏló	ma-sóló	'mushroom'
găngala	ma-kángala	'wooden frame'
βɔ̆φa	ma-φɔ́φa	'word'

This variation of CT effects is also found in the Austronesian language, Jabem. It can be represented as the mirror-image of the phonological process in Suma.

(22)

Notice that in Yaka, the implosives, prenasalized stops, and sonorants do not alternate because whether they are prespecified with [L/voice] or they become so specified through this rule, there is no change in their surface realization. There is no contrast between these types of consonants based on the feature [L/voice]. This finds a parallel in Kotoko, a Chadic language with the most liberal class of depressor consonants found so far.

When it comes to depressor consonants, voiced obstruents are always included in the set. In some languages, the set is extended to include sonorants, but implosives are generally excluded. In Kotoko, the set of depressors includes not only voiced obstruents and sonorants, but also implosives and glottal stop. Any consonant which can be specified as [L/voice] without a change in surface realization acts as a depressor consonant in this language. This set turns out to be all consonants other than the voiceless obstruents. Depressing behavior is seen for the full set of potential depressors in Kotoko in the recent past tense, as reported in Odden 2002. In this tense, M is assigned to the verb root and it is lowered when the initial consonant is anything other than a voiceless obstruent or *h*. Vowels without tone markings are M in the following.

(23) *Recent Past Tense in Kotoko (Odden 2002)*

D	gə̀ɗ-ə́m	'open'	T	pay-ə́m	'bury'
	zàk-ə́m	'beat'		sap-ə́m	'chase'
R	yèy-ə́m	'call'	H	her-ə́m	'bite'
	làb-ə́m	'tell'	D'	ɗə̀h-ə́m	'write'
ʔ	ʔə̀kf-ə́m	'approach'		ɓàl-ə́m	'dance'

A further typologically unusual twist found in Kotoko is that depressors can influence a preceding tone. In the case where the M tone is not lowered because of the initial consonant, it can be lowered by a following voiced obstruent. Odden 2002 provides the rule: M → L / ___ [+voice, -sonorant]

(24) sàb-ə́m 'grow' sxàj̀ì-ə́m 'be able' (recent past)

Although typologically unusual, this alternation is simply represented with the multiplanar [L/voice] feature. The lack of phonetic motivation for this kind of phonological process, coupled with its theoretical simplicity, argues for the importance of the division between phonetics and phonology.

(25)

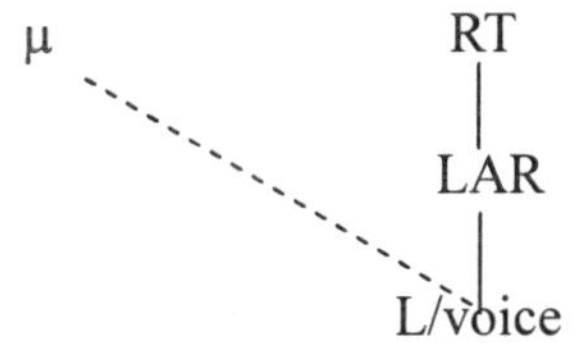

5. Languages with no alternation effects

In languages like Shanghai Chinese and the Chadic language, Mulwi, we find evidence of a lexical correlation between voiced obstruents and L tone without a phonological process of CT interaction, and in this they differ from languages like Suma. In languages with only a lexical correlation, the tone change which leads to the correlation does not enter the phonology because there is no phonologically relevant alternation which will take it in that direction.

The generalization in Mulwi, according to Tourneux 1978, is that any word in which the initial consonant is a voiced obstruent will have a L tone on the vowel following that consonant. In Mulwi, it doesn't matter if the initial voiced obstruent is preceded by a vowel or not. The set of voiced obstruents which condition this generalization does not include implosives or prenasalized stops.

(26)

zì	'to do'	gǎr	'collective hunt'
bàrà	'termite hill'	àvěk	'grass'
dìdìmì	'to dance'	ávùrvùlí	'whirlwind'

Verbs in Mulwi are divided lexically into H and L toned verbs. H-toned verbs with an initial voiced obstruent bear the tones LH.

(27)	bìzì	'spend the year'	bìzí	'apply pressure'
	kì	'flow'	kí	'accompany'

Thus, we can postulate that the tone change leading to the lexical regularities observed consists of inserting a L tone after a voiced obstruent in initial position (*H > LH/ D__), just as in Suma.

6. Diachronic but not synchronic: 3 way splits

Because of the nature of the phonological representation which consists of a monovalent feature, synchronic CT interaction can only involve a 2-way contrast in tonal effects. This makes clearer why depressor consonants can include more than just voiced obstruents. Since every consonant must be a depressor or nondepressor, it is not surprising that that division of the consonant inventory should show some variation from language to language. Diachronic CT interaction, unlike synchronic often involves 3-way splits in tonal effects.

In tonogenesis in Vietnamese, for example, Haudricourt 1954 proposed that the original split was into 3 tones based on the ending of the monosyllabic word. When the ending was a vowel or nasal, the tone was level. When it was a consonant (except for *s*) including glottal stop, the tone was rising. When it was *s*, the tone was falling. At a later stage, the 3 way split divided again into higher and lower registers yielding a system with 6 tones that contrast in height and contour.

(28) *Vietnamese (Haudricourt 1954, cited in Thurgood)*

	Tonogenesis	*Register Split*	
CV, CVN	level	pa	H
		ba	L
CVC, CVʔ	rising	pak	high rising
		bak	low rising
CVs	falling	pas	high falling
		bas	low falling

In Vietnamese, the original 3-way split is based on the existence and nature of a following consonant. It is not unknown in the synchronic phonology to have a CT effect triggered by a following consonant, as we have seen from Kotoko. But the nature of the consonants triggering the effect differs. Synchronically, the relevant feature is [L/voice], diachronically, the relevant features, if we choose to talk about diachronic phenomena in terms of features, would be features such as [consonantal], [sonorant] and/or [continuant]. In fact, it is most likely a mistake to think of diachronic sound change in terms of phonological features, not because features don't ultimately change, but because it tends to obscure the phonetic nature of the change itself.

Another 3-way split is apparent in the tone changes proposed in Burling 1967 for the Lolo-Burmese language, Maru. Proto-Lolo-Burmese is reconstructed as having five different tone patterns: 3 associated with open syllables (ending in vowels or nasals) and 2 associated with stopped syllables (ending in voiceless obstruents). Although no CT effect is found among the tones that were historically associated with open syllables, among the tones associated with stopped syllables, those with voiced obstruent onsets are now level L in tone and those with voiceless nonglottalized obstruent onsets are now level H. The latter onsets are aspirated voiceless when they are stops. Stopped syllables with glottalized obstruent or glottalized nasal onsets are considered toneless. In (28), tones are not marked in Proto-Burmish apparently because the nature of the original tones could not be reconstructed due to lack of consistency among the comparative forms. *w* and *y* which pattern with the voiced obstruents, are described by Burling as continuants produced with considerable friction. *y* is described as the voiced counterpart of *s*. It seems likely that these should be considered fricatives. (Although even if they were classified as sonorants they could be expected to pattern with voiced obstruents, as 28b shows.)

(29)		*Proto-Burmish*	*Maru (Burling 1967)*	
	a.	daʔ	dòʔ	'ascend'
		gyaʔ	gyòʔ	'cold'
		byok	byòk	'disappear'
		yaʔ	yòʔ	'lick'
		waʔ	wòʔ	'carry on shoulder'
	b.	mut	màt	'blow'
		mik	màk	'bamboo shoots'
		lok	lòk	'maggots'
	c.	phyik	chāphyák	'chili'
		tshat	tshéʔ	'deer'
		šok	šók	'drink'
		sik	sák	'new'
	d.	kʔyok	kʔyuʔ	'dry'
		nʔut	nʔat	'mouth'
		tʔap	tʔeʔ	'attach'

A 3-way tone split provides evidence that diachronically, unlike in the synchronic phonology, the triggering factor in change is not limited to the feature [voice] or even its surface equivalent. Diachronically, a number of factors can trigger change and a number of changes can be triggered. The repertoire of the synchronic phonology is much more restricted, and this allows us to develop a more constrained theory. Diachronic sound change, in common with phonetics, does not allow for a constrained theory to the same extent.

7. Sensitivity to other phonetic effects

The triggers for diachronic CT interaction are qualitatively different from those for phonological CT interaction. Phonological effects are limited to consonants which can be specified featurally with [L/voice]. Historical effects, on the other hand, have been claimed for voiced and voiceless obstruents, implosives and ejectives, laryngeal, aspirated and unaspirated voiceless stops, breathy voiced stops and voiced and voiceless sonorants. This can be attributed to the fact that historical change reflects salient phonetic effects of consonant on tone and not phonological effects. That is, it appears that consonants with shared laryngeal characteristics act together to induce tone change. However, it is not entirely clear that only these sorts of consonants are active in tonogenesis.

(30) Consonantal Factors in Tonogenesis and their corresponding features

-voicing	[L/voice]
-aspiration	[spread glottis]
-breathy voicing	[spread glottis, L/voice]
-glottalization	[constricted glottis]

Another tonogenetic effect, reported by Wayland & Guion, involves colloquial Phnom Penh Khmer which has diverged from standard Khmer and appears to be acquiring a falling-rising tone contour on some monosyllabic words. The trigger is identified as a trilled *r* in a consonant cluster, which is lost, much as voicing is lost in many languages in the process of tonogenesis, and the preceding consonant becomes aspirated. Wayland & Guion also report that the aspirating of the preceding consonant is not present in every dialect of colloquial Khmer where a tone contour is appearing with the loss of trilled *r*. Although it is not clear that phonemic tone is present in colloquial Khmer, the suggestion that tone changes can be triggered by trills is an unusual one, and indicates the freedom with which consonants interact with pitch in the diachronic realm.

(31)	*standard*	*colloquial*	(Guion & Wayland)
	pram	p^hẹăm	'five'
	trɨw	t^hɨ̂̌w	'correct'
	kru	k^hŭ	'teacher'

(32) Tone changes in colloquial Khmer

*#TrV(V)(C) > # T^hv̂́ (V)(C)

r > ø

T > T^h

ø > falling rising pitch

If we consider effects on consonants in the vicinity of a L tone, as in Jabem and Yaka, we find diachronically that the most common case is one in which voicing is lost when a L tone is generated after a voiced consonant. This has been postulated for Vietnamese, Chinese and other Asian languages. There is no equivalent in synchronic sound alternations whereby a consonant becomes voiceless before a L tone. Nor does there seem to be a diachronic case in which obstruent voicing is analyzed as resulting from the presence of a L tone. This gap may be due to a prejudice against that kind of an analysis, as suggested by Teil-Dautrey 1999. She claims that there is evidence for CT interaction in proto-Bantu and that it is not possible to tell if consonants triggered L tone effects or if L tones triggered consonant voicing effects. The evidence Teil-Dautrey cites relies on Guthrie's comparative lists of verbs and nouns and various reconstructions of proto-Bantu. She finds that lexically H tones predominate after voiceless obstruents, while L tones predominate after voiced obstruents. For example, using Guthrie's comparative lists of verbs and nouns, she finds that after *d approximately 35% of tones are H and 65% are L, while after *t approximately 70% of tones are H and 30% are L. This tonal situation is mirrored in words beginning with *k and *g, while those beginning with *y are more evenly split tonally, with about 55% H and 45% L. Problems are posed by *p/*b and *c/*j, but these are attributed to the possible existence of an implosive bilabial in the former case, and a question about the reconstructions in the latter.

In summary, there are major differences between the triggers found in phonological CT interaction and those found in diachronic CT interaction. Any category of consonantal laryngeal activity has been argued to trigger tone change, and considering the trilled *r* in Khmer, it is possible that any consonant or any consonantal attribute is capable of acting as a trigger. Within the synchronic phonology, only consonants which bear the feature L/voice can trigger CT interaction. A comparison of tonal effects on consonants also yields differences between diachrony and phonology. Diachronically, it is common for voicing to be lost once a tonal split occurs. Thus, the appearance of a L tone is synchronized with the disappearance of voicing. This is an effect that has never been reported in the literature on phonological CT interaction. Conversely, the acquisition of voicing by obstruents before a L tone, which is seen synchronically, has not been reported in the historical literature. Although this may be a function of the preference for an analysis in which L tone is generated over one in which voicing is generated, it may also be related to notions of what is phonetically more natural and thus provide another example of the close ties of diachronic change to the phonetic realm and the need to make a distinction between those areas and that of phonology.

8. Conclusion

It is true that the phonology and the phonologist have something to say about diachronic sound change. However, what there is to say is rather simple and straightforward in nature. Sound change takes place at the surface, in the realm of phonetics, and only enters the phonological rule system if it can be represented by means of viable feature configurations. In the case of CT interaction, sound change that cannot be expressed by the use of the multiplanar L/voice feature does not result in rules of phonological interaction. Diachronic CT interaction can enter the lexicon and affect the language, introducing tones initially as in tonogenesis, or affecting tone patterns of a language, such as reintroducing LH contours in Suma or introducing a third tone, as in Siswati. The phonology of a language can be indirectly affected by such lexical changes, but the rules that arise are those resulting from a reinterpretation of surface alternations affected by the changes.

The quest to find something meaningful to say about diachrony from a phonological perspective is one that should be undertaken with great care. If phonological theory is altered to account for diachronic patterns that do not occur synchronically, then the theory will be rendered ineffective in its predictive ability and in its ability to capture true synchronic generalizations about phonological processes.

A further question that could be raised is whether there is any explanation for patterns found in language families that might be due to phonological or phonetic factors endemic to those families. For example, a look at the Gbaya languages reveals that the M tone was introduced in at least 2 independent cases (Suma and the Eastern group) and in both cases it seems to be tied to the LH tone contour. Furthermore, CT interaction has been introduced in 2 different independent cases (Suma and Gbaya ɓokota). We might ask why a language like Siswati or Ewe introduces a third tone as a division in the non-high tone triggered by depressor consonants while in the Gbaya languages, where depressor effects are also fated to occur, the third tone is the result of the lowering of a H after L or the intermediate pitch quality of a rise in tone. Both changes are natural, but it is not clear why one predominates in one family, and another in a different family. Investigation into such questions may provide further insight into the nature of diachronic sound change.

References

Bradshaw, M. 1999. A Crosslinguistic Study of Consonant-Tone Interaction. Ohio State dissertation.

Bradshaw, M. 1996. The independent development of mid tone in Suma. OSU Working Papers in Linguistics 46. 1-15.

Burling, Robbins. 1967. Proto-Lolo Burmese. International Journal of American Linguistics 33(2):part 2. Bloomington: Indiana University.

Duanmu, S. 1990. A Formal Study of Syllable, Tone, Stress and Domain in Chinese Languages. MIT dissertation.

Guion, S & R. Wayland. Aerodynamics of [r] in tonogenesis. Ms.

Halle, M. & K. Stevens. 1971. A Note on Laryngeal Features. RLE Quarterly Progress Report 101: 198-312. MIT.

Hombert, J. 1978. Consonant types, vowel quality and tone. Tone: A Linguistic Survey, ed. By V. Fromkin, 77-112. New York: Academic Press.

Kutsch-Lojenga, C. 1998. Depressor consonants and rising tones in Yaka (C10). Paper presented at the 28th Conference on African Languages and Linguistics. Leiden

University.
Monino, Y. 1988. Lexiques Comparatif des Langues Oubanguiennes. LACITO, Paris.
Monino, Y. 1987. La determination nominale en Gbaya-Manza: Choix a la carte ou menu impose? In P. Boyeldieu (ed.) La Maison du Chef et la Tete du Cabri. Paris: Geuthner.
Monino, Y. 1981. De deux a trois tons, l'evolution tonale dans les Langues gbaya-Manza-Ngbaka. Tons et Accents dans des Langues Africaines, ed. by Guarismo. LACITO, Paris.
Odden, D. 2002. The verbal tone system of Zina Kotoko. In Schmidt, Odden & Holmberg (eds), *Some aspects of the grammar of Zina Kotoko*, 15-34. Lincom Studies in African Linguistics 54. Munich: Lincom Europa
Roulon, P. 1987. La determination nominale en Gbaya Kara ɓodoe. In P. Boyeldieu (ed.) La Maison du Chef et la Tete du Cabri. Paris: Geuthner.
Samarin, W. 1970. Sango: Langue de l'Afrique Centrale. Leiden: EJ Brill.
Samarin, W. 1966. The Gbɛya language. Berkeley & Los Angeles: University of California Press.
Teil-Dautrey, G. 1999. Notes sur l'interaction consonnes-tons en Proto-Bantou. In J. Blanchon & D. Creissels (eds.) Issues in Bantu Tonology.
Thurgood, Graham. Ms. Vietnamese and tonogenesis: revising the model and the analysis.
Tourneux, H. 1978. Le mulwi ou vulum de Mogroum, Tchad: langue du groupe musgu, famille tchadique: phonologie, elements de grammaire. Paris: SELAF
Wayland, R. & S. Guion. (to appear). Tonogenesis in Khmer. Papers from the Twelfth Annual Meeting of the Southeast Asian Linguistics Conference. Chicago.

Comments on "Synchronic Perspective on Diachronic Tone Change in Suma and Other Languages" by Mary Bradshaw

Yasuko Nagano-Madsen
Department of Oriental and African Languages,
Göteborg University, Sweden
Yasuko.madsen@japan.gu.se

Introduction

The ultimate question Dr. Bradshaw addresses in her paper is the relationship between phonetics and phonology. She attempts to answer this question by comparing the nature of diachronic and synchronic tone change in relation to consonant-tone interaction (hence forth CT interaction). She concludes that diachronic sound change differs qualitatively from that found in synchronic sound change, the former being a matter of phonetics and the latter phonology, so that it is not justified to alter phonological rules to explain diachronic sound change. Dr. Bradshaw's stance of separating phonetics and phonology is further reinforced by a number of irregular cases of CT interaction where phonetic predictions are not borne out. Since the core part of Dr. Bradshaw's paper deals with CT interaction, I have chosen to comment on her phonological theory of CT interaction as represented by the feature [L/voice] from the perspective of phonetic realization of [+voice]. However, before doing so, I will briefly comment on the language situation around Suma and other languages in the Central African Republic (hence forth CAR) that may be relevant for the present topic.

Suma and surrounding languages

The proto-Gbaya as well as the large majority of the dialects of Gbaya are attested as having a two-tone system, while the Suma dialect (Central group) and some dialects of the Eastern group have evolved to a three-tone system. The evolution of Suma tone change is analysed by Dr. Bradshaw as having two major steps, the first of which was the introduction of a M tone by eliminating the LH sequence. At some point after the change *LH>M, another tone change occurred in which a L tone was introduced as a result of CT interaction. Mid tone was introduced both in Suma and in the Eastern group, while the CT interaction took place only in Suma and Gbaya ɓokota. In this connection, Dr. Bradshaw raises an interesting question as to whether there is any explanation for patterns found in language families that might be due to phonological or phonetic factors endemic to those families. I would like to note at this point, that Gbɛya and Gbaya ɓozom (for the location of these dialects, see Fig. 1), the two dialects of Gbaya that are supposedly totally mutually intelligible with the Suma dialect (Monino 1995: 45), have not evolved to a three-tone system (cf. the phoneme inventories of these languages in Monino 1995: 143,162). The tone change in Suma may well have been induced by phonetics or phonology, but it will be worth noting the ethnically and linguistically complicated situation to which Suma is exposed (cf. Thornell forthcoming). Recall the cases for Trans New Guinea languages (Donohue, this volume) and The Bodish languages (Mazaudon, this volume) in which the areal, rather than the genetic model, of tonality was demonstrated.

Suma is situated on the northernmost border of CAR where the Gbaya language is spoken. It shares its northern border with Sara, a Nilo-Saharan language, and shares its southern border with Gbɛya, another dialect of Gbaya with which Suma is said to be totally mutually intelligible. It is known that the Suma people are ethnically mixed with the Sara people and Sumas are said to be bilingual in the Sara language (Sammy-Macfoy 1984: 41, Monino 1995: 16). This complex linguistic situation is also reflected in Suma's vocabulary. The word *bákàrà* 'cow' which is said to be one of the exceptional cases where the CT interaction has not taken place in Dr. Bradshaw's data of Suma, is a loan word from Arabic and is likely to have come into Suma through Sara. The majority of the Gbaya languages, on the other hand, have [ndae] for 'cow' (cf. Hilberth, 1952), which is also likely to be a borrowed word since such an animal as 'cow' is not indigenous to CAR. However, this word has also not been borrowed from Arabic. Alternatively, the word *bákàrà* might have been adopted from the lingua franca Sango that is used for TV and radio broadcasting, as evidenced by the fact that Sango has this word in its lexicon. Thornell (1998: 34), citing (Tchakongo 1988), reports that 70% of the radio broadcasting in CAR is in Sango.

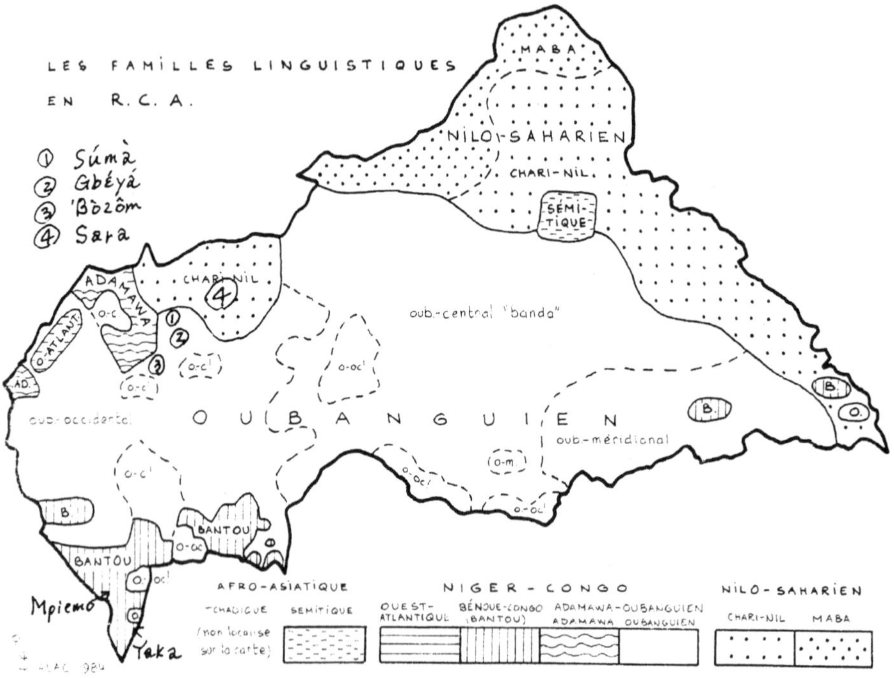

Figure 1. The language map of CAR and the location of Suma and other dialects/languages.

Dr. Bradshaw's data and analysis reveal that the tonal change in Suma is an internally induced one, but I wonder if there is any influence from Sara on this tonal pattern. I was not able to have access to the Sara phonology but the Genesis transcription of Sara indicates it has a three-tone system (/http://www.language-museum.com/s/sar.htm). There has been encouragement to study exactly which of its own features Suma abandons and which features of Sara it adopts (Sammy-Macfoy 1984: 41), but studies on Suma are extremely limited to date. Dr. Bradshaw's data on Suma tone, therefore, is a valuable contribution not only to phonetic and phonological theories but also to sociolinguistic research in CAR. Whether those dialects of Gbaya that have developed a three-tone system can eventually be analysed as a two-tone system is another area that deserves further research.

The Multiplanar Representation of consonant-tone interaction

In the earlier part of her paper, Dr. Bradshaw presents her theory of phonological CT interaction represented by a single monovalent feature [L/voice]. Closely related to the phenomenon of CT interaction is the group of consonants which are referred to as depressors. Classical use of the depressor consonants is found in southern Bantu languages where some consonants have a significant lowering effect on the tone of a following vowel (both H and L tones). Later, the use of the term depressor became more general and even consonants such as voiced obstruents with an intrinsic phonetic effect on the F0 of a following vowel were called depressors. Typical depressor consonants are voiced obstruents but sometimes other voiced consonants can also be depressors.

Since Roman Jakobson proposed the distinctive features, all of his features and the consequently refined ones have been defined by phonetic properties, either in articulatory or acoustic terms. The phonetic correlate of the feature [voice] is assumed to be presence or absence of vocal cord vibration. From time to time, a question has arisen as to why sonorants and implosives are not depressors since they are 'voiced'. Particularly problematic is the case of implosives as they not only do not act as depressors but can raise the F0 instead, in the same way as voiceless obstruents do.

In order to exemplify the phonetic realization of [+voice], I will show how voicing is realized for prenasalized stops, implosives, and voiced stops in Mpiemo, a language also spoken in CAR. Mpiemo is a Bantu language (A86c by Guthrie's classification) and shares its border with the Gbaya language. The consonant inventory of Mpiemo is pretty similar to that of the Gbaya language and the doubly articulated /g͡ɓ/ are only found in loan words from the Gbaya language. In Suma, depressor consonants are the voiced obstruents, excluding the implosives and the prenasalized stops. I am not quite sure about the phonemic status of these consonants in Suma, but in Mpiemo, the implosives and non-implosives are allophonic and there is no CT interaction. I have, however, no reason to claim that the realizations of the consonants are the same in Suma or in any other languages. These are only a handful of tokens to demonstrate the realization of voicing and its inconsistency in matching with the feature [voice]. For the details of the speaker's background and other information, readers are referred to Thornell and Nagano-Madsen (2004).

Figure 2 shows the mono-syllabic word spoken in word isolation form. Comparison of the voicing of the implosive [ɓɛ](/bɛ/) and the prenasalized stop [mbɛ](/mbɛ/) indicates a clear difference in the type of voicing. In the case of prenasalized stop [mb] (to the right in Figure 2), there is an even and regular voicing for a nasal, indicating that the dominant acoustic phonetic (but not perceptual) property of [mb] in this language is [+sonorant]. The obstruent nature that might be expected from /b/ is not evident. This observation agrees with our inductive prediction from the past data that prenasalized stops are usually not depressors, as also seen in Suma.

As for the implosive [ɓ], the voicing is not constant but instead increases followed by a burst at the release which has caused perturbation at the onset of the following vowel. The reason why an implosive (or a glottalic ingressive stop) is usually voiced is explained by Ladefoged (1975: 116) by the fact that the glottis is not usually totally closed when pulled downwards (perhaps for physiological reasons) but allows airflow from the lungs to keep coming up so that the vocal cords can vibrate. Notice, however, that by feature definition (through phonetic correlates), implosives are not voiced as they are [+constricted glottis] 'vocal cords are closed' (Halle and Clements 1983), i.e. they are not in vibration. The successive increase in voicing such as that observed in Figure 2 (left) for [ɓ] indicates perhaps that the glottis is closed initially but as it is pulled downwards, more and more air flows up through the glottis.

Difference in voicing is further demonstrated in Figures 3 and 4. In the words [aɗaro] and [adiβiç], compare the voicing for the implosives [ɗ] and the pulmonic voiced stop [d]. For the word [aɗaro], after the initial vowel, there is a state of voicelessness, indicating that the glottal ingressive initiaion is in preparation (glottis closed). This is followed by an increasing amplitude of voicing, as we have seen in Figure 1. Note that during this voicing while the occlusion in the alveolar region is held, the F0 value increases. It should be noted that this increase in the F0 value was caused most likely by the increased air pressure in the oral cavity rather than by the activation of cricothyroid muscles that are responsible for regular pitch control. This phase is followed by a burst (alveolar closure is released) and the voicing of the vowel follows. In the case of [d] in the word [adiβiç], we see the exact opposite. After the initial vowel, the vocal cords' vibration continues for some time but then gradually diminishes. By the time of the alveolar release for [d], there is virtually no vocal cord vibration left because the air pressure behind the oral closure becomes high and the air from the lungs cannot continue to flow to the glottis to allow them to vibrate. This explains why long (geminate) voiced stops are not common. The difference in [ɗ] and [d] have also affected the adjacent vowels differently. The initial vowel that precedes [ɗ] decreases in its F0 value, and at release there is increased F0 during the voicing phase of the occlusion, followed by a perturbation before the regular course of F0 manifestation on the vowel. These edge effects cannot be attributed to vocal cord vibration per se. Note that neither of the edge effects that arise from the implosive are observed in the case of [d].

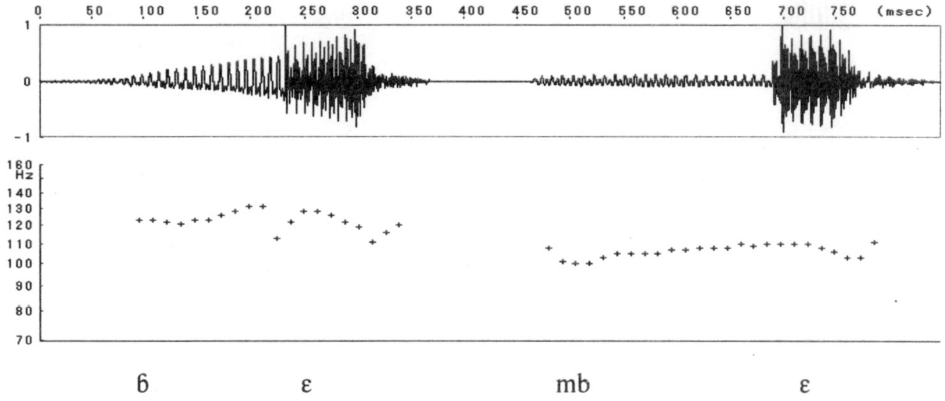

Figure 2. Sound wave and F0 contour for the word [ɓɛ] versus [mbɛ] in Mpiemo.

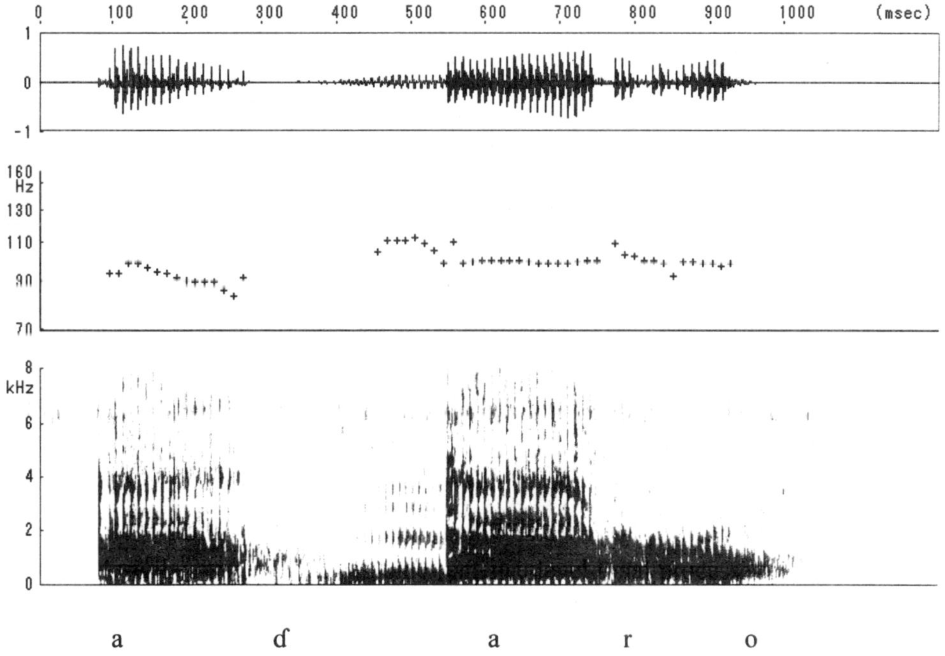

Figure 3. Sound wave, F0 contour, and spectrogram for the word [àɗáró] 'slick' in Mpiemo, illustrating the word medial implosive.

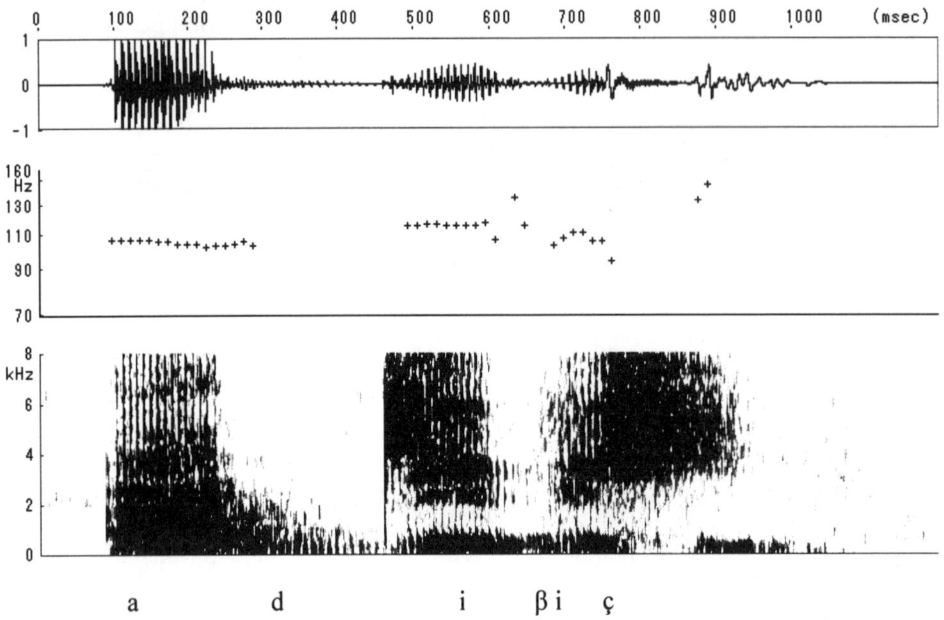

Figure 4. Sound wave, F0 contour, and spectrogram for the word [àdíβíç] 'open' in Mpiemo.

Although laryngeal features are defined as the physiological property of the larynx, research on the laryngeal activity in relation to voicing (and tone production) is methodologically difficult and thus still limited to date. Phonetic theories of voicing have mostly concentrated on the voicing distinction in the perceptual-acoustic dimension. It has been known for a long time that the contrastive voicing judgment lies critically at the region of voice onset time (VOT) rather than the presence or absence of vocal cord vibration (recent studies include Diehl, Castleman, and Kingston 1995, Castleman and Diehl 1995, Kim 2000). The feature [L/voice], which associates the articulatory dimension and the prosodic dimension, departs from the traditional feature [voice] defined as the 'presence or absence of vibration at glottis', making it closer to the phonetic findings. Indeed, a number of cases have been reported in which the only phonetic cue to signal the voicing distinction is a raised/lowered F0. Even though Dr. Bradshaw's theory is a representative one and will not be affected by phonetic details, it would be more revealing if future phonetic research clarifies the relationship between voicing and the tone production mechanism fully.

Finally, I agree with Dr. Bradshaw's stance of keeping the distinction between phonetics and phonology. Even my own study on how Japanese listeners perceived vowel duration with a varied F0 contour (Nagano-Madsen 1990) showed that listeners perceive such an effect through their mother tongue phonology. Although in many languages the changing

F0 is matched with longer duration, it is not simply the case that changing F0 results in different vowel duration percepts. Only when that patterning is incorporated into a listener's mother tongue phonology, will he perceive it as longer. Here, we may talk of intrinsic versus phonologized cases respectively. The final decision is made by phonology. At the same time, however, I feel there is a significant amount of data to support phonetic naturalness. What is needed then, is an explicitness to state when and exactly how the two dimensions may differ, as Dr. Bradshaw has shown us in her paper.

Reference

Castleman, W.A. & R.L. Diehl. (1995) Effects of fundamental frequency on medial and final [voice] judgments. *Journal of Phonetics* 24, 383-398.

Diehl, R.L., W.A.Castleman, & J. Kingston. (1995) On the internal perceptual structure of phonological features: The [voice] distinction. *The Journal of the Acoustical Society of America*, May 1995, Volume 97, Issue 5, 3333-3334.

Donohue, M. (In this volume). Tone and the Trans New Guinea languages.

Halle, M. & G.N. Clements. (1983) *Problem Book in Phonology. A Workbook for Introductory Courses in Linguistics and in Modern Phonology*. MIT.

Hilberth, J. (1952) *Vocabulaire Gbaya-Français*. AB Littorin Rydén Boktryckeri: Örebro.

Kim, M-R. (2000) Intrinsic versus interaction effects on F0. *The Journal of the Acoustical Society of America*, May 2000, Volume 197, Issue 5, p.2804.

Ladefoged, P. (1975) *A course in Phonetics*. Harcourt Brace Jovanovich, Inc.:New York.

Mazaudon, M. (In this volume) On tone of Tamang and neighboring languages.

Monino, Y. (1995) *Le Proto-Gbaya. Essai de linguistique comparative historique sur vingt-et-une langues d'Afrique centrale*. Peeters: Paris.

Nagano-Madsen, Y. (1990) Influence of fundamental frequency pattern on the perception of the vowel mora in Japanese. Phonum, 1, 31-35.

Sammy-Macfoy, P. (ed.) (1984) *Atlas Linguistique de l'Afrique centrale (ALAC). Situation linguistique en Afrique centrale: inventaire preliminaire: la Republique Centrafricaine.* Agence de Coopération Culturelle et Technique: Paris.

Tchakongo, C. (1988) *Le sango des medias à Bangui. Mémoire de licence*. Unpublished ms. L'Université Boganda: Bangui.

Thornell, C. (1997) *The Sango Language and Its Lexicon (Sêndâ-yângâ tî sängö)*. Lund University Press: Lund.

Thornell, C & Y. Nagano-Madsen. (2004) Preliminaries to the Phonetic structure of the Bantu language Mpiemo. *Africa & Asia* 4, 163-180. Department of Oriental and African Languages, Göteborg University.

Thornell, C. (forthcoming) Central African Republic: Language Situation. (ed.) K. Brown. *Encyclopedia of Language and Linguistics* (ELSEVIER) 2nd Edition.

Pitch Accent in Karitiana•

Luciana R. Storto & Didier Demolin*°*

*Linguistics Department/Museu de Arqueologia e Etnologia, Universidade de São Paulo**
Phonology Laboratory, Université Libre de Bruxelles°

1. Introduction

Our goal is to describe phonetic and phonological characteristics of pitch accent in Karitiana, an indigenous language of the Arikém family, Tupi stock, spoken today by approximately 350 people in the state of Rondônia, Northwestern Brazil. The language shows interesting interactions between stress and pitch, in a system in which both are predictable, and where the distribution of pitch is dependent on stress.

Karitiana is the first fully described pitch accent system within the Tupi stock (Storto 1999). Tupi languages have an important contribution to make to a better understanding of tone typology and universals, because within the stock there are tonal languages, pitch accent languages, and toneless languages (Moore 1998). It is an open question whether Proto-Tupi was a tonal language or not. Tonal systems (combinations of level H and L tones) have been reported in two out of the ten Tupi families: Mondé (Moore 1984, 1998), and Munduruku (Crofts 1985, Picanço 1999, 2003). In Ramarama tone and stress interact, but in an unpredictable way (Gabas Júnior 1999). In a fourth family, Juruna, tone has been reported as being unpredictable (Fargetti 1992), with stress depending on tone. Since these four families of languages are not more closely related to each other than to other Tupi languages, one could imagine that tone is not a recent development within the Tupi stock. Languages in which tone is reported as unpredictable are underlined in the diagram below[1]:

• This research was sponsored by CNPq PROFIX grant number 540532/01-0, by a visiting professor CNPq grant number 303770/03 (IE), by the Projeto Tupi Comparativo, funded by The Wenner-Gren Foundation for Anthropological Research, by Leiden University's Spinoza Project 'Lexicon and syntax', by FAPESP grant number 03/09930-9, and by an ARC. convention 98-02 n°226 of the Belgian ministry of scientific research.

[1] Gavião differs from Zoró, Cinta-Larga and Aruá mainly in tonal patterns. These four dialects could be classified as a single language since they are intelligible (personal communication, Denny Moore).

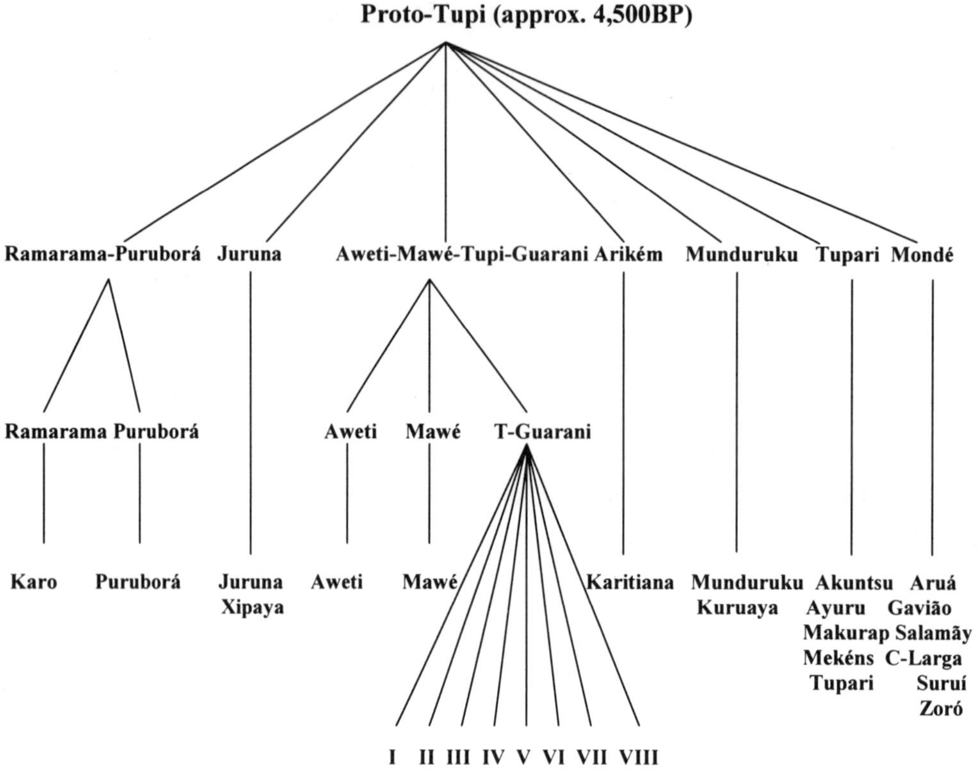

The Mawé-Aweti-Tupi Guarani macro-family does not have any tonal languages (Rodrigues, A. 1964, 1985, 1986, 1999, 2000, Lemle 1971, Jensen 1999, Schleicher 1998, Mello 1992, Franceschini 1999). Puruborá is an incognita, because the language has not been used for more than 50 years, and the remaining speakers have not reported any minimal pairs. Xipaya certainly displays pitch contours (Rodrigues, C. 1990, 1995), in what seems to be a pitch accent system, but it may be the case that this system will never be described, given that there are only 2 speakers remaining. The Tupari family has a few descriptions (Alves 1991, Braga 1992, Galúcio 2001), and none so far have mentioned tonal phenomena. However, in his fieldwork on Ayuru (a Tupari language spoken by 7 people), Didier Demolin has observed tonal patterns. It is yet unclear whether the language is tonal or pitch accent. To conclude, the only grouping inside the Tupi stock that certainly does not display any tonal phenomena is the Mawé-Aweti-Tupi Guarani macro-family. All of the others have either unpredictable tone (Mondé and Munduruku), unpredictable pitch accent (Ramarama and Juruna), or predictable pitch accent (Arikém). This picture is consistent with the hypothesis that Proto-Tupi was a tonal language and that the Mawe-Aweti-Tupi-Guarani macro-family was the only one in which pitch was lost completely. It remains to be determined whether any Tupari language has tone or pitch accent.

Most Tupi languages display another interesting suprasegmental phenomenon possibly related to tonogenesis: glottalization. Demolin & Storto (2004) have reported that in Tupi languages glottal stops (and related sounds such as laryngealized vowels and voiced glottal approximants) often have a marginal status as segments, in that their distribution is dependent on larger phonological units such as the syllable or the prosodic word. Since these larger units are the units to which suprasegmentals such as stress and tone are assigned, it is possible that glottalization plays a role in tonogenesis in Tupi. It is necessary to investigate all of the languages before we understand the implications of such facts for the reconstruction of Proto-Tupi. However, there is strong indication that Proto-Tupi may have used degrees of glottal constriction to mark suprasegmental phonological distinctions. Glottalization phenomena linked to structures higher than the segment are found both in families of languages that have glottal stops in their phonemic inventories and in those that arguably do not. In the first group are, at least, Aweti, Mawé, Puruborá, Ramarama, and Munduruku, and in the latter are, at least, Arikém, Tupari, and Mondé.

2. Descriptive Aspects of Pitch Accent in Karitiana

Materials and method

Recordings of Karitiana words and sentences have been made with three speakers. The data, based on the material presented in Storto (1999), have been collected with a *senhiszer* head microphone in order to avoid intensity variations due to possible movements of the speakers' heads. The recording of each sentence or word whistled has also been done. Then the data were processed with the *Signal Explorer* software. Fo curves have been made with the *Comb* method.

2.1. Stress

The assignment of stress in Karitiana is predictable based on phonological and lexical information. The stressed syllable in a root is always the rightmost, unless a heavy syllable is present (that is, a syllable with a long vowel), in which case, the heavy syllable will bear stress, as in (2). In case a root has more than one heavy syllable, as in (4), the rightmost heavy syllable is stressed[2] (Storto 1999):

1. 'grasshopper'

```
      *  line 2
      *) line 1
  (*  *  line 0
  pasen
```

2. 'alligator'

```
   *      line 2
   *)     line 1
  (*) *   line 0
  saara
```

3. 'to see'

```
       *  line 2
       *) line 1
  (*   *) line 0
  so'oot
```

4. 'owl'

```
          * line 2
   *      *) line 1
  (*)     *) line 0
  pyypyyp
```

The grid representations given in this paper are descriptive devices of our phonological analysis. They represent stress prominent syllables with an asterisk in line 1, and show primary stress in line 2.

---

[2] Karitiana has twenty distinctive vowels, but only five different vowel qualities: i, e, a, o, ɨ (long and short, oral and nasal). The consonantal inventory is: p, t, k, m, n, ɲ, ŋ, β, ɾ, s, h. The transcription used in this paper is orthographic. It differs from the phonemic transcription in a few aspects, namely: the high central vowel ɨ is represented as y; long vowels are represented as two vowels of the same quality; glottal stops, which are not considered phonemic for being limited to the onset of stressed syllables, are represented as '; the oral and nasal allophones of /ɲ/ are represented as j and j, respectively; nasal vowels contiguous to nasal consonants are not marked with a tilde; pre and/or post oralized allophones of nasal consonants are represented as preceded and/or followed by voiced stops with the same point of articulation as the nasals; /ŋ/ is represented as ng; the tap is represented as r and β is represented as w. Stressed syllables are marked here by bold. Syllables are formed minimally of a short nucleus, and maximally of an onset, a long nucleus and a coda. The onset of a syllable has no restrictions as to the quality of the consonants allowed, but codas do not allow any of the following segments: s, ɾ, β and h.

5.   *   line 2   *'gnat (mosquito)'*
       *)   line 1
      (*   line 0
    kyr<y>k

Example (5) is representative of a class of disyllabic roots with word initial stress. This class of roots at first sight seems exceptional in terms of stress, since the language usually assigns stress to the last syllable in a root. However, on closer inspection, it is possible to describe these examples as involving epenthesis of the final vowel (marked henceforth by <v>). Evidence in favor of this hypothesis comes from the fact that all disyllabic roots with initial stress, without exception, have the same vowel quality in the first and last syllable. Also, there is prevalent use of vowel epenthesis elsewhere in the language (between a root and its affixes, and in lexical compounds and other complex nuclei formed by combining a lexical and functional item) driven by resyllabification and restrictions on syllable well-formedness (Storto 1999). Therefore, we will assume that (5) is to be represented phonemically as /kyrk/. Epenthetic vowels are transparent for stress assignment purposes.

Derived and inflected words may involve more than one accented unit, because affixes may be inherently stressed. Compounds are always formed by at least two roots, all of which are stressed. In case more than one stressed lexical item is present in a word, primary stress is assigned to the rightmost stressed unit without exception.

2.2. Tone

Tone is predictable based on stress according to the following assignment conventions: from right to left (R→L), a tone is assigned to a syllable nucleus and spreads (leftward) only if that nucleus in unaccented (Storto 1999). That is, if a tone is associated to a stressed nucleus, it cannot spread. In this case, a different tone is assigned to the nucleus to the left of a stressed syllable, and spreads until an accented nucleus gets a tone, and so on, until the end of the word. For descriptive purposes, we will refer to the syllables through which a single tone spreads as a "tone domain". Words in isolation always bear a declarative boundary L (L%) at the end, unless they are affirmative imperatives, in which case the boundary tone is H (H%). In the figures given below, tones linked to stressed syllables are marked by an asterisk:

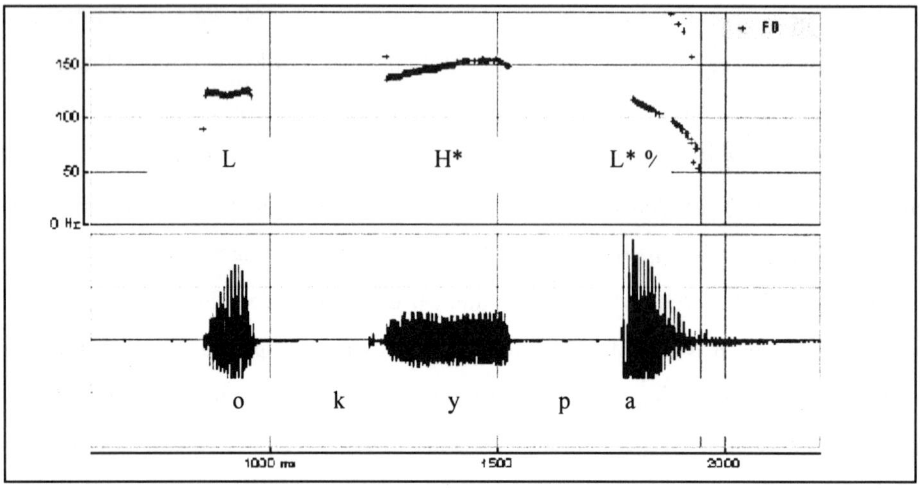

Figure 1. Fo contour and audio waveform of the word o**kypa** 'killing instrument'

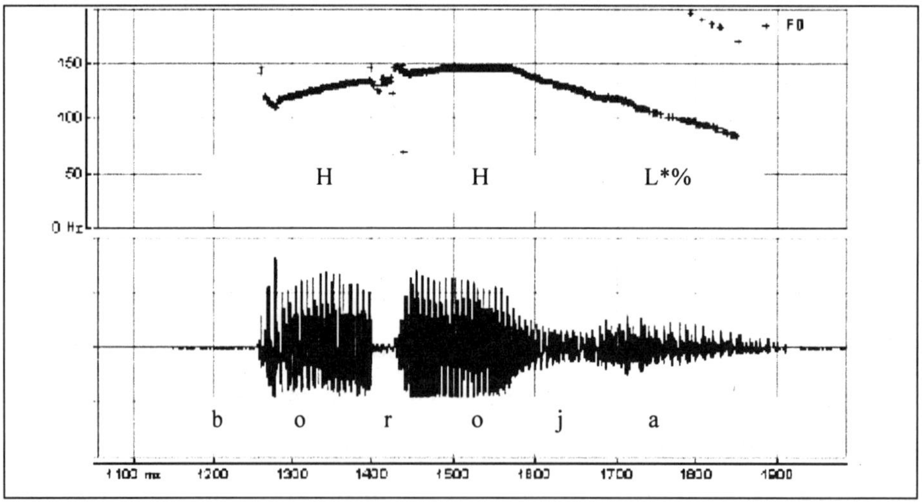

Figure 2. Fo contour and audio waveform of the word boro**ja** 'snake'.

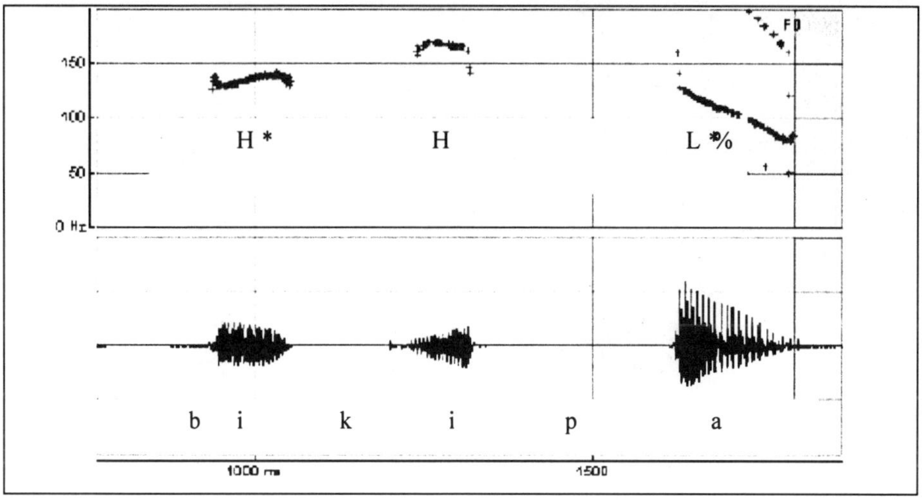

Figure 3. Fo contour and audio waveform of the word **bikipa** ‘bench’.

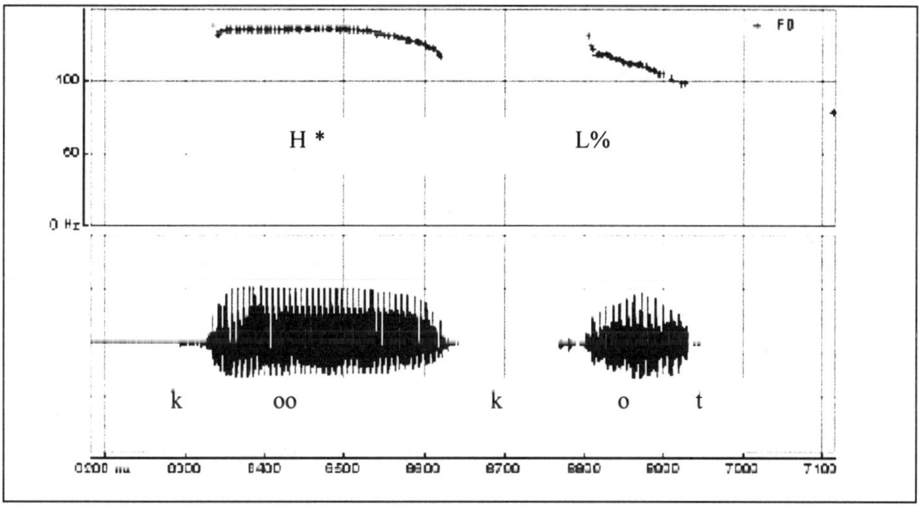

Figure 4. Fo contour and audio waveform of the word **koo**kot ‘to pass’.

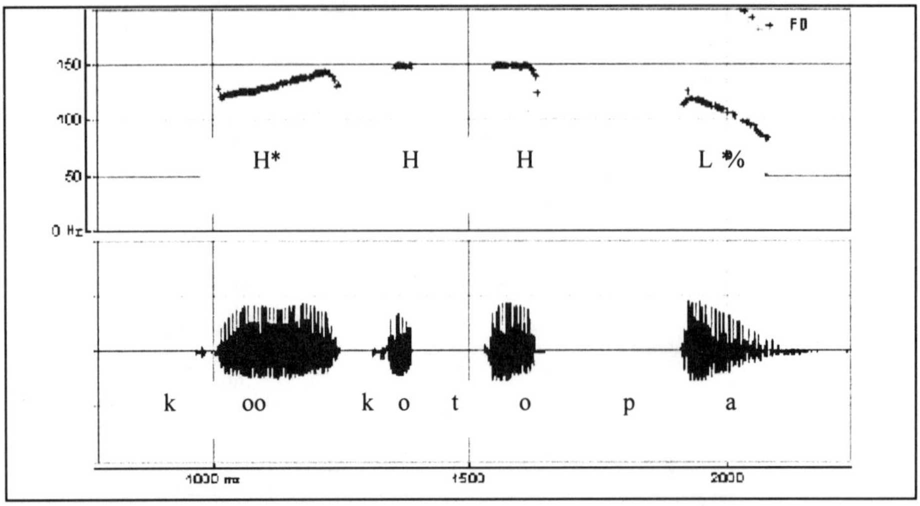

Figure 5. Fo contour and audio waveform of the word **koo**koto**pa** 'bridge'.

Nouns derived with the suffix "**-pa**" have two stresses: one from the nominalizing suffix and one from the verb root. Primary stress falls on the suffix, and secondary stress falls on the stressed syllable of the root. The tonal effects of such stress facts are: words like "**koo**koto**pa**" (HHHL) (Figure 5) derived from "**koo**kot" (HL) (Figure 4) and "**bik**<i>**pa**" (HHL) (Figure 3, derived from "**bik**" + "**-pa**") have a L boundary tone at the end, which does not spread to the left because a tone linked to a stressed syllable cannot spread. Then, a H tone spreads right-to-left through all other syllables, ending in the next stressed syllable. In the case of the monomorphemic word "boro**ja**" (Figure 2), a word with a single final stress, the pattern is the same: HHL. In words like "o**kypa**" (Figure 1, derived from "o**ky**" + "**-pa**"), where the second syllable of the root "o**ky**" is accented, we have a change in tone pattern from the second to the first syllable, generating LHL, because a tone cannot spread leftward if it is linked to a stressed syllable.

In Figure 6 below we have two unstressed affixes; the imperative suffix "–a" and the second person singular agreement prefix "a-". As such, they do not affect the tone patterns of the final word, which is LHH, because the only stressed syllable present comes from the root. The last tone is H because affirmative imperatives have a H boundary tone (H%). It spreads until it reaches a stressed syllable, and the tone assigned to the following tone domain is a default L.

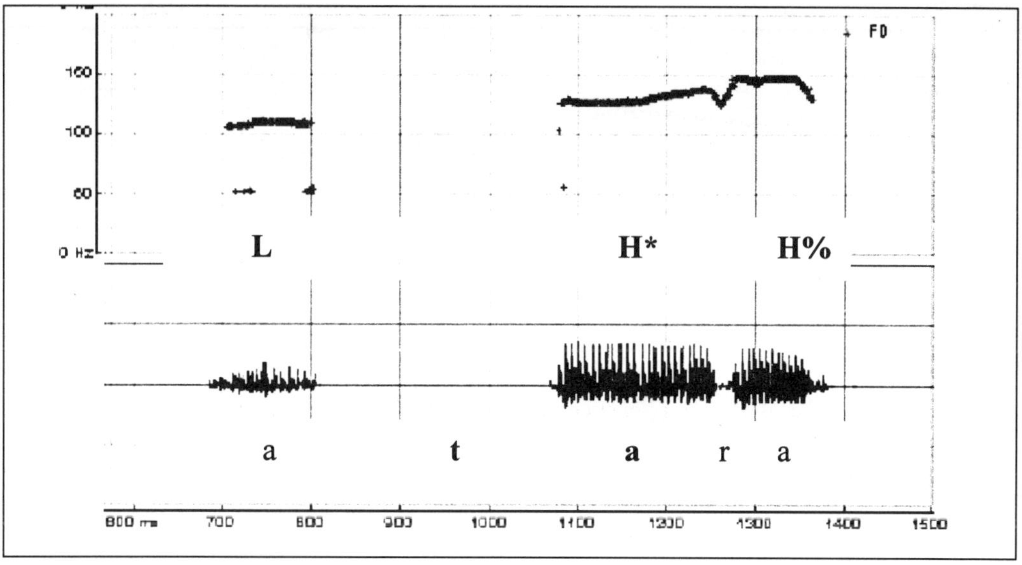

Figure 6. Fo contour and audio waveform of the word a**ta**ra 'go!'.

One may wonder where the H tone comes from in disyllabic words such as "**koo**kot". We assume that a H tone is always available for each root, associated to the stressed syllable (H*). When a L boundary tone is available and links to the last syllable, which is usually stressed (L* %), the H tone associated to that syllable becomes available to associate to other syllables in the next adjacent tone domain to the left. The result is a HL pattern for all disyllabic words in isolation regardless of their stress structure. In other types of words, all L tones other than the L boundary tone are given by default. There is no need to posit any other H tones than the ones which are required lexically in the stressed syllables of roots and stressed affixes.

Disyllabic words pronounced in isolation (Figures 7, 8, 9, 10) are somewhat exceptional, in that they do not follow the conventions described above. In such words, tone is always HL, regardless of the stress pattern. This can be explained if we assume that all declarative utterances must necessarily realize the L boundary tone (L%) at the end, as well as the H tone linked lexically to the stressed syllable of every root (H*). Note that the prohibition of spreading a tone linked to a stressed unit is respected even in these cases.

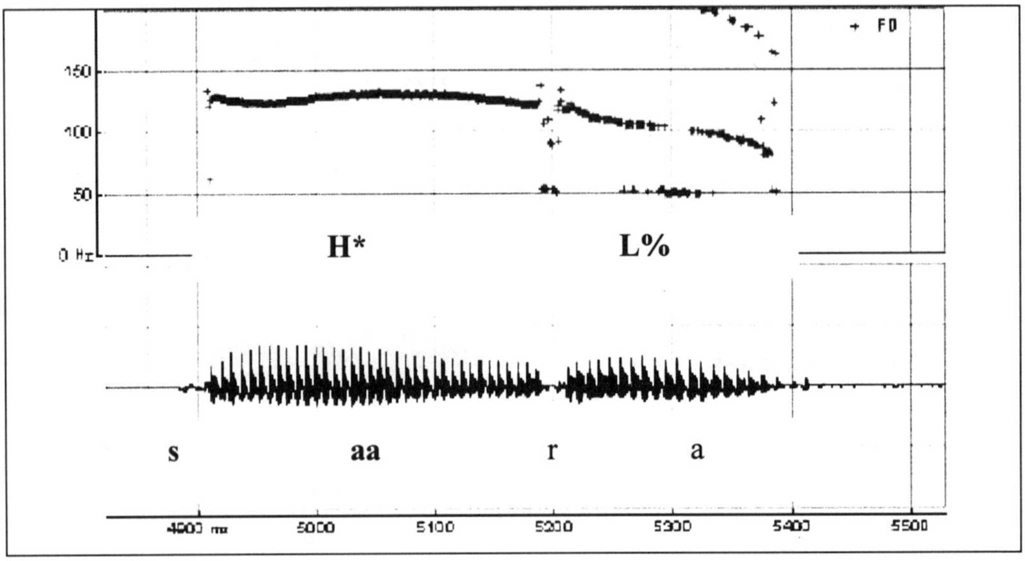

Figure 7. Fo contour and audio waveform of the word **saara** 'alligator'.

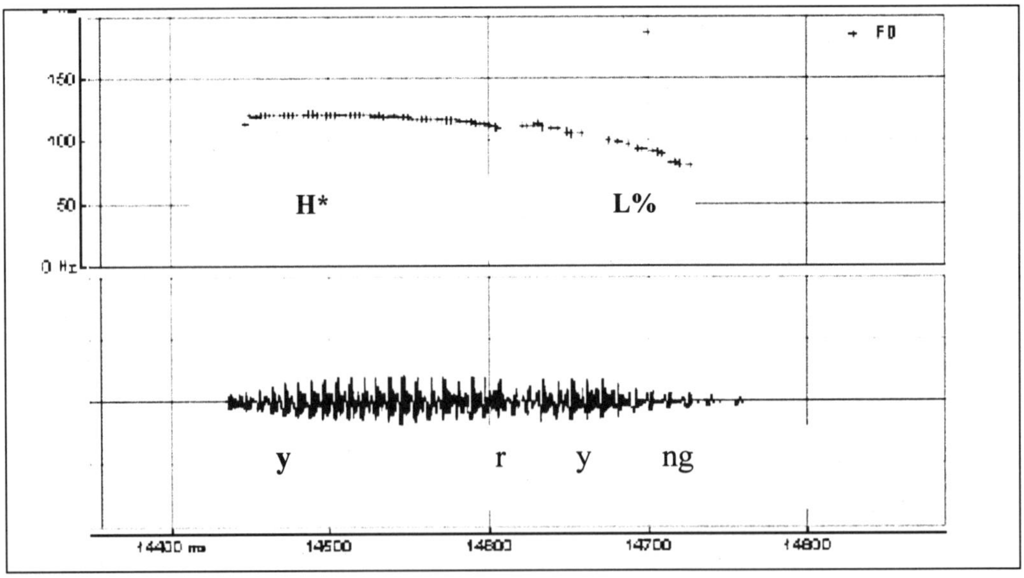

Figure 8. Fo contour and audio waveform of the word **yryng** 'cicada'.

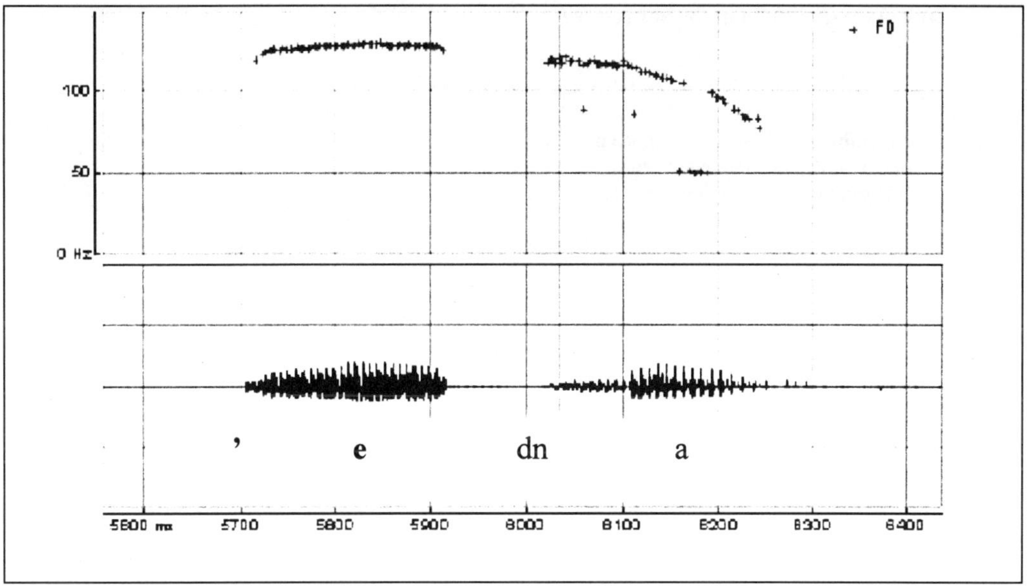

Figure 9. Fo contour and audio waveform of the word ’**e**dna ‘pregnant’.

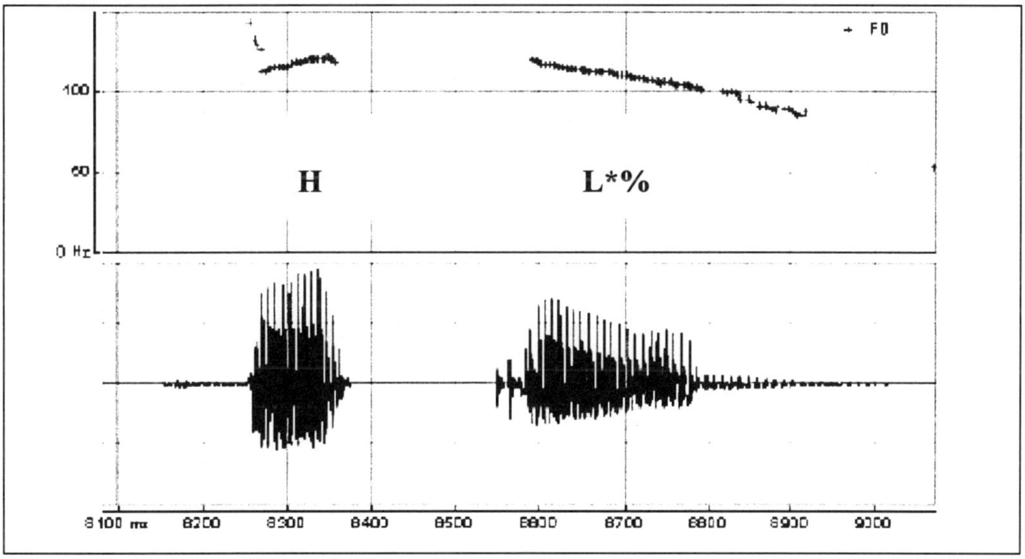

Figure 10. Fo contour and audio waveform of the word do**kon** ‘skunk’.

3. Pitch Accent Patterns in Sentences

Within sentences, words usually have a final H tone[3]:

6. na+**ambo** **saryt** go**kyp**
decl-raised ind.evid. sun
'the sun raised (to the sky), they say'

```
     *     *     *              *     *      *
     *)    *)    *)             *)    *      *)
* (* *  (* *  (* *    →    (*  *  * (*  *  (*   *
     |     |     |          \/    | | |  |    |
     H     H     H          L     H L H  L    H
  naambo saryt Gokyp       naambo  saryt  gokyp
```

In this excerpt from a sentence taken out of a text entitled "Gokyp" ('the sun'), each word has a H tone at the end, and the tone associated to that last syllable does not spread to the left because all of the words in question have final stress. As we have seen above, a tone associated to a stressed syllable does not spread, and a default L tone is inserted is the tone domain to the left of the H tone domain in each word.

Alternatively, when the stress of a word falls on a non-final syllable, as in "**pa**dni" ((7) below), all syllables to the right will have the same tone value as the stressed syllable:

```
7.   iaoky   padni          i+a+oky          padn+i
     \| / |   | |           3-passive-kill   neg-suffix
      L  H*  H* H           'He wasn't killed'
```

Words end in L tone when a boundary L tone is present at the end of a sentence (L in declaratives, interrogatives, negative imperatives and H in affirmative imperatives). For instance, the sentence from which excerpt (6) above was taken has a L boundary tone at the end.

---

[3] Abbreviations used in this paper: decl = declarative mood; ind.evid = indirect evidential (hearsay); 1s = 1st person singular agreement; 2s = 2nd person singular agreement; 3 = 3rd. person agreement or cliticized pronoun; neg = negation; impfve = imperfective aspect; aux = auxiliary; nfut= non-future tense (present and past); 2pron = pronoun of 2nd person singular; aff.imp = affirmative imperative; neg.imp = negative imperative; caus = causative; refrtl = referential aspect; obl = oblique Case; wh = interrogative wh word; vblzr = verbalizer.

8.

mora**song**, naa**mbo** sa**ryt** Go**kyp**, a**toop**, iri'**aj**

```
 \/    |       \/  |   |   |   |    |      |   |   \/ |
L    H*     L  H* L H* L   H*   L   H*  H  L* %
```

'Then, the sun raised up to the sky (they say) up it went'

The following example (Figure 11) makes explicit the presence of a L boundary tone in sentence final position:

9.

taso na+o**pĩ**+t omba**ky** 'the man cut the jaguar'
man decl-cut-nf. jaguar

```
  *        *          *                  *        *          *
  *)       *)         *)         →       *)       *)         *)
(* * * (* *      (* * *                 (*  *  * (*  *    (* * *
  |        |          |                  |  |  \ /   |      \/  |
  H        H          H                  L  H   L  H        H  L
```

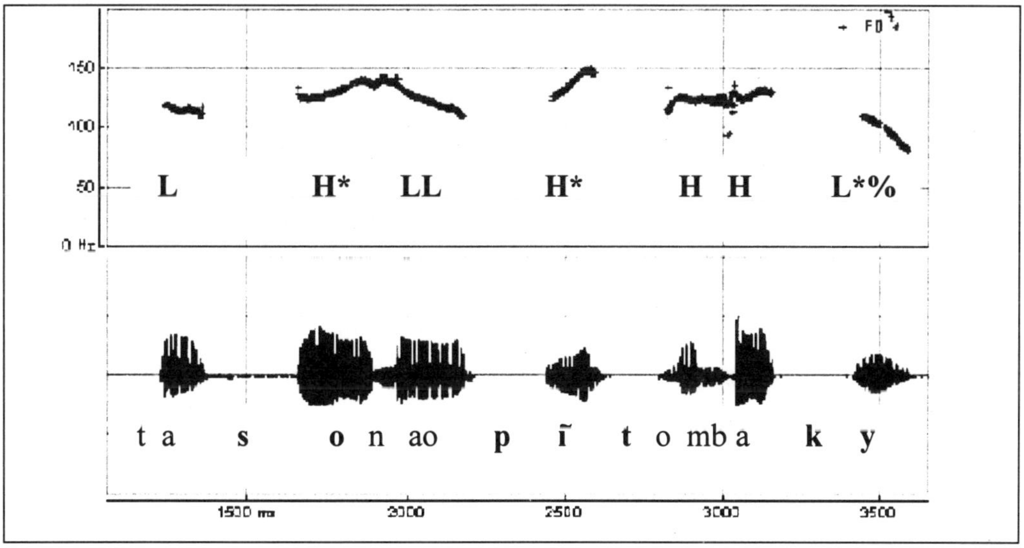

Figure 11. Fo contour and audio waveform of the sentence "ta**so** naop**ĩt** omba**ky**" 'the man cut the jaguar'

4. A Phonological Process involving Pitch Accent: Destressing

The example below (whose F0 curve is presented in Figure 12) is a case of stress deletion or destressing, an optional phonological process taking place between two words that may form a prosodic unit together, such as a verb and an aspectual auxiliary ("i'a tykat" in (10) below).

10.

yj**xa** pi**tat** **i'a** ty**kat,** irika . raj .
yj**xa** pi**tat** i+**'a** ty+**ka**+**t** i+ri+ka . raj)
human really 3-be impfve-aux-obl 3-cit-think

'"He was really human", he thought'.

```
     *     *             *         *    *      *
     *)    *)    *)      *         *)   *      *)
 (*  *   (* *  * (*  (*  * → (*  * (*  *    * (* (*   *
     |     |     |       |     |   |   |  |   |  |   \ /
     H     H     H       H     L   H   L  H   L  H    L
   yjxa  pitat  i'a   tykat  yjxa    pitat    i'a  tykat
```

The result of destressing is that the verb ("i'**a**") keeps its stress and the aspectual auxiliary ("ty**kat**") loses it. This causes the loss of the H tone associated to the stress of the destressed unit. A boundary L tone then spreads throughout the destressed word "tykat", because when the stressed syllable is lost, the prohibition against spreading a tone to the left is also lost.

The explanation for stress deletion seems to be that in the new prosodic unit [verb+aspectual auxiliary], the verb is the nucleus of the syntactic constituent and it keeps its stress (Storto 1999):

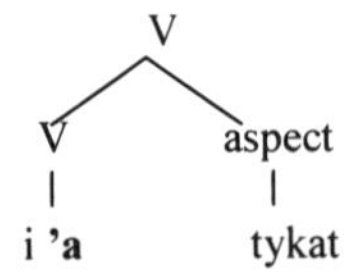

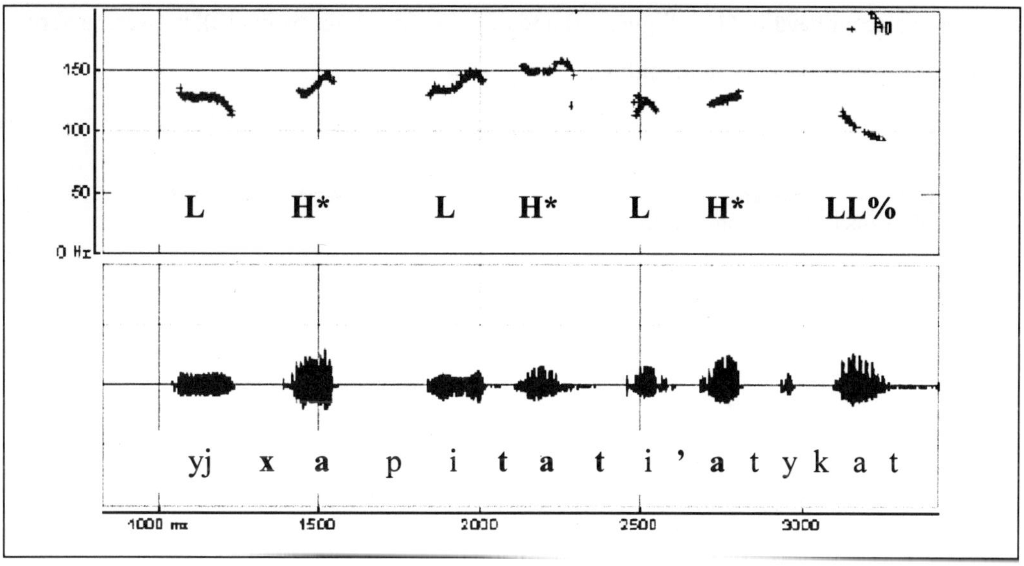

Figure 12. Fo contour and audio waveform of the sentence "yj**xa** pi**tat** i'**a** tykat 'he was really human'.

The syntactic environments in which destressing was found in the data presented by Storto (1999) are between two heads in compounds, or between a clitic and its host. The environments between a clitic and its host include verb-negation, verb-evidential, verb-aspect, noun-postposition, noun-adverbial, wh-word and adjacent head, and a verb plus oblique object. In the data digitally recorded for this paper we have no examples of destressing between a verb and an evidential or between a noun and a postposition, but Storto (1999) has recorded examples of such cases. The process of deletion is optional because these syntactic units are mapped into the phonology as phonological phrases just in case the speaker chooses to pronounce them as a phonological unit. Alternatively, in case the pronunciation is carried out on a word by word basis, the tonal patterns of each word in the unit are kept and destressing does not take place.

Interrogative sentences in Karitiana do not impose a H boundary tone as in many languages, but have a final L instead. The cases of stress deletion in interrogatives available in our data set are limited to two syntactic environments: between a wh-word and an adjacent head in (11) (Figure 13) and in polar questions, as in (12), between a verb and the negative polarity item "**mini**".

11.

ti+hoo+t a+aka an+o 'Where do you live?'
wh-aux-obl. 2s-aux 2pron-emph.

```
   *     *  *       *         *
   *)    *) *)      *)        *)
 * (*   (* * (*  →  * (*   * (*   (* *
   |     |  |       |    \ |  /     \/
   H     H  H       L      H        L
 tihoot a ka ano  ti hoot  a ka    a no
```

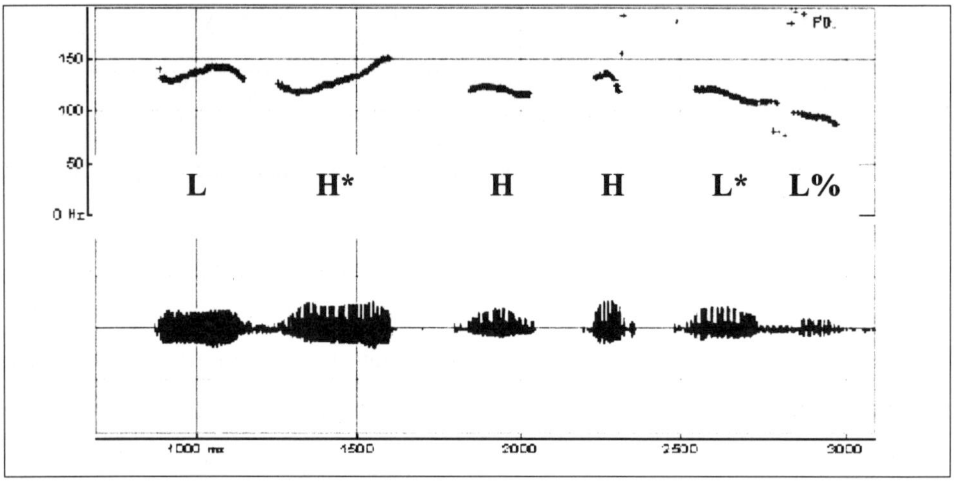

Figure 13. Fo contour and audio waveform of the sentence "ti**hoot** aka **a**no" 'where do you live?'

In (11) above, the loss of a stressed syllable in the auxiliary "**aka**" results in a HH configuration. We have argued above that the H linked to the destressed syllable was lost in the process of stress deletion. The HH tone of "aka" seems to have resulted in this case from another source, namely from the rightward spreading of a H tone attached to the wh-word "tihoot". There are restrictions on what kind of H can spread rightward in destressing environments. It seems to be a fact of the language that when a stressed syllable is lost, you only get spreading of the H linked to a preceding syllable if that syllable bears the main stress of that phonological phrase.

In the following example, we also have a change in the expected tone patterns. Instead of getting a HH pattern in "**mi**ni", we get a LL. The explanation is that "**mi**ni" loses its stress when it becomes a single prosodic unit with the verb, and because of this the H tone is lost. As in the case discussed above, the default L is inserted. There is no spreading of a preceding H because the preceding H is not linked to a stressed syllable.

12.

a+**tat**<a> **min**+i **an** yj+[a+**kan**] 'You are going to the village, aren't you?'
2s-go neg.pol-suff. 2s 1p-[there-place]

```
                                    *
         *     *     *      (* *              *              *        *  *
         *)    *)    *)      *)*)             *)             *)      (*  (*
      * (*  * (* *  (*   *  (*(*    →    (*   *   *    (* *   (*   (*  (*( *
         |     |     |       | |          |   \ /       \/     |     |   | |
         H     H     H       H H          L    H        L      H     L   H L
atata  mini    an   yjakan
```

Note that the compound word "a**kan**" is formed by two roots, and for that reason has two stressed syllables (the last one with primary stress), which accounts for the LHL pattern.

In the next two examples, we have evidence of the optionality of stress deletion. In the same syntactic environment, that is, between a verb and the negative word "**pa**dni" we have stress deletion in the verb in one case (13a) (Figure 14) and no deletion in the other (13b), where the verb keeps a H tone linked to its stressed syllable (Figure 15). The reason why the verb is destressed is the same as the one given for the [verb-aspectual auxiliary] unit in Figure 12: the syntactic head of the unit keeps its stress. The syntactic unit in this case is one in which the verb moves syntactically to adjoin to the functional category negation:

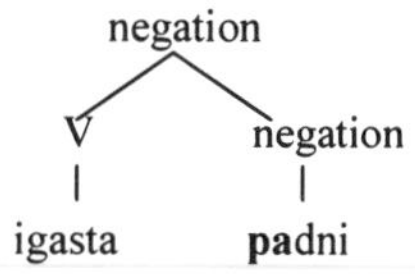

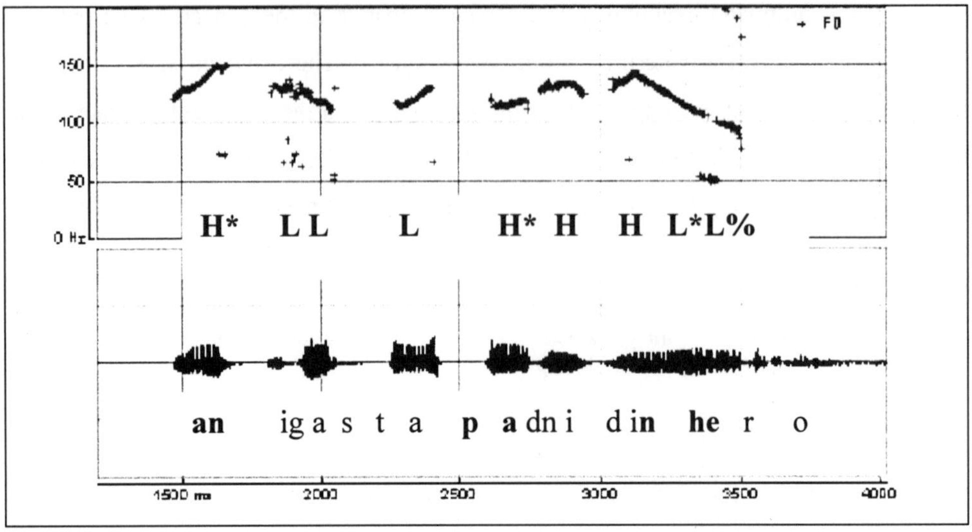

Figure 14. Fo contour and audio waveform of the sentence "**an** igasta **pa**dni din**he**ro" 'don't spend the money'.

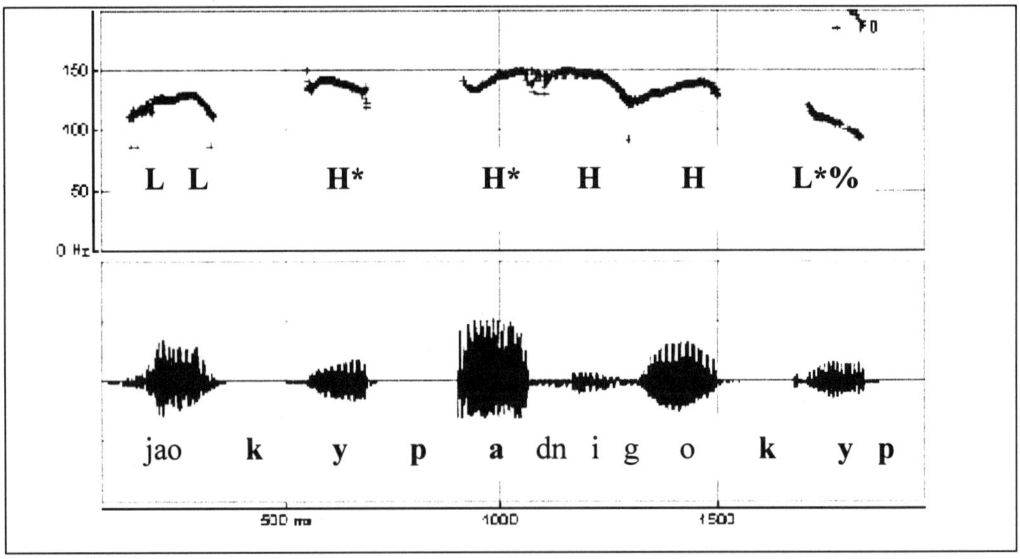

Figure 15. Fo contour and audio waveform of the sentence **an** iao**ky** **pa**dni go**kyp** 'gokyp was not killed'.

13a.

```
     an     i-gasta   padn-i      dinheiro                  'Don't spend money'
     2pron  3-spend  neg.-suff   money

     *        *   *       *         *              *         *
     *)       *)  *)      *)        *)             *)        *)
     (*  *(*  *   (*   (* *  *  →   *    * (*  *  (*  *   (*  *  *
     |        |   |       |         |      \ | /   \ /      | \ /
     H        H   H       H         H        L        H      H   L
     an   igasta padni dinheiro     an   igasta   padni  dinheiro
```

13b.

```
     iaoky    padni    Gokyp             i+a+oky          padn+i          Gokyp
     \ | / |    \ /      | |             3-passive-kill   neg-suffix
      L  H*     H*      H L*%            'Gokyp wasn't killed'
```

As mentioned before, affirmative imperatives end in H tone, whereas negative imperatives end in L tone. Therefore, the differences in pitch in the examples below come from the fact that the affirmative imperative ends in a H boundary tone, whereas the negative imperative ends in a L boundary tone. Note that the stressed syllable is the same in both cases:

14.

```
     a+tat+a                    'Go'
     2s-go-aff.imp.

       *              *
       *)             *)
     * (*  *   →    * (*  *
     |              | \ /
     H              L  H
     a  ta ra       a ta  ra
```

15.

```
     a+tat<y>                   'Don't go'
     2s-go-neg.imp.

        *               *
        *)              *)
     *  (*  *   →   *  (*  *
        |           |   \ /
        H           H    L
     a  tat y       a  ta ty
```

Negative imperatives are formed by a verb inflected with absolutive agreement (subject agreement if intransitive, object agreement if transitive), and followed by the negation word "padni", which is often omitted, as in (15) above. When the verb root ends in a voiceless stop, an epenthetic vowel is inserted between the verb and the negation word by the application of epenthesis. The quality of the vowel in this case is not determined by assimilation of the features of a preceding vowel, as in other epenthesis cases, but is listed in the lexicon as the high central vowel, orthographically represented as <y>. Note that even when the negation word is dropped, the epenthetic vowel remains. This occurs in all [verb-padni] units in the language if the verb ends in a voiceless stop, because there is a prohibition in the language against clusters of voiceless stops word internally or inside compounds and other complex heads. If the verb root of a negated imperative ends in a nasal consonant or in a vowel, predictably, no epenthesis takes place, and the verb stem is unmarked for imperative mood.

16.

an	y+mi	'Don't hit me'
2pron	1s-hit	

```
 *       *        *        *
 *)      *)       *)       *)
(*   *  (*   →    *    *  (*
 |       |        |    |   |
 H       H        H    H   L
 an  y  mi        an   y   mi
```

Examples (16) to (19) are negated imperatives. The negation word "**pa**dni" is elided in (16) and present in (17). No epenthesis takes place in those examples between the verb and the negation word because the verb ends in a vowel. In (18) and (19) the epenthetic vowel is present because the root ends in a voiceless stop. Note that even when the negation word is elided the epenthetic vowel <y> appears. This is evidence that when a negation morpheme is not visible in a negative sentence in Karitiana, it had been present and was subsequently elided.

17.

a+piso padn+i   'Don't step on it'
2s-step neg-sufix

```
 *   *           *   *
 *)  *)          *   *)
*(* *  (* * →  * (* *  (*  *
 |     |        \ /  |  \ /
 H     H         L   H   L
api so padn     a pi so  pa dni
```

18.

an   i+m+sembok<y>   'Don't get wet'
2pron   3-caus-wet-neg.imp

```
 *        *            *        *
 *)       *)           *)       *)
(*   * * ( *  *    → (*     * (* *  *
 |        |            |     \ /  \ /
 H        H            H      H    L
an  imsemboky
```

19.

an   i+atot<y>   'Don't take it'
2pron   3-take-neg.imp

```
 *        *          *          *
 *)       *)         *)         *)
(*    * * (* *   → (*      * ( * *  *
 |        |          |      \ /  \ /
 H        H          H       H    L
an   iatoty
```

Affirmative imperative verbs are marked by the suffix "-a", which occurs with a consonant-final root. When the root ends in a vowel, there is no morphological mark for the imperative. It is interesting to notice that negated imperative verbs ending in a vowel (such as (16)) would be phonetically indistinguishable from affirmative imperatives ending in a vowel if it weren't for the intonation difference between them.

Examples (20) to (23) are affirmative imperatives. All of the roots involved end in a consonant, and in that phonological environment the affirmative suffix is the allomorph "-a".

20.

```
     y+hit+a                                 'Give it to me'
     1s-give-aff.imp

       *           *
       *)          *)
    * (* *  →  *  (*  *
    |          |   \/
    H          L   H
   yhira
```

21.

```
     a+pom+a          andyk+a          'Go play!'
     2-play-aff.imp   refrtl-aff.aff.imp

       *     *         *       *
       *)    *)        *       *)
    * (*  * * (* *  → * (* *  (*   *  *
       |     |         | \ /   |   \ /
       H     H         L  H    L    H
    a poma andyka
```

22.

```
     a+pongyp+a                              'Shut up'
     2-be.quiet-aff.imp

          *               *
          *)              *)
   * (*   *   *  →   *  (*  *   *
          |          \ /    \ /
          H           L      H
   apongywa
```

23.

```
     bawak  a+haadn+a                        'Speak low'
     Low     2s-speak-aff.imp

      *    *        *          *
      *)   *)       *)         *)
    (*  *(* * →   (*  *    *  (*   *
      |    |        \ /    |   \ /
      H    H         H     L    H
    bawak ahaadna
```

Examples (24) and (25) are cases of imperatives with verb roots formed by compounding, and for that reason the bracketing shows two stressed units to begin with. The rightmost syllable in compounds gets main stress because destressing deletes secondary stress in these cases. For that reason, the tone linked to the second syllable can spread to the first:

24.

```
          a+pyt+'y                      'Don't eat'
          2s-something-eat

           *
    (*     *              *
      *  )* )             *)
  * (* (*    →    * (* (*
      |   |          \/   |
      H   H          H    L
  apyt  'y
```

25.

```
          a+py+so                 'Don't touch it (literally, 'don't be hand-aware')'
          2s-hand-aware

             *
    * (*     *              *
    *   *)  *)              *)
  (* (*  (*   →    *  (*  (*
        |             \ /   |
        H             H     L
  a  py   so
```

In (27) (Figure 16) the verb is followed by an oblique object and in the phonological phrase formed by these two units the verb gets destressed.

26.

```
          a+amy   ka+t     y+hot                 'Buy me this'
          2s-buy  this-obl. 1s-to

          *     *      *                  *        *
          *)    *)     *)                 *)       *)
  (*      *    (*     *(*   →   (*   *   (*      * (*
          |     |      |          \  /    |      |  |
          H     H      H           L      H      L  H
  a      my   kat   y hot       a  my   kat    y  hot
```

27.

```
    ōwā      hor<o>t   taka+'oot              saryt   Gokyp   'Gokyp began like a child, they say'
    child    like       decl-inceptive aux.   ind.evid

      *   *             *           *         *
      * ) *)            *)          *)        * )              →
  (*  *  (*  *     * * ( *      (*  *     (*  *
      |   |             |           |         |
      H   H             H           H         H
```

```
   *              *            *        *
   *)             *)           *)       * )
(*  *  (*  *    *  *  ( *    (*    *    (*   *
 \/     \/       \ /   |      |    |     |   |
 L      H        L     H      L    H     H   L
```

This final example of destressing is one in which a noun and the adverbial “**hor<o>t**” form a phonological phrase. The unit that loses its stress in such a case is the noun. As we have seen before, when destressing takes place, the H tone attached to the stressed syllable is deleted and a default L tone is inserted.

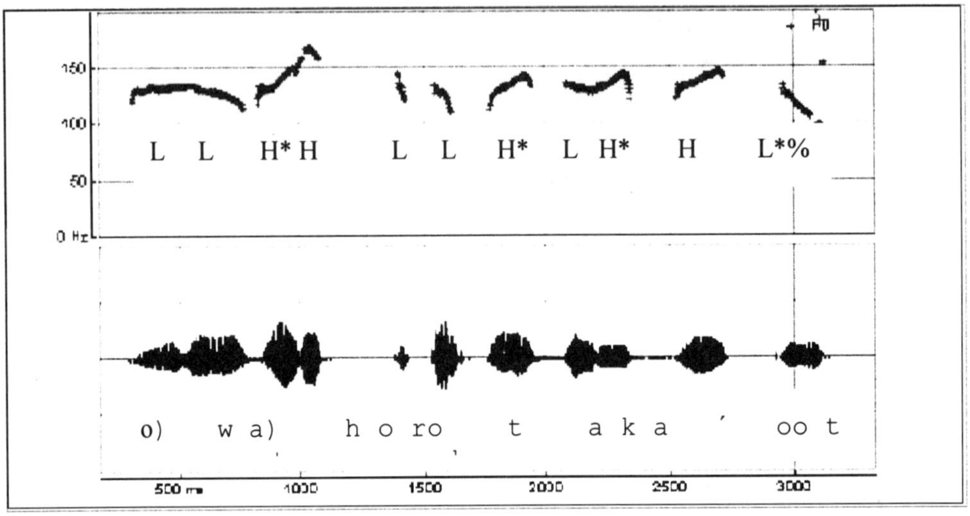

Figure 16. Fo curve and audio waveform of the sentence “õ**wã** horot taka‘**oot** sa**ryt** Go**kyp**” ‘Gokyp began like a child, they say’.

5. Observations on pitch realization in Karitiana

Although a more systematic account of the realization of pitch in Karitiana remains to be done, some observations can already be made with the data upon which this work has been done.

When initial and not stressed, a high tone (H) is slightly rising (Figures 2 and 10). When stressed in initial position a H is rather stable (Figures 4, 7, 8, 9), sometimes with a short falling end (Figures 4 and 7). In this position, it can also be rising but in this case its duration is shorter. A H with a rising contour can also be observed when it is in non-initial position. An interesting observation for H tones is that when there are sequences of H tones (2 or more), the last tones of the sequence are always higher than the first (Figures 2, 3, 5, 6, 11, 13, 14, 15). However between words, there is occasionally a downstep of the pitch (Figures 11, 13, 15).

When initial, a low (L) tone has a level contour (Figures 1, 6, 11, 12, 13). When final there is always a sharp falling contour, whether it is in a stressed syllable or not (Figures 1-5, 7-16). Sequences of L tones show a clear downdrift effect except in initial position (Figures 11, 13, 14). After a H tone, a L always has a falling contour (Figures 1-5, 7-16). When followed by a H in a stressed syllable a L tone is always raised and can have various contours (Figures 12, 13, 14). This effect of L rising seems to be quite frequent in the language and should be explored more systematically.

6. Conclusion

This paper described the pitch accent system of Karitiana, the last surviving language of the Arikém family, Tupi stock. It was shown that both stress and tone are predictable in Karitiana, and that both phenomena interact, the latter depending on the former. One phonological process was shown to operate inside prosodic units larger than words: destressing. We have provided acoustic data showing that stress is realized as length or intensity, and pitch is realized as a difference in fundamental frequency with an ambitus ranging from 80 to 170 Hz. Pitch curves show that downdrift acts on sequences of L tones in Karitiana.

References

ALVES, P. 1991. *Análise Fonológica Preliminar da Língua Tupari*. MA. Thesis. Univeridade de Brasília, Brazil.

BRAGA, A. 1992. *A Fonologia Segmental e Aspectos Morfofonológicos da Língua Makurap (Tupi)*. MA. Thesis. Universidade Estadual de Campinas (UNICAMP), Brazil.

CROFTS, M. 1985. *Aspectos da Língua Mundurukú*. Brasília: SIL.

DEMOLIN, D. & L. STORTO 2004. The Phonetics and Phonology of Glottalization in Tupi. Paper presented at XIX Meeting of the Associação Nacional de Pós Graduação em Letras e Lingüística. Maceió. June 28th to July 2nd.

FARGETTI, C. 1992. *Análise Fonológica da Língua Juruna*. MA. Thesis. Universidade Estadual de Campians (UNICAMP), Brazil.

FRANCESCHINI, D. 1999. *La Langue Sateré-Mawé: description et analyse morphosintaxique*. Ph.D. Dissertation. Universite Paris VII.

GABAS JR. 1999. *A Grammar of Karo*. Ph.D. Dissertation. University of California: Santa Barbara.

GALÚCIO, A. V. 2001 A *Morphosyntax of Mekéns*. Ph.D. Dissertation. University of Chicago.

JENSEN, C. 1999. Tupi-Guarani. In *The Amazonian Languages*, R.M.W. Dixon & A. Aichenvald (eds.), 125-163. Cambridge: Cambridge University Press.

LACERDA, M. 2004. Phonétique et phonologie du Surui. Mémoire de DEA, Université Libre de Bruxelles.

LADD, R. D. An introduction to intonational phonology. In Docherty, G. J. & R. Ladd (editors) *Papers in Laboratory phonology II: Gesture, Segment, Prosody*. 321-334. Cambridge University Press.

LEMLE, M. 1971. Internal Classification of the Tupi-Guarani Linguistic Family. *Tupi Studies I.* Norman: SIL.

MELLO, A. 1992. *Estudo Comparativo do Léxico da Família Lingüística Tupi-Guarani.* MA Thesis. UFSC.

MOORE, D. 1998. Tonal System of the Gavião Language of Rondônia, Brazil, In Tupian Perspective. *Cross Linguistic Studies of Tonal Phenomena.* 297-310. Tokyo: ILCAA.

________ 1984. *Syntax of the Language of the Gavião Indians of Rondônia, Brazil.* Ph.D. Dissertation. City University of New York.

PICANÇO, G. 1999. *Estudo Preliminar da Fonologia da Lingua Munduruku.* BA Monograph. UFPA.

________ 2002. O sistema tonal de Munduruku revisitado. Línguas Indígenas Brasileiras; Fonologia, Gramática e História; Atas do I Encontro Internacional do Grupo de Trabalho sobre Línguas Indígenas da ANPOLL, Tomo I, org. por A. S. A. C. Cabral e A. D. Rodrigues, pp. 243-253. Belém: Editora Universitária UFPA.

________ 2003. Tonal polarity as phonologically conditioned allomorphy in Munduruku. In Julie Larson & Mary Paster (editors), *Proceedings of the XXVIIIth Annual meeting of the Berkeley Linguistic Society*. 237-250. Berkeley Linguistics Society.

RODRIGUES, A. 1964. A Classificação do Tronco Lingüístico Tupi. *Revista de Antropologia 12*: 99-104. São Paulo.

_________ 1985 Relações Internas da Família Lingüística Tupi-Guarani. *Revista de Antropologia 27/28.*

_________ 1986. *Línguas Brasileiras - para o conhecimento das linguas indigenas.* São Paulo: Loyola.

_________ 1999. Tupi. In *The Amazonian Languages*, R.M.W. Dixon & A. Aichenvald (eds.), 125-163. Cambridge: Cambridge University Press.

_________ 2000. Hipóteses Sobre as Migrações dos Três Subconjuntos Meridionais da Família Tupi-Guarani. CD-Rom *II Congresso Internacional da ABRALIN e XIV Instituto Lingüístico*. Florianópolis.

RODRIGUES, C. 1995. *Etude Morphosyntaxique de la Langue Xipaya (Bresil)* Ph.D. Dissertation. Universite Paris VII.

_________ 1990. *Langue Xipaya, Etude Phonologique.* MA.Thesis. Universite Paris VII.

SCHLEICHER, C. 1998. *Comparative and Internal Reconstruction of Proto-Tupi-Guarani.* Ph.D. Dissertation. University of Wisconsin, Madison.

STORTO, L. 1999. *Aspects of a Karitiana Grammar.* Ph.D. Dissertation. Massachusetts Institute of Technology.

Comments on "Pitch accent in Karitiana" by Luciana R. Storto & Didier Demolin

Elsa Gomez-Imbert

This paper presents the pitch accent system of the Karitiana language from Brazil. Karitiana is described as having stress and tone, both predictable after lexical and phonological information. The presentation concentrates not only on stress and tone assignment of isolated words but also on sentence patterns. The acoustic data provided show the realization of both stress and tone in isolated words and in sentences. These two aspects, that are not available in most descriptions, are important to understand the whole system.

Roots have no lexical stress — their last syllable becomes prominent — while affixes can be inherently stressed. When a word has several prominent syllables, the rightmost receives primary stress. The system is sensitive to syllable weight, but only CVV syllables attract stress. Thus, bisyllabic words are accented on the last syllable, except when the first is CVV; also when the last vowel is epenthetic. A metrical grid is built for stress assignment, where stress prominent syllables are represented by an asterisk on line 1, and primary stress corresponds to a line 2 asterisk on the rightmost prominent syllable. In a derivational perspective, stress assignment must precede vowel epenthesis because epenthetic final vowels remain unstressed.

H tones are assigned to syllable nuclei represented by asterisks on lines 1 and 2. Unaccented syllables receive a default L that can spread to adjacent unaccented syllables creating a "tone domain". Words combined in sentences do not always exhibit the patterns described so far because some sentence level tonal processes modify their pitch accent patterns: boundary final tones and destressing.

A L boundary tone appears at the end of declarative, interrogative, and negative imperative sentences and produces the shift of the final H to the left. Words in isolation receive the boundary declarative L tone also which changes, for instance, the LH pattern of dissyllabic isolated words into HL. A H boundary tone is assigned to affirmative imperatives, establishing a contrast with negative imperatives which receive final L.

Destressing is an optional process that creates a new prosodic unit by deletion of the accent of the word in second position, between constituents such as: verb and auxiliary, the two heads in a compound, a clitic and its host (verb-negation, verb-evidential, verb-aspect etc.). Destressing seems to indicate dependency relations.

Karitiana is the second language of the Tupi linguistic stock and the third of South America to be presented at these Tokyo tonal symposia. From a typological perspective, these three languages are quite different, even if they share the fact of having two tones, H and L, as most South American known tonal languages do (Moore 1999, Yip 2002). Gavião (Moore 1999) is a purely tonal language where tones have a lexical distinctive function; tones are not predictable. Barasana (Gomez-Imbert 2002) is a restricted tonal language where tones have also a lexical distinctive function and typical tonal processes such as polarization; tones are predictable to a certain degree, a characteristic that renders a pitch accent analysis possible, even if we need two pitch accents (Gomez-Imbert & Kenstowicz 2000). Karitiana has a predictable stress system; it exhibits also a predictable distribution of H and L tones in terms of prominence. Stress and tone have no distinctive function at all. Sensitivity to syllable weight is another cue indicating that it is a stress, not a tonal system. The acoustic data are welcome because they show different correlates for stress and tone.

Concerning the typological issue, if one refers to the typological diagnostic of stress versus tone in Odden (1999: 210), no doubt that Karitiana has a stress and not a tonal system. Recognized common properties of stress systems describe well Karitiana: "The stressed syllable does not usually have to be identified in the lexicon, but is generally picked by a counting algorithm that starts from one end of the word and selects, for example, the second-to-last syllable, or the first syllable, as the stressed one. Other factors, such as syllable size and morphological structure, may also affect stress placement, but in the typical stress language it is not lexically marked." (Yip 2002: 4). If Karitiana is considered a pitch accent language, one wonders whether it could enter in the continuum going from accent to tone and fit Hyman's definition of a tone language, quoted by Yip: “A language with tone is one in which an indication of pitch enters into the lexical realization of at least some morphemes.” Boundary tones are not usually part of stress systems.

Even if Tupian is one of the most important linguistic South American stocks concerning the number of internal subdivisions and of surviving languages — together with Arawakan — few systematic and reliable studies of prosodic systems are available today. The authors underline the important contribution that Tupi languages can make for a better understanding of tone typology and universals, with families and macro-families inside the stock having no tonal languages reported (Tupi-Guarani), others with only tonal representatives (Mondé, Munduruku), unpredictable pitch accent (Ramarama, Juruna), or with tone and stress interacting in a predictable way (Karitiana). We must yet keep in mind that most of the research on these prosodic systems remains to be done (Tupari).

The need for good and urgent research covers all South America and mainly the lowland languages of Amazonia, where tones seem to concentrate. There is urgency of documenting these languages not only for typology but over all because hundreds of them are endangered languages condemned to disappear in this century if nothing is done. Studies such as the one been done in Karitiana can play an essential role in revitalization of a 350 speakers comunity, via the use of vernacular languages at school. Several cases in Brazil and other South American countries indicates this issue as promising.

A question related to tonogenesis is mentioned by the authors. Tonal languages found in the stock are probably not a recent development and tonogenesis is probably related to glottalization — glottal stops, laryngealized vowels and voiced glottal approximants — which often has a marginal status as segments and whose distribution is dependent on the syllable or the prosodic word. But again, it is necessary to investigate all the languages. Nevertheless, they make the hypothesis that Proto-Tupi may have used degrees of glottal constriction to mark suprasegmental phonological distinctions.

REFERENCES

GOMEZ-IMBERT Elsa. 2001. More on the tone versus pitch accent typology: evidence from Barasana and other Eastern Tukanoan languages, in KAJI Shigeki (ed.). *Proceedings of the Symposium Cross-Linguistic Studies of Tonal Phenomena. Tonogenesis, Japanese Accentology and other Topics*. ILCAA, Tokyo University of Foreign Studies: 369-412.

GOMEZ-IMBERT Elsa, KENSTOWICZ Michael. 2000. Barasana tone and accent. *International Journal of American linguistics*66.4: 419-463.

MOORE Denny. 1999. Tonal system of the Gavião language of Rondônia, Brazil, in Tupian perspective, in KAJI Shigeki (ed.). *Proceedings of the Symposium Cross-Linguistic Studies of Tonal Phenomena. Tonogenesis, typology, and Related Topics*. ILCAA, Tokyo University of Foreign Studies: 297-308.

ODDEN David. 1999. Typological issues in tone and stress in Bantu, in KAJI Shigeki (ed.). *Proceedings of the Symposium Cross-Linguistic Studies of Tonal Phenomena. Tonogenesis, typology, and Related Topics*: 187-215.

YIP Moira. 2002. *Tone*. Cambridge, Cambridge University Press.

An Acoustic-Phonetic Descriptive Analysis of Kagoshima Japanese Tonal Phenomena *

Shunichi Ishihara †

Shunichi.Ishihara@anu.edu.au

The Japan Centre & Phonetics Laboratory, the Australian National University

and

Department of Computing, Macquarie University

Abstract

In this paper, the accentual effects of Kagoshima Japanese accentual contrast are investigated on the basis of acoustic–phonetic descriptions of Kagoshima Japanese tonality. The logarithmic z–score normalisation technique is adapted to acoustically–phonetically describe Kagoshima Japanese tonality using a multiple number of speakers. Based on the descriptions, it will be demonstrated in this paper that Kagoshima Japanese Type A triggers so–called 'accentual boost'; 'accentual fall' and 'downstep', like accented words in Standard Japanese. Some possible acoustic–phonetic differences between Kagoshima and Standard Japanese are also discussed in this paper by referring to the descriptive results.

1 Introduction

The main aim of this study is to investigate how the contrastive accentual patterns observed in Kagoshima Japanese (KJ) differ from each other. The accentual contrast of KJ has been well documented (Hirayama 1951; Kibe 1997; Kibe 2000), and there has been a lot of discussion of how its surface forms are derived within different phonological frameworks (Haraguchi 1977; Shibatani 1990; Smith 1997; Hayata 1999; Lawrence 1999). However, little attention has been paid to the accentual contrast in terms of its acoustic–phonetic realisation in fundamental frequency (F0). As a result, although we know how the accentual patterns of KJ are contrastive at the auditory level, we do not know how they are acoustically-phonetically realised.

The accentual contrast of KJ has been traditionally understood to have two pitch patterns: one has a fall in pitch and the other does not (refer to §1.1). Like the accentual behaviour of Standard Japanese (SJ) (Poser 1984; Pierrehumbert and Beckman 1988; Kubozono 1993; Vance 1995; Warner 1995), recent instrumental approaches to KJ prosody revealed that the accentual type of so–called Type A initiates not only global rises but also drops in F0

*This research is supported by a Research Support Grant through the Faculty of Asian Studies, the Australian National University.

†Postal Address: The Japan Centre, Faculty of Asian Studies, The Australian National University, ACT 0200 AUSTRALIA

(Kubozono and Matsui 1996). The results of the above instrumental research indicate that the mapping from phonological pitch description, whereby a sequence of conventional (H)igh and (L)ow are used, to phonetic F0 realisation is not straightforward.

Taking Kubozono and Matsui's (1996) findings, which are summarised in §1.2, as the first step, the current study further investigates the F0 realisation difference and the behaviour of KJ's accentual contrast on a larger scale. Specifically, the following two points will be closely looked at in this study to achieve the above–mentioned research aim.

1. How KJ's accentual contrast itself is realised acoustically–phonetically; and
2. How juxtaposed accentual units affect each other.

Two experiments (Experiments 1 and 2) were conducted to investigate the above two points. The first point is investigated on the basis of the results of Experiments 1 and 2. The second point is investigated on the basis of the results of Experiment 2. Possible differences between KJ and SJ will also be discussed by referring to the results of Experiments 1 and 2.

In order to pursue the aim of this study, a proper acoustic–phonetic description of KJ's accentual contrast is needed. All analyses and discussions in this study are based on the quantitative acoustic–phonetic descriptions of KJ's accentual contrast using a small group of four informants and a normalisation technique to extract and specify the linguistic–tonetic features of their accentual contrast.

In this section, the accentual nature of KJ is explained in §1.1, and previous studies on KJ are summarised in §1.2, focusing on the research of Kubozono and Matsui (1996). In §2, the general methodology used to conduct the two experiments is explained. The results of Experiments 1 and 2 are analysed and discussed in §3 and §4, respectively. §5 summarises and concludes this study.

1.1 Kagoshima Japanese Accentual Contrast

As can be seen from the fact that KJ is often referred to as a 'two–pattern' type dialect, KJ exhibits two contrasting accentual patterns. The two-pattern dialect is different from SJ, in that all words exhibit only two-way accentual oppositions. Table 1 contains some examples showing the two-way contrast KJ exhibits:

In the words in the left column of Table 1, only the penultimate syllable of the word has a high pitch, and every other syllable has a low pitch. In the words in the right column, only the last syllable of the word has a high pitch, and every other syllable before it has a low pitch. That is, the two-way contrast is realised in KJ as [$L^{(n)}$HL] and [$L^{(n)}$H] where n = positive integers or zero.

As can be seen by this, the details of KJ's accentual contrast can be easily expressed, although scholars use different terms to characterise these two oppositions (Hirayama 1957;

Table 1: *The accentual contrast of KJ.*

number of syllables	$L^{(n)}HL$		$L^{(n)}H$	
two	hana HL	nose	hana LH	flower
three	sakura LHL	cherry blossom	usagi LLH	rabbit
four	kagaribi LLHL	watch fire	kakimono LLLH	document

Hirayama 1960; Haraguchi 1977; Kobayashi 1975; Shibatani 1990). Some Japanese linguists refer to the [$L^{(n)}HL$] type as the 'accented type' and the [$L^{(n)}H$] type as the 'unaccented type' in the same sense as the accentual contrast of SJ. This is simply because a pitch fall is observed in the former type, and no such pitch fall is observed in the latter type. However, Hirayama's (1960, 1957) terms—Type A for [$L^{(n)}HL$] and Type B for [$L^{(n)}H$]—are used in this study. The reason for choosing to use these neutral terms is that they are the most widely used in accentual dictionaries of Japanese dialects. Also I would like to avoid the impression which comes from the terms 'accented' and 'unaccented' that 'accented' implies such that 'an accent location' needs to be represented in the lexicon, and that an accented word is marked, i.e. it has something that an unaccented word does not.

1.2 Previous Studies on Kagoshima Japanese

Kubozono and Matsui (1996) conducted an experiment to investigate whether the type of 'accentual boost (ACB)', 'accentual fall (ACF)' and 'downstep (DNS)' (Kubozono 1993) found in SJ are also observed in KJ. They used one male native speaker of KJ and 11 pairs of target utterances (sentences and possessive phrases) which consisted of two accentual units (either Type A or Type B). Table 2 contains one of the utterance pairs which were statistically compared in their study. The paired utterances, which are sentences, given in Table 2 are as follows. one is the combination of a Type A accentual unit and a Type B accentual unit (AB), and the other is that of a Type B accentual unit and a Type B accentual unit (BB). They are segmentally identical, and the difference is only the accentual type of the first accentual unit (Type A vs. Type B). Note that the combination of a noun and a particle is recognised as one accentual unit in KJ, inheriting the accentual type of the noun.

F0 values were sampled at the peak and the valley points of the utterances in their study. These peak and valley points are: the F0 peak associated with the first accentual unit (P1); the F0 valley between the first and the second peaks associated with the first and the second accentual units (V1); and at the F0 peak associated with the second accentual unit (P2). The F0 sampling points of the pair given in Table 2 are illustrated in Figure 1. The amount of F0 fall between P1 and P2 (P1–P2) was also calculated in their study.

As can be seen from the F0 values given in Table 2, these two sentences exhibit different mean F0 values at the sampling points. The differences between the AB and the BB sequence observed from Table 2 are: 1) the AB sequence shows a higher F0 realisation at

Table 2: *Examples of F0 values from KJ utterances differing in the accentuation of the first accentual unit (after Kubozono and Matsui (1996, p105)). P1 = the peak value at the initial high pitched syllable, and V1 = the valley value between the initial peak and the second peak value, P2 = the peak value of the second high pitched syllable and P1–P2 = the amount of F0 fall from P1 to P2. The numerals are the mean F0 values (Hz) at these sampling points. SUB stands for a subject marker.*

Type	Gloss	P1	V1	P2	P1-P2
a:(AB)	hana-ga takai (LHLLH) nose-SUB tall Nose is tall.	153.7	120.4	130.0	23.7
b:(BB)	hana-ga takai (LLHLH) flower-SUB expensive Flower is expensive.	146.7	126.5	135.3	11.4

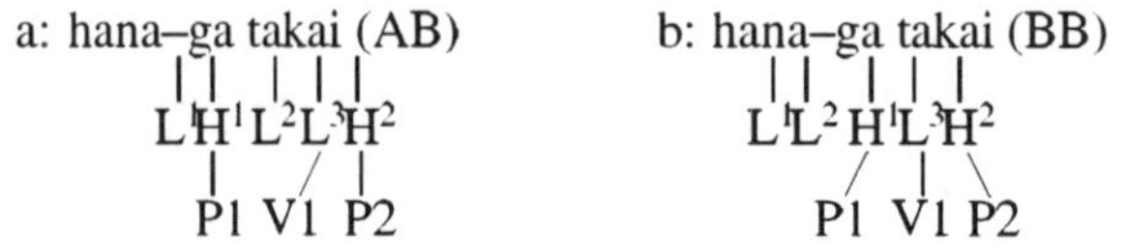

Figure 1: *Pitch configuration of the example utterances given in Table 2.*

the P1 point than the BB sequence; 2) the AB sequence is realised lower in F0 than the BB sequence at the V1 point; 3) the AB sequence has a lower F0 value than the BB sequence at the P2 point; and 4) the slope between P1 and P2 is steeper in the AB sequence than the BB sequence. These differences, although small in the case of the pair given in Table 2, are statistically significant (two–tail t–test, $p < 0.05$). Difference 1) supports ACB associated with Type A of the first accentual unit; difference 2) supports ACF associated with Type A of the first accentual unit, and differences 3) and 4) support DNS. As a whole, out of a total of 11 comparisons, a significant difference was observed in 6 comparisons at P1 and V1; in 7 comparisons at P2; and in 8 comparisons for P1–P2. On the basis of these results, Kubozono and Matsui (1996) concluded that the contrast between Type A and Type B in KJ corresponds to that of accented and unaccented words in SJ, and Type A induces ACB, ACF and DNS.

Although the differences observed by Kubozono and Matsui (1996) between utterances consisting of different accentual combinations were statistically significant, there is a possibility that they might to a certain extent have been influenced by the effect of declination (Umeda 1982; Ladd 1988). This is because the sampling points of the utterances that were compared were not time-aligned. The utterances given in Table 2 have the pitch configurations shown in Figure 1. According to the representations shown in Figure 1, for the AB sequence, only one syllable (L^1) precedes the high pitched syllable (H^1) from which the P1 value was sampled, whereas for the BB sequence, two syllables (L^1L^2) come before the high pitched syllable (H^1) from which the P1 value was sampled. That is, the P1 value of the BB sequence is exposed to a possible declination effect longer than that of the AB sequence. Similarly, two low pitched syllables (L^2L^3) follow the high pitched syllable (H^1) for the AB sequence, while only one low pitched syllable (L^3) follows the high pitched syllable (H^1) for the BB sequence. That is, again, there is more time for F0 to fall in the two low pitched syllables (L^2L^3) of the AB sequence than the one low pitched syllable (L^3) of the BB sequence.

One might argue that since the accentual effect is phonologically associated with the accentual type (either Type A or Type B), the effect of declination onto the second accentual unit (or at V1 and P2) is identical because the pitch configuration of the second accentual unit is identical. However, phonetically speaking, since ACF and DNS are initiated by a pitch fall after the first high pitched syllable (H^1), there is a clear durational difference between H^1 and H^2 when one compares the AB sequence and the BB sequence of Figure 1. Further, regarding the declination effect, there might be still an argument that since the sentences given in Table 2 share the same segmental structure, the declination effect at L^3 and H^2—where the V1 and P2 values are sampled—is identical as a whole in both sentences. However, there is a possibility that the declination effect is not identical at L^3 and H^2 because the pitch configuration coming before L^3 and H^2 is not identical. Therefore, ACB, ACF and DNS in KJ need to be reinvestigated in an environment where the magnitude of the declination effect is ideally controlled.

As illustrated in Table 2, the ACB associated with Type A was demonstrated in Kubozono and Matsui (1996). However, precisely speaking, what they investigated is only the ACB appearing at the high pitched syllable of the first accentual unit. Therefore, we still do not know how Type A influences the low pitched syllables appearing before the high pitched syllable. This point is important because KJ is subject to having a long sequence of low pitched syllables before a high pitched syllable (i.e. **LLLLHL**). Therefore, in this study, the effects of KJ's accentual contrast are investigated not only at the high pitched syllable but also at the low pitched syllable(s) preceding the high pitched syllable.

Furthermore, as Kubozono and Matsui (1996, p106) acknowledge, their results need to be confirmed by using multiple speakers as well. This point is particularly germane to this thesis because data collected from multiple speakers is necessary for linguistic–phonetic descriptive work.

1.3 Acoustic–Phonetic Descriptions of Tones

As mentioned in §1, this study is based on acoustic–phonetic descriptions of KJ's accentual contrast (Type A and Type B). KJ's Type A and Type B have phonologically contrastive features—which can be phonologically represented in various ways (Hirayama 1951; Haraguchi 1977; McCawley 1977; Shibatani 1990). However, what we are concerned with in this study is to describe/identify the acoustic–phonetic realisation differences of KJ's Type A and Type B. In order to identify the acoustic–phonetic realisation differences between Type A and Type B, linguistic–phonetic representations of these contrastive features are inevitable (refer to §2.3 for linguistic–phonetic representations using normalisation), otherwise not only can we not compare the linguistically important F0 realisation differences of Type A and Type B due to large between–speaker differences, but also we cannot compare KJ's Type A and Type B with the accentual/tonal features of other

Japanese variations or other languages.

For example, the falling tone and the high level tone of Mandarin Chinese and Standard Thai can be phonologically represented as HL and H, respectively (Gandour 1974; Yip 2002; Gussenhoven 2004). However, although the falling tone (HL) and the high level tone (H) phonologically share the same H tone, it does not necessarily mean that the F0 realisation of the H tone is the same between the falling tone and the high level tone. Furthermore, although Mandarin Chinese and Standard Thai have a falling tone which can be phonologically represented as HL, this does not necessarily mean that the F0 realisation of the high falling tone (HL) is identical between the two languages.

2 Experiments

As mentioned in §1, taking the findings of Kubozono and Matsui (1996) as a starting point, two experiments (Experiments 1 and 2) were conducted in this study to investigate the F0 realisation differences of KJ's accentual contrast and its effects on the neighbouring environments.

In Experiment 1, I investigated how KJ's Type A and Type B polysyllabic words are acoustically–phonetically realised. By investigating the F0 realisation difference between Type A and Type B words, in return, a clear picture of KJ's accentual effect (i.e. ACB) can be obtained at a word level. In Experiment 2, the points that Kubozono and Matsui (1996) examined in their study will be further looked at with more complex data.

This section describes and explains the various techniques used to obtain the data. Included are the personal information of the informants who participated in the recordings and a description of the recorded materials and the digitisation procedure used in the experiments. With respect to the information about elicitation methods and methods of measurement, since different methods are used for the two different experiments, they will be explained at the beginning of each relevant experiment (§3 and §4).

2.1 Informants

Four informants (2 male and 2 female) participated in this study. This sample size is short of the minimum of three people for each sex required for quantified phonetic work as suggested by Ladefoged (1997, p140). However, four informants were the maximum number that could be handled by a single person within the time constraints of this study. Since the target words/utterances were recorded at least five times by each informant and were selected by keeping comparisons of them in mind, the data is statistically comparable. Table 3 contains the personal details of the four informants who participated in this study.

The informants were all born and raised in Kagoshima city. Both parents of the informants were also born and raised in Kagoshima city. None of the informants have residential experience outside of Kagoshima city. All of them have completed up to secondary education. TYM, TTF, and NKF went to the same primary school (6–11 years of age) and junior high school (12–14 years of age), and they are still living in the same neighbourhood. There-

Table 3: *Personal details of informants. Note that the informants' initials are followed by either an M (= male) or an F (=female).*

Sex	Names	Age	Education
Male	TYM	35	secondary
	YNM	26	secondary
Female	TTF	34	secondary
	NKF	35	secondary

fore, this group of informants can be considered to be a homogeneous set.

2.2 Recorded Materials

Two corpora were arranged for recording respectively for the two experiments in this study. Each corpus consists of target words/utterances for analysis and some dummy words. Corpus 1 (for Experiment 1) consists of monosyllabic and polysyllabic words. However, the relevant words for this study are only polysyllabic words. Corpus 2 (for Experiment 2) consists of three types of target utterances (sentences, noun phrases and possessive phrases) together with some dummy utterances. A full description of target words/utterances of Corpora 1 and 2 is given in the Appendix.

These corpora were written in the usual Japanese orthography: a mixture of Chinese characters and the hiragana/katakana syllabaries. The pronunciation of all Chinese characters was written above them in the hiragana syllabary, which disambiguates any confusion in the readings of the Chinese characters.

The elicitation sessions were conducted in 1999 in Kagoshima city in an adequately quiet room, but under non-laboratory conditions. The recording materials were recorded on high-quality normal position tapes using a SONY TCM-5000EV tape recorder and a SONY ECM-D8 microphone. No noise reduction and no compression were applied.

The raw recorded signal was digitised with CSL hardware (©Kay Elemetric Corp, Computerised Speech Laboratory). The signal was digitised using 16 bit quantisation at a sampling rate of 10 KHz. This fairly low sampling rate, 10 KHz, only allows digitisation of frequencies up to 5,000 Hz due to the Nyquist principal, and thus causes some audible quality loss from the original recording. It was chosen, however, to facilitate F0 extraction by the package's software algorithm. The CSL manual recommends this rate for the purpose of formant and F0 extraction (©Kay Elemetric Corp 1994, p384).

2.3 Normalisation

According to Ladefoged and Maddieson (1986, p1), there are two major aims in linguistic phonetics. These are the identification of the phonetic features which specify the sounds within a given language or variety, and the identification of those features which underly sound contrast between varieties. However, the identification of the specific phonetic features of a given language or variety is not an easy task because different speakers have different acoustic outputs for what is perceived to be the same linguistic information. This is because '[t]he acoustic properties of the radiated speech wave are a unique function of a speaker's vocal tract anatomy, and since speakers' vocal tracts differ, so will their acoustic output—even for phonetically the same sound' (Rose 1987, p343). Therefore, individual differences of this type need to be factored out as much as possible by a process of normalisation in order to specify the acoustic correlates of linguistically the same sound (Disner 1980; Rose 1991). Normalisation is crucial in this study because multiple informants are involved.

In this study, logarithmic z–score normalisation and intrinsic normalisation parameters are used because they perform very well in tonal normalisation (Zhu 1994). The log z–score normalisation expresses the same thing as the linear z–score normalisation, but in logarithmic terms. Log z–score normalised values (z_i') can be obtained using the formula defined in (1) (Zhu 1994, p58).

$$z_i' = \frac{y_i - m_y}{s_y} = \frac{log_{10}x_i - \frac{1}{n}\sum_{i-1}^{n} log_{10}x_i}{\sqrt{\frac{1}{n-1}\sum_{i-1}^{n}(log_{10}x_i - \frac{1}{n}\sum_{i-1}^{n} log_{10}x_i)^2}} \quad (1)$$

In (1), $y_i = log_{10}x_i$, m_y and s_y are the arithmetic mean and standard deviation (sd) of y_i ($i = 1, 2, \cdots, n$), respectively. Intrinsic normalisation parameters were acquired from the words to be normalised.

2.4 Terminology

When the F0 contours of Type A and Type B are described in this paper, the syllable associated with a high phonetic pitch (= the penultimate syllable for Type A and the ultimate syllable for Type B) is referred to as the peak syllable, and the syllables appearing before the peak syllable as the pre–peak syllables. The final syllable of Type A words is referred to as the post–peak syllable.

3 Experiment 1

In this section, the F0 realisations of Type A and Type B are compared using polysyllabic words consisting of CV syllable structures.

The specific methodology that is used for Experiment 1 is explained in term of elicitation methods and methods of F0 measurement. The relevant corpus to Experiment 1 is Corpus 1. General methods that are applicable to both experiments are as explained in §1.2.

3.1 Recording Materials and Recording Procedure

The target polysyllabic words of Corpus 1 consists of 20 Type A polysyllabic words (4 disyllable, 4 trisyllable, 5 four–syllable, 5 five–syllable, 1 six–syllable and 1 seven–syllable words) and 19 Type B polysyllabic words (4 disyllable, 4 trisyllable, 5 four–syllable, 5 five–syllable, and 1 six–syllable words). Refer to Table 12 of the Appendix for a detailed description of these target words. The syllable structure of these polysyllabic target words is CV.

Although the informants were simply asked to read Corpus 1 six times (including one practice to get used to recording), they were also instructed to make sufficient pauses between each word in order to avoid any listing effect. Before recording, the informants were allowed to practise until they felt confident, and during recording, the informants were allowed to correct themselves by repeating if necessary.

3.2 Measurement Procedure

Three F0 measurement procedures were used for the analysis. In the first procedure (Procedure 1), F0 was sampled at the onset and at every 20% point of the duration of each syllable nucleus. This procedure makes it possible to show in detail the F0 time course in each word. In Procedure 2, F0 was sampled at the 50% point of the duration of each syllable nucleus. Procedure 2 enables us to collect F0 values that are the least consonantally perturbed. In Procedure 3, the minimum F0 value was sampled from each low pitched syllable nucleus, and the maximum F0 value from the high pitched syllable nucleus.

3.3 Normalisation Parameters

On the basis of raw F0 values obtained from Corpus 1, log intrinsic normalisation F0 parameters (arithmetical mean and standard deviation) were derived for log z–score normalisation procedure. Table 4 contains log intrinsic normalisation F0 parameters (arithmetical mean and standard deviation of samples) together with some basic statistics.

Table 4: *Log intrinsic F0 statistics of the four informants from Corpus 1 ($\bar{x}$ = mean value; sd = standard deviation; N = number of F0 samples).*

Informant	$\bar{x}$ (log Hz)	sd (log Hz)	skew	N
TYM	2.012	0.060	-0.604	9270
YNM	1.994	0.037	-0.501	9270
TTF	2.263	0.088	-0.690	9270
NKF	2.211	0.054	-1.182	9270

In Experiment 1, therefore, the mean log F0 and the sd values of the samples given in Table 4 are used as the normalisation parameters.

3.4 Analysis of Normalised Data

In this section, the realisation of Type A and Type B polysyllabic words is compared on the basis of F0 normalised data. Judging from the results of Kubozono and Matsui (1996), the expected F0 pattern from the results of Experiment 1 is the higher F0 value associated with the peak syllable of Type A compared to that of Type B.

Five different comparisons—Type A three syllable word vs. Type B two syllable word; Type A four syllable word vs. Type B three syllable word; Type A five syllable word vs. Type B four syllable word; Type A six syllable word vs. Type B five syllable word; and Type A seven syllable word vs. Type B six syllable word—are possible in Experiment 1. Note that these pairs have been arranged in order to factor out the declination effect (refer to §1.2).

Figure 2 contains the mean normalised F0 values of Type A and Type B words. Figure 2a has the mean normalised F0 values of Type A words having 3 and 4 syllables compared with the values of Type B words having 2 and 3 syllables. Figure 2b contains the mean normalised F0 values of Type A words having 5 syllables compared with the values of Type B words having 4 syllables. Figure 2c contains the mean normalised F0 values of Type A words having 6 syllables compared with the values of Type B words having 5 syllables. Figure 2d shows the mean normalised F0 curves of a Type A word having 7 syllables compared with the values of a Type B word having 6 syllables.

As can be seen from Figure 2, in addition to the fact that Type A falls in F0 at the end and Type B does not, other differences between Type A and Type B are not only that the peak syllable of Type A is associated with higher normalised F0 values than that of Type B, but also that all the pre–peak syllables of Type A are associated with higher normalised F0 values than those of Type B.

An important point that can be easily seen in Figure 2 is that normalised F0 declines around the mean (= 0 SD[1]) in the pre–peak syllables. That means that although the pre–peak syllables are traditionally associated with a low phonetic pitch, it is more accurate to say that they are associated with a mid surface phonetic pitch from the narrow transcription and perceptual points of view.

The F0 realisations of Type A and Type B on polysyllables are statistically compared on the basis of the log z–score normalised F0 values which were converted from the raw F0 values sampled by means of Procedures 2 and 3. As noted before, Type A and Type B polysyllabic words having the same number of pre–peak syllables are compared in order to factor out the declination effect.

In the case of comparing a Type A seven syllable word and a Type B six syllable word, for example, a t–test (unpaired, two–tailed) was conducted at six different locations as shown in Figure 3 for both sets of values collected by means of Procedure 2 and Procedure 3. That is, a pair of comparable Type A and Type B words was compared one syllable to one syllable starting from the left.

[1] Standard deviation (SD) is used as the unit for normalised F0 value because normalisation is based on the SD of the sample.

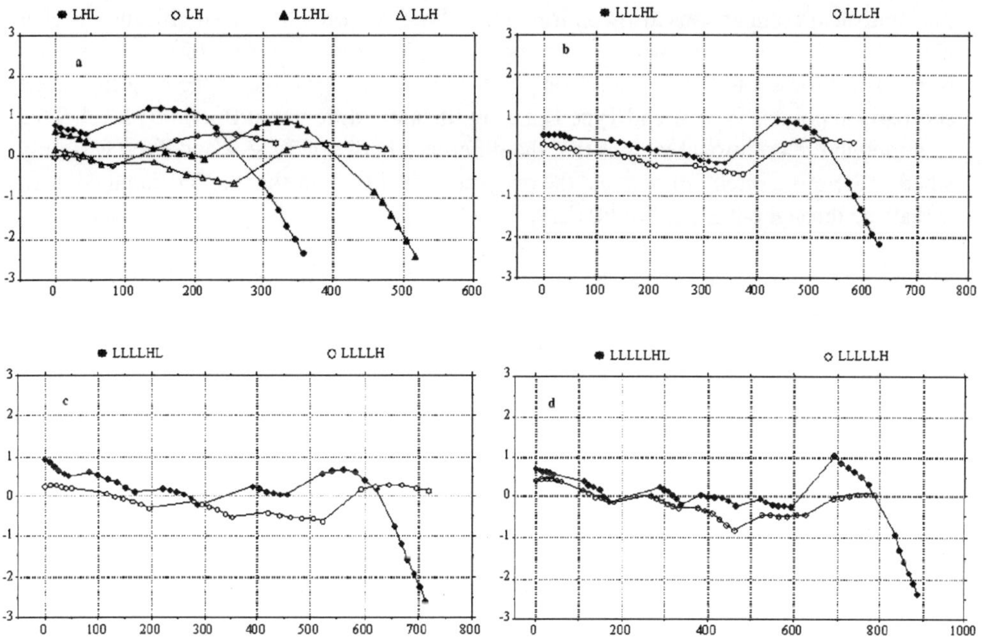

Figure 2: *Mean normalised F0 curves of Type A and Type B words, showing the realisation difference between the two accentual types. X–axis is duration (msec) and Y–axis is log z–score value (SD). The filled symbol is Type A and the empty symbol is Type B.*

Type A: 7 syllable word								Type B: 6 syllable word					
σ	σ	σ	σ	σ	σ	σ		σ	σ	σ	σ	σ	σ
|	|	|	|	|	|	|		|	|	|	|	|	|
L	L	L	L	L	H	L		L	L	L	L	L	H
|	|	|	|	|	|			|	|	|	|	|	|
1	2	3	4	5	6			1	2	3	4	5	6

Figure 3: *Statistical comparison points between Type A and Type B words.*

The statistical comparisons also confirmed that Type A words have a significantly higher normalised F0 realisation than the corresponding Type B words ($p < 0.05$) at all comparisons except for a couple of comparison points in the longest words. At the majority of the comparison points, Type A and Type B are significantly different at $P < 0.001$ level. That is, although the traditional view is that the difference between Type A and Type B is only whether there is a pitch fall or not at the end, these results show that the accentual contrast is realised throughout the entire F0 curve.

The term 'Accentual Boost' (ACB) was used in Kubozono and Matsui (1996) for the F0 rising observed in Type A compared to Type B. In the current study, two different terms are used to specify the location where the F0 raising effect of Type A is observed. One is 'Peak Accentual Boost' (PAB) which refers to the higher F0 values at the peak syllable of Type A, and the other is 'Initial Accentual Boost' (IAB) which refers to higher F0 values observed in the pre–peak syllables within the same phrase. However, it needs to be noted that although the terms IAB ('initial accentual boost') and PAB ('peak accentual boost') were chosen to be used in this study, it is not known yet whether the cause of the above demonstrated difference between Type A and Type B in KJ is an 'accent' or not in the same sense as in SJ.

Table 5 shows the average magnitude of the differences in normalised F0 between Type A and Type B words. As far as the average magnitude based on Procedure 2 is concerned, the magnitude of the difference between the pre–peak syllables and the peak syllables is only 0.027 SD (= 0.390 SD – 0.363 SD). That is, it can be said that the magnitude of the difference caused by the accentual contrast is almost identical between the pre–peak and peak syllables. In other words, the effect of IAB and that of PAB are almost identical in Procedure 2. However, if it is compared on the basis of Procedure 3, the magnitude is greater in the peak syllables (0.537 SD) than the pre–peak syllables (0.369 SD). Considering the fact that the onset and the offset F0 value of each syllable will often be perturbed by the preceding and the following consonant, respectively, it is more sensible to consider that the magnitude calculated on the basis of Procedure 2 gives the more accurate picture of KJ's accentual effect. This is considered to be appropriate also because no drastic F0 change was observed within each of the pre–peak and peak syllables.

Table 5: *Average magnitude of difference caused by Type A and Type B accentual contrast for the pre–peak (IAB) and peak (PAB) syllables.*

Procedure 2		Procedure 3	
pre-peak (IAB)	peak (PAB)	pre-peak (IAB)	peak (PAB)
0.363	0.390	0.369	0.537

3.5 Discussion

As explained in §1.1, KJ's Type A has been referred to as 'accented' by some researchers mainly because there is a pitch fall, and Type B as 'unaccented' because there is no pitch fall. Although it is not certain at this stage whether the concept of accent is necessary in KJ, the results of Experiment 1 demonstrate that Type A words have similar acoustic–phonetic characteristics to those found in the accented words of SJ with respect to the F0 raising effect.

Regarding the higher F0 of the peak syllable in Type A words as compared to Type B words, there still seems to be a possible argument that the peak syllable is realised relatively lower in Type B than Type A words in the current data because the final syllable (= peak syllable) of Type B words is directly associated with a boundary tone of a higher intonational level—more specifically, the tone which causes sentence–final–lowering (Fujisaki 1983; Liberman and Pierrehumbert 1983; Poser 1984; Pierrehumbert and Beckman 1988). Therefore, the F0 realisation in the final syllable might have been pulled down in Type B because of this final boundary tone. Although the magnitude of the final–lowering is not known (including whether it has only local effect on the final syllable (Poser 1984) or a wider effect (Pierrehumbert and Beckman 1988)), it is not appropriate to ignore its possible effect. However, as has been clearly demonstrated in Figure 2, a difference in F0 values was also observed in the pre–peak syllables between Type A and Type B words, regardless of the length of the words. This observation seems to imply that there is indeed an F0 realisation difference indeed caused by the accentual types (even if the final–lowering effect is taken into consideration) because the boundary tone would be associated with both Type A and Type B. If there is an F0 realisation difference, it can be understood that the accentual difference between Type A and Type B does not have a limited effect only on local regions, such as only on peak syllables, but rather globally affects the whole word. An interesting point is that the accentual effect of Type A is very pervasive so that the F0 raising is observed throughout the pre–peak syllables regardless of the length of a word.

As explained in §3.4, Type A and Type B words which are time–aligned were statistically as well as visually compared in Experiment 1. In all cases, the actual length of the words that were compared is different in terms of syllable number: the Type B word is shorter by one syllable than its Type A counterpart. Some studies report that the initial F0 value of an utterance increases as a function of the utterance length (Cooper and Sorensen 1981; Lindau 1986). In fact, Ishihara (2004) using the same dataset as Experiment 1 reports that the longer a Type B word, the higher in F0 it starts with, whereas word length does not affect initial F0 value in Type A words. Although the fact that those Type A and Type B words that were compared do not have the same word length might have influenced Experiment 1 due to the different onset F0 values as a function of word length, the possible effect coming from this is miniscule compared to the effects resulting from the accentual contrast of Type A and Type B (Ishihara 2004, pp237–238).

4 Experiment 2

In this section, the differences between Type A and Type B are further investigated using utterances consisting of two accentual units, e.g. *amaka nimono*, 'sweet stew' ([amaka LHL] 'sweet'; [nimono LHL] 'stew'). Specifically speaking, this section examines pairs of strings of different accentual units having the same pitch configuration sequence. For example, a string consisting of Type A and Type B accentual units (LLLHL.LLH) and a string consisting of two Type B accentual units (LLLH.LLLH) can have the same pitch sequence. In this section, it is investigated how two such strings can be distinguished in the light of F0 realisation.

In this subsection, the specific methodology that is used for the analysis of Experiment 2 is explained. The relevant corpus to Experiment 2 is Corpus 2.

4.1 Recording Materials and Recording Procedure

Corpus 2 was compiled for Experiment 2. The target utterances of Corpus 2 consists of 24 utterances. These utterances can be classified into three types according to their syntactic structure. The first type is Sentence (S) with an internal structure of Noun + Particle + Verb. The second type is Noun Phrase (NP) with an internal structure of Adjective + Noun. The third type is Possessive Phrase (PossP) with an internal structure of Noun + *no* (possessive marker) + Noun.

All utterances listed in Corpus 2 consist of two accentual units (either Type A or Type B). Therefore, four accentual permutations are possible: Type A + Type A (AA), Type A + Type B (AB), Type B + Type A (BA) and Type B + Type B (BB).

In Experiment 2, as well, those utterances which have an identical pitch configuration when they are time–aligned are compared in order to factor out any declination effect. For the sake of convenience, a concise transcription and pitch configuration of each utterance is presented in Table 6. Refer to Table 13 of the Appendix for a full description of the target utterances used in Corpus 2.

The convention used in Table 6 work in this way. NP5BA, for example, means that this is a Noun Phrase (NP) consisting of a Type B word and a Type A word (BA). The numeral is a reference number and those utterances sharing the same reference number were statistically compared.

The utterances of Corpus 2 were read in the carrier sentence given in Table 7 11 times including one practice. The informants were instructed not to make a pause utterance–internally, but to make sufficient pause between each utterance. The informants were encouraged to repeat the utterances as many times as they wished if they were not satisfied with their performance.

4.2 Measurement Procedure

F0 samples are taken from valley and peak points, which are assumed to be the manifestation of KJ's accentual effects. An audio speech waveform, a spectrogram and a superimposed F0 trace of [*saru–no atama* LLH.LLH] 'monkey's head' (PossP9BB) (YNM) are presented in Figure 4 as an example for the F0 measurement procedure.

In the example given in Figure 4, F0 samples are taken from 4 different points: V1, P1, V2 and P2. V1 is the minimum F0 value observed before the first high pitched syllable. P1 is the maximum F0 value observed in the first accentual unit. V2 is the minimum F0 value observed between the first and the second high pitched syllable. P2 is the maximum

Table 6: *Target utterances of Corpus 2 for investigation of the effect of accentual difference in longer utterances. S, NP and PossP stand for sentence, noun phrase and possessive phrase, respectively. Period = an accentual boundary.*

S			**PossP**		
S1AA	hana–ga naru	LHL.HL	PossP9AB	kimono–no nuno	LLHL.LH
S1BA	e–ga narabu	LH.LHL	PossP9BB	saru–no atama	LLH.LLH
S2AB	sakana–ga nigeru	LLHL.LLH	PossP10AA	kimono–no gara	LLHL.HL
S2BB	hana–ga nagareru	LLH.LLLH	PossP10BA	yama–no sakura	LLH.LHL
S3AB	kimono–o naderu	LLHL.LLH	PossP11AA	himago–no kimono	LLHL.LHL
S3BB	kazu–o shiraberu	LLH.LLLH	PossP11BA	mago–no tabemono	LLH.LLHL
S4AA	minami–ni mukeru	LLHL.LHL	PossP12AB	himago–no megane	LLHL.LLH
S4BA	umi–ni tobikomu	LLH.LLHL	PossP12BB	mago–no hakimono	LLH.LLLH
NP					
NP5AA	nagaka kami	LHL.HL			
NP5BA	yoka sakana	LH.LHL			
NP6AA	amaka nimono	LHL.LHL			
NP6BA	yoka tabemono	LH.LLHL			
NP7AB	nagaka tamago	LHL.LLH			
NP7BB	yoka kudamono	LH.LLLH			
NP8AB	nagaka kudamono	LHL.LLLH			
NP8BB	yoka yudetamago	LH.LLLLH			

Table 7: *The carrier sentence used in Experiment 2*

Naomi–wa ——	to	itta	gayo.
L H L	L	HL	H L
name–TOP ——	QUOTE	say–past	SFP

Note: TOP, QUOTE and SFP stand for topic marker, quotation and sentence final particle, respectively.

F0 value observed in the second accentual unit. In terms of accentual effects, V1, P1, V2 and V2 correspond to IAB, PAB, ACF and DNS, respectively.

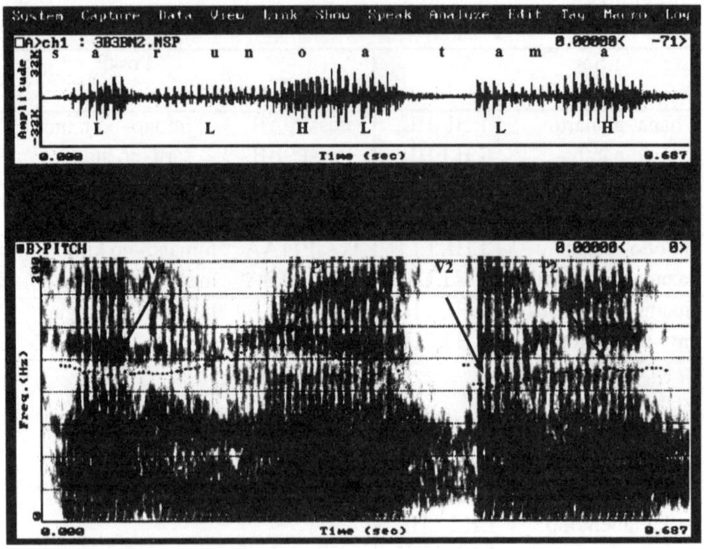

Figure 4: *Audio-speech waveform, wide band spectrogram and superimposed F0 trace of the Type B + Type B phrase [saru–no atama] 'monkey's head' (YNM), showing how F0 was sampled. V1 = the first valley point, P1 = the first peak point, V2 = the second valley point, P2 = the second peak point.*

4.3 Normalisation Parameters

On the basis of raw F0 values sampled from Corpus 2, normalisation parameters were calculated for Experiment 2. Table 8 contains log intrinsic normalisation F0 parameters (arithmetical mean and standard deviation) together with some basic statistics.

Table 8: *Log intrinsic F0 statistics of the four informants from Corpus 2 ($\bar{x}$ = mean value; sd = standard deviation; N = number of F0 samples).*

Informant	$\bar{x}$ (log Hz)	sd (log Hz)	skew	N
TYM	2.118	0.059	0.212	4530
YNM	2.047	0.040	0.061	4530
TTF	2.338	0.059	-0.195	4530
NKF	2.284	0.048	0.192	4530

In Experiment 2, therefore, the mean log F0 and the sd values given in Table 8 are used as the normalisation parameters.

4.4 Analysis of Normalised Data

On the basis of the normalised F0 values obtained at V1, P1, V2 and P2, the realisation difference of Type A and Type B words in first accentual unit (i.e. IAB and PAB) and the influence of the accentual type of the first accentual unit on the second accentual unit (i.e. ACF and DNS) are statistically analysed using unpaired two–tail t–tests. Table 9 contains relevant basic statistics and the results of the overall statistical comparisons. In Table 9, each pair is statistically compared at V1, P1, V2 and P2, and the number of significant differences is counted at each sampling point across all pairs in order to compare with Kubozono and Matsui's (1996) results.

Table 9: *Overall statistical comparisons using unpaired two–tail t–test at V1, P1, V2 and P2. *** stands for $P < 0.001$, ** for $0.001 < P \leq 0.01$, * for $0.01 < p \leq 0.05$, ∽ for no significant difference ($p > 0.05$). Shading = significant difference.*

		V1	P1	V2	P2			V1	P1	V2	P2
AA	F0	-0.20	1.46	-0.28	1.12	AB	F0	-0.54	1.58	-1.66	0.71
S1		***	∽	*	∽	NP7		*	*	∽	∽
BA	F0	-0.76	1.37	-0.13	1.25	BB	F0	-0.78	1.39	-1.53	0.41
AB	F0	-0.71	1.35	-1.72	0.52	AB	F0	-0.52	1.62	-1.75	0.42
S2		∽	∽	*	∽	NP8		*	*	∽	∽
BB	F0	-0.57	1.46	-1.56	0.68	BB	F0	-0.72	1.43	-1.82	0.68
AB	F0	-0.24	1.66	-1.62	0.49	AB	F0	-0.29	1.48	-1.21	0.82
S3		***	∽	*	∽	PossP9		*	∽	∽	∽
BB	F0	-0.73	1.55	-1.45	0.70	BB	F0	-0.73	1.49	-1.32	0.74
AA	F0	-0.64	1.55	-1.26	1.42	AA	F0	-0.31	1.37	-0.92	0.98
S4		∽	∽	***	∽	PossP10		***	∽	**	*
BA	F0	-0.73	1.45	-0.72	1.46	BB	F0	-0.82	1.48	-0.35	1.36
AA	F0	-0.71	1.37	-0.63	1.30	AA	F0	-0.54	1.62	-0.81	1.12
NP5		∽	∽	∽	∽	PossP11		***	*	∽	∽
BA	F0	-0.82	1.40	-0.38	1.33	BA	F0	-0.80	1.42	-1.12	1.17
AA	F0	-0.73	1.60	-1.17	1.23	AB	F0	-0.55	1.55	-1.80	0.61
NP6		∽	∽	∽	∽	PossP12		***	∽	***	*
BA	F0	-0.81	1.43	-1.01	1.17	BB	F0	-0.94	1.45	-1.34	0.85

V1	P1	V2	P2
8/12: A>B	3/12: A>B	6/12: A<B	2/12: A<B

Merely looking at the overall mean normalised F0 values presented in Table 9 for each sampling point (V1, P1, V2 and P2), the following observations can be made: 1) a higher mean V1 value is observed in the utterances having a Type A word as the first accentual unit than those having a Type B word in 11 out of 12 comparisons; 2) for the mean P1 values, utterances with a Type A word as the first accentual unit show a higher P1 value than those with a Type B word in 8/12 comparisons; 3) for the mean V2 values, utterances having a Type A word as the first accentual unit show a lower V2 value than those having a Type B word in 9/12 comparisons; and 4) a lower mean P2 value is obtained when the first accentual unit is a Type A word than a Type B word in 9/12 comparisons.

However, unlike the above simple comparisons based on the mean normalised F0 values, statistical comparisons present a slightly different picture. At the V1 point, as a whole, the higher F0 realisation of Type A words compared to Type B words was statistically confirmed in 8 out of 12 comparisons. At the P1 point, however, the higher F0 realisation of Type A words was statistically confirmed in only 3 comparisons. At the V2 point, the lower F0 realisation when the first accentual unit is a Type A word was statistically confirmed in 6 comparisons. At the P2 point, the suppressed F0 value of the second accentual unit when preceded by a Type A word was confirmed only in 2/12 comparisons.

As can be seen by these comparisons, the difference at the V1 point (or the IAB effect) is very frequently observed. Moreover, it is far more frequent than the difference at P1 (the PAB effect) and the difference at P2 (the DNS effect).

A statistical comparison was conducted pairwise in Table 9 to get an informal picture of the accentual effect. Therefore, in order to obtain a true picture regarding the accentual effect, a two–factor ANOVA (factor one = accentual type; factor two = syntactic type) was conducted at each sampling point. Table 10 contains the results of overall comparisons regarding the accentual effect at each sampling point (two–factor ANOVA).

Table 10: *Results of ANOVA for the accentual effect. *** stands for $P < 0.001$, ** for $0.001 < P \leq 0.01$, * for $0.01 < p \leq 0.05$, ~ for no significant difference ($p > 0.05$).*

a	V1	P1	V2	P2
Accent Type (A, B) Variance	*** 83.61	** 7.25	*** 19.61	* 4.75
Accent Syntax Variance	** V1	~ P1	~ V2	~ P2

The statistical results given in Table 10 show that there is a significant difference ($p < 0.03$) triggered by the accentual contrast at each of the sampling points (V1, P1, V2 and P2). That is, as a whole, the effects of IAB, PAB, ACF and DNS are significantly observed in KJ.

4.5 Discussion

Conforming to the results of Kubozono and Matsui (1996), the statistical results given in Table 10 confirm the effects of IAB, PAB, ACF and DNS in KJ, as a whole. That is, like SJ accented words, KJ Type A causes IAB, PAB, ACF and DNS. However, some points need to be discussed regarding these accentual effects of KJ below.

It was demonstrated in Experiment 1 that the pre–peak syllables and the peak syllable of an isolated Type A word have higher F0 values than those of an isolated Type B word in almost all comparison points, and also that the magnitude of the accentual effect is almost identical at the pre–peak (IAB) and peak syllables (PAB) when it is compared at the 50% point of each syllable nucleus. Comparing the results of Experiment 2 with those of Experiment 1 in terms of IAB and PAB, some different results can be observed between Experiments 1 and 2. These differences are: 1) the magnitude and the occurrence of IAB and PAB are almost identical in Experiment 1 while the magnitude and the occurrence of IAB are larger and more frequent than those of PAB in Experiment 2; and 2) the magnitude and the occurrence of IAB and particularly PAB are weaker and less frequent in Experiment 2 than Experiment 1.

Table 11 contains the magnitude of the accentual difference in normalised F0 realisation at each sampling point. Note that these values are the overall average values of all target utterances. The differences in the magnitude of the IAB and PAB effects between Experiments 1 and 2 can be clearly observed from Tables 5 and 11. The magnitude of the PAB effect and that of the IAB effect are weaker in long utterances (Experiment 2) (0.256 SD for IAB; 0.083 SD for PAB) than in isolated words (Experiment 1) (0.363 SD for IAB; 0.390 SD for PAB).

Table 11: *Magnitude and sd (in bracket) of the accentual difference appearing at each sampling point.*

V1 (IAB)	P1 (PAB)	V2 (ACF)	P2 (DNS)
0.256 (0.231)	0.083 (0.100)	0.176 (0.270)	0.089 (0.180)

It was pointed out in §3.5 for Experiment 1 that the offset low boundary tone associated with the final syllable of a Type B word might have caused or exaggerated the difference observed at the peak syllable. In other words, the peak syllable of an isolated Type B word has a lower F0 realisation than that of an isolated Type A word possibly because the offset low tone which is anchored to the final syllable of an isolated Type B word pulled down the F0 realisation of Type B compared to Type A at the peak syllable.

The result from Experiment 2—which is free from the influence of the low boundary tone—indicates that the boundary tone possibly has influenced or exaggerated the differences observed between isolated Type A and Type B words in Experiment 1 to a certain extent, otherwise the magnitude of the accentual effect should also have been observed equally at V1 and P1 in longer utterances. That is, judging from the frequency and the magnitude of the accentual effect, the PAB effect is possibly weaker than the IAB effect in KJ.

Furthermore, since the results of Experiment 1 are based on isolated words and those of Experiment 2 are based on longer utterances embedded in a carrier sentence, it is possible that the differences in the magnitude of the accentual effect between Experiments 1 and 2 have something to do with the differences between eliciting isolated words and eliciting words combined together in a larger context. It has been pointed out in conjunction with prosodic behaviour that isolated words behave differently from running speech (Kratochvil 1998). It is well known that not only tonal target but also segmental articulatory target tend to be 'undershot' in running speech (Clark and Yallop 1990; Harrington and Cassidy 1999). Therefore, it can be considered that due to the F0 undershoot, the F0 differences in magnitude and frequency between the accentual types of KJ are not as evident in Experiment 2 as in Experiment 1.

Comparing the results presented in Table 9 with those presented in Kubozono and Matsui (1996), it is noticeable that significant differences at P1 and P2 (the PAB and the DNS effects) are far less frequently observed in the current study. In their experiment, 6 comparisons showed a significant difference at P1, and 7 comparisons at P2 out of a total of 11comparisons. In Experiment 2, as shown in Table 10, a significant difference was confirmed in only 3 and 2 comparisons out of 12 at P1 and P2, respectively. Since the declination effect was not controlled in Kubozono and Matsui's experiment, one could say that the accentual effect was possibly exaggerated in their experiment. That is, there is a possibility that some of the accentual effects are indeed weaker than reported in Kubozono and Matsui (1996).

As can be seen in Tables 10 and 11, although the effects of ACF and DNS are statistically significant, the occurrence and the magnitude of these effects are less frequent and weaker than those of the IAB effect. According to Table 10, a significant difference was observed only in 2 comparisons at P2 despite the fact that a significant difference was observed in 6 comparisons at V2. That is, the ACF effect—which is the initial stage of DNS—is more frequently observed than the DNS is significantly observed. Although it is not acknowledged by Kubozono and Matsui (1996), only one utterance shows significant differences simultaneously at all comparison points in their study, which contrasts with Kubozono's (1993) study on SJ in which the accentual effects (ACB, ACF and DNS) are simultaneously observed at the different comparison points in many cases. In fact, this agrees with the result in Experiment 2 in which no target utterances show significant differences at the same time at all points of comparison. Reflecting these points, one could argue that although the ACF and DNS are statistically significant, they may be too weak in KJ (compared to SJ) to cause a significant difference on some occasions.

In Experiment 1, it was demonstrated that the IAB effect is very pervasive in the pre–peak syllables of Type A polysyllabic words. Judging from the results of Experiments 1 and 2, it appears that the IAB effect is indeed strong in KJ (not only compared to the PAB effect but also to the ACF and the DNS effect). In SJ, on the other hand, Kubozono (1993, p89–90) reported that the IAB effect is weaker than the other accentual effects. The strength of the IAB effect is therefore another possible difference between KJ and SJ.

One possible explanation for the strong IAB effect can be drawn from the accentual nature of KJ. Because of its accentual nature, KJ words are subject to having a sequence of low pitched syllables (e.g. **LLLLLH**(L)) before a high pitched syllable. That is, only one high pitched syllable per accentual unit is permitted in KJ. Therefore, although the contrast is primarily located at the end of a word in terms of whether there is a pitch fall or not, the accentual contrast is more perceptually salient if a clear acoustic difference is made in the sequence in question, because the sequence accounts for the major portion of a word.

The results of Experiments 1 and 2 tell that although KJ and SJ are significantly different in their accentual systems, when it comes to intonational phenomena, they share much similarity in that KJ's Type A words and SJ's accented words trigger IAB, PAB, ACF and DNS. On the other hand, some possible differences between KJ and SJ have been discussed in this paper at the F0 realisation level. Although the nature of the F0 realisation of the accentual effects in KJ and SJ need to be compared in mutually comparable environments to verify the above possible differences, if there is a difference between KJ and SJ at the acoustic–phonetic realisation level, this shows that a linguistic feature shared by two languages or varieties at one level does not necessarily behave identically at another level.

5 Conclusion

It has been demonstrated in this study that Type A triggers ACB (IAB and PAB), ACF and DNS, like the accented words of SJ. This similarity between KJ's Type A and SJ's accented words tells that although KJ and SJ are significantly different in their accentual systems, the behaviour of their accentual contrast is very similar at the intonational level. However, some possible differences between KJ and SJ have also been discussed at the phonetic realisation level. These possible differences are: 1) PAB, ACF and DNS may be generally weaker in KJ compared to SJ, 2) IAB is stronger than the other accentual effects in KJ whereas the IAB is weaker than the other accentual effects in SJ.

6 Acknowledgments

I thank Dr Phil Rose at the Australian National University and Professor Haruo Kubozono at University of Kobe for giving valuable comments on this research.

References

Clark, J. and C. Yallop (1990). *An Introduction to Phonetics and Phonology*. Oxford: Blackwell Publishers.

Cooper, W. E. and J. M. Sorensen (1981). *Fundamental Frequency in Sentence Production*. Berlin: Springer–Verlag.

©Kay Elemetric Corp (1994). *CSL Instruction Manual 'Computer Speech Lab' Model 4300B, Software Version 5.X*. ©Kay Elemetric Corp.

Disner, S. (1980). Evaluation of vowel normalization procedures. *Journal of Acoustical Society of America 67*(1), 253–261.

Fujisaki, H. (1983). Dynamic characteristics of voice fundamental frequency in speech and singing. In P. MacNeilage (Ed.), *The Production of Speech*, pp. 39–55. New York: Springer–Verlag.

Gandour, J. (1974). On the Representation of Tone in Siamese. *UCLA Working Papers in Phonetics 27*, 118–146.

Gussenhoven, C. (2004). *The Phonology of Tone and Intonation*. Cambridge: Cambridge University Press.

Haraguchi, S. (1977). *The Tone Pattern of Japanese: An Autosegmental Theory of Tonology*. Tokyo: Kaitakusha.

Harrington, J. and S. Cassidy (1999). *Techniques in Speech Acoustics*. Kluwer Academic Publishers.

Hayata, T. (1999). *Onchoo no taiporojii*. Taishuukan shoten.

Hirayama, T. (1951). *Kyuushuuhoogen onchoo no kenkyuu*. Gakkai no shihyoosha.

Hirayama, T. (1957). *Nihongo onchoo no kenkyuu*. Tokyo: Meiji shoin.

Hirayama, T. (1960). *Zenkoku akusento jiten* (1st ed.). Tokyo: Tookyoodoo.

Ishihara, S. (2004). *An Acoustic–Phonetic Descriptive Analysis of Kagoshima Japanese Tonal Phenomena*. Ph. D. thesis, The Australian National University.

Kibe, N. (1997). *Kagoshimaken no kotoba: Nihon no kotoba siriizu*, Volume 46 of *Nihon no kotoba siriizu*. Meijishoin.

Kibe, N. (2000). *Seinanbu kyuushuu nikeiakusento no kenkyuu*. Tokyo: Bensei Shuppan.

Kobayashi, C. (1975). *Japanese Dialects: Phonology and Reconstruction of the Proto–Accentual System*. Ph. D. thesis, Cornell University.

Kratochvil, P. (1998). Intonation in Beijing Chinese. In D. Hirst and A. D. Christo (Eds.), *Intonation Systems*, pp. 417–431. Cambridge University Press.

Kubozono, H. (1993). *The Organization of Japanese Prosody*. Tokyo: Kuroshio Publishers.

Kubozono, H. and M. Matsui (1996). Nihongo no akusentojakka to intoneeshon. In the Phonetic Society of Japan (Ed.), *Proceedings of the 10th General Meeting of the PSJ*, pp. 101–106.

Ladd, D. (1988). Declination 'reset' and the hierarchical organisation of utterances. *Journal of Acoustical Society of America 84*(2), 530–544.

Ladefoged, P. (1997). Instrumental techniques for fieldwork. In W. J. Hardcastle and J. Laver (Eds.), *The Handbook of Phonetic Science*, pp. 137–166. Blackwell Publishers.

Ladefoged, P. and I. Maddieson (1986). Some of the sounds of the world's languages: Preliminary version. *UCLA Working Papers in Phonetics 64*, 1–26.

Lawrence, W. P. (1999). Comments on Prof. Hayata's paper "Accent and tone: Towards a general theory of prosody". In S. Kaji (Ed.), *Proceedings of the Symposium: Cross–Linguistic Studies of Tonal Phenomena, Tonogenesis, Typology, and Related Topics*, Institute for the Study of Languages and Cultures of Asia and Africa, Tokyo University of Foreign Studies, pp. 235–236.

Liberman, M. and J. B. Pierrehumbert (1983). Intonational invariance under changes in pitch range and length. In M. Aronoff and R. T. Oehrle (Eds.), *Studies in Phonology Presented to Morris Halle*, pp. 157–233. Cambridge, Massachusetts: MIT Press.

Lindau, M. (1986). Testing a model of intonation in a tone language. *Journal of Acoustical Society of America 80*(3), 757–764.

McCawley, J. D. (1977). Accent in Japanese. *Studies in Stress and Accent: Southern California Occasional Papers in Linguistics 4*, 261–302.

Pierrehumbert, J. and M. Beckman (1988). *Japanese Tone Structure*. Cambridge, Massachusetts, London, England: MIT Press.

Poser, W. (1984). *The Phonetics and Phonology of Tone and Intonation in Japanese*. Ph. D. thesis, MIT.

Rose, P. (1987). Considerations in the normalisation of the fundamental frequency of linguistic tone. *Speech Communication 6*, 343–351.

Rose, P. (1991). How effective are long term mean and standard deviation as normalisation parameters for tonal fundamental frequency? *Speech Communication 10*, 229–247.

Shibatani, M. (1990). *The Languages of Japan*. Cambridge University Press.

Smith, J. (1997). Noun faithfulness: Evidence from accent in Japanese dialects. *Japanese/Korean Linguistics 7*, 611–627.

Umeda, N. (1982). F0 declination is situation dependent. *Journal of Phonetics 10*, 279–290.

Vance, T. (1995). Final accent vs. no accent: Utterance-final neutralization in Tokyo Japanese. *Journal of Phonetics 23*, 487–499.

Warner, N. (1995). Japanese final-accent and unaccented phrases. *Journal of Phonetics 25*, 43–60.

Yip, M. (2002). *Tone*. Cambridge: Cambridge University Press.

Zhu, X. (1994). *Shanghai Tonetics*. Ph. D. thesis, the Australian National University.

Appendix

	Type A			Type B		
2	buta	豚	pig	baka	馬鹿	stupid
	kagu	家具	furniture	kagi	鍵	key
	mune	胸	chest	kogu	漕ぐ	to row
	take	竹	bamboo	mimi	耳	ears
3	kakuho	確保	security	gakubu	学部	department
	kimono	着物	clothes	megane	眼鏡	glasses
	komimi	小耳	ears	tamago	卵	egg
	sakana	魚	fish	yubiwa	指輪	ring
4	getabako	下駄箱	shoe box	demakase	でまかせ	lie
	kanimiso	蟹味噌	crab paste	kakimono	書き物	document
	kagaribi	篝火	bonfire	miminari	耳鳴り	ringing in the ears
	kimusume	生娘	maid	nanohana	菜の花	rape blossoms
	mamagoto	ままごと	playing house	yamanami	山脈	mountain tops
5	kamibasami	紙バサミ	scissors	hanamizake	花見酒	appreciate flowers
	kamiyasuri	紙ヤスリ	sandpaper	kamikazari	髪飾り	hair–ornament
	machiyakuba	町役場	town hall	katatsumuri	カタツムリ	snail
	minamigawa	南側	south side	mimizawari	耳障り	irritating noise
	minamimura	南村	south village	miyagemono	土産物	present
6	terebikamera	テレビカメラ	TV camera	niwatorigoya	鶏小屋	hen house
7	kamikiribasami	紙切りバサミ	scissors			

Table 12: *Target polysyllabic words of Corpus 1*

Sentences: Noun + Particle + Verb			
S1AA	hana–ga naru LHL HL	鼻が鳴る。	Nose makes noise.
S1BA	e–ga narabu LH LHL	絵が並ぶ。	Pictures line up.
S2AB	sakana–ga nigeru LLHL LLH	魚が逃げる。	Fish escape.
S2BB	hana—ga nagareru LLH LLLH	花が流れる。	Flowers flow.
S3AB	kimono–o naderu LLHL LLH	着物を撫でる。	(Someone) rubs clothes.
S3BB	kazu–o shiraberu LLH LLLH	数を調べる。	(Someone) checks number.
S4AA	minami–ni mukeru LLHL LHL	南に向ける。	(Someone) turns (something) to the south.
S4BA	umi–ni tobikomu LLH LLHL	海に飛び込む。	(Someone) dives into the sea.
Noun phrases: Adjective + Noun			
NP5AA	nagaka kami LHL HL	長か紙	long paper
NP5BA	yoka sakana LH LHL	よか魚	good fish
NP6AA	amaka nimono LHL LHL	甘か煮物	sweet stew
NP6BA	yoka tabemono LH LLHL	よか食べ物	good food
NP7AB	nagaka tamago LHL LLH	長か卵	long egg
NP7BB	yoka kudamono LH LLLH	よか果物	good fruit
NP8AB	nagaka kudamono LHL LLLH	長か果物	long fruit
NP8BB	yoka yudetamago LH LLLLH	よかゆで卵	good boiled egg
Possessive phrases: Noun + Particle (*no*) + Noun			
PossP9AB	kimono–no nuno LLHL HL	着物の布	texture of cloth
PossP9BB	yama–no sakura LLH LHL	山の桜	cherry blossoms on the mountain
PossP10AA	kimono–no gara LLHL LH	着物の柄	colour of cloth
PossP10BA	saru–no atama LLH LLH	猿の頭	head of monkey
PossP11AA	himago–no kimono LLHL LHL	曾孫の着物	clothes of great–grandchild
PossP11BA	mago–no tabemono LLH LLHL	孫の食べ物	food of grandchild
PossP12AB	himago–no megane LLHL LLH	曾孫の眼鏡	glasses of great–grandchild
PossP12BB	mago–no hakimono LLH LLLH	曾孫の履物	shoes of grandchild

Table 13: *Target utterances of Corpus 2*

Comments on Shunichi Ishihara's Paper on Tonal Phenomena in Kagoshima Japanese

Haruo Kubozono (Kobe University)

Summary

This commentary consists of four sections. In section 1, I would like to sketch some salient prosodic features of Kagoshima Japanese (KJ) in comparison with those of Standard Tokyo Japanese (TJ). Understanding these features is essential if one wants to assess Ishihara's work on KJ prosody properly. Section 2 summarizes the main points of Ishihara's paper with focus on its merits. Section 3 provides some arguments in support of Ishihara's claim that the two distinctive tonal patterns in KJ —Type A and Type B— resemble accented and unaccented patterns in TJ. Section 4 lists an agenda for future work regarding the phonetics and phonology of KJ.

1. Prosodic Differences between Tokyo and Kagoshima Japanese

KJ is a regional dialect spoken in the south of Japan. This dialect displays some prosodic properties that are not present in TJ and many other dialects of Japanese (Hirayama 1960, Kibe 2000, Kubozono 2004). First of all, KJ has a two-pattern prosodic system: that is, it has only two tonal patterns irrespective of the length of words. These patterns are called Type A and Type B in this paper. Words of Type A have a high tone on the penultimate syllable, while those of Type B have a high tone on the final syllable. In either case, every word has only one high-toned syllable, with all other syllables low-toned, when pronounced in isolation. It is implicitly assumed in the literature that the two tonal patterns contrast in the location of high tone (Hirayama 1960, Kibe 2000, Kubozono 2004). This two-pattern system is strikingly different from the multi-pattern system of TJ, where the number of contrastive patterns is supposed to increase as the word becomes longer [see Note 1]. Some examples are given in (1), where NOM means nominative particle.

(1) Multi-pattern system of TJ and two-pattern system of KJ

Word	namida-ga	kokoro-ga	otoko-ga	sakana-ga
Gloss	eyedrop-NOM	heart-NOM	man-NOM	fish-NOM
Tokyo	námida-ga (initial accent)	kokóro-ga (medial accent)	otokó-ga (final accent)	sakana-ga (unaccented)
Kagoshima	Type B (high tone on the final syllable)			Type A (high tone on the penult)

A second salient feature of KJ is that its system is based on the syllable rather than the mora. As is well known, TJ and most other dialects of Japanese are so-called 'mora languages' (or 'mora dialects'), in which the mora serves many crucial roles. In accentuation, for example, TJ assigns an accent by counting the number of moras from the end of the word. KJ is similar to TJ in computing accentuation from the right edge of the word but is different in measuring phonological distance in terms of the syllable rather than the mora. Thus, this dialect assigns a high tone on the penultimate *syllable* (i.e. Type A) in most loanwords. TJ generally assigns an accent on the antepenultimate *mora* in this type of word. This is illustrated in (2), where capital letters and dots indicate high tones and syllable boundaries, respectively.

(2) Loanword accent/tone in TJ and KJ

Word	in.do	gi.ri.sya	doi.tu	ha.wai
Gloss	India	Greece	Germany	Hawaii
Tokyo	ín.do	gí.ri.sya	dói.tu	há.wai
Kagoshima	IN.do	gi.RI.sya	DOI.tu	HA.wai

A third feature characteristic of the prosodic system of KJ concerns its compound accent/tone rule. In this dialect, the prosodic structure of compounds is determined by their initial member. If compounds begin with a Type A morpheme, they take Type A tonal pattern — i.e. high tone on the penult. If, on the other hand, compounds begin with a Type B morpheme, they take Type B tonal pattern — i.e. high tone on the final syllable. Compound words thus inherit the tonal pattern of their initial member, either Type A or Type B, with the result that the two contrastive patterns are never neutralized no matter how long a word may be. This is illustrated in (3).

(3) A.ka + sin.GOO → aka-SIN.goo 'red signal'
a.O + sin.GOO → a.o-sin.GOO 'green signal'

Interestingly, this compound tone rule can be extended to basic phrases generally called 'bunsetu'. Thus, phrases take Type A or Type B depending on whether their initial element is a Type A or Type B morpheme. The phrases in (4a) bear a high tone on the penult since their initial element takes a high tone on the penult when it is pronounced in isolation. The phrases in (4b) take a high tone on it's the final syllable since their initial element is a Type B morpheme.

(4) a. ka.ri.fo.ru.NI.a 'California'
ka.ri.fo.ru.ni.A-ga 'California-NOM'
ka.ri.fo.ru.ni.a-KA.ra 'from California'

ka.ri.fo.ru.ni.a-ka.RA.mo 'from California, too'

b. a.me.ri.KA 'America'
   a.me.ri.ka-GA 'America-NOM'
   a.me.ri.ka-ka.RA 'from America'
   a.me.ri.ka-ka.ra-MO 'from America, too'

2. Ishihara's Findings

Ishihara's main finding is that the distinction between Type A and Type B in KJ corresponds to the distinction between accented and unaccented words in TJ in phonetic terms. In other words, words of Type A in KJ exhibit essentially the same pitch behavior as accented words in TJ. Similarly, words of Type B in KJ show the same pitch patterns as unaccented words in TJ. To understand this point, let us first look at the tonal differences between accented and unaccented words in TJ.

As is well known, accented words crucially differ from unaccented words in showing an abrupt pitch drop at the phonetic output. Thus, accented words like *u'mai* 'tasty' and *nomi'mono* 'drink' involve a sudden pitch fall, whereas unaccented words like *amai* 'sweet' and *yamaimo* 'yam (potato)' do not exhibit such a pitch fall. Indeed, the presence or absence of such a sudden pitch fall is supposed to be the distinctive feature of accented words as opposed to unaccented ones in TJ.

However, accented words differ from unaccented ones in several other ways as well. As shown clearly in the literature (Poser 1984, Kubozono 1988), accented words begin with a higher pitch than their unaccented counterparts. Moreover, the former exhibits a higher F0 peak than the latter. These two differences can be attributed to an 'accentual boost' exhibited by accented words (Kubozono 1988). In addition to this, accented words crucially differ from their unaccented counterparts in exerting a lowering effect of pitch (or pitch range) on following words. Thus, a word/phrase, whether lexically accented or unaccented, is phonetically realized at a lower pitch level when it follows a lexically accented element than when following a lexically unaccented element. This effect is called 'catathesis' (Poser 1984, Pierrehumbert and Beckman 1988) or 'downstep' (Kubozono 1988, 1989, 1992; Selkirk and Tateishi 1991). The second term is used in this paper.

The effects of accentual boost and downstep are illustrated in Figure 1. A solid line shows the typical pitch contour of an accented element followed by another accented element. In contrast, a dotted line shows the typical contour of an unaccented element followed by an accented element.

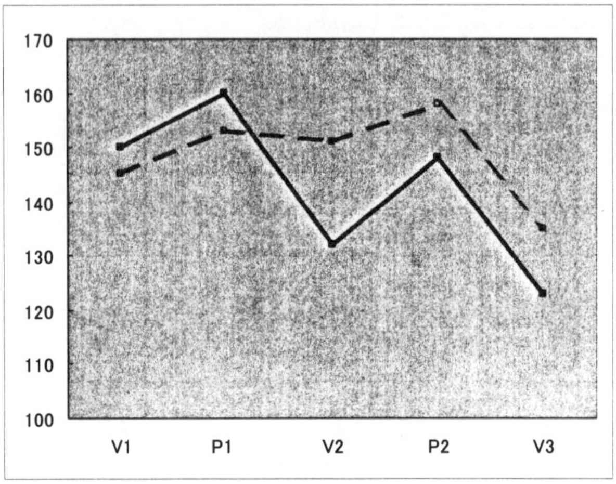

Figure 1 Typical pitch contours of a sequence of lexically accented words (solid line) and a sequence of unaccented and accented words (dashed line).

What Ishihara has shown in his paper/presentation is that words belonging to Type A in KJ display basically the same pitch behavior as accented words in TJ. First, words of Type A exhibit a higher pitch than those of Type B both at their onset and at their pitch peak. Second, these words show a lower pitch when they follow a Type A word than when they follow a Type B word. The latter point had previously been pointed out by Kubozono and Matsui (1996), but Ishihara confirmed this by properly removing a possible effect of mechanical declination.

It is worth emphasizing that KJ exhibits very striking phonetic similarities to TJ despite all the prosodic differences described in section 1 above. It is interesting indeed that the two tonal patterns in KJ —Type A and Type B— display essentially the same tonal behaviors as accented and unaccented words in TJ although they are generally supposed to differ in the location of a high-pitched syllable.

3. Additional Evidence for Ishihara's Arguments

As mentioned above, Ishihara has shown that Type A in KJ exerts the same pitch effects as accented words in TJ. This implies that the distinctive feature of Type A as opposed to Type B is the presence of a pitch fall; that is, Type A and Type B crucially differ in that the former, but not the latter, involves a pitch fall. Stated conversely, it implies that the location of pitch rise is not a primary feature distinguishing one tonal pattern from another in KJ. In this section, I would like to provide some additional evidence for this idea by drawing on data from my own fieldwork.

In my recent paper (Kubozono 2003), I discussed ongoing tonal/accent changes in KJ. This study has shown that some words of Type A have turned to Type B, while other words have changed in the other direction in the speech of young speakers of KJ. Interestingly, these bi-directional changes are observed in highly restricted types of words. The change from Type A to Type B is predominantly observed in words that are 'unaccented' in TJ. Similarly, the change from Type B to Type A is largely observed in words that are pronounced as accented words in TJ. In other words, words tend to change their tonal pattern (from Type A to Type B or otherwise) in KJ if they differ in the presence or absence of a sudden pitch fall between KJ and TJ. Some examples are given in (5) and (6). In TJ, words in (5) are lexically unaccented: that is, they are pronounced with a rather flat pitch.

(5) bu.ra.ZI.ru → bu.ra.zi.RU 'Brazil' (Tokyo: bu.ra.zi.ru)
ka.E.de → ka.e.DE 'maple' (Tokyo: ka.e.de)
sya.KAI.too → sya.kai.TOO 'Socialist Party' (Tokyo: sya.kai.too)

(6) doo.na.TU → doo.NA.tu 'donut' (Tokyo: dóo.na.tu)
mo.mi.ZI → mo.MI.zi 'autumn leaves' (Tokyo: mó.mi.zi)
a.o.sin.GOO → a.o.SIN.goo 'green signal' (Tokyo: a.o.sín.goo)

The words in (5) traditionally belong to Type A (with a pitch fall) in KJ, but are pronounced as unaccented words (without a pitch fall). These words are now pronounced by young KJ speakers as Type B (without a pitch fall). In contrast, those in (6) traditionally belong to Type B (with no pitch fall) in KJ, but are pronounced as accented words (with a pitch fall). These words belong to Type A (with a pitch fall) in young KJ speakers' speech. Note that the new KJ tonal patterns in (5) and (6) are not exactly identical to the tonal patterns in TJ: e.g. /doo.na.tu/ 'donut' has a high tone on /do/ in TJ, whereas it has a high tone on /na/ in the new KJ pattern. However, the two types of tonal pattern now agree in the presence or absence of a pitch fall. This is the crucial point in which the new KJ patterns resemble the TJ patterns.

While young speakers of KJ exhibit bi-directional tonal changes illustrated in (5) and (6), they do not show similar changes in words that agree in the overall pitch shape between KJ and TJ. Thus, words like those in (7) do not tend to show the kind of tonal change illustrated in (5) and (6): words in (7a) are accented in Tokyo, while those in (7b) are unaccented.

(7) a. gi.RI.sya 'Greece' (Tokyo: gí.ri.sya)
aka.SIN.goo 'red signal' (Tokyo: a.ka.sín.goo)
b. a.me.ri.KA 'America' (Tokyo: a.me.ri.ka)
zi.yuu.TOO 'Liberal Party' (Tokyo: zi.yuu.too)

The tonal changes illustrated in (5) and (6) can be summarized as (8).

(8) Words produced with a pitch fall in TJ tend to be produced as Type A by young speakers of KJ now; those produced without a pitch fall in TJ tend to be pronounced as Type B by

young speakers of KJ.

The tonal changes summarized in (8) can be attributed to two independent factors. First of all, they can be attributed to the strong influence of TJ. Young native speakers of KJ are sensitive to a sudden pitch fall in accented words in TJ and introduce a sudden pitch fall in their own pronunciation of the same words in KJ. If they do not hear a sudden pitch fall in certain words in TJ speakers' pronunciation, they tend to produce the same words without a sudden pitch fall when they pronounce them in their native dialect.

This perceptual influence of TJ does seem remarkably profound in the speech of young KJ speakers, but it does not fully account for the tonal changes sketched in (5) and (6). What is important here is that young speakers of KJ still employ their native tonal patterns even though they deviate from the traditional pronunciations. Namely, young KJ speakers produce a 'wrong' tonal pattern when they pronounce the words in (5) and (6), but they almost never assign a tonal pattern other than Type A or Type B. The fact that they show a deviation *within* their native two-pattern system indicates that a phonological factor is at work here: tonal changes are tolerated within the prosodic system of KJ. This restriction imposed by the native prosodic system together with the perceptual factor mentioned above provides a sufficient account of the precise output patterns that are observed in (5) and (6). Young native speakers of KJ determine the overall pitch shape of words by copying the pitch shape of those words in TJ, while being constrained by their native phonology as to the precise output patterns.

Having understood that the ongoing bi-directional tonal changes summarized in (8) are attributable to two factors — the perceptual influence of TJ and a phonological restriction from KJ itself, let us go one step further to ask what lies behind the perceptual factor. As mentioned above, young native speakers of KJ simply pick up a sudden pitch fall in the speech of TJ. Seen conversely, this means that they are not attentive to any pith change other than a pitch fall.

Why are they not attentive to the location of a pitch rise? One plausible answer to this question is that the location of a pitch rise is a non-distinctive phonetic feature in the native prosodic system of KJ. In other words, Type A and Type B are not distinguished from each other by the location of a high-pitched syllable, as is generally assumed (Hirayama 1960, Kibe 2000, Kubozono 2004); rather, they are distinguished in terms of the presence or absence of a pitch fall in KJ just as are accented and unaccented words in TJ. This is in accordance with Ishihara's experimental results discussed above, i.e. the claim that Type A and Type B in KJ correspond, respectively, to accented and unaccented words in TJ.

4. Problems for Future Work

Ishihara's work is important in that it has opened a door to many interesting questions for future work on KJ prosody. One such question concerns the influence of syntax on prosody. Experimental work on TJ has shown that intonational structure is strongly influenced by syntactic structure (Kubozono 1988, Selkirk and Tateishi 1991). For example, different branching structures —left-branching and right-branching— are known to yield different intonation patterns. It is worth exploring if the same effect is observed in KJ, too.

Another interesting question that remains unanswered concerns the interface between prosody and discourse. In TJ, it is known that pragmatic focus on a certain element changes intonational patterns and, hence, prosodic structures. Similar work should certainly be done on KJ. It is expected that work on focus prosody in KJ and its comparison with similar work on TJ and other dialects/languages will illuminate the central question in focus prosody —the question of what is actually changed by the presence of focus.

Finally, KJ is known to exhibit peculiar patterns of question prosody (Kibe 2000). Specifically, questions —yes/no questions as well as Wh questions— in this dialect are typically indicated by a pitch fall rather than a pitch rise. Thus, the one-word sentence in (9) is taken as a declarative sentence if it is pronounced with its lexical pattern, whereas it is regarded as an interrogative sentence if an extra low pitch is added to the lexical pattern. (H and L indicate high and low tones, which are tentatively assigned to each syllable here).

(9) a. declarative sentence
amerika. 'America'
LLLH
b. interrogative sentence
amerika? 'America?'
LLLH**L**

This is a unique prosodic feature of KJ that is not shared by TJ or many other dialects of Japanese. Details of this peculiar pattern of question prosody need to be explored in the future.

Note

1. This generalization may not be supported in statistical terms since accented patterns do not occur as frequently as each other. Rather, nouns tend to be accented on the antepenultimate mora (or on the non-final, rightmost foot) if they are accented at all in TJ. This fact suggests that the prosodic system of TJ is very close to a two-pattern system at least in statistical terms. Not surprisingly, most of the minimal pairs of words that are accentually distinguished do contrast between accented and unaccented patterns, not between two different accented patterns.

Selected References

Hirayama, Teruo 1960. *Zenkoku Akusento Ziten* (All Japan Accent Dictionary). Tokyo: Tookyoodoo.

Kibe, Nobuko 2000. *Seinanbu Kyuushuu Nikei Akusento no Kenkyuu* (Studies on the two-class-accent dialects of Southwest Kyuushuu). Tokyo: Benseisha.

Kubozono, Haruo 1988. *The Organization of Japanese Prosody.* Ph.D. dissertation, University of Edinburgh.

Kubozono, Haruo 1989. Syntactic and rhythmic effects on downstep in Japanese. *Phonology* 6-1: 39-67.

Kubozono, Haruo 1992. Modeling syntactic effects on downstep in Japanese. In G. J. Docherty and D. R. Ladd (eds.) *Papers in Laboratory Phonology II: Gesture, Segment, Prosody.* 368-387. Cambridge: Cambridge University Press.

Kubozono, Haruo 2003. Accentual changes in Kagoshima Japanese. (in Japanese) *Kokubungaku* 48-4: 46-52.

Kubozono, Haruo 2004. What does Kagoshima Japanese tell us about Japanese syllables? In T. Kageyama and H. Kishimoto (eds.) *Nihongo no Bunseki to Gengo Ruikei* (Analysis of Japanese and Language Typology). 75-92. Tokyo: Kurosio Publishers.

Kubozono, Haruo and Michinao Matui (1996) Accent reduction and intonation in Japanese. Paper presented at the annual meeting of the Phonetic Society of Japan. (*Proceedings of the 10th general meeting of the PSJ*, pp.101-106).

Pierrehumbert, Janet and Mary Beckman 1988. *Japanese Tone Structure*. MIT Press.

Poser, William (1984) *The Phonetics and Phonology of Tone and Intonation in Japanese*. Ph.D. dissertation, MIT.

Selkirk, Elizabeth and Koichi Tateishi 1991. Syntax and downstep in Japanese. In C. Georgopoulos and R. Ishihara (eds.) *Interdisciplinary Approaches to Language : Essays in Honor of S.-Y. Kuroda*, 519-544. Dordrecht : Kluwer.

Tone Patterns of Matengo Nominals

Yoneda, Nobuko
(Osaka Jogakuin College)
yoneda@wilmina.ac.jp

1. Introduction

Matengo is a Bantu language spoken in the southern part of Tanzania. Although Matengo has lost tone contrast in verb stems, nouns still show a tone contrast. This paper will discuss the various tone patterns which can be seen in Matengo nouns and divide them into groups.

1.1. Vowels and Consonants

Vowels:

Short vowels	/ i, e, ɛ, a, u, o, ɔ /	
Long vowels	/ iː, eː, ɛː, aː, uː, oː, ɔː /	

Consonants:

Stops	/ p, b, t, k, g /	
Fricatives	/ s, h /	
Affricates	/ dʒ /	(→ dz / nasal __)
Nasals	/ m, n, ɲ, ŋ /	
Approximants	/ l /	(→ d / nasal __)
Semi-vowels	/ w, j /	

1.2. Length of vowels

Matengo has phonemic long vowels, and vowels automatically appear as long in the following contexts.

(1) a. vowel in the penultimate syllable of the tone phrase
/ kibega / [kibeːga]
cf. / kibega kinjahi / [kibega kinjaːhi]
b. vowel followed by NC (mb, nd, ndz, ŋg)
/ bombola / [boːmboːla]
c. vowel proceeded by Cw or Cj
/ tweleka / [tweːleːka]

Syllables with a long vowel have two moras, and other syllables have one mora. Long vowels, however, only appear in the antepenultimate, penultimate or final syllables in any word. Long vowels before the antepenultimate syllable are shortened.

Examples are seen in (2). It is to be noted that although the unit of the rule "vowel in the penultimate syllable becomes long vowel" is the tone phrase, the unit of shortening of long vowels in the antepenultimate syllable is the word (compare (2b) and (2c)).

(2)	a.	/-dʒo:ba/	[dʒo:ba]	"to peel"
	b.	/-dʒo:beka/	[dʒo:be:ka]	"to peel for"
	c. cf.	/-dʒo:beka likalatasi /	[dʒo:beka likalata:si]	"to peel paper for"
	d.	/-dʒo:batoka/	[dʒobato:ka]	"to peel off "

1.3. Tone (Accent)

The tone bearing unit is the mora. Only High (H) tone is marked and others, i.e. -H, appear as Low (L). Therefore, although I use the term "tone", it may more accurately be called "accent". Falling (F) or Rising (R) tones also appear in two-mora syllables as the combination of H and L. A two-mora syllable which has H in the first mora appears as F. One which has H in the second mora appears as R. If R is proceeded by L, H in the R syllable spreads to the left mora and the syllable appears as a long H syllable as seen in (3c). Underlining represents a two mora syllable, ●= H, and ○=L, as seen below.

(3)	a.	first mora is H	●○		F
	b.	second mora is H	● ○●		R
	c.		○ ○●	> ○ ●●	H

mípě:pi	*mípé:pi	"fins"
mítɔpǐ:tɔ >	mítɔpí:tɔ	"a tree of cherimoya"

F, R, or long H syllables can only appear in antepenultimate, penultimate or final syllable position, because these are the only positions where a two-mora long vowel may occur. In this paper, I use the symbol ":" not only for the phonemic long vowels but also for all the vowels which appear as long vowels. The tone marks on long vowels are: á: = áá, â = áa, ǎ = aá.

1.4. Noun Construction

One of the significant characteristics of Bantu languages is the "Noun class" system, which is grammatical gender. Matengo has 16 noun classes[1] and each noun class has its own class prefix (See Table 1). Matengo nouns are basically constructed with a noun class prefix and a noun stem[2], as seen below.

---

[1] In addition to these 16 classes, Matengo has 3 locative noun classes.
[2] Some nouns are constructed in different ways from this.

(4)	NCP -	noun stem		
a.	lí-	hi:mba	líhi:mba	“ a lion (5)”
b.	ú-	to:pi	úto:pi	“ clay (11)”
c.	ḿ-	po:ŋga	ḿpo:ŋga	“ rice (3)”

2. Observations

2.1. Tone of Noun class prefixes

Nouns that have the same stem usually appear with the same tone pattern irrespective of the class. However this is not always the case for class 5. For example, when adding different noun class prefixes to the stem “-lenda”, they appear as HRL, but only class 5 appears as LHL.

(5) L-HL

li-lé:nda	“ a trap (5)”

H-RL

má-lě:nda	“ traps (6)”
mi-le:nda	“ big traps (4)”
ká-lě:nda	“ a tiny trap (12)”
tú-lě:nda	“ tiny traps (13)”
gú-lě:nda	“ a big trap (20)”

The tone patterns of HRL can be seen in every noun class except class 5. On the other hand, the tone pattern of LHL can only be seen in this one noun class. There are other tone patterns as well which can be seen in every noun class except class 5, such as H-LFL and H-LHL, or which can only be seen in class 5 such as L-LHL.

(6) a. H-LFL

ń-sokô:lo	“a grandchild (1)”
á-sokô:lo	“ grandchildren (2)”
ń-tɔŋgâ:na	“ a mulberry tree (3)”
mí-tɔŋgâ:na	“ mulberry trees (4)”
má-dʒɔdʒɔ̂:la	“ lungs (6)” cf.) li-dʒɔdʒɔ̂:la “a lung (5)”
kí-dʒalî:la	“ burned rice (7)”
hí-dʒalî:la	“ burned rice pl.(8)”
ndzéŋgasê:gi	“ kind of beans (9/10)”
lú-pɛlɛ̂:la	“ nose cavity (11)”
ká-hombê:la	“ a shoal (12)”
tú-hombê:la	“ shoals (13)”
ú-kɔlɔ̂:ŋgu	“ bigness (14)”

b. H-LHL

ń-nabá:na	“son’s wife (1)”

á-nabá:na "son's wives (2)"
ń-tɔpí:tɔ " a tree of cherimoya (3)"
mí-tɔpí:tɔ " trees of cherimoya (4)"
má-tɔpí:tɔ " cherimoyas (6)" cf.) li- tɔpí:tɔ "a cherimoya(5)"
kí-hɔpɔ́:la " an unborn baby (7)"
hí-hɔpɔ́:la " unborn babies (8)"
ŋgámbugá:mbu "a kind of grasshopper (9/10)"
lú-pulí:ka "a kind of ant (11)"

Because of these facts, the noun class prefix of class 5 is considered to have a different underlying tone from the other classes. In the tone patterns which can be seen in all the noun classes except class 5, the noun prefixes are H, and in the tone patterns which can be seen only in class 5, the noun prefixes are L. Therefore it is clear that the prefixes of all classes except class 5 are +H, and the class 5 noun prefix is underlyingly -H, which appears as L.

Table 1 : Noun class prefixes

sg.			pl.			
class	prefix	noun	class	prefix	noun	gross
1	mu- / N-	múbe:hi ntâ:mu	2	ba- / a-	ábe:hi atâ:mu	"hunter" "sick person"
3	N-	ḿpa:lu nsî:pu	4	mi-	mípa:lu misî:pu	"animal trail" "sneeze"
5	li-	líhu:pa likɔ̂:lɔ	6	ma-	máhu:pa makɔ̂:lɔ	"bone" "cave"
7	si- /ki-	sîndu kímulî:la	8	hi- / i-	hîndu ímulî:la	"thing" "bat"
9	ø, in-, n-	íŋɔ:ma imbɛ̂:la	10	ø, in-, n-	íŋɔ:ma imbɛ̂:la	"drum" "top"
11	lu-	lúmu:li lubɔ̂:la	10	ø, in-, n-	ímu:li imɔ̂:la	"torch" "sting of bee"
12	ka-	kálo:si kalɛ̂:la	13	tu-	túlo:si tulɛ̂:la	"stream" "footpath"
14	u-	úto:pi úŋă:ga				" clay" "foolishness"
15	ku-	kú-bɔ:ku	6	ma-	má-bɔ:ku	"arm"
20	gu-	gú-li:bu	4	mi-	mí-li:bu	"big rock"

N = syllabic nasal

2.2. Tone of noun stems

The nouns with three-syllable stems, which have the greatest diversity of tone patterns, show six different patterns in isolation. In this paper I call these "tone groups

I ~VI". As mentioned above, all of the noun class prefixes except class 5 behave the same as the noun class prefix of class 6. In order to compare the influences of the different tones of noun class prefixes, the nouns of class 5 and class 6 are used as examples. A is the tone pattern of class 6, thus "the prefix of all classes except class 5", which is underlyingly H. B is the tone pattern of class 5, which is underlyingly L.

(7) **In Isolation**

I .	A	H-LL̲L	má-tɛlɛ:ku	" clay pots (6)"
	B	L-HL̲L	li-tɛ́lɛ:ku	" a clay pot (5)"
II .	A	H-LL̲L	má-tala:bu	" flat stones (6)"
	B	H-LL̲L	lí-tala:bu	" a flat stone (5)"
III .	A	L-HL̲L	ma-sɛ́ta:ni	" dragonflies (6)"
	B	L-HL̲L	li-sɛ́ta:ni	" a dragonfly (5)"
IV .	A	H-LF̲L	má-tutû:ma	" waterfalls (6) "
	B	L-LF̲L	li-tutû:ma	" a waterfall (5)"
V .	A	H-LH̲L	má-tɔpí:tɔ	" cherimoyas (a kind of fruit) (6) "
	B	L-LH̲L	li-tɔpí:tɔ	" a cherimoya (5) "
VI.	A	L-LF̲L	ma-gasɛ̂:ti	" newspapers (6) "
	B	L-LF̲L	li-gasɛ̂t:i	" a newspaper (5) "

These surface tones alternate depending on whether a word follows, in which case it matters what the tone of the next word is.

(8) **Followed by H** : noun + -ílihaha " bad …" (H - LLL)

I.	A	H-LLL	HLL̲L	má-tɛlɛku gíliha:ha	"bad clay pots"
	B	L-LLL	HLL̲L	li-tɛlɛku líliha:ha	"a bad clay pot"
II.	A	L-LLL	HLL̲L	ma-talabu gíliha:ha	"bad flat stones"
	B	L-LLL	HLL̲L	li-talabu líliha:ha	"a bad flat stone"
III.	A	L-HLL	HLL̲L	ma-sɛ́tani gíliha:ha	"bad dragonflies"
	B	L-HLL	HLL̲L	li-sɛ́tani líliha:ha	"a bad dragonfly"
IV.	A	H-LHL	HLL̲L	má-tutúma gíliha:ha	"bad waterfalls"
	B	L-LHL	HLL̲L	li-tutúma líliha:ha	"a bad waterfall"

V.	A	H-LLL HLL̲L	má-tɔpitɔ gíliha:ha	"bad cherimoyas"
	B	L-LLL HLL̲L	li-tɔpitɔ líliha:ha	"a bad cherimoya"
VI.	A	L-LHL HLL̲L	ma-gasɛ́ti gíliha:ha	"bad newspapers"
	B	L-LHL HLL̲L	li-gasɛ́ti íliha:ha	"a bad newspaper"

(9) **Followed by L** : noun + -njáhi "good …" (L - FL)

I.	A	H-LLL LF̲L	má-tɛlɛku manjâ:hi	"good clay pots"
	B	L-LLL LF̲L	li-tɛlɛku linjâ:hi	"a good clay pot"
II.	A	L-LLL LF̲L	ma-talabu manjâ:hi	"good flat stones"
	B	L-LLL LF̲L	li-talabu linjâ:hi	"a good flat stone"
III.	A	L-HLL LF̲L	ma-sɛ́tani manjâ:hi	"good dragonflies"
	B	L-HLL LF̲L	li-sɛ́tani linjâ:hi	"a good dragonfly"
IV.	A	H-LHL LF̲L	má-tutúma manjâ:hi	"good waterfalls"
	B	L-LHL LF̲L	li-tutúma linjâ:hi	"a good waterfall"
V.	A	H-LLH LF̲L	má-tɔpitɔ́ manjâ:hi	"good cherimoyas"
	B	L-LLH LF̲L	li-tɔpitɔ́ linjâ:hi	"a good cherimoya"
VI.	A	L-LHL LF̲L	ma-gasɛ́ti manjâ:hi	"good newspapers"
	B	L-LHL LF̲L	li-gasɛ́ti linjâ:hi	"a good newspaper"

Table 2 : Tone patterns of three syllable stem nouns

Tone Group		3-syllable stem nouns	Isolated form	+ - íliha:ha (HLL̲L)	+ - nja:hi (LF̲L)	gross
I	A	má-tɛlɛ:ku	H-LL̲L	H-LLL HLL̲L	H-LLL LF̲L	clay pots
	B	li-tɛ́lɛ:ku	L-HL̲L	L-LLL HLL̲L	L-LLL LF̲L	a clay pot
II	AB	má-tala:bu lí-tala:bu	H-LL̲L	L-LLL HLL̲L	L-LLL LF̲L	flat stones a flat stone
III	AB	ma-sɛ́ta:ni li-sɛ́ta:ni	L-HL̲L	L-HLL HLL̲L	L-HLL LF̲L	dragonflies dragonfly
IV	A	má-tutû:ma	H-LF̲L	H-LHL HLL̲L	H-LHL LF̲L	waterfalls
	B	li-tutû:ma	L-LF̲L	L-LHL HLL̲L	L-LHL LF̲L	a waterfall
V	A	má-tɔpí:tɔ	H-LH̲L	H-LLL HLL̲L	H-LLH LF̲L	cherimoyas
	B	li-tɔpí:tɔ	L-LH̲L	L-LLL HLL̲L	L-LLH LF̲L	a cherimoya
VI	AB	ma-gasɛ̂:ti li-gasɛ̂:ti	L-LF̲L	L-LHL HLL̲L	L-LHL LF̲L	newspapers a newspaper

Nouns in tone group VI are mostly loan words from Swahili, which doesn't have a tonal contrast and always has the accent on the penultimate syllable. Non-loan words in this group appear in both tone groups IV and VI in free variation. Since group VI are mostly loans from Swahili, group VI is excluded from the following discussion.

3. Underlying Tones and Rules

We can make the following observations about the marked H tone in this language.

(10) Appearance of H
- H never appears as the phrase-final tone.
- There are one or two Hs in isolation.
- The number of Hs in the noun stem is one or less.

The following rules can also be presumed.

(11) 1. Tone groups III and V:
When two H's appear next to each other at a boundary, the left H is deleted.
2. Tone groupV:
H on the phrase final mora shifts to its left.

Regarding tone group I, when the noun prefix is H or the following word has a H, the stem has no H. Only when the noun prefix is L and there is no following word, which must always have at least one H, does the second mora of the word appear as H[3]. Therefore at least one H is required, and the unit that requires at least one H is not the word but the tone phrase. Thus, the following rule can be presumed.

(12) 3. Tone group I:
When there is no H in the tone phrase, the second mora becomes H.

---

[3] It is possible to think that this H is stem-initial rather than the second mora of the word. However, this follows the same pattern that is seen in verbs. In the following example we see that the second mora becomes H regardless of the kind of morpheme it is:

L-LLLL	→	L-HLLL	
tu- butuki:la	→	tu-bútuki:la	" We run after."
SM1pl.-"run after"			
L-L-LLLL	→	L-H-LLLL	
tu- dʒi- butuki:la	→	tudʒíbutuki:la	" We run after it. "
SM1pl-OM(9)-"run after"		(SM=subject marker, OM=object marker)	

Considering each tone group with these rules, the underlying tones of group I, III, IV and V can be determined as in (13).

(13) Tone group I : no H
Tone group III : H on the stem initial
Tone group IV : H on the right next to the stem initial
Tone group V : H on the stem final

The next question is how to analyze tone group II. If we see the tone pattern of a noun with a following word in this group, the noun stems seem to have no H. But if so, some reason is needed to explain why the class 5 prefix form becomes H in isolation. We have just presumed a rule whereby the second mora becomes H when there is no H in the tone phrase, but now H appears in initial position.

Let us consider that the position of this H not on the word-initial mora but "immediately before the stem". That is, the stem in this group appears as L, but there is a H in front of the stem. This H links to its left mora (noun class prefix) and surfaces as H.

(14)
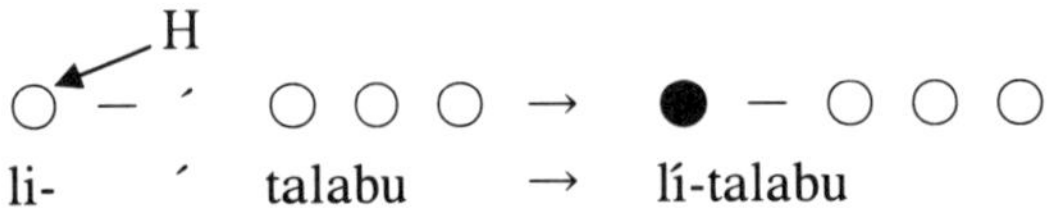

Considering it this way, the next issue to come up in this tone group is the form of the noun followed by another word. When the noun is followed by another word, the noun class prefix appears as L. Even the class 6 prefix, which is underlyingly H, appears as L. This means that the prefix H is deleted at the stage of being attached to the stem of tone group II nouns[4], and the H which the group II stem has in front of it makes the noun class prefix H as seen in (15).

(15)
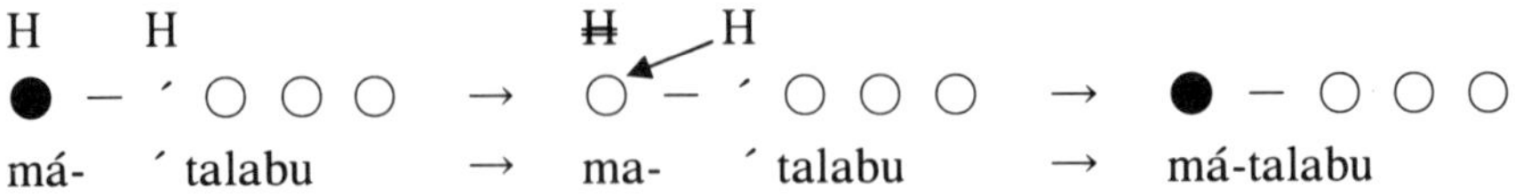

Moreover, although the H in front of the stem always causes the H to its left to delete, it makes the left mora H only when there is no H in the tone phrase.

[4] Professor Odden accounts for this deletion of H as the restatement of rule 1 (the left H is deleted when two Hs appear next to each other at the boundary) in his comments.

(16)

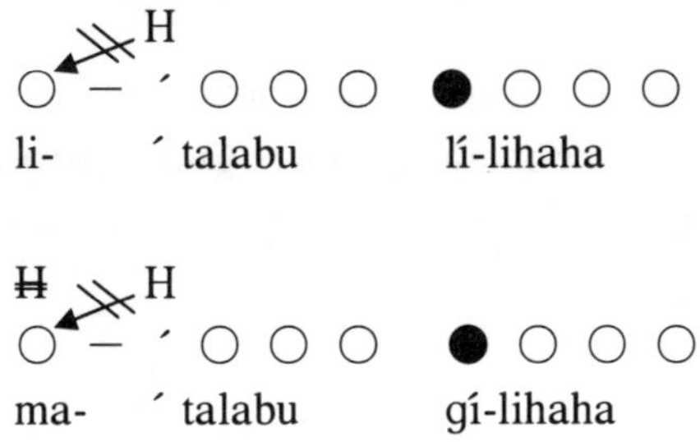

Below is a summary of the tonal phenomena discussed thus far.

(17) ◆Underlying tone of noun class prefixes

noun class prefixes except class 5	: H
noun class prefix of class 5	: L (-H)

◆Underlying tone of the noun stem of each tone group

	location of II
Tone group I: no H	(ø)
Tone group II: H immediately before the stem	(-1)
Tone group III: The stem initial is H	(0 / initial)
Tone group IV: The mora right next to the stem initial is H	(+1 / penult)
Tone group V: The stem final is H	(+2 / final)

◆Rules

Rule 1: When two Hs appear next to each other at a boundary, the left H is deleted.

Rule 2 : A phrase-final H tone shifts to the mora to its left.

Rule 3 : When there is no H in the tone phrase, the second mora becomes H.[5]

As we have seen above, the tone of the noun stem is classified according to the location of H in the stem. This means that the number of tone groups is the number of syllables of the stem (*n*) plus 2, "no H (ø)", and "H immediately before the stem (-1)", i.e. "*n* + 2"[6].

---

[5] This is the case for the nouns with more than three syllables. When the noun has three syllables or less, the word initial mora becomes H.

[6] Theoretically tone groups such as "the third from the stem initial is H" or "the fourth from the stem initial is H" are possible when the number of syllables in the stem increases. Namely it can be considered that other tone groups can exist between tone group IV and V of Table 3. Such examples are not found, though, because the number of nouns whose stems have more

4. Application of the rules

With these rules, let us interpret the surface tones of the nouns in each tone group shown in Table 3. ●=H, ○=L, ○ = one-mora syllable, ○○ = two-mora syllable, □ = where the rules are applied.

I. The noun stems have no H

A H noun class prefix

In isolation

Underlying tone		Surface tone	
●−○ ○	→	●−○○ ○	má-bɛːli
●−○ ○ ○	→	●−○ ○○ ○	má-tɛlɛːku
●−○ ○ ○ ○	→	●−○ ○ ○○ ○	má-ŋgɛŋgalɛːma
●−○ ○ ○ ○ ○	→	●−○ ○ ○ ○○ ○	má-tondalakoːu

Followed by H

●−○ ○ ● ○ ○ ○	→	●−○ ○ ● ○ ○○ ○	má-bɛli gíliha:ha
●−○ ○ ○ ● ○ ○ ○	→	●−○ ○ ○ ● ○ ○○ ○	má-tɛlɛku gíliha:ha
●−○ ○ ○ ○ ● ○ ○ ○	→	●−○ ○ ○ ○ ● ○ ○○ ○	má-ŋgɛŋgalɛma gíliha:ha

Followed by L

●−○ ○ ○ ● ○	→	●−○ ○ ○ ●○ ○	má-bɛli manjâ:hi
●−○ ○ ○ ○ ● ○	→	●−○ ○ ○ ○ ●○ ○	má-tɛlɛku manjâ:hi
●−○ ○ ○ ○ ○ ● ○	→	●−○ ○ ○ ○ ○ ●○ ○	má-ŋgɛŋgalɛma manjâ:hi

B L noun class prefix

In isolation

		(Rule 3)	
○−○ ○	→	●−○○ ○	lí-bɛːli
○−○ ○ ○	→	○−● ○○ ○	li-tɛ́lɛːku
○−○ ○ ○ ○	→	○−● ○ ○○ ○	li-ŋgɛ́ŋgalɛːma
○−○ ○ ○ ○ ○	→	○−● ○ ○ ○○ ○	li-tóndalakoːu

Followed by H

○−○ ○ ● ○ ○ ○	→	○−○ ○ ● ○ ○○ ○	li-bɛli líliha:ha
○−○ ○ ○ ● ○ ○ ○	→	○−○ ○ ○ ● ○ ○○ ○	li-tɛlɛku líliha:ha
○−○ ○ ○ ○ ● ○ ○ ○	→	○−○ ○ ○ ○ ● ○ ○○ ○	li-tóndalakou líliha:ha

Followed by L

○−○ ○ ○ ● ○	→	○−○ ○ ○ ●○ ○	li-bɛli linjâ:hi

---

than four syllables are actually very limited.

○−○ ○ ○ ○ ● ○ → ○−○ ○ ○ ○ ●○ ○ li-tɛlɛku linjâ:hi
○−○ ○ ○ ○ ○ ● ○ → ○−○ ○ ○ ○ ○ ●○ ○ li-tóndalakou linjâ:hi

II. H immediately before the stem

A H noun class prefix

(◎ denotes that there is a H immediately before it)

In isolation

●−◎ ○ → ●−○○ ○ má-dʒa:bu
●−◎ ○ ○ → ●−○ ○○ ○ má-tala:bu
●−◎ ○ ○ ○ → ●−○ ○ ○○ ○ má-sɔŋgulɛ:la

Followed by H

●−◎ ○ ● ○ ○ ○ → ○−○ ○ ● ○ ○○ ○ ma-dʒabu gíliha:ha
●−◎ ○ ○ ● ○ ○ ○ → ○−○ ○ ○ ● ○ ○○ ○ ma-talabu gíliha:ha
●−◎ ○ ○ ○ ● ○ ○ ○→ ○−○ ○ ○ ○ ● ○ ○○ ○
má-sɔŋgulɛla gíliha:ha

Followed by L

●−◎ ○ ○ ● ○ → ○−○ ○ ○ ●○ ○ ma-dʒabu manjâ:hi
●−◎ ○ ○ ○ ● ○ → ○−○ ○ ○ ○ ●○ ○ ma-talabu manjâ:hi
●−◎ ○ ○ ○ ○ ● ○ → ○−○ ○ ○ ○ ○ ●○ ○
má-sɔŋgulɛla manjâ:hi

B L noun class prefix

In isolation

○−◎ ○ → ●−○○ ○ lí-dʒa:bu
○−◎ ○ ○ → ●−○ ○○ ○ lí-tala:bu
○−◎ ○ ○ ○ → ●−○ ○ ○○ ○ lí-sɔŋgulɛ:la

Followed by H

○−◎ ○ ● ○ ○ ○ → ○−○ ○ ● ○ ○○ ○ li-dʒabu líliha:ha
○−◎ ○ ○ ● ○ ○ ○ → ○−○ ○ ○ ● ○ ○○ ○ li-talabu líliha:ha
○−◎ ○ ○ ○ ● ○ ○ ○→ ○−○ ○ ○ ○ ● ○ ○○ ○
lí-sɔŋgulɛla líliha:ha

Followed by L

○−◎ ○ ○ ● ○ → ○−○ ○ ○ ●○ ○ li-dʒabu linjâ:hi
○−◎ ○ ○ ○ ● ○ → ○−○ ○ ○ ○ ●○ ○ li-talabu linjâ:hi
○−◎ ○ ○ ○ ● ○ ○ ○→ ○−○ ○ ○ ○ ○ ●○ ○ lí-sɔŋgulɛla linjâ:hi

III. H on the stem initial

A H noun class prefix

In isolation (Rule 1)

●−● ○ → ○−●○ ○ ma-hî:na

●−● ○ ○ → ○−● ○○ ○ ma-sɛ́ta:ni

●−● ○ ○ ○ → ○−● ○ ○○ ○ ma-pwátaki:la

Followed by H (Rule 1)

●−● ○ ● ○ ○ ○ → ○−● ○ ● ○ ○○ ○ ma- hína gíliha:ha

●−● ○ ○ ● ○ ○ ○ → ○−● ○ ○ ● ○ ○○ ○ ma-sɛ́tani gíliha:ha

●−● ○ ○ ○ ● ○ ○ ○→ ○−● ○ ○ ○ ● ○ ○○ ○

ma-pwátakila gíliha:ha

Followed by L (Rule 1)

●−● ○ ○ ● ○ → ○−● ○ ○ ●○ ○ ma- hína manjâ:hi

●−● ○ ○ ○ ● ○ → ○−● ○ ○ ○ ●○ ○ ma-sɛ́tani manjâ:hi

●−● ○ ○ ○ ○ ● ○ → ○−● ○ ○ ○ ○ ●○ ○ ma-pwátakila manjâ:hi

B L noun class prefix

In isolation

○−● ○ → ○−●○ ○ li-hî:na

○−● ○ ○ → ○−● ○○ ○ li-sɛ́ta:ni

○−● ○ ○ ○ → ○−● ○ ○○ ○ li-pwátaki:la

Followed by H

○−● ○ ● ○ ○ ○ → ○−● ○ ● ○ ○○ ○ li-hína líliha:ha

○−● ○ ○ ● ○ ○ ○ → ○−● ○ ○ ● ○ ○○ ○ li-sɛ́tani líliha:ha

○−● ○ ○ ○ ● ○ ○ ○→ ○−● ○ ○ ○ ● ○ ○○ ○

li-pwátakila líliha:ha

Followed by L

○−● ○ ○ ● ○ → ○−● ○ ○ ●○ ○ li-hína linjâ:hi

○−● ○ ○ ○ ● ○ → ○−● ○ ○ ○ ●○ ○ li-sɛ́tani linjâ:hi

○−● ○ ○ ○ ○ ● ○ → ○−● ○ ○ ○ ○ ●○ ○ li-pwátakila linjâ:hi

IV. H to the right of the stem initial

A H noun class prefix

In isolation

●−○ ● ○ → ●−○ ●○ ○ má-tutû:ma

●−○ ● ○ ○ → ●−○ ● ○○ ○ má-kɛlábɛ:la

●−○ ● ○ ○ ○ → ●−○ ● ○ ○○ ○ kí-pɛlápatɛ:la

Followed by H

●–○ ● ○ ● ○ ○ ○ → ●–○ ● ○ ● ○ ○○ ○ má-tutúma gíliha:ha

●–○ ● ○ ○ ● ○ ○ ○ → ●–○ ● ○ ○ ● ○ ○○ ○ má-kɛlábɛla gíliha:ha

●–○ ● ○ ○ ○ ● ○ ○ ○ → ●–○ ● ○ ○ ○ ● ○ ○○ ○ kí-pɛlápatɛla gíliha:ha

Followed by L

●–○ ● ○ ○ ● ○ → ●–○ ● ○ ○ ●○ ○ má-tutúma manjâ:hi

●–○ ● ○ ○ ○ ● ○ → ●–○ ● ○ ○ ○ ●○ ○ má-kɛlábɛla manjâ:hi

●–○ ● ○ ○ ○ ○ ● ○ → ●–○ ● ○ ○ ○ ○ ●○ ○ kí-pɛlápatɛla manjâ:hi

B L noun class prefix

In isolation

○–○ ● ○ → ○–○ ●○ ○ li-tutû:ma

○–○ ● ○ ○ → ○ ○ ● ○○ ○ li-kɛlábɛ:la

Followed by H

○–○ ● ○ ● ○ ○ ○ → ○–○ ● ○ ● ○ ○○ ○ li-tutúma líliha:ha

○–○ ● ○ ○ ● ○ ○ ○ → ○–○ ● ○ ○ ● ○ ○○ ○ li-kɛlábɛla líliha:ha

Followed by L

○–○ ● ○ ○ ● ○ → ○ ○ ● ○ ○ ●○ ○ li-tutúma linjâ:hi

○–○ ● ○ ○ ○ ● ○ → ○–○ ● ○ ○ ○ ●○ ○ li-kɛlábɛla linjâ:hi

V. H on the word final

A H noun class prefix

In isolation (Rule 2)

●–○ ● → ●–○● ○ má-hǐ:na

●–○ ○ ● → ●–○ ○● ○

→ ●–○ ●● ○ má-tɔpí:tɔ

Followed by H (Rule 1)

●–○ ● ● ○ ○ ○ → ●–○ ○ ● ○ ○○ ○ má-hina gíliha:ha

●–○ ○ ● ● ○ ○ ○ → ●–○ ○ ○ ● ○ ○○ ○ má-tɔpitɔ gíliha:ha

Followed by L

●–○ ● ○ ● ○	→	●–○ ● ○ ●○ ○	má-hiná manjâ:hi
●–○ ○ ● ○ ● ○	→	●–○ ○ ● ○ ●○ ○	má-tɔpitɔ́ manjâ:hi

B L noun class prefix

In isolation

		(Rule 2)	
○–○ ●	→	○–○● ○	
	→	○–●● ○	li-hí:na
○–○ ○ ●	→	○–○ ○● ○	
	→	○–○ ●● ○	li-tɔpí:tɔ

Followed by H

		(Rule 1)	
○–○ ● ● ○ ○ ○	→	○–○ ○ ● ○ ○○ ○	li-hina líliha:ha
○–○ ○ ● ● ○ ○ ○	→	○–○ ○ ○ ● ○ ○○ ○	li-tɔpitɔ líliha:ha

Followed by L

○–○ ● ○ ● ○	→	○–○ ● ○ ●○ ○	li-hiná linjâ:hi
○–○ ○ ● ○ ● ○	→	○–○ ○ ● ○ ●○ ○	li-tɔpitɔ́ linjâ:hi

Table 3 : Tone group according to the number of syllables of the noun stem

	2 syllables	3 syllables	4 syllables	5 syllables
I A	H - LL má-bɛ:li "breasts" H - LL HLLL H - LL LFL	H - LLL má-tɛlɛ:lu "cooking pots" H - LLL HLLL H - LLL LFL	H - LLLL má-ŋgɛŋgalɛ:ma "leg bells" H - LLLL HLLL H - LLLL LFL	H - LLLLL má-tondalako:u "stomachs" H - LLLLL HLLL H - LLLLL LFL
B	H - LL lí-bɛ:li "a breast" L - LL HLLL L - LL LFL	L - HLL li-tɛ́lɛ:lu "a cooking pot" L - LLL HLLL L - LLL LFL	L - HLLL li-ŋgɛ́ŋgalɛ:ma "a leg bell" L - LLLL HLLL L - LLLL LFL	L - HLLLL li-tóndalako:u "a stomach" L - LLLLL HLLL L - LLLLL LFL
II A B	H - LL má-dʒa:bu lí-dʒa:bu "kassaba" L - LL HLLL L - LL LFL	H - LLL má-tala:bu lí-tala:bu "flat stone" L - LLL HLLL L - LLL LFL	H - LLLL má-sɔŋgulɛ:la lí-sɔŋgulɛ:la "aloe" L - LLLL HLLL L - LLLL LFL	
III A B	L - FL ma-hî:na li-hî:na "stem" L - HL HLLL L - HL LFL	L - HLL ma-sɛ́ta:ni li-sɛ́ta:ni "dragonfly" L - HLL HLLL L - HLL LFL	L - HLLL ma-pwátaki:la li-pwátaki:la "tomato" L - HLLL HLLL L - HLLL LFL	

IV A		H - LFL má-tutû:ma "waterfalls" H - LHL HLLL H - LHL LFL	H - LHLL má-kɛlábɛ:la "(a kind of) birds" H - LHLL HLLL H - LHLL LFL	H - LHLLL kí-pɛlápatɛ:la "a mat" H - LHLLL HLLL H - LHLLL LFL
B		L - LFL li-tutû:ma "a waterfall" L - LHL HLLL L - LHL LFL	L - LHLL li-kɛlábɛ:la "(a kind of) bird" L - LHLL HLLL L - LHLL LFL	
V A	H - RL má-hǐ:na "names" H - LL HLLL H - LH LFL	H - LHL má-tɔpí:tɔ "cherimoyas" H - LLL HLLL H - LLH LFL		
B	L - HL li-hí:na "a name" L - LL HLLL L - LH LFL	L - LHL li- tɔpí:tɔ "a cherimoya" L - LLL HLLL L - LLH LFL		
VI A B	L - FL ma-lû:ka li-lû:ka "shop" L - HL HLLL L - HL LFL	L - LFL ma-gasêti li-gasêti "newspaper" L - LHL HLLL L - LHL LFL	L - LLFL ma-kalatâ:si li-kalatâ:si "paper" L - LLHL HLLL L - LLHL LFL	Isolation "gross" followed by H followed by L

5. Tone of the nouns which structure is not "noun class prefix – stem"

5.1. Nouns without the noun class prefix

There are nouns without a noun class prefix in class 9 and 10 (most of them are loan words). When the noun has three syllables or more, the first syllable behaves as the noun class prefix and the remaining syllables behave as the stem, but when the noun has only two syllables this does not happen and both syllables remain in the stem.

(18) ϕ - Noun Stem

				tone group
a.	sô:ma	"bead"	soma injâ:hi	I / II
b.	pɛ́:ti	"ring"	pɛtí injâ:hi	V
c.	hálǎ:bu	"driver ant"	hálabú injâ:hi	V

5.2. Nouns whose stem begins with the vowel

When the stem begins with a vowel, the boundary disappears, and the vowel of the noun class prefix and the stem initial vowel merge with each other. In this case, if the noun has only two syllables, both syllables behave as the stem. If the noun has three syllables or more, the first syllable behaves as the noun class prefix, i.e. it can even be H when there is another H next to it, and the remaining syllables behave as the stem.

(19) Noun Class Prefix / Noun Stem

						tone group
a.	li-	inu	lî:nu	"a tooth"	linu linjâ:hi	I / II[7]
b.	ma-	inu	mî:nu	"teeth"	minu manjâ:hi	I / II
c.	li-	ina	lî:na	"a pit trap"	lína linjâ:hi	III
d.	ma-	ina	mî:na	"pitfall"	mí:na manjâ:hi	III
e.	li-	uŋgula	ljuŋgû:la	"a frog"	ljuŋgúla linjâ:hi	III
f.	si-	ɛmbɛmbi	sɛ́:mbɛ̌:mbi	"a pit of stomach"	sɛ́:mbɛ:mbí kinjâ:hi	V

5.3. Nouns with an augment

When the noun stem is monosyllabic, an augment "i-" is added in front of the noun class prefix.

(20) i - Noun Class Prefix - Noun Stem

				tone group
a.	í-ma:-bu	"stones"	imabu manjâ:hi	II
b.	í-li:-bu	"a stone"	ilibu linjâ:hi	II
c.	i-mâ:-ta	"spittle"	imáta manjâ:hi	III
d.	i-lî-hu	"ash"	ilíhu linjâ:hi	III

Considering that the augment bears the tone which the noun class prefix usually bears, "stone" can be realized as having the tone pattern of tone group II, and "ash" and "spittle" of tone group III. Thus regarding the tone, the augment behaves as the noun class prefix, and the noun class prefix and stem together behave as a disyllabic stem.

5.4. Locative nouns

The noun class prefixes of locative class 16, 17 and 18 are pu-, ku-, and mu- respectively[8]. They are added in front of other nouns. Regardless of the tone or tone

[7] The difference between tone group I and II are only seen on the noun class prefix. Therefore we can't distinguish if a noun belongs to tone group I or II in this case.

[8] When the locative class prefixes are added to nouns, the vowel of the noun class prefix is inserted between the locative class prefix and the noun. Each locative class prefix refers to

groups of the nouns to which the locative is added, the locative noun class prefixes always appear as L and they do not affect the tone of the nouns. Therefore they are underlyingly -H like the class 5 prefix.

(21) Locative Noun Class Prefix – Noun Class Prefix – Noun Stem

tone group I				
a.	pu-	má-tɛlɛ:ku	pwamátɛlɛ:ku	"at the clay pots"
b.		li-tɛ́lɛ:ku	pwilitɛ́lɛ:ku	"at the clay pot"
c.	ku-	má-tɛlɛ:ku	kwamátɛlɛ:ku	"around the clay pots"
d.		li-tɛ́lɛ:ku	kwilitɛ́lɛ:ku	"around the clay pot"
e.	mu-	má-tɛlɛ:ku	mwamátɛlɛ:ku	"in the clay pots"
f.		li-tɛ́lɛ:ku	mwilitɛ́lɛ:ku	"in the clay pot"
tone group II				
g.	pu-	má-tala:bu	pwamátala:bu	"on the flat stones"
h.		lí-tala:bu	pwilítala:bu	"on the flat stone"
i.	ku-	má-tala:bu	kwamátala:bu	"around the flat stones"
g.		lí-tala:bu	kwilítala:bu	"around the flat stone"
tone group III				
k.	pu-	ma-hî:na	pwamahî:na	"on the stems"
l.		li-hî:na	pwilihî:na	"on the stem"
m.	ku-	ma-hî:na	kwamahî:na	"around the stems"
n.		li-hî:na	kwilihî:na	"around the stem"
tone group IV				
o.	pu-	má-tutû:ma	pwamátutû:ma	"at the waterfalls"
p.		li-tutû:ma	pwilitutû:ma	"at the waterfall"
q.	ku-	má-tutû:ma	kwamátutû:ma	"around the waterfalls"
r.		li-tutû:ma	kwilitutû:ma	"around the waterfall"
tone group V				
s.	pu-	má-tɔpí:tɔ	pwamátɔpí:tɔ	"on the cherimoyas"
t.		li-tɔpí:tɔ	pwilitɔpí:tɔ	"on the cherimoya"
u.	ku-	má-tɔpí:tɔ	kwamátɔpí:tɔ	"around the cherimoyas"
v.		li-tɔpí:tɔ	kwilitɔpí:tɔ	"around the cherimoya"

References

Yoneda, Nobuko 2000. *A Descriptive Study of Matengo, a Bantu Language of Tanzania.* Unpublished Ph.D. Dissertation of Tokyo university of foreign studies.

---

different aspects of a location, pu- refers to a specific place "on, at", ku- refers to a general place "around", and mu- refers to an internal place "in".

Comments on Nobuko Yoneda, "Tone Patterns of Matengo Nominals"

David Odden
Ohio State University

Professor Yoneda's paper provides much-needed descriptive data on a sector of the Rufiji-Ruvuma group within Bantu. In addition to providing information that yields a deeper understanding of the relation of Matengo to other Bantu languages, her description provides novel data which may have a broader theoretical impact. First, her presentation brings to light a number of interesting parallels between the prosody of Matengo and that of other Bantu languages spoken in Southern Tanzania. Matengo is quite similar to Kimatuumbi in restricting vowel length to the last three syllables of the stem. The consequence of that restriction in Kimatuumbi is that there is an alternation of length within roots, depending on how many affixal moras follow.

(1)	*Matengo*	<u>jo:</u>be:ka	'to peel for'	j<u>o</u>bato:ka	'to peel off'
	Kimatuumbi	áandika	'to write'	ándikiya	'to make write'
		káata	'to cut'	kátanika	'to be cuttable'
		tyátyaakiya	'plaster'	tyátyatyakiyilwa	'to be plastered'
		tɪ́ila	'fear'	tɪ́ilana	'fear e.o'
				tɪ́laanga	'fear pl.'

In Kimatuumbi, this restriction is not exceptionless on the surface, because syllable readjustments such as glide formation can lead to long vowels in any position, and there are other exceptions such as the perfective stem infix which contributes a mora but does not trigger preantepenultimate shortening.

(2)	chatwáacholɪ́té	'what we drew'	/cha-tú-a-cholɪ́té/
	tuunkálaangiile	'we fried for him'	/tu-mu-kálaang-i-ile/

Kimatuumbi does not automatically lengthen penultimate syllables, so learning whether a vowel is underlyingly long is not particularly challenging in that language. The situation in Matengo seems to be rather different, because on the face of it there would only seem to be one position where a child can observe contrastive vowel length, namely in the antepenult. This gives vowel length a low functional load and makes it likely that the language will eventually lose length entirely. To the extent that vowel length interacts with tone, the distribution of tone may have consequences for tonal contrasts in the language. The length data that are considered from Matengo are almost totally restricted to predictable length, and in order to have the full picture of tone and stress issues in this part of Bantu, it will be important to consider how length interacts with tone, beyond the retraction of final H's to long syllables.

Such a restriction on vowel length may tempt one to invoke metrical feet, such that one disyllabic non-final foot is constructed at the right edge of a word, and long vowels must appear within that foot.

(3)
```
       *                        *
    * (* *) *                (*  *)  *
    jo̱bato:ka                jo̱:be:ka
```

This formal imposition may seem somewhat artificial, but the proposal will receive additional support as we consider other facts of the language.

It is also very interesting that there is an epenthetic vowel before the noun class prefix, just in case the root is monosyllabic. Epenthetic vowels are found in a number of languages when a word is too short, for example in Mohawk, monosyllables are made into disyllables by epenthesis of *i*, as they are also in Makonde.

(4)	*Mohawk*	/k-tats-s/	→	iktats	'I offer'
	Makonde	/lya/	→	íi-lya	'eat'
				cf. píima	'measure!'

However, in Matengo, the unaugmented word itself would already be bisyllabic. While this usually counts as 'long enough' in other languages, it does not in Matengo, as seen in the examples in (5).

(5)	í̱-ŋɔ:ma	'drum' (cl. 9)	/ŋɔma/	cf. ndéngasê:gi	'sp. beans'
	í̱-ma:-bu	'stones' (cl. 6)	/ma-bu/	cf. má-hu:pa	'bones'
	í̱-li:-bu	'stone'(cl. 5)	/li-bu/	cf. lí-hu:pa	'bone'

In terms of the metrical structure hypothesis, a two-syllable word could not have a non-final, disyllabic foot, and thus epenthesis could be seen as a means of enabling foot structure.

(6)
```
                   *
    * *          (* *) *
    li-bu  →     i-li-bu
```

There is an interesting areal analog to Matengo's special treatment of disyllables as being in some sense "too short", coming from the treatment of preconsonantal nasals in the phrasal phonology of Mwera, illustrated in (7). The Class 9 prefix of Mwera is not generally tone bearing, so when a H tone is assigned to the beginning of a word after certain words in phrasal context, the H goes to the noun class prefix if it has a vowel, and goes to the stem-initial syllable if the prefix is the nonsyllabic class 9-10 prefix *n*-. Thus we would assume that preconsonantal nasals are not generally moraic.

(7)	mi-kóongo	'trees'	tuveeye míkóongo	'that we carve trees'
	ma-jela	'hoes	kúúpíme májela	'come measure hoes'

n-domoóndo 'hippo' vulaga n-dómoóndo 'kill a hippo!'
n-gweena 'crocodile' ayi n-gwéena 'this crocodile'

But just in case the stem has two or fewer morae, the nasal prefix does bear tone, thus an exceptional mora is present (as is the case with an epenthetic vowel).

(8)	m-bwá	'dog'	akáápéleka ḿ-bwá	'he is not sending a dog'
	n-jété	'salt'	akáápéleka ń-jété	'he is not sending salt'
	n-guvo	'cloth'	shiinjóne ń-guvo	'I will wear cloth'

Thus there are parallels to Matengo's trisyllabic minimal word requirement to be found in neighboring languages. To this we may add the fact in Chingoni, H is regularly assigned to the antepenultimate syllable, and in Kinga, H almost exclusively appears either in the pre-stem or antepenult positions, as evidence that the antepenultimate syllable has a special status in the languages of the area.

There are some interesting points of similarity between tone in Matengo and tone in Yao, Mwera and Kimatuumbi. One is the retraction of word-final H tone to a long penult via Rule 2, sometimes referred to as Heavy Syllable Retraction, which creates a rise vs. fall contrast in the phrasal penultimate syllable.

(9)	*Matengo*	má-hiiná	→ máhiína	(máhiná manjâ:hi)	'good names'
	Kimatuuumbi	mboopó	→ mboópo	(mbopó inaánnogá)	'good knife'
	Yao (also Mwera)	chipuulá	→ chipuúla	(chipuulá cháámbóne)	'good knife'

Another similarity, held with Kimatuumbi, is the tonal peculiarity of the class 5 prefix, which is that in contrast to the other prefixes, it does not have a H tone. The class prefixes are not themselves H toned in Kimatuumbi as seen in (10), but they exhibit a correlation with H tone, namely that a H tone appears at the beginning of a stem that is preceded by a mora-bearing noun class prefix. Thus an unprefixed noun such as *sipitaáli* will take a H tone on the first mora when a prefix such as class 6 *ma-* precedes, and the root *ngalawá* similarly receives a H tone when the cl. 6 prefix is added or after the class 12 & 13 prefixes. However, the class 5 prefix *li-* does not cause the appearance of this H tone. There are other tonal peculiarities of the class 5 prefix, as indicated in the last set of examples, where the class 5 form lacks a H tone found in related forms of the noun.

(10)	a.	sipitaáli	'hospital'	ma-sípitaáli	'hospitals' (c. 6)
		ngalawá	'canoe' (cl. 9)	ma-ngálawá	'canoes'
		ka-ngálawá	'little canoe'	tu-ngálawá	'little canoes'
	b.	li-ngalawá	'huge canoes' (cl. 5)		
	c.	ma-tóbó	'holes' (cl. 6)	lii-tóbo	'hole' (cl. 5)
		ma-túutá	'planting ridges'	li-tuutá	'planting ridge'

The Matengo tone contrasts associated with class 5 are analogous, in that Kimatuumbi *li-* does not *contribute* a H tone and Matengo *li-* does not *have* a H tone.

(11) li-lé:nda 'a trap' (cl. 5) má-lě:nda 'traps' (cl. 6)
but: ngámbungá:mbu ← /ń-gambungambú/ (cl. 9)

However, the parallelism is broken with the class 9 prefix, which does not contribute a H tone in Kimatuumbi, but does in Matengo.

Turning to the matter of the contrasts in nominal tone pattern, the question arises how the patterns which Professor Yoneda has described might be be accounted for in terms of a formal model, such as one with autosegmental representations and rules. A theoretically interesting question emerging from consideration of the Matengo facts is how the contrasting patterns are to be represented in a grammar: what exactly does the child learning the language memorize? Some languages in this area have more tonal contrasts than one would expect from the simple combinatoric considerations that operate more widely in Bantu, which at most allow any stem syllable to have an underlying H tone. That predicts a maximum of 4 tone classes for disyllabic stems, but contrary to this widely observed pattern, Shimakonde has almost twice as many contrasts than that.

(12)	li-doôdo	'leg'	lí-jáanga	'stone'
	li-laála	'coconut'	lí-páápa	'broken basket'
	lú-ngaau	'net'	mi-mpiila	'balls'
	li-káaya	'village'		

Hehe similarly has 5 tone-class contrasts.

(13)	mu-guúnda	'field'	mu-víifu	'gloomy person'
	mú-teela	'stirring stick'	lú-fwíili	'hair'
	ki-tóofú	'potato'		

Professor Yoneda describes 6 tone patterns attested in Matengo for trisyllabic stems: this presents a similar problem of having too many contrasts for a conventional analysis of noun tone in a Bantu language, since we would predict a maximum of 4 tonal types assuming a limit of one underlying H within the stem. The size of the problem is reduced somewhat by the fact that class VI which has penult fall and no prefixal H is apparently populated only by loanwords, so they might be treated as exceptions. Of course, it is important to know what they are exceptions to, but we might assume that they are exceptions in requiring deletion of the prefixal H.

Certain conclusions about underlying representations in Professor Yoneda's analysis are secure. One is that the noun class prefixes except for class 5 have underlying H tones; indeed the prefixes do have a surface H tone in many cases except for group VI and group III. Stems whose initial syllable is always H toned would, most reasonably, be assumed to have an initial H tone, so Group III with a stem initial vowel poses little problem, given rule 1 where the prefixal H is deleted because of the stem H.

(14) Group III: má-séta:ni → ma-séta:ni

Group I nouns have no underlying stem H's, and in classes other than class 5, the class prefix H is the only H in the word. Since the class 5 prefix has no H, the combination of such a stem with the prefix *li* would yield a word that is entirely toneless.

(15)	Group I	má-tɛlɛ:ku	má-tɛlɛ:ku gíliha:ha
		li-tɛ́lɛ:ku	li-tɛlɛ:ku gíliha:ha

The appearance of a H tone in phrase-final position is then a way to guarantee that nouns always have a H tone. Kimatuumbi presents a similar set of data, in that all words have a stem H tone prepausally, but some words are underlyingly toneless. In Kimatuumbi, a H is assigned to the stem initial mora of a toneless noun in prepausal position.

(16)	ki-wíkɪlyo	'cover' (cl. 7)	/ki-wɪkɪlyo/
	nga ki-wɪkɪlyo lí	'it isn't a cover'	
	ma-tógolo	'waterbucks' (cl. 6)	/ma-tógolo/
	nga ma-tógolo lí	'it isn't waterbucks'	

The same assignment of H to an otherwise toneless word also seems to be taking place in Matengo, except that the surface position of the H varies somewhat. In some cases the H is on the stem initial syllable, and sometimes, just in case the stem is disyllabic, the H is on the prefix.

(17)	má-bɛ:li	má-tɛlɛ:ku	má-ŋgɛŋgalɛ:ma	má-tondalako:u
	lí-bɛ:li	li-tɛ́lɛ:ku	li-ŋgɛ́ŋgalɛ:ma	li-tóndalako:u
	*li bɛ̂:li			

Thus it would appear that the language shifts an assigned tone off of the penult. A number of languages in the area show signs of avoiding H toned penults. Shimakonde blocks an otherwise general rule of tone doubling if the target is the penult, and Hehe has an entirely analogous leftward shifting rule. In Hehe (18), H is assigned to the root initial mora in certain tenses like the negative future, but it is shifted to the left when that mora is the penultimate mora.

(18)	situ-lóot-a	'we won't dream'
	situ-táwul-a	'we won't give'
	situ-púundul-a	'we won't shoot'
	situ-fúungulaang-a	'we won't untie'
	sitú-lim-a	'we won't cultivate'

It is interesting to see that Matengo has a very similar avoidance of the penult for tone assignment, especially in light of the evidence from epenthesis and vowel restrictions that there is something special about the antepenult.

One final point regarding the assignment of tone in prepausal toneless words is that Professor Yoneda indicates there may be some evidence for assigning tone to the second syllable of the word, rather than the first syllable of the stem, based on verbal forms. It will be very interesting to consider data on verb tone assignment, since we know that the verbal tonologies of Kimatuumbi, Yao, Makonde and Makua are very complex, indicating the possibility of analogous complexity in Matengo. A close analysis of the facts of Kimatuumbi shows that the assigned prepausal H is assigned to the stem-initial mora, but then shifts rightward in some contexts, just in case the H would be on the word-initial syllable. More information on Matengo verbs could thus tell us how close the parallelism is with Kimatuumbi, in terms of where the prepausal H is assigned.

A somewhat challenging set of stems are those in group II, where a H is assigned to the pre-stem mora. This poses a representational puzzle, because such nouns don't have an underlying H on some stem syllable such as the first or last syllable, but they also can't be underlyingly toneless since the toneless class of nouns fall into the behaviorally distinct Group I. In terms of exploiting possible underlying forms, there remains one further tonal possiblity, that stems could have a floating H, one that is present but not linked to a particular vowel underlyingly. This then provides us with a representational basis for distinguishing group II from other groups.

(19)

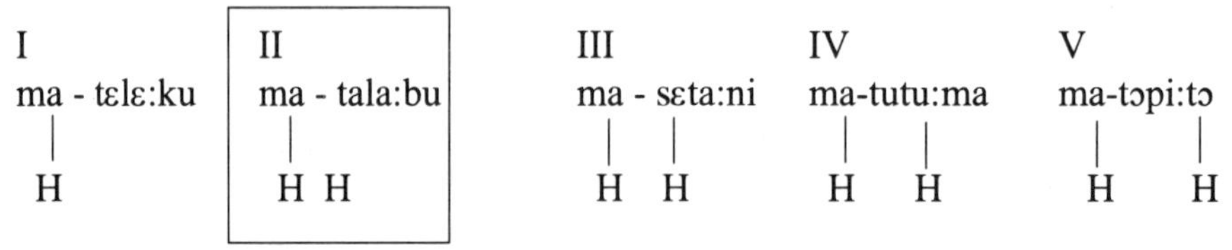

However, group II nouns have other puzzling properties. We have seen that the H tone of the class prefix is stable in phrase medial position: like other underlying H tones, it is present in prepausal and phrase-medial positions alike.

(20)	má-tɛlɛ:ku	má-tɛlɛku gíliha:ha	má-tɛlɛku manjâ:hi
	má-kɛlábɛ:la	má-kɛlábɛla gíliha:ha	má-kɛlábɛla manjâ:hi

It is only the toneless noun stems, and only the class 5 forms, which are entirely toneless in phrase medial position. In comparison we see that group II nouns of all classes, both those with H toned class prefixes and those with toneless class prefixes, are toneless phrase medially.

(21)	má-tala:bu	matalabu majâhi
	lí-tala:bu	litalabu lijâhi

Thus we need to understand both what happened to the floating stem H, if that is the right analysis of this group of nouns, and what happened to the prefixal H, in phrase medial position.

The necessary mechanism is available in Professor Yoneda's account, in her Rule 1, which states that the first of two consecutive H tones is deleted — a process commonly known as Reverse Meeussen's Rule. This rule not only accounts for the deleting of word final H before a modifier having an initial H, but also explains the lack of prefixal H tone in nouns of group III which have a root initial H. Further, drawing from some work on the theory of adjacency, we can restate the condition for deletion, so that a H is deleted before a H, as long as the H's are not on non-adjacent syllables.

```
(22)  H's not separated                        H's separated by a syllable
         ma - tala:bu        ma - sɛta:ni        ma-tutu:ma      ma-tɔpi:tɔ
            |                   |    |            |   |            |    |
      ∅ ← H H             ∅ ← H    H            H   H            H    H
```

Stated that way, a floating H can cause the prefix H to delete, even though it is not on the next syllable or any syllable, for that matter. What remains for this account of the group II nouns is to explain why the H systematically appears on the prefix syllable, and only prepausally. Recognition of this fact can be made via a rule that links a floating H tone to the beginning of word prepausally.

Though most of the data we have on Matengo come from nouns in classes that have surface moraic or tone-bearing prefixes, there is some interesting data from class 9-10 which speaks to the prosodic status of NC sequences in the language. On the surface, some preconsonantal nasals are tone bearing, for example classes 1 and 3.

(23) ń-sɔkô:lo 'grandchild' (cl. 1) ń-tɔngâ:na 'mulberry tree' (cl. 3)

With respect to minimality and vowel epenthesis, these prefixes count as syllables, since we do not find epenthesis when the stem is disyllabic. That contrasts with the class 9 prefix, which as we have seen does not provide the necessary antepenultimate syllable.

(24) n-tâ:mu 'sick person' (cl. 1) n-sî:pu 'sneeze'
i-m-bɛ̂:la 'top' (cl. 9)

But there is evidence that class 9-10 is underlying a mora-bearing or tone-bearing prefix, because class 9-10 nouns provide the only examples of stems with two H tones. This makes sense if the prefix has a H, which is transferred under desyllabification to the following vowel.

(25) háhǎ:bu /ń-halabú/
ndzéngasê:gi /ń-dzengaségi/
ngámbungá:mbu /ń-gambungambú/

This is a point of difference with Kimatuumbi, in that the class 9 prefix behaves tonally the same as the class 5 prefix does, in not contributing a stem initial H.

(26) ngoongoní 'hartebeest' ma-kóongoní 'hartebeests'

In summary, Professor Yoneda has made a valuable contribution to the study of Bantu and general phonlogy via her description of Matengo prosody, and I look forward to learning more about the structure of this very interesting language.

List of Contributors

Mary **Bradshaw**	Kyungpook National University, South Korea
Didier **Demolin**	University of São Paulo, Brazil & University of Brussels, Belgium
Mark **Donohue** University	Australian National University, Australia and National of Singapore, Singapore
San **Duanmu**	University of Michigan, U.S.A.
Elsa **Gomez-Imbert**	Centre National de la Recherche Scientifique (CNRS), and Université Toulouse Le Mirail, France
Norihiko **Hayashi**	Kyoto university, Japan
Osamu **Hieda**	Osaka University of Foreign Studies, Japan
Shunichi **Ishihara**	Australian National University, Australia
Chiyuki **Ito**	ILCAA, Tokyo University of Foreign Studies, Japan
Ray **Iwata**	Kanazawa University, Japan
Shigeki **Kaji**	Kyoto University and ILCAA, Tokyo University of Foreign Studies, Japan
Michael **Kenstowicz**	Massachusetts Institute of Technology (MIT), U.S.A.
Charles **Kisseberth**	Tel Aviv University, Israel
Tomoyuki **Kubo**	Kyushu University, Japan
Haruo **Kubozono**	Kobe University, Japan
James **Matisoff**	University of California at Berkley (emeritus), U.S.A.
Martine **Mazaudon**	Centre National de la Recherche Scientifique (CNRS), Paris, France
Daniel **Mkude**	University of Dar es Salaam, Tanzania & ILCAA, Tokyo University of Foreign Studies, Japan
André **Motingea**	Institut Pédagogique National (IPN), Democratic Republic of the Congo & ILCAA, Tokyo University of Foreign Studies, Japan
Yasuko **Nagano-Madsen**	University of Götcborg, Swcdcn
David **Odden**	Ohio State University, U.S.A.
Masao **Okazaki**	Ibaraki University, Japan
Robert **Ramsey**	University of Maryland, U.S.A.
Ruth **Roberts-Kohno**	ILCAA, Tokyo University of Foreign Studies, Japan
Malcolm **Ross**	Australian National University, Australia
Tadahiko **Shintani**	ILCAA, Tokyo University of Foreign Studies, Japan
Jennifer **Smith**	University of North Carolina, U.S.A.
Luciana **Storto**	University of São Paulo, Brazil
Nobuko **Yoneda**	Osaka Jogakuin College, Japan

Proceedings of the Symposium
CROSS-LINGUISTIC STUDIES OF TONAL PHENOMENA
Historical Development, Tone-Syntax Interface, and Descriptive Studies

---

2005（平成17）年12月14日　発行

編　集　梶（かじ）　茂樹（しげき）
発　行　東京外国語大学アジア・アフリカ言語文化研究所
〒183-8534 東京都府中市朝日町3-11-1
TEL 042-330-5600　FAX 042-330-5610
印　刷　三鈴印刷株式会社

© Shigeki Kaji 2005　ISBN 4-87297-917-6